UNDERSTANDING CRIME IN CANADA

AN INTRODUCTION TO CRIMINOLOGY

SECOND EDITION

Edited by
NEIL BOYD

emond ▪ Toronto, Canada ▪ 2019

Emond Montgomery Publications Limited
1 Eglinton Avenue E., Suite 600
Toronto ON M4P 3A1
http://www.emond.ca/highered

Printed in Canada.
Reprinted November 2020.

We acknowledge the financial support of the Government of Canada.   Canadä

Vice president, publishing: Anthony Rezek
Publisher: Mike Thompson
Director, development and production: Kelly Dickson
Developmental editor: Joanne Sutherland
Production supervisor: Laura Bast
Production editor: Natalie Berchem

Copy editor: Cindy Fujimoto
Permissions editor: Monika Schurmann
Typesetter: SPi Global
Text designer: Tara Agnerian
Proofreader: Marg Anne Morrison
Indexer: Marnie Lamb
Cover image: Rynio Productions/Shutterstock

Library and Archives Canada Cataloguing in Publication

Boyd, Neil, 1951-, author
   Understanding crime in Canada : an introduction to criminology / Neil
   Boyd. — Second edition.

Includes index.
ISBN 978-1-77255-400-7 (softcover)

   1. Criminology—Canada—Textbooks.   2. Crime—Canada—Textbooks.   3. Crime—Canada—Case studies.   4. Textbooks.   I. Title

HV6807.B67 2019   364.971   C2018-905879-X

Brief Contents

PART ONE Foundations of Criminology

PART TWO Theories of Crime

Contents

PART THREE   Types of Crime

Figures and Tables

Preface

For the past 40 years, I have taught in the School of Criminology at Simon Fraser University. During that time, I have seen criminology studied from many different vantage points. I have seen a range of psychological, sociological, and biological analyses of crime; I have seen crime conceptualized as a matter of choice, and I have seen, in quite a different vein, feminist critiques and critical analyses of both crime and the creation of law, again from a range of perspectives.

All of these perspectives have helped me to improve my understanding of crime, and it is, accordingly, a breadth of perspectives that I am hoping to convey within this textbook. When I first began teaching criminology courses in the late 1970s, I was somewhat more narrowly focused, mostly interested in the continuing evolution of law and attempts to understand its twists and turns—sometimes over centuries and sometimes within the space of a decade.

But the great benefit of having spent virtually all of my professional life in the School of Criminology at Simon Fraser has been the exposure to a range of theories and studies of substantive types of crime. I suppose this text reflects my education over the past four decades, and if there is a message in its content, it is that criminology is a realm of study that can usefully house many disparate perspectives.

My colleague Rob Gordon, the former director of the School of Criminology, has always been fond of referring to a "big tent" approach to the study of crime, noting that all credible forms of inquiry are to be welcomed. But, he has always been quick to add, please don't burn the tent down; if you try that approach, you will no longer be welcome within it.

Professor Gordon's admonition flows from his knowledge of the many conflicts that have emerged within criminology: positivist versus critical criminology, quantitative versus qualitative methodologies, crime control versus due process, and so on. Most of these conflicts have been healthy and stimulating—depending, of course, on the tolerances of those who hold opposing points of view.

Disagreements among criminologists over the very definition of the term "terrorism" provide yet another example of the type of conflicts and debates referred to above. This debate is discussed in Chapter 19, 21st-Century Crimes: Cybercrime and Terrorism, new to this edition. The subject of cybercrime is both important and troubling, as it is clear that we have not yet begun to even count credit card theft, identity theft, hacking, and attempts to defraud via telephone and email as the crimes that they are: predatory acts that are not typically reported to police but have significant negative consequences for those who are victimized.

I am indebted to the many authors who have contributed to this text, bringing carefully constructed overviews of their topics to introductory students and reflecting a substantial range of viewpoints. My message to students is that there is no singular criminology, and that they will benefit from understanding different theoretical perspectives, different methodological approaches, and different types of crime. This book will have accomplished its purpose if students emerge from their reading of it with the sense that the world of crime is not black or white but is better analyzed and understood as flowing from a rich and, I hope, satisfying mix of competing values, perspectives, theories, and methodologies.

Neil Boyd
Professor
School of Criminology
Simon Fraser University

Acknowledgments

The publisher and author wish to thank the following people for providing reviewer feedback and suggestions on the first edition of this book: Heidi Currie (Douglas College and Columbia College), Cindy Gervais (Fleming College), Deborah Landry (University of Ottawa), Michael Seredycz (MacEwan University), Eva Silden (Camosun College), and Andreas Tomaszewski (Mount Royal University). Special thanks to Barry Cartwright (Simon Fraser University) for his editorial assistance.

For Instructors

For additional information and resources, please visit the accompanying website for this book at http://emond.ca/crim2. The "Updates" tab on this site provides links to current news stories, commentary, legislation, cases, and other relevant information to enhance and update the content of this book.

For information on obtaining the teaching resources available to instructors who have chosen this book for their courses, visit the "For Instructors" tab on this book's website. These resources include PowerPoint slides, test bank, sample syllabus, image bank, additional case studies, and more.

About the Authors

Neil Boyd (lead author and editor) is a professor in the School of Criminology at Simon Fraser University, where he teaches courses related to law, crime, and criminal justice policy. He is a frequent media commentator on crime-related subjects, and is the author of seven books, along with numerous government reports and academic articles. He is the recipient of several awards, including Honorary Director of the B.C. Civil Liberties Association and the President's Award for Contributions to the Media and Public Relations from Simon Fraser University.

Valerie Steeves is a professor in the Department of Criminology at the University of Ottawa. **Trevor Scott Milford** is a sessional lecturer in the Department of Sociology and Anthropology at Carleton University.

Craig Jones is a professor in the Faculty of Law at Thompson Rivers University.

Hilary Kim Morden is a sessional lecturer and graduate researcher in the School of Criminology at Simon Fraser University. **Ted Palys** is a professor in the School of Criminology at Simon Fraser University.

Hannah Scott is a professor in the Faculty of Social Science and Humanities at the University of Ontario Institute of Technology.

Barry Cartwright is a senior lecturer in the School of Criminology at Simon Fraser University.

Jonathan Heidt is an associate professor in the School of Criminology at the University of the Fraser Valley.

Gail S. Anderson is a professor and associate director of undergraduate programs in the School of Criminology at Simon Fraser University.

Fiona M. Kay is a professor in the Department of Sociology at Queen's University.

Jeff Shantz is a professor in the Criminology Department at Kwantlen Polytechnic University.

Graham Farrell is professor of International and Comparative Criminology at the School of Law, Leeds University. **Tarah Hodgkinson** is a PhD candidate in the School of Criminology at Simon Fraser University.

Sara Thompson is an associate professor in the Department of Criminology at Ryerson University and associate director of the Canadian Network for Research on Terrorism, Security and Society.

Lisa Murphy is coordinator of the Sexual Behaviours Clinic, Integrated Forensic Program, at the Royal Ottawa Mental Health Centre. **J.P. Fedoroff** is director of the Sexual Behaviours Clinic at the Royal Ottawa Mental Health Care Group and head of the Division of Forensic Psychiatry at the University of Ottawa.

Bill O'Grady is a professor in the Department of Sociology and Anthropology at the University of Guelph. **Ryan Lafleur** is a recent Sociology PhD graduate from the University of Guelph and has taught at King's College and the University of Guelph.

Andrew D. Hathaway is an associate professor in the Department of Sociology and Anthropology at the University of Guelph. **Amir Mostaghim** is an assistant teaching professor in the Faculty of Social Science and Humanities at the University of Ontario Institute of Technology.

Scot Wortley is graduate coordinator and an associate professor of criminology at the Centre for Criminology and Sociolegal Studies at the University of Toronto. **Adam Ellis** is a PhD candidate and Vanier Scholar at the Centre for Criminology and Sociolegal Studies at the University of Toronto.

Poonam Puri is a professor at Osgoode Hall Law School, York University. **Simon Kupi** is a regulatory lawyer at Dentons Canada LLP in Calgary.

Ryan Scrivens is an assistant professor in the School of Criminal Justice at Michigan State University. **Martin Bouchard** is a professor at the School of Criminology, Simon Fraser University and director of the CaIN Lab (Crime and Illicit Networks Laboratory).

PART ONE

Foundations of Criminology

Criminology in Action: The Legalization of Cannabis

After being illegal for almost a century, cannabis has now been legalized in Canada. The new law, the *Cannabis Act*, was given royal assent in June 2018, and retail sale of cannabis began in October 2018.

As the following chapter notes, the criminalization of certain kinds of conduct has changed over time—the distribution of alcohol is no longer a crime, nor is homosexual conduct, and

Former chief of the Ontario Provincial Police and Toronto Police Service Julian Fantino (middle) celebrates the opening of his cannabis business. Fantino was previously known for his tough-on-crime stance, including support for drug prohibition.

neither is a physician's act of performing an abortion or the act of a physician in assisting in the death of a terminally ill patient. At the same time, we have seen new forms of criminalization over the past few decades—penalties for child sexual exploitation on the Internet, offences relating to violations of the confidentiality and availability of computer data, identity theft, and identity fraud.

How are we to understand what happened with the legalization of cannabis? The drug was criminalized by Canada in 1923, with no discussion taking place in the House of Commons regarding the new law. The only mention was a single statement: "There is a new drug in the schedule." (*Debates*, p. 2124) In 1923, cannabis was virtually unknown in Canada. An Edmonton magistrate, Emily Murphy, wrote a book in 1922 called *The Black Candle*, in which she condemned the traffic in cocaine and opium, linking their distribution to the Chinese and to Black people in America. This was described in racist terms as an attempt to injure "the bright browed races of the world" (p. 88). One chapter in *The Black Candle* was titled "Marijuana—The New Menace." She told her readers that marijuana use could lead to unimaginable violence and was also likely to produce insanity in its users.

From 1923 to 1961 penalties related to cannabis (and to cocaine and opiates) escalated dramatically. All were described in the *Narcotic Control Act of 1961* as "narcotics," though only opiates actually fit such a pharmacological description. And the *Narcotic Control Act of 1961* provided a maximum term of life imprisonment for those who distributed these "narcotics," an increase from the maximum penalty of 14 years' imprisonment that had been set out in 1954.

It was perhaps ironic that just five years later, in 1966, cannabis use increased dramatically in Canada, in the face of the most severe penalties our country had ever enacted. The initial response of the judiciary, when faced with an annual toll of 1,000 convictions for possession of cannabis, was to sentence about half of all those convicted to significant terms of imprisonment.

This "get tough" approach to cannabis was not successful. By 1975, there were 40,000 convictions annually for cannabis possession, and fines, probation, and absolute and conditional discharges were handed down in more than 90 percent of cases; imprisonment became a rarity.

In the late 1960s and throughout the 1970s, cannabis was an export-import business in Canada. Very little cannabis was produced domestically, and both cannabis and hashish were exported from many different countries around the globe: hashish from Lebanon and Afghanistan, cannabis from Thailand, Mexico, the United States, and Colombia. By the late 1980s, however, the export-import industry began to give way to domestic production, both indoors and outdoors. Cannabis of higher potency was produced, along with a greater variety of strains. A similar transformation took place in the United States and in many other Western nation-states.

Government responses to these kinds of changes first began in 1969, with the appointment of the LeDain Commission by then Prime Minister Pierre Trudeau. The Commission reported back to the federal government in 1972, recommending both the elimination of criminal penalties for possession and support for permitting cultivation for personal use. These changes were not acted upon by the federal government, but the judiciary and the police gradually began to change societal responses to cannabis use through police discretion in not always bringing charges forward and through the judicial imposition of much less punitive sentences after conviction.

By the 1990s, the domestic production of cannabis was well established and a variety of advocacy groups had formed, urging the legalization of cannabis and holding annual rallies in Vancouver (for example, the 4/20 event held on April 20), at which cannabis was openly consumed by thousands of individuals.

It had become clear, not only through scientific inquiry but also through the knowledge of millions of experientially informed consumers, that cannabis was much less of a threat to public health than more commonly used and legal recreational drugs, notably alcohol and tobacco.

During the federal election campaign of 2015, the Liberal party, led by Justin Trudeau, promised to legalize cannabis if elected. When they became government in the fall of that year, with a strong majority, they began to set in motion the steps that would lead to legalization. The government indicated that they wanted legalization to accomplish two objectives: the elimination of the illicit market and a reduction in youth access to cannabis. A task force was constructed, and it reported to government in the fall of 2016, recommending a system that would monitor the supply of the drug to avoid pesticides and other contaminants, provide labelling to indicate the potency of the product in terms of both THC and CBD levels, and avoid advertising or promotion of the product. All cannabis was to be produced by "licensed producers" who would have the ability to sell their products across the country via mail order. Individual provinces would determine the age required for purchase and the kind of retail, beyond mail order, that might be provided. The task force recommended that cannabis and alcohol not be sold from the same store, given the synergistic impacts of consuming both drugs. The task force also recommended that a maximum of four plants could be grown in individual dwellings.

The *Cannabis Act* was introduced in the House of Commons in April 2017 and made its way through both the House and the Senate, and a significant number of committee hearings before receiving royal assent in June 2018. Most of the recommendations of the task force are embodied in the legislation. The federal government has control of the supply chain; only the products of licensed producers may be sold, via mail order or through provincial systems of retail. The provinces set the age for purchase (it will vary from 18 to 19 years of age, depending on the province) and determine, usually along with municipalities, what kinds of retail (private or public stores) will be allowed.

Canada is only the second country in the world to legalize cannabis, following Uruguay's lead in 2013. More important, however, has been the experience in a number of US states. Washington and Colorado legalized cannabis, and sales have been taking place since 2014. More recently, California and Oregon have legalized it, meaning that almost 25 percent of Americans now live in jurisdictions where cannabis is legal.

What should we be studying as legalization unfolds in Canada? There are many interesting and important questions. Will the illicit market slowly disappear? How much enforcement and regulation will be required to encourage the disappearance of this market? Will youth access increase, decrease, or stay about the same? Will adult use increase? Will driving impaired by cannabis increase, decrease, or stay at about the same level? And finally, what will happen to the criminal records of the hundreds of thousands of Canadians who were convicted of cannabis possession? Will these records be expunged, allowing these individuals to escape from the travel and employment disabilities that often follow from criminal conviction? As criminologists, we will want to study a range of impacts of this significant change in criminal justice policy.

Before You Read Chapter 1

- What kinds of criminological study are mentioned in this case study?
- Why is this a worthwhile case study for criminologists to examine? What larger questions or issues does it raise for anyone studying crime?
- What other kinds of current crimes might be decriminalized or legalized in the future?
- Is the criminalization of cannabis analogous to the criminalization of other currently illegal drugs?

What Is Criminology?

LEARNING OUTCOMES

After reading this chapter, students will be able to:

- Identify the various disciplines and areas of study that formed the foundation of modern criminology.

- Explain the social, cultural, and demographic trends in the 20th century that led to the rise in prominence of criminology as an area of study.

- Identify the range of subjects that criminologists study and the corresponding range of approaches they take to study crime.

CHAPTER OUTLINE

Introduction

The *Oxford Reference Dictionary* defines criminology quite simply as the "scientific study of crime." More specifically, the word "crime" is derived from the Latin word "crimen," and the "-ology" tacked onto our English "crimin" refers us to the study of crime.

The behaviours that are at the heart of crime have been a part of human conduct for as long as we have lived on the planet as *Homo sapiens*. In pre-state societies, there were assaults, robberies, thefts, and homicides—the kinds of activities that we regard today as criminal and punishable by the state.

But **criminology**—the scientific study of crime—is a relatively recent development. Although one can point to the Code of Hammurabi or the pronouncements of the Roman republic as examples of early codifications of crime, or to the work of an 18th century philosopher of punishment such as Cesare Beccaria, the study of crime itself did not really begin in any systematic way until the 19th century (Rafter, 2009). And even then there was not a great deal of coherence within the field, a phenomenon that arguably continues in the present. The German psychiatrist Krafft-Ebing wrote of sexual deviations, the Italian anthropologist Lombroso wrote of criminal man, and the French sociologist Durkheim wrote much more broadly of the normalcy of crime in all human societies. It's also fair to note that criminology began, within a global context, as a subset of the discipline of sociology.

criminology
The study of crime and criminal behaviour, which are defined by reference to criminal law.

Criminology as an Academic Discipline

In Canada, the study of crime in universities began during the 1950s, at the University of British Columbia. The new program in criminology was announced in 1954, originating from the division of sociology within the Department of Economics, Political Science and Sociology. The spur for the development of the new program was an emerging sense that correctional efforts—the rehabilitation of offenders—were going to be assisted by an accumulating body of knowledge (Parkinson, 2008). The proponents of the program argued that offenders could no longer be seen as "born criminals," and they pointed to the local Haney Correctional Centre as the site of an emerging progressive correctional administration that was concerned about developing educational and vocational programs, maintaining family and community ties for offenders, and developing programs of probation and parole.

Although this program was short-lived, closing in 1959 and becoming part of the School of Social Work, the impetus for the study of crime in Canada, and in other Western nation-states, was clearly building. In 1963, Denis Szabo declared the arrival of "a new discipline" and "a new profession" at the Université de Montréal. Similarly, also in 1963, the Centre of Criminology at the University of Toronto was established as a research entity by J.L.J. Edwards. In 1967, Tadeusz Grygier established the Department of Criminology at the University of Ottawa as an applied interdisciplinary program, with courses to be offered in both English and French. And in 1973, Simon Fraser University's School of Criminology, led by a former faculty member of the Université de Montréal, Ezzat Fattah, began to offer its program, again interdisciplinary in structure. Additionally, from the 1960s to the present, criminology programs emerged within departments of sociology at many universities, focused on understanding crime as a form of **deviance** and then studying the processes of defining criminal law, the social precursors to involvement in crime, and the potential range of appropriate and/or effective responses to law breakers.

deviance
Behaviour that differs from accepted social norms; it may include acts that violate specific rules (crime), sexual behaviours, or non-criminal acts that challenge accepted values.

The Emergence of Criminology in the Postwar Era: The Social Backdrop

These developments necessarily raise the question of why, during the 1960s and 1970s, the study of crime emerged as a subject of scholarly inquiry, no longer limited to the relatively exclusive purview of philosophers, theologians, and politicians. Canada was not the only nation-state in which this kind of rapid growth of the discipline occurred. In both the United States and the United Kingdom, the study of crime emerged as both a burgeoning and contested form of academic inquiry (Laub, 2004; Taylor, Walton, & Young, 1973).

Urbanization and industrialization were key features of social life in Canada, the United Kingdom, and the United States during the late 19th and early 20th centuries. There was substantial migration from rural areas to urban areas and the creation of new categories of crime, which were often directed at the behaviours of the urban poor: new proscriptions against vagrancy, drunkenness, and prostitution. The early 20th century also witnessed the beginnings of globalization—immigration in the form of inexpensive labour arriving from China, Japan, and the developing world. And these new immigrants represented an economic threat to established labour. They also brought long-established parts of their cultures with them to their new world—smoking opium from China, hashish from India, and coca and cocaine from South America. These alternatives to tobacco and alcohol were resisted and criminally prohibited, and laws were passed to aid deportation of "foreign drug pedlars" and to restrict immigration.

Put differently, the culture was changing. It was more urban and more global, and these changes created tensions. With increased literacy and increased access to information there were also challenges for the perpetuation of long-established institutions. The practice of capital punishment began to be criticized, public executions moved behind closed doors, out of sight of the population, and reformers began to urge more humane treatment of law breakers, and to ask for more economic support for the urban poor.

By the end of the Second World War, social conflicts had become social threats. Global annihilation now appeared as a possibility, underlined by the Cold War between two dominant global powers, the United States and the Soviet Union. And so began the 1960s. Crime rates began to escalate in a time of youth rebellion. Young people were urged to "make love, not war" in the wake of the US entry into Vietnam, while Timothy Leary urged experimentation with a counter-cultural grouping of mind-active drugs. "Tune in, turn on, and drop out" was his rallying cry. There was also a **demographic** shift of some relevance. The percentage of young men within the populations of Canada, the United States, and the United Kingdom increased dramatically, beginning in the mid-1960s. The so-called baby boomers, born between 1946 and 1964, entered their crime-prone years (between the ages of 15 to 29) in the mid-1960s. In every era of human history, and in every part of the world today, young men commit a disproportionate amount of crime relative to other age cohorts. It was perhaps not surprising, then, that in the postwar era, with this explosion in the relative contribution of young men to national populations, that crime rates should rise, though there has also been considerable debate within criminological literature as to the statistical importance of this demographic shift (Fox, 2000; Marvell & Moody, 1991).

demographics
Statistical data relating to characteristics of a population, such as relative size of age groups, gender balance, or any other measurable information.

correlation
The finding that two measurable phenomena occur together, suggesting a relationship, but not necessarily one of direct cause and effect.

BOX 1.1

Correlates of Crime

As we will see in Chapter 4, Measuring Crime, a full understanding of the prevalence of crime is highly dependent on how crime is defined and how it is then reported to, processed, and counted by police. It is safe to say, however, that young men—not just in Canada today, but in most times and places throughout history—tend to commit a disproportionate amount of crime, as Figure 1.1 illustrates. Both age and sex can be seen in this figure as important **correlates** of crime; that is, they are factors that do not *cause* crime, but they are strongly linked to criminal behaviour. Simply put, young men make contributions to crime statistics that are remarkably disproportionate to the size of their population in Canada, the United States, the United Kingdom, and elsewhere.

Several other correlates of crime will be discussed at relevant points in this book, including, for example, the disproportionate representation of poverty, race, and income inequality within certain criminal justice statistics. The difficult task for criminologists is to try to understand the significance of these correlations. They do not express cause-and-effect relationships, but responding to this information, and understanding the meanings of these relationships, is important in the construction of an effective criminal justice policy.

FIGURE 1.1   Cases Completed in Adult Criminal Court, by Age Group and Sex of the Accused, Canada, 2014–2015

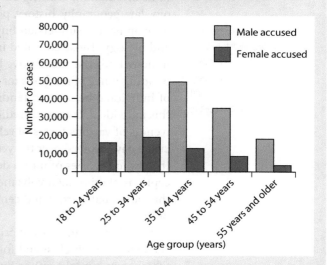

Source: Maxwell (2017, Chart 9).

At the same time, alcohol consumption was increasing dramatically, approximately 50 percent per capita between 1966 and 1975. The birth control pill had also dramatically changed male–female relationships with its emergence in the mid-1960s, allowing women to experiment with sex without the risk of pregnancy and outside of marriage. Not surprisingly, rates of divorce, aided by more social acceptance of the dissolution of marriage, increased four-fold, again within the space of a decade. Added to that social upheaval, young women were leaving the family or marital home for the workplace. In Canada, the number of women in the labour force increased from 2.2 million in 1966 to more than 5.5 million in 1975. These were dramatic social changes for both men and women, and they weren't always easy to accept, particularly for men (Boyd, 1988).

Crime rates—perhaps understandably, given this backdrop—were increasing dramatically (see Figure 12.2 in Chapter 12, Crime Choice Theory). There were many ways in which the social changes of the 20th century, particularly those of the post–Second World War era, created the social conditions in which criminology emerged as an academic discipline. What was to be done about the use of cannabis and these other drugs, flowing from far-flung regions of the globe? What was to be done about the conflict between youth and the generation of their parents? What was to be done about the increasing disintegration of marriage and the problems of domestic violence? What was to be done about the new roles of women? Criminology entered the fray with multiple and sometimes conflicting agendas: controlling crime, reducing conflict, emancipating women and youth, and evaluating policies that might best respond to these new realities.

Criminology: A Discipline or a New Home for Already Established Disciplines?

What does it mean to be a criminologist? The field has typically been interdisciplinary in its orientation, drawing on long-established disciplines such as sociology, psychology, law, geography, history, political science, and economics, and more recently, with developments in understanding DNA and **forensic entomology**, the fields of chemistry and biology. Those educated in all of these realms tend to bring to the study of criminology both the substantive base of knowledge from their disciplines and a corresponding range of methods for undertaking academic inquiry. Psychology, as the study of individual behaviour, tends to focus on the criminal individual, often classifying this individual, trying to predict the risk of reoffending, and then evaluating the effectiveness of various forms of rehabilitation or treatment. Psychological explanations of crime have evolved over the years, moving from Freudian psychoanalysis to personality theory, to theories of moral development, and, more recently, to developmental conceptions of criminal involvement (Moffitt, 1993). In all of these constructions of crime, the individual is front and centre: An individual's psyche and behaviours are the focus of the study of crime.

Sociological analyses of crime are, not surprisingly, focused on the social order—the extent to which social forces work to define crime, and to create conditions in which crime might either flourish or diminish. Sociological analyses of crime are essentially trying to understand how the social context of our lives works to create law and certain kinds of crime and crime rates, as well as to point to social and structural

forensic entomology
The study of insects to assist in legal investigations; insects found on a corpse can help identify facts about the time and place of the victim's death.

changes that might be made in order to effectively respond to the challenges that crime presents. Sociology has, historically, been the dominant paradigm within criminology, giving rise, among other conceptions, to social control theory, labelling theory, differential association, notions of anomie, and, more recently, to a range of critical theories of crime: moral panics and the culture of control, Marxian and neo-Marxian analysis, Foucaldian perspectives, and post-modern conceptions of **criminality**. For as long as criminology has been a subject for academic inquiry, social analyses of crime, law, and deviance have tended to be pre-eminent. Crime and criminal conduct have been regarded as more likely to be driven by social conditions than by individual aberrations.

criminality
The state of being criminal; criminal acts or practices.

BOX 1.2

Shifting Concepts of Deviance

All societies define some behaviours as deviant, and some of these deviant behaviours are also regarded, through the further step of criminalization by the state, as crimes. These shifting definitions of deviance and crime can differ markedly across societies. For example, some nations regard alcohol consumption as both deviant and criminal; others regard sexuality outside of marriage as deviant and, in some circumstances, as criminal and deserving of severe penalties.

The history of crime teaches us that deviance, and crime itself, are both malleable constructions. In late 19th-century Canada, homosexuality was illegal and punishable by imprisonment. Today, however, gay marriage is legal, and we have openly gay politicians, celebrities, and an ever-growing number of athletes and other public figures. (Meanwhile, in some countries, particularly several in Africa, punishment for homosexuality has recently grown *more* severe, including life imprisonment—which illustrates how tolerance and definitions of deviance can trend in the opposite direction.)

Similarly, doctors who performed abortions in 19th-century Canada were subject to criminal conviction and even faced the possibility of a death sentence. Canadians have also debated in recent years whether some kinds of illegal drug use should properly be regarded as criminal and/or deviant. This debate culminated in the recreational use of cannabis becoming legal in Canada in 2018 after the Liberal Party made legalization one of their campaign promises in the 2015 election campaign. It had become clear, as countless politicians and other "law-abiding" people admitted to smoking pot, that the general public

no longer considered this to be criminal behaviour. Today, cannabis is largely considered to be like alcohol and tobacco—a potential risk to an individual's health that should be subject to some regulation, but not generally considered a crime deserving of punishment, and not a deviant act in the opinion of most people.

Michael Leshner and Michael Stark celebrate a court's decision allowing them to wed. In 2003, they became the first legally married same-sex couple in Canada. This landmark decision was one clear illustration of how social attitudes had shifted in recent decades.

The study of law is also central to the study of criminology, as it defines the landscape of crime, setting out the specifics of prohibited behaviours and the penalties that may attach to various acts of law breaking. The history of law provides insight into the changing nature of crime, allowing students to come to terms with the malleable nature of some forms of deviance, and the evolving nature of what might be viewed as appropriate responses to crime. A consideration of the evolution of criminal law provides insight into the creation of new forms of criminality. For example, legal analysis allows for discussion of the emergence of a global prohibition of certain mind-active drugs in the early 20th century, an experiment that began as a moral crusade against intolerable harms, but is now facing difficult challenges to both its empirical logic and its corresponding moral underpinnings. Similarly, study of the history of criminal law allows students to view changing responses to long-established and universally condemned forms of conduct. For example, in Canada in the latter half of the 19th century, capital punishment was regarded in law as an appropriate punishment not only for murder but for many other crimes. Study of subsequent amendments to criminal law, and the debates that surrounded these amendments, allows students to reflect on not only changing approaches to the punishment of crime, but also on the logic and utility of these changing approaches.

The disciplines of history, geography, political science, and economics have, historically, been less central to the study of criminology than psychology, sociology, and law, but they have each made different kinds of contributions. The social and spatial geography of crime have been critical to the development of programs of crime prevention through environmental design, and to the tracking of serial predatory offenders across time and space (Brantingham & Brantingham, 1984; Rossmo, 1999).

Detailed histories of crime, law, and criminal behaviours have permitted greater understanding of the utility of law and a range of various legislative and policy initiatives, and of the kinds of variables that might either foster crime or serve to diminish it. More recently, the discipline of economics has also made important contributions to criminology, permitting evaluative analyses of the costs and benefits of various crime reduction initiatives. With recent developments in the utility of gathering DNA at crime scenes, and in studying key elements of the decomposition of bodies to determine time of death (forensic entomology), the fields of chemistry and biology have both become a significant part of criminology, providing evidence that can be both inculpatory and exculpatory.

Is there, however, a discipline of criminology that will, in time, displace or unite all of these long-established disciplines? Or is criminology better described simply as the study of crime, and, as such, wholly dependent on the methods and literatures of sociology, psychology, law, and other disciplines? There are now many universities across the Western world that offer MA, MSc, and PhD programs in criminology. In Canada alone, the Université de Montréal, the University of Toronto, and Simon Fraser University all currently offer doctoral programs in criminology. But can any of these institutions claim ownership of a new academic discipline?

The faculty in departments and schools of criminology do appear to represent a variety of disciplines: law, psychology, sociology, economics, and geography, and also the natural sciences. But they also have individuals with doctorates in criminology.

BOX 1.3

Why Study Crime?

Before embarking on an in-depth examination of the many aspects of criminology covered in the chapters that follow, it is worthwhile to stand back and consider several general questions about the *value* of studying crime. Thinking about these issues helps one appreciate the role that criminology plays in defining and shaping our society, and why it is important and beneficial—both for individuals and society—to understand crime and criminal behaviour.

What to criminalize and how to respond to crime?

First, we need to think about what we as a society should criminalize. The power to define a person as criminal, and then to be able to deprive that person of liberty, is an extraordinary power. We learn from the history of crime that its content is highly malleable—in Canada alone, within the past century, we have come to regard some previously criminal acts as tolerable behaviours and some forms of punishment as inappropriately harsh and counterproductive. We also know that the powers of the police and the criminal justice system have often been abused or misapplied. The questions of how the state defines and responds to crime say a great deal about our culture, and they are deserving of careful consideration.

What does the best evidence tell us about our responses to crime and their effectiveness?

There are some forms of crime that have always been defined as such: Physical offences against persons, theft, and fraud come quickly to mind. But how effective are the typical responses to these crimes? Does imprisonment for certain kinds of crime have significant impacts on crime rates—that is, is it an effective deterrent? What about probation, fines, or conditional sentences? Can

neighbourhoods and communities be designed in ways that will reduce opportunities for crime, and therefore crime itself? Do the media influence our responses to crime, and do they give us an accurate understanding of crime? These are all important questions, and criminological research can provide important insights into the utility of various approaches and the creation of sound policies.

Can the study of crime help us to respond to emerging challenges?

Since the beginning of the 21st century we have witnessed significant social changes in Western society. Concerns about terrorism since the attacks of September 11, 2001 have led to expanded security measures and surveillance, which have in turn raised fears about compromised privacy and human rights. More generally, we have seen the proliferation of the Internet and of telephones that are also computers and cameras. What are the implications of these changes for crime and crime detection? We must now contend with identity theft, Internet and telephone fraud, and more, all of it within a virtual and global context. On any given day, we all face the possibility of being victims of these new kinds of crimes. How can we effectively respond to these new challenges?

Furthermore, while crime rates have dropped in most Western nations, there is a great deal of ongoing debate about why this has happened: A simple demographic shift? A cultural shift? Improvements in technologies for combatting crime? More effective policing? Or is a large proportion of crime simply shifting to a new, virtual terrain? If we are to understand both the present and the future of our society, and determine how best to deal with these challenges, these are some of the key questions we must attempt to answer.

Perhaps the difficulty for those who argue that criminology is a separate discipline, rather than simply a particular focus of study, is, however, one of demonstrating a set of theories and methods that are specific to criminology and quite separate from those other disciplines. Some of the most recent and arguably innovative approaches within criminology—life course development theory, geographic profiling, DNA profiling, and critical criminology—can be seen to have origins in psychology, geography, chemistry, and sociology, respectively.

Criminology: What Do We Study?

As criminology is home to a host of disciplines, it is not surprising that the questions that criminologists ask tend to vary significantly, and this in part depends on the field of their training and in part depends on the lens or framework through which they understand the realities of crime. This issue of what to study takes us back to the social and political backdrop against which the study of criminology emerged in the 1960s and 1970s. Crime rates were rising, and the social conflicts described earlier in this chapter did set the stage for a more rigorous analysis of crime. Perhaps not surprisingly, though, the questions of what to study and how to study produced multiple responses, as they still do today.

criminalization
To define an act as a crime and thereby subject that act to formal punishment.

For example, the process of **criminalization** itself has been subject to considerable scrutiny. The criminalization of the possession and distribution of certain kinds of drugs is an ongoing process that has produced a considerable amount of research, as has the criminalization and subsequent decriminalization of abortion and the contested criminalization of the trade in sexual services. In each of these instances, criminologists have examined the legal history of criminalization and its consequences, but they have also considered the effectiveness of the law, its intended and unintended consequences, the harms imposed by these illegal activities, and the harms imposed by the laws that control these activities.

In these contested terrains of criminal law, the disciplinary background of the criminologist remains critical. A historian will canvass and catalogue the emergence of law and legal amendments in substantial detail, attempting to explain the social, political, and economic context of changing law. A psychologist will consider the harms to the individual, not only from involvement in these typically consensual activities, but also from the law itself. An economist will consider the cost effectiveness of various sanctions. Does, for example, the provision of a supervised injection site for injection drug users reduce health care costs through avoidance of HIV and hepatitis C infections?

But once we move away from the contested terrains of crime—from those forms of conduct that might be viewed as socially tolerable and capable of regulation rather than as unacceptable behaviours deserving of the possibility of imprisonment—the focus of inquiry becomes quite different.

Crime Rates: Why Do They Go Up? Why Do They Go Down?

Since 1960, we have amassed a considerable amount of data reported by police (for example, the Canadian Uniform Crime Reporting Survey [UCR]) that documents the extent of particular types of crime. We are now able to look back for decades from the present, using data from dozens of nation-states, in order to determine whether specific types of crimes have increased or decreased over time within specific jurisdictions. We can also compare different nation-states over time to determine whether the trends observed are crossing national boundaries.

For more on the UCR Survey, see Chapter 4.

We have learned that the reliability of these police data vary: Reports of homicides do tend to have a very close relationship to the actual number of homicides committed in most jurisdictions. But police reports of theft, assault, and even sexual assault may represent a minority of all such incidents, depending on willingness to report the particular crime, perceived significance of the incident, and both individual and societal attitudes toward involvement with police and the **criminal justice system**. Fortunately, we also have a considerable amount of additional data generated by surveys of individual victimization that documents the extent of crime experienced by a random selection of citizens in a given jurisdiction (for example, the *General Social Survey* [Statistics Canada, 2013]). The combination of police reports of crime and ongoing surveys of criminal victimization provides a more complete and nuanced understanding of changing crime rates.

Criminologists study these changing crime rates in order to provide explanations for increases and decreases. Put differently, what variables produce an increase in certain kinds of crime, and, more important, having understood what drives crime rates up, what can we do to push them in the opposite direction? Alternatively, once crime rates have fallen, what can we attribute this to? And how can we produce more of the same? Much has been written, for example, about the crime drop experienced in Canada and the United States from the 1990s to the present (Blumstein & Wallman, 2000; Farrell, Tilley, Tseloni, & Mailley, 2011; Pinker, 2011).

What we have learned is that patterns of increase and decrease in crime rates are not universal; the explanations for these increases or decreases vary for different types of crime and are not consistent across nation-states. For example, motor vehicle theft has dropped significantly over the past 15 years, largely because improvements in motor vehicle alarm and access technology have made the possibility of theft much less likely (Kriven & Ziersch, 2007).

But why have homicides in Canada and the United States dropped to almost half the rates experienced in the late 1970s? There are many different explanations (Pinker, 2011; Zimring, 2006) but no universally accepted accounting for this change. We can point to a vast amount of correlational data regarding crime rates and other variables, but cause–effect descriptions and conclusions are simply not possible. Nonetheless, the tracking of crime and attempts to explain increases and decreases, notably the increases of the late 1960s and the early 1970s, and the decreases of the past 20 years, are a critical focus for criminology. If we are to reduce the impact that crime has on our everyday lives, we need to understand how and why particular kinds of crime increase and decrease over time. It is, for example, not surprising to learn that while many forms of personal and property crime have declined markedly over the past 20 years, online victimization, identity theft, and credit card fraud have all dramatically increased (United Nations Office on Drugs and Crime, 2013). Further, credit card companies do not typically report these fraudulent activities to police, leading us to underestimate one critical area of increase in property crime.

Studying Criminals and Their Pathways to Crime

An important part of criminology, beyond understanding the creation of criminal law and concomitant penalties, and beyond understanding changing crime rates, is the task of understanding why particular individuals commit crime and, in some circumstances, continue to do so. What, for example, are the characteristics of those convicted of crime, and why do some people commit a significant amount of crime, while others do not?

criminal justice system
The various institutions and processes through which an offender passes, such as the police, the courts, and correctional facilities and programs.

FIGURE 1.2   Criminology, Criminal Justice, and Deviance

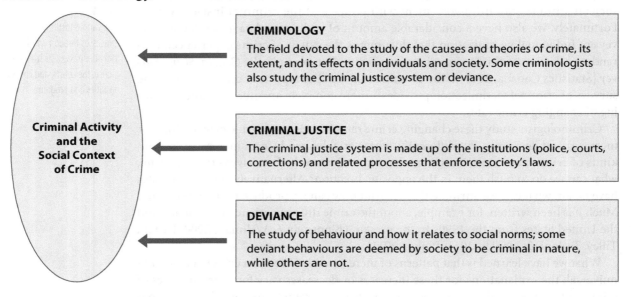

CRIMINOLOGY
The field devoted to the study of the causes and theories of crime, its extent, and its effects on individuals and society. Some criminologists also study the criminal justice system or deviance.

CRIMINAL JUSTICE
The criminal justice system is made up of the institutions (police, courts, corrections) and related processes that enforce society's laws.

DEVIANCE
The study of behaviour and how it relates to social norms; some deviant behaviours are deemed by society to be criminal in nature, while others are not.

We've learned that most people convicted of crime are male and relatively young (typically between the ages of 15 to 34); they also tend to have few resources and little education. Early criminologists like Cesare Lombroso argued for the heritability of crime—a conception of a "born criminal," while William Sheldon argued in the mid-1950s that body type or somatotyping is strongly linked to criminal behaviour, with well-muscled mesomorphs more likely to commit criminal offences. Neither of these conceptions linking biology to criminality were able to find much empirical support, but research in the past 20 to 30 years has begun to regard criminal conduct as a complex mix of both biology and environment.

traits
Those attributes or features that distinguish or characterize an individual.

It appears that some individuals have personality **traits** and characteristics that predispose them to crime (Raine, 2013), but biology does not predetermine criminality. A series of studies of adopted children and identical twins raised apart have prompted some rethinking of the relative significance of environment in predisposing individuals to involvement in crime. When Sarnoff Mednick, William Gabrielli Jr., and Barry Hutchings (1984) discovered, after considering a sample of more than 14,000 Danish adoptions, that these children were significantly more likely to commit crime if their biological fathers had criminal records—trumping the influence of the criminal records held by the adopted fathers who raised them—the findings were denounced in some quarters and met with disbelief in others. But other research has served to confirm the thrust of this finding. Although our tendency has been to view crime as environmental in origin, research data suggest that our biology can also create challenges and predispositions that can, in some circumstances, outweigh environmental influences. Again, while biology may not be determinative, we are learning that it is not as unimportant as was once thought. Just as intellectual and athletic abilities are widely acknowledged to have a genetic backdrop, we are now accepting that difficult personalities can have a biological origin (Raine, 2013).

We have also learned that acquired trauma can have a significant impact on predispositions to crime. Frontal lobe damage, for example, has now been clearly linked to an increase in the likelihood of impulsively aggressive behaviour (Brower & Price, 2001). And the prevalence of brain injuries in prison populations has been very clearly identified as both disproportionate to the general population and a significant risk factor for reoffending (Raine, 2013).

In studying the criminal and pathways to crime, criminologists have come to appreciate the complex mix of biological predisposition and environmental influences, permitting a more nuanced analysis of the genesis of crime. We now tend to regard biological risks, whether in the realm of a psychopathic personality, brain injury, or the complex mix of mental health and substance abuse difficulties, as having a synergistic relationship with a dysfunctional environment, a social backdrop often characterized by physical and emotional abuse and neglect.

Further, study of the criminal has also allowed us the opportunity to understand that there is often little **empirical** support for some of our populist conceptions. Just as during the 1960s and 1970s we came to reject the simplicity of Lombroso's criminal man and Sheldon's somatotyping, we have more recently come to realize that adult sex offenders are not specialists in that particular kind of crime—that is, men who predominantly commit a relatively narrow range of predatory sex offences.

empirical
That which is understood or verified through experiment, measurement, or direct observation; as opposed to theoretical.

Sex offenders are, rather, a much more diverse population, their crimes encompassing a range of offences, from incest and inappropriate touching to predatory attacks on strangers; predatory attacks on strangers are actually very rare events (Bonnar-Kidd, 2010; Bonnycastle, 2012). Sex offenders (with the notable exception of pedophiles) also tend not to specialize in sex offences; they are more accurately classified as antisocial deviants who commit a range of crimes, some of which happen to be sex offences (Lussier, Tzoumakis, Cale, & Amirault, 2010). We've also learned that most sex offenders have relatively low rates of reoffending, again contrary to populist conceptions (Hanson & Bussière, 1998). These findings raise important questions, for example, about the empirical logic of a sex offender registry. Why, we might ask, do we have a sex offender registry that houses such a varied range of offenders, particularly when the rates of reoffending for most of these kinds of crime are actually much lower than for other crimes?

It's clear, then, that much can be learned through the study of offenders, sometimes leading to findings that conflict with popular misconceptions and societal biases. And although those who study the individual offender are often criticized for failing to take account of social conditions and thereby inadvertently demonizing and **stigmatizing** offenders, it can also be argued that this kind of research can serve to create an improved understanding of the difficulties that offenders face, and the challenges that we have, correspondingly, in responding appropriately and humanely to their circumstances. Studies focused on offenders can also allow us to understand when young men and women are at risk of involvement in crime, and this understanding may help us find ways to prevent the harms that these individuals are likely to impose upon others and upon themselves.

stigmatize
To strongly disapprove of a person or behaviour; to find disgraceful.

Technologies of Crime Control: Criminology in Aid of Detection and Avoidance of Crime

The study of criminology has also produced innovative and potentially valuable technologies for the control of crime; a rich academic literature has developed within this realm, documenting not only the techniques, but also their costs, benefits, and potential limitations.

Crime prevention through environmental design (CPTED) is a term that was originally set out by the late criminologist C. Ray Jeffery (Jeffery, 1971). It is, essentially, a multidisciplinary approach, and almost all of these **interventions** appear in an urban environment, using, among other initiatives, landscape and lighting design to increase natural surveillance. Crime prevention through environmental design seeks to manage crime by decreasing both the opportunity for a crime to occur and an individual's motivation to commit crime, and by simultaneously increasing the risk to the offender if the crime is to be committed. There is a considerable body of empirical evidence demonstrating the utility of this approach (Casteel & Peek-Asa, 2000; Cozens, Saville, & Hillier, 2005; Felson, 1987). Further, many criminology programs now offer courses focused on the practicalities of this approach, and encourage students to both investigate and solve specific problems faced by local communities (Brantingham & Brantingham, 1993). Critics of CPTED argue, however, that environmental design can only displace crime into less-protected environments, and does not address the root causes or motivations that underlie the commission of criminal offences. Further, some critics suggest that CPTED shifts the responsibility for crime prevention away from the state and onto the individual, expecting citizens "to become prudent consumers of crime prevention advice or else face moral and/or ethical sanction for not holding up their end of the proverbial bargain" (Parnaby, 2007, p. 73).

Geographic profiling is aligned with crime prevention through environmental design, drawing upon an understanding of urban environments, the behaviours of serial predatory offenders, and using mathematical tools to determine the likely home residence of a given offender. Developed by Dr. Kim Rossmo, a former detective with Vancouver police, it is a method that focuses an investigation of serial crimes into a relatively small geographic area, through looking at the spatial patterns of such crimes and the specific hunting behaviours of the offenders (Rossmo, 1999). Although geographic profiling only considers the spatial behaviour of serial offenders, it has a demonstrated success in specific cases, and has spawned a literature that builds on the accuracy of its projections (Levine & Block, 2011).

Electronic monitoring, also known as electronic tagging, typically involves an offender wearing an electronic device that allows his or her location to be monitored through a control centre. Electronic monitoring permits both pre-trial release back into the community and the serving of a sentence within the community, often referred to as home detention. The advantages of electronic monitoring can be significant; the process avoids the costs of placing the offender in a correctional facility, and the well-documented negative impacts of incarceration on the individual. The concerns expressed regarding electronic monitoring have to do with its potential for **net widening**—imposing a form of control on individuals who might otherwise not be subject to such control—and its potential for demeaning intrusions into personal privacy. Additionally, there is the practical issue of how to respond quickly and effectively when an offender either removes the monitor or travels outside the permitted range.

Empirical studies of the effectiveness and consequences of electronic monitoring have revealed, however, that it is a technology that does not appear to be used to widen the net of control over offenders. Rather, it seems that it is an effective public safety alternative to the use of imprisonment, reducing reoffending for the population placed under such surveillance (Padgett, Bales, & Blomberg, 2006).

The trial of O.J. Simpson for the murder of his wife Nicole Brown Simpson focused global attention on the use of DNA evidence in criminal trials. Deoxyribonucleic acid

interventions
Strategies intended to shape the physical environment to mitigate crime; also various programs targeting individual offenders, offering alternatives to criminal behaviour.

geographic profiling
A tool that permits police officers to focus on the likely residence of offenders in cases of serial crimes.

net widening
Imposing a form of control on individuals who might otherwise not be subject to such control.

is a molecule that encodes genetic instructions in all living organisms. It is akin to a fingerprint when used to identify an individual, and, in fact, is often referred to as genetic fingerprinting. The forensic science of DNA testing has had considerable advances during the past 25 years and is now widely used in criminal trials in order to link an accused to a crime scene and a particular victim or victims (and to exclude an accused from a crime scene). In the O.J. Simpson case, the defence team poked holes in the handling of the DNA evidence, arguing that it could have been contaminated at several different points, leading to physical evidence that was unreliable. However, although police mishandling of the evidence was problematic in many ways, the evidence still pointed to Simpson's guilt—his blood was found at the crime scene, the blood of his wife was found on his sock, and the blood of his other victim, Ron Goldman, was found in his car.

Although DNA evidence can be mishandled and inappropriately ignored (as in the Simpson case), it has become a very valuable tool in the detection of crimes, allowing conclusions regarding guilt that are both inculpatory and exculpatory. In Canada, both Guy Paul Morin and David Milgaard have been compensated for their wrongful convictions, largely due to the contribution of DNA evidence.

The Study of Crime: What Theories, What Methods?

As the preceding sections of this chapter demonstrate, criminologists employ a significant range of approaches in studying crime—from a detailed examination of the legal history of the criminal law, to evaluation of the effectiveness of various criminal sanctions and geographic profiling. When one looks at the content of university courses in criminology, whether at the graduate or undergraduate level, it appears that courses on theory and methods are pre-eminent. There are many other courses in the curricula of criminology schools and departments: policing, corrections, criminal law, sentencing, penology, juvenile delinquency, drugs and crime, white collar crime, and criminal investigations. But at the heart of the criminological enterprise are courses that are focused on theory and methods.

What theories guide criminology and criminologists? Some theorists, who might describe themselves as critically inclined, focus on the power of the state and its potential for abuse; others might describe themselves as rational choice theorists, arguing that crime occurs as a consequence of rational choices made by willing (or largely willing) actors. Still others use learning theory as a guide for their scholarly analysis. One prominent department of criminology focuses on teaching theories related to anomie, differential association, social control, social disorganization, routine activities, deterrence, and developmental approaches. A theory course in another department of criminology has a somewhat overlapping agenda that includes labelling theory, differential association, Marxist theories of crime, and moral regulation.

With the issues of methods to be employed by criminologists there is a similar breadth, though most discussions of methods tend to focus on a distinction between **qualitative** and **quantitative** approaches. It's a distinction that is, at least to some extent, rooted in particular disciplines. Lawyers and sociologists are generally more likely to employ qualitative methods of analysis. In contrast, psychologists and economists are more likely to employ quantitative frameworks.

But these distinctions also have some elasticity; there are sociologists who conduct research that is very much quantitative, relying on the analysis of large sets of data,

qualitative
The study of phenomena based not on measurement but on an exploration of the reasons for human behaviour and the qualities of subjective experience.

quantitative
Relating to the measurement of something—its quantity—rather than its qualities.

and there are psychologists who focus on qualitative approaches to crime and criminal behaviour by interviewing offenders and their victims. The combination of quantitative and qualitative methods, also known as a mixed methods approach, has gained popularity during the past 20 years. Adam Trahan and Daniel Stewart (2013) argue, for example, that the current divide between quantitative and qualitative research is restricting our ability to develop a coherent understanding of crime and criminal justice, and that mixed methods—combining qualitative and quantitative approaches in a single study—provides a way out of this difficulty. (See Box 1.4, below.)

But before we embark on any discussion of the relative merits of quantitative, qualitative, and mixed methods approaches, we must think first about the nature of the questions we ask about crime, law, and offenders and their victims. Let's suppose that we want to know whether the extent, nature, or character of homicide has changed in Canada over a 50-year span—between 1964 and 2014. Statistics Canada can provide us with a substantial amount of quantitative data from police-generated forms, filled out after a homicide has been uncovered. We can document changing rates, any changes over time in the methods used to commit such crime, the gender and age of victims and suspects, provincial and municipal differences in prevalence, and potentially changing motivations for these killings.

BOX 1.4

Qualitative and Quantitative Approaches to Studying Crime

The study of crime has been dominated by quantitative analyses of crime. Richard Tewksbury (2009) notes that only 10 to 15 percent of all articles published in peer-refereed criminological journals use qualitative methods. He goes on to make the bold claim that this is lamentable, as qualitative methods—interviews, field observations, and participant involvement—have superior value in "the creation of criminological and criminal justice knowledge" (p. 38). We do not have to agree with Tewksbury's claim, however, to see the value of both approaches, sometimes used in isolation of one another and most profitably used in combination.

Both quantitative and qualitative methods have their limitations. With quantitative methods, there is often a justifiable fear that the method dominates the inquiry—that increasingly sophisticated statistical manipulations of data may add little to our understanding of a particular phenomenon. Put differently, the questions we ask are at the heart of the criminological enterprise, and the quantitative responses we receive from quantitative study inevitably point to correlations, not cause–effect relationships. For example, even the startling finding by Mednick et al. (1984) that adopted male children are more likely to commit crime if their biological fathers (rather than their adopted fathers) had criminal records, is not without its

limitations. We don't really know what specific behaviours or attributes have been inherited and what impact these attributes might have on the development of criminality over time. The Mednick et al. (1984) data also revealed a strong genetic link with property crime but not with violent crime. With quantitative data, the methodology employed is always open to criticism, and our abilities to explain the variations that exist between two variables are typically quite limited. For example, David Weisburd and Alex Piquero (2008), after examining empirical tests of criminological theory in criminology between 1968 and 2005, concluded:

> The overall level of variance explained is often very low, with 80 or 90 per cent unexplained. There has been no improvement over time … . Criminologists will need to pay much more attention to what is not explained in criminological modeling if they are to make significant advances in understanding crime. (p. 453)

What sorts of things do you believe qualitative research can tell us about crime and criminal behaviour that quantitative methods might not? Conversely, what would quantitatively oriented criminologists cite as the shortcomings of research that is too reliant on qualitative approaches?

A significant part of the answer to this question depends, then, on the use of quantitative methods—engaging in a systematic empirically based inquiry, using numerical data, and depending on mathematical, statistical, or computational techniques. But this question could also benefit from qualitative research. Two possible examples are interviews with police officers who have investigated homicide during this time span and interviews with individuals convicted of homicides during this time span. These interviews could add much detailed and rich information about the potentially changing nature of homicide, complementing the rigour of quantitative analysis.

While the insights obtained from qualitative data may be useful contributions to building knowledge within a given field, they cannot be assumed to apply to a much larger group of individuals. In part, this is because the techniques—field observations or semi-structured interviews—are more subjective and more likely to be affected by the differing approaches and potential biases and inclinations of individual interviewers. But what also contributes to a lack of reliability with qualitative data is the typically small number of interviews (or number of data points). There is an irony here—the value of qualitative data usually increases as its similarities to quantitative data increase. For example, if one researcher conducts four interviews with users of crystal meth regarding the origins of their use of the drug, current patterns of consumption, reasons for using, and their hopes for the future, the results may be somewhat useful, perhaps even illuminating. But if 10 different researchers each conducted 20 interviews of a similar kind, in 10 Canadian provinces, the finding would have much more relevance and utility. One might argue that this is the Achilles heel of qualitative research. In order to achieve a greater legitimacy and respect within the discipline of criminology, it must, at least in some important ways, begin to more closely resemble its older and more established brother, quantitative methods.

The Big Tent: Toward an Inclusive Criminology

Robert Gordon, the former Director of the School of Criminology at Simon Fraser University, refers to the philosophy of his approach in relation to research, teaching, and practice in the field of criminology as one that embraces a "big tent." What he means to convey with the term "big tent" is that all credible approaches are welcome—from crime prevention through environmental design to critical analysis of the history of laws, practices of enforcement, and sentencing rationales; from understanding how and why individuals commit crimes to what can be done to make a continuing trajectory of crime less likely. Criminology can comfortably house subjects as diverse as improving our understanding of the hunting patterns of serial sex offenders, documenting and explaining the resilience of illegal markets, understanding what drives the spatial and temporal distribution of crime in urban neigbourhoods, and using forensic entomology to determine time of death in homicide investigations.

Professor Gordon also typically expresses a caveat that goes along with his "big tent" vision of the School of Criminology. "You are all welcome here," he has said, "just don't try to burn the tent down." Put differently, this is a call for tolerance. We are best served by an inclusive criminology, one that is worthy of support and remains mindful of the many conflicts that have hampered—and stimulated—our field over time. As you read through the following chapters, I hope you will find work that will challenge you and encourage you to look at the subject matter of crime and criminology through many different lenses. This is the challenge that criminology offers: a problem in search of multiple solutions, with many avenues of approach available.

SUMMARY OF KEY POINTS

- Although crime has been a part of societies throughout history, the serious scientific and academic study of crime is a relatively recent development.
- Criminology has typically been a very interdisciplinary field of study, drawing on disciplines as diverse as law, sociology, psychology, geography, political science, economics, gender studies, and more.
- All societies define some behaviours as deviant, and some of these deviant behaviours become subject to criminalization by the state. These definitions of deviance and crime can differ markedly across societies but can also be quite malleable. Consider, for example, recent changes in public attitudes and legal responses relating to cannabis and homosexuality in North America in only the last decade.
- Criminology can play a valuable role in determining how society copes with many new 21st-century challenges, including those relating to the current revolution in communications technologies.
- The findings of criminologists often provide information that serves to correct popular misconceptions or societal biases about the nature of crime and criminals.
- There are two categories of methods—qualitative and quantitative—that are used to study crime, each with its own advantages and disadvantages, depending on the context or goal of the research. Many criminologists now see a fusion of quantitative and qualitative methods as a particularly compelling approach to the study of crime.

QUESTIONS FOR CRITICAL DISCUSSION

1. Can you imagine a time in which criminology will be regarded as an entirely distinct discipline, such as psychology, law, or sociology? Give reasons for your answers.
2. Given that most data gathered by criminologists are correlational, how much explanatory power does criminological research actually have? Does the use of correlational data represent a serious limitation for the field?
3. What do you think are the main reasons for the increase in crime rates in Canada from the late 1960s to the early 1970s? And, correspondingly, what do you think are the main reasons for the general decrease in crime rates that occurred in Canada over a quarter century, from the early 1990s to circa 2015?

SUGGESTED FURTHER READINGS

Canadian Journal of Criminology and Criminal Justice: https://www.ccja-acjp.ca/pub/en
Criminology (journal): https://onlinelibrary.wiley.com/journal/17459125
Journal of Law and Society: https://onlinelibrary.wiley.com/journal/14676478
Journal of Research in Crime and Delinquency: http://jrc.sagepub.com
The Yale Law Journal: http://www.yalelawjournal.org

Websites

The American Society of Criminology: http://www.asc41.com

CASE STUDY 2.1

Immigration, Public Safety, and Criminal Activity

Syrian immigrants, who fled from violence, make a new home in Canada.

In April 2014, an organization by the name of Immigration Watch Canada distributed a flyer in the city of Brampton targeting the Sikh community. The flyer featured two photos, the top one a group of mostly white Canadians and the bottom photo a group of Sikhs. "Is this what you really want?" asked the flyer, underneath the second photo. In April 2018, the same organization criticized the city of Vancouver for making an apology to its Chinese citizens for the ways in which they were discriminated against near the beginning of the 20th century. The organization claimed it was "probably one of the most outrageous acts ever committed against its European-based population," adding that the apology "comes after immigrants, particularly Chinese from Mainland China, have driven housing costs into the stratosphere for hundreds of thousands of Metro Vancouver residents" (Immigration Watch Canada, 2018).

Concerns about Canada's immigration system, while not as intemperate as these remarks, have also been expressed by Andrew Scheer, the leader of Canada's Conservative party. In July 2018, he tweeted, "Canadians expect our immigration system to be safe, orderly and compassionate. They expect the government to take a border crisis of their own creation seriously. For months our @CPC_HQ team has been asking to see Justin Trudeau's plan, but it's clear he doesn't have one" (AndrewScheer, 2018). A poll undertaken by EKOS Research in August 2018 found that while only 12 percent of Liberal supporters and 17 percent of NDP supporters believe that too many visible minorities are immigrating to Canada, 73 percent of Conservative supporters say that there are too many of these people coming to our country (VoiceOfFranky, 2018).

Candice Malcolm, a syndicated columnist, writing in the *Toronto Sun* in November 2017, complained that "our immigration system seems to put the desires of newcomers and the whims of political elites ahead of the well-being of all Canadians. Trudeau wants more refugees, with less security. He wants more immigration, but with less of a focus on integration and national unity. The Trudeau government's immigration agenda is a dangerous combination, and it's one that Canadians are understandably rejecting" (Malcolm, 2018).

Are these fears legitimate? Are Canada's refugees a significant source of criminal activity? Is our collective security being compromised? Is our system of immigration, as Scheer has implied, unsafe, disorderly, and lacking compassion? Statistics Canada reports that from 2006 to 2014, when Conservative leader Stephen Harper was prime minister, the number of immigrants coming into Canada averaged about 250,000 annually. Since the Liberal government of Justin Trudeau came to power in 2015, the average annual number of immigrants has been about 275,000 (from 2015 to 2017), an increase of about 10 percent. Immigration Minister John McCallum stated in 2016 that he wanted to boost immigration levels to "help alleviate the demographic challenges of an aging population." The *Globe and Mail* reported in May 2018 that the significant number of immigrants from Syria, Canada's compassionate response to a humanitarian crisis in that country, largely explains the slightly unusual increase in the 2016 calendar year (Grant, 2016).

Are Canada's immigrants a threat to law and order? A 2014 study in the Department of Economics at the University of British Columbia found no immediate relationship between immigration and property crime, but noted that over time, through the creation of changing neighbourhood characteristics, there was a net reduction in crime committed by immigrants to Canada (Zhang, 2014). A Statistics Canada study from 2004 focused on rates of violent victimization, finding that immigrants were significantly less likely to report such victimization than were native born Canadians (Perrault, Sauvé, & Burns, 2009). And perhaps the most comprehensive attempt to improve our understanding of this relationship is to be found in *The Oxford Handbook of Ethnicity, Crime and Immigration*. Although there are difficult methodological issues involved in understanding the relationship between immigration and crime, there is little evidence of higher crime rates caused by immigration into either Canada or the United States (Bucerius & Tonry, 2014). In sum, while there may be occasional violence committed by recent immigrants to Canada, even a conservative reading of the best available evidence suggests there is no greater threat to public safety than that which comes from native-born Canadians.

Before You Read Chapter 2

- Who serves to gain from the misleading characterizations of immigration described here? In what ways might they benefit?
- What is the purpose of this kind of coverage of this issue? Why might a media organization, like the *Toronto Sun*, engage in such inflammatory rhetoric?
- Can you think of similar cases in which the media play a role in influencing public opinion on a controversial issue?
- What role *should* the media play in describing, reporting, or commenting on crime and the criminal justice system?

The Media: Shaping Our Understanding of Crime

LEARNING OUTCOMES

After reading this chapter, students will be able to:

- Explain how media producers and audiences negotiate the meaning of the images of crime and violence that are found in news stories, movies, shows, and music videos.

- List the important questions one should consider when taking a critical-thinking approach to viewing the media.

- Define "moral panics" and identify the social actors and conditions that produce them.

- List Goode and Ben-Yehuda's five characteristics of moral panics.

- Explain the different ways the media tend to treat victims and offenders, based on race, class, or gender.

CHAPTER OUTLINE

Introduction

Students often come to the study of criminology with a predefined set of attitudes, beliefs, and perceptions about crime and the criminal justice system. In many cases, those ideas have been shaped by the television shows and films they have watched, the video games they have played, and the news stories they have read. Consider the following statistics: The average child spends approximately five hours a day in front of a screen, watching television or movies, listening to music, surfing the Internet, or playing video games (Carnagey, Anderson, & Bartholow, 2007; Common Sense Media, 2015), and more than two-thirds of what they see on that screen involves violence (Federman, 1998). As members of a media-rich culture with constant access to networked devices, we all consume a variety of media that provide us with a continuous stream of images and stories about crime, many of them violent.

This chapter explores the ways in which media images and stories can inform or affect our understanding of crime and the workings of our criminal justice system. For our purposes, *the media* includes any means of mass communication—including newspapers, magazines, radio, television, film, video games, music videos, and social media. Across these media you will find both real-world crime reporting by different types of news organizations and countless fictional stories centred around crime, such as police television shows, forensic television dramas, and action films. Thus, before exploring the many aspects of criminology that are examined in the chapters that follow, this chapter provides an opportunity to step back and consider the ways in which many of our attitudes and opinions are formed and the often complex relationship that exists between media and crime.

Perspectives on Media and Crime: A Brief Overview

When social scientists first began to seriously study crime and media in the 1960s and 1970s, psychologists and sociologists sought to measure the impact of media consumption on aggression. These studies, which focus on **media effects**, suggested that children who watched a lot of violence on television, for example, were more likely to act violently toward others.

media effects
The concept that exposure to media has an effect on behaviour. For example, young people exposed to violent media will behave aggressively.

Although many social scientists have rejected the media effects approach because of methodological concerns, some criminologists have continued to be interested in the effects of exposure to media violence. For example, Matt DeLisi, Michael Vaughn, Douglas Gentile, Craig Anderson, and Jeffrey Shook (2012) have argued the following:

> The consumption of violent media is far from innocuous, and when violent media consumption in the form of video games is viewed by adults as a "reward" for youth to spend their free time, it can be problematic. Youth with pre-existing psychopathology are particularly at risk for the deleterious effects of violent video games, and much more research is needed on correctional samples of youth to ascertain the severity of violent video games and related media factors as risk factors for their behavioural problems (p. 139; see also Gentile & Bushman, 2012).

Others, such as Ray Surette (2013), suggest that media images of crime expose viewers to anti-social behaviours and that these behaviours may be copied by youth who are already predisposed to violence. From this perspective, "the association between exposure to media crime and criminal behavior has been more often viewed as one of instructional sources, as crime catalysts and rudders, rather than as crime generating triggers" (p. 394).

active audiences
The concept that audiences are not passive recipients of information or meanings but are instead active in the process of creating meaning.

However, many criminologists have moved away from considering the effect of the media on crime to instead examine the cultural meaning of media violence. Much of this work is based on the cultural studies concept of **active audiences**. This concept suggests that people do not passively consume media messages, as implied in some of the media effects literature. Instead, the meaning of the messages is negotiated or constructed by an interaction between the persons who produced the image and the audiences who consume it. From this perspective, audience members do not simply *absorb* a violent image; they *make* their own meaning of it according to their own perspectives and values. This approach has led to the emergence of the subdiscipline of "cultural criminology," which explores the links between culture, crime, and crime control in contemporary social life (Ferrell, 1999). From this perspective, news media and popular culture are *social sites* where people collectively negotiate the meaning of crime, violence, victimization, justice, and community. As much as crime generates media stories, those media stories themselves also create narratives that provide the context for our understanding of criminal events. Media narratives are therefore excellent cultural artifacts for criminologists to examine, because they provide a window into the social construction of the meaning of crime.

Criminological studies of media emphasize the need for **critical thinking** in our interactions with news and other types of media (see Box 2.1). As we will see below, media narratives of crime contribute to shaping our society; they can either help promote tolerance for and public engagement with the issues of the day, or reinforce stereotypes and limit the range of public debate. These realities suggest that we must acquire the skills to interpret and understand the many messages embedded in the media we consume and critically assess our roles as audience members.

critical thinking
The process of evaluating information, claims, or arguments through careful questioning and the application of reason.

The Case of the Columbine High School Shootings

As we begin to explore the complex ways in which audiences construct the meaning of crime, let's consider a particularly well-known case.

On April 20, 1999, Eric Harris and Dylan Klebold walked into Columbine High School in Colorado and started shooting, killing 15 people before turning their guns on themselves. Within minutes of the first shot being fired, journalists were camped outside the school and graphic images of bodies, escaping students, and a grieving community began to flood the news media. At the height of the incident, over 400 reporters, between 75 and 90 satellite trucks, and 60 television cameras were on the scene, including at least 20 television crews from foreign countries (Jefferson County Sheriff's Department, n.d.). The coverage was so extensive that the story was ranked the largest US news story for 1999 and the seventh-largest story of the 1990s (Muschert, 2009, p. 165).

BOX 2.1

Thinking Critically About Media

In order to develop an ability to think more critically about media coverage of actual crime or fictional depictions of the criminal justice system, it is important to consider the following questions:

- Who created the media product, and what is its purpose?
- What assumptions or beliefs do its creators appear to have, as reflected in the content?
- What is the commercial purpose of the media product (in other words, how will it help someone make money)? What influence might this factor have on the content and on how it is being communicated?

- How might different people see the media product in different ways?
- Who and/or what is shown in a positive light? In a negative light? Why might these people or issues be shown this way?
- Who and/or what is not shown at all?
- What conclusions might audiences draw about an event or an issue based on the facts being presented in the news story or narrative?

Source: MediaSmarts (2018).

Within days, the news coverage shifted from reporting the facts and garnering reaction to discussing root causes of the violence. The most common explanations involved the lack of gun control and, interestingly for our purposes, the role of popular media; a number of pundits argued that Harris and Klebold's actions were a result of their interest in video games, Marilyn Manson's music, and the movie *The Matrix*. A headline from a National Public Radio online article was typical of much of the discussion:

Students flee Columbine High School during the shooting.

"Columbine High School Shootings and How the Internet, Video Games and Violence on TV and in the Movies May Contribute to Teen-Age Violence" (Muschert, 2009, p. 167). Popular media were not only singled out as potentially responsible for causing the Columbine shootings; Columbine itself was incorporated into a variety of popular media products. Most famously, filmmaker Michael Moore's 2002 documentary, *Bowling for Columbine*, examined politics and power relationships, and took issue with the argument that popular media causes crime. The film cited statistics that indicate that other countries with high video game consumption, for example, do not have elevated levels of shooting violence. The film also incorporated an interview with rocker Marilyn Manson, who defended himself against the accusation that his music was central to Harris's and Klebold's motivations. In an interesting twist, Manson pointed the finger instead at a different kind of medium: advertising containing fear-based messages.

Other media creators appropriated images of the shooting for their own purposes. For example, the closed-captioned video coverage of Harris and Klebold in the school cafeteria, which was posted to the Internet shortly after the shooting, is featured in the highly controversial video game *Super Columbine Massacre RPG!* In the game, players re-enact Harris and Klebold's attack, proceeding through the school to kill students with names like "Preppy Girl" and "Jock Type." Danny Ledonne, who created the game in 2005, maintains that he did so to help explore his own experience with bullying as a teen, to explore the shooters' motivations, and to provide a social critique of the news media's sensationalization of the massacre. Many people attacked Ledonne for being insensitive to the victims' families and seeking to profit from the tragedy. However, the game does underline the power of media images, and it draws attention to the negotiation that occurs between producers and audiences about what, exactly, these media representations of violence mean.

In perhaps the most interesting example of the complex interplay between crime and media, it was discovered that Harris and Klebold had made videos of themselves before the shootings in which they reflect on how famous they would become and wonder whether Steven Spielberg or Quentin Tarantino would direct the film that would tell their story. Klebold concluded:

> Directors will be fighting over this story. I know we're gonna have followers because we're so f**ing God-like. We're not exactly human—we have human bodies, but we've evolved into one step above you, f**ing human s**t. We actually have f**ing self-awareness. (Jefferson County Sheriff's Office, n.d.)

The Columbine incident is an excellent illustration of how media stories about crimes shape our understanding of those crimes, and how our understanding of crime shapes the kinds of media stories we produce. In this sense, media and crime are mutually constituted—each works to shape the other. For example, the real-world crimes committed during the Columbine shootings generated a great deal of news coverage, and that news coverage shaped our attitudes—and, arguably, our policies—relating to similar real-world incidents for years to come (Muschert, Henry, Bracy, & Peguero, 2014). The shooters themselves sought to impact others' perceptions of the real-world incident by creating a media record of their thoughts before the rampage began and anticipated that they would continue to "live on" in other media after the incident. In this sense, their media story shaped the way we saw the real-world incident. And others, like Danny Ledonne, created different media narratives around the incident to tell different stories. All of these narratives continue to compete for the attention of media audiences, who interpret them in a variety of ways for their own purposes. And, as we shall see below, these media narratives also determined which issues would be widely discussed and which ones would not.

Media, Crime, and the Problem Frame

A brief perusal of a local newspaper or television news program demonstrates that crime is central to the production of Canadian news media. Clearly, journalists consider crime to be newsworthy and often focus on it to the exclusion of other kinds of stories. At the same time, crime is also a central component of entertainment; it grips the collective imagination of television viewers, theatregoers, Internet browsers, and readers of true-crime books as few other topics can (Dowler, Fleming, & Muzzatti, 2006, p. 837).

David Altheide (1997) suggested that violence is treated in this way because both news organizations and popular media producers are primarily focused on entertainment and are, accordingly, looking for clear, unambiguous stories. Ideally, these stories will garner immediate attention yet be easily resolved at some time in the future. He argues that media stories about crime are therefore cast through a **problem frame** because such a frame helps generate a narrative that is easily understood and likely to sell. The problem frame focuses on the existence of something extraordinary and "bad" that affects many people. An ideal story concerns a crime that is unambiguously bad and calls out for a solution that can be pointed to in the future when an organization (usually the government, the police, or some other arm of the state) responsible for fixing the problem will do so.

problem frame
A narrative that is easily understood because it focuses on the existence of something extraordinary and "bad" that affects many people, and identifies unambiguous solutions that can be implemented in the future.

Applying the problem frame to the Columbine incident, media stories focused on the exceptional nature of school shootings (the extraordinary and easily identifiable bad thing) and the horror it generated in the community, the nation, and beyond (affecting many people). An immediate response was required to fix the problem of school shootings, and an attempt was made to identify an unambiguous and easily resolved cause, such as violent video games. The government "solved" the problem by holding a series of consultations on youth consumption of violent media and enacting legislation requiring rating labels and content warnings for media content.

This type of morality play provides a simplistic version of events that complies with the need to quickly and easily identify and punish the bad person responsible for the crime. But it also serves to create boundaries around the event, determining what can and cannot be discussed. The Columbine incident, for example, generated a great deal of discussion about young people's consumption of violent media, but broader questions about gun control, mental health, and the need for better services for young people in crisis were not a significant part of the debate.[1]

For more on mental illness and crime, see Case Study 7.1 and Case Study 8.1.

Challenging the problem frame and opening up space to discuss new issues can be difficult. Students who survived the 2018 mass shooting at Marjory Stoneman Douglas High School (MSD) in Parkland, Florida banded together to create the Never Again MSD movement. They publicly challenged the view that school shootings are exceptional and called on news media and policy-makers alike to stop talking about "gore" and instead focus on changing gun laws that "make it easier for people like Nick Cruz [the MSD shooter] to acquire an AR-15" (Witt, 2018). Students across the country organized local and national protests in support, with a goal to hold over 500 town halls and other events in 30 districts to call elected representatives to account for their position on gun control (Beckett, 2018).

As with previous school shootings, any attempts by the media to focus attention on lax gun laws in the immediate aftermath of the MSD shooting quickly drew criticism from various quarters—notably, powerful interest groups such as the National Rifle Association and conservative media outlets like Fox News—for attempting to politicize a tragedy (Beckett, 2018). The success of this pushback is yet to be determined. Florida, for the first time in 30 years, passed legislation to restrict gun sales, including raising the minimum age and lengthening the wait period to purchase a firearm, as a direct response to the Never Again MSD movement. However, national efforts have stalled. And, tragically, just five months after the MSD shooting, a high school student shot 10 people to death at Sante Fe High School in Texas (Martin, 2018).

Moral Panics

Stories about school shootings—which focus on sensational events that are horrifying and likely to evoke a strong emotional reaction—may sell media stories, but they also link crime storytelling to fear, which in turn distorts our understanding of crime and deviance. Dowler et al. (2006) wrote:

> The selective nature of crime news, for example, with its emphasis on violence and sensationalism—essentially crime as a product, playing to the fears, both imagined and real, of viewers and readers—has produced a distorted picture of the world of crime and criminality. (p. 839)

A distorted picture of crime and criminality can have real policy consequences. *Policing the Crisis: Mugging, the State and Law and Order* (Hall, Critcher, Jefferson, Clarke, & Roberts, 1978), a classic analysis of the relationship between the media and the criminal justice system, demonstrates how media stories about a new "crime wave" of muggings in London in the 1970s encouraged politicians to devote more police resources to catching the perpetrators, which led to more arrests and more convictions. Judges then quoted the news stories to justify higher sentences for offenders. After a period of time, the politicians reported that the problem was solved, so fewer resources were devoted to catching muggers, and the number of arrests dropped. However, the actual number of robberies did not change throughout the entire "war on mugging."

Hall et al. (1978) cited Stanley Cohen's notion of **moral panic**—when a "condition, episode, person or group of persons emerges to become defined as a threat to societal values and interests" (Cohen, 1972/1980, p. 9)—to explain how the belief that a particular

moral panic
Phenomena—socially constructed by the media, politicians, and "moral entrepreneurs"—in which certain people or groups are labelled or stigmatized as the cause of a perceived social problem, resulting in widespread public alarm.

crime is on the rise justifies a change in activities (such as devoting more police resources to arresting perpetrators) that in turn makes it look like the crime is on the rise even when it is not. They concluded that the "rising crime rate equation" plays a conservative ideological role in maintaining the status quo by creating public support for more policing to bring the "crisis" back under control. This dynamic underlines how the narratives around crime have real consequences; they shape our understanding of who should be protected, who should protect them, and whom they should be protected from.

moral entrepreneur
A person, group, or organization that takes the lead in identifying certain behaviour as deviant and in need of legal sanctions.

BOX 2.2

Cohen on Social Problems and Moral Panics

Stanley Cohen explored the relationship between the media and moral panics in his 1972 book *Folk Devils and Moral Panics: The Creation of the Mods and Rockers*. A year later, Stanley Cohen and Jock Young published *The Manufacture of News: Social Problems, Deviance, and the Mass Media*. These books, along with the 1973 book *The New Criminology: For a Social Theory of Deviance* (Taylor, Walton, and Young, 1973), as well as 1978's *Policing the Crisis: Mugging, the State and Law and Order* (Hall et al., 1978) are considered landmark works in the field of critical criminology (a topic explored in detail in Chapter 10, Critical Criminology). The evolution of cultural criminology—and, indeed, studies on the relationship between the media and crime—can be traced back to these writings of the 1970s.

In *Folk Devils and Moral Panics*, Cohen (1972/1980) drew on Edwin Lemert's 1951 book *Social Pathology*, in which Lemert discussed primary and secondary deviance. According to Lemert, *primary deviance* occurs when an individual (or group) engages in disapproved behaviour, without seeing that behaviour as necessarily "deviant" or "criminal." *Secondary deviance*, on the other hand, results from the social reaction to primary deviance. In other words, individuals may come to view themselves as "deviant" or "criminal" because they are subjected to stigmatization and social control. Cohen also drew upon Howard Becker's 1963 book *Outsiders: Studies in the Sociology of Deviance*. Becker, the most well known of the labelling theorists (discussed in Chapter 9, Sociological Approaches), pinpointed the role of **moral entrepreneurs** (or "moral crusaders") in the social construction of deviance. Moral entrepreneurs are members of society who have wealth, power, and political clout, not to mention sufficient time and energy to pursue their moral crusades. Becker argued that unless a certain type of behaviour was

deemed to be deviant or criminal by these moral entrepreneurs, and as a consequence became the target of rule making and rule enforcement, then that behaviour would likely be tolerated by society or, if not, then at least ignored.

Cohen (1972/1980) identified the mass media as a crucial factor in stirring up moral panics. He said that when there is no news to report, the media engage in their own moral crusading or moral entrepreneurship, acting "as agents of moral indignation." The media, according to Cohen, actively search for social "problems" to sensationalize and individuals or groups to demonize. More often than not, the media single out youth culture—hippies, skinheads, punks—and present them as the next big threat to the social order.

The Mods and Rockers of 1960s Britain were not new, but as Cohen (1972/1980) says, they were presented as "new" by the media in order to justify their inclusion in news reports. Despite the sudden attention brought to bear on their activities by the media in the mid-1960s, these two loosely organized youth groups had been in existence for years. The Mods and Rockers dressed differently, listened to different kinds of music, and occasionally clashed in "rumbles" in seaside resort towns. The British media exaggerated and distorted the seriousness of these occasional clashes, referring to the Mods and Rockers as screaming mobs and describing their activities as "orgies of destruction." In reality, the so-called troublemakers were often outnumbered by the crowds, who turned out in the hope of seeing some action on an otherwise boring long weekend. Nobody was killed, few incidents of serious violence occurred, and relatively little property damage took place. As is the case with most moral panics, the concern about the Mods and Rockers lost momentum and quickly faded from the public imagination.

The "Bad Guys"

Hall et al. (1978) also argued that crime news reflects society's shared values, linking the ideological role of the "rising crime rate equation" in 1970s London to rising racial tensions between the police and London's Black community. Media-driven moral panics were used to strengthen public and political support for increased policing. Increased arrests and convictions were then used to restrict the freedom of the supposed criminals (the **folk devils** referred to by Cohen, 1972/1980) at the heart of these moral panics: Black Londoners accused of mugging.

folk devils
Originating in images from folklore, this term refers to people or groups presented in media as deviant outsiders and the cause of social problems.

Media Depictions of Race and Gender

In news and entertainment media today, stories about crime often continue to reflect these deep-seated social tensions. Rodanthi Tzanelli, Majid Yar, and Martin O'Brien (2005) wrote that crime stories "as a whole can be seen to make use of, exemplify and give voice to wider assumptions, concerns and anxieties about social life, social disorder and social change" (p. 98). These assumptions, concerns, and anxieties are brought to the forefront when we consider how certain types of offenders are **stereotyped** in media representations.

stereotyping
The simplistic and often belittling representation of a person or group, using exaggerations of traits that the larger group supposedly possesses.

In popular media portrayals, people of colour are commonly represented in derogatory and unflattering ways (Dickerman, Christensen, Beatriz, & McClain, 2008). Racialized populations are often portrayed as criminal: In news media, the subjects of stories about crime are between three and four times more likely to be Black than white (Coogan, 2012).

The field of sports media offers some examples of this difference in media coverage. For example, in 2007, NFL quarterback Michael Vick was charged with operating an illegal interstate dog-fighting ring; in 2009 and 2010, Ben Roethlisberger, also an NFL quarterback, was accused of two counts of sexual assault. Vick and Roethlisberger were both top-tier players, but one important distinction between the two men is their race: Vick is Black; Roethlisberger is white. In news coverage on ABC, CBS, and Fox News, far more airtime was dedicated to Vick's case than Roethlisberger's (in fact, Fox News ignored Roethlisberger's case entirely). News stories emphasized that Vick's case reflected a subculture of violence more than Roethlisberger's. Characterizations of Vick were visceral and dehumanizing, using words like "barbaric" and "evil." Meanwhile, characterizations of Roethlisberger were sympathetic and understanding. As one commentator pointed out, "Certainly the media have convicted Vick" (Coogan, 2012, p. 142).

While there is no doubt that white youth, such as the Mods and Rockers and Columbine shooters, can sometimes be the source of moral panic, it is more common for racialized offenders (particularly Black offenders) to be portrayed as violent, aggressive "thugs and toughs" (Carter, 1988, p. 420). As Coogan (2012) writes, "In influencing perceptions and attitudes, race represents a salient factor for viewers" (p. 129). Coogan also argues that the overwhelming media portrayal of Black people as perpetrators of crime can have real social consequences, resulting in viewers or readers perceiving that group as more dangerous than other groups and substantiating existing racist misconceptions of Black men as dangerous or violent.

The Media Coverage of Hurricane Katrina

One of the best-known examples of moral panics occurred in the aftermath of Hurricane Katrina, which struck the southern US coast in August 2005 and left the city of New Orleans devastated. In their examination of the hurricane's aftermath, Timothy

Brezina and Herbert E. Phipps (2010) drew on Cohen's (1972/1980) work on "folk devils and moral panics" (see Box 2.2) and Erich Goode and Nachman Ben-Yehuda's formula for evaluating moral panics (see Box 2.3) to demonstrate how the interactions between news reporters, politicians, and public officials created a media story that greatly exaggerated the urban chaos and violent crime that took place in New Orleans. Brezina and Phipps stated that this exaggeration was due to false statements from the police and public officials who were caught off guard by the extent of the damage caused by the hurricane (and the federal government's inaction in the face of the crisis, which has had a lasting negative effect on the reputation of then President George W. Bush). Authorities in New Orleans responded by feeding misinformation to the media, who in turn fed gruesome tales to the public, no doubt certain that they would attract huge audiences. The result was that powerless, low-status hurricane refugees had the blame shifted to them as they became cast as the "villains" by police, politicians, and media.

As the hurricane survivors congregated in their urgent search for safety and shelter, the media painted a picture of a city (including the Superdome, a football stadium converted into a shelter) rife with lawlessness and rampant murder. However, much of the crime reported in the media, including the alleged rape of babies, did not in fact occur (Brezina & Phipps, 2010, p. 100).

The media's distortion of events can be explained by several factors, including breakdowns in communication, class and racial stereotyping, and narratives that had been established, such as "civil unrest" and "urban warfare." Kathleen Tierney, Christine Bevc, and Erica Kuligowski (2006) examined the role that such narratives and "disaster myths" played in the news coverage following Hurricane Katrina:

> These reports (of rampant murder) were later found to be groundless, but they were accepted as accurate by both media organizations and consumers of news because they were consistent with the emerging, myth-inspired media narrative that characterized New Orleans as a "snake pit of anarchy," a violent place where armed gangs of Black men took advantage of the disaster, not only to loot, but also to commit capital crimes. (p. 68)

Other Stereotypes

Muslim persons accused of crimes have also frequently been the subjects of discriminatory media representations, especially in the years after the September 11, 2001 attacks. Muslims are commonly constructed in various popular media as terrorists, jihadists, and sexual deviants (Hickman, Thomas, Silvestri, & Nickels, 2011; Puar & Rai, 2002). These constructions help incite or perpetuate deep-seated Islamophobia. They also help justify more punitive action against Muslim offenders in the name of anti-terrorism and the preservation of Western sensibilities. Consider the 2010 incident in which a small plane was flown into a government building in Austin, Texas. Initial reports speculated that this event was another case of terrorism. However, when it was revealed that the pilot was a white man with a grievance against the tax policies of the US government, the narrative of a "terror attack" quickly disappeared. This was perhaps surprising, given that the incident so clearly replicated the airplane attacks of September 11, 2001 on the World Trade Center and the Pentagon—acts that are now considered synonymous with "terrorism."

discourses
Refers to forms of language, representation, and practices and how meaning is created and shared. Discourses take place within specific cultural and historical contexts.

Media **discourses** also commonly represent youth and young offenders as "dangerous others" who are prone to violence and crime and do not consider the consequences of their actions, often allegedly led astray by violent music or video games (as was suggested in the case of the Columbine shooters) (Mahari & Conner, 2003).

BOX 2.3

Goode and Ben-Yehuda on Moral Panics and Social Construction

Erich Goode and Nachman Ben-Yehuda (1994) set out criteria to distinguish between legitimate social problems worthy of public concern and moral panics stirred up by moral entrepreneurs and the media. According to Goode and Ben-Yehuda, a moral panic is characterized by the following five features (which usually appear sequentially):

Concern. A "heightened level of concern" about the "problem," often fanned by media attention, action groups, or legislative initiatives.

Hostility. An "increased level of hostility" toward the targeted group, with the group's behaviour characterized as harmful or threatening to the values, beliefs, and morals of "normal" society.

Consensus. Some sort of fairly widespread "consensus" (agreement) among members of the society that the threat posed by the wrongful behaviour is real and serious.

Disproportionality. A level of concern that is disproportionate to the actual seriousness of the threat; figures may be exaggerated, and there may be little or no evidence of a real threat.

Volatility. The sudden appearance and then disappearance of the "threat" without any valid explanation for why it became such a big problem one day and was no longer a problem the next day.

Goode and Ben-Yehuda also proposed three theories to explain why moral panics emerge:

- *Grassroots theory* suggests that moral panics begin with genuine public concern about a problem (real or imagined) and that politicians and the media become involved in response to this public concern. Most proponents of the grassroots model would acknowledge that involvement of the media, action groups, and politicians is necessary in order for a moral panic to develop fully.

- *Elite-engineered theory* suggests that small, powerful groups deliberately set out to create moral panics to divert public attention away from truly serious social problems, where the solutions to those problems might negatively impact the interests of the elite groups themselves. Goode and Ben-Yehuda point to Hall et al.'s 1978 book *Policing the Crisis* as an example of the elite-engineered model, where the wealthy and powerful in British society used the media and the legislative/law-enforcement apparatus to generate public fear about a non-existent increase in muggings.

- *Interest group theory*—based on Howard Becker's (1963) work on how moral crusades are launched by moral entrepreneurs—is the most common perspective on moral panics. It suggests that interest groups such as the media, politicians, professional groups, and religious organizations may act independently rather than in consort with one another. While the moral panics generated by these interest groups may seem self-serving, the groups might genuinely believe that they are acting in the best interests of society.

Goode and Ben-Yehuda concluded that a blend of all three theories is required in order to properly understand moral panics. Concern must be present at the grassroots (public) level, but this concern requires articulation by the media, politicians, and interest groups. The elite may be able to "engineer" a moral panic, but to do so successfully, some genuine public fear must exist. Moreover, the elite need a degree of cooperation from the media, legislators, and law enforcement officials. Interest groups may be able to focus attention on a social "problem," and argue for enhanced rule making and rule enforcement. However, to create a moral panic, they need to strike a resonant chord with the public, and with the media and politicians (who ultimately respond to public opinion).

Female offenders are often seen as particularly worrisome and commonly described as *predatory* or *promiscuous* (Ringrose, 2006). Women, and especially marginalized women, are often harshly judged and constructed as deviant (or as offenders) for departing from stereotypical feminine ideals such as being passive, self-restrained, or pretty. Those who do depart from these ideals face an "explosion in arrest rates and incarceration of girls and women, in spite of decreases in violent crime" (Chesney-Lind & Eliason, 2006).

The stereotypes perpetuated in media representations come together to portray society in a way that constructs certain groups as the norm and acceptable, and other groups as deviant and unacceptable. As we have seen, portrayals of criminals are more likely to include social minorities, whether in terms of ethnicity, religion, gender, or age. These portrayals have the effect of preserving majority social values and constructing the **other** as inherently transgressive. As we will see below, this has real implications for how we deal with crime and victimization in Canadian society.

other
A person or group of people defined as fundamentally different, or even deviant, by the dominant culture, often through stereotyping.

The Victim

We have established that crime media tend to reflect dominant social values. As the previous section pointed out, media influence how we think about offenders. They also affect how we think about victims. Like media representations of offenders, media representations of victims revolve around deeply entrenched social stereotypes. As Dowler et al. (2006) write, "The common statement 'If it bleeds, it leads' is not entirely truthful, as it really depends on who is bleeding" (pp. 840–841).

The concept of the "ideal victim" was first suggested by Norwegian criminologist Nils Christie (1986). According to Christie, an ideal victim is "a person or a category of individuals who, when hit by crime, most readily are given the complete and legitimate status of being a victim" (p. 18). The more characteristics of an ideal victim an individual has, the more readily victim status will be conferred upon that individual.

In media portrayals, the ideal victim intersects with values surrounding race, religion, gender, age, and other social characteristics. Portrayals of victims are often strongly affected by racism, Islamophobia, ageism, ableism, homophobia, and misogyny. As a rule, victims with a minority status are constructed as less ideal than victims with a majority status. Victims characterized as deviant—whether because they engage in deviant activities or because they come from a social minority—are also constructed as "less innocent" than other victims. As Dowler et al. (2006) point out, "Minority crime victims receive less attention and less sympathy" (p. 840).

Race and gender are two major components of media portrayals of victims. A crime story involving a white victim or a minority offender will commonly play on racist stereotypes; meanwhile, victims of crime who are racial minorities are frequently ignored (Dowler et al., 2006). Consider the amount of press coverage typically given to a crime against a white person (such as the alleged attack by Black male youth on the white female "Central Park Jogger," referred to in Box 2.4), versus the murder of a young man or woman of colour in a housing project. Clearly, crimes committed *by* racial minorities receive more news coverage than crimes committed *against* them. And crimes against white victims are almost always considered to be more newsworthy than crimes against minorities.

BOX 2.4

The Ideal Victim

According to Christie (1986), an ideal victim is:

1. Weak in relation to the offender: either female, sick, very old, very young, or a combination thereof.
2. Going about routine, respectable, and legitimate (read as "legal") daily activities when she or he is victimized.
3. Blameless for what transpired.
4. Unrelated to and unacquainted with the person who committed the offence.
5. In a submissive or subordinate position to the perpetrator, who can easily be described in negative terms.
6. Someone with enough influence, power, or sympathy to assert "victim status" without threatening the broader political status quo.

The 1989 assault and rape of the Central Park Jogger, a young white woman, caused widespread public hysteria, which was fuelled by the police and the media. Five young men—four of them Black, one Hispanic—were wrongfully convicted in the case.

Female victims, meanwhile, are more newsworthy than male victims, provided that they can be characterized as innocent, virtuous, and honourable (Dowler et al., 2006). Problematic and sexist media portrayals result, with female victims characterized as either "innocent" or "blameworthy." "Innocent" victims are constructed as submissive and passive recipients of male violence; "blameworthy" victims are constructed as responsible for their victimization. This shift of responsibility onto the victim reduces or eliminates the responsibility of the perpetrator and portrays these victims as less deserving than victims who are "innocent." As Dowler et al. (2006) wrote, such portrayals send a message that "violence against women is devalued, while the female victim is depersonalized, objectified, and dehumanized" (p. 841).

The "Good Guys"

Media portrayals can also impact viewers' or readers' perceptions of police. Police in news media and reality television are commonly portrayed as crime-fighting, heroic, no-nonsense law enforcers who are hypercompetent, hard-working, and "tough on crime" (Doyle, 2003; Inciardi & Dee, 1987). As Doyle (2003) points out, crime media "offer a very particular and selective vision of policing ... best seen as 'reality fiction'" (p. 34). The relationship between police and news media sources is complex. In news media, journalists can face pressures to report stories about police in a positive way since a positive relationship with police ensures access to interviews or news tips. The same constraints play out in popular media as well. In reality TV shows like *Cops*, for example, television networks give police ultimate control over what footage makes a final broadcast. Giving police editorial control is necessary to ensure that film crews continue to have access to ride-alongs, ongoing investigations, and other footage that requires police permission and cooperation. As a result, the transparency of footage that makes a final broadcast is compromised, and only footage that portrays police in a positive light makes the final cut (Doyle, 2003).

Media portrayals can also inaccurately represent the nature of police work, misconstruing what it means to work in law enforcement. News media and reality TV (as well as fictional police dramas) "promote the idea that fighting crime is the chief function of police, as opposed to preventing crime, directing traffic, and keeping the peace" (Inciardi & Dee, 1987, p. 100). Since news media and reality TV shows function as informal recruitment and training materials for those beginning or considering careers in policing (Doyle, 2003), glamourized media portrayals of policing also have very real implications beyond general public sentiment toward police.

In addition, by portraying police as hypercompetent, depictions of police in news media and reality television can create exaggerated public expectations for real-life police performance. At the same time, they can also conceal the darker side of policing, rarely focusing on police brutality, abuses of power, or police incompetence. A general lack of negative real-world portrayals of police can build pro-police sentiment among the public when there is no corresponding documentation of their flaws and shortcomings.

Certainly, news media reports about police abuse have helped bring incidents of abuse of power to the forefront in the past. For example, coverage of both the fatal tasering of Robert Dziekański at Vancouver Airport in 2007 and the use of excessive force during mass protests at the G20 summit in Toronto in 2010 was followed by a storm of public debate and demands for increased accountability. But these incidents are also good examples of the power of **sousveillance** to make abuse of power more visible so police can be held to account.

Sousveillance occurs when an activity is recorded by a participant in that activity or by a bystander (Mann, Nolan, & Wellman, 2003). Unlike **surveillance**, which is a "top down" phenomenon where a central authority uses technology (such as a security camera) to watch those "below" it—sousveillance is a "bottom up" form of watching and documenting events. It involves ordinary citizens who record events and share their recordings with others as a way to hold those in positions of power accountable for their actions.

With the explosion in use of social media tools such as Twitter, Facebook, and YouTube, sousveillance has become a much more common way to attempt to challenge police abuse. The #blacklivesmatter campaign, for example, organized a series of mass protests after bystanders posted videos of New York Police Department officers arresting Eric Garner for allegedly selling loose cigarettes. The videos showed officers putting Garner in a stranglehold and forcing him to the ground. Garner told the officers 11 times that he could not breathe, but his pleas were ignored and he was later declared dead at the hospital (Goldstein & Schweber, 2014). The most widely viewed video of Garner's arrest has been viewed more than 3 million times on YouTube, and thousands of protestors marched after the court failed to indict the officers involved.

sousveillance
The recording, by a citizen participant or witness, of an incident or activity, to hold a bureaucratic organization to account. It can be used to record incidents in which police may be seen abusing their power.

surveillance
The monitoring of individuals or populations for the purposes of control and/or care (Lyon, 2001).

Sousveillance may potentially shift media constructions of crime and criminality by providing a way for regular citizens to tell their own stories. However, social media is not a panacea. Because online advertising models reward stories that attract attention, clickbait and fake news can overwhelm both mainstream and alternative perspectives (Rochlin, 2017). In addition, the search algorithms that drive people to online media content can create "filter bubbles" that surround individuals with news and other media stories that support their pre-existing ideological positions; rather than democratizing access to media resources, this can polarize groups of people (Spohr, 2017) and weaken public debate about the meaning of crime and criminality.

Conclusion

Many criminologists argue that the stories about crime that we watch or read are more than news or entertainment; they are one way in which we collectively construct the meaning of criminals, victims, police, and other justice officials. They are also one way we negotiate who is part of "us" and who is the "other," or one of "them." Therefore, criminology students need to approach media representations critically to better identify the many messages about crime and criminality embedded in the media they consume, and to question the assumptions and biases the media often contain.

SUMMARY OF KEY POINTS

- *Media effects*, an early focal point in the study of media and crime, suggested that exposure to media could determine behaviour, most notably aggression. For instance, children who watched a lot of violence on television were more likely to act violently toward others. (The approach subsequently came under scrutiny from some criminologists who questioned its methodologies.)

- Many criminologists shifted their focus away from the effect of the media on crime to instead examine the cultural meaning of media violence. The concept of "active audiences" suggests that people do not passively consume media messages; rather, meaning is constructed by an interaction between the persons who produced the image and the audiences who consume it.

- When examining how the media cover crime, it is essential to engage in "critical thinking." This involves a rigorous, logical evaluation of the claims and arguments being presented, and a questioning of both the messages embedded in the media we consume, and our role as audience members.

- Crime is presented in the media not only as news content, but also as a central component in many forms of entertainment. It often takes the form of simple narratives or "problem frames," which are often not accurate representations of complex reality.

- "Moral panics" tend to arise when a person or group of persons "becomes defined as a threat to societal values and interests" (Cohen, 1972/1980). The media often play a central role in the diffusion of moral panics, along with, in some cases, politicians, the police, and "moral entrepreneurs."

- According to Erich Goode and Nachman Ben-Yehuda (1994), a moral panic is characterized by the following five features (which usually appear sequentially) (1) concern, (2) hostility, (3) consensus, (4) disproportionality, and (5) volatility.

- As illustrated by the examples of news coverage of Hurricane Katrina, or the legal problems of NFL quarterbacks Michael Vick and Ben Roethlisberger, the media can often reflect deep-seated social tensions in society relating to race, class, or other issues.

- Nils Christie (1986) suggested that the media often confer victim status on an individual based on certain characteristics he or she possesses that relate to race, gender, class, etc.

NOTE

1. Mark Leary, Robin Kowalski, Laura Smith, and Stephen Phillips (2003) have noted that in 13 of 15 school shootings between 1995 and 2001, acute or chronic rejection of the shooter was prominent. Furthermore, all of the shooters had one or more of three risk factors: a significant interest in firearms or bombs, a fascination with death, and psychological problems of depression, impulse control, and/or sadism.

QUESTIONS FOR CRITICAL DISCUSSION

1. Over the next several days, take note of the kinds of stories about crime that are contained in the news you read or hear, and the shows and movies you watch. Who is the victim? Who is the perpetrator? How do the police interact with the people involved in the crime? How do these stories shape your own assumptions about who commits crime, who is victimized by crime, and how the police intervene?

2. Can you think of an example of an "ideal victim" that appeared in any media you watched or listened to recently? What made the victim seem "innocent"? How was this "innocence" conveyed? What kinds of images or words were used to describe the victim?

3. In what ways do different media outlets cover the same story? Try the following exercise: Seek out news stories from multiple sources on the policing of the G20 Summit in Toronto in 2010. You can search the CBC (http://www.cbc.ca), the Canadian Press (http://www.thecanadianpress.com), the *Toronto Sun* (http://www.torontosun.com), and The Media Co-op, an alternative news site run by activists from across Canada (http://www.mediacoop.ca). How does coverage by these different sources differ? What kinds of assumptions are made about the role of the police by each source?

4. How does the media portray the #blacklivesmatter and the #metoo movements? What kinds of images or words are used to describe each movement and its members? What are the similarities between the two? What are three differences? Celebrities have become involved in both movements. Does celebrity involvement help or harm a movement?

5. Look up section 163 of the *Criminal Code*, where it states that it is a crime to make, print, publish, distribute, or sell a crime comic. You can read the parliamentary debate at http://parl.canadiana.ca/view/oop.debates_HOC2101_01/514?r=0&s=3. Is this legislation the result of a moral panic? Why or why not? If so, which groups do you think lobbied for the legislation? Why?

6. What implications does sousveillance have for the ways we think about police? How do you think sousveillance affects the public's relationship with the police? Should it be legal to film police and post those videos online? Why or why not?

SUGGESTED FURTHER READINGS

Cohen, S. (1980). *Folk devils and moral panics: The creation of the mods and rockers*. Oxford, UK: Basil Blackwood. (Original work published 1972.)

Greer, C. (Ed.). (2010). *Crime and media: A reader*. Oxford, UK: Routledge.

Hall, S., Critcher, C., Jefferson, T., Clarke, J.N., & Roberts, B. (1978). *Policing the crisis: Mugging, the state and law and order*. London, UK: Macmillan.

Surette, R. (2010). *Media, crime, and criminal justice* (4th ed.). Belmont, CA: Wadsworth.

Websites

Center for Media Literacy: https://www.medialit.org

MediaSmarts: http://mediasmarts.ca

Legislation

Criminal Code, RSC 1985, c C-46.

The Bountiful Polygamy Case: Section 293 of the Criminal Code of Canada

Winston Blackmore of Bountiful, British Columbia.

"Polygamy" is the term used to describe a marriage involving more than two people. Anthropologists and historians tell us that, almost without exception, it takes the form of "polygyny" (that is, one man with more than one wife), although "polyandry" (the opposite arrangement) also occurs in some societies. Usually, polygamy is founded on, or at least supported by, particular religious doctrines or deep cultural tradition.

Canada's concern over polygamy dates back to the early days of Confederation. In 1887, Mormon elder Charles Ora Card led a vanguard of Mormon settlers into Western Canada, fleeing persecution of the polygamous group by an increasingly intolerant US government. The federal government already held a lingering concern over polygamy as practised by some First Nations peoples in the Northwest Territory (as Canada's western provinces of today were then known). To make matters worse, a mischievous Vancouver Island politician named Anthony Maitland Stenhouse converted to Mormonism and noisily declared that no Canadian law prohibited polygamy, so he would (if he could find two willing women) marry plurally. A criminal law was seen to be the solution to polygamy, and in 1890, *An Act Further to Amend the Criminal Law* was passed.

Canada's legislative approach to polygamy seemed to deter it for a while. In fact, polygamy did not take hold in a significant way in Canada until the 1940s, when a handful of excommunicated Mormons from Card's Alberta colony moved onto a large piece of land in southern British Columbia, which became known as Bountiful. Eventually, Bountiful became a community of about 1,000, isolated and mysterious. As the decades wore on, complaints surfaced about child brides, "lost boys," and an (apparently increasingly) abusive patriarchy that served the interests of church elders and no one else.

When the *Canadian Charter of Rights and Freedoms* was introduced in 1982, it was not surprising that the polygamy prohibition was identified by constitutional lawyers as a criminal law that could not be justified. The prohibition surely was a Victorian anachronism, perpetuated through bigotry and inattention, a way to isolate and marginalize (mostly) religious minorities such as Muslims, Canada's small but persistent band of fundamentalist Mormons, and a small number of African immigrants from nations where this traditional practice continues. Uncertain of the constitutional validity of the prohibition, British Columbia's attorney general openly refused to enforce it against the senior men of Bountiful, including bishop Winston Blackmore, who at one time claimed to have 24 wives.

But the problem of polygamy was not going away, and even if Bountiful remained a small outpost, newspaper stories reported that polygamy was spreading among immigrant populations in Ontario and elsewhere. Some certainty around the law was needed.

The matter finally came for adjudication before the Supreme Court of British Columbia through a constitutional reference case in 2010–2011 (a reference case is a rare form of proceeding in which the government may ask the court to settle a controversial issue without the traditional, purely adversarial process). Would the criminal prohibition survive modern scrutiny?

After 42 days of often intense hearings and submissions, Chief Justice Robert Bauman decided that the law infringed on the religious freedoms of polygamists, which was contrary to section 2(a) of the Charter, but that the infringement was justified as reasonable, given the significant harms associated with polygamy. Relying on what he referred to as "the most comprehensive judicial record on the subject ever produced," Bauman set out in a 357-page decision his conclusions that polygamy caused harm to women and children as well as society at large (*Reference re Section 293 of the Criminal Code of Canada*, 2011). In his reasons for judgment, Bauman referred to the international experience with polygamy and noted that in societies where the practice was most prevalent, the rights of women and children (and many men) suffered accordingly. He decided that it was likely that such negative effects were *caused* by the social structure that polygamy promotes and reinforces, and were not simply coincidental. And for every negative effect predicted by the expert witnesses, Bauman found plenty of corroborating evidence from individuals who had experienced the problems firsthand in the polygamous communities of Canada and the United States.

After the law against polygamy was upheld in the reference case, a special prosecutor brought charges against the two competing "bishops" of Bountiful, Winston Blackmore and James Oler. After a 12-day trial and a renewed constitutional challenge, both were convicted, and in June 2018 were sentenced to house arrest for periods of six and three months, respectively.

The polygamy reference case was unusual in many ways: It was the first reference case heard by a trial court, with live witnesses, instead of by an appeal panel relying on counsel's submissions alone; some witnesses were permitted to offer their evidence anonymously; an *amicus curiae* ("friend of the court") was hired to argue against the government's position that the law should be upheld; and a large number of groups were permitted to appear as "interested persons" to argue for or against the law. These features are not common to an ordinary criminal process.

In its exploration of the appropriate role of criminal law in addressing social harm, morality, and the clash of rights, *Reference re Section 293 of the Criminal Code of Canada* (2011) remains a very useful takeoff point for a discussion of the ideas underlying criminal law.

Before You Read Chapter 3

- To what extent do you believe the state (via the police, the courts, or provincial or federal legislatures) has the right to impose laws on an isolated or traditional community and its unconventional family or marriage practices?
- Are there social norms or practices that should always be "off limits" for the state?
- How would you define the "crime" described in this case? What makes this case an interesting topic for exploring the intersection of criminology and the law?
- During the BC hearings, what arguments do you imagine were made by those witnesses who supported this community's right to practise polygamy?

Criminal Law in Canada

Introduction: What Is Criminal Law?

Criminology is the study of crime and criminal behaviour, which are defined by reference to **criminal law**. What is crime, and how do we decide what behaviour is criminal and what is not?

All societies have developed mechanisms for the collective enforcement of group norms in service of what might be called a "public purpose." Where these mechanisms take the shape of a **prohibition** coupled with a *penalty*, they are legitimately regarded as elements of a criminal legal system. In modern nation-states, near-universal characteristics separate criminal law from other aspects of the legal system. Unlike violations of social norms that are embodied in the law of contract or tort, criminal behaviour is addressed by state, not individual, action and the penalties that may be imposed often, although not always, involve periods of imprisonment in state institutions.

The Origins of Criminal Law

Crime is prosecuted by the state because it is considered to be a violation of public order (which was once referred to as "the king's peace") rather than an infringement on the rights of another citizen. However, the distinction between private and public criminality has not always been so clear. For much of Western history, incarceration or state-enforced servitude could be imposed for private debts, and breaches of public

criminology
The study of crime and criminal behaviour, which are defined by reference to criminal law.

criminal law
The entire set of principles, procedures, and rules established by governments through the courts and criminal legislation in order to ensure public safety. It includes definitions of crimes, criminal responsibility, punishments, and defences to a criminal charge.

prohibition
A law forbidding a specific act.

The author is grateful to Neil Boyd and Micah Rankin for their thoughtful suggestions and editorial contributions, and to Graham Hudson for his assistance.

obligations were generally left to be prosecuted by the affected private individuals, usually victims and their families. The ancient world's most famous recorded criminal trials were framed as private undertakings: The prosecution that led to the execution of the Greek philosopher Socrates in 399 BCE was initiated and conducted in large part by Meletus, a poet, and some centuries later, Cicero's prosecution of Gaius Verres for corruption was initiated on behalf of deprived Roman citizens. Indeed, "private prosecutions" are technically available in Canada to this day.

By the Age of Enlightenment in 18th-century Europe, a number of factors had combined to create what we now recognize as a modern system of criminal law: the emergence of the government as a meaningful source of central authority and a mechanism of collective action, which supplemented and eventually displaced the Church (which, in many European countries, had its own law, its own police, and its own prisons); the growth of professional state police services; and the ever-increasing complexity of social interaction. The modern system of criminal law required a body of **penal law** that was comprehensive, codified (whether in written laws or in courts' decisions), and—in theory at least—subject to consistent enforcement.

Most of the "core" criminal prohibitions in Canada—such as murder, robbery, trespass, and assault—originate in ancient history and were inherited in more or less their modern form along with the laws of England in a process that began in the 18th century and continued until the *Statute of Westminster* in 1931 (which saw the Supreme Court of Canada become the court of last resort for criminal matters). By the time most of the remaining British North American colonies and territories merged into Canada in the late 19th century, the basic elements of the criminal justice system—police, courts, prisons, and legislation—were firmly in place. However, unlike Great Britain, where **common law** (or "judge-made") offences continued in force, Canada adopted its own *Criminal Code* in 1892. The effect of this Code was to substantially codify existing English offences. That said, Canada retained the power to create common law offences until the 1950s.

Criminal Law in Canada

We would be forgiven if we thought of the criminal process as either a provincial or a local affair. After all, provincial or municipal police forces investigate most crimes, and prosecutors working for the provincial governments prosecute most offenders. Nevertheless, by the terms of section 91(27) of Canada's *Constitution Act, 1867*, the federal Parliament determines what acts are criminal and which available punishments apply, as well as the procedures associated with investigating and prosecuting crimes.

The federal government may enact any criminal laws necessary to protect "public peace, order, security, health, and morality" (*The Canadian Federation of Agriculture v The Attorney-General of Quebec and Others*, 1950; more recently, see *Reference re Assisted Human Reproduction Act*, 2010). Thus, some laws that might not be regarded as truly "criminal," such as those that restrict the sale of tobacco products (*RJR-MacDonald Inc v Canada (AG)*, 1995) have been considered by the courts to be valid exercises of the federal power.

However, the laws that most people think of as "criminal laws," and the laws that consume virtually all of the efforts of the criminal courts and the corrections systems, are found mainly in two pieces of federal legislation: the *Criminal Code* and the *Controlled*

penal law
A law that imposes punishment, as opposed to (for instance) a law that provides only the right of a victim to compensation.

common law
A body of law defined primarily through successive decisions of judges, as opposed to through legislation.

Drugs and Substances Act. Others are the *Youth Criminal Justice Act* and the *Crimes Against Humanity and War Crimes Act* (examined in Box 3.1).

Criminal offences generally fall into one of two categories: summary offences or indictable offences. A **summary offence** (known in many US states, and historically in Canada, as a "misdemeanour") is the less serious type. It generally carries a penalty of no more than six months in prison or a $5,000 fine. More serious offences, referred to in some other countries (and historically) as "felonies," are called **indictable offences** in Canada. While the most serious crimes, such as murder, are only prosecuted by way of indictment, the majority of indictable offences may also result in summary convictions, and so are known as "hybrid offences." The distinction between summary and indictable offences has procedural consequences as well.

summary offence
A relatively minor offence, punishable by a fine or a maximum jail sentence of six months.

indictable offence
A serious offence, such as murder or rape, which carries a severe penalty. An "indictment" is the formal process of setting out a criminal charge in a document for serious, "indictable" offences.

BOX 3.1

The Crimes Against Humanity and War Crimes Act

Canada's *Crimes Against Humanity and War Crimes Act* (CAHWCA) is an especially interesting criminal law statute, because it gives domestic legal effect to international criminal law. Under this Act, Canadian courts are authorized to assume jurisdiction over crimes against humanity, war crimes, genocide, and any other crime recognized under international law, even if the crime took place in another country and did not involve any Canadian citizens—a power referred to as "universal jurisdiction." The CAHWCA also allows courts to assume jurisdiction over international crimes committed within Canada or abroad by Canadian citizens and state officials. This suggests that international law can take its place alongside the common law, statutes, and the Constitution as a source of criminal law in Canada.

In 2009, Désiré Munyaneza, a Rwandan national with permanent resident status in Canada, became the first person charged and convicted under the CAHWCA. After being recognized by members of the Rwandan diaspora

in Toronto, Munyaneza was prosecuted in Quebec. The Quebec Superior Court found him guilty of genocide, war crimes, and crimes against humanity during the Rwandan genocide, and sentenced him to life imprisonment with no possibility of parole for 25 years.

In the larger international arena, the International Criminal Court (ICC), located in The Hague in the Netherlands, has a mandate under the provisions of public international law to prosecute genocide and other crimes against humanity. More than 120 countries are members of this "court of last resort," which will try serious cases in those situations where a national court proves unable or unwilling to do so. Notably, several powerful nations, including the United States, Israel, China, and Russia have refused participation in the ICC, and have often been critical of it. A number of African nations have, in recent years, threatened to withdraw from the ICC, asserting that it is biased against the states of that continent.

The Criminal Courts

The adjudication of Canada's criminal cases is divided between two levels of court in the provinces and territories (with the exception of Nunavut, which has a single territorial court)—and these levels have developed considerable overlap.[1] Provincial superior courts are administered by the provinces, but their judges are appointed federally. These courts are tasked with the adjudication of the most serious matters, civil and criminal. They have their own powers and are independent; that is, they are not "creatures of statute" (created by Parliament). While the federal and provincial governments can legislate the processes and administration of these courts, they can't impair the courts' fundamental powers or jurisdiction (*MacMillan Bloedel Ltd v Simpson*, 1995).

FIGURE 3.1   Hierarchy of Courts

Supreme Court of Canada
(National Court)

Provincial Court of Appeal

Superior Trial Court
(e.g., Superior Court
of British Columbia)

Presides over more serious
offences, such as murder.

Provincial Trial Court
(e.g., Provincial Court of
British Columbia)

Presides over most criminal and
youth justice bails, trials, and
preliminary hearings.

civil law
A system in which the law is
primarily set out in legislation,
and judges' discretion is limited
to interpretation and application
of those written provisions.

Each province may structure its courts as it sees fit, but the common design divides the superior court into a trial court (called the Supreme Court in British Columbia, the Court of Queen's Bench in Alberta, and the Superior Court of Justice in Ontario) and a court of appeal.

Each province also has its own provincial court, which is sometimes referred to as the "inferior court," and which again may be variously named (for example, it is called the Court of Justice in Ontario and the Provincial Court in British Columbia). Provincial Court judges are appointed by the provincial government and generally have jurisdiction over matters considered to be less important than those that occupy the superior courts. However, describing the Provincial Court as "inferior" is somewhat misleading, at least with respect to criminal law, because every criminal prosecution begins in Provincial Court and the overwhelming majority are concluded there as well. In recent years, Canadian constitutional law has developed to recognize substantial, fundamental powers even in these "inferior" entities, to the point now where their independence has received constitutional recognition virtually equivalent to that of superior courts (*Reference re Remuneration of Judges of the Provincial Court (PEI)*, 1997).

At a national level, the Federal Court and the Federal Court of Appeal deal mainly with matters of exclusively federal interest, and the Supreme Court of Canada can hear and provide final decisions on appeals from all the other courts.

Criminal courts are responsible for applying the *Criminal Code* or relevant regulatory statute to the facts of a particular case. Doing so necessarily involves a substantive interpretation of the law. Moreover, because judges traditionally give written reasons for their decisions, the courts themselves are a significant source of criminal rules. As a result, commentators sometimes describe the Canadian legal regime as a common law (that is, a judge-made law) system. However, this description is incomplete, at least with respect to criminal justice. While judges can exercise varying degrees of discretion in their decisions, and while they are bound by precedent (that is, they must generally follow decisions made by superior courts), they remain constrained by legislation in the same way as judges in countries that use the continental European, or **civil law**, system. The difference, if any, is mostly of degree. The Canadian criminal law tradition stands in stark contrast to the English tradition and its numerous "common law crimes"—that is, crimes that were defined (if not invented) by judges, often over generations and even centuries. It might surprise the North American reader to learn that the prohibition on murder, for instance, is not founded on any English statute (although legislation may establish defences, procedures, and modify punishments). Common law crimes persist in some Commonwealth jurisdictions; in Canada, however, they were abolished[2] at the time of the consolidation of the *Criminal Code* in 1953.

One way in which Canadian criminal law differs sharply from the continental European tradition is in its complete reliance on an adversarial, rather than inquisitorial, model. In many European countries, the judge may play a role as an active investigator, along with the prosecutorial lawyers of the state. In Canada and other countries based on English tradition, the judge is an impartial arbiter between the state on the one hand, usually represented by a public prosecutor, and the individual and his or her lawyer on the other.

Criminal Justice Process

Typically, a crime is investigated by police officers employed by municipal or provincial police forces (or, in the case of RCMP officers, by a federal force contracted out to provinces and municipalities). When the police have gathered sufficient evidence to support a charge, they then (in most provinces) provide a report to the public prosecutor's office (a semi-independent branch of the attorney general's ministry generally known as Crown counsel), who then approves the charge based on an assessment of whether the evidence will support a conviction and whether prosecution is in the public interest. Much is made of the fact that some jurisdictions still allow the police to "press charges" without prior approval. However, in practice, cases cannot proceed without prosecutorial support, so little practical difference exists between one approach and the other.

In all provinces, the prosecution begins with the swearing of an information before a justice of the peace. Usually, the swearing is done by a police officer or another public official. The police officer recounts his or her belief that a crime has been committed, and the justice of the peace orders the charge. Private prosecutions (whereby a layperson, rather than a police officer or other public official, swears the information and initiates the prosecution) are still technically possible under the *Criminal Code*. However, they are now almost always taken over by Crown counsel, who may pursue or (far more often) stay charges (that is, suspend or terminate the prosecution).

Once a person is arrested, he or she is usually released on a promise to appear in court at an appointed time. In more serious matters, the police may choose to hold the accused in custody. In such cases, the accused must be brought before a justice of the peace within 24 hours for a bail hearing, at which the Crown must demonstrate a reason for continued custody or the conditions for interim release. Usually the accused is granted bail, often with conditions such as the posting of a bond, a curfew, or orders that the accused avoid certain places or people.

In more serious cases, where the Crown proceeds by way of **indictment**, a preliminary inquiry is usually held at which a judge of the Provincial Court decides whether sufficient evidence exists to proceed to trial. If evidence is insufficient, then the accused is discharged (subject to the Crown's right to restart the prosecution if more evidence becomes available or, in extraordinary cases, to proceed by direct indictment). If sufficient evidence exists, a trial date is set.

indictment
A formal written accusation, usually reserved for more serious crimes.

In cases where the Crown is pursuing a summary conviction, no preliminary inquiry takes place and the matter proceeds directly to trial in the Provincial Court.

Under section 11 of the Charter, the accused has a right to choose trial by judge and jury for any offence that could result in a sentence of five years or more. In any other case, the trial will be by judge alone, whether in the superior court or Provincial Court. In jury trials, a panel of laypeople determines the accused's guilt or lack thereof (it should be noted that "innocent" is not an available verdict in Canada). The judge makes peripheral decisions such as those governing the admissibility of evidence and the setting or modification of bail conditions. The judge also guides the jury on the legal rules it is to apply through comprehensive instructions.

FIGURE 3.2   The Criminal Justice Process in Canada

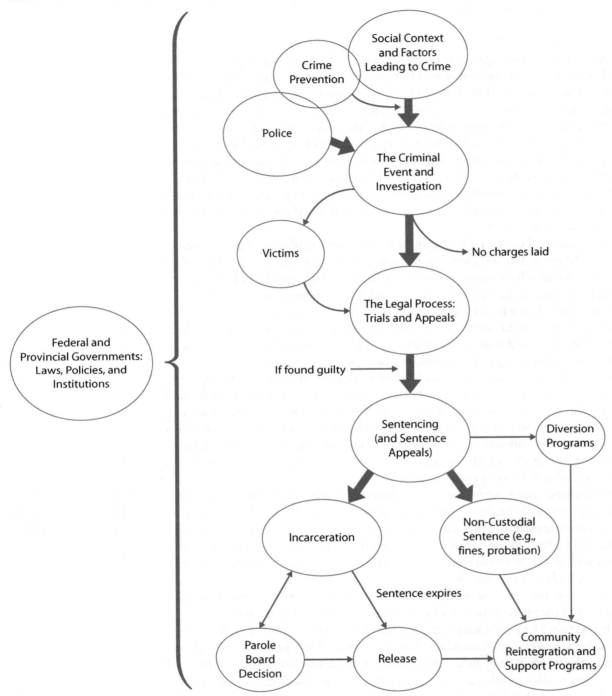

Throughout a trial, the accused may sit mute, exercising the right to silence and forcing the state to prove every element of the case against him or her beyond a reasonable doubt. Nonetheless, prosecutions that proceed to trial usually conclude with a conviction, either through trial or through an accused's plea of "guilty" (often the result of a pre-trial bargain for a lesser sentence). Of course, a trial may also result in an acquittal (after which an accused may not be retried, unless the Crown successfully appeals), a stay of proceedings (a suspension of charges), or a mistrial (where the trial is aborted but may begin anew at a later date).

Arthur Lucas (left) and Ronald Turpin were the last two people executed in Canada, on December 11, 1962, at Toronto's Don Jail.

Once convicted, an accused faces a sentence that can range from an absolute or conditional discharge (whereby an accused is essentially forgiven for the offence, either immediately or following a period of good behaviour) to imprisonment for periods up to life. However, the parole system in Canada generally releases prisoners under supervision after they have served one-third of their sentences (with the exception of murderers, who are ineligible for parole for 10 to 25 years). Sentences of less than two years are served in provincial correctional institutions. Sentences of two years or more are served in federal penitentiaries. The death penalty for murder was abolished in Canada in 1976; by that time, Canada had not carried out an execution in 14 years. Although a few attempts have been made to lobby for the reintroduction of the death penalty, Supreme Court of Canada decisions regarding the rights of accused facing extradition to death-penalty jurisdictions suggest that no such law could withstand a constitutional challenge (*United States v Burns*, 2001).

The Elements of a Crime

As described above, in Canada a crime is described in a federal statute, which sets out the prohibition and the associated penalty. These provisions typically contain a description of the prohibited acts (collectively known by the Latin term ***actus reus***) coupled with some element of mental culpability (***mens rea***).[3] The basic offence of theft, for instance, is described in section 322 of the *Criminal Code* as follows:

> 322(1) Every one commits theft who fraudulently and without colour of right takes, or fraudulently and without colour of right converts to his use or to the use of another person, anything, whether animate or inanimate, with intent
> (a) to deprive, temporarily or absolutely, the owner of it, or a person who has a special property or interest in it, of the thing or of his property or interest in it; ... .

actus reus
The criminal act or personal conduct relating to a crime; it may include a failure to act but does not include the mental element of a criminal offence.

mens rea
The mental element of a criminal offence or the state(s) of mind of the offender; it is the intent to commit a criminal act.

What follows in the *Criminal Code* are a number of clarifications designed to provide some guidance to the courts. When does the theft occur? For instance, is a person guilty of shoplifting when he picks up the item from the shelf? When he conceals it in a pocket? When he walks out of the store? Section 322(2) of the *Criminal Code* provides some guidance:

> 322(2) A person commits theft when, with intent to steal anything, he moves it or causes it to move or to be moved, or begins to cause it to become movable.

In theory, then, the theft has occurred when the item is taken from the shelf. However, each element of the offence must be proven by the Crown beyond a reasonable doubt. Practically speaking, how can one prove the "intent to steal" without the accused actually leaving the store without paying, or at least without him or her concealing the item or otherwise signalling a criminal purpose? Nevertheless, the law as it is defined allows the police to intervene and the Crown to prosecute at the earliest stages, where an intent to steal is coupled with some concrete action.

Note that criminal *intent* changes an ambiguous act (such as picking up an item from a shelf) into an act that can result in arrest and imprisonment (such as stealing). As such, the concept of a guilty mind (*mens rea*) is central to our understanding of most criminal sanctions. Proof beyond a reasonable doubt of mental culpability is a necessary element of every serious criminal offence and most less-serious ones. The exceptions are criminal or penal negligence and strict liability offences (where, once the Crown has proved the prohibited acts, or *actus reus*, the onus switches to the defendant to show that he or she *did not* have a criminal intent by establishing, for instance, due diligence). In even rarer situations, absolute liability (where the commission of the act alone is sufficient to support conviction) may be permissible where no potential for imprisonment exists. Generally speaking, the more serious the crime and its consequences, the higher the requirement that intent be proven: Murder requires proof of a subjective intent to kill a victim, or at least the reckless intent to create a situation where death is likely to occur. On the opposite end of the spectrum, some offences of a regulatory nature do not require intent. For example, a car's registered owner might be fined for a parking violation, even if his or her car had been illegally parked by a thief.

Criminal Defences

One other significant feature of Canadian criminal law is the availability of defences. The most common criminal defence is simply that the Crown has failed to establish the elements of an offence. As described above, to prove an offence, the Crown must establish beyond a reasonable doubt that the accused committed the prohibited act or made the omission that the offence prohibits (the *actus reus*), as well as any associated mental elements of the offence (the *mens rea*). Where the prosecution fails to establish any of the elements of the offence, or the defendant can disprove an element of the offence, there will be no criminal liability. Thus, a defence such as an alibi, or a partial defence such as **intoxication**, would be used simply to cast doubt on the Crown's proof of a required element of the offence.

More formal defences—often called "true defences"—are also available to an accused. A true defence is a set of circumstances that, if proven by the accused, will excuse him or her of the crime. The defence of insanity is one example. The *Criminal Code* itself sets out certain defences that, if proven on a balance of probabilities, absolve behaviour that would otherwise be considered criminal. Section 34 of the *Criminal Code*, for example, provides that a person is not guilty of a crime if he or she acts reasonably in his or her own defence or the defence of another.

The courts themselves have crafted still other defences—these common law defences are incorporated into the *Criminal Code* by virtue of section 8(3).[4] The defence of **duress** is one such common law defence that is available to any crime except murder. It provides that where an accused committed an act under threat of death or serious injury, and had no reasonable alternative, he or she will escape liability provided that the crime committed was not disproportional to the threat. If a defence such as duress is raised by an accused, the burden is on the Crown to prove that one or more of its elements is not present.

For more on criminal defences and liability, see Case Study 6.1, Sentencing for Manslaughter.

intoxication
A potential defence in which drugs or alcohol may prevent an accused from forming the necessary intent to commit a particular crime.

duress
An unlawful threat or coercion used by one person to induce another to perform some act against his or her will.

The Public Purpose of Criminal Law

A criminal law is not simply a prohibition coupled with a penalty: To be considered valid, a criminal law must also serve a public purpose.

This public purpose may evolve over time, usually as new mischiefs—harms to be avoided—are perceived. But which harms does criminal law implicitly recognize? How direct must they be?

To explore this question, let's return to the idea of theft in a more explicitly modern context than the shoplifting example discussed earlier: What does "theft" mean in the age of telecommunications? What behaviour can the criminal law be used to control?

Almost everyone knows someone who has "stolen" cable or satellite signals. Should society treat this act as criminal theft? For most of Canada's history, radio (and later television) programming had been available to anyone with a receiver, free over the public airwaves. The development in the 1960s of various technologies for delivering television broadcasts only to *paying* subscribers led some to circumvent the subscription restriction and obtain the service for free (for instance, by splicing into their neighbour's cable connection). Courts might well disagree on whether this is "theft" under the traditional definition: Certainly, the cable hacker is converting something to his or her own use (to the extent that a pattern of modulation of electrical signals is a "thing") without the legal right to do so, but is the cable hacker truly intending to deprive anyone of it? In the 1970s, the following crime was added to the *Criminal Code*:

> 326(1) Every one commits theft who fraudulently, maliciously, or without colour of right, ...
>   (b) uses any telecommunication facility or obtains any telecommunication service.

The reasons for the addition are not difficult to imagine. Cable companies and other controlled-subscription broadcasters (such as satellite TV providers) invest in an infrastructure and expect a return. Customers provide that return through their subscriptions. Allowing free riders to piggyback on the system deprives the service provider of income and forces paying users to effectively subsidize the system's hackers. However, these harms, even if economically significant, are indirect. Unlike murder or robbery, the moment at which telecommunications theft is committed nobody is hurt, and it is unlikely that anyone even knows the crime has occurred. But indirect harms are no less real: The innocent and obedient cable subscriber *will* pay more, even a few pennies more, as an indirect result of piracy.

Some have attempted to restrict criminal law only to areas where direct harm has occurred ("My right to swing my fist ends only where another's nose begins"). Yet courts have consistently rejected the "harm principle" as providing a clear boundary on criminal law (*R v Malmo-Levine; R v Caine*, 2003). In fact, the harm principle, at least to the extent that it requires some immediate, apparent, or direct harm to justify criminalization, isn't even very helpful as a descriptive, let alone prescriptive, norm. Criminal laws justified, in whole or in part, on indirect or even speculative effects are surprisingly common. How else to explain the various possession offences? The criminal law, for instance, prohibits the possession of high-capacity pistol magazines (even if never loaded), child pornography (even if computer simulated), and burglary tools (even if never used); it also controls the keeping or distribution of hundreds or even thousands of other things, from drugs to dangerous or endangered animals to some kinds of writing (*Regulations Prescribing Certain Firearms and Other Weapons, Components and Parts of Weapons, Accessories, Cartridge Magazines, Ammunition and Projectiles as Prohibited or Restricted*, 1998; *R v Sharpe*, 2001; *Mihalchan v The King*, 1945).

Possession offences are not the only crimes aimed at acts whose commission may not be immediately harmful to anyone. Incest is a crime almost everywhere, even when it occurs between adults raised in separate households, and even when (due to sterility, age, or contraception) there is no possibility of conception (and thus no danger of birth defects). As was discussed in Case Study 3.1 that precedes this chapter, polygamy (being in a marriage with more than one person at a time) is also a crime, even when those directly affected view their acts as harmless or even positively good. Dangerous driving and other forms of recklessness can be criminal even if no accident results. Less notoriously, and perhaps surprisingly, *Criminal Code* section 143 states that it is a crime in Canada to publish an advertisement that offers a reward for the recovery of a lost or stolen item and promises there will be no questions asked.

The justification for criminalizing activities with indirect or speculative effects can only be that, while they are not necessarily *individually* harmful, the acts increase the *risk* of social harm in society. For example, the proliferation of high-capacity pistol magazines or burglary tools increases the *risk* of mass shootings or breaking-and-entering incidents; permitting even consenting adults to engage in safe incestuous relationships increases the *risk* that girls (who are overwhelmingly the victims of sexual abuse in the home) will be targeted and groomed as sexual partners by male household members; and "no questions asked" reward posters create a marketplace for stolen goods and therefore increase the *risk* of thefts. In each case, the law intervenes early by criminalizing activity that *might* lead to more serious crimes or other harm.

All countries, even the most notoriously abusive, have sought to justify their laws, asserting that they serve the public good and address harms, whether real or imagined. So, naturally, there must be limits to the power to criminalize on the basis of *speculation* of indirect harm or risk. Nevertheless, Canadian courts have generally deferred to Parliament in making the determination, holding that Parliament's apprehension of future harm must only be "reasonable," not demonstrable or actual. Although there have been important exceptions with significant social repercussions (as in laws relating to abortion, homosexuality, and assisted suicide), judges have overwhelmingly accepted a parliamentary determination that a criminal prohibition is justified. It is hoped, of course, that this deference is also the result of Parliament's own respect for the limits of the criminal power, and its concomitant restraint when crafting laws.

The Purpose and Function of Criminal Law
Denunciation and Retribution

deterrence
A principle of sentencing or punishment intended to discourage citizens from offending or reoffending.

denunciation
A formal expression that conduct is unacceptable.

retribution
Punishment for transgressions.

The most frequently cited justifications for criminal penalties are **deterrence**, **denunciation**, and **retribution**. The last two, denunciation and retribution, are almost redundant in a system dedicated to imposing penalties for activities deemed objectionable by society. What benefits do denunciation and retribution offer beyond their deterrent effects?

Denunciation and retribution could be considered as social goods in themselves. Participating in denunciation and retribution—whether verbal or physical—against those who violate social norms probably increases humans' sense of positive well-being.

Punishing is, as countless psychological experiments have shown, often pleasurable. But this pleasure can be achieved whether the target of social ire is guilty or innocent (consider the crowds taunting Jesus on his walk to crucifixion or the Puritans of the Salem witch trials). Presumably, we evolved (biologically and culturally) to gain satisfaction from punishing transgressors because doing so provided positive benefits to the group and, consequently, to its individual members through the elimination of group-diminishing behaviour.

The fact that our criminal law system goes to great lengths to ensure that its targets have *actually* transgressed suggests that denunciation and retribution must be directed at actual wrongdoing; in this sense, their main value seems to lie in their ability to guide behaviour and prevent crime.

Deterrence

Whether the prospect of criminal punishment actually modifies behaviour in convicted individuals (specific deterrence) or in others who learn of it (general deterrence) has been repeatedly called into question. Some go so far as to say that the criminal law by and large simply codifies what people would do anyway, and so little or no deterrence actually occurs. A good account of the deterrence debate can be found in Paternoster (2010).

By contrast, deterrence advocates argue that most people comply with the law as they understand it and respond to its changes. So, for instance, when the Canadian government introduced a criminal prohibition on the possession of an unregistered firearm, coupled with significant penalties for non-compliance, most gun owners registered their weapons or disposed of them through gift, sale, or surrender. Thus, the targeted activity (possession of an unregistered firearm) was undeniably—and, in the unique circumstances, measurably—deterred.

Those who contemplate engaging in criminal activities are rarely "rational actors"—that is, they are not people who make subtle cost–benefit assessments and govern themselves accordingly. Certainly, people who are only occasionally tempted to commit a crime are likely deterred by the threat of exposure, arrest, and prosecution. However, habitual criminals are a fairly distinct population—generally poor, often sick with drug addiction or underlying (often undiagnosed) mental illness, and almost always suffering from deficiencies in impulse control. They are also overwhelmingly young and male, a cohort that is, perhaps for evolutionary reasons, disproportionately driven to taking risks and inclined to violent acts as a means of improving social status. General deterrence has been shown to have little effect on habitual criminals: The path of criminality of teenaged boys, for instance, does not appear to change on the birthday they become subject to greater penalties as "adult offenders."

Some have concluded that changes to the law have no deterrent effect, but surely this is going too far, for the reasons discussed earlier. Nevertheless, we might concede that for habitual criminals, the penal justice system behaves more as a regulator of opportunity to commit crime than a moral force; it acts mainly to disrupt criminal behaviour (because a prisoner is temporarily prevented from committing most crimes, and the activities of organized crime or conspiratorial criminal networks are impaired through the rotating arrest and prosecution of even a minority of its members). In this view, members of the "criminal class" are *managed* through the period of their greatest anti-social tendencies, and the public absorbs the associated expenses as a significant but acceptable social cost. These issues and related themes will be explored in greater detail in Part Two, Theories of Crime.

The federal government's gun registry program sparked a highly charged debate across Canada. It was supported by police, but many opponents felt it was far too costly and would have no effect on deterring criminals. The national registry was eventually cancelled, although Quebec still maintains its own. Here, Montreal police seize weapons after consulting the registry during a standoff with an armed man.

The Limits of Criminal Law: Revolution and Evolution

Any successful society exists in a tension between the liberty of individuals and the power of the state. Individual fulfillment requires freedom to direct one's own path in life, subject to limitations in the interest of the collective good. But this borderline is a battleground. On the one side, individuals strive for their own success, even if doing so sometimes places the collective good at risk. On the other side, the group—and by extension the state—prefers the preservation of public order above almost all else, particularly where the activities it restricts are not those in which the majority of the public engages. The two sides, therefore, are constantly at odds. Nowhere is this more apparent than in the interplay between *constitutional law*, which restrains government and enforces individual rights, and *criminal law*, which provides crude coercive weight to the will of the majority.

The following section provides a brief introduction to the idea of "rights" in the criminal law context and an exploration of their limits "in a free and democratic society" (*Canadian Charter of Rights and Freedoms*, 1982, s. 1).

The Development of the Rights of Criminal Defendants

The idea that criminal defendants should have rights has grown alongside the development of the modern nation-state and, perhaps ironically, in response to the spread of democratic power within populations.

After the Norman Conquest of 1066 in England, the series of revolutions, compromises, and agreements that eroded the power of the king empowered lesser nobles and, over time, led to an increasingly representative Parliament. Not coincidentally, one of the means by which the Crown's power was diminished was through the recognition of fundamental rights of citizens faced with criminal accusations, and a number of English history's landmark legal tracts, most famously the *Magna Carta* ("great charter") in 1215, began to refer to the inalienable right of individuals to a minimum standard of due process.

Once **parliamentary supremacy**—something resembling the **rule of law**—took hold, it became clear that removing the power to arbitrarily punish from the king and transferring it to Parliament did not necessarily advance the cause of justice. Democracy alone was no defence against the abuse of prosecutorial authority. Elected assemblies had shown themselves to be just as capable of the arbitrary imposition of capital or penal sanctions as any warlord or king, and, given a legislature's sensitivity to the popular will, perhaps even more so. Just consider the Six Generals' trial in ancient Athens (Socrates' "other trial") and the notorious "Bills of Attainder" and "Bills of Pains and Penalties" passed by the English Parliament to effectively convict and punish named individuals. The ancient English right of *habeas corpus* (literally, "you have the body"), which permitted a prisoner to challenge the lawfulness of his or her confinement, didn't help if the law under which he or she was detained was itself capricious, corrupt, or unfair. The increasing popular demand to establish fundamental rights in the law became one of the forces that drove the development of constitutionalism. What was needed was a body of laws that would restrain the power of democracy itself.

The birth of the United States at the close of the 18th century, and in particular the codification of the Bill of Rights in the US Constitution, firmly and famously established the idea that the power of the collective and the state must be balanced against the rights of the individual, because only constitutional law could constrain the legislature.

England, from which Canada largely derives its criminal justice system, never adopted a written constitution. However, the notion of citizens' rights against the prosecutorial state has remained a powerful unwritten norm throughout the British Commonwealth. When Canada's *Charter of Rights and Freedoms* ("the Charter") was introduced in 1982, it set out a number of rights specific to an accused that in large part mirror those in the then 200-year-old American Bill of Rights. The Charter produced no radical upheaval in criminal justice outcomes in this country, in part perhaps because these fundamental ideas were already so firmly entrenched (Roach, 2008).

The Charter grants a number of rights to criminal defendants. Some are extremely general, such as the guarantee in section 7 that one will not be deprived of life or liberty except in accordance with the principles of fundamental justice. Others are more specific, such as the right in section 8 "to be secure against unreasonable search or seizure," to be free from "cruel or unusual treatment of punishment," and to be tried "within a reasonable time" (pursuant to s. 11). Still other rights, such as the provision of an interpreter where necessary (s. 14), are very specific. Most, such as the right of *habeas corpus* and the right to remain silent upon arrest, served to enshrine long-standing, even ancient, rights of Anglo-Canadian tradition.

parliamentary supremacy
The concept that the legislative body is superior to other institutions, including the executive and the courts.

rule of law
The principle that governments, individuals, and corporations must follow the law; governments may take actions that limit the activities or rights of citizens only in accordance with substantive and procedural requirements prescribed by law.

habeas corpus
The right of an accused (in the form of a "writ") to appear before a court and not be detained without just cause.

Limitations on Rights

The vulnerability of criminal defendants makes them members of a minority for whom special protection is warranted, and so it's not surprising that defendants' rights were the earliest fundamental rights enumerated in the laws of Athens, Rome, and England (and in numerous other countries and cultures; however, our focus is on the Canadian system's most immediate legal forebears). As the law progressed, other vulnerable minorities were also recognized as worthy of legal (and later constitutional) protection: first, members of political and religious groups, then those of disadvantaged races and women (although not technically a minority, women were historically underrepresented in the democratic power structure so as to make them similarly vulnerable). Ideally, the goal of the law is to treat all citizens equally except where differential treatment (or differential impact) can be objectively justified (as it might be in the case of children, for instance). Efforts to build a more just and equal society, which often conflict with individuals' desire to do as they please, have strongly influenced the development of criminal law in Canada and elsewhere.

Rights, even fundamental rights, have never been without qualification. For example, although the right of free speech has often been regarded in the West as nearly absolute, it does not protect communications that are immediately harmful (such as in US Justice Oliver Wendell Holmes' famous example of shouting "fire" in a crowded theatre [*Schenck v United States*, 1919]). In reality, the near-absolute right of free speech has often succumbed to criminal law as the notion of what constitutes sufficiently imminent danger changes. Criminal conspiracies may be nothing more than conversations that never manifest in damage or injury, but their prohibition has never been seriously controversial. Even mildly critical speech in wartime has been deemed seditious and has resulted in imprisonment of notional traitors in the United States (which had constitutional protections for free speech), no less than in England and Canada (which didn't have such protections). Art and literature that have been deemed obscene, depending on the morals of the day, were also made criminal, and only a vocal few have objected. Ongoing examples are numerous. The trend in Western democracies has been to liberalize speech laws, but not without the occasional considered retreat. One example is the introduction (and successful constitutional defence) in Canada of criminal prohibitions on certain forms of hate speech, such as the advocacy of genocide. One of Canada's landmark freedom of expression cases, *R v Keegstra*, is examined in Box 3.2.

Similarly, religious practices have also been prohibited where they are considered to be harmful, although religious beliefs have been persistently protected. Political affiliation is no longer a ground for imprisonment, but affiliation with a criminal organization may be.

This discussion erodes the simplistic view expressed at the beginning of this section that society is a binary struggle between individual and state. We can now appreciate that laws are made in the context of a constantly changing soup of various interests, both group and individual. As a result, the struggle to define the limits of criminal law has become complex, both for legislators and courts.

A main difficulty in setting limits on criminal law is determining when a law serves legitimate social purposes or instead is simply the handmaiden of an outdated paternalism or empty morality. For example, the criminal law against homosexual sodomy has persisted in one form or another throughout our history and arguably lingers to this day (inasmuch as the age of consent is different from that which applies to "normal" sexual acts).[5] Some say that other criminal prohibitions relating to sexual intimacy, such as the ban on consensual adult incest or multi-party marriage (polygamy), are similarly irrational vestiges of Victorian puritanism. But weighing individual rights against the public interest is a tricky business: In a society where both prostitution and its criminalization have been held as unacceptable violations of women's dignity, what is a lawmaker or a constitutional court to do?

BOX 3.2

The Limits of Free Expression

In *R v Keegstra* (1990), the Supreme Court of Canada reviewed the constitutionality of criminal laws prohibiting hate speech. Section 319(2) of the *Criminal Code* states the following:

> Every one who, by communicating statements, other than in private conversation, wilfully promotes hatred against any identifiable group is guilty of
> > (a) an indictable offence and is liable to imprisonment for a term not exceeding two years; or
> > (b) an offence punishable on summary conviction.

This provision was used to arrest, charge, and prosecute James Keegstra, an anti-Semitic high school teacher. Keegstra taught his classes that Jewish people were responsible for depressions, anarchy, chaos, wars, and revolution. According to Keegstra, Jews "created the Holocaust to gain sympathy" and, in contrast to the open and honest Christians, were said to be deceptive, secretive, and inherently evil. Keegstra expected his students to reproduce his teachings in class and on exams, and they were given poor grades if they didn't. Keegstra argued that hate speech laws unjustifiably infringed his Charter right to freedom of expression in section 2(b), which states:

> Everyone has the following fundamental freedoms:
> ...
> > (b) freedom of thought, belief, opinion and expression, including freedom of the press and other media of communication.

The government replied that the Charter protects equality, human dignity, and multiculturalism, as well as freedom of expression, and that hate speech laws are designed to protect the rights of victims as well as important public values. For those reasons, it argued, the laws are justified in a free and democratic society.

Not all such problems are necessarily vexing. Increasingly, courts and—perhaps more sluggishly—legislators have become attuned to historical patterns of prejudice and have begun to view criminal law, and even criminal procedure, in that light. The particular challenges faced by victims of sexual assault, for instance, led to changes in the criminal process to protect against revictimization of women and children in a number of ways. Lately, and belatedly, the recognition of the woeful overrepresentation of Indigenous peoples in the prison system has led to extensive rethinking of sentencing, in both process and substance, among numerous other legal and social reforms.

Conclusion: The Future of Criminal Law

Criminal justice faces many challenges in the years ahead. The increasing emphasis on rights and due process has contributed to a system that many regard as cumbersome, inefficient, and overly expensive. Trials, which historically would generally last days or (in particularly complex cases) a couple of weeks now often take months or, in some cases, years. State funding of defence counsel, increasingly viewed as fundamental to a fair trial, has nevertheless become concentrated on the most serious cases, and a growing number of criminal defendants are left with little or no recourse to legal advice. In all this, judicial resources are stretched thin in an age of fiscal austerity, resulting in delays and abandoned prosecutions. Many are calling for a fundamental rethinking of the entire justice system, but the direction that this will take is far from certain.

And while criminal law has struggled to accommodate the post–Second World War "rights revolution," it now finds itself stymied in the face of the other great postwar phenomenon: globalization. In the age of international industry and commerce, easy travel, and the Internet, many criminal activities, from child exploitation to securities fraud and environmental crimes, are inherently **interjurisdictional**. Yet investigation and prosecution have remained firmly rooted in individual countries, provinces, states, and municipalities. Interjurisdictional cooperation in everything from policing to extradition has improved but is far from adequate; international criminal courts, where they are effective at all, concern themselves with breaches of international law such as genocide, not with ordinary crimes.

The prescription for the problem is far from clear. Even if a truly international criminal court were established, whose law would it apply, for instance, to Internet gambling? Surely, we cannot expect online activity to be held to the lowest common denominator, with so many countries imposing hideous restrictions on their own citizens' speech and other liberties.

At its core, criminal law is deeply entrenched, calcified, and resistant to change or sudden movement. However, at its periphery, it is constantly evolving, sometimes quickly, in response to political and social trends. Criminal law is the product of humans, and, like them, it is both brilliant and inevitably, deeply flawed. However one views the role of criminal law, one thing is clear: It is impossible to understand criminal law without an understanding of its historical, sociological, political, and psychological context.

interjurisdictional
Relating to crimes, legislation, or other legal issues that cross the boundaries of nations, provinces, or other jurisdictions.

SUMMARY OF KEY POINTS

- All societies have developed mechanisms for the collective enforcement of group norms in the service of what might be called a "public purpose." Unlike violations of social norms that are embodied in the law of contract or tort, criminal behaviour is addressed by state, not individual, action.

- Most of the core criminal prohibitions in Canada—such as murder, robbery, trespass, and assault—originate in ancient history and were inherited in more or less their modern form along with the laws of England. However, the Canadian criminal law tradition differs from the English tradition in several important ways.

- The laws that most people think of as "criminal laws," and the laws that consume virtually all of the efforts of the criminal courts and the corrections systems, are found mainly in two pieces of federal legislation: the *Criminal Code* and the *Controlled Drugs and Substances Act*.

- The concept of a guilty mind (*mens rea*) is central to our understanding of most criminal sanctions. Proof beyond a reasonable doubt of mental culpability is a necessary element of every serious criminal offence and most less-serious ones.

- Whether the prospect of criminal punishment actually modifies behaviour in convicted individuals (specific deterrence) or in others who learn of it (general deterrence) has been repeatedly called into question and is the subject of ongoing debate in Canada.

- Any successful society exists in a tension between the liberty of individuals and the power of the state. Individual fulfillment requires freedom, subject to limitations in the interest of the collective good. The borderline between these two forces is the subject of ongoing legal, political, and social debate.

NOTES

1. The territories have similar courts, but they vary somewhat from those in the provincial model. For the sake of simplicity, the territorial systems will not be addressed in this chapter.

2. The one exception to this is "criminal contempt of court," by which courts may impose penalties, including incarceration, for disrespectful or abusive behaviour that is nowhere defined in statute. Even this, though, is authorized by the *Criminal Code* (s. 9).

3. Latin terms, most of which originated millennia ago in Roman law, recur frequently in the legal lexicon. In recent years, a "plain language" movement has replaced many of these terms with ordinary English terms, but a number of them, such as *actus reus* and *mens rea,* have survived in common use.

4. Section 8(3) of the *Criminal Code* reads:

    > Every rule and principle of the common law that renders any circumstance a justification or excuse for an act or a defence to a charge continues in force and applies in respect of proceedings for an offence under this Act or any other Act of Parliament except in so far as they are altered by or are inconsistent with this Act or any other Act of Parliament.

5. At the time of writing, the federal government had introduced Bill C-39, which, among other things, repealed the sodomy provision of the *Criminal Code.* At the same time, the government issued a public apology for its historical persecution of LGBTQ citizens.

QUESTIONS FOR CRITICAL DISCUSSION

1. How does an understanding of criminal law and its related processes affect one's understanding of criminology?
2. Is it possible to study criminology without any consideration of criminal law?
3. What are the primary purposes of criminal law?

4. Is criminal law shaped by society's values, or are our values shaped by criminal law?
5. Is it the role of criminal law to promote social changes? Or should it serve primarily to uphold established, traditional notions of justice?
6. Why has the United States, among other countries, refused to be part of the International Criminal Court?

SUGGESTED FURTHER READINGS

Brown, D.H. (1995). *The birth of a criminal code: The evolution of Canada's justice system.* Toronto: University of Toronto Press.
Cameron, J., & Stribopoulous, J. (Eds.). (2008). *The Charter and criminal justice: Twenty-five years later.* Toronto, ON: LexisNexis.
Katz, H. (2011). *Inside wrongful convictions in Canada.* Toronto: Dundurn Press.

Websites

Canadian Legal Information Institute: http://www.canlii.org
Department of Justice Canada: http://www.justice.gc.ca
International Criminal Court: https://www.icc-cpi.int

Legislation

An Act Further to Amend the Criminal Law (1890), 53 Vict, c 37, s 8.
Canadian Charter of Rights and Freedoms, Part I of the Constitution Act, 1982, being Schedule B to the Canada Act 1982 (UK), 1982, c 11.
Constitution Act, 1867 (UK), 30 & 31 Vict, c 3, reprinted in RSC 1985, Appendix II, No 5.
Controlled Drugs and Substances Act, SC 1996, c 19.
Crimes Against Humanity and War Crimes Act, SC 2000, c 24.
Criminal Code, RSC 1985, c C-46.
Regulations Prescribing Certain Firearms and Other Weapons, Components and Parts of Weapons, Accessories, Cartridge Magazines, Ammunition and Projectiles as Prohibited or Restricted, SOR/98-462.
Youth Criminal Justice Act, SC 2002, c 1.

Cases

Canadian Federation of Agriculture v The Attorney-General of Quebec and Others, [1950] UKPC 31, [1951] AC 179.
MacMillan Bloedel Ltd v Simpson, [1995] 4 SCR 725, 1995 CanLII 57.
Mihalchan v The King, [1945] SCR 9, 1944 CanLII 28.
R v Keegstra, [1990] 3 SCR 697, 1990 CanLII 24.
R v Malmo-Levine; R v Caine, 2003 SCC 74.
R v Sharpe, 2001 SCC 2.
Reference re Assisted Human Reproduction Act, 2010 SCC 61.
Reference re Remuneration of Judges of the Provincial Court (PEI), [1997] 3 SCR 3, 1997 CanLII 317.
Reference re Section 293 of the Criminal Code of Canada, 2011 BCSC 1588.
RJR-MacDonald Inc v Canada (AG), [1995] 3 SCR 199, 1995 CanLII 64.
Schenck v United States, [1919] 249 US 47.
United States v Burns, 2001 SCC 7.

Measuring Crime: How Much Can Chart 4.1 Tell Us?

A first glance at Chart 4.1 on page 64 suggests that crime in Canada increased quite dramatically between 1962 and the mid- to late 1980s. The trend appears to be particularly noticeable for property crime, but violent crime also increased significantly during the same time period. And then, in sharp contrast, between the early 1990s and circa 2015, all forms of crime declined.

As the chapter that follows will tell you, there are a number of important limitations or caveats that must be introduced in response to such observations. First, these are the crimes that were reported to police; there may be many crimes that are not reported to police for a variety of reasons. Additionally, there may be crimes not witnessed by the police and some crimes that the police, in exercising their discretion, may choose not to report. And finally, different police departments may have different policies with respect to the reporting of crime, leading to potentially erroneous conclusions about the amount of crime that exists in a given jurisdiction.

When we look more deeply into specific kinds of crime, we can also appreciate, for example, that homicides are almost always reported, whereas, in contrast, relatively minor assaults in playgrounds might most often not be reported as criminal actions. As the authors of the following chapter note, one way of trying to correct these anomalies is to survey members of the public with respect to their victimization by crime. Canada's General Social Survey asks Canadians a range of questions regarding social characteristics, and notably, for those of us who study crime, a series of questions about their victimization in relation to eight different crime types. When we correlate the results of the victimization survey with police-reported crime, a more nuanced and accurate portrait of crime in Canada emerges.

But what accounts for the crime drop that we have witnessed, beginning in the early 1990s and continuing until roughly 2015? And similarly, what accounts for the crime increase that occurred in Canada between the early 1960s and the late 1980s? There have been a number of different explanations for both of these relatively dramatic changes.

With respect to the increase, it has been noted that there were many more young men in the Canadian population in the late 1960s than there were in the early 1990s—and in every era of human history (and in every jurisdiction) young men have committed a disproportionate share of crime within our societies. The percentage of young men in the Canadian population was at about 17 percent in the late 1960s, but that figure dropped to about 9 percent by the early 1990s.

CHART 4.1   Police-Reported Crime Rates, Canada, 1962–2017

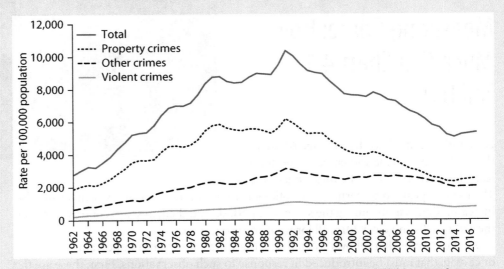

Note: Information presented in this chart represents data from the Uniform Crime Reporting (UCR1) Aggregate Survey, and permits historical comparisons back to 1962. New definitions of crime categories were introduced in 2009 and are only available in the new format back to 1998. As a result, numbers in this chart will not match data released in the new UCR2 format. Specifically, the definition of violent crime has been expanded. In addition, UCR1 includes some different offences in the "Other Crimes" category. Populations are based upon July 1st estimates from Statistics Canada, Demography Division.

Source: Allen (2018, Chart 2).

The 1960s and 1970s were also a time of significant social conflict, with anti-war movements, calls for sexual liberation, and an emerging industry of illegal drug distribution and use, an industry where disputes could not be settled in courts or systems of arbitration, but through the occasional use of predatory violence. This was also a time of conflict between men and women, and a time in which both men and women were consuming more alcohol. Between 1966 and 1975 the divorce rate in Canada increased by 400 percent, and alcohol consumption rose by 50 percent per capita. These social changes appear to have some utility in explaining the increase in crime: destabilization of relationships, increased use of alcohol and other drugs, and social conflict over unpopular wars.

But how to explain the decrease of the next 25 years? Farrell, Tilley, Tseloni, and Mailley, cited in the following chapter, suggest that the best explanation is the "security hypothesis." In a nutshell, crime has become more difficult to commit because of enhanced security in a number of important spheres. Automobile immobilizers have made both the theft of automobiles and theft from automobiles more difficult. Security systems and video cameras have made thefts and robberies of retail outlets and banks more difficult.

There is a good deal of merit in this argument, but how to explain the decrease in violent crimes and, most notably, homicide? It might be argued that the enhanced security in relation to property has had something of a spillover effect on the realm of violent crime, but, in fact, most homicide is quite removed from security issues surrounding property and property crime.

The psychologist Steven Pinker argues in his 2011 book, *The Better Angels of Our Nature: Why Violence Has Declined* that we have lived through a number of "rights revolutions" in most Western cultures over the past 40 years, changes that can explain the drop in violent crime. Simply put, in Pinker's view, we have become a more civilized society, less tolerant of violence. Pinker points to the issues of racial equality, women's rights, gay rights, children's rights, and animal rights as examples of fundamental change (Pinker, 2011). It is no longer permissible, for example, for teachers to punish students in elementary or high school with physical force.

But before we conclude with certainty that all is well on the crime front, with both personal and property crimes declining, let's consider some changes that have emerged in the past 25 years—a dramatic surge upward in credit card fraud, identity theft, and fraud perpetrated through Internet access. Put simply, this is the realm of cybercrime and most of it is not reported. Most of us who have Internet access can attest to many attempts to defraud us, and those of us who use credit cards are, again, not unfamiliar with attempts, sometimes successful, to use our card numbers without our consent.

Most banks do not report these violations to police, and, in fairness, policing these crimes is exceedingly difficult. The perpetrator is often online in a jurisdiction far away from where the crime takes place. It is not an easy matter to track the precise locations of those who commit these crimes. And then there is the problem of carrying out both arrest and extradition. Both the technology and the resources for enforcement are not available. On March 19, 2015, for example, the *London Telegraph* reported that a study from the city of London police had concluded the following:

> The scale of under-reporting is significant. In 2013–2014, Action Fraud and the National Fraud Intelligence Bureau recorded 211,000 crimes in England and Wales with a reported loss of £2.2 billion. But the City of London Police estimated that a further 1,160,500 crimes, with a loss worth £12.1 billion, were not reported by individuals and businesses (Barrett, 2015).

Put differently, there are many good reasons to believe that property crime is not actually decreasing in Canada. With the advent of the Internet and a series of technologically based frauds, it seems most likely that property crime is increasing. We are just not counting or measuring the changes that we have experienced.

Before You Read Chapter 4

- Review the chart on page 64. What can we conclude from it? What remains uncertain?
- Why are statistics valuable? What uses do you think they serve?
- As a citizen, do you pay attention to crime statistics? Do they affect your opinions about crime in particular places? Should they have more impact than they do?

CHAPTER 4 / HILARY KIM MORDEN AND TED PALYS

Measuring Crime

LEARNING OUTCOMES

After reading this chapter, students will be able to:

- Understand the theoretical nature of crime statistics and the four perspectives (structuralist, positivist, constructionist, and integrationist) through which crime may be identified, interpreted, and counted.

- Understand how crime statistics are constructed, what they do and do not show, and the social factors that guide their production.

- Understand the process by which a behaviour that is perceived as a crime becomes an official crime statistic.

- Identify the strengths and limitations of the different data gathering measures used to collect crime data, including the UCR2, victimization surveys, and the Crime Severity Index.

- Identify specific ways in which the Internet has altered existing crime and created new opportunity for crime, as well as how these crimes are discovered and measured.

CHAPTER OUTLINE

Introduction

If criminology comprises the study of crime and responses to it, then it is clearly important to know how much crime takes place. Any consideration of crime—including what causes it, who it victimizes, what its general social impacts are, and what should be done about it—requires the ability to assess how it varies from place to place and increases or decreases depending on changes to crime control policies and practices.

The kinds of crime statistics that you typically see referred to in the media and used in much criminological research are often referred to as **quantitative** data, which generally refers to data that are represented in numeric form and generated by methods that are highly structured and seek to aggregate as many cases as possible. Quantitative data are often contrasted with **qualitative** data, which tend to involve fewer cases that go into greater depth, focus on people's words, and often use methods such as interviewing that emphasize interaction with research participants to find the meaning they associate with events.

quantitative
Relating to the measurement of something—its quantity— rather than its qualities.

qualitative
The study of phenomena based not on measurement but on an exploration of the reasons for human behaviour and the qualities of subjective experience.

Qualitative and quantitative methods should be seen as complementary, rather than rivals. Quantitative data help show overall patterns, and their consistent structure allows for comparisons to be made between groups, times, and places. Qualitative observations serve to strengthen statistical results and help to put them into context; when we understand the meaning that people attach to different phenomena, it can help us understand *why* the aggregate results are the way they are. While there is often much made of the differences between qualitative and quantitative research methods, the social sciences benefit far more from an approach that uses multiple methods or a mixed methodology (Palys & Atchison, 2014). Combining methods, sometimes referred to as "triangulation" (Denzin, 2017), can give us a more comprehensive understanding of a phenomenon and result in research that is more complete, holistic, and contextual (Jick, 1979).

This chapter is a case in point. Although crime statistics are typically conceived as "quantitative data," understanding the prevalence of crime, and what crime statistics can tell us, has benefited from research that involves both qualitative and quantitative traditions. This is because counting the number of criminal acts that occur is not as straightforward as counting phenomena in other areas of study; for example, a health researcher might look at numbers of hospital admissions or how often antidepressants are prescribed, while a political scientist might look at voting records to determine how many Canadians voted in the last federal election. Two factors contribute to the complexity of measuring crime: (1) the inherently theoretical nature of crime as a construct and (2) the practical challenge of knowing where crime occurs, what to count, and how to count it.

Crime as a Theoretical Construct

Once we embrace the goal of trying to measure the volume of crime, our first challenge is to agree on which acts are "criminal" and which are not. Muncie (2001) offered 11 bases on which an act might be seen as "criminal," including prohibition based in law (that which is prohibited by the state and punishable by law), violation of moral values (that which violates norms of religion and morality and is punishable by a supreme being), violation of social convention (that which violates cultural norms and customs and is punishable by the community), and an act that has behavioural consequences (that which harms others). No doubt all of these and more play a role in how what is "criminal" comes to be defined in any society. Stated another way, the concept of crime is socially defined and hence inherently intertwined with theory.

Whatever its basis, the starting point for any discussion of crime in Canada is typically the *Criminal Code*, a federal statute that first came into force on July 1, 1893. Following that, an examination of the frequency and distribution of crime often involves the consideration of "crimes known to the police," which form the basis for crime statistics released periodically by Statistics Canada. We will examine below how these statistics are gathered and generated, but the inherently theoretical nature of crime requires that we first consider the meaning that supporters of different schools of thought attribute to crime statistics. It is important to do so because how crime statistics are conceived has significant implications for the kinds of research conducted, which, in turn, informs areas of concern to those who support the different schools of thought. The four general approaches we will review are the "structuralist," "positivist," "constructionist," and "integrationist" approaches. Note that these crime theories are discussed in much greater detail in Part Two of this book, but the following serves as a preview to how various theories relate to the practical question of how crime is measured.

Structuralist Perspectives

Structuralist perspectives fall within the general scope of **conflict theories**. Examples of structuralist perspectives include Marxist theories, which focus on inequities in the distribution of capital in society, and feminist theories, which focus on gender inequity in societies organized on largely patriarchal lines. Researchers who follow these and other structuralist perspectives pay particular attention to power structures and ideological influences that play out in a wide array of social contexts. They tend to view the *Criminal Code* not as a reflection of some neutral social consensus about what a particular society prohibits, but rather as a contemporary scorecard that reflects who has the power to create the laws that define what is and is not criminal. Crime statistics from that perspective are less useful as a measure of how much crime there is in society, and more a reflection of the extent to which those with power recognize and deal with activities they identify as criminal.

Certainly, a good deal of evidence supports the reasonableness of a structuralist point of view. When Indigenous communities and corporations come into conflict over the latter's interest in a development project on traditional Indigenous territory, why is it that the police seem to protect corporate rights and interests instead of those of the Indigenous community? Why are the possession and consumption of intoxicants favoured by the Western European people who first colonized Canada—alcohol, in particular—legal, while the intoxicants associated with "minorities"—coca, peyote, and opium—remain illegal? Why is it that when an individual kills someone we call it "murder" and look for a criminal charge, but when a corporation demonstrates neglect or follows a policy that results in a death, that death is considered a civil matter? Is it also a mere coincidence that minorities are incarcerated at higher rates than one would expect, given their proportion in the population?

With respect to gender issues, feminists have been at the forefront of various social debates and justice system challenges regarding the legality and illegality of particular acts. Feminists fought to institutionalize women's control over their own bodies in abortion debates and succeeded in making legal what was formerly illegal. They also exposed the blind eye that society had turned to wife assault and succeeded in making illegal what had formerly been tolerated.

The "political" and structural nature of these and other changes are sometimes highlighted when there are significant shifts in government, as occurred in Canada when Conservative Prime Minister Stephen Harper was succeeded by Liberal Prime Minister Justin Trudeau and in the United States when Donald Trump succeeded Barack Obama as president. In both cases, the new leaders sought to "undo" initiatives set in place by their predecessors. In Canada, examples include getting rid of many of the mandatory minimum sentences that Harper had introduced, increasing the environmental regulations that Harper had reduced, and paying greater heed to Indigenous rights than Harper had done. The United States went in the opposite direction: In the first year of his presidency, Trump appointed a new justice to the Supreme Court who was expected to be supportive of gun laws and limited access to abortion; began the criminalization and deportation of "dreamers"—the children of illegal immigrants to the United States for whom Obama had offered a road to full citizenship; and eliminated many environmental regulations, which made acceptable what had previously been illegal.

conflict theories
Theories, originating primarily with Marx, that focus on the unequal distribution of power in society—for example, due to class, race, or gender. Conflicts between classes or groups are driven to a large extent by this unequal power and unequal access to resources.

A pro-pot rally on Parliament Hill in Ottawa. Alcohol, the preferred intoxicant of mainstream Canadian culture, has been legal in all parts of the country since approximately 1920 (after a brief period of prohibition), yet cannabis, an arguably less harmful substance, remained illegal for recreational use until 2018. A "conflict" perspective would see this discrepancy in what gets counted as "crime" as evidence of the ideological power structures that dominated Canada throughout most of the 20th century. By contrast, a "consensus" view would attribute both the previous criminalization of cannabis and current legalization as evidence of Canada's legislators showing deference to shifts in public attitudes and a new social consensus.

One thing you should start to see is that the way you conceptualize or theorize "crime" and how you measure it will have implications for where you look and what you look at. For a structuralist who believes that the *Criminal Code* is where those with opposing ideologies battle over institutionalizing society's conception of right and wrong, the official crime statistics are useful for what they impart about the distribution of power in society more so than what they impart about the distribution of misconduct. Research from this perspective tends to focus not on crime statistics but on the activities around the creation and implementation of laws, and/or on what happens in the absence of law that the structuralist views as desirable. Those who advocate for legal reform from a structuralist perspective strive to make changes that do not unfairly advantage or disadvantage identifiable groups based on factors such as gender, culture, race, or socio-economic status.

Positivist Perspectives

Positivist perspectives fall within the general scope of **consensus theories**. Unlike conflict theorists, who see the *Criminal Code* as a battleground influenced by differential access to power, positivists tend to take the *Criminal Code* as a reflection of societal consensus about what is and is not criminal. Positivists assume that the *Criminal Code*

consensus theories
In opposition to conflict theories, consensus theories, which originate with Durkheim, hold that society functions through social bonds and collective beliefs, and is characterized by widespread acceptance of values, norms, and laws.

is a reflection of a society's collective social values, and therefore consider crime statistics, generated by the criminal justice system and governmental agencies such as Statistics Canada, unbiased measures of societal crime and criminality.

Crime statistics are gathered by most justice agencies and have been for a very long time. As John Lowman and Ted Palys (1991) note, "Such records are still the most lengthy time-series crime data available to us, having been collected in parts of Europe and North America since the early nineteenth century." It is also arguably the case that, in democratic societies at least, the *Criminal Code* really does represent something of a general societal consensus on what defines crime. Certainly that is so with the major categories of crime that get the preponderance of attention from crime analysts and the media. Is there anyone who does *not* think that actions such as assault, robbery, break and enter, theft, fraud, and murder warrant being treated as crimes? We may debate what we think should be done with people who commit those acts, or how we might prevent them, and the line between criminality and legality may shift back and forth depending on the political winds of the day, but positivists would suggest there are some core underlying values in any society that actually thinks of itself as one. And if that is the case, and the *Criminal Code* is in some ways the embodiment of that consensus, then looking at crime statistics based on those crime categories—which will tell us things like how much crime there is, whether it is increasing or decreasing, and who its perpetrators and victims are—seems like a very reasonable thing to do.

In Canada, police-recorded crime statistics have been collected and published since 1921 (Fetter, 2009). However, the early data were highly inconsistent due to the small number of police agencies that submitted information and the lack of consistency from year to year and place to place for crimes reported. Standardized and comprehensive practices were developed later, the most significant of which occurred in 1962, when Canada implemented the Uniform Crime Reporting Survey (UCR). The goal was to generate police-reported crime statistics that were complete, accurate, and standardized to facilitate temporal (time-to-time) and spatial (place-to-place) comparisons (Fetter, 2009). Ongoing research shows that these statistics have their imperfections—variations between police departments in how crime data are collected and counted, even when they were standardized, produced results that seemed to confuse and in some cases obscure what was *really* going on. However, the process of reviewing and attempting to improve on these statistics has continued.

As well, the **dark figure of crime**—crimes that occur that are never reported to police—has always been a problem in measuring crime. It makes the collected data both incorrect *and* incomplete. Accordingly, Statistics Canada and the agencies that report to it have constantly looked for ways to create even greater standardization, resolve inconsistencies, and increase clarity in crime statistics. Although positivist researchers acknowledge that the reported crime statistics are imperfect, they argue that these statistics are still useful. Paul Brantingham and Patricia Brantingham (1984), for example, compare these statistics to a miscalibrated bathroom weigh scale that always reads 10 kilograms too light. Even though the weight readings are incorrect (invalid), they can still be used to measure *changes* in weight or to compare different people, as long as we can assume the error is constant.

dark figure of crime
Refers to the variation between the number of crimes that occur and the number of crimes that are actually reported to the police. This figure highlights the large number of unreported crimes.

Constructionist Perspectives

Implicit in positivist approaches to measuring crime is the notion that the challenge of creating better crime statistics is primarily a *technical* problem that can be overcome by identifying sources of error and finding ways to correct, or at least minimize, them. **Constructionist** theorists do not disagree with the wisdom of trying to minimize error, but suggest that we cannot fully understand crime and its causes and consequences unless we also accept that the identification, coding, and counting of crime is a human and, thus, social process that says as much about our society and justice system as it does about the amount of "crime" that occurs. Constructionists differentiate between the laws that are made—which is of great interest to the structuralists, as we saw—and the way those laws on the books are implemented. Do the police implement all laws, or just some of them? Do they respond equally to everyone, or to some people more or less than others? Stated another way, is justice truly blind? Or is justice more accessible to some than others?

> **constructionist**
>
> Constructionist perspectives emphasize the idea that life does not come with categories and labels, and that we understand and define the world on the basis of our socialization and interactions with others.

In 2017, Robyn Doolittle, a reporter with Canada's *Globe and Mail* news agency, sought to determine whether police do indeed implement all laws equally. She examined police data on complaints that were formally dismissed as unfounded (crimes police determine not to have occurred). Requests were made to all police agencies in Canada and data was received for 873 of 1,100 jurisdictions, covering 92 percent of the country's population. Analysis showed that indeed, not all crimes in Canada are treated equally, with more than 5,000 complaints of sexual assault, or one in five, closed as unfounded. Unlike other serious violent crime, such as physical assault, which has a 10.84 percent unfounded rate, complaints to police regarding sexual assaults are more than twice as likely to be closed as unfounded and three or more times as likely to be written off that way than any other crime in Canada.

Depending on where you live in Canada, you have a varying likelihood of being believed by police if you make a complaint of sexual assault. Cities such as Winnipeg, Surrey, and Windsor have fewer than 10 percent of these cases deemed unfounded, yet there are 115 other communities where the likelihood of a case being deemed unfounded is one in three, or even one in two. Clearly, when complaints of a single type of crime are dismissed with such high frequency it shows deep flaws in our policing processes that highlight problems of inadequate training, flawed interviewing techniques, and biased attitudes against a specific class of victims.

Inflated unfounded rates have a number of serious consequences. First, if police declare an allegation unfounded, then they have little reason to caution the perpetrator, which may lead the perpetrator to believe the behaviour is acceptable, or if the perpetrator knows the actions are criminal, the perpetrator may believe that he or she can get away with it and continue or even increase the behaviour, which will lead to there being more victims. Second, if police deem no crime was committed, then there will be no arrest or conviction. Statistics Canada shows that just 42 percent of those investigated for sexual assault are charged for the crime, yet when unfounded cases are factored in, this rate drops to 34 percent. Third, unfounded cases create a false impression of safety with the illusion that there are fewer sexual assaults than there actually are. And finally, when police fail to believe the complainant, it is likely that the victim will lose faith in the ability of the police to do their job. Given that it is currently estimated that only one in ten victims of sexual assault report to police, if they think the police are not going to believe them and won't investigate the crime, or that they will be blamed for making a false complaint, then it is unlikely these crimes will be reported in the future.

Constructionist theorists argue that crime and crime rates cannot be fully understood unless we understand the social processes by which our laws are implemented. Indeed, one of the more extreme positions in this perspective, asserted by Jason Ditton (1979), is that crime statistics have little to do with the amount of crime that really exists and are instead primarily measures of police activity. According to this view, police literally "produce" crime statistics by virtue of the calls for service they respond to, the proactive efforts they make to find crime, and the discretion they exercise in reporting it once they find it. Not surprisingly, those who subscribe to such a view have spent considerable time researching the police in the belief that understanding police theories of crime and criminality is integral to understanding the crime rates their behaviour generates. In this view, "profiling" is no more than institutionalized stereotyping that can create self-fulfilling prophecies by the selective attention police pay to particular groups they view as troublesome. The more attention paid to a particular group, the more members of that group will be caught in illegal activity, while similar activities of other groups will escape attention. As a result, the stereotype associated with the group is supported, leading to even more police attention and stronger stereotypes about groups of people that legitimizes the attention police pay to this group. Indeed, police closely observe people they believe are "out of place" in certain settings: the visible minority in a predominantly white neighbourhood; the single woman standing for an extended period on a street corner; the young person wearing a hoodie and driving an expensive, newer car (for example, Sacks, 1972).

Integrationist Perspectives

A fourth perspective, referred to as **integrationist** (Lowman & Palys, 1991), sees some merit in all three of the other perspectives. An integrationist approach suggests that any criminological theory that seeks to offer a complete explanation of crime and its causes and consequences should include both (1) a philosophy and sociology of law that focuses on the development and change in laws, incorporating an analysis of whose interests are served; and (2) an empirical study of crime and deviance focused on not only how the criminality revealed by crime statistics is distributed in society, but also how these categories are interpreted and managed by those who control the development and implementation of law. And while individual researchers and theorists will follow their own priorities and interests, an integrationist approach suggests that the discipline of criminology as a whole would sell itself short if it lacks any of the perspectives noted here.

We can take almost any area of interest to criminologists and see how the various theoretical perspectives described above would connect to certain ways of looking at that area. Let's take prostitution, for example, a profession or activity that has been the subject of considerable debate in Canada in the past decade about how it should be dealt with in law:

integrationist
A combination of structuralist, positivist, and constructionist approaches in criminology facilitating the inclusion of philosophy and sociology of law, the empirical study of crime, and its interpretation by those who control and implement the law.

- The structuralist might start by taking a look at who is involved in prostitution and would see that it is highly gendered—women are by far the most common service providers, while men are the most common clients. Structuralists would also focus on the role that race plays, with visible minorities far overrepresented among those at the "survival sex" segment of the profession that is characterized by high violence and most likely to encounter difficulties with justice personnel, and underrepresented among higher paid "escorts" who are also better protected and less likely to have run-ins with legal authorities.
- The positivist would be more likely to take arrest statistics involving prostitutes and their clients and analyze them to see who is most commonly arrested, what penalties are put in place, and what outcomes are associated with those penalties (for example, in terms of displacement or recidivism).
- The constructionist, in turn, would be highly suspicious that arrest statistics related to prostitution would not be evenly distributed throughout society, and would find those at the lower echelons of the trade, and the clients who frequent them, would be far more likely to be arrested than prostitutes and clients of higher status, suggesting that the picture that emerges by looking at arrest statistics is likely to be highly unrepresentative of the sex trade as a whole. Constructionists also would be more likely to do field research to try to get a better sense of how police discretion is implemented, and how decisions to check or arrest are made.
- The integrationist would look to all three of the other perspectives and think of them not as perspectives competing to see which was "correct," but rather that each of them puts different aspects of the sex trade under the spotlight, and that all three are needed to put together a comprehensive understanding of how prostitution and its regulation functions in contemporary society.

This fourth perspective guides the rest of our discussion in this chapter. We continue by analyzing how crime statistics are constructed, which in turn will help us see what they do and do not show, as well as identify the social factors that guide their production.

Deconstructing the Crime Statistic

Figure 4.1, which is adapted from Wesley Skogan (1975), shows a simplified model of the events that must occur before behaviour contrary to the *Criminal Code* (a "crime") will make its way into the crime statistics reported by Statistics Canada. Of course, by adopting this model, we have bypassed the debate about whether the behaviour in question *should be* considered a crime. We leave that to others in this text and elsewhere to consider. On the left side of this figure, one can see that a number of steps occur from the time a criminal act takes place to the point that it becomes—or does not become—a statistic. This is known as a **crime funnel**. Moving through this process step by step, the number of acts that will eventually be registered as an official statistic is reduced.

crime funnel
A model indicating that the actual total quantity of crime is much higher than the decreasing proportion that is detected, reported, prosecuted, and punished.

Crimes Witnessed by the Public

The left side of the figure shows the process that must occur for a criminal event to be brought to the attention of the police by a member of the general public. The first thing that must happen is that a person must recognize an event as "a crime." Even if an event is criminal, if somehow the person does not notice it (for example, money is stolen from a person, but that person doesn't realize it or thinks that he or she might have lost it) or does not consider the event to be "criminal" (for example, a physical interaction is viewed as "roughhousing" rather than "assault"), then clearly that will be the end of it.

FIGURE 4.1   The Processes by Which a Behaviour That Is a "Crime" According to the Criminal Code Becomes an Official "Crime Statistic"

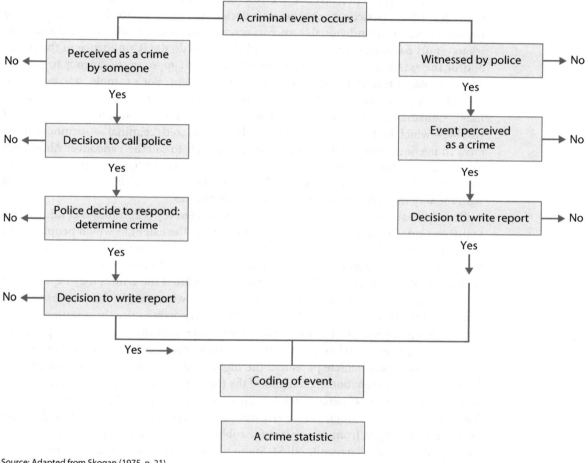

Source: Adapted from Skogan (1975, p. 21).

Understanding this first step in the process also allows us to consider other human factors that might influence whether the event is dismissed or moves to the next step in the process. Certainly, one's knowledge of the criminal justice system could play a role here; however, with more than 40,000 laws on the books, it is doubtful that any of us knows all of the "crimes" that might be committed. Cultural differences could also play a role in the interpretation of events. For example, years ago one author of this chapter was involved in research that involved visiting RCMP detachments in different parts of the country (see Dutton, Boyanowsky, Palys, & Heywood, 1982). It very quickly became apparent that different communities had different standards for defining "assault." In northern mining communities such as Flin Flon, Manitoba, a certain amount of "roughness" was tolerated that might well be considered "assault" in an urban centre such as Winnipeg. This finding suggests that it would be reasonable to compare the rate of assault in Flin Flon at two different points in time because the local interpretation of what constitutes "assault" is likely to be the same. However, it would be problematic to compare the rate of assault in Flin Flon and Winnipeg because the meaning of "assault" is not the same in the two communities.

Even if an event *is* perceived as a crime, it will never become a statistic unless an individual who experiences or witnesses it decides to call the police. Many factors come into play here. Some individuals—such as teachers and social workers—have legal duties to report particular kinds of crimes, while others do not. Confidence in the police and/or the extent to which one sees the police as the "appropriate" agency to contact will also play a role in the decision to report an event. For example, one author of this chapter has done research with an Indigenous justice program that operates in a major Canadian city (Palys, Isaac, & Nuszdorfer, 2012). Over time, for many forms of trouble—which include acts that might well be considered "criminal"—members of the city's Indigenous community have become more likely to call the Vancouver Aboriginal Transformative Justice Services Society (VATJSS), the city's Indigenous justice program, than to dial 911. They prefer the way that the program deals with offenders compared with the way the police and Canadian justice system do.

Broad social surveys, such as the General Social Survey (GSS) that is conducted by Statistics Canada every five years, help shed light on the extent to which people fail to call police and a few of the reasons why. Statistics Canada regularly finds that most individuals fail to report criminal victimization to police. In 2014, on average, only one in five Canadians of those polled in the GSS had reported the crimes they experienced to the police; this percentage was down from 2004 when one in four reported their victimization (Perreault, 2015). Declining rates of reporting raise the question of why an increasing percentage of Canadians decide not to report the crimes they experience.

Reporting rates are related to the type of crime. Break and enter and theft of motor vehicle or motor vehicle parts had the highest rate of reporting at 54 percent and 50 percent respectively, and even higher if the theft of the motor vehicle was completed (the car was taken) at 90 percent, while sexual assaults were least likely to be reported, at 5 percent (Conroy & Cotter, 2017; Perreault, 2015). Reporting for other types of violent victimization ranged from 45 percent for robbery and break-ins, down to 38 percent for physical assault (Perreault, 2015). Some of the most common reasons for not reporting violent crimes include "not important enough" (78 percent); "it was a personal matter" (63 percent); "did not want to get the offender in trouble" (27 percent); "feared revenge" (18 percent); and "did not want to bring shame or dishonour to their family" (12 percent). For non-violent crimes the most common reason for not reporting was that victims had low expectations for police response; 66 percent "believed the police would not consider the incident important enough," 65 percent felt police "would not be able to identify the perpetrator or find the property stolen," and 61 percent thought "there was a lack of evidence for meaningful police action" (Perreault, 2015). In sum, despite being recognized as a "crime," many criminal events never become crime statistics because they are never reported to police.

For more on this study, see Figure 5.1 in Chapter 5, Victims of Crime.

Rather than contacting a municipal or provincial police department, many Indigenous people prefer to contact their local Indigenous justice program, such as the VATJSS office in Vancouver pictured here. This is one example of how the reporting of crime through various channels can have an influence on what is included in, and left out of, official government statistics.

Citizens' expectations about the prospective outcome of their interaction significantly affect whether they will call the police. For example, years ago, after "Operation Identification" was first implemented—a program that encouraged individuals to engrave identifying information on precious items to make it easier to recognize them as stolen and thereby easier to potentially foil and convict thieves—crime rates *increased*. It appears that this increase had nothing to do with the actual frequency of break and enters and theft, but rather with people's belief that it was now worth calling police because the program was advertised as increasing the chance of getting stolen goods back (Lowman, 1982).

Even if the police *are* called, the first decision they make is whether to respond. This involves deciding whether the call involves a "police matter" and whether it is worthwhile for them to attend the scene. For example, years ago, Bruce Levens and Donald Dutton (1980) found that when one major Canadian police department received calls from women who had been or were being assaulted by their husbands, it sent out officers to investigate less than 50 percent of the time. More recently, many police departments have adopted mandatory attendance policies for domestic disputes. Clearly, this change in policy will affect the extent to which such events will appear in crime statistics.

If the police do respond when called, they still have considerable discretion about what to do when they get to the scene. Research by Donald Black (1970) and Donald Black and Albert Reiss (1970) has shown that a variety of factors influence whether the police decide to write a report instead of simply issue a warning, confiscate illicit goods (for example, flushing illegal drugs down the toilet), interrupt some escalating activity (for example, by separating combatants in a bar fight and sending them off in separate taxis), or undertake some other non-processed alternative. They found that police officers were *less* likely to write reports when the relationship between the perpetrator and the victim was close, believing that such incidents were less likely to end up in court; and they were *more* likely to write a report when the complainant was deferential or someone of high social status.

If anything, police officers these days are required to keep even more detailed records and fill out even more forms for any given incident, and we have yet to meet a police officer whose favourite part of the job is the paperwork. Every time the police encounter an incident, they weigh the pros and cons of "making a case" or letting it go, depending on aspects of the crime (Is it serious enough? Is it clearcut enough to generate a conviction?), the offender (Is the individual known to police? Is the individual deferential and apparently a "good" person?), and the complainant or witness (Is the person a "good witness"? Is culpability clearcut, vague, or perhaps shared?).

Crimes Witnessed by the Police

The right side of Figure 4.1 shows the process the police follow when they witness a criminal event either because they have gone looking for it (for example, they drive through areas where sex workers might ply their trade; they set up drinking-and-driving roadblocks) or because they are out and happen to be where one takes place (for example, they pass by a bar as it empties and a fight breaks out or a shooting occurs; they turn a corner and come upon individuals consuming or dealing illicit drugs).

The proactive aspect of this side of Figure 4.1 immediately invites the methodological concern of whether some increases (or decreases) in a particular crime rate are due to increases (or decreases) in criminal behaviour or are simply indicative of greater police attention that, in turn, produces more arrests (see Cohen, 2002). In Vancouver, for example, street prostitution brought about a media frenzy in the 1980s and 1990s—both because of citizen concern about the visibility of sex worker–client exchanges and because of feminist concerns that the clients (mostly men) were being violent against vulnerable women. The result was a concentrated police campaign to "shame the johns" by arresting them for soliciting in a public place, which at that time was against the law. The result was a huge increase in the number of charges laid, not because of any change in activity, but because of the increased police attention.

As all these examples suggest, police influence on crime statistics extends beyond the level of individual patrol officers or detectives to jurisdictional differences in the way certain crime categories are addressed from one detachment to another and from one municipality to another.

Many of the factors that influence whether an act becomes a crime statistic on the right side of Figure 4.1 mirror those already mentioned on the left side of the figure. The police must witness the event, must determine that the event is "criminal," and must make a decision to intervene in some formal way that will require them to process the individual(s) involved and write a report. After these steps are taken on both sides of the figure, the event is then categorized and processed.

Categorizing and Processing the Event

We have seen how various filters may intervene between the occurrence of a criminal event and its being archived as a crime statistic, with some proportion of events passing through to the point of being officially recorded and processed. Remember that crime statistics are meant to enumerate the amount of crime that occurs in different categories. Single crimes that involve a single perpetrator and single victim are dealt with easily enough, but what happens when we have multiple crimes and/or multiple perpetrators and/or multiple victims? Under the UCR Survey rules that went into effect in 1962, the first key distinction in counting was whether the crime was a crime of violence or a crime of property. The general counting rules were as follows (Dauvergne & Turner, 2010):

1. for crimes of violence, one counts the number of victims;
2. for crimes of property, one counts the number of events; and
3. for mixed or multiple offences, only the most serious offence is recorded.

To illustrate, imagine two perpetrators enter a store, steal some candy bars, rob the proprietor and a customer, shoot a police officer who tries to apprehend them, set the store on fire, and jaywalk as they return to their getaway car. The event includes both crimes of property (theft under $5,000) and crimes of violence (armed robbery and murder), which makes it a "multiple offence." However, the UCR Survey counts only the most serious offence. Accordingly, despite the various crimes that were involved, the police would report that "one murder" was committed. As Skogan (1975) suggests, the effect of such counting rules was to enhance reliability—different police forces would all use the same rules and presumably all count in exactly the same way—but they did so at the expense of validity. The resulting crime statistic failed in two notable respects: (1) it failed to capture the true nature of the event; and (2) because of the counting bias that favoured the reporting of violent crime, it would consistently underestimate the amount of property crime and give a distorted (inflated) picture of the relative amount of violent crime in Canada.

CompStat
COMPuter STATistics; the name given to the New York City Police Department's accountability process that was introduced in the 1990s to facilitate a reduction in crime.

clearance rates
The proportion of criminal incidents solved by the police. A crime is cleared when the police believe they have found its perpetrator.

BOX 4.1

Distortions in Crime Measurements: Three Examples

United Kingdom: Jurisdictional differences affecting reported volumes of crime were presented by David Farrington and Elizabeth Dowds (1985) in a study on the disparity of officially recorded crime rates in Leicestershire, Nottinghamshire, and Staffordshire. While police-reported statistics showed Nottinghamshire to have significantly higher crime rates, victimization surveys demonstrated that they were only one-third to one-quarter the difference suggested by official statistics.

United States: New York City also experienced reporting errors after the introduction of **CompStat**, a computer-based, real-time mapping system that allowed tracking of serious index crimes such as homicide and rape in New York City in the mid-1990s. Commanding officers in each of the boroughs would be called into a CompStat meeting every Friday morning and, in front of politicians and other police officers, asked to explain what CompStat showed regarding index crimes (crimes included in the FBI's annual crime index) in their area. Pay raises and promotions, as well as demotions and public shame, were doled out as a result of CompStat's crime statistics. In 1994, after adopting the use of CompStat, New York police recorded a 12 percent decline in crime, a further drop of 16 percent in 1995, and another drop of 16 percent in 1996. Despite this amazing reduction in reported crime, later studies showed that patrol officers were pressured to "write down" crime—record lower-level offences rather than higher-level index crimes—and to disregard witness statements to ensure that crime dropped in their boroughs (Eterno & Silverman, 2010).

Australia: The police department in Victoria was exposed as having a "significant and cumulative" distortion of crime data related to underreporting crime (the department failed to disclose up to 15,000 of the 380,000 annual crimes) and overreporting **clearance rates** (Rood, 2011). Political pressure, public outrage, and police funding all have been shown to have an effect on police activity and their reported crime statistics (MacDonald, 2002).

Other Ways to Count Crime

If there is one certainty about crime, it's that it is multi-faceted and complex. Thus, it is highly unlikely that any one measure of crime will capture its complexity. Every crime statistic has strengths as well as limitations that place some aspects of crime beyond its reach. Accordingly, researchers, statisticians, and policy-makers have sought other ways to measure crime to get a more complete picture of the crime that does exist.

Victimization Surveys

We saw from the left side of Figure 4.1 that a number of steps exist between a citizen experiencing or witnessing a criminal act and its being processed by the police in such a way as to become a crime statistic. Those steps—the "crime funnel"—see the police gradually reduce the number of events that achieve official recognition through the application of different filters. Some of these reductions are reasonable; for example, if we want to count *Criminal Code* "crime," then it seems appropriate to ensure that non-criminal events are set aside. But other reductions are not, such as those based on personal interest (for example, reducing the amount of paperwork one has to deal with), pragmatic considerations regarding conviction (for example, getting the victim to withdraw a complaint because of the low likelihood of gaining a conviction), or other policy considerations (for example, downgrading crimes in order to intentionally reduce crime rates in the area). Another way researchers have attempted to look at crime is through social surveys in which a sample of citizens is asked to divulge information about their experiences with crime and the criminal justice system.

Canada produces a number of victimization surveys, including the Canadian Urban Victimization Survey, the Violence Against Women Survey, and the commonly cited General Social Survey (GSS) conducted by Statistics Canada. The GSS is used more generally to gather data on social trends to allow the government to monitor changes in living conditions and the well-being of Canadians over time. However, one portion of the survey is dedicated to victimization and eight crime types are targeted in the survey. A sample of Canadians aged 15 and over is polled to gain a better understanding of how Canadians perceive crime, the justice system, and personal experiences of victimization (Statistics Canada, 2014). The GSS uses a cross-sectional design and, in 2009, surveyed approximately 19,500 households. Starting in 2014, the GSS used Statistics Canada's new telephone sampling frame that, for the first time, included cellphone numbers from the census and other administrative sources provided to Statistics Canada. Rather than collecting the survey data via the phone call, respondents were directed to an electronic questionnaire (Statistics Canada, 2014).

The GSS provides an important complement to official crime statistics by bringing to light information on crimes that individuals fail to report or police fail to discover. It also allows us to ask respondents about victimizations and any reasons why they did not report their victimization to the police. Victimization surveys are not without their own limitations, however. Figure 4.2 shows the steps that must be taken before a criminal event becomes a "crime statistic" reported to and recorded by an interviewer as well as sources of errors that affect results.

FIGURE 4.2   The Construction of Crime Statistics via Victimization Surveys

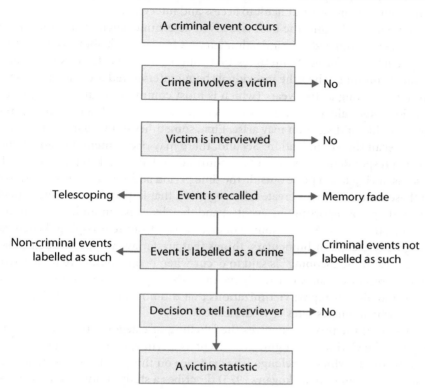

Source: From Palys/Atchison. Research Decisions, 4E. © 2008 Nelson Education Ltd. Reproduced by permission.

Again, we start with a "criminal" event, something that is really a crime. The first filter indicates that the event must involve a victim because people are unlikely, for example, to spontaneously admit to having consumed illicit drugs or to having solicited the services of a prostitute (often referred to as **victimless crimes**). A related issue identified by Skogan (1982) revolves around our often erroneous assumption that crimes are discrete, one-time events, such as a robbery or a murder. He points out that some criminal acts are ongoing and almost continuous—such as child abuse or partner abuse—which may make them less likely to be reported when or if a survey is constructed in such a way as to ask about discrete events.

Next comes the **sampling** issue. Victimization surveys typically seek a representative sample of the population—sometimes of residents of a particular urban centre—although national samples are more likely to be sought these days, as is the case with Statistics Canada's GSS and similar US and UK surveys. Given that victimization rates are actually relatively low, particularly for more serious offences, samples must be huge in order to find enough people who have actually experienced certain forms of victimization as well as to ensure subsamples of interest—for example, members of minority groups and vulnerable or marginalized populations—so that analyses based on those subsamples are both generalizable and meaningful. Yet, as Skogan (1982) points out,

victimless crimes
Actions (often perpetrated consensually) that are ruled illegal but do not directly violate or threaten the rights of other individuals.

sampling
In statistics, the selection of a subset of the population in such a way that will allow the results of one's research to be generalizable to the population as a whole.

victimization is not equally distributed across society, and those who are the most vulnerable are often also the most difficult to access and interview.

Once the interview begins, the next issue is to determine whether the interviewee has, indeed, been victimized. Victimization surveys typically ask about victimization within a specific time frame. Sometimes that time frame is as short as six months (which is most common when the individuals being interviewed are known victims); other times it is as long as two years (which is most common in surveys of the general population, especially in countries where crime rates are very low). Three different sources of invalidity or distortion may arise. First, sometimes individuals are not aware of or able to recall the victimization. Second, there may occur **memory fade**, which happens when respondents forget about a victimization that has taken place or recall it erroneously as having taken place outside the time period addressed in the survey. Note that both these sources of error create false negatives; that is, people who were actually victimized end up not reporting the event(s) and thereby cause an underestimation of actual victimization rates. A third source of error arises from **telescoping**. When you look through a telescope or binoculars, things that are far away appear much closer; in the survey realm, "telescoping" is said to occur when people recall events as having occurred more recently than was actually the case. This type of error creates false positives; that is, individuals report victimizations that did not actually occur during the study period, which inflates rates of victimization.

The next step in the process involves the labelling or categorization of the crime, which requires the victim to recognize the event as a crime, and to correctly identify the crime category to which it belongs. The evidence on this point suggests that interviewees can do this quite well; Skogan (1975) describes a study conducted in San Jose, California that found legal authorities and interview participants classified an event in the same way 88 percent of the time.

Finally, even when each of the filters above has been passed, the victim must be willing to tell the interviewer about the event. Skogan (1982) suggests that this may well be the biggest tripping point in the entire process, not only because different crimes are more likely to be reported than others, but also because there are so many ways that the recollection of the particulars of the event are subject to error: forgetting, misremembering, lying (particularly in situations where the victim bears some complicity in the event), and the differential reconstruction of events (persons unaccustomed to violence may see events as more menacing than do those who are more accustomed to violence, so that the former are more likely and the latter less likely to report the event to the interviewer).

Notwithstanding all of these prospective difficulties, victimization surveys succeed in offering a different view of crime and, in particular, help explain the how and why of people's decisions to report crimes to police. These data, in turn, help interpret official crime statistics.

Developing "Better" Crime Statistics
Uniform Crime Reporting Survey 2

The original Uniform Crime Reporting Survey (UCR) that Canada adopted in 1962 included a number of reported offences, actual offences, offences cleared by charge, and offences cleared by other means (Government of British Columbia, 2015). It did not ask police to report victim or incident characteristics, had a limited number of offence

---

memory fade
The phenomenon whereby a survey participant forgets about a victimization that has taken place.

telescoping
The phenomenon whereby a survey participant recalls events as having occurred more recently than is actually the case.

codes, and had no ability to add offence codes for new crimes (such as cybercrime) created through legislation. As new crimes came into existence—including criminal harassment, extortion, and offences against the administration of justice—they were merely categorized under "Other" (Government of British Columbia, 2015). In the late 1980s, Statistics Canada moved to adopt a more detailed reporting and collection system: the Uniform Crime Reporting Survey 2 (UCR2). This survey was slowly adopted over the following three decades and became the standard for most police services across Canada by 2007. UCR2 has been the official police-reported crime survey nationally since 2009.

UCR2 uses a set of nationally set scoring rules, created and managed by the Canadian Centre for Justice Statistics. It includes the same data collected under UCR—thereby ensuring some degree of comparability with the older UCR data—but adds detailed information on individual criminal incidents reported to the police, including victim, accused person, and incident characteristics. UCR2 also allows for the entry of up to four different offences for each incident, which provides a better understanding of multiple-event occurrences, and a wider list of offence categories to better reflect the nature of criminal offences. The "violent crime" category was revised to include events such as criminal harassment, sexual offences against children, forcible confinement/kidnapping, extortion, uttering threats, and threatening/harassing phone calls, while the "property crime" category was revised to include mischief and arson.

Other changes to UCR2 will undoubtedly alter future statistics, making it even more difficult to compare data from year to year. Robbery, which was historically counted by incident, will now be tabulated by number of victims, with each new victim counting as a new crime. Other violations that have been added as categories of crime since 2011 are assault with a weapon, causing bodily harm to a peace officer, aggravated assault on a peace officer, robbery to steal a firearm, kidnapping, forcible confinement, sexual exploitation of a person with a disability, break and enter to steal a firearm, break and enter to steal a firearm from a motor vehicle, and identity theft and fraud. These changes will alter counts of historic crimes as Statistics Canada backdates the data to reflect these changes in policy. Similarly, future statistics will be affected, because some crimes will now be recorded under different categories. British Columbia's Ministry of Justice warns, "police services are able to utilise the new codes as their records management systems are updated to allow it. As a result, these data should be interpreted with caution" (Government of British Columbia, 2015).

Crime Severity Index

The vast majority of crime in Canada tends to be of the non-severe type, which means that UCR2 is dominated by less serious crimes. To complement the URCR2, Statistics Canada developed a Crime Severity Index (CSI), which is designed to distinguish the severity of crime, and not simply violations of the *Criminal Code* (Government of British Columbia, 2015). CSIs were instituted in 2009 and include "Overall CSI" (based on the total volume of police-reported federal statute offences—a measure of the relative severity of overall crime); "Violent CSI" (based on the total volume of police-reported violent federal statute offences—a measure of the relative severity of violent crime); "Non-Violent CSI" (based on the total volume of police-reported federal statute offences not considered violent in nature—a measure of the relative severity of non-violent crime); and "Youth CSI" (based on the number of youth accused of crime—a measure of the relative severity of overall youth crime). CSIs are based on the total volume of federal statute crimes (including those listed in the *Criminal Code*) and are designed to measure both year-to-year changes in crime volume as well as crime seriousness (Wallace, Turner, Matarazzo, & Babyak, 2009). Each crime is weighted according to seriousness; for example, a serious offence such as murder is weighted at a value several hundred times higher than a less-serious offence such as mischief. By weighting crimes, the CSI allows more-serious but lower-volume offences to have a greater impact on the crime rate than high-volume, less-serious offences.

While the CSI allows more-serious crimes to be weighted more heavily than other crimes, more-serious crimes are not weighted on the basis of an objective determination of their seriousness, but rather on the basis of court sentencing, thus relying on the subjectivity of the judge imposing the sentence (Dauvergne & Turner, 2010). Using sentencing to weight crime has significant limitations. One problem is that data related to time served on remand (the amount of time a person serves in jail prior to sentencing) are not collected and not included in the weighting of the CSI. While judges often factor remand time in their sentencing decisions, the CSI survey data cannot show the entire sentence length (days in jail including remand time or days in jail excluding remand time) (Wallace et al., 2009). Furthermore, repeat offenders, youth offenders, and life sentences can all skew the weightings, given that judges often take into consideration a person's prior criminal record when determining a sentence. Also, information related to recidivism is not collected for the CSI. As well, conditional sentences are viewed as non-prison sentences for the purposes of the CSI weighting model. Moreover, a life sentence cannot be measured in terms of actual time but is estimated at a value of 25 years (Wallace et al., 2009). Additional limitations on the usefulness of year-to-year comparisons in the CSI arose when weights were updated in 2013 (for the first time since the introduction of this measure), reflecting court data from 2006 to 2011 and altering the prior published CSI ratings (Wallace et al., 2009).

Trying to Capture a Moving Target

In the 2009 *Star Trek* film, Scottie becomes the starship *Enterprise*'s chief engineer and explains the difficulty involved in transporting ("beaming") someone from a fixed location to another starship that is moving in space. He says, "The notion of transwarp beaming is like trying to hit a bullet with a smaller bullet, whilst wearing a blindfold, riding a horse." Statisticians who try to improve crime statistics face an analogous complexity. While previous research can tell us about potential sources of error and the limitations of existing statistics that have implications for how they might be improved, society itself is changing, which means that one is always trying to capture, in a fixed way, a target that is always moving.

UCR and UCR2 have focused on traditional types of crimes, including violence and property offences, despite the creation and common use of the Internet in the late 20th century. The Internet is used to commit both crimes of a traditional nature and new crimes; crime committed over the Internet or a computer network is known as **cybercrime** (Smyth, 2010). Although the Internet started to be used commercially in the 1990s and was rapidly adopted by criminals and non-criminals alike, Canada did not begin to collect statistics on cybercrime until 2005 (Griffiths, 2019).

cybercrime
Crime committed over the Internet or a computer network.

Understanding Societal Change: Crime Drop or Crime Swap?

As shown in Chart 4.1, for almost three decades, industrialized countries worldwide reported dramatic decreases in some police-reported crimes (FBI, 2012; Home Office, United Kingdom, 2013; Perreault, 2012). Researchers have begun to offer some explanations for these decreases. For instance, crimes such as automobile theft, at least by less-skilled thieves, may have dropped due to the installation of government-mandated disabling and anti-theft devices in all new cars. The idea that a change in the level and quality of security leads to a decrease in crime has been coined the "security hypothesis" by Graham Farrell, Nick Tilley, Andromachi Tseloni, and Jen Mailley (2011).

According to the United Nations Crime Trends Survey for developed countries, worldwide levels of homicide also have fallen, whereas levels of assault have increased (Gruszczyńska & Heiskanen, 2012). While no one is quite certain why these changes have occurred, competing explanations include the following:

1. Improvements have been made in emergency medical care, which have led to an increased number of assault victims surviving their assault rather than dying as they would have 20 or 30 years ago.
2. Young adults have become less risk-tolerant, which has led to safer behaviours and a reduction in potential victimization (Mishra & Lalumière, 2009).
3. The advent of commerce on the Internet led a greater number of young adults (males, particularly) to stay home playing online video games (ComScore, 2011), removing them from potential harm as victims (they are safe at home) and offering a substitute for excitement and risky behaviour that otherwise could lead to fatal assaults.

The Effect of the Internet on Crime Measurement

The question remains: Has crime really dropped? By examining Figure 4.1, we are able to offer avenues by which to explore this issue by placing rival plausible explanations in the decision-making framework. This allows us to explore the idea that crime has not necessarily dropped but some types of traditional crime have merely been displaced by cybercrime. Although crimes such as identity theft and identity fraud have been directly linked to the growth in Internet adoption and usage, Canada only drafted and tabled related legislation, such as Bill C-13—the *Protecting Canadians from Online Crime Act*—which received its first reading in November 2013 and was assented to in December 2014. With the exception of child pornography and child luring, cybercrimes have been entirely excluded from UCR2 until now. Not only are new crimes emerging due to the Internet, but also, as the RCMP report, almost any traditional crime can be perpetrated via computer (RCMP, 2016).

Recall that for crime to make its way into police-recorded statistics, it must first be noticed. Crimes in the virtual space of the Internet are often far less visible than those that happen in the face-to-face world. It is much easier to be certain that you have been mugged than to know that your bank account was hacked or your identity stolen—especially immediately after these crimes have occurred. Once a crime is noticed, the police must then be called. But how many people know to call the police for an Internet-related crime? When most people notice an error on their bank or credit card statement, they are more likely to call their bank than the police. When their computer is hacked, people are more likely to take the computer in for servicing or call the technical support number of their computer's manufacturer.

Cybercrime includes a wide variety of offences against computer data and systems. It includes money laundering; corruption; offences against confidentiality, integrity, and availability of computer data and systems—including unauthorized entry into computers or the unauthorized use or manipulation of electronic systems—data and/or software—including illegal downloading of data and programs; as well as crimes against persons such as harassment, bullying, child luring, and child pornography. Despite the lack of police-reported statistics, regular news reports highlight the vast number and pervasiveness of these cybercrimes.

Despite the numerous possible difficulties in dealing with cybercrime, according to data collected by Kaspersky Lab and B2B International, a Canadian anti-virus and software company that conducted a survey of Canadian computer users in 2014, cybercrime is highly prevalent in Canada: 62 percent of respondents reported experiencing at least one attempt by cybercriminals to steal their personal financial information, and 41 percent reported that they had lost money they were unable to retrieve (Kaspersky Lab, 2014).

For the police, handling cybercrime can be complicated. Finding a perpetrator who is anywhere on earth is much more difficult than finding a perpetrator who is somewhere in one's own town (even then, the task is a challenge). If the perpetrator is found, where should the crime statistic be recorded? In the country of the victim? In the country of the perpetrator? Where the Internet service provider is stationed? These are all questions that law enforcement agencies are grappling with today. Historically, crime was a local phenomenon. Thinking of routine activity theory, the perpetrator and victim met in time and space in the absence of a capable guardian. For cybercrime, how do we measure time and space? Finally, if the crime is noticed and reported, does it even exist as a crime, and how will the police respond? Defining, discovering, and prosecuting cybercrime (both traditional crime that takes place online and strictly Internet-related crime) poses challenges for law enforcement agencies related to jurisdictional boundaries and domains as well as police practices and the gathering and processing of Internet-related evidence.

> For more on these topics, see Chapter 18, White-Collar Crime.

Conclusion

Measuring crime statistics involves multiple steps and processes of interpretation and understanding—with each one adding complexity and the possibility for measurement error, both deliberate and accidental. Although they appear in official Statistics Canada reports and are typically treated as objective measures of crime, you should see that the categories and numbers of crimes are affected by far more than the actual amount of crime out there. They also are influenced by the attitudes and opinions of the officers, policies, and procedures of the police; legislation passed by government, at multiple levels; and larger societal influences. The interpretation of crime statistics is equally nuanced, often reflecting the opinions and beliefs as well as the general philosophy of the researcher. Structural, positivist, constructionist, and integrationist approaches to understanding crime statistics all reflect different world views and affect not only the understanding of how crime is measured and recorded but what gets measured and why. While government and police agencies have worked over the years to improve the quality of crime statistics, inherent weaknesses remain that, at least at this time, simply cannot be fixed. Victimization surveys help fill in some of the missing information on crime, but they also have weaknesses. The current, apparent drop in crime witnessed in most industrialized countries has presented a puzzle for criminologists, not only because it appears as though human behaviour may have radically changed, but that the Internet poses challenges to measuring crime statistics that may take years to address effectively.

SUMMARY OF KEY POINTS

- The theoretical nature of crime, its identification, interpretation, and statistical enumeration are examined through four perspectives: structuralist, positivist, constructionist, and integrationist.
- Understanding the theories and perspectives through which crime statistics are constructed allows the individual to consider what they do and do not show and the social factors that guide their production.
- Understanding the process by which a behaviour is perceived to be a crime and eventually becomes a crime statistic must take into account the crime funnel—the process through which the actual quantity of crime is reduced in stages such that only a small proportion of total crime is detected, prosecuted, and punished.
- A number of data-gathering measures are used in Canada to collect crime data, including the UCR2, victimization surveys, and the Crime Severity Index. Although each measure has its own strengths and weaknesses, it is hoped that by collecting the different measures, statisticians might be able to determine a more accurate count of crime in Canada.
- Changes in the way in which Canadians live, including Internet use, have vastly altered the landscape of crime and offending, creating both new opportunities for crime and new ways to commit traditional crimes. Currently, most developed countries are grappling with ways in which to discover and measure these crimes.

QUESTIONS FOR CRITICAL DISCUSSION

1. What is meant by the terms "structuralist," "positivist," "constructionist," and "integrationist"? How do these perspectives influence the construction of crime statistics?
2. What are the strengths and weaknesses of our various measures of crime (including the UCR2, the General Social Survey, and the Crime Severity Index)?
3. Discuss how the Internet has influenced crime (both new and traditional crime) and how it has made the discovery and counting of crime much more complex than crime committed in the physical world.
4. Explain the process of the crime funnel. What are some of the factors that affect the reduction of crime at each stage?

SUGGESTED FURTHER READINGS

Adorjan, M. (2012). The lens of victim contests and youth crime stat wars. *Symbolic Interaction*, *34*(4), 552–573. https://doi.org/10.1525/si.2011.34.4.552

Cook, A.N. (2012). Tough on crime reforms: What psychology has to say about the recent and proposed justice policy. *Canadian Psychology*, *53*(3), 217–225. https://doi.org/10.1037/a0025045

Websites

BC Ministry of Justice Police Services Division: https://www2.gov.bc.ca/assets/gov/law-crime-and-justice/criminal-justice/police/publications/statistics/2013-police-resources.pdf

Employment and Social Development Canada: https://www.canada.ca/en/employment-social-development.html

Juristat: https://www150.statcan.gc.ca/n1/pub/85-002-x/index-eng.htm

Legislation

Criminal Code, RSC 1985, c C-46.

Protecting Canadians from Online Crime Act, SC 2014, c 31.

Appendix 4.1   Researching Crime Online
Statistics Canada

As readers will notice from many of the figures and tables seen throughout this text, the primary source of detailed data on crime in Canada is Statistics Canada. This federal government agency gathers data at the national as well as provincial levels, and also presents some data at the municipal level ("CMA," or census metropolitan area).

Homepage for Statistics Canada: Crime and Justice:

https://www.statcan.gc.ca/eng/subjects-start/crime_and_justice

Crime statistics are released annually. Reports written related to crime statistics and trends do not have a regular release date other than those labeled "annual." These include:

Police Reported Crime Statistics offer annual updates for Canada and the individual provinces. The following statistics and severity indices are usually available between six months and two years after end of the year for which statistics have been gathered:

- Annual crime rate.
- Annual Crime Severity Index.
- Police Reported Crime per 100,000 population.
- Violent Crime Severity index.
- Youth crime rate.
- Non-violent Crime Severity Index.
- Homicide victims.
- Homicide rate per 100,000 population.

TIP: It is important to think critically about information you come across and to understand what is being measured. For instance, in late 2018, the media reported that Toronto had set a record for murders in a year, breaking the record set in 1991, and suggesting the city was becoming more violent. The number of murders cited was correct; however, the city's population had grown significantly over that quarter century, meaning that the actual homicide *rate*—that is, the number of murders per capita—remained lower in 2018 than 1991.

Correctional Services Canada presents statistics and reports including coverage of:

- Adult correctional services.
- Youth correctional services.
- Outcomes of probation and conditional sentences and restorative justice programs, etc.

Courts: Statistics Canada data focusing on adult criminal courts, civil courts, legal aid, and youth courts.

Crimes and Offences: General information from police reported crime including topics such as police reported sexual assault before and after #MeToo, economic profiles of offenders by province, firearm related violent crime, and more:

- Crime rates reports including incident-based crime statistics by crime type and province.
- Crime Severity Index (CSI).
- Hate crimes.
- Homicides.
- Sexual assaults.

Police Services: Personnel and resources, ranks, perception of performance, etc.

Victimization: Includes data on family violence, victimization of children and youth, seniors or women, and other content related to victimization.
Other Statistics Canada data covers, for example, overdose deaths from illicit drugs, cybercrime, sentencing patterns, organized crime, and more.

Some Statistics Canada information is presented less frequently: **The General Social Survey** consists of six core social themes or *cycles* (one of which is crime victimization) that are reported on in five-year intervals and archived. Additional themes or phenomena are often examined.
https://www150.statcan.gc.ca/n1/en/catalogue/89F0115X

Violence Against Women Survey (VAWS): This one-time survey conducted in 2007 examined Canadian women's safety inside and outside the home, and examined perceptions of fear, sexual harassment, sexual violence, and threats by strangers, boyfriends, and dates.
http://www23.statcan.gc.ca/imdb/p2SV.pl?Function=getSurvey&SDDS=3896

Other Online Surveys and Studies

International Crime Victims Survey (ICVS): An annual survey comparing levels of victimization and perceptions of quality of life across the European Union.
http://www.unicri.it/services/library_documentation/publications/icvs/

United Nations Office on Drugs and Crime: A variety of studies and articles, which includes 150 surveys conducted in 80 countries since 1989.
https://www.unodc.org/unodc/index.html?ref=menutop

National Longitudinal Study of Adolescent to Adult Health (Add-Health): A school-based study of health-related issues relating to deviancy and criminal behaviours of American adolescents.
https://www.cpc.unc.edu/projects/addhealth

Inter-University Consortium for Political and Social Research (ICPSR): An international consortium of more than 750 academic institutions and research organizations, the ICPSR hosts 21 specialized collections of data in education, aging, criminal justice, substance abuse, terrorism, and other fields.
https://www.icpsr.umich.edu/icpsrweb/content/about/

Encyclopedias

Online reference sources provide basic information and context around your research topic, and numerous criminology encyclopedias covering various subtopics have been published. They are a useful place to start when looking for biographical information or introductions to criminological theories.

> **TIP**: There are a number of encyclopedias at libraries (print and online) with biographical entries on criminals, however their tables of contents are sometimes not indexed by search tools. Thus, a library keyword search for your topic may not reveal everything available. To find these "hidden" encyclopedias, you will need to search by more general terms such as *criminals encyclopedias* (or similar combinations) and then manually check to see if an encyclopedia has the entry you are looking for.

Finding Books

When searching library catalogues to find books on your topic, you can use the word "and" to combine search terms, for example: "murder and profiling." Once you find a book that meets your needs, take a look at the subject heading links in the catalogue record below the location and status information. These links will list other books on the same topic.

While there may not be a whole book about the criminal you are searching for, you may find a book chapter within a broader-themed book that treats your criminal in detail. Keep in mind that many of the books you come across may not be considered academic. Nevertheless, these may be the only source of biographical information available.

> **TIP**: It may be worth checking if Google Books (https://books.google.ca) provides full or partial access to a book you are looking for.

Internet and Database Searches Using Boolean Search Protocols

Boolean searches use quotation marks or words (and, or) to more effectively narrow, or widen, the topic one is searching for. Boolean search protocols are as follows:

- When searching for a single keyword, no quotation marks or brackets are needed:
  - crime
- If searching for two or more words that you want to appear in a specific order, you must use quotation marks:
  - "sexual crime"
  - "females who commit sexual crime"

  Remember, the above searches will only return documents that contain those words in the exact order, form, and spelling as they are input.

- If you are searching for two or more words in a document and they do not have to appear together, use (and) or AND. Boolean search protocols vary, depending on the code used when setting them up in private or academic search forms:
  - sexual (and) crime
  - sexual AND crime
  - female (and) sexual (and) crime
  - female AND sexual AND crime

  These will return documents that contain those words anywhere within them, and in any order, appearing together or separately.

- This type of search is often widened using the (or) OR function:
  - sexual (and) crime (or) deviance
  - sexual AND crime OR deviance

  This will return documents that have the words sexual and crime or sexual and deviance anywhere in the body.

Most of these requirements are typically met by the search forms in online libraries for academic use, but if you are using Google or an academic online library where there is a single line of blank space for entering search parameters, then one must use Boolean protocols.

Be particularly careful about using information found on the web or via Google. The topic of serial murder, for instance, has a great deal of biased, inaccurate, out of date, and misleading websites devoted to it. As part of your research, read up on how to evaluate web-based resources for reliability, and do not rely on Wikipedia for your primary information.

Finding Journal Articles

Articles in academic journals are a valuable source of information. Some widely used criminology databases are listed below, but here are some search tips before you begin:

- As discussed above, you can use Boolean search protocols to narrow your search using the word "and." A search for *"dental records" and murder* will bring back only articles that match both of those keywords, for example.
- Combine your search terms using the word "or" to bring back articles with *either* term. This technique is good for searching synonyms. Place your synonyms separated by the word "or" between brackets to avoid getting irrelevant results. Example: *"serial murder" and (child or children or youth or teenager).*
- Use quotation marks to find an exact phrase like "dissociative identity disorder" or "Henry Lee Lucas."
- Try searching for name variants of your criminal's name.
- As you search, modify your search terms and look for relevant keywords in article titles and abstracts you read.
- Keep in mind that it may be difficult to find academic-level psychological analysis of a particular criminal, especially for obscure or very recent cases, as these may never have been written. You may need to generalize your searches to similar crimes/criminals or psychological conditions.

Suggested Databases

- **Criminal Justice Abstracts (EBSCO)** covers crime trends, crime prevention and deterrence, juvenile delinquency, juvenile justice, police, courts, punishment, and sentencing.
  https://www.ebsco.com/products/research-databases/criminal-justice-abstracts
- **PsycINFO** is the core database for research in Psychology, providing article citations for over 1300 journals.
  https://www.apa.org/pubs/databases/psycinfo/
- **DSM-V: Diagnostic and Statistical Manual of Mental Disorders** is the standard diagnostic tool used by mental health professionals.
  https://doi.org/10.1176/appi.books.9780890425596

Recommended Journals

- Journal of Criminal Justice: An International Journal.
- International Criminal Justice Review.
- The Forensic Examiner.
- Homicide Studies.
- Journal of Police and Criminal Psychology.

Other Useful Resources

- **Oxford Bibliographies Online** lists core readings on a wide range of criminological theories.
  http://www.oxfordbibliographies.com
- Graduate theses and dissertations may contain uniquely in-depth information on your criminal. You can search the theses of thousands of universities using the database by searching under **ProQuest Dissertations and Theses Abstracts and Index**.

Finding Newspaper Articles

Newspaper articles can be an excellent source for factual background information. Newspaper articles may also provide important coverage of court proceedings and criminal sentences not necessarily available in case law. Check to see if your library provides access to online archives for some of these news sources:

- **Canadian Newsstream** provides full-text articles in major Canadian newspapers.
  https://www.proquest.com/products-services/canadian_newsstand.html
- **CBCA Complete** (Canadian Business and Current Affairs) Canadian newspapers, newswires, newsmagazines, as well as television and radio transcripts.
  https://www.proquest.com/libraries/academic/databases/cbca.html
- **The Globe and Mail** maintains archives dating from 1844.
- **The New York Times**.
- **LexisNexis** features US and world news, with a legal emphasis.
  https://www.lexisnexis.com/en-us/product-sign-in.page
- **Factiva** has full-text access to thousands of news sources from 1951.
  https://www.dowjones.com/products/factiva/

Amanda Todd

In October 2012, 15-year-old Amanda Todd hanged herself at her home in Port Coquitlam, British Columbia. One month earlier, she had posted a nine-minute YouTube video entitled "My story: Struggling, bullying, suicide and self-harm." The video showed Amanda using a series of flash cards, without any audible commentary, to tell her story.

Students observe a moment of silence in memory of bullying victim Amanda Todd.

"I've decided to tell you about my never-ending story," she began. "In 7th grade I would go with friends on webcam ... I got called stunning, beautiful, perfect, etc. They wanted me to flash ... so I did."

About a year later, she continued, she received a message from someone on Facebook saying, "If you don't put on a show for me I will send ur boobs." The young man knew her name, address, and her friends. A short time later, Amanda received a knock on her door at 4 a.m. from the police; the photo had been sent everywhere online.

Amanda felt sick and began to suffer from anxiety, depression, and panic disorder. She moved to another school and became involved with drugs and alcohol. The topless photo followed her to this new location, and her difficulties worsened. She did not have any friends, was called names, and concluded that the photo was "out there, forever."

Amanda started cutting herself; at school, she sat alone at lunch—and then moved schools again. Things were better for a while, although she still ate lunch alone. About a month later, she started texting with "an old guy friend" who "liked me, led me on, he had a girlfriend."

She went over to his house and had sex with him while his girlfriend was on vacation. "Big mistake," she said. A week later, she received this text: "get out of your school." A group of young teens approached her, with the support of the young man she had had sex with. One of them, a young girl, threw her to the ground and punched her several times; a few kids filmed the event.

"I thought he really liked me," she continued in the video, "but he just wanted the sex." She lay in a nearby ditch until her father came to pick her up. "I wanted to die so bad," she wrote, "when he brought me home, I drank bleach." She thought she was going to die, but the ambulance came, brought her to hospital, and flushed the bleach from her system.

Facebook posts were unrelenting and unkind: "She deserved it" was a common theme. Amanda moved again, to another city, to be with her mother. She decided against pressing charges, just wanting to move on with her life. But the commentaries on Facebook continued—with posted photos of bleach and ditches. One comment went so far as to suggest a hope that she would actually kill herself next time.

"Life's never getting better," she said, adding, "I can't meet or be with people ... am constantly cutting. I'm really depressed." She went to counselling and was placed on anti-depressants, but nothing seemed to improve her mood. She overdosed and ended up in hospital.

"I have nobody; I need someone," her video concluded, along with a photo of her arm, revealing a series of bloody slashes. A month later, she was dead.

The media response to the death of Amanda Todd was international in scope. Her YouTube video has now attracted more than 13 million viewers, and shortly after her death more than 1 million Facebook users reported that they "liked" her Facebook page. But some negative sentiments persisted. Among the mostly positive commentaries on Facebook were some continuing attacks from students claiming to be former classmates. And ABC News reported from the United States that a number of fraudulent websites had been set up, linked to the tragedy, to solicit donations on behalf of Amanda Todd.

Technology has clearly changed both the scope and nature of victimization. Social media can work to amplify harm and to distribute harmful material to literally anyone with a computer and access to the Internet. This case provides a clear example of a type of victimization that simply did not exist until the last decade.

Before You Read Chapter 5

- What can be done in law and policy and in our schools to diminish the likelihood of this kind of tragedy?
- What is it about social media that amplifies this sort of victimization?
- We may typically think of "victims of crime" as somehow different from people who commit suicide. How does the case of Amanda Todd suggest otherwise?

Victims of Crime

LEARNING OUTCOMES

After reading this chapter, students will be able to:

- Describe the differences between criminology and the study of victims.
- Understand issues surrounding the researching of victim experience, including who we define as a victim and issues related to measuring victim experience.
- Understand common responses to victimization and victim resilience.
- Understand who is most vulnerable to victimization.
- Describe the victim-blaming process and problems with the victim precipitation model.
- Understand the role of Victim Impact Statements and the *Canadian Victims Bill of Rights*.

Introduction: Victimology in Canada

Think about the last news story you heard or read about that involved a criminal act. If you cannot think of such a story, go to your favourite news website and find one. Now think about what you know about the victim from that story. Do you know more about the victim experience or the criminal and what the criminal did to the victim? Chances are, if the story came from the media, you know significantly more about the criminal than the victim. Consider, for example, that the average Canadian has probably heard of mass murderers Paul Bernardo and Karla Homolka, Robert Pickton, Marc Lépine, Clifford Olson, and Bruce McArthur, but likely cannot name any of their victims. But when we know someone who has been victimized, whether a family member, friend, or even the friend of a friend, we tend to want to know about his or her experience, not the offender's. Moreover, we tend to discuss with others what we know about the victim experience (what happened, to whom, at what time of day, what the victim was doing when it happened, how badly the victim was hurt, and so on) so that we can learn from it, and perhaps bring some understanding to our own experiences or determine how to avoid victimization ourselves.

It is critical for anyone studying victims of crime to recognize that without the victim's courage to report a criminal act, very few criminals would ever be apprehended. Victims often exhibit heroic actions after their own victimization. After experiencing something traumatic, victims must invoke the criminal justice system (i.e., call the police). Often, the state can only pursue charges if a victim exists and is willing to report the crime(s) against him or her. In some cases, the victim must also be prepared to testify in court about the experience. Without the victim, the criminal justice system would grind to a halt. The decision to come forward can be a very difficult one. Victims may hesitate to report a crime for many reasons. With more serious crimes, these reasons could include fear of repercussion, or concerns that many others would learn about their experience, which in turn may lead to stigmatization. In some cases, victims who have come forward have reported poor treatment by police or medical personnel at critical junctures in their victim process: when providing evidence to police or when seeking help for injuries inflicted by the offender. In light of all this, changes have recently been made to enhance legislation to protect current and future victims.

While other chapters in this book focus on criminology (i.e., the study of crime), this chapter will focus instead on **victimology** (i.e., the study of victims). Victimologists study the victim experience and larger victimization trends. Table 5.1 lists some of the ways in which victimology differs from criminology. In this chapter, we will use the term "victimizer" interchangeably with "offender," which is consistent with a victim-centred approach.

victimology
The study of victims.

TABLE 5.1   A Comparison of Victimology and Criminology

Victimology	Criminology
• It focuses on the study of victims.	• It focuses on the study of criminals.
• It emphasizes a victim-centred approach to analyzing crime.	• It emphasizes an offender-centred approach to analyzing crime.
• It seeks to understand challenges facing victims of crime.	• It seeks to understand challenges facing criminal offenders.
• It is an emerging discipline.	• It is an established discipline.
• It emphasizes personal solutions to dealing with victims.	• It emphasizes dealing with the criminal via the criminal justice system.
• Victims initiate the criminal justice response by calling the police and deciding to report a crime.	• The police apprehend a criminal based on a victim report.
• Prior victimization has been found to increase the likelihood of subsequent victimization, as well as a criminal lifestyle in some individuals.	• A criminal lifestyle has been shown to increase the risk of being victimized.
• Victims are represented by a Crown counsel at trial.	• Offenders are represented by their own personal attorney.
• Victim rehabilitation is rarely financially supported by the state.	• Criminal rehabilitation is often financially supported by the state.
• Data on victims are collected using victimization surveys. The surveys ask members of the public about victimization experiences they have had and include both crime reported and not reported to police.	• Data on criminals are collected by police, the courts, and the corrections system and include only those crimes reported to those agencies.

Victimology as an Emerging Discipline

As you read through this chapter, keep in mind that victimology is an *emerging discipline*. In other words, this area in the study of crime is relatively new. Traditionally, crime studies, as well as theories that developed from this early research, were predominantly concerned with how people, especially males, became criminals (Naffine, 1987). Early questions centred on whether criminals were simply born bad (suggesting a biological root cause for their offending) or pushed, in some way, into a life of criminal activity. Early Chicago School theorists (such as Robert Park, Ernest Burgess, Clifford Shaw, and Henry McKay), who focused on crime in Chicago from the 1920s to the 1940s, wrote about the acts of male offenders. The victims of crime were of little interest.

Until the 1970s, only a handful of academics engaged in studying the victim experience. Research on victims emerged out of human rights campaigns, such as the civil rights and women's movements in both Canada and the United States. Like criminology, victimology's theoretical roots are American. More recently, a growing number of universities and colleges around the globe are teaching more victim-centred courses within their criminology and criminal justice programs, including courses in victimology, domestic and/or family abuse, the impact of hate crimes, and understanding the importance of the role of victim. In your own studies, how many of your projects have focused on the victim as the subject of inquiry?

Who Is a Victim?

Many people believe they have a clear idea of who a victim is. Ask any number of people to define "victim" and the answers will probably be fairly similar. According to the *Oxford English Dictionary* (n.d.), a **victim** is "a person harmed, injured, or killed as the result of a crime, accident, or other event or action." For example, an individual can be a victim of spousal violence or a fraud or hoax. As well, an individual can identify as a victim when that person feels helpless and develops a victim mentality. Animals, too, can be victims of various types of abuse, and it is worth remembering that cruelty to animals is a criminal offence (see ss. 444 to 447 of the *Criminal Code*).

victim
A person harmed, injured, or killed as a result of a crime, accident, or other event or action.

On the left is Andrea Constand, the Canadian who, in 2018, accused Bill Cosby of sexual assault and won her case against him. On the right is a missing persons poster for Andrew Kinsman, one of Bruce MacArthur's victims.

Even with this apparently clear definition, how we come to identify a victim is complex. Let us take the example of a car accident. Imagine that one car hits another in an intersection. Each car has a driver and a passenger. Both drivers are seriously injured, but both passengers receive only minor scratches and bruises. Directly after the accident, people who witnessed the collision called for emergency services and tried to help the victims as best they could while awaiting the arrival of first responders. The two drivers and two passengers were taken to hospital, and the cars were towed away. Family and friends were notified about the accident and met the injured parties at the hospital.

Deciding who is and is not a victim can be a challenge. In the example of the car accident, who were the victims? Each of the four people involved experienced some form of injury, even if the passengers' injuries were only minor. Typically, a person's status as a victim is tied to the idea of **culpability**. For example, your assessment of which driver was a victim may be affected by the knowledge that one driver was attentive and obeying the traffic signal, while the other was distracted. What if one driver intentionally drove through the intersection, knowing that halfway through the light would turn red? Does it matter to you whether one or both of the drivers had consumed alcohol or cannabis before they got behind the wheel? If one driver intentionally drove through a red light, is that driver a victimizer instead of a victim? The circumstances surrounding an event are critically important when addressing victimization issues. For the purposes of this example, we will assume that no one was at fault.

In victimology, there are many levels of victimization and victimization experience. Back to our example, all drivers and passengers experienced physical injuries, which makes them **primary victims** in the accident. Primary victims are the most easily identifiable victims because they are directly affected, and often physically injured, in an event. But what about the other people who witnessed the accident and called emergency services? Anyone who has ever witnessed a car accident knows that it can be traumatizing, especially when victims are seriously injured. These witnesses are **secondary victims**, in that they did not directly experience the accident but were present at the scene when it took place and may have been hurt psychologically by the unfolding events. Family members who were not at the scene of the accident but met the injured parties at the hospital were also probably saddened and worried about the primary victims. Moreover, some family members will have to physically and emotionally support the victims while they recover from their injuries and, therefore, their lives also become disrupted as a result of the accident. These individuals are **tertiary victims**, in that they were not directly victimized and may not have witnessed the event but will suffer negative repercussions as a result of it.

In addition, we can categorize victims based on their direct or indirect involvement with the event. Individuals who were directly involved and suffered as a result of it are called **direct victims**. Back to our example, all of the people who were in the vehicles and were hurt as a result of the accident are direct victims. Those who were not directly involved in the event, such as witnesses to the event and people who showed up at the hospital to be with the victims, are called **indirect victims**. These individuals experienced negative indirect consequences as a result of the event.

We can also categorize victims based on whether they undergo the victimization themselves or feel traumatized by the victimization of others and undergo many of the same emotional experiences that the actual victims do. Individuals who directly

culpable
Deserving of blame; guilty of wrongdoing.

primary victim
A person who is directly harmed as a result of a victimizing experience.

secondary victim
A person who is not directly impacted by the harmful effects of a victimizing event but may witness the event or have to deal with the after-effects of a victimizing event, such as supporting a victim in recovery.

tertiary victim
A person who may suffer repercussions of victimization even though they are not directly involved in or witness to the harmful event.

direct victim
A person who is present at the time of victimization and experiences harm.

indirect victim
A person who is not immediately affected by victimization but nonetheless suffers in some way as a result of it.

experience an event are **actual victims**. Those who experience trauma just by being aware of an event that has befallen others are **vicarious victims**; they can become fearful and anxious and sometimes suffer the same symptoms as those who have had the actual experience. In our car accident example, those in the car who were injured are the actual victims. However, those who saw the accident or supported the victims after the accident would be vicarious victims if they had heightened anxiety or became fearful of driving because they felt scared that they might get into a similar accident. Applying this to crime, Figure 5.1 shows how fear and anxiety over victimization can affect people's daily behaviour. While most people who have been victimized routinely lock their doors at night, fewer avoid places and people, and some have so much fear and anxiety that they resist leaving their houses at night. Figure 5.1 also demonstrates that these behaviour changes are significantly and more often felt by women, as compared to men.

Therefore, it is possible for individuals involved in an event to be categorized as multiple types of victims. In our example, both the drivers and the passengers can be considered to be direct, primary, and actual victims. We can draw this conclusion because no driver was at fault, and neither driver intended to hurt anyone in the accident. All four individuals in the cars witnessed the accident and witnessed other people being hurt. Both passengers and drivers, because they witnessed each other get injured, are primary victims and secondary victims in that they witnessed victimizations other than their own. Because of the many roles that victims can play in a single victimizing event, victimization can also be compounded, depending on the circumstances of the event.

actual victim
A person who is the direct target of victimization.

vicarious victim
A person who does not experience direct victimization but nonetheless responds as if they had been victimized directly after learning of the event.

FIGURE 5.1 Use of Protective Behaviours, by Sex, Canada, 2014

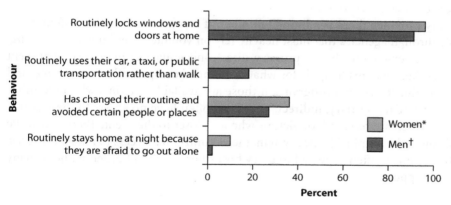

*Significantly different from the reference category p < 0.05.

†Reference category.

Source: Adapted from Perreault (2017, Chart 5).

Victim status is also based on the perceptions of those directly involved in a victimizing act. Consider whether two people involved in a criminal act would agree on the level of harm experienced as a result of a victimization event, or even whether one or the other was hurt. For example, imagine two people are arguing. They become angry and start shouting at each other. Others start to notice the argument. Sometimes, these events can turn violent and one person will hit the other. The physically injured person may choose to retaliate in kind and attempt to hurt the attacker in some way. The initial victim then becomes an attacker as well. In the end, who becomes the ultimate victim in this incident depends on the outcome of the altercation. These situations can be resolved in a number of ways. The individuals may choose to stop victimizing one another or someone (a witness) may attempt to break up the fight. Alternatively, the police might be called and could charge one or both of the victimizers with assault.

Who we identify as a victim can be extremely important, as this has a number of consequences (Quinney, 1972). Quinney notes that who we call a victim changes over time, can be pressured by the political landscape, affected by advances in medicine, and other social phenomena. For example, Hinch (1985) noted that prior to the reforms to Canadian sexual assault laws in 1983, women who were married could not be raped by their husbands. Likewise, men could not be victims of rape because rape could only legally be considered a crime when it happened to women and girls. More recently, as we have developed laws around hate crime, gender has only newly been added as a category that is eligible under hate crime victimization. The #metoo, #beenrapednever-reported, #timesup, and #annetdonahue—who famously tweeted "When did you first meet YOUR Harvey Weinstein? I'll go first"—are all social media movements that shine a light on the everyday acts of violence that women routinely endure. Actions that were previously considered commonplace and part of working and social experiences are no longer acceptable. Victims who were previously silent about these experiences for a number of reasons are now speaking out about the violence they have experienced because these social media movements assert that predatory acts are inappropriate and criminal. These changes illustrate that how we describe and recognize criminal behaviour dictates how we respond to it.

In every province there is a limited number of resources for victims, often made available through agencies that must heavily rely on volunteers and unstable funding. Therefore, agreement on who is a primary, direct, and actual victim of a criminal event also allows those victims to apply for whatever limited compensation is available, and become eligible for certain programs, if those are available. Victims who hold other statuses (secondary, tertiary, indirect, vicarious) often have no access to these scarce resources, which are reserved for victims who are closer to the event. Therefore, while going through the criminal justice system, the victimizer has access to many resources, while the victim is often expected to carry his or her essential burden without many additional supports.

> For more on disparities between men and women in criminal justice, see Chapter 10, Gender and Crime.

BOX 5.1

Victims and Offenders

As noted in Table 5.1, those who lead a criminal lifestyle face an increased risk of victimization. In other words, there is a correlation between being a victim of crime and engaging in criminal activity. Young men are both the group most likely to commit criminal offences and, as Table 5.3 confirms, the group most at risk of victimization.

Criminologists have known for many years that the risk of being a victim of crime is not randomly distributed across populations in Canada, the United States, or other Western nations. Rates of criminal victimization are somewhat like rates of offending: They tend to be at their highest among young men and in geographic areas that have a significant amount of "social disorganization" (this will be discussed in more detail in Chapter 9, Sociological Approaches). As a result, this finding has prompted the conclusion that victims of crime and offenders are often quite similar and are largely overlapping populations.

There is some logic and some empirical evidence to support this conclusion. Victims are, statistically, more likely to have a history of criminal offending and risk-taking behaviour than are non-victims. Those who are inclined toward "routine activity theory" and "self-control theories" (which will be discussed in Part Two) for understanding criminality argue that young males who have little self-control typically engage in high-risk lifestyles and activities that expose them to the possibility of criminal involvement, both as offenders and as victims. One recent study of particular incidents of homicide, for example, found that victims tended to share similar demographic and behavioural characteristics with

their victimizers (Lauritsen & Laub, 2007). It should also be noted that this behavioural risk is truer for men than it is for women. As Figure 1.1 in Chapter 1, What is Criminology? clearly demonstrated, women are far less likely to engage in criminal activity, thereby suggesting that women are far less likely to be victimized than men. (See also Box 1.1, "Correlates of Crime," in Chapter 1.) Despite this fact, women, as we shall see below, are more likely to report violent victimization (see Table 5.3).

However, victims and offenders are also far from uniformly overlapping populations. Not surprisingly, crime victims without a criminal history tend to be much less likely to resemble criminal offenders in their characteristics. And while it is important to note the overlap between victims and offenders, it is also important not to blame victims for this correlation.

Source: Lauritsen & Laub (2007).

Rainer Strobl (2010) argues that for people to be classified as victims, some agreement must exist between people's subjective view of their victim status and the interpretation of that status by others. Strobl identifies four types of victim experiences, shown in Table 5.2. To illustrate how they apply, let us use the example of a physical altercation that occurs at a bar. Two people, Jack and Alex, engage in a short fist fight, and the fight is broken up. The "actual victim" is the person who believes he or she was victimized and the person others believe was victimized. In our example, if Alex believes that he was victimized and others agree, he is the clearly identifiable actual victim. This is our most common understanding of victimization. If Jack and Alex agree that neither one was victimized and others agree that no victims exist in the altercation, Jack and Alex both become "non-victims"; perhaps the fight was rationalized as a way of releasing aggression and resolving a dispute. (This scenario is reminiscent of the discussion in Chapter 4, Measuring Crime, in which it was noted that in northern mining communities such as Flin Flon, Manitoba, a certain amount of "roughness" is tolerated, but the same behaviour might be considered assault in an urban centre such as Winnipeg.)

TABLE 5.2 Strobl's Self and Other Victim Classification

	Others do regard the individual as a victim	Others do not regard the individual as a victim
Individual does regard himself or herself as a victim	Actual victim	Rejected victim
Individual does not regard himself or herself as a victim	Designated victim	Non-victim

Source: Strobl (2010, p. 6).

In some cases, others who observe an event will designate a person as a victim, even when that person does not agree that he or she has been victimized. In our example, this classification might be made if Alex is too injured to continue the fight, and the fight was stopped. Alex, as the "designated victim," may want to keep fighting, but others agree that a clearly larger harm exists for him than for Jack if he continues. Finally, if Jack claims that he has been hurt and is a victim, yet others do not agree, Jack becomes a "rejected victim." When people are classified as rejected victims or designated victims, the victims and others surrounding them may end up with bitter feelings about their non-victim status after the event.

How Do We Measure Victimization?

As we saw in the previous chapter, criminologists measure crime in a number of ways. The Canadian criminal justice system collects data on many aspects of the victimizer experience. Government statistics on offenders relate to such events as calls for service, any charges laid, whether they were arrested, court verdicts, admissions to correctional facilities, and some elements of the correctional experience. However, measuring victimization is more difficult because the data must come from the victims themselves. Victims are a vulnerable population, and although we may be interested in their experiences, we cannot just go up to victims and ask them how they were victimized. Doing so could be traumatic for them for many reasons, and academic ethical requirements insist that harm to research participants be minimized. The question is, how can we learn about victim experience without causing victims undue harm? The answer, for some, is to conduct victim surveys.

The two main sources of crime data are (1) the annual Uniform Crime Reporting Survey (UCR2), which records microdata on incidents, victims, and the accused based on police reports and (2) self-reported victimization surveys. Although self-reported victimization surveys can be conducted in a number of ways, all of them entail victims reporting their victimization experiences to researchers. Although most self-reported victimization surveys are undertaken with small, non-random groups and focus on a specific victimizing experience, every five years the Canadian government carries out a large-scale victimization survey as part of the annual General Social Survey (GSS). The GSS, which began in 1985, uses a random sample of the Canadian population and asks them a number of questions about their quality of life, as well as victimization experiences and feelings of safety. The latest version of the GSS that includes a cycle on victimization experience and perceptions of safety was conducted in 2014 (Statistics Canada, 2014). The unique advantage of the GSS is that it includes data on victimizing events that were reported and *not reported* to the police. The next cycle of the GSS concerned with victimization will be conducted in 2019, and initial results will become available in 2020.

According to the GSS (Perreault, 2015), not all victims of crime wish to involve the police after they have been victimized. The most common reason cited was that the incident was not considered important enough for police involvement (78 percent). Violent crimes (excluding homicide) were less likely (64 percent) to be reported than household victimization (53 percent not reported). Sexual assault was least likely to be reported to authorities (78 percent not reported). Reasons why sexual assaults were not reported include that the respondent felt the crime was minor and not worth taking the time to report (71 percent), the incident was a private or personal matter and was handled informally (67 percent), and no one was harmed (63 percent).

A Profile of Victimization in Canada

The GSS collects hundreds of variables on victimization, only a small portion of which we will show here. Some results from the 2014 survey are found in Table 5.3. The table shows that those who are most at risk for violent crime victimization are young adults aged 15 to 24 and single people (15–24: 163/1,000; single: 139/1,000); they are also the most at risk for theft of personal property (15–24: 110/1,000; single: 97/1,000). Other factors that put individuals at risk for violent crime are having a household income under $20,000 (79/1,000), identifying as Aboriginal (160/1,000), being homosexual (207/1,000), and/or having experienced physical or sexual assault by an adult before the age of 15 (125/1,000). According to the GSS (Perreault, 2015), when we look at the rate of violent incidents self-reported, females are more likely to report violent victimization than males (females: 85/1,000; males: 67/1,000).

TABLE 5.3 Personal Victimization Incidents Reported by Canadians, by Type of Offence, History, and Selected Demographic and Socioeconomic Characteristics, 2014

Characteristics	Sexual assault Number (thousands)	Rate[1]	Robbery Number (thousands)	Rate[1]	Physical assault Number (thousands)	Rate[1]	Total—violent incidents Number (thousands)	Rate[1]	Theft of personal property Number (thousands)	Rate[1]
Sex										
Female[†]	553	37*	77[E]	5[E]	636	43*	1,266	85*	1,609	72
Male	80[E]	5[E]	113[E]	8[E]	786	54	979	67	1,085	75
Age										
15 to 24[†]	321	71	82[E]	18[E]	334	74	737	163	494	110
25 to 34	159[E]	32[E*]	37[E]	8[E*]	388	78	585	118*	479	97
35 to 44	49[E]	10[E*]	F	F	257	55	319	68*	446	95
45 to 54	69[E]	13[E*]	30[E]	6[E*]	261	50*	360	69*	382	73*
55 to 64	18[E]	4[E]	F	F	139	30*	177	38*	232	50*
65 and over	F	F	F	F	43[E]	8[E*]	68[E]	13[E*]	121	23*
Marital status										
Married[†]	83[E]	6[E]	33[E]	2[E]	470	32	585	40	916	62
Common law	F	F	F	F	235	73*	303	94*	282	88*
Single	641[E]	57*	141[E]	14[E*]	553	68*	1,128	139*	783	97*
Widowed	F	F	F	F	13[E]	9[E*]	22[E]	16[E*]	27[E]	19[E*]
Separated/ divorced	37[E]	20[E*]	19[E]	10[E*]	150[E]	79[E*]	207	108*	146	77

Table 5.3 is concluded on next page.

Characteristics	Sexual assault Number (thousands)	Sexual assault Rate[1]	Robbery Number (thousands)	Robbery Rate[1]	Physical assault Number (thousands)	Physical assault Rate[1]	Total—violent incidents Number (thousands)	Total—violent incidents Rate[1]	Theft of personal property Number (thousands)	Theft of personal property Rate[1]
Household income										
Less than $20,000[†]	NA	NA	NA	NA	NA	NA	90	79	49	43
$20 to $59,999	NA	NA	NA	NA	NA	NA	291	60	218	45
$60 to $99,999	NA	NA	NA	NA	NA	NA	288	56	321	63[*]
$100 to $139,999	NA	NA	NA	NA	NA	NA	225	59	283	75[*]
$140 to $179,999	NA	NA	NA	NA	NA	NA	118	54	183	84[*]
$180,000 or more	NA	NA	NA	NA	NA	NA	168[E]	69[E]	206	84[*]
Aboriginal identity										
Aboriginal people[2]	54[E]	58[E*]	F	F	81[E]	87[E*]	149	160[*]	95	102[*]
First Nation	F	F	F	F	59[E]	135[E*]	95[E]	216[E*]	33[E]	75[E]
Métis	F	F	F	F	23[E]	50[E]	55[E]	119[E]	61[E]	131[E*]
Non-Aboriginal people[†]	577	20	175	6	1,337	47	2,089	74	2,055	72
Immigrant status										
Immigrant[†]	69[E]	10[E*]	23[E]	3[E*]	200[E]	30[E*]	292	44[*]	322	49[*]
Non-immigrant	564	25	167	7	1,222	54	1,953	86	1,832	80
Visible minority										
Visible minority	104[E]	21[E]	F	F	133[E]	27[E*]	271[E]	55[E*]	292	59[*]
Non-visible minority[†]	498	21	155	7	1,267	53	1,920	80	1,843	77
Sexual orientation[2]										
Heterosexual[†]	443	17	136	5	1,245	47	1,824	69	1,915	72
Homosexual or bisexual	74[E]	102[E*]	F	F	57[E]	79[E*]	150	207[*]	67	93
Physicially or sexually assaulted by an adult before age 15 (total)										
No[†]	285	15	79[E]	4[E]	710	36	1,073	55	1,245	63
Yes	312	36[E]	109[E]	12[E*]	676	77[*]	1,097	125[*]	861	98[*]

* Significantly different from reference category (p < 0.05).

† Reference category.

E = Use with caution.

F = Too unreliable to be published.

1. Rates are calculated per 1,000 population age 15 years and older.

2. Includes those who self-identified as First Nation, Métis, or Inuit.

Note: Excludes responses of "Don't know and not stated." Excludes data from the Northwest Territories, Yukon, and Nunavut.

Source: Adapted from Perreault (2015, Table 4, p. 33; Table 5, pp. 34–35; Table 6, p. 36).

Males are more likely to report experiencing a robbery (males: 8/1,000; females: 5/1,000) and significantly more likely to report physical assault (males: 54/1,000; females: 43/1,000), and are slightly more likely to report theft of personal property (males: 75/1,000; females: 72/1,000). Women are over seven times more likely to self-report being sexually assaulted (females: 37/1,000; males: 5/1,000). When compared to 2009 (Perreault & Brennan, 2010), rates of victimization for all groups have dropped, in most cases, significantly. Of note is that those who reported being visible minorities or new to Canada were less likely to self-report victimization when compared to their counterparts.

Reactions to Victimization: The Aftermath of Crime

Victims react to victimization just as people do to other traumas, as Figure 5.2 shows. Self-reported emotional responses to violent and household victimization in the GSS indicate that those who experience violence, unsurprisingly, report a more heightened emotional response when compared to those who self-reported household victimization. The most common emotional consequence is anger (violent: 34 percent; household: 32 percent), followed by being upset, confused, or frustrated (violent: 23 percent; household: 21 percent). Even though some may expect victims to have a more subdued response, such as shock, confusion, or disbelief, these responses are less common overall, but higher for those reporting a violent experience (violent: 13 percent; household: 5 percent). One of the most common reactions to victimization, whether one is a direct victim or hears about a victimizing incident, is fear (violent: 17 percent; household: 6 percent). Fear is a fairly typical reaction to a threat. Ferraro (1996) suggests that fearful reactions differ depending on the crime under consideration. For example, a person may feel less fear about having his or her bike stolen and more fear about violent crime, such as murder and sexual assault. When people are asked about their fear of being the victim of crime, many refer to "stranger danger," meaning that they fear being attacked by someone they do not know. However, both victimization and police data show that, in most cases, the victimizer and the victim know each other (Scott, 2003). But even here, gender dictates different experiences. While men are more likely to be victimized by an acquaintance, women are more likely to be abused by someone close to them, such as an intimate partner or other family member (Perreault, 2015). Who victimizes a target, and under what circumstances, has profound implications for recovery.

Another common response to victimization is stress. However, the way in which stress manifests itself differs from experience to experience and from person to person. For this reason, symptoms of stress can be difficult to identify. For example, some people may stop communicating with people and/or eating when they are stressed, while others may increase their communication levels and/or food intake.

Sometimes the reaction to stress can be particularly severe. Some individuals who have experienced a severe traumatic event have reported symptoms that align with **post-traumatic stress disorder (PTSD)**. This condition occurs when "people experience an event which is so unexpected and so shattering that it continues to have a serious effect on them, long after any physical danger involved has passed" (Canadian Mental Health Association, n.d.). Symptoms of PTSD are often seen in those who have served in combat; experienced severe victimization, including assault and sexual assault both inside and outside the family; lived through natural disasters; and/or survived terrorist acts.

post-traumatic stress disorder (PTSD)
A set of symptoms that emerge as a result of the stress of experiencing severe trauma. Symptoms may include recurring nightmares, jumpiness, agitation, trouble sleeping, trouble concentrating, and social isolation.

FIGURE 5.2   Emotional Reactions Following Victimization, by Type of Offence, 2014

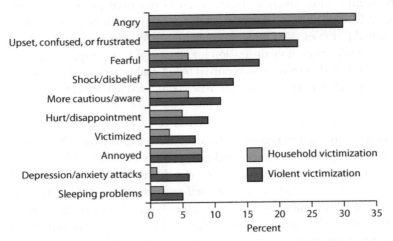

Note: Respondents were able to give more than one answer. Violent victimization includes sexual assault, robbery, and physical assault, but excludes incidents of spousal sexual and physical assault. Household victimization includes break and enter, theft of motor vehicle (or parts), theft of household property, and vandalism.

Source: Perreault (2015, Chart 11).

rape trauma syndrome (RTS)
A set of PTSD symptoms that have been linked specifically to those who have experienced severe violence in the form of sexual assault.

According to the *Diagnostic and Statistical Manual of Mental Disorders*, symptoms of PTSD in adults can include feelings of intense fear, helplessness, or horror (American Psychiatric Association, 2013). Victims may have intense, vivid, and repeated recollections of the event; trouble sleeping and recurrent nightmares; jumpiness; agitation; feelings of detachment or estrangement from others; difficulty concentrating; and difficulty functioning. Victims may also engage in reckless and self-destructive behaviour, act aggressively, or be hypervigilant. Acute PTSD can last for up to three months, while chronic PTSD can last for much longer. **Rape trauma syndrome (RTS)** (Frazier & Borgida, 1992; Giannelli, 1997) is a unique set of PTSD symptoms that have been linked specifically to victims who have survived more severe forms of sexual assault.

In an effort to capture the effects of trauma, the GSS asked Canadian respondents about some of the long-term psychological effects of their victimization experience. Figure 5.3 illustrates that, predictably, those who experienced violent victimization had considerably higher levels of symptoms associated with PTSD. One-quarter of those who had experienced violence reported hypervigilance, while slightly fewer stated that they made efforts to not think about the incident. Just under one-fifth stated that they continued to have nightmares about the incident, while just under one-eighth of the sample stated that they felt detached from other people and activities going on around them. Just over one-eighth of the respondents who reported victimization in this study stated that they had experienced at least three or more long-term effects. In comparison, those who experience household victimization were less likely to report symptoms of PTSD.

FIGURE 5.3 Long-Term Psychological Consequences, by Type of Offence, 2014

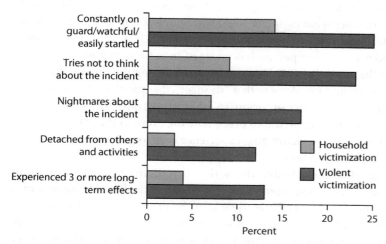

Note: Respondents were able to give more than one answer. Violent victimization includes sexual assault, robbery, and physical assault, but excludes incidents of sexual and physical assault between spouses. Household victimization includes break and enter, theft of motor vehicle (or parts), theft of household property, and vandalism.

Source: Perreault (2015, Chart 12).

Victim Precipitation

In his study of 588 homicides in Philadelphia between 1948 and 1952, criminologist Marvin Wolfgang (1958) declared that in some homicides, the eventual victim was the initial aggressor. Specifically, in about one-quarter of the homicides he reviewed, the victim appeared to have engaged in actions that contributed to his or her own death. The idea that victims could somehow influence the outcome of their own victimization was termed **victim precipitation**. Wolfgang's work in this area became very well known, and the idea of victim precipitation was extended to other crimes, most notably sexual assault (Amir, 1971). Menachem Amir, in his early research on sexual assault, was one of the first researchers to assert that victims of sexual assault could behave in such a way as to bring about their own victimization—for example, by dressing provocatively, using provocative language, or engaging in risky situations. These assertions drew significant criticism from other researchers, who argued that Amir and others who followed this line of thinking were reinforcing **rape myths** as well as engaging in **victim blaming**.

Helen Eigenberg (2003) identified five major issues with the attempt to blame victims for their own victimization. First, Eigenberg notes that victims are no different from non-victims, except for the fact that they have been victimized. Research has not been able to identify distinct characteristics of victims as compared with non-victims because they do not exist. The *process* of victimization is the factor that leads one person to become a victim and not another. The behaviours of a prospective victim only matter if that person is victimized. The reasoning behind victim precipitation, Eigenberg

victim precipitation
The problematic assumption that victims can somehow influence or bring about their own victimization by exhibiting behaviours that provoke a victimizer.

rape myths
Stories that reflect belief systems that reveal incorrect assumptions about the causes of sexual assault.

victim blaming
A process whereby a victim is found at fault for his or her own victimization, in whole or in part.

argues, is tautological, or circular. For example, consider the idea that it is inadvisable that we should spend time alone with strangers because this may leave us vulnerable to victimization. Now consider what happens when two people are in a dating situation: They often seek time alone to get to know one another better. If the date is successful, we would not consider that either person has engaged in actions that would precipitate victimization. If the same date involves one person harming the other, rather than blame the victim for seeking time alone with a "stranger," the question should be what *process* may have brought on this victimization. In other words, only after being victimized does one look to what the victim did to precipitate the event. If the experience was positive (i.e., it did not result in a victimizing experience), we would not be putting any of the victim's behaviours in question.

Second, Eigenberg (2003) asserts that the notion that victims are either guilty or totally innocent is problematic. She asserts that on one end of the **blame continuum**, a totally guilty victim essentially means that there must be no victimizer, given that the victim holds total responsibility for his or her own victimization. On the other end of the continuum, a totally innocent victim does not exist because everyone, whether they have experienced direct or indirect victimization, could identify preventive actions to avoid harm had they suspected they were going to be victimized.

Third, the insinuation that victims hold blame for their victimization suggests that they have absolute control over the actions of others, which is not the case.

Fourth, if we accept the problematic premise that victims can be blamed, then Eigenberg (2003) argues that we are creating culturally legitimate victims. If we consider that some individuals engage in risky behaviour and that they must accept the risk of victimization, such a view could be applied more collectively. If society accepts the existence of culturally legitimate victims, police and court systems might also adopt this view and, as a result, legitimate victims would become more vulnerable to victimization because they would be systematically discriminated against by the police and the law. For example, the #metoo movement has demonstrated that sexual assault in the workplace, especially of women, was acceptable for many years in that it was difficult for victims to find help to take action against offenders and have offenders' actions identified as criminal. This now appears to be changing.

Fifth, if victims are to blame for their victimization, then it follows, according to Eigenberg, that victimizers are absolved of responsibility for their criminal behaviour. The idea of victim precipitation is oddly comforting, in that it supposes that people are empowered to control whether they are victimized. If we accept this idea of control, then it means that we do not have to spend time concerning ourselves with why victimizers are motivated to harm others and target individuals.

Resilience and Victimization

How people recover from victimization is important, and a key factor is the resilience of victims after a trauma. **Resilience** has several facets. According to Masten and Powell (2003), resilience involves the ability not only to resist trauma but also to cope and recover from such events successfully. This ability to recover from trauma and the stress that accompanies trauma is not as rare as once suspected (Bonanno, 2004). We now understand that traumatizing and stressful events, such as victimization, are not rare. Most, if not all, people experience some type of trauma during their lifetime,

blame continuum
The range of blaming possibilities, from total guilt to total innocence, of both the victim and the victimizer.

resilience
The ability to successfully recover from trauma.

such as personal injury due to an accident, ill health, or the death of a loved one. However, most of us are unlikely to experience serious criminal victimization during our lifetime.

How we recover, or "bounce back," from traumatic events depends on our "protective mechanisms." These protective mechanisms act as **insulators** from the victimization experience as well as from the negative effects of victimization, enhancing the recovery process. Protective mechanisms are those characteristics or resources that victims have access to that help in the victimization/trauma recovery process. These protective mechanisms can be divided into two broad categories: **personal protective factors** and **community and social support factors**. Personal protective factors are the characteristics an individual possesses to help deal with stress (Bergeman & Wallace, 1999). These factors include coping skills, the ability to handle new situations, and strong social skills (the ability to communicate effectively and solve problems). The basic premise is that having effective coping skills, the ability to handle new situations, and good communication strategies can have a positive effect on how quickly and how well we recover from traumatic events (Garmezy, 1991). Ong, Bergeman, Bisconti, and Wallace (2006) found that routine daily positive emotions can enhance resilience by moderating the effects of stress. In other words, those who are more effective in recovering from traumatic events seem to have more positive thoughts and emotions throughout the day. These researchers suggest that positive emotion cognitive therapies, which introduce positive emotions to those who have suffered trauma, may be an effective way of bolstering resilience in those suffering the stressful effects of victimization.

Community and social support factors include the people and resources that support the individual experiencing traumatic stress. They involve supportive acts by bystanders after the victimization has occurred, the kindness of neighbours, the emotional support of family and friends, as well as community supports that might help the individual work through the impact of the stressful event. Rienick, Mulmat, and Pennell (1997) found that those who had strong social supports had fewer emotional problems after they had experienced violent crime. Davis, Lurigio, and Skogan (1999) found that people were more likely to use these informal support networks in the initial aftermath of their victimization experience, such as talking to family members and close friends. As the victims' needs became more focused later on in the recovery process, the more likely victims were to use formal support systems, such as victim assistance programs.

Changes to Canada's Criminal Justice System Favouring Victims

In recent decades there have been several changes within Canada's criminal justice system intended to address some of the burdens victims take on as a result of their experiences. One of the most significant has been the introduction, in 1988, of the **victim impact statement (VIS)**. A VIS is a written or oral statement by the victim that gives him or her the opportunity to demonstrate the physical, financial, and emotional impacts of victimization. Victims can choose to write a VIS without introducing new evidence into the case in their statements. The statement can be introduced at various stages as the victimizer is processed through the criminal justice system. In both the

insulators
Social and psychological factors that protect an individual from being harmed.

personal protective factors
The characteristics an individual possesses to help deal with stress, including coping skills, the ability to handle new situations, and social skills.

community and social support factors
The people and resources that support the individual experiencing traumatic stress; that is, community members, family, and friends that serve to insulate the community and its members from traumatizing events through prevention and/or by fostering resilience.

victim impact statement (VIS)
A written document describing the harm done to the victim as a result of victimization that may include statements about physical, emotional, or financial impact(s).

Canadian and the American systems, VISs are allowed at sentencing hearings and may be allowed at other stages, such as bail and parole hearings and in plea-bargaining sessions, depending on the procedures followed in different provinces or states.

These statements have both positive and negative impacts. VISs allow the victim to be humanized, may increase the use of restitution/compensation orders, and help to demonstrate that the victim is committed to the process (Summer, 1987). Statements also allow the court to see how the victimization has affected the victim and tend to be a factor in making sentences more appropriate (Erez & Rogers, 1999).

Conversely, there is concern that VISs may make the court less objective in its decision-making process, because the court will hear the more "subjective" impacts of a crime as experienced by the victim. The victim may also have to defend his or her VIS to defence counsel in some jurisdictions. Furthermore, it is conceivable that if the victim does not choose to prepare a VIS, the court may see the victim as less committed to the outcome of the case (Ashworth, 1993). Learning about the VIS process also differs among jurisdictions. Some victims may receive a form or a pamphlet from police, while others may be referred to a Victim Services Unit. Training for victims with regard to how to write VISs is also not standardized across jurisdictions. This can lead to VISs being edited by the court before they are entered into proceedings, omitting large parts of the victim perspective, leaving many victims frustrated because they are unclear as to what may or may not be admissible in their statements.

Another significant change in the criminal justice system is the creation of the *Canadian Victims Bill of Rights* (2015). The goal of this legislation, like others before it, is to entrench the rights of victims into law at the federal level. A major concern with this type of legislation is ensuring that the rights of the victim do not interfere with the rights of the victimizer, which are protected under sections 7 through 14 of the *Canadian Charter of Rights and Freedoms*. Although the rights of victims have been violated by victimizers, our government prioritizes the protection of the rights of all citizens, especially when the accused is being threatened with the removal of some of those rights by the state. Therefore, the state must prove, beyond a reasonable doubt, that the victimizer has done harm before it removes any of those rights through penalties and/or imprisonment.

Conclusion

This chapter has focused on the victim rather than the victimizer (or offender). The average criminal act takes a very short time—the time it takes to grab someone's purse, wallet, or cellphone, or engage in a fight at a bar. Those students who will become more involved with criminology will probably have classes that predominantly focus on victimizers. However, it is the victim who often identifies that a crime has occurred, and it is the victim who initiates the involvement of others, such as the criminal justice system, in order to apprehend a victimizer. We expect victims to provide evidence about their own harm to help in investigations, then face their victimizer in court to testify about the truth of the evidence they have provided. Victims are asked to do this while dealing with the effects of the harm done to them, with little support when compared to what we offer offenders. Readers of this chapter should be aware that without care, concern, and protection of the victim, the structures of law and order become significantly weakened.

SUMMARY OF KEY POINTS

- Victimology looks at crimes from a victim-centred approach, understanding the victim experience. Victims are seldom afforded the same resources to deal with the victimization experience as are the victimizers, who can have legal representation and rehabilitation efforts provided through public funds.

- The concepts of victim and victimization, like criminal and criminal activities, are socially constructed, and they change over time to reflect the changing worldview on vulnerability and harm.

- Conducting research about the victim experience can be difficult because the population is vulnerable. Victims can also carry multiple statuses; they may be primary victims of an event and, if they witness others being victimized, they may be secondary victims and have other victimizing experiences. Furthermore, doing larger studies on victims is difficult because many individuals may not want to talk about their victimizing experience. Research must be conducted carefully when trying to understand these issues.

- Responses to victimization can vary significantly from victim to victim. Surprising to many, the most common response to victimization is anger. This may conflict with our ideas on how victims should respond. Likewise, resiliency among victims is more common than we understand it to be, given that most individuals have experienced or will experience at least some form of victimization over their lifetimes.

- Vulnerability to victimization varies over one's lifetime and varies with life experiences. General trends show that those most at risk for violent victimization are young, single males, followed closely by young, single women. Those with lower incomes are also at highest risk for violent victimization yet have the fewest resources for recovery.

- We must guard against seeking to blame the victim for their own victimization. Many problems exist with this common practice, most notably that it assumes that the victim is somehow culpable in the crimes committed against them. Victim blaming also assumes that the victim can control his or her environment and must be watchful against victimization at all times. If we blame victims, we run the risk of creating culturally legitimate victims, which goes against Canadian social values of equality and fairness for all.

NOTE

For more relevant information on victimization, go to the Updates & Videos tab for this book at https://emond.ca/crim2.

QUESTIONS FOR CRITICAL DISCUSSION

1. When we think of people as *victims*, what other themes are associated with this word? Do we make assumptions about people when we identify them as victims? Are there both positive and negative associations with the word *victim*? Can you think of other words that could also identify this experience that would change the way we think about victims?

2. Look up the word "victim" in the thesaurus of your word-processing software. What synonyms for victim come up? Now, in the same thesaurus, look up another word that you have chosen as a better word that describes "victim." Repeat this exercise, but online: Look up the word "victim" in your favourite online dictionary or thesaurus. What synonyms for victim come up? Now look up on the same online thesaurus another word that you believe is a better word that describes "victim." How do your word processor's thesaurus and your online source differ in their descriptions of "victim" and the synonym you chose for "victim"?

3. Identify the victim experience: In today's newspaper or on an online news website, find a story in which a victim is identified. Most news stories focus on the offender. Is this story offender-focused or victim-focused? Now, try to understand what the victim experienced that day, before, during, and after the victimization experience.

4. Protective mechanisms: What protects individuals against victimization? How many insulators can you think of? Why do you think these insulators help protect individuals against victimization?

5. Blaming the victim—identifying rape myths: Rape myths are defined as untrue assertions surrounding rape and/or sexual assault. Many colleges and universities discuss these myths as part of student awareness campaigns. What are some of these myths? Why do you think these myths emerged, and how do these myths blame victims for their own assaults?

SUGGESTED FURTHER READINGS

Bonanno, G.A. (2004). Loss, trauma, and human resilience: Have we underestimated the human capacity to thrive after extremely adverse events? *American Psychologist, 59*(1), 20–28. https://doi.org/10.1037/0003-066X.59.1.20

Eigenberg, H. (2003). Victim blaming. In L. Moriarty (Ed.), *Controversies in victimology* (pp. 15–24). Cincinnati, OH: Anderson.

Perreault, S., & Brennan, S. (2010). Criminal victimization in Canada, 2009. *Juristat.* Statistics Canada Catalogue no. 85-002-X. Retrieved from http://www.statcan.gc.ca/pub/85-002-x/2010002/article/11340-eng.htm

Scott, H. (2011). *Victimology: Canadians in context.* Don Mills, ON: Oxford University Press.

Websites

Canadian Crime Victim Foundation: http://www.ccvf.net
Canadian Resource Centre for Victims of Crime: http://crcvc.ca
Mothers Against Drunk Driving (Canada): https://www.madd.ca
Office for the Federal Ombudsman for Victims of Crime: http://www.victimsfirst.gc.ca

Legislation

Canadian Charter of Rights and Freedoms, s 1, Part I of the *Constitution Act, 1982*, being Schedule B to the *Canada Act 1982* (UK), 1982, c 11.
Canadian Victims Bill of Rights, SC 2015, c 13.
Criminal Code, RSC 1985, c C-46.

PART TWO

Theories of Crime

CASE STUDY 6.1

Sentencing for Manslaughter: Two Opposing Views

Osgoode Hall in Toronto, site of the Ontario Court of Appeal.

On a summer afternoon in 1996, after having lunch with his 71-year-old mother, Olive, 47-year-old Robert Turcotte went with her to the Royal Canadian Legion to drink beer. The mother and son were there from about two in the afternoon until 11 that night. Robert estimated that he drank about 16 pints of beer—when blood alcohol readings were taken later that night, he had more than 230 milligrams of alcohol in 100 millilitres of blood. Robert drove his mother back from the Legion to the apartment that they shared; his mother had also been drinking excessively, and she fell several times just walking from the car to the apartment. As he was preparing for bed, his mother confronted him with a knife (she often became aggressive after drinking).

Robert removed the knife and put it away, but shortly afterward his mother went after him with her bare hands. He does not recall anything that happened after that, until he saw his mother lying on the floor, with blood coming from her nose. He soon understood that he had strangled her with a television cable cord and a telephone cord, and he called police. After a trial for second-degree murder, Robert Turcotte was ultimately convicted of manslaughter. The Crown suggested a sentence of 10 to 12 years; the defence asked for a conditional sentence, to be served in the community.

The majority of the Ontario Court of Appeal, in determining this case, quoted approvingly from the trial judge, Mercier J (who had imposed a conditional sentence of two years less one day, to be served in the community):

> What does society stand to gain by such a sentence? Who benefits from this type of sentence? The daughters of the victim do not benefit; they have made that clear. The offender would not benefit. His rehabilitation would be greatly hindered, if not totally destroyed, by such a sentence. Society or the community gains nothing. It will end up supporting the offender while in prison and may well be faced with a person whose rehabilitation will have been seriously negatively affected when he is eventually released. (*R v Turcotte*, 2000, para. 22)
>
> This offence was committed under very specific difficult conditions unlikely to ever reoccur. This offender has expressed sincere remorse for his actions. This offender has taken very extensive and positive steps towards his rehabilitation and it is most important that his treatment and counselling be continued without interruption. This offender's siblings, the surviving victims of the offence, understand the circumstances under which the offence occurred and wish him to be allowed to continue his rehabilitation. This offender presents no risk to the community. Robert Turcotte will then be permitted to serve his sentence in the community. (para. 23)

Consider, however, the view of MacPherson JA, the dissenting judge in this decision. MacPherson JA asked, "Was the sentence imposed by the trial judge, namely, a conditional sentence of two years less day, 'demonstrably unfit'?" (para. 27a). He responded to his question as follows:

> With great respect for the trial judge ... I have reached the reluctant conclusion that the conditional component of the sentence he imposed was demonstrably unfit. I reach this conclusion for several reasons.
>
> First, this was a violent and terrible crime. The victim was a thoroughly drunk 71-year-old woman. The offender was her adult son. Mrs. Turcotte was completely defenceless. The son used not one, but two, cords ... to strangle his mother. He tied half-knots in one of the cords. He wrapped them so tightly around his mother's neck that the police officers had trouble removing them when they arrived at the scene. The strangulation went on for several minutes and was accompanied by the mother's screams. Neighbours testified that between midnight and 12:20 a.m. they heard banging noises and a woman's cries: "Help," "help me, please help me," "Bobby stop. Don't, Bobby, please." (paras. 29a–30a)

MacPherson JA noted:

> Later, when he turned to considering whether he should impose a conditional sentence, the trial judge said nothing about denunciation. The focus of this later part of his reasons is almost entirely on the rehabilitation of Mr. Turcotte. (para. 31a)

MacPherson JA quoted approvingly from a previous judgment of the Ontario Court of Appeal (*R v Inwood*, 1989) on the matter of sentencing in the context of family violence:

> This court has acted on the principle that where there is a serious offence involving violence to the person, then general and individual deterrence must be paramount considerations in sentencing in order to protect the public. In my opinion, this principle is applicable not only to violence between strangers but also to domestic violence. Domestic assaults are not private matters, and spouses are entitled to protection from violence just as strangers are. This does not mean that in every instance of domestic violence a custodial term should be imposed, but that it should be normal where significant bodily harm has been inflicted, in order to repudiate and denounce such conduct. (para. 42)

MacPherson JA concluded by suggesting that Turcotte receive a custodial sentence of two years less a day in prison.

Before You Read Chapter 6

- Consider these sharply contrasting decisions—the majority and the dissent. How might you summarize both positions, in a sentence or two each?
- Which decision do you think most closely reflects the notion of "free will"? Which most closely reflects "determinism"?
- Keep these decisions in mind as you read Chapter 6, and then return to this case study. What theoretical approaches, or ways of analyzing crime, are represented in these decisions: Classical? Positivist? Other approaches?

Theories of Crime: A Brief Introduction

LEARNING OUTCOMES

After reading this chapter, students will be able to:

- Explain why theories are important and identify the characteristics of a good theory.

- Distinguish between Classical School and Positivism and provide examples of theories associated with each school of thought.

- Explain how theories are influenced by their social context.

- Assess how theories could potentially affect criminal justice system policy and practices.

- Distinguish between consensus and conflict theories.

CHAPTER OUTLINE

Introduction

The major theoretical perspectives of crime and deviance are based on biological, psychological, and sociological explanations. However, many of the theories encountered in Part Two cannot be classified easily as biological, psychological, or sociological in origin. Contemporary social learning theory, for example, involves a combination of sociological, psychological, and, in some instances, biological thinking (Akers & Sellers, 2009; Tremblay, 2012). Classical School theory, in contrast, is neither sociological, psychological, nor biological, but premised on 18th-century notions of free will, hedonism, and utilitarianism (Mutchnick, Martin, & Austin, 2009).

This chapter provides a general introduction to these and other key concepts as well as the main historical currents in criminological thought.[1] After reading it, you will be prepared to explore in more detail the various theories that follow in Chapters 7 through 12.

Why Do We Need Theories?

We have all heard expressions such as "theoretically speaking" or "it sounds good in theory," which imply that theory does not necessarily work in practice. That said, all of the chapters in this book—not just those in Part Two—have theoretical underpinnings, even though they may not be readily apparent at first glance. Without a theoretical foundation, we could soon find ourselves advancing ungrounded, fragmented opinions rather than a disciplined, scientific approach to exploring and explaining crime and deviance. And, of course, not all theories have similar methods or frameworks of analysis. Put differently, conceptions of science vary across theoretical perspectives.

Former Justice Minister Rob Nicholson unveils the Canadian government's "tough on crime" legislation in 2011. Criminologists often find that popular solutions for reducing crime are not supported by research findings.

If you asked your family and friends what causes crime or why certain individuals become criminals, most would be able to offer some sort of explanation, even if it was unrefined and based mostly on truisms or what they had heard in the media. They might suggest that crime is the result of poor child-rearing, that criminals suffer from mental illness, or that crime rates are high because of soft-on-crime laws and lax enforcement on the part of the criminal justice system (Lilly, Cullen, & Ball, 2015). Some might even insist that we could reduce crime by imposing lengthier sentences or by bringing back capital punishment, despite a dearth of evidence demonstrating that harsher punishments work to deter or reduce crime (Donohue & Wolfers, 2009; Piquero & Blumstein, 2007).

In a sense, explanations that state crime is caused by poor child-rearing or by mental illness are theories about crime, except that both explanations are overly simplistic and lack the critical elements required to be "good" theory (Williams & McShane, 2018). Most individuals who experience poor parental control and role modelling during their youth eventually turn out to be law-abiding adults, whereas individuals from seemingly ideal family backgrounds sometimes go on to become adult criminals (Sampson & Laub, 1992). Relatively few mentally ill individuals become criminal offenders, while any number of "sane," rational individuals may engage in crime if given a good opportunity, especially when it looks like little chance exists of being caught and punished (Clarke & Cornish, 2001). As we shall see, most well-travelled criminological theories are quite complex, even when they attempt to explain only one type of crime. For example, Chapter 13, Violent Crime observes that interpersonal violence typically involves a blend of biological, psychological, sociological, and personal factors.

Thinking Critically

To be good, a theory must be logical, with a valid structure—that is, it must follow the most basic rules of critical thinking and logic, such as the requirement that premises be provided that support a conclusion. It must also help us make sense of reality: A good theory should make statements or propositions about reality that can be *tested*, so that the theory can be accepted or rejected on the basis of solid evidence. Otherwise, it becomes difficult to distinguish a logical argument that supports a true theory from a simple *opinion*. Good theories should also be parsimonious. This term is a fancy way of saying that if two theories explain the same phenomenon equally effectively, scientists should prefer the one that offers the simplest and most straightforward explanation (this tenet is known as "Occam's razor"). Simpler theories are also easier to test. Those that have earned widespread acceptance have usually been tested (successfully) on many occasions and under many different circumstances. Social disorganization theory, social control theory, and social learning theory—all discussed in Part Two—have been successfully tested multiple times, in many different countries, at different periods in history.

That said, it is not always possible to adequately test a new theory when it is first proposed (Williams & McShane, 2018). For instance, if someone in the 18th century had proposed the big bang theory for the origin of the universe, that person likely would have been ridiculed. Astronomers required the type of large, sophisticated telescopes and isolated observatories not available until the 20th century in order to confirm that other galaxies existed and were moving apart from one another.

A parallel exists in criminology. Advances in self-report surveys and victimization surveys during the 1970s persuaded criminologists to examine new dimensions of crime—victim characteristics, immediate environmental opportunities, lifestyle choices—that went beyond the characteristics and motivations of individual offenders (Sacco & Kennedy, 2011). Routine activity theory, lifestyle exposure theory, opportunity theory, and rational choice theory all came onto the scene at this time. Recent developments in genetic research and brain-imaging techniques have subsequently challenged the neoclassical notions of rational choice and free will that are commonly associated with rational choice theory, routine activity theory, and lifestyle exposure theory, causing some criminologists to re-examine the degree to which free will and rational choice are actually components of offender decision-making.

See Chapter 12, Crime Choice Theory for more on these theories.

The Significance of Social Context

All theories—and the theorists who propose them—are affected to one degree or another by their social, political, economic, and historical circumstances (Cullen, Jonson, Myer, & Adler, 2011). The **Positivist School** notion of criminality as an inherited (genetic) propensity was a reflection of what was going on in the mid- to late 1800s, intellectually linked to Charles Darwin's 1859 theory of evolution, Gregor Mendel's 1865 work on genetics, and then current developments in the fields of physical anthropology, medicine, and psychiatry (Wortley, 2011). The **Chicago School** view of criminality as a product of the social environment was shaped by the rapid urbanization that took place around the globe in the late 1800s and early 1900s, by the emergence of the discipline of sociology in the 1890s, and by social forces such as the Progressive Movement (Lilly,

Positivist School
A school of thought that attributed criminal behaviour to biological or psychological factors; often referred to as the "Italian School."

Chicago School
The first school of sociology in the United States; contributed to social disorganization theory, cultural transmission theory, differential association theory, subcultural theory, the sociology of deviance, and symbolic interactionism.

Cullen, & Ball, 2015). Theories do not emerge in isolation but, rather, reflect what has gone on in the past and what is happening at the time they are being proposed.

Even theories originating in the so-called hard sciences—chemistry, physics, and biology—are influenced by social and historical circumstances. On occasion, scientists can even be persuaded to discard or repudiate perfectly good theory. To illustrate, we need look no further than Galileo, who was forced by religious authorities (under threat of death) to recant his observation that the Earth and the planets revolved around the sun because, at that time, established religious doctrine held firmly to the belief that the sun and planets revolved around the earth.

As we examine criminological theories, we should always ask ourselves how certain ideas about criminals come to be regarded as self-evident or true. In other words, we should remember to think critically (Young, 2002). Why are we currently hearing slogans or phrases such as "the war on drugs," "get tough on crime," "zero tolerance," "truth in sentencing," and "three strikes and you're out" (Garland, 2001)? Where did these sayings come from, when did they first appear in public discourse, and why do they seem to have struck such a resonant chord with politicians and members of the public? Why have certain criminological theories become popular in their time, only to be consigned to the dustbin of history? At one point during the infancy of criminal psychology, for example, it was widely held that most serious criminals were morally insane—that is, they were considered psychopaths (Rafter, 2009b). Today, while the notion of criminal **psychopathy** still exists, it is believed that most criminals are not psychopaths, and that many so-called normal people who might meet the definition of psychopathy are not necessarily criminals (Andrews & Bonta, 2010).

Criminological Theory and Public Policy

While theories may at times appear to be fanciful ideas conjured up by people sitting in armchairs in ivory towers, the fact remains that criminological theories have had, and continue to have, a substantial impact on public policy. The **Classical School of criminology** recommendations regarding the need for due process, the use of imprisonment as a form of punishment, and limitations on the severity of punishment found their way into a number of laws and policies, including the US Constitution, the *English Penitentiary Act*, and the French criminal code (Lilly, Cullen, & Ball, 2015). Early Positivist School theorists also had a major impact on the criminal justice system. Cesare Lombroso endorsed the "medical model"—the notion that criminals were sick and in need of treatment. This idea gave rise to a number of prison reforms and a new emphasis on rehabilitation (Rafter, 2009a). Social disorganization theory, put forward by Chicago School theorists Clifford Shaw and Henry McKay in the early 1940s, resulted in the ongoing Chicago Area Project, which focuses on redesigning (reorganizing) socially disorganized slums through the creation of community organizations, cleaning up neighbourhoods, and reviving community pride (Williams & McShane, 2018).

Lawrence Cohen and Marcus Felson's 1979 routine activity theory, Michael Hindelang, Michael Gottfredson, and James Garofalo's 1978 lifestyle exposure theory, and Derek Cornish and Ronald Clarke's 1986 **rational choice theory** have contributed to the development of a number of crime prevention programs that are currently in use around the world, such as situational crime prevention, target hardening (designing out crime), and community (or problem-oriented) policing (Felson & Clarke, 2010).

psychopathy
A personality disorder characterized by a lack of empathy, egocentrism, manipulation of others, and a tendency toward anti-social and criminal behaviour.

Classical School of criminology
A body of work that emerged in Europe in the 17th and 18th centuries that argued people have the capacity to think rationally; contemporary deterrence theory is rooted in this school of thought.

rational choice theory
A modern version of Classical School thinking originating in economics; it assumes that humans are rational and have free will, and that offenders make conscious choices to commit crime based on a cost–benefit analysis.

Examples of such measures abound, including improved street lighting, burglar alarms, CCTV cameras, automobile immobilizers, GPS tracking, secure parking lots with barriers, boutique-style community police stations, and bike patrols by police (Clarke, 2009; Farrell, 2010). Routine activity theory, rational choice theory, pattern theory, situational crime prevention, and their influence on public policy and crime reduction strategies are described in greater detail in Chapter 12.

Many of today's successful correctional rehabilitation programs are premised, in part, on the tenets of Ronald Akers' social learning theory, which in turn are premised on the tenets of Edwin Sutherland's **differential association theory** (Cullen, Wright, Gendreau, & Andrews, 2003). During the early 20th century, when others were describing criminals as "psychopaths," "feeble-minded," "genetically inferior," or "evolutionary throwbacks," Chicago School theorist Edwin Sutherland (1947/1994) proclaimed, through his differential association theory, that criminal behaviour was learned, not inherited. He argued that criminality was learned in the same manner as other normative behaviour (for example, tying your shoes, reading, and writing)—that is, by learning the necessary techniques, values, and attitudes through social interaction with family members, peers, and significant others (teachers or role models). In his social learning theory, Akers built on Sutherland's notion that criminal behaviour is learned through social interaction, adding that processes of reinforcement and punishment were critical, in accordance with the principles of B.F. Skinner's operant conditioning and Albert Bandura's work on imitation and modelling behaviour, both emanating from the field of psychology (Akers & Jensen, 2003). Social learning theory—often delivered in the form of cognitive behavioural programs targeting anti-social associations and anti-social values—has been proven to deliver results superior to other programs, notably in reducing offender recidivism (Akers & Jensen, 2006; Cullen et al., 2003).

We should remember that public policy and public opinion continue to play a role in shaping criminological theory. If the public and politicians believe that crime is caused by a poor social environment—as was believed to a large extent during the 1940s, 1950s, and 1960s—then we can expect a wellspring of sociological theories explaining crime in those terms, buttressed by public support and public policy, and aimed at eradicating "criminogenic" (crime-causing) social conditions. On the other hand, if the crime rate is going up exponentially—as it was throughout the 1960s, 1970s, and 1980s—we can expect to see growing public support for conservative politicians such as Ronald Reagan in the United States and Margaret Thatcher in the United Kingdom. Conservative politics and public perceptions of rising crime rates can in turn lead to greater demand for rational choice theories, deterrence theories, or theories that support the incapacitation of "life-course-persistent offenders." Or, to express this shift differently, theories that put the blame back on the offenders, rather than on society (Williams & McShane, 2018).

We noted above that the Positivist School view of criminality as an inherited or genetic predisposition was influenced by developments in the mid-19th century, in fields such as evolution and genetics. In the following sections of this chapter, we will see how similar historical circumstances—social, political, scientific, or intellectual—gave rise to various theories. We will examine them in roughly chronological order, beginning over two centuries ago with the Enlightenment (or Age of Reason), which gave rise to Classical School thinking.

differential association theory
Sutherland's theory that criminal behaviour is learned through the process of social interaction and that the process includes the learning of criminal skills, motivations, attitudes, and rationalizations.

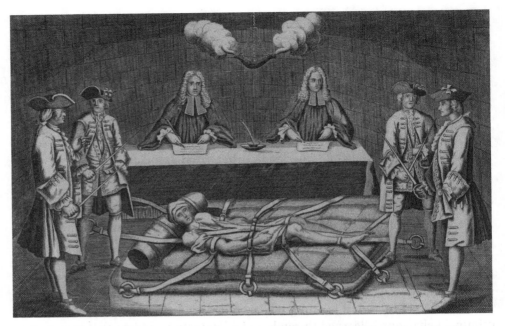

Found guilty of the attempted assassination of King Louis XV of France in 1757, Robert-François Damiens was subjected to grotesque public torture. His fate influenced Cesare Beccaria's 1764 treatise, *On Crimes and Punishments*, as well as Michel Foucault's 1975 book, *Discipline and Punish*.

The Classical School of Criminology

The Classical School of criminology was not a "school" in the sense that we may think of schools today. To illustrate, the three most well-known members of the Classical School were French philosopher Baron de Montesquieu (1689–1755), Italian philosopher Cesare Beccaria (1738–1794), and widely influential English philosopher Jeremy Bentham (1748–1832). They lived at different times and in different countries. Essentially, the Classical School consisted of a group of European social philosophers who lived during the 18th-century Enlightenment (Zeitlin, 2001). Members of the Classical School were social reformers who challenged the way criminals were dealt with, criticized the absence of due process, and argued against the death penalty and the use of torture to extract confessions.

Before the Classical School

Prior to the emergence of the Classical School, it was generally believed that criminals were possessed by evil spirits, or demons. This view of crime is referred to as "demonology" or "spiritualism." Demonology was essentially a theological (religious) theory about crime. It took the position that individuals who behaved in a socially disapproved manner had succumbed to temptation, becoming evil as a result. Even the mentally ill were thought to be possessed by evil spirits (Einstadter & Henry, 2006).

The prescribed remedies for criminality and insanity were also of a religious nature, typically involving confession (under interrogation and torture), repentance, and then execution. The means of torture or execution often involved fire, considered an essential ingredient in the purification ritual. Accused "witches" would be burned at the stake, while the bodies of condemned criminals who had been executed by hanging and/or dismemberment would often be burned following their execution (Pfohl, 1985).

During this "demonic" period, when spiritualistic explanations and remedies held sway, accusations, interrogations, and executions were often carried out by religious authorities. When they were not, they were carried out by the aristocracy (for example, kings and queens) or their official delegates. Such procedures were generally not governed by written law (at least, not written law as we know it today), nor were any safeguards in place to protect the rights of the accused. It was assumed that individuals accused by the aristocracy or the religious authorities were already guilty (otherwise, they would not have been accused in the first place), that it was simply a matter of getting them to confess to their guilt through interrogation and torture, and that executing them was the most logical way to rid the Earth of their presence.

Cesare Beccaria (1738–1794)

The Social Context of the Classical School

The Classical School emerged during the 18th-century Enlightenment, bracketed by the English Revolution of 1689 at one end and the French Revolution of 1789 at the other, with the American Revolution of the 1770s in-between. Clearly, this era was marked by great social and political turmoil. England lost control of America, its former colony, and the French aristocracy lost their heads to the guillotine. It was also during this period that Sir Isaac Newton discovered the laws of gravity, Voltaire argued against superstition (i.e., religion), Jean-Jacques Rousseau wrote about "the social contract," and Adam Smith inquired into "the nature and causes of the wealth of nations" (Yar, 2010; Zeitlin, 2001).

Jeremy Bentham (1748–1832)

Cesare Beccaria and Jeremy Bentham

While de Montesquieu, Voltaire, and English prison reformer John Howard were arguably members of the loosely defined "Classical School," the two most well-known Classical School theorists of relevance to criminology were Cesare Beccaria and Jeremy Bentham. Their works make extensive mention of **hedonism**, **utilitarianism**, **free will**, and human beings as rational, logical actors. The term hedonism refers to the view that humans will naturally seek pleasure and avoid pain. Utilitarianism suggests that the actions of governments and individuals should be measured in terms of their utility—how much pleasure they bring, and how many people benefit (derive pleasure) from those actions (DiCristina, 2012a).

In *On Crimes and Punishments*, Beccaria argued against secret accusations and the use of torture, insisting instead that accused individuals should have the right to know their accusers and the right to a fair trial. He opposed the death penalty, arguing that punishment should be proportional to the crime. Consistent with the concept of the social contract, Beccaria pointed out that when people agreed to join society, they did not agree that society should be able to kill them if they misbehaved (Mutchnick, Martin, & Austin, 2009). Beccaria also argued fervently against religious dogma and the authority of the Church, causing his treatise on crimes and punishments to be placed on the Catholic Church's list of prohibited readings, where it remained until the mid-20th century (DiCristina, 2012a). Nevertheless, Beccaria's recommendations regarding presumed innocence, trial by jury, restraints on judicial authority, and limitations on the severity of punishment—things that we take for granted today—formed the basis for new criminal codes in the United States and France, following the American and French Revolutions (Bernard, Snipes, & Gerould, 2010; Einstadter & Henry, 2006).

hedonism
The view that pleasure is the primary good; the pursuit of pleasure.

utilitarianism
A philosophy that suggests reasoned decisions will produce the greatest good for the greatest number.

free will
A will whose choices are not conditioned or determined by factors external to itself; also, the doctrine that free will exists.

Bentham is most well known for his argument that humans are rational, free-willed actors, and that their behaviour is governed by a hedonistic (pleasure–pain) calculus. Bentham argued that individuals would make a rational choice—a hedonistic calculation—about whether or not to commit crime, based on the anticipated amount of pleasure they would derive from their crime and the anticipated amount of pain they might suffer if they were caught and punished (O'Malley, 2010). According to Bentham, excessive punishment was evil in itself. Extreme and unnecessary punishment was not thought to deter crime, and might even cause the public to view the criminal justice system as tyrannical. He argued that punishment should be restricted only to the amount required to achieve **deterrence**, that the prescribed punishment should be made widely known to the public in advance, and that certainty and swiftness of punishment were more important for deterrence than the severity of the punishment (DiCristina, 2012b).

deterrence
A principle of sentencing or punishment intended to discourage citizens from offending or reoffending.

The Legacy of the Classical School

We can still find many examples of Classical School thinking in our modern criminal justice system, such as the codification of criminal offences (and a well-articulated list of possible penalties or sentences for violating the law), the presumption of innocence, the right to a fair trial, the right to know the case against you, and the right to be tried by a jury of your peers (DiCristina, 2012a). The legal concept of *mens rea* (or criminal intent)—which is essential to a finding of guilt in criminal court—is linked to Classical School notions of free will, rational choice, and individual culpability (Wortley, 2011). Our contemporary prison system is also a reflection of Classical School thinking. Before the Classical School, relatively few prisons resembled those we know now; prisons were generally used to hold accused people while they were being interrogated and tortured and then while they were awaiting execution (Foucault, 1979). Contemporary prisons are based more on the notion of imprisonment as a form of punishment, with prescribed limitations on the duration and severity of the punishment.

See Chapter 3, Criminal Law in Canada for more on *mens rea*.

Classical School thinking has enjoyed something of a revival in recent decades, with the emergence of contemporary deterrence theory, rational choice theory, and situational crime prevention theory. All of these approaches have their roots in Classical School thinking about free-willed individuals making rational choices to engage in or refrain from crime, based on an economic calculation of the perceived pleasure (benefit or gain) if they get away with it, and the perceived pain if they are caught and punished.

These topics are canvassed in detail below, in Chapter 12, Crime Choice Theory and Chapter 15, Property Crime.

The Positivist School

The term "Positivist School" is often used interchangeably with "Italian School," primarily to describe three 19th-century Italian theorists—Cesare Lombroso, Raffaele Garofalo, and Enrico Ferri—who attempted to apply what they regarded as a "scientific" method to the study of crime and deviance (DiCristina, 2012c; Walsh, 2012). These members of the Positivist School did not, however, invent the term **positivism**. Henri de Saint-Simon, an Enlightenment philosopher, is credited with first using the term positivism in his call for the use of scientific method to study human society (Zeitlin, 2001). The birth of what is commonly known as the Positivist School was also preceded by August Comte, a sociologist who wrote about positivism, "positive philosophy," and "positive politics" in the mid-1800s (Mutchnick, Martin, & Austin, 2009). Basically, the term positivism refers to the application of the scientific method to the study of society,

positivism
The application of the scientific method to the study of society, including the study of crime and criminals.

including the study of crime and criminals. Most social scientists—for example, sociologists, psychologists, and criminologists—try to develop logical, scientific theories and test the validity of those theories through systematic observation and measurement (Sacco & Kennedy, 2011). In fact, of the three members of the Positivist School, only Lombroso could be described as a medical doctor or "scientist"; Garofalo was more concerned with moral and legal matters, while Ferri was trained in psychology and criminal law (Mutchnick, Martin, & Austin, 2009).

The Social Context of the Positivist School

As noted above, the Positivist School was influenced by Darwin's theory of evolution and Mendel's study of genetics. A number of other 19th-century fields of study contributed to Positivist School thinking, among them physiognomy, phrenology, and psychiatry. Physiognomy—which had been around for centuries but enjoyed something of a revival during the 18th and 19th centuries—proposed that facial features could reveal an individual's inner characteristics, such as cowardice, deceitfulness, or propensity to engage in violence and crime (DiCristina, 2012c). Phrenology, sometimes referred to as "craniometry," held that abnormalities or anomalies in the shape of the skull were indicative of a person's morality and intelligence (Bradley, 2010). Psychiatry, with its increasing interest in moral insanity (psychopathology), was a precursor to the Positivist School view of habitual (incorrigible) criminals as insane, genetically unfit, or intellectually inferior (Rafter, 2009b). Essentially, the Positivist School rejected the main tenets of the Classical School, arguing that individuals did *not* exercise free will or make rational choices. Instead, members of the Positivist School claimed that behaviour was predetermined by genes, and/or by an individual's evolutionary circumstances.

Cesare Lombroso and the Atavistic Man

Cesare Lombroso has often been referred to as the father of modern criminology because he was the first to attempt to systematically apply scientific method to the study of criminality (Williams & McShane, 2018). Lombroso worked at different times as an army doctor, a psychiatrist, and as a university professor in medical jurisprudence, psychiatry, and anthropology (Mutchnick, Martin, & Austin, 2009). In the course of his duties, he measured and classified the skulls and body types of many prisoners and inmates confined to insane asylums. Lombroso concluded from his studies that criminals were **atavistic**—that they were degenerate, evolutionary throwbacks.

In his 1879 book *On Criminal Man*, he argued that criminals exhibited distinguishing features much like those of apes or Neanderthals—retreating foreheads, large ears, large jaws, and long arms—which, according to Lombroso, demonstrated their primitive evolutionary condition (DiCristina, 2012c). He also wrote about "insane criminals," such as kleptomaniacs (compulsive thieves), nymphomaniacs (sex addicts), and pederasts (older males who engaged in sexual relations with teenage males) (Mutchnick, Martin, & Austin, 2009). Lombroso went on to co-author the 1903 book *The Female Offender*, in which he and his son-in-law Gugliemo Ferrero described female offenders as "physically deformed" with "degenerative traits"—evolutionary throwbacks, similar to their male counterparts (Akers & Sellers, 2009). While Lombroso later added social and environmental factors to his theory, he is primarily known for his characterization of criminals as being like cavemen, cavewomen, or apes (Bradley, 2010).

atavism
A term associated with Cesare Lombroso and the Positivist School of thought; the notion that criminals are less evolved than "normal" humans.

Cesare Lombroso (1835–1909)

Enrico Ferri and Raffaele Garofalo

Enrico Ferri and Raffaele Garofalo were both trained initially in law, and later became students of Cesare Lombroso at the University of Turin in Italy (DiCristina, 2012c; Mutchnick, Martin, & Austin, 2009). Ferri was active in politics, and was at one time a Marxist and a member of the Socialist Party. He later became aligned with Benito Mussolini's fascist government, and was at one point invited to help redraft the Italian criminal code (Lilly, Cullen, & Ball, 2015). Although a member of the early Positivist School, Ferri employed a blend of anthropology, psychology, and biology, and wrote in the area of sociological criminology (DiCristina, 2012c). It was Ferri—not Lombroso— who first talked about "the born criminal." Nevertheless, Ferri also acknowledged the influence of age, gender, ethnicity, and social class on criminality. In particular, Ferri was known for his vehement rejection of Classical School notions of free will and rational choice, and his insistence that criminal behaviour was determined by a combination of biological, political, economic, and social factors (Lilly, Cullen, & Ball, 2015; Williams & McShane, 2018).

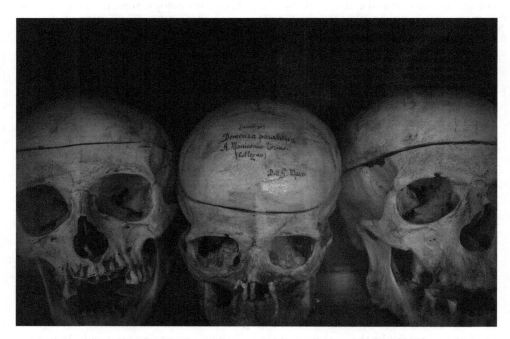

Some specimens from Lombroso's collection of hundreds of human skulls, whose size and shape he carefully studied in his attempts to understand criminality. Though this research was badly flawed, it did represent a serious attempt to apply scientific methods to the study of crime, and also reflected the growing influence of Charles Darwin's theory of evolution at the time.

Garofalo was, at different times throughout his career, a prosecutor, a magistrate, and a member of the Italian Senate (DiCristina, 2012c). Consistent with his experience in law and politics, he focused on "social defence" and what he regarded as "natural crimes." For Garofalo, there were certain "natural crimes" that all societies would instantly recognize as abhorrent, such as murder or the sexual abuse of children. He believed that societies had a right to defend themselves against offenders who committed such crimes through execution, transportation to another (distant) country, or incapacitation through imprisonment (Mutchnick, Martin, & Austin, 2009). Garofalo argued against the Classical School notion of free will, claiming that criminal thinking was inherited or "organic," and not the result of environmental factors or logical thinking.

Free Will Versus Determinism

Early Positivist School theorists rejected the Classical School view that individuals exercised free will and made rational choices, arguing instead that the behaviour of individuals was primarily predetermined by their inherited genetic makeup, which in turn affected the inner working of their minds. According to Positivist School thinking, then, criminals were born, not made. Positivist School adherents felt this to be the correct, "scientific" approach to understanding criminal behaviour, as it was rooted in the burgeoning disciplines of medicine, psychiatry, and biology, and based on scientific methods of observation, measurement, and classification (Pfohl, 1985). According to this medical model, criminality was a disease that could best be studied, understood, and "treated" by medical doctors and scientific "experts" (Foucault, 1979; Pfohl, 1985).

This debate between free will and **determinism** has raged on for centuries. Until quite recently, those who supported the deterministic perspective (for example, evolutionary biologists) insisted that human behaviour was predetermined by genes—that it was inherited, in the same fashion that animal behaviour was inherited. Those who traditionally favoured the free-will perspective argued, to the contrary, that humans were born without instincts—that human behaviour was socially constructed through interaction with the social environment (Fishbein, 1990). This debate hinged on the issue of whether nature or nurture played the largest role in the shaping of individual characteristics. Presently, evolutionary biologists are more likely to accept the existence of an interplay between genes and the environment, with both factors contributing to criminality in different ways (Anderson, 2007). Similarly, sociologists have gradually come to accept that certain characteristics—intelligence, physical abilities, and perhaps even problematic personalities—are at least partially heritable.

determinism
The doctrine that one's will is not the sole cause of choices, but that those choices are conditioned or determined by factors external to one's will.

Criticisms of the Positivist School

Members of the Positivist School were roundly criticized for their simplistic assumptions about "the born criminal," the existence of identifiable criminal body types, and their unfounded belief that "innate" anomalies such as immorality, deceitfulness, or low intelligence could be ascertained by examining a person's skull or facial features. They were also criticized for discounting the relationship between crime and social factors like poverty, lack of education, and lack of employment opportunities (Akers & Sellers, 2009). Members of the Positivist School tended to view impoverished individuals as genetically inferior, when in fact most were poor because they were born into the lower social classes and had no way to rise up through the social ranks. Positivist School theorists would also describe uneducated, illiterate people as "feeble-minded," when most simply lacked exposure to the kind of public schooling system that we have today.

More than anything, Positivist School adherents were criticized for their support for the so-called science of *eugenics*—the misguided notion that the bad genes that led to "diseases" like feeble-mindedness, homosexuality, and criminality could and should be eliminated from the human gene pool through selective breeding; that is, through sterilization, segregation, and (if necessary) extermination. People whose only crime was vagrancy (being poor and homeless) found themselves being locked up indefinitely, while those designated as feebleminded (usually the uneducated or illiterate) found themselves subjected to enforced sterilization, or castration, so that they could not procreate (Lilly, Cullen, & Ball, 2015). As recently as 1976, some states in the United States still permitted involuntary sterilization of habitual criminals, epileptics, the mentally ill, and those deemed to be mentally "retarded" (Pfohl, 1985).

Note that this "scientific" approach was very much in keeping with the Social Darwinist perspective that was prevalent during the late 1800s and early 1900s, and the concomitant belief that society is a reflection of what goes on in the animal kingdom. To follow the logic of Social Darwinism, those who were on the bottom-most rungs of society—the poor, the "feeble-minded," the physically deformed—were evolutionary throwbacks. Those who were on the uppermost rungs—the wealthy, the educated, the politically powerful—were at the very pinnacle of evolution, having arrived there through the processes of "natural selection" and "survival of the fittest" (Lilly, Cullen, & Ball, 2015). It was reasoned that the rich and powerful deserved their elevated position in society due to their advanced stage of evolution, whereas the poor deserved to be poor (and even to be eliminated), because of their lower, primitive evolutionary status. This view worked well for those who were born into wealth and title, such as the aristocracy, but not so well for those who were born into poverty.[2]

The Legacy of the Early Positivist School

Despite numerous criticisms, the tradition set in motion by the early Positivist School persisted for many years. Examples of early and mid-20th-century Positivist School thinking include Earnest Hooton's "hierarchy of degeneration" and William Sheldon's **somatotyping**. In his 1939 study, Hooton examined 17,000 inmates in a variety of correctional institutions and concluded that prisoners had distinctive and inferior characteristics—lower intelligence, mixed eye colours, and sloping foreheads (Akers & Sellers, 2009; Lilly, Cullen, & Ball, 2015). He described a hierarchy of degeneration, descending from sane civilians to sane criminals, and from insane civilians to insane criminals, with decreasing intelligence, increasing insanity, and more physical "deformities" the further you went down the scale (Deutschmann, 2002). In 1949, Sheldon's somatotyping theory, premised on 19th-century biological and psychiatric thinking, described three distinct (unusual) body types: the *ectomorph*, who was skinny, frail, and prone to nervous disorders and anxiety; the *endomorph*, who was rotund (overweight), sociable, and loved to eat; and the *mesomorph*, who had a muscular, triangular torso and was competitive, aggressive, and prone to violence (Bartol, 1999). Sheldon claimed that delinquents were more mesomorphic than non-delinquents, thus attempting—like Lombroso before him—to link a person's body type to their supposed propensity for criminal behaviour. Sheldon and Hooton both enthusiastically endorsed eugenics as a means to eliminate crime and criminals (Deutschmann, 2002).

somatotyping
A research technique that links behavioural characteristics to body types, such as mesomorphy.

FIGURE 6.1   Sheldon's Somatotypes

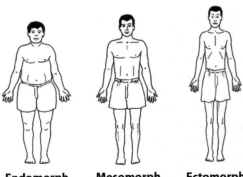

Endomorph   **Mesomorph**   **Ectomorph**

As was the case with the Classical School, early Positivist School thinking has had a significant impact on criminal justice policy. If it was assumed that individuals became criminals due to circumstances beyond their control—poor genes, inbred feeble-mindedness, inferior body type—then logically, they could not be held accountable for their behaviour. Nothing would be accomplished by punishing (deterring) criminals, because their behaviour was predetermined. Instead, crime was seen as a disease, requiring treatment by medical professionals (Cohen, 1985; Pfohl, 1985). Greater emphasis was given to treatment, rehabilitation, and the use of indeterminate sentences to ensure that criminals had been cured prior to their release into society.

Sigmund Freud (1856–1939)

We still see vestiges of this medical model in the Canadian court system today, where lawyers argue that their clients deserve special consideration because of psychological disorders, diminished mental capacity, or inability to understand the nature of their actions. Experts testify at trial as to the degree of physical or mental incapacity, and judges weigh this expert testimony prior to sentencing. The same applies to the Canadian correctional system, where transfer to a reduced security institution or release on parole routinely involves psychiatric and psychological reports, that is, "expert" opinion. The "dangerous offender" designation is intended to incapacitate "untreatable" criminals indefinitely, while the "long-term offender" designation is intended to extend and increase the level of control over chronic offenders who have not responded adequately to repeated attempts at "treatment."

Psychology, Psychobiology, Criminology, and Positivism

During the 19th and early 20th centuries, theories of criminal behaviour proposed by psychiatrists and psychologists were similar to—and in many cases overlapped with—Positivist School thinking. Both approaches viewed (and continue to view) criminality through a medical lens—as a disease or abnormality that can be cured if diagnosed and treated properly by scientific experts. Also, both approaches applied the "scientific" method to the study of criminality. Sigmund Freud, the founder of psychoanalysis and a forerunner of modern-day psychiatry, typifies the 19th-century positivist. Freud, a medical doctor specializing in neurology, was also interested in psychology, biology, and anthropology (Lemert, 1993). Freud's psychodynamic theory postulated that human psychology was shaped by biological processes (instincts), family dynamics, and early childhood experiences. Although Freud did not specifically focus on criminality in his own work, Freudian thinking presaged much of the contemporary work in psychological explanations of crime and deviance, such as psychopathology, social learning, and the relationship between frustration and aggression (Andrews & Bonta, 2010).

The 1950 book *Unraveling Juvenile Delinquency*, written by husband and wife team Sheldon and Eleanor Glueck, is a prime example of psychobiology, or biopsychology. In their study of 500 delinquent and 500 non-delinquent boys, the Gluecks observed that delinquent boys were more mesomorphic than non-delinquent boys. This conclusion is reminiscent of William Sheldon's 1949 work on somatotyping (see above) and hearkens back to Cesare Lombroso's earlier characterization of criminals as atavistic (Lilly, Cullen, & Ball, 2015). At the same time, the Gluecks stated that delinquent boys had a greater number of psychological or temperamental problems (Glueck & Glueck, 1950/1994), implying that delinquents displayed characteristics normally associated with psychopathy.

Contemporary criminal psychology is considerably more sophisticated and is often grounded in "cohort studies" that measure the development of large birth cohorts over a period of many years. One of the most well-known of these cohort studies—*Cambridge Study in Delinquent Development [Great Britain], 1961–1981*—was spearheaded by psychologist David Farrington (Farrington et al., 2006). In his article "Criminological Psychology in the Twenty-First Century," Farrington (2004) calls for a discipline that embraces an array of explanations, including biological factors (low intelligence and cognitive disabilities), sociological factors (poverty, family conflict, delinquent peers), and psychological factors (individual differences in impulsivity, attentiveness, and learning). He even adds rational choice theory and routine activity theory to the mix. Contemporary work in the area of psychobiology is exemplified by Terrie Moffitt's study on "life-course-persistent" (LCP) offenders and "adolescent-limited" (AL) offenders. According to Moffitt, LCP offenders and AL offenders are two entirely different groups, each warranting its own theoretical explanation. She says that LCP offending can best be explained by heritable factors, such as cognitive deficits, and by prenatal and neonatal trauma (maternal alcohol or drug abuse during pregnancy, deprivation of affection following birth). AL offending, on the other hand, can best be explained in terms of social learning—the type of peer pressure, peer approval, or peer rejection routinely experienced by teens (Moffitt, 1993).

The Schism Between Sociology and Biology

Historically, psychology and sociology have shared a fruitful—if at times uneasy—relationship. While sociology searches for the causes of criminal behaviour in social structure, social institutions, and social interaction, psychology searches for causes of criminal behaviour in the characteristics of individual offenders. However, the two disciplines have traditionally recognized that an interplay exists between the social environment and the inner workings of the mind (Andrews & Bonta, 2010; Wortley, 2011). Akers's social learning theory and Agnew's general strain theory are both excellent examples of "social psychology," a blend of sociology and psychology.

The same cannot be said for the fractious relationship between sociology and biology. French sociologist Émile Durkheim was highly critical of the early Positivist School, particularly with respect to its characterization of crime as "abnormal" or "pathological" (Walsh, 2002). Durkheim pointed out that all societies had crime, that crime had existed throughout history, and that crime had not been weeded out through evolutionary processes. Therefore, Durkheim concluded that a certain amount of crime must be normal (Durkheim, 1964). He objected to the Positivist School portrayal of criminality as a disease invading an otherwise healthy organism, and to the notion that human beings should be quarantined, sterilized, and even eradicated to prevent them from spreading the disease of criminality. Durkheim argued that a limited amount of crime actually served a social function by reinforcing social values and demonstrating what might happen to those who refused to play by society's rules (Erikson, 1962).

See Chapter 12 for more on these theories.

Moffitt's whose work is discussed in Chapter 7, Biological Approaches and Chapter 8, Psychological Approaches.

See Chapter 9, Sociological Approaches for more on social learning theory and general strain theory.

Edwin Sutherland (1883–1950)

This divide, or "schism," between sociology and biology was widened further by Edwin Sutherland's withering attack on the 1950 work of Sheldon and Eleanor Glueck, whose thinking was in turn influenced by William Sheldon's somatotyping, and by prison psychiatrist Bernard Glueck, the older brother of Sheldon Glueck (Laub & Sampson, 1991; Rafter, 1997). William Sheldon, a supporter of eugenics, claimed that violent criminals could be identified through their mesomorphic body type. Bernard Glueck was convinced that most criminals were psychopaths and should be committed to psychiatric institutions for life (Rafter, 1997). Edwin Sutherland, a Chicago School sociologist, ridiculed such notions. He argued that criminal behaviour was learned through interaction with the social environment, and observed that crime existed in the supposedly "normal" middle and upper classes, as well as among members of the lower classes (Sutherland, 1940, 1947/1994, 1950). Between the 1920s and the 1970s, biological explanations of criminal behaviour fell into disfavour and were largely supplanted by sociological explanations, many emanating from the Chicago School.

See Chapter 9 for more on this development.

The Rebirth of the Positivist School

After decades of being discounted, biological and psychological explanations enjoyed something of a revival during the 1970s and 1980s, in part because society started to view the social solutions to crime as ineffective. In the 1950s, crime rates were relatively low; however, in the 1960s, crime rates started to rise in the United States, Canada, and the United Kingdom. This trend continued until the early 1990s. During the mid-1970s, people started to lose faith in the criminal justice system as well as the social theories that formed the basis for the penal-welfare system (Garland, 2001). In criminology, socially oriented theories, such as the labelling perspective, conflict theories, critical criminology, and Marxist theories, had come to dominate the field. Ironically, the criticisms levelled by socially oriented critical criminologists and Marxist criminologists against traditional mainstream criminology—and its alleged focus on measuring and "treating" only those whom the state defined as "criminal"—caused many criminologists to begin to re-evaluate sociological theories of crime and deviance. Eventually, positivist contributions from biology began to re-enter criminological theorizing (Jeffery, 1978).

In 1976, Samuel Yochelson and Stanton Samenow—who worked at a forensic psychiatric institution—published *The Criminal Personality*, in which they argued that criminals were born with abnormal thought patterns that affected their ability to make normal decisions (Williams & McShane, 2018). Beginning in 1977, Sarnoff Mednick and Karl Christiansen (working with a variety of colleagues over the years) disseminated the results of a series of studies on disturbances in the autonomic nervous system and low cortical arousal in high-risk offenders, suggesting that serious criminal offending was linked to biological processes (Lilly, Cullen, & Ball, 2015). In 1985, James Wilson and Richard Herrnstein published *Crime and Human Nature*, in which they asserted that constitutional factors such as mesomorphy were indeed related to criminality (Paternoster & Bachman, 2001). In 1994, Richard Herrnstein and Charles Murray took this one step further, arguing in *The Bell Curve* that a relationship existed between criminality and low intelligence (Lilly, Cullen, & Ball, 2015).

During the 1990s, a number of evolutionary biologists made a concerted effort to mend fences with sociology and restore biology to what they considered to be its rightful place in criminology (Ellis & Walsh, 1997). Emerging knowledge about DNA, neurotransmitters, the human genome, and the use of MRIs for brain imaging have added significantly to biology's contribution to the study of criminal behaviour (Beaver, Ratchford, & Ferguson, 2009; Raine & Yaralian, 2001). Biology's stature in criminology has also been enhanced by its abandonment of eugenics, the search for a specific crime gene, and the search for an identifiable criminal body type (Lilly, Cullen, & Ball, 2015).

Chapter 7 examines a number of contemporary biological explanations of criminal behaviour.

Theoretical Integration in Criminology

At some point, students may come to the realization that there are dozens (if not hundreds) of factors that can be useful in understanding and explaining crime and criminal behaviour. This suggests that one simple (unicausal) theory cannot adequately explain all types of crime and criminal behaviour. Thus, it seems that theorists would be better advised to draw upon a variety of known criminogenic factors from various disciplines (for example, sociology, psychology, biology, etc.) (Bernard & Snipes, 1996). Indeed, during the 1980s and 1990s, criminology became embroiled in a debate about how best to approach this issue of theoretical integration (Elliott, Ageton, & Canter, 1979; Meier, 1985; Messner, Krohn, & Liska, 1989). Some have argued that this movement generated a lot of heat, but not much light. They also warned that too much theoretical integration runs the danger of creating a "theoretical mush," which could ultimately fail to provide an enhanced understanding of the processes and mechanisms associated with criminal behaviour (Akers, 1989). Travis Hirschi, known for his work on social bond theory and low self-control theory, insisted at the time that major theories should be kept separate from each other, because their underlying assumptions were fundamentally incompatible with each other (Hirschi, 1979, 1989). Nevertheless, theoretical integration remains an important development in criminological thinking, and continues to have an impact to this day (Agnew, 2011; Bruinsma, 2016).

It would be impossible to do justice to integrated theories in an introductory chapter of this nature. Examples of respected and well-travelled integrated theories abound. As noted earlier in this chapter, Ronald Akers's social learning theory includes elements of Sutherland's (sociological) differential association theory, Skinner's (psychological) work on operant conditioning, and Bandura's (psychological) work on imitation and modelling behaviour, resulting in what might best be described as a combined social-psychology approach (Akers & Jensen, 2003). Terrie Moffitt's (1993) dual taxonomy of adolescent-limited and life-course-persistent offenders contemplates an array of variables, including neuropsychological deficits such as cognitive disabilities (thought to be at least partially heritable, consistent with psychobiological theorization), plus factors such as social class and peer reinforcement (consistent with sociological thinking).

Further information on Akers's social learning theory can be found in Chapter 9.

Further information on Moffitt's dual taxonomy can be found in Chapter 8.

One integrated theory that appears to offer considerable promise is Cullen and Colvin's social support and coercion theory. According to Cullen, the United States exhibits higher rates of serious crime because it is a less supportive society than comparable industrialized nations (Cullen, 1994). Cullen describes two main types of social support: instrumental support and expressive support. Instrumental support means, for example, being able to rely on others for help with paying tuition fees, or for help in finding a job. Expressive support refers to receiving love and affection, feeling included, and being able to share sentiments with, and express frustrations to, significant others. These types of social support can come from parents, spouses, friends, social networks/relationships, and even government agencies. Among the reasons that Cullen proffers for the diminishment of social support in American society are the culture of individualism, the rampant social inequality, and the mean-spirited attitude of its welfare agencies (Cullen, 1994; Lilly, Cullen, & Ball, 2015). According to Colvin, coercion is a primary cause of crime. Coercion consists of controls such as punitive discipline, negative commands, critical remarks and humiliation in the family setting, and similarly harsh controls encountered in the school and work settings. The sense of being "coerced" can also arise from the social and economic pressures of poverty, unemployment, and the competitive nature of capitalist society (Colvin, Cullen, & Vander Ven, 2002; Lilly, Cullen, & Ball, 2015). In their integrated theory, Colvin and Cullen argue that coercion and social support are distinct and inversely related variables—coercion promotes crime, whereas social support can prevent crime. Moreover, they propose that the existence of consistent social support may lessen the use of coercion, while consistent (and especially erratic) coercion may in turn weaken social support (Colvin, Cullen, & Vander Ven, 2002).

Conflict Versus Consensus: Karl Marx and Émile Durkheim

While neither was a criminologist, both Karl Marx and Émile Durkheim had a profound influence on the development of criminological theory. Marx was a political philosopher and economist, and although a prolific writer, did not say much about crime in his writings. To the extent that Marx touched on the topic, it was mostly in reference to crime as a byproduct of the social inequality and class struggle that he associated with the capitalist mode of production (Renzetti, Curran, & Carr, 2003; Williams & McShane, 2018). While Durkheim touched occasionally on the subject of crime, it was not his main focus (Passas, 1995). Rather, Durkheim was more concerned with articulating what he felt to be a scientific approach to the understanding of society. Nevertheless, the conflict tradition in criminology is typically associated with the thinking of Marx, whereas the consensus tradition is typically associated with Durkheim (Burtch, 2003). Most criminological theories can generally be classified as either conflict or consensus theories, although a number admittedly fall somewhere in-between.

Conflict theory posits that society and its laws and legal system are rooted in social, political, and economic conflict. Those who have wealth and power get to decide what will be against the law and who will be targeted by the legal authorities. Examples of conflict theory include "cultural criminology," "labelling theory," "critical constructionism," "critical criminology," and many branches of feminist criminology. Some of these perspectives are not necessarily Marxist in origin, but most conflict-oriented theorists would agree that an ongoing struggle, albeit not necessarily explicit, exists between the rich and powerful and the poor and powerless, with the rich and powerful largely getting their own way and ultimately imposing their will over the poor and powerless (Lilly, Cullen, & Ball, 2015; Reiman, 2003). Thus, both law and the criminal justice

Karl Marx (1818–1883)

Émile Durkheim (1858–1917)

conflict theories
Theories, originating primarily with Marx, that focus on the unequal distribution of power in society—for example, due to class, race, or gender. Conflicts between classes or groups are driven to a large extent by this unequal power and unequal access to resources.

system do not reflect widely held social values and beliefs but, rather, the attitudes, values, and beliefs of those who have the power to make and enforce laws. Instead of asking why certain individuals become criminals, conflict theorists argue that we should question why certain individuals end up being criminalized while others do not, and who benefits most from this criminalization process.

Consensus theory, on the other hand, argues that society and its laws are rooted in the shared values and beliefs of its members. Society is viewed as a natural, organic entity that works to the benefit of all its constituents. Those who do not share the values and beliefs of society, and who behave in a socially unacceptable manner, are regarded as deviant or criminal (abnormal) and therefore legitimately subject to punishment, incapacitation, or "treatment." In other words, the role of the criminal justice system (and criminologists as well) is to protect society. Examples of consensus theory include anomie-strain theory, social control theory, and rational choice theory, although all three theories acknowledge that socio-economic inequalities and social conflict are factors in criminal motivation and in social reactions to crime (Williams & McShane, 2018). Psychological and biological theories could also be regarded as consensus theories, in that they begin with the assumption that such a thing as "normal" behaviour exists, and then set about to study (and cure) what they deem to be "abnormal" behaviour (Pfohl, 1985).[3] As you read the rest of the chapters in Part Two, or those in other parts of this book, try to identify which perspectives are conflict-oriented, which are consensus-oriented, and which fall somewhere in-between.

consensus theories
In opposition to conflict theories, consensus theories, which originate with Durkheim, hold that society functions through social bonds and collective beliefs, and is characterized by widespread acceptance of values, norms, and laws.

Conclusion: The Future of Criminological Theory

Given its rather chaotic past, it is difficult to predict with precision what lies ahead for criminological theory. With the rapid development of the biological sciences, it seems safe to assume that biosocial explanations of criminal behaviour will experience vibrant growth in the foreseeable future. New discoveries in genetics and evolutionary theory, accompanied by the use of new tools and technology (for example, brain scans), will surely contribute to more research and further theoretical contributions from this area (cf. Raine, 2013). Recent developments in the field of "epigenetics"—which examines how stimuli in the immediate environment can alter the functioning of genes without changing the basic structure of DNA—have presented a challenge to those who favour more socially oriented explanations (Beaver et al., 2009; Lilly, Cullen, & Ball, 2015). At the same time, it can be anticipated that sociologists and critical criminologists will respond to the theoretical challenges raised by biological and psychobiological criminology, attempting to provide ever-stronger empirical evidence to demonstrate that society, culture, politics, and the economy play a larger role than inherited genes when it comes to the shaping of criminal behaviour (Duster, 2006).

White-collar and corporate crime are other areas that have been receiving increasing attention from criminological theorists in recent years. The collapse of the savings and loan industry during the 1990s, the Enron scandal in the early 21st century, and the meltdown of the stock market in 2008 have generated extensive media coverage, drawing increasing public attention to the crimes of the rich and powerful. Social strain theory has traditionally been used to explain white-collar and corporate crime (Lilly, Cullen, & Ball, 2015), but labelling, differential association, social control, rational

See Chapter 17, Organized Crimes and Gangs.

choice, and opportunity theories have also been applied to this problem (Benson & Simpson, 2009; Sutherland, 1940).

The same can be said for cybercrime. The Internet has expanded exponentially over the past 20 years, arguably becoming one of the predominant social domains (Alpert & Hajaj, 2010; Netcraft, 2010). It competes for time and space with the family (household), workplace, and leisure domains that have been front and centre in earlier iterations of criminal event theory and routine activity theory (Cohen & Felson, 1979; Sacco & Kennedy, 2011). Cyberspace is a place where many people go to commit crime such as identity theft, credit card fraud, the distribution of child pornography, the luring of children for sexual purposes, and even cyberterrorism (Broadhurst, 2006; Walsh & Wolak, 2005). To date, most studies in the area of cybercrime tend to be atheoretical, in the sense that they focus more on describing the various types of cybercrime, quantifying the costs of cybercrime, examining the laws (or lack thereof) in cyberspace, and exploring ways in which to prevent cybercrime and track down cybercriminals. However, it seems likely that socially oriented criminology will soon devote more attention to cybercrime, given that cyberspace is socially constructed and is primarily grounded in the type of symbolic interaction first identified by members of the early Chicago School.

In the past decade, interest in theoretical integration has continued within criminology. Using ideas from several different disciplines, these "integrated theories" attempt to fuse explanations across the micro and macro levels. In many cases, these theories attempt to explain both crime rates and patterns of individual criminality by incorporating ideas from biology, psychology, sociology, ecology, and economics. Future research efforts will likely seek to specify interactions between the variables suggested by each discipline (Agnew, 2005; Robinson & Beaver, 2008), including (but not limited to) genes, cognition, social structure, the social environment, and the exercise of individual choice (free will).

SUMMARY OF KEY POINTS

- The major theoretical perspectives of crime and deviance are based on biological, psychological, and sociological explanations. However, some theories do not fall squarely within one of those three. Contemporary social learning theory, for example, involves a combination of sociological, psychological, and, in some instances, biological elements.

- A good theory must follow basic rules of logic, and must help us make sense of reality. A good theory can be accepted or rejected on the basis of solid evidence. Otherwise, it becomes difficult to distinguish a simple opinion from a logical argument that supports a true theory.

- All theories are affected to one degree or another by their social, political, economic, and historical circumstances. For example, the Positivist School reflected what was going on in the latter 19th century, such as Darwin's theory of evolution. The Chicago School's views were shaped by, among other things, the rapid urbanization that took place around the turn of the 20th century.

- We can still find many examples of Classical School thinking in our modern criminal justice system, such as the codification of criminal offences, the presumption of innocence, the right to a fair trial, the right to know the case against you, and the right to be tried by a jury of your peers.

- The Positivist School rejected the main tenets of the Classical School, arguing that individuals did not exercise free will or make rational choices. Instead, members of the Positivist School claimed that behaviour was predetermined by genetics and evolution.

- While sociology searches for the causes of criminal behaviour in social structures and interactions, psychology examines the characteristics of individual offenders. These two disciplines have traditionally recognized an interplay between these factors. In contrast, the relationship between sociological and biological theories has been much more contentious.

- Conflict theory posits that society and its laws and legal system are rooted in social, political, and economic conflict. It is typically associated with the thinking of Marx. Consensus theory holds that society and its laws are rooted in the shared values and beliefs of its members, and is typically associated with Durkheim. Most criminological theories can generally be classified as either conflict or consensus theories, although a number fall somewhere between the two.

NOTES

1. Note that while definitions of several key terms are provided in this chapter, a number of terms relating to specific theories are defined within their respective chapters.

2. Like many applications of evolutionary theory that emerged during this time, this line of reasoning is based on a misinterpretation of Darwin's ideas. Evolutionary theory states that organisms develop different traits that allow them to survive in their surroundings. It might be more accurate to argue that some forms of criminality (for example, drug dealing, white-collar crime) actually provide evolutionary advantages that help criminals thrive in their environments. Further, in some cases, law-abiding behaviour does not seem to be very adaptive, since it really provides no clear evolutionary advantages, especially if the likelihood of being caught and punished for committing a crime is very low.

3. Examples of "pure" conflict and consensus theories are few and far between. Even Durkheim, the forefather of consensus theory, would acknowledge that conflict exists between individual wants and aspirations, and the social institutions and regulations that restrain individual conduct. Some biologists accept the notion that the law is a product of social conflict, rather than consensus. While they might argue that biology trumps the environment in producing criminality, biologists could still be skeptical of state definitions of criminal behaviour and the moral legitimacy of state sanctions.

QUESTIONS FOR CRITICAL DISCUSSION

1. Which theories seem to have stood the test of time and continue to be influential or broadly accepted? Which ones have not?
2. How have various theories influenced one another? Provide some examples.
3. What accounts for the most heated debates among criminologists, such as sociological versus biological approaches, or consensus versus conflict approaches? Can you imagine these debates ever being resolved? What other key debates can you identify in this chapter?
4. What are the external disciplines that appear to have had the most influence on criminological theories?
5. Is it possible for any single theory to adequately explain crime?
6. What does a theory require in order to be considered useful, or valid? How does one judge the merit of a given theory?

SUGGESTED FURTHER READINGS

Agnew, R. (1985). A revised strain theory of delinquency. *Social Forces, 64*(1), 151–167.

Broadhurst, R. (2006). Developments in the global law enforcement of cyber-crime. *Policing: An International Journal of Police Strategies and Management, 29*(3), 408–433. https://doi .org/10.1108/13639510610684674

Burgess, R.L., & Akers, R.L. (1966). A differential association-reinforcement theory of criminal behaviour. *Social Problems, 14*(2), 128–147.

Duster, T. (2006). Comparative perspectives and competing explanations: Taking on the newly configured reductionist challenge to sociology. *American Sociological Review, 71*(1), 1–15. Retrieved from http://www.jstor.org/stable/30038973

Ellis, L., & Walsh, A. (1997). Gene-based evolutionary theories in criminology. *Criminology, 35*(2), 229. https://doi.org/10.1111/j.1745–9125.1997.tb00876.x

Farrington, D.P. (2004). Criminological psychology in the twenty-first century. *Criminal Behavior and Mental Health, 14*(3), 152–166. https://doi.org/10.1002/cbm.583

Jeffery, C.R. (1978). Criminology as an interdisciplinary behavioral science. *Criminology, 16*(2), 149–169.

Laub, J.H., & Sampson, R.J. (1991). The Sutherland-Glueck debate: On the sociology of criminological knowledge. *American Journal of Sociology, 96*(6), 1402–1440.

Piquero, N.L., Tibbetts, S.G., & Blankenship, M.B. (2005). Examining the role of differential association and techniques of neutralization in explaining corporate crime. *Deviant Behavior, 26*(2), 159–188.

Sampson, R.J., & Groves, W.B. (1989). Community structure and crime: Testing social-disorganization theory. *American Journal of Sociology, 94*(4), 774–802.

Sutherland, E.H. (1940). White-collar criminality. *American Sociological Review, 5*(1), 1–12.

Cases

R v Inwood, 1989 CanLII 263, 32 OAC 287 (CA).

R v Turcotte, 2000 CanLII 14721, 48 OR (3d) 97 (CA).

Crime and Mental Disorder: The Tragic Case of Matthew de Grood and His Five Victims

The parents of Matthew de Grood, who was found not criminally responsible for the deaths of five young adults in Calgary in 2016.

In the early morning of April 15, 2014, University of Calgary student Matthew de Grood stabbed five young adults to death at a house party. The victims were four men and one woman, all between the ages of 21 and 27. Three of the victims died at the scene and the other two died soon after in hospital. All had received multiple stab wounds. Matthew de Grood was an invited guest to this end-of-the-school-year party. He had been successful in gaining admission to law school for the fall of 2014.

Shortly after arriving at the home, he found a large knife. After a frenzied few minutes of stabbing, he fled the house on foot, only to be captured less than an hour later by police.

In the weeks before the killings, both de Grood's parents and his classmates noticed that his behaviour had started to change. He had posted what were termed "bizarre" updates on Facebook, and on the evening prior to the stabbings, he had sent text messages to his parents indicating that he was going to harm himself.

Charged with five counts of first-degree murder, he went to trial in May 2016 and was found not criminally responsible. The expert witnesses who assessed Matthew de Grood testified that he was "clearly psychotic" at the time of the killings, and the suggested diagnosis from one of the two forensic psychiatrists was schizophrenia. Psychologist Dr Andrew Haag said, "He did suffer from a disease of the mind. ... At the time of the index offences, my professional opinion is that he likely suffered from schizophrenia" (Hixt & Tucker, 2016).

In September 2018, de Grood's case came before the Alberta Review Board ("the Board") for its third annual review. (All of those who are found not criminally responsible have their cases reviewed each year by a provincial board.) At a previous review in 2017, the Board had ruled that de Grood could take supervised walks around the grounds of the Alberta Forensic Psychiatric Centre, a move opposed by the families of his victims. In 2018, his psychiatrist recommended that de Grood receive two additional privileges: one-on-one supervised passes to attend malls near the facility in which he is confined and supervised passes to go to Calgary for further treatment programming. Family members of the victims jeered at the hearing when Dr. Sergio

Santana told the Board that de Grood was "a model patient ... doing everything he can." Santana added that both de Grood's schizophrenia and post-traumatic stress disorder were in remission and had been treated with appropriate medication (Graveland, 2018).

The response from the five families was not supportive. They told CBC News in a written statement, "We, the five families of Lawrence Hong, Joshua Hunter, Kaiti Perras, Zackariah Rathwell and Jordan Segura, remain steadfast in our position that Matthew de Grood should be institutionalized indefinitely." They went on to add, "We strongly defy anyone that suggests this risk is manageable or acceptable. The absolute evil and heinous nature of the crime he committed cannot be overstated and the prospect of this person being re-integrated into our community is beyond comprehension" (Dormer, 2018).

Brendan McCabe, a lifelong and close friend of Matthew de Grood, arrived at the home that night as his friend was disappearing down the street, after the stabbings. He has a somewhat different take on this tragedy, writing in Vice in 2017, "A single 24-hour period that occurred three years ago has become fodder for media, idle office chatter, dinner table conversations, and social media feeds across Canada and the world. While understandable, I find the conclusions drawn are regressive, short sighted, and will in no way work to aid in healing survivors, the families of the victims, Matthew de Grood, or the one of every two Canadians who will experience a mental illness by the age of 40."

McCabe argued, "At this point Matt is beyond the criminal justice system: he's a *ward* receiving treatment, not a criminal being punished. Yet for the past three years I have seen this case discussed as a testament to the institutional failings of our judicial system; as if it is somehow unfair that Matt is not being treated as a criminal. He committed an unimaginable act, but I know that based on every shred of evidence and personal history that Matt did not commit murder in the first degree."

And McCabe concluded, "Many headlines last month have told you that Matthew de Grood is now being granted 'extra freedoms.' This is true to an extent, but these are an established and routine part of his rehabilitation programs. The language used is crafted to provoke a reaction, not begin a discussion of the complex nuances of Matt's treatment plan and life, nor the elements of rehabilitation in Canada" (McCabe, 2017).

Before You Read Chapter 7

- Would you say that Matthew de Grood was under the influence of a mental illness at the time that he stabbed these five young people? Is this a good example of nature, rather than nurture, producing criminal conduct? What other explanations might explain his behaviour?
- Is this better thought of as a case in which both environment and the individual's illness are in play, influencing one another? Or as a case in which an individual's untreated illness best explains the events that unfolded?
- Are the feelings of the victims' families also deserving of serious consideration: that the prospect of reintegrating someone who has committed this kind of crime poses an unacceptable risk? How does one assess the nature of the risk?

Biological Approaches

Introduction

Criminologists, law enforcement, and the general public have tried for millennia to understand why people commit crime. Environmental, psychological, and sociological explanations for criminal behaviour are readily accepted, but biological explanations have, in the past, been considered highly controversial. This is, in part, due to a lack of understanding of biology and to the appalling atrocities that have been committed in the past because of just such a lack of understanding and the abuse of biology. In the last decade, however, there has been a major shift in interest in what is now often coined biological or biosocial criminology (Rocque & Posick, 2017), with a greater emphasis on genetic and neurological explanations for criminal behaviour, and their increased presentation in court as mitigating or aggravating factors.

In the early days of criminology, most early criminogenic theories postulated biology to be the *single* causal agent for crime. Franz Gall (1758–1828) believed that a criminal could be identified by the shape of the skull, and **phrenology** developed a massive following. In the late 1890s, pioneering Italian criminologist Cesare Lombroso described certain physical features, or **atavisms**, of criminals. He considered people who exhibited such atavisms to be less developed, more primitive, and more violent. Today, it seems absurd that anyone would believe such unscientific theories, yet we are all inclined to judge individuals by the way they look or dress, so one can understand how people could accept such theories at the time. Thankfully, these theories fell out of favour as they had no scientific backing whatsoever.

phrenology
The study of the shape and size of the skull as a supposed indication of character and mental abilities. This theory has been discredited.

atavism
A term associated with Cesare Lombroso and the Positivist School of thought; the notion that criminals are less evolved than "normal" humans.

Charles Darwin's theory of evolution (Darwin, 1859) explained how certain *genetic* characteristics can lead an individual to be more or less successful, or fit, in some environments than others (a theory that influenced Lombroso's ideas). Although Darwin's work had nothing to do with crime, due to a lack of understanding of genetics at that time, contemporaries began to suggest that many *non-genetic* factors could be inherited, such as poverty, promiscuity, and crime (Niehoff, 1999). This terrifying misunderstanding led to the **eugenics** movements in North America, the racial policies of the German Third Reich (1933–1945), and the subsequent Nazi genocide of European Jews during the Second World War. This frightening past has led people to forget that, at the time, scientists frequently explained that no scientific basis existed for these assumptions whatsoever; in fact, science proved the opposite. However, politicians abused the public's lack of understanding, with appalling consequences.

eugenics
Methods to improve populations by controlling breeding to increase the occurrence of desirable heritable characteristics.

Nature and Nurture

Today it is important to look at the true science behind biology and crime, and realize, as scientists always have, that behaviour, whether criminal or otherwise, is not caused by one single entity but by a combination of many factors that *include* biology as part of the equation. Anyone who does not believe that biology can impact behaviour has clearly never known a newborn baby or experienced a biological change such as puberty. Any parent will tell you that their baby was not born as a total nonentity, but instead immediately exhibited (often while still in the womb) a distinct personality. This personality, of course, will be greatly influenced by the environment the child grows up in, but the way a child's personality responds to that environment is based on the child's biology. Puberty, with its massive change in hormones, often results in behaviour changes and mood swings in adolescents. Past scholarly arguments have often spoken of "nature versus nurture." Biologists have recognized for years that such a phrase is incorrect and that it should be nature *and* nurture.

It is truly unfortunate that biological explanations for crime are not better understood, as they often offer much greater hope for rehabilitation than environmental explanations for crime. It is often considered that a person's DNA is a person's destiny, and that they are "born that way" and so cannot be changed. This assertion is very far from the truth. We alter our genetic future all the time. For example, a person who has a family history of heart disease may greatly decrease his or her own risk with diet and exercise.

Genetic Predispositions for Criminal Behaviour

Studying human genetics for any purpose is ethically, numerically, and biologically difficult. Even in large-scale studies, such as drug trials, every person is influenced by different biological and **environmental** (for example, diet, lifestyle) factors. Ideally, a good experiment requires a large number of identical animals, but cloning large numbers of people for experiments is not possible or ethical. However, fortunately, clones do exist in nature in the form of twins. Two types of twins exist. Dizygotic (DZ) twins are the result of two sperm fertilizing two eggs. They are no more genetically similar than any other pair of full siblings. Monozygotic (MZ) twins, however, are the result of a single sperm fertilizing a single egg, which then cleaves into two separate zygotes shortly after fertilization, resulting in two genetically identical babies.

environment
The external conditions, resources, and stimuli a person interacts with.

Twin Studies

Full siblings and DZ twins are said to share 50 percent of their DNA. This assertion is incorrect because all humans share about 99 percent of the same DNA that controls functions such as digestion, respiration, and physical makeup. So, DZ twins share 50 percent of the approximately 1 percent of human DNA that explains variations in characteristics. However, 100 percent of the DNA of MZ twins is the same; MZ twins are natural clones. Both types of twins are considered to share 100 percent of their environment, as they are reared together and are the same age. Therefore, comparing a trait in MZ and DZ twins allows us to consider that trait in a natural, non-experimental situation. Most studies use **concordance rates** to compare the traits of MZ and DZ twins. For example, if the concordance rate for a trait in MZ twins is determined to be 85 percent, then, because they are identical, we expect both twins to have an 85 percent chance of developing the trait. If the concordance rate for the same trait is only 15 percent in DZ twins, then the trait most likely has an inherited component because the twins that are identical are more likely to exhibit it than the twins who have less genetic similarity. If, on the other hand, the concordance rate for a trait is 85 percent in both DZ and MZ twins, then it is more probable that the trait relates to the environment because the greater genetic relationship does not impact concordance rates. A scientist could then go further and look at the trait in other, unrelated people. If the trait were found to occur much less in unrelated people, that would suggest the trait has both an environmental and a genetic component or is specific to a twin environment.

A wide variety of twin studies have been conducted over the last 100 years, including research on a range of criminal activities (with many long-term studies still ongoing). Concordance rates vary in studies and by type of crime but, overall, a much greater concordance rate for criminal behaviour is seen in MZ twins than in DZ twins, which indicates a strong genetic basis for criminal behaviour.

Twin studies have been very valuable in showing behaviours that are not only linked to genetics but also influenced primarily by the environment, because one cannot study one without the other. Such studies have been conducted in many countries, over many years, and by a variety of researchers. So, the results can be considered robust but some concerns remain (Anderson, 2007). We assume that the environment is the same for both DZ and MZ twins. However, as DZ twins may be of different sexes and MZ twins look identical, it is possible that pairs of MZ twins are treated more similarly than pairs of DZ twins, or, alternatively, that MZ twins deliberately try to be individually distinct, all of which would impact the assumptions related to environment. Also, MZ twins, although genetically identical, may have other biological differences due to the gestational environment or birth complications that are more common in twins.

Adoption Studies

Possibly the biggest concern with twin studies is the similarity of environments in which the twins live. This concern is eliminated with a more powerful natural genetic study type: an adoption study. In adoption studies, researchers compare the criminal behaviour of people who were adopted by non-family members with that of their adoptive

MZ twin brothers Reginald and Ronald Kray, who were notorious London gangsters in the 1950s and 1960s.

concordance rate
In a random sample of pairs, the proportion of pairs that share a certain characteristic.

and biological parents. This approach is much more effective in separating genetic and environmental influences and does not rely on an assumed identical environment for two people (twins). If adoptees who commit crimes have a statistically higher number of criminal biological parents, then this finding would suggest that criminal behaviour has a genetic basis. However, if adoptees who commit crimes have a statistically higher number of criminal adoptive parents, then this finding would suggest that criminal behaviour has an environmental basis. Many adoption studies have shown a higher level of anti-social or criminal behaviour in adoptees with criminal biological parents (see the review in Anderson, 2007).

More recent adoption studies have shown that adopted children are significantly more likely to be arrested multiple times and incarcerated if their biological parents had a criminal background (Beaver, 2011).

Is Violence Heritable?

heritability
The statistical estimate of the amount of variance in a trait that is due to genetics.

As violent crime is rare, most studies have not been able to look specifically at the **heritability** of violence, but a Danish adoption study (see Box 7.1) was so large that a comparison could be performed between violent offenders and those that had committed only property offences (Mednick, Gabrielli, & Hutchings, 1987). In the Danish study (as in the twin studies), property crime had a very significant genetic component, but violent crime was not significantly impacted by genetics.

Although early genetic studies showed a heritable basis for petty and non-violent crimes, later twin and adoption studies have shown a heritable basis for aggression. This finding makes sense, as aggression was a vital part of survival for early humans, and violence is simply misplaced aggression. In a study of rhesus monkeys, female offspring were taken from aggressive mothers and placed with non-aggressive females and vice versa to determine whether female aggression was inherited or merely copied. Over a three-year period, it was clear that offspring exhibited the aggressive or non-aggressive behaviour of their biological mothers, and the behaviour of the adoptive mothers had little impact (Maestripieri, 2003). Several studies on humans have found similar results. For example, in a large twin study in Britain and Sweden, aggressive behaviour (such as fighting and bullying) and non-aggressive behaviour (such as truancy and petty theft) were studied in both males and females. A highly heritable basis for aggressive behaviour was found in both sexes, but non-aggressive behaviour was significantly heritable in girls but less so in boys (Eley, Lichtenstein, & Stevenson, 1999). Both countries yielded similar results, which speaks to the robustness of the findings.

It has become clear that many genes can, when integrated with the environment, lead to violent behaviour, with approximately half of the variance being attributed to genetics and half to the environment, with the environment modifying the expression of the genes, referred to as GxE (Laucht, Brandeis, & Zohsel, 2014). This means that a person with a certain genotype may or may not exhibit violent behaviour, depending on the environment to which they have been exposed. Molecular studies have identified a number of genes that relate to aggression or disorders that frequently result in violence, such as alcoholism, schizophrenia, anti-social personality disorder (ASPD), and conduct disorder (CD) (Laucht et al., 2014).

What Can Adoption Studies Tell Us About Criminal Behaviour?

One of the largest adoption studies was conducted in Denmark and examined 14,427 non-familial adoptions (Mednick, Gabrielli, & Hutchings, 1984). Denmark maintains complete records on its citizens, so researchers were able to access extensive data on adoptees and their adoptive and biological parents. Criminal convictions were used as an index of criminal behaviour, and data on the crime, the date of the crime, and the sentence were obtained. Demographic data for adoptees and adoptive and biological parents were also examined, including date and place of birth, sex, address, occupation, and size of local community. These data could be used to imply socio-economic status as well as whether the child grew up in a city or in the country. The study showed that if a male child's adoptive and birth parents had never been convicted of a crime, then only 13.5 percent of the male adoptees received a conviction. If only the adoptive parents had a criminal record, then 14.7 percent of the adopted sons also received a conviction. However, if only the biological parents had a criminal record, then the percentage of convicted sons jumped to 20 percent. If both sets of parents had a criminal record, then the conviction rate in the sons reached 24.5 percent (Mednick et al., 1984). This shows a genetic basis for crime, but one that is influenced by the environment. Obviously, it was rarer for adoptive parents to have criminal records, as it is unusual for a couple to be allowed to adopt a child if they have a criminal background.

However, when the data were further refined to eliminate families in which an adoptive parent had a record, the relationship remained, with biological parents having a genetic influence on offspring criminality. The number of criminal convictions of adoptees with biological parents who had multiple convictions increased with the level of biological parent recidivism. In some cases, a parent gave up more than one child for adoption, which allowed a comparison of siblings and half siblings raised in different adoptive homes.

Overall, the data indicated that the chance any two randomly picked adoptees would both have a criminal record was 8.5 percent (so, this percentage was considered a baseline). Concordance rates for criminal records were 12.9 percent for half siblings, 20 percent for full siblings, and 30.8 percent if the biological father also had a criminal record—again, clearly indicating that a genetic relationship increases concordance. The number of females who had criminal records was much lower than males, but the researchers did investigate just female offenders and found that the pattern remained. Interestingly, the relationship between biological mother and female adoptee was actually statistically stronger than that between biological father and male adoptee, although the sample size available was small (Mednick et al., 1984). Adoption studies more clearly show the relationship between biology and crime, while also indicating the additive impact of the environment.

Alcoholism

Other adoption studies have looked at not only criminality but also the interrelationship between crime, alcoholism, and mental illness. A large, ongoing Swedish study found a high **correlation** of both criminal behaviour and alcoholism between biological fathers and biological sons who were adopted, indicating a genetic relationship between both criminality and alcoholism (Bohman, 1996). Moreover, two forms of alcoholism have been identified: Type I is found in both males and females, begins later in life, and is influenced by both the environment and genetics. Type II is almost always found in men, begins early in life, and is almost entirely genetic (Begleiter, 1995). Since the time of the Swedish study, several genes have been identified that contribute to the risk of alcoholism, as well as some that protect against it, together with a number of GxE interactions (Zhu, Hu, & Soundy, 2017).

Research has shown that alcoholic criminals commit repeated violent offences, whereas non-alcoholic criminals commit property offences and are more likely to have

correlation
The finding that two measurable phenomena occur together, suggesting a relationship but not necessarily one of direct cause and effect.

biological parents who committed petty offences only (Bohman, 1996). When only criminal behaviour was considered, if both biological and adoptive parents were not criminals, then there was less than a 3 percent risk of criminality in male offspring. When only the adoptive parents were criminals, this figure increased to 6.7 percent, and when only the biological parents were criminals, it reached 12.1 percent. However, when both biological and adoptive parents were criminals, the risk of criminality in male offspring jumped to 40 percent, which shows the interactive and additive effects of genetics and the environment (Bohman, 1996). As well, research has shown that a three-fold increase in the rate of schizophrenia occurs in both male and female adoptees of violent biological fathers. Interestingly, environment had differing effects on male and female adoptees. Long-term institutional care increased the risk of criminal behaviour in females, but not males. Meanwhile, many short-term stays in homes of low socio-economic status greatly increased the risk of criminal behaviour in males but not females. Overall, low socio-economic status alone did not increase the risk of criminal behaviour in males, but unstable homes, repeated institutionalization, and having stayed in a large number of foster homes did increase the risk of alcoholism and petty criminality (Bohman, 1996). (See also the related discussion concerning fetal alcohol spectrum disorder [FASD] later in the chapter.)

Attention Deficit Hyperactivity Disorder and Personality Disorders

Anti-social behaviour in youth is sometimes a prelude to criminal behaviour later in life. Twin and adoption studies have shown that **attention deficit hyperactivity disorder (ADHD)** and many personality disorders, such as CD, and borderline personality disorder (BPD), have strong genetic bases. Twin studies have shown a heritability rate of 68 percent for CD and 63 percent for BPD (Coolidge, Thede, & Jang, 2001). Researchers using four independent sources of data on anti-social behaviour in young twins (mothers, teachers, researchers, and twins' self-reports) found that anti-social behaviour identified by all four sources was highly heritable (82 percent). However, anti-social behaviour reported by only one of the four sources ranged from 33 to 71 percent, suggesting that very clear anti-social behaviour had a strong genetic basis, but milder behaviours may relate more to the situation or environment (Arseneault et al., 2003).

Children who suffer from ADHD generally do not do well in school, with over 25 percent of children with ADHD exhibiting reading disabilities. A lack of education and appropriate peer models will compound the genetic predisposition for ADHD. An analysis of almost 5,000 twins and adoptees has shown that reading success and reading disability are highly heritable (70 percent) (Kirkpatrick, Legrand, Iacono, & McGue, 2011). Studies have also identified genetic factors for ADHD on chromosomes 10, 16, and 17, and genetic factors for reading disabilities on chromosomes 2, 8, and 15 (Loo et al., 2004). The better the understanding we have of the actual biological deficit, the better chance we have of treating the condition. For example, ADHD has been linked to a variant of the **dopamine** transporter gene (Cook et al., 1995) as well as several dopamine receptor genes (Stergiakouli & Thapar, 2010). This finding is very important, as many of the drugs found to be beneficial to children with ADHD work by inhibiting the dopamine transporter system. Preliminary research has shown that in some cases, differences in siblings' contacts with the criminal justice system can be partly explained by differences in their dopamine-processing systems (Schwartz & Beaver, 2014). Breaking down the criminal act can allow researchers to understand which specific behaviour is

attention deficit hyperactivity disorder (ADHD) A condition that includes a combination of behaviours, such as difficulty sustaining attention, hyperactivity, and impulsive behaviour.

dopamine A neurotransmitter that controls the reward and pleasure centres of the brain.

responsible for it and, thus, how it can be ameliorated. Genetic studies have been able to indicate not only whether some behaviours are heritable but also which disorders are heritable and which *alleles* (or variants of a gene) actually control them, allowing for specific treatments.

Schizophrenia

Schizophrenia is a severely debilitating psychiatric disease that can include delusions, hallucinations, and cognitive disabilities (Rees, O'Donovan, & Owen, 2015). There are many factors that can contribute to schizophrenia, although more and more studies suggest a genetic basis (Rees et al., 2015) and many studies have suggested a polygenic basis for the inheritance of schizophrenia (Rees et al., 2015). Large-scale dataset genome sequencing has identified over 100 loci for alleles that contribute to risk for schizophrenia, with levels of risk varying from mild to high (Foley, Corvin, & Nakagome, 2017). As well, de nova mutations, which occur during life and so are not heritable, have also been shown to be involved in schizophrenia (Rees et al., 2015), as well as epigenetics (Shorter & Miller, 2015), in which the genes themselves are not changed but their expression or function changes. Several genes involved in schizophrenia appear to be specifically responsible for the cognitive deficiencies sometimes seen in schizophrenia and other psychiatric disorders (Lencz et al., 2014). Genetic studies have shown that schizophrenia shares many alleles with other psychiatric disorders including BPD and ADHD (Rees et al., 2015).

Many studies have shown a link between schizophrenia and violence, although the actual relationship is unknown but appears to also relate to socio-economic and socio-demographic factors (Bo, Abu-Akel, Kongerslev, Haahr, & Simonsen, 2011). In a large-scale longitudinal study in Sweden, 13.2 percent of patients with schizophrenia had committed at least one violent crime in comparison with 5.3 percent in the general population, with the risk increase greater in patients comorbid with substance abuse (Fazel, Langstrom, Hjern, Grann, & Lichtenstein, 2009).

Protective Factors

Many genetic studies have identified several protective factors that can ameliorate or prevent anti-social behaviour. Early studies showed that a good, stable environment can offset a genetic predisposition for crime (Bohman, 1996; Mednick et al., 1984), and this continues to be shown in more recent studies (Kendler, Morris, et al., 2016a; Kendler, Ohlsson, Sundquist, & Sundquist, 2016b). Genetic factors can also impact educational outcomes and lack of academic achievement, as well as externalizing behaviours or "acting out," even in very young children, although shared environments (as opposed to genetics) also play a major role (Newsome, Boisvert, & Wright, 2014). Many genetic predispositions relate to impulsivity, lack of attention, and poor peer relations, which can result in anti-social behaviour and dropping out of school. Conversely, good academic achievement has been shown repeatedly to be protective against anti-social behaviour and criminal outcomes (Bennett, 2018; Wertz et al., 2018). These findings could mean that a greater understanding of a specific behaviour and how environmental factors can shape it may help in allocating resources to ensure a more protective environment. The link between academic outcomes and acting out (Newsome et al., 2014), as well as school engagement (Snyder & Smith, 2015), suggests that improving one will improve the other.

The Brain

When considering a biological basis for criminal behaviour, one must ask exactly what part of the behaviour is under genetic control? Clearly, one does not inherit a desire to steal cars or strike out violently. However, criminal behaviour may be controlled by various factors, such as impulsivity, an inability to understand consequences, the need for immediate gratification, lack of empathy, anxiety, depression, or reduced cognitive ability. In a twin study (Eley et al., 1999), the researchers suggested that genetic predisposition for violent behaviour is related to brain chemistry and the functionality of various **neurotransmitters**, such as serotonin, dopamine, and norepinephrine (see Figure 7.1).

neurotransmitter
A substance that carries signals from cell to cell.

FIGURE 7.1   Neurotransmitters

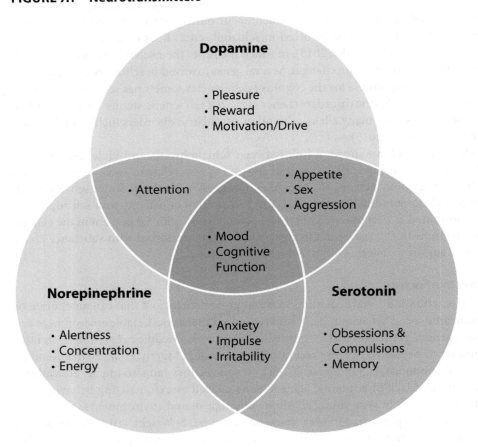

Brain Chemistry

The body contains two major types of communication systems that allow us to function: the hormonal system and the nervous system. The *hormonal system* works through chemicals released into the bloodstream and therefore acts relatively slowly. In contrast, communication between nerve cells in the brain and throughout the *nervous system* is extremely rapid, occurring in nanoseconds or less. Neurochemistry is a very complex subject and is rarely discussed outside biology, but it is an area that is very important for criminology as it controls much of our behaviour. To simplify greatly, much of the communication between our nerve cells involves chemical messengers, or neurotransmitters, which are released by one nerve cell and received and acted upon by another (for a more detailed explanation, see Anderson, 2007). These neurotransmitters are the basis for behaviour. The actual neurotransmitter is made up of amino acids (or precursors), which are converted into a neurotransmitter by specific enzymes. Once its message is delivered, the neurotransmitter is broken down into specific metabolites. Therefore, researchers can measure the levels of neurotransmitters at any one of these four areas: precursor, neurotransmitter, enzyme, or metabolites. These chemicals can be measured in cerebrospinal fluid, blood, and urine, with decreasing levels of invasiveness.

Serotonin

One of the most studied neurotransmitters is **serotonin** (5-HT or 5-hydroxytryptamine). Serotonin has been repeatedly shown to play a major role in impulsive-aggressive behaviour. It is a behavioural inhibitor, so high levels of serotonin *reduce* impulsive-aggressive behaviour. Therefore, problems occur in people who have low or irregular serotonin levels. Many studies have linked low serotonin levels to violent methods of suicide, an inability to cope with stress, aggression, anti-social personality disorder, and impulsivity.

serotonin
A neurochemical that plays an important role in depression, anxiety, and bipolar disorder. Also involved in brain development, serotonin dysfunction could lead to an increase in impulsiveness.

In order for serotonin to be produced, a person must possess adequate levels of its precursor, tryptophan, which is obtained from food. The production of serotonin occurs over many stages, and a defect in any stage could result in low serotonin levels. A person may simply have an inadequate or irregular diet, so does not possess enough of the precursor to produce adequate levels of serotonin. Or they may have a condition that prevents or reduces the uptake of dietary tryptophan. Such problems can sometimes be treated with something as simple as a dietary change or, more controversially, with drugs that can increase the dietary uptake of tryptophan. In order to have an effect, neurotransmitters must bind to receptor sites in the receiving cells, and studies have shown that some people have fewer binding sites than normal, which influences the overall effect of even adequate levels of serotonin (da Cunha-Bang et al., 2017).

In most cases, a biological predisposition may only impact behaviour under certain environmental conditions. The serotonin transporter gene (5-HTT) involved in the recycling of serotonin has been shown to be important in handling stress. Humans have two alleles, or versions, of the 5-HTT gene: a long version that helps a person handle stress and a short version that makes a person much more susceptible to stress. In a long-term study of individuals who had suffered multiple life stresses, those with the short version were much more likely to develop depression (43 percent) than those with the long version (17 percent). Of those who did develop depression, 11 percent of those with the short version attempted suicide in comparison with only 4 percent of those with the long version (Caspi et al., 2003). Variation in the 5-HTT gene was also shown to impact the responses of children who were bullied, with bullying causing emotional problems that were moderated by variations in the gene, indicating a protective factor in some variants (Sugden et al., 2010). These findings highlight the interaction between biology and the environment. Many behaviours have a biological basis that may only show an effect in certain environments.

Dopamine

Many studies have also shown that neurotransmitters such as dopamine and norepinephrine can have adverse effects on behaviour (including increased aggression) when they are at higher-than-normal levels (Grigorenko et al., 2010). Dopamine is a "happy" neurotransmitter that creates pleasurable sensations when we eat, experience feelings of love, and have sex. It is often released by illicit drugs to produce sensations of euphoria (Dos Santos et al., 2018). Some people do not get enough stimulation from natural pleasurable activities, and consequently are more likely to become addicted to drugs that increase the high. Research has shown that differences in sibling criminality may relate to differences in dopamine-related alleles, with some variants being more commonly linked to anti-social behaviour and criminal outcomes (Schwartz & Beaver, 2014). Altered dopamine synthesis and release has long been related to the onset of schizophrenia, and other psychoses and drugs that alter the function of the dopamine transporter gene can reduce aggression in violent people (Howes, McCutcheon, Owen, & Murray, 2017).

MAOA

The enzymes monoamine oxidase A (MAOA) and monoamine oxidase B (MAOB) break down several neurotransmitters, and so they too impact the levels of neurotransmitters in the body. The genes that control both MAOA and MAOB are found on the X chromosome, so they are sex linked. Therefore, any variants are expressed mostly in men. The original interest in these enzymes began with the study of a large Dutch family in which several males but no females exhibited a specific behavioural condition (Brunner, Nelen, Breakefield, Ropers, & van Oost, 1993). The affected males, who could be identified in childhood, were slightly mentally challenged, verbally and physically aggressive, fire setters, and responsible for committing many violent crimes. An examination of this family showed that affected males carried a variant of the normal MAOA gene, which influenced their ability to metabolize neurotransmitters (Brunner et al., 1993).

More recently, a much more interesting discovery related to MAOA helps to partially explain a major conundrum in criminology. Often, violent and dangerous men have suffered an extremely abusive childhood, and the later criminality is usually blamed on the earlier abuse. However, many boys who suffer similar abuse do not become criminals. So, the conundrum is this: Why do some abused boys become violent men and others do not? One explanation was offered in a series of studies from New Zealand (Caspi et al., 2002). The authors assessed a large number of male adults who had been abused as boys to determine whether they had a normal allele of the MAOA gene or a lower-functioning variant. Eighty-five percent of the severely abused men who carried the lower-functioning allele later exhibited violent behaviour. However, those men who had the normal gene rarely exhibited any form of violence or criminal activity, even if they had suffered severe physical childhood abuse. This finding clearly shows a link between a genetic trait, a lower-functioning MAOA gene, and the environment—which, in this case, included childhood abuse (Caspi et al., 2002).

This discovery also indicates that a normal MAOA genotype (the genetic constitution of an individual) has protective effects, although some studies have shown that the normal MAOA genotype is not protective in cases of extreme childhood abuse

(Weder et al., 2009). Further work has shown that the anti-social behaviour in abused children with a lower-functioning variant could be seen in children as young as seven (Kim-Cohen et al., 2006). The presence of the lower-functioning variant also greatly increased the risk of CD developing in children who were abused, but the presence of the gene had no deleterious effects in children who were not abused (Foley et al., 2004). More recent studies have found that a specific level of childhood violence is required before adult violence is triggered (Ouellet-Morin et al., 2016). These studies pave the way to explain the interaction between genes and the environment. The genes create the basic blueprint, but the environment shapes the final outcome. People born with this genetic variant are "designed" to live normal lives, unless they experience abuse, which then changes the normal outcome. It has been estimated that approximately 40 percent of violent crimes in the United States are committed by offenders with the lower-functioning MAOA gene (Wiberg, 2015).

It is vital that we continue to explore the relationship between genes and the environment because it is becoming more and more common for biological or neurological disorders to be presented in court as a defence or at least a mitigation. Testimony regarding a defendant's MAOA has been used by both the defence and prosecution in a number of cases, primarily in the United States and Italy (Bernet, Vnencak-Jones, Farahany, & Montgomery, 2007). In at least one case, a reduction in charge was made due to the presence of the lower-functioning MAOA gene, but whether the defendant had also suffered childhood abuse was not addressed, despite the fact that scientific research shows that the allele is *only* harmful under such circumstances (Bozanich, 2013). In a study of US and Italian cases from 1995 to 2016, evidence of the presence of the lower-functioning MAOA gene was used in the sentencing phase in four cases, one of which ended with a lesser sentence (McSwiggan, Elger, & Appelbaum, 2017), and it has been suggested that such evidence could be used to indicate diminished responsibility (Gavaghan & Bastani, 2014).

In a study of juror perceptions, 600 mock jurors were presented with a case study that could potentially result in a death sentence, together with mitigating evidence that included environmental factors such as child abuse, a genetic factor, a combination of gene and environmental factors, or no mitigating factors. The results show that the gene-environment scenario had no impact on whether the jury decided on the death penalty, but the jury were more likely to choose capital punishment if they perceived a high risk of future dangerousness (Gordon & Greene, 2018).

Changes in Brain Chemistry

Changes in brain chemistry can result from genetic and environmental factors, and usually through an interaction of both factors. We often relate childhood environmental conditions such as poverty and abuse to later criminal behaviour. From an understanding of basic brain chemistry, we can now see how environmental conditions interact with criminal behaviour. Poverty often leads to a poor diet, which may be low in the essential amino acids that act as precursors to building proper neurotransmitter levels. A poor diet may also contain other substances that can block the uptake of vital precursors. A poor diet during pregnancy may impact the fetus, and damage caused during pregnancy and early childhood may be permanent. The presence of lead, a known neurotoxin, can cause serious cognitive and behavioural problems, particularly in

Be Safe: Have an alcohol-free pregnancy

Drinking alcohol during pregnancy can cause birth defects and brain damage to your baby. The safest choice in pregnancy is *no* alcohol at all. In fact, it is best to stop drinking *before* you get pregnant.

For more information:
1-877-FAS-INFO
www.alcoholfreepregnancy.ca

Brochures about alcohol and pregnancy are available at LCBO stores.

LCBO   *best start meilleur départ*)

Drinking during pregnancy is a major concern due to the damage alcohol can cause to the developing brain of the fetus—damage that is known to result in potentially serious behavioural problems.

fetal alcohol spectrum disorder (FASD)
The range of disorders that can arise in a child if the child's mother drank alcohol while pregnant. It is a leading cause of preventable developmental disability in Canada.

children where the brain is still developing. It frequently leads to poor performance in school as well as risky and potentially criminal behaviour (Amato et al., 2013), and its effects are often closely linked to socio-economic status (Beckley et al., 2018). It is unfortunate that lead is still a problem, because although it is still pervasive in many areas in such things as old paintwork and piping, it can easily be removed from the body and its effects reversed (Billings & Schnepel, 2018).

Women who consume alcohol during pregnancy put their babies at risk of developing **fetal alcohol spectrum disorder (FASD)**. Depending on the timing of the alcohol consumption, different organs of the fetus can be damaged, with the brain being the most vulnerable. FASD children have many disabilities, including reduced IQ, facial anomalies, reduced cognitive ability, inability to understand the consequences of their behaviour, and an increased response to stress. FASD results in low self-esteem, low levels of education, poor peer relationships, low job expectancy, and a desire to please people. People with FASD are disproportionally represented in the criminal justice system in Canada and other countries (Fast, Conroy, & Loock, 1999) and there is growing awareness of the issues related to FASD within the court system (Fast & Conry, 2009). In a study of 25 sentencing judgments involving people with FASD in Canada, FASD was considered to be a mitigating circumstance in 68 percent (Kim, 2016).

Imbalances in brain chemistry also affect cognitive abilities such as reasoning and memory, so affected individuals may misinterpret a situation and react violently and impulsively when such a reaction is not warranted, or they may be unable to remember punishment and thus will repeat mistakes. The effects of imbalances in brain chemistry highlight the interaction between a person's genetic background and the environment. They clearly indicate that investing in child protection and measures to provide suitable social and health care, education, and mentorship are not just socially valuable, but may have previously unconsidered benefits that reduce anti-social behaviour and crime.

Brain Injuries

All behaviours, whatever their basis, are controlled by the brain. Therefore, any damage to the brain is likely to lead to a change in behaviour. This is particularly true of a child's brain because it is still developing. Traumatic brain injuries (TBIs) are extremely common in society and often occur in children—during play, sports, or due to child abuse—and may also occur during childbirth. We have only recently become aware of the permanent damage that can be caused by repeated mild concussions during sports. The area of the brain damaged and the timing of the injury will affect the behavioural outcome. For example, our frontal lobe is mostly involved in internal control and is one of the latest parts of the brain to complete development. Therefore, damage to this area in childhood will have a much greater effect on social interaction, impulsivity, and innate control than it will on an adult who has already learned acceptable social behaviours.

The frontal lobe is responsible for many aspects of our behaviour, such as self-control, inhibition, judgment, patience, reasoning, problem solving, self-esteem, using and understanding appropriate social skills, and the ability to comprehend the results of our actions. Thus, it is clear how damage in this area will not only impact personality and the ability to interact with others, but also lead to anxiety, hostility, impulsivity, edginess, and a lack of regard for consequences, all potentially predisposing to anti-social behaviour.

Much of our behaviour and our personality is controlled in the frontal lobe, which is also an area very easily injured as it is at the front of our head (just behind our forehead) and therefore most readily damaged in a fight or accident. The classic case of Phineas Gage provides a chilling description of the potential results of frontal lobe damage. In 1848, young Phineas Gage was a railroad construction crew supervisor when an accident resulted in a metal rod going through his left cheek and up through his brain, exiting the top of his head, completely pulverizing his frontal lobe. Amazingly, he survived and his memory, intelligence, and ability to do his job had not changed, but friends and family simply said he was "no longer Gage" (Damasio, Grabowski, Frank, Galaburda, & Damasio, 1994, p. 1102). His personality (what made him

meta-analysis
A quantitative statistical analysis of several similar experiments or studies to test for statistical significance.

"Gage") was destroyed. He had previously been a polite and considerate man, but after the accident he lost all his social graces and became violent and irritable. Since then, many examples have been documented of similar injuries that do not destroy memory or abilities (such as the ability to do one's job), but instead destroy social abilities and personality, which is very difficult for family and friends to deal with.

Many studies have linked TBIs with later criminal behaviour. It could be argued that a person who has suffered a TBI may be predisposed to violence and so was injured in a violent confrontation; in other words, the head injury was a result of a violent lifestyle rather than violence being a result of head injuries. However, this is not the case as most TBIs are caused by accidents or sports rather than violence. In studies of adult and juvenile death-row inmates, all inmates were found to have suffered a severe TBI *prior* to committing their offences (Lewis et al., 1986, 1988). In Australia, 82 percent of men in prison self-identified as having received a prior TBI (Schofield et al., 2006). A **meta-analysis** of several studies of males who committed domestic violence showed that 53 percent suffered from TBI (Farrer, Frost, & Hedges, 2012). We usually think of TBI as a physical trauma, but the developing brain can be damaged in other ways, for instance, by disease (for example, syphilis, meningitis, a tumour), stroke, emotional trauma, or a lack of appropriate nutrition. In a study on rats, separating rat pups early from their mothers resulted in damage to the hippocampus, part of the temporal lobe, suggesting that early childhood trauma may affect the developing brain (Andersen & Teicher, 2004). Childhood physical and sexual abuse as well as neglect have been shown to result

Phineas Gage was an American railroad crew supervisor who suffered a gruesome head injury in 1848. He is pictured here with the steel rod that pierced his skull. He is famous in the annals of neurology and psychology because of the effects that this injury had on his behaviour and personality.

NFL player Jovan Belcher committed a murder–suicide in December 2012. His family launched a lawsuit claiming that his violent behaviour was caused by head trauma suffered while playing football (a condition known as chronic traumatic encephalopathy [CTE]).

computer tomography
A medical technique combining X-rays taken at many different angles and computer technology.

magnetic resonance imaging
A medical diagnostic technique that uses a powerful magnet, radiofrequency waves, and computer imaging to produce images of tissues.

positron emission tomography
A recording of body images via a radioactive isotope injected into the blood that can be followed in the body during activities. It is commonly used to study the functioning of parts of the brain.

single-photon emission computed tomography
A recording of body images via a radioactive isotope injected into the blood that provides a 3D image of tissues. It is commonly used to measure brain blood flow.

in reduced development of several parts of the brain, in particular the corpus callosum (Teicher et al., 2004).

In many cases, the TBI may be compounded by the environment in which it occurred; for example, an environment of child abuse not only results in physical injury, but also is a hostile and damaging environment. Understanding the damage is important in developing treatment programs and routines that can help people gain greater control over their behaviours. Even mild head injuries can create problems, so it is important that offenders are properly assessed (many offenders are unaware that they have received a TBI). Information on a head injury may be important in court, particularly during sentencing and in developing treatment programs. Experiments with mock jurors indicated that defendants with TBIs were considered to be less guilty of their crimes and should receive lesser punishment than those without TBIs, suggesting that further understanding of TBI may result in it being used as a mitigating factor in court (St. Pierre & Parente, 2016).

Although we do not yet fully understand the functioning of the brain, many recent imaging techniques are helping us make great strides in understanding brain function. **Computer tomography** and **magnetic resonance imaging** allow us to see the structure of the brain in a minimally invasive manner, while **positron emission tomography** and **single-photon emission computed tomography** allow us to understand functional changes or deficits. Many studies have been conducted using these techniques and have identified differences in brain function and structure between non-criminals and a variety of offender populations. It is hoped that once we can identify specific areas of brain deficits, we will have much greater success in treating or ameliorating damage. This has resulted in a new area called neurolaw, which is currently an area of great interest in criminal law (Meynen, 2016).

Body Chemistry

The brain is the seat of all behaviour, so it is obvious that brain chemistry can affect behaviour. But many other chemicals, or hormones, in our body also impact our behaviour. The very word "hormone" is itself derived from a Greek word that means to excite or to put in motion. Hormones are released directly into the blood system or stored in glands and released in a controlled manner later. Because the blood stream reaches every cell in our body, hormones are circulated everywhere. However, only certain target cells respond to certain hormones. Hormones control many aspects of our lives, including growth, metabolism, development, and behaviour. Some hormones fluctuate naturally in the body, and others—antagonistic hormones—work to regulate body conditions within acceptable limits. For instance, high blood sugar is dangerous, as are wide swings in blood sugar levels, so when the blood sugar level reaches a certain high, a hormone (insulin) is released from the pancreas to bring the sugar level down. However, when the blood sugar level drops too low, an antagonistic hormone (glucagon) is released to bring the sugar level back up. The two hormones work together to keep our blood sugar level as even as possible, despite the fact that we regularly intake sudden large amounts of sugar when we eat.

Changes in a hormone itself, the cells involved in its production, the antagonistic hormone, or the target cells can all affect how the body responds; and because hormones work in very tiny quantities, even a slight shift can greatly affect behaviour and mood. The first hormone that comes to mind when we consider crime is testosterone. Innumerable studies have looked at testosterone levels in violent and non-violent offenders, as well as the effects on the body of increasing and decreasing testosterone. The results have been mixed. Studies assessing testosterone levels in incarcerated populations have shown a link between testosterone levels and violent crime, rule violations, and negative parole board decisions in both men (Dabbs, Frady, Carr, & Besch, 1987) and women (Dabbs & Hargrove, 1997). Some studies have linked testosterone levels with domestic abuse and also with alcohol use, so it is hard to determine whether the link is to alcohol, a known predisposer for crime, or directly to testosterone (Soler, Vinayak, & Quadagno, 2000). A meta-analysis of 45 separate studies showed a weak positive relationship between testosterone levels and aggression in males and females (Book, Starzyk, & Quinsey, 2001).

Testosterone levels fluctuate constantly and, interestingly, many studies have suggested that competition rather than aggression is what heightens testosterone levels (Archer, 1991). For instance, testosterone levels in male judo competitors pre- and post-fight were correlated with aggression within the fight, although the same researchers also found an earlier positive correlation between testosterone levels and vigorous exercise (Salvador, Suay, Martinez-Sanchis, Simon, & Brain, 1999). Even more intriguing is that an increase in testosterone levels also occurs in people watching a fight or even a sporting event. Testosterone levels were measured in two groups of sports fans before and after a game (Bernhardt, Dabbs, Fielden, & Lutter, 1998). The first group watched a live basketball game between rival university teams, and the second group watched a televised World Cup football match between two national teams. Dramatic differences in testosterone levels were recorded between sports fans in each group, with an increase in the testosterone levels of fans of the winning side and a decrease in the testosterone levels of fans of the losing side. The authors attributed these results to self-esteem and status, which could suggest an adaptive evolutionary response—that is, in our evolutionary past, success in a competition over resources or a mate was extremely important. In a more modern context, these results might explain the violent confrontations that frequently occur after large sporting events.

Although some studies have shown higher levels of testosterone in violent men, no proof exists that this relationship is causal. Moreover, many men with high levels of testosterone are not violent. Another way to look at the situation is to compare the activities of individuals who have had their testosterone levels deliberately increased, for instance, elderly men, those suffering from sexual dysfunction, and athletes illegally using anabolic steroids. Several studies have shown that although sexual appetite and mental acuity may improve with a higher level of testosterone, no correlation exists between a higher level of testosterone and increased violence. Finally, and more controversially, we can look at individuals in whom testosterone has been removed, by either surgical or chemical castration, thereby removing the source of the testosterone. Studies have shown a dramatic reduction in sexual crimes after castration, but no difference in non-sexual recidivism (Wille & Beier, 1989).

For more on gender-related violence, see Chapter 10, Gender and Crime.

Testosterone does not act in isolation, and high testosterone levels are often correlated with low serotonin levels as well as alcoholism, which individually are linked to anti-social behaviour. Testosterone certainly relates to sex drive and has been shown to have an indirect link to violence, but no direct causal relationship has been proven. It is probable that many factors interact to provide an indirect link with violence. Other gonadotrophic hormones have recently been shown to correlate more closely with self-reports of hostility than testosterone in a large population of convicted sex offenders up to 20 years post-release (Kingston et al., 2012). Although still not well understood, scientists now recognize that testosterone can regulate both anti-social and pro-social behaviours and acts in different ways (depending on the social situation) when a person faces a low or high threat (Van Honk, Terburg, & Bos, 2011).

Cortisol, another well-studied hormone, is released during stress and is also involved in autonomic arousal. Those with low cortisol levels may respond much more negatively to stress and will not respond to the concept of punishment or cause and effect. Cortisol levels can be impacted by numerous things such as neurotransmitters, other hormones, and brain injury. A study of salivary levels of testosterone and cortisol in children hospitalized in a child psychiatric ward indicated a link between cortisol levels and number of aggressive incidents, with testosterone levels linked to the severity of the incident (Barzman et al., 2013). Research suggests that there is a strong link between testosterone and cortisol, with cortisol providing an ameliorating effect (Mehta & Josephs, 2010). Finally, thyroid hormones and adrenalin also have an impact on our behaviour, and abnormal levels have been linked to anti-social behaviour as well as various clinical disorders, although, again, no direct causal link has been shown.

Hormones clearly impact our behaviour; that is one of their normal functions. But do they cause violent or anti-social behaviour? So far, no direct causal relationship has been found between hormones and violent or anti-social behaviour, but it is clear that hormones interrelate with many other factors (such as neurotransmitter levels) that are fundamentally under genetic control. Interestingly, one area in which a biological predisposition for homicide has been consistently accepted in our court system is hormonal imbalance. Infanticide, the killing of a baby under the age of one year by the biological mother, is considered by our legal system to be entirely different from the murder of the child by someone else or by the mother after the age of one, due to the acceptance that postnatal depression, caused by hormones, can affect the mother's behaviour beyond her control.

Conclusion

This chapter has sought to clarify that although biology does *not* cause a person to be criminal, it can impact behaviours that can *predispose* a person to commit a criminal act. Biology does not act in a vacuum and is greatly influenced by our experiences and environment. Our personality, behaviour, and the experiences that shape us affect the way we handle situations. Research into biological predispositions has also shown us the protective and advantageous role a stable environment can have on those who are predisposed to anti-social behaviour. For example, researchers studying youth in the Netherlands have shown that childhood delinquency is affected by the interaction of gender attitudes, child abuse, parental connectedness, and socio-economic status, with children who suffer from less parental monitoring and greater parental rejection significantly more likely to engage in delinquent behaviour (Lahlah, Lens, Bogaerts, & van der Knaap, 2013). Cognitive and developmental behaviour programs are being developed (including developmental intervention and prevention strategies), beginning at the prenatal stage or age two and continuing through the school years (Rocque, Welsh, & Raine, 2012). Many behavioural changes occur due to very small shifts in biochemical balance and, when understood, might be corrected easily. Also, understanding what protective factors are most advantageous in certain situations may help guide resource allocation.

SUMMARY OF KEY POINTS

- It is important to recognize that behaviour, whether criminal or otherwise, is not caused by one single entity but by a combination of many factors that *include* biology as part of the equation.

- Studies of human genetics require a large number of identical animals, which is why twin studies have been important in this area. Two types of twins exist: dizygotic (DZ) twins (non-identical) and monozygotic (MZ) twins (identical). Concordance rates vary in studies and by type of crime, but, overall, a much greater concordance rate for criminal behaviour is seen in MZ twins than in DZ twins, which indicates a strong genetic basis for criminal behaviour.

- In adoption studies, researchers compare the criminal behaviour of people who were adopted by non-family members with that of their adoptive and biological parents. This approach seeks to separate genetic and environmental influences and does not rely on an assumed identical environment for two people (twins).

- Criminal behaviour may be controlled by various factors, such as impulsivity, an inability to understand consequences, the need for immediate gratification, lack of empathy, anxiety, depression, or reduced cognitive ability. Researchers have suggested that genetic predisposition for violent behaviour could be related to brain chemistry and the functionality of various neurotransmitters, such as serotonin, dopamine, and norepinephrine.

- Damage to the brain is likely to lead to a change in behaviour. Damage to the frontal lobe will not only affect personality and the ability to interact with others, but also lead to anxiety, hostility, impulsivity, edginess, and a lack of regard for consequences, all potentially predisposing to anti-social behaviour.

- Hormones such as testosterone and cortisol can affect behaviour. Although no direct causal relationship has been found between hormones and violent or anti-social behaviour, it is clear that hormones interrelate with many other factors (such as neurotransmitter levels) that are fundamentally under genetic control.

QUESTIONS FOR CRITICAL DISCUSSION

1. Genetic studies show a predisposition for petty crime. What evolutionary value might there be for this trait?
2. Many studies are done on incarcerated volunteers. Consider the ethical and experimental issues involved with investigating such a population.

3. Why is infanticide treated differently by our criminal courts than other biologically predisposed crimes, such as those predisposed by FASD?
4. Consider protective factors involved in preventing someone who is genetically
predisposed to commit a crime. How might we exploit these?
5. Consideration of biological bases for criminal behaviour often results in two
main schools of thought that can be encapsulated as "he could not stop himself, so he should not be held responsible" and "she can never be treated, so we
should lock her up and throw away the key." Envision trying to explain to people
in these two camps a more rational approach based on this chapter.

SUGGESTED FURTHER READINGS

Anderson, G.S. (2007). *Biological influences on criminal behavior*. Boca Raton, FL: CRC Press.

Beaver, K.M., Barnes, J.C., & Boutwell, B.B. (Eds.). (2015). *The nature versus biosocial debate in criminology: On the origins of criminal behavior and criminality*. Los Angeles, CA: Sage.

Boyd, N. (2000). *The beast within: Why men are violent*. Vancouver: Greystone Books.

Glenn, A.L., & Raine, A. (2014). *Psychopathy: An introduction to biological findings and their implications*. New York: New York University Press.

Raine, A. (2013). *The anatomy of violence: The biological roots of crime*. New York: Pantheon Books.

Cases

R v de Grood, 2016 ABQB 294.

CASE STUDY 8.1

The Mask of Sanity: Colonel Russell Williams

Convicted killer Russell Williams.

Note to the reader: This case involves offences that some readers may find disturbing. The study of such cases should be approached with sensitivity and respect.

Colonel Russell Williams was charged in February 2010 with two counts of first-degree murder, sexual assault, forcible confinement, and breaking and entering. At the time, he was the 46-year-old commander of Canadian Forces Base Trenton, apparently happily married, and enjoying a remarkably successful military career.

However, at some point during his forties, Williams had begun breaking into homes, entering women's bedrooms, dressing in the lingerie he found there, and masturbating. He took photos of himself clad in their underwear, and these became important "trophies," which he carefully catalogued when he returned home. From that point, his criminal conduct escalated. He broke into homes where women were sleeping, committing two brutal sexual assaults, and then two sexually motivated murders. After police traced tire treads from his car to tire treads near the home of the victim of his second murder, he was brought in for questioning and, during a ten-hour interview, confessed to dozens of crimes. He was convicted of two counts of first-degree murder and is currently serving a life term in a Canadian prison.

Is Russell Williams a psychopath? Dr. Brad Booth, a forensic psychiatrist based in Ottawa, has indicated that Williams might be properly classified as such, noting that psychopathy is "marked by charming behaviour and a complete disregard for the feelings of [the] victims" (Mulholland, 2012). Anne McIlroy and Erin Anderssen, writing in the *Globe and Mail*, seem to agree:

> Though never officially diagnosed as a psychopath, Mr. Williams appears to fit the profile. The way he toyed with his victims like playthings, unable to offer mercy: "Have a heart," one pleaded, as he unflinchingly duct-taped her nose to suffocate her. The singular attention with which he catalogued photos and video of his crimes. The fleeting shows of remorse. (He feels "disappointed," he tells police in his confession, about what he's done.) All the while, he wore the mask of sanity, in place for so long and so well, that he tortured and killed, and then went to work to discuss whether the military should buy a new aircraft transport. That's also the measure of a cunning psychopath: He's often the last guy you'd ever suspect. (McIlroy & Anderssen, 2010)

And yet Timothy Appleby, in his account of the case in his book *A New Kind of Monster*, argues that Williams is not best understood as a psychopath. Appleby notes that Williams could demonstrate genuine concern and compassion for friends and colleagues and was also capable of feeling shame. Appleby suggests that Williams is best understood as a sexual deviant: He had a sexual preoccupation with non-human objects, he was focused on sexually oriented suffering and humiliation, for both himself and others; he had a sexual interest in children; and he also participated in violent sex with an unwilling partner.

How are we to make sense of the murderous conduct of Russell Williams? What explanations might we find in the realm of psychological theories of crime for this sort of behaviour? We can say, as Appleby has, that Williams has a mental disorder—an amalgamation of sexual deviance with obsessive-compulsive disorder. We can suggest, alternatively, that he is a heartless psychopath, unable to feel compassion for others, except in circumstances where such a display might work in his self-interest, to present his actions in a more positive light.

It is possible that Russell Williams is all of the above and more, a reminder that the science of mental disorder and the science of psychopathy cannot always describe and dissect individuals and events with an unerring precision.

Before You Read Chapter 8

- Does it seem improbable that someone like Williams could rise to such a position of prominence and responsibility in his career? Why or why not?
- Do you think psychological explanations of crime are sufficient for explaining this sort of behaviour?
- After reading Box 8.1, under the heading "Psychoanalysis and Crime: From Personality to Thought Patterns" in this chapter, return to this case study and reread it. How might the definition of "psychopathy" apply to Williams, if at all?

Psychological Approaches

LEARNING OUTCOMES

After reading this chapter, students will be able to:

- Understand and define the key psychological theories of crime causation.
- Discuss the research on IQ and criminality.
- Describe the differences between psychoanalytic and learning approaches to criminal behaviour.
- Explain how moral development relates to an understanding of criminal behaviour.
- Identify some of the integrated explanations of criminal behaviour offered by psychologists.
- Describe the clinical tools used by the criminal justice system to evaluate offenders.
- Understand the relationship between mental illness and criminal behaviour.
- Evaluate the approaches used by the criminal justice system to deal with mentally ill offenders and addiction.

CHAPTER OUTLINE

Introduction

Psychological theories examine a number of factors thought to contribute to criminality and criminal behaviour. The discipline of psychology is composed of several different (and often competing) perspectives that include psychoanalysis, behaviourism, social cognitivism (or social learning), and developmental psychology. These different approaches have produced numerous psychological theories that seek to explain criminal behaviour or certain aspects of criminal behaviour. It would be a mistake to lump all of the psychological explanations of criminal behaviour together and consider them as a single theory because various psychological theories of criminal behaviour exist (Bartol & Bartol, 2011; Einstadter & Henry, 2006).

Studies linking intelligence (or **IQ**) to criminality have been a staple of psychological research on crime dating back to the early 1900s. In fact, links between low intelligence and criminality can be found all the way back to the work of Cesare Lombroso (1835–1909), an individual many consider to be "the father of modern criminology." Other more recent

IQ (intelligence quotient)
A standardized measure of intelligence used by psychologists.

theories and research have also considered the importance of IQ and its relationship to criminality (Eysenck, 1964; Hirschi & Hindelang, 1977; Wilson & Herrnstein, 1985). Contemporary theories also examine various aspects of brain function, which often involves aspects of intelligence (see, for example, Farrington, 1992; Moffitt, 1993).

There are many branches of psychological theory that are relevant to criminology, including those that examine individual differences that may result in criminality (for example, certain personality traits like aggression, impulsivity, and low empathy) and theories that focus on socialization, conditioning processes, learning experiences, and psychological development.

The Intelligence–Criminality Connection

feeble-mindedness
A term used in the 19th century to describe individuals with low intelligence or low IQ.

Early positivist criminologists (i.e., those concerned with finding objective statistical and scientific ways to understand crime) noted that there were connections between **feeble-mindedness** (or low intelligence) and criminality. A well-known example of this early line of research is Henry Goddard's (1913) longitudinal study of the Kallikaks. The Kallikaks were two families fathered by the same man. One of the wives was a Quaker woman, and the other was, in Goddard's words, a "tavern wench." Goddard found that the side of the family mothered by the Quaker woman exhibited very little criminality, while the other side exhibited a great deal of criminality. Interestingly, he did not jump to the conclusion that criminality was a result of heredity. Instead, he thought that feeble-mindedness was inherited, and suggested that less intelligent people were at greater risk for criminality.

Approximately two decades after this research, Edwin Sutherland (1931), the founder of differential association theory, argued that the research linking intelligence to criminality was flawed. He claimed that the tests were biased and unreliable, and that similar rates of intelligence were likely found in criminal and non-criminal populations. Because of his influence on the field of criminology, research in this area fell into disfavour for several decades.

Differential association theory is further discussed in Chapter 9, Sociological Approaches, which discusses sociological approaches to criminology.

Almost 50 years after Sutherland's dismissal of the connection between IQ and criminality, Travis Hirschi and Michael Hindelang (1977) resurrected interest in this area with their article "Intelligence and Delinquency: A Revisionist Review." They argued that intelligence does not have a *direct* impact on criminal behaviour; rather, it affects criminality indirectly, through poor school performance. In other words, doing poorly in school can lead to other problems, including problematic behaviour, punishment, and possibly negative labelling and weakened social bonds. In addition, opportunities for future employment are cut off, which reduces one's pro-social options later in life. According to Hirschi and Hindelang, trouble in school seems predictive of problems later in life. Figure 8.1 describes Hirschi and Hindelang's positivist view of the link between IQ and crime.

William Herrnstein and Charles Murray's (1994) theory on race, IQ, and criminality is perhaps the most controversial work in this area. Herrnstein and Murray start out by citing research that suggests a link between criminality and IQ. Next, they refer to the fact that certain racial minorities (i.e., Black people) tend to test much lower on IQ tests than white and Asian people. They then state that Black populations are typically overrepresented in official crime statistics. Based on this information, they argue for a racial connection to criminality by way of low IQ.

FIGURE 8.1   The Positivist View on IQ and Crime

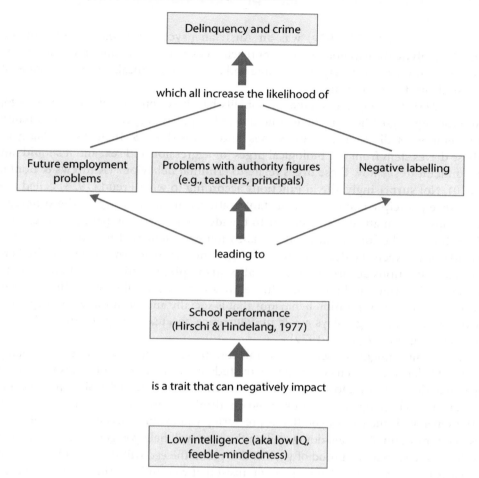

Herrnstein and Murray's (1994) line of argument raised a variety of issues. To summarize the objections: The authors disregarded numerous studies that link social class to both IQ scores and criminal opportunities. Perhaps the most damning criticism of this theory is the fact that IQs have steadily risen over time, a phenomenon known as the "Flynn effect." In the 1980s, James Flynn was able to demonstrate that IQ rates had been rising for at least 60 years, and these increases could not be attributed to changes in genetics as Herrnstein and Murray (1994) would have us believe (Bernard, Snipes, & Gerould, 2010). More recent research seems to indicate that IQ is an important *correlate* of crime; however, the *causal connection* is not readily apparent. In most cases, theories that rely on race to explain crime and/or IQ are misguided because they often fail to consider factors such as socio-economic status, criminal opportunities, and the interactions between biological factors and social context. For example, people living in poverty-stricken areas often face challenges accessing proper nutrition and prenatal care, and may even risk exposure to environmental toxins because of poor living conditions. All of this can affect early brain development, which later affects IQ (Robinson & Beaver, 2008).

Psychoanalysis and Crime: From Personality to Thought Patterns

Sigmund Freud (1856–1939) was an Austrian psychiatrist and founder of the **psychoanalytic** (or psychodynamic) approach. While Freud's writings are quite extensive, he had very little to say about crime and deviance specifically. However, some of his students did study crime.

Freud (1920, 1923) claimed that personality has three components: The id, the ego, and the superego. The **id** is the instinctual and impulsive aspect of one's personality that embodies all of our desires, wishes, and drives (Redl & Toch, 1979). Many of these drives stem from our biological urges for aggression and sex, and it should not be difficult to see how these urges relate to criminal behaviour (Andrews & Bonta, 2010). Not surprisingly, the id functions according to what Freud (1923) called the **pleasure principle** and demands instant gratification of these urges. The **superego** develops as we mature and is similar to the idea of a moral compass or conscience; it embodies all of our values and socialization experiences. The **ego** serves as the regulator between the demands of the id and the superego. This aspect of the personality functions according to the **reality principle**, meaning that it attempts to delay gratification until it can be achieved in socially acceptable ways. The ego may also serve to stop or prohibit behaviour that is socially and/or morally unacceptable. Consequently, the ego plays a role in deterrence because it helps distinguish right from wrong (Redl & Toch, 1979).

An example might be useful to illustrate how these components of one's personality control behaviour: When confronted with studying for an exam, your id is the part of you that does not want to study. You may be tempted to watch television, play a computer game, check up on Facebook, or go out drinking with friends at the pub instead. The superego is the part of you that is pressuring you to study because you want to do well on the exam. After all, doing well on the exam will help you get a better mark and will make your parents proud of you. At this point, the ego will step in and attempt to balance out the situation. Your ego might insist that you study for three hours and then have a nice meal and relax for the rest of the evening.

In most cases, Freudian criminologists attribute criminality to problems in childhood resulting from poor parenting practices. Given their emphasis on family and early childhood development, it should come as no surprise that most Freudian criminologists (including Freud's own daughter, Anna) studied juvenile delinquency (see also Aichhorn, 1925; Alexander & Healy, 1935; Redl & Wineman, 1951).

Psychoanalytic theorists have identified a number of different paths to criminality (see Figure 8.2). First, people with an overactive superego are said to experience increased levels of guilt. These **neurotic** offenders, as they are sometimes called, commit crime to be punished in order to lessen negative feelings arising from this guilt (Freud, 1920, 1923).

Second, some people are thought to have a weak ego that fails to control behaviour. In these cases, the id is unregulated, and the individual has an impulsive personality and behaves hedonistically.

Third, Freudians believe that criminal behaviour could stem from deviant self-identification (Blackburn, 1990). In this case, the superego develops normally, but the

psychoanalysis
A therapeutic technique in psychiatry and philosophy pioneered by Sigmund Freud.

id
An aspect of Freud's theory of personality; the impulsive part of one's personality.

pleasure principle
The notion that one should maximize pleasure and minimize pain.

superego
An aspect of Freud's theory of personality; one's moral compass, conscience, and ethical principles.

ego
An aspect of Freud's theory of personality; the aspect of personality that helps negotiate the demands of the real world.

reality principle
The notion that one should assess the demands of the real world and act accordingly.

neurotic
According to psychoanalytic theory, a condition that results from an overactive superego.

person identifies with and forms a close bond to someone who is a criminal (in most cases, a parent). People who have undergone the process of deviant self-identification are sometimes referred to as sociopaths or anti-social offenders (Andrews & Bonta, 2010; Serin et al., 2011).

FIGURE 8.2   Psychoanalytic Theories of Crime

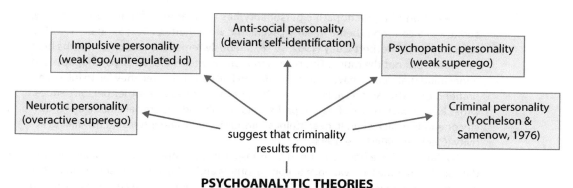

Fourth, the psychopathic personality results when the superego fails to develop properly. Psychopaths lack a conscience and have an inability to feel empathy for others (Andrews & Bonta, 2010). See Box 8.1 for a discussion of the modern conception of **psychopathy**.

psychopathy
A personality disorder characterized by a lack of empathy, egocentrism, manipulation of others, and a tendency toward anti-social and criminal behaviour.

BOX 8.1

Psychopathy: Misunderstandings and Misconceptions

What name comes to mind when you hear the word "psychopath"? Often, the answer is a historical figure such as Adolf Hitler, Joseph Stalin, Mao Zedong, or Saddam Hussein, or a serial killer such as Charles Manson, David Berkowitz (the "Son of Sam" killer), Ted Bundy, or Clifford Olson. Examples of movie and television characters abound: Norman Bates (*Psycho*), Hannibal Lecter (*Silence of the Lambs*), Mr. Blonde (*Reservoir Dogs*), the title character from *Dexter*, and Walter White from *Breaking Bad* (for more on psychopaths in the media, see Blair, Mitchell, & Blair, 2005; Cleckley, 1964; and Hare, 1993). It has been suggested that in the business world, people such as Bernie Madoff and Steve Jobs are psychopaths. Some have even claimed that political figures such as Margaret Thatcher, Bill Clinton, and George W. Bush resemble psychopaths based on their calculating natures and lack of empathy in certain situations. However, after learning more about the definition of psychopathy and the psychopathy checklist, you will realize that very few if any of these examples really fit the profile of a psychopath (Blair, Mitchell, & Blair, 2005; Dutton, 2012). One of the foremost experts on psychopathy, Robert Hare (1993) provides the following advice:

> *Psychopathic* killers ... are not mad, according to accepted legal and psychiatric standards. Their acts result not from a deranged mind but from a cold, calculating rationality combined with a chilling inability to treat others as thinking, feeling, human beings. ... As disturbing

as this is, we must be careful to keep some perspective here, for the fact is that the majority of psychopaths manage to ply their trade without murdering people. By focusing too much on the most brutal and newsworthy examples of their behavior we run the risk of remaining blind to the larger picture: psychopaths who don't kill but who have a personal impact on our daily lives. We are far more likely to lose our life savings to an oily-tongued swindler than our lives to a steely-eyed killer. (p. 6)

The notion of a psychopathic personality has been around for at least a century, and it was a common theme in early psychiatric work (Rafter, 2008; Serin et al., 2011). John Johns and Herbert Quay (1962, p. 18) famously remarked that psychopaths hear the words, but not the music. This means that on an intellectual level, psychopaths can understand that people have emotions and can feel pain; however, they fail to fully comprehend empathy and have an inability "to put themselves in another person's shoes." Other key characteristics of psychopaths include glib and superficial charm, egocentricity or egotism, lack of guilt, deceitfulness, impulsiveness, and interest in risk-taking activity (Cleckley, 1964; Hare, 1993).

Psychopaths have been described as intraspecies predators that manipulate, intimidate, and sometimes use violence to control others and fulfill their own selfish goals. It is important to keep in mind that not all psychopaths are criminals; psychopaths are found in politics, the legal profession, and the business world (Babiak & Hare, 2006; Dutton, 2012; Hare, 1996). At the beginning of this section, one important misconception about psychopathy was identified: Psychopaths are not all serial killers, or even violent; many work in more subtle ways. A number of other common misunderstandings exist about this phenomenon.

First, psychopaths are not psychotic, mentally ill, or "sick" in the legal sense of the term (Hare, 1993); that is, the disorder does not "[render] the person incapable of appreciating the nature and quality of the act or omission or of knowing that it was wrong" (*Criminal Code*, s. 16). In contrast, *psychotics* refers to people who are mentally ill in a legal sense and often have hallucinations and delusions that spur on their abnormal behaviours; for example, they may suffer from schizophrenia.

Second, the terms "psychopathy," "anti-social personality disorder," and "sociopathy" are often used interchangeably (often by criminologists who should know better), despite the fact that they refer to different (and sometimes outdated) classifications (Babiak & Hare, 2006). Psychopathy and sociopathy were once considered to be the same disorder; however, this idea changed when revisions were made to the Diagnostic and Statistical Manual of Mental Disorders (DSM-II) in 1968 (Hare & Cox, 1978). "Sociopathy" was changed to **anti-social personality disorder (APD)**. Later, psychiatrists attempted to distinguish psychopathy from APD (Hare, 1996). It should be noted that the term "sociopathic personality disorder" is no longer in use; however, the term "sociopath" is sometimes used to refer to those with APD. The main difference between individuals with APD and those with psychopathy is that APD is thought to result from one's environment, whereas true psychopaths seem to have physical and mental abnormalities (such as lower resting heart rates, less fear response, and structural brain abnormalities).

The varying prevalence of psychopathy and APD also helps set them apart. According to Hare (1996), psychopaths represent about 1 percent of the general population and may comprise as much as 25 percent of the prison population. Meanwhile, APD is seen in about 6 to 9 percent of the general population and roughly 50 to 75 percent of inmates. These figures imply that psychopaths represent a small subset of people with APD. Thus,

anti-social personality disorder (APD)
A personality disorder characterized by a lack of morality, impulsivity, and aggressive behaviour; individuals with APD often have a history of criminal behaviour.

almost all psychopaths have APD, but only a small subset of those diagnosed with APD would qualify as psychopaths (Hare, 1996).

The modern conception of the psychopath was heavily influenced by Hervey Cleckley's seminal work, *The Mask of Sanity* (1964). Hare (1970; Hare & Cox, 1978) used this research to develop his psychopathy checklist, a scale that can reportedly measure levels of psychopathy in individuals. This scale has been revised and adjusted numerous times (see, for example, Hare, 2003) and is commonly used in corrections work to estimate risk of reoffending. However, the scale has also been used in other arenas, such as university campuses.

The Psychopathy Checklist: Are You Sitting Beside a Psychopath?

Some notable attempts have been made to apply the Psychopathy Checklist-Revised (PCL-R) to groups of non-criminal and mentally normal individuals. Kevin Williams, Delroy Paulhus, and Robert Hare's (2007) research study on psychopathy in the university environment is one example. These researchers administered a version of the PCL-R to a group of undergraduate students at a large Western university. The goal was to gain insights into the applicability of the psychopathy checklist to non-clinical and non-forensic populations. In other words, these researchers were seeking to develop a scale that could detect non-criminal psychopaths in university and possibly workplace settings.

Williams and colleagues (2007) claimed that self-report psychopathy measures are the most practical way of capturing information on non-clinical and non-forensic populations. This conclusion seems unusual because in his book *Without Conscience* (1993), Hare offers the following emphatic cautionary note about using the psychopathy checklist:

> The *Psychopathy Checklist* is a complex clinical tool for professional use. What follows is a general summary of the key traits and behaviors of psychopaths. **Do not use these symptoms to diagnose yourself or others.** A diagnosis requires explicit training and access to the formal scoring manual. [Emphasis in original.] (p. 34)

While self-report measures are not exactly the same as untrained assessments, the stern warning above might well apply to self-reports too. It seems at least important to acknowledge the potential for self-report research to lead to some very misleading data.

The researchers also used several questionable measures as indicators for the various factors in their model of psychopathy, especially if we consider that their sample was composed of college students. For instance, the indicators of the erratic lifestyle index (for example, breaking rules, taking risks, and drinking) all seem to capture behaviour that is quite common among college students. Moreover, the indicators of the offensive activity dimension (for example, listening to aggressive music, watching violent movies, and playing violent video games) seem to be highly susceptible to cultural influences. Consider the widespread popularity of gangsta rap during the mid-1990s or the current popularity of violent video games among a very large, diverse cross-section of young people.

These points might lead us to ask some important questions about this research: Does more attention need to be paid to defining typical undergraduate behaviours? Is it common for a larger percentage of people to be irresponsible during their college years? Is it reasonable to conclude that we can differentiate between psychopaths and non-psychopaths by investigating the types of music they listen to or the types of movies they watch? Is it reasonable to assume that psychopaths prefer violent and aggressive media more than other people do?

Fifth, Samuel Yochelson and Stanton Samenow's (1976) theory of the criminal personality explains criminal behaviour based, in part, on psychoanalytic thought. These theorists examined the thinking patterns and problematic cognitions apparent in criminals. The sample for their study was a group of serious offenders imprisoned in a hospital for the criminally insane. According to Yochelson and Samenow, the offenders studied were self-centred, impulsive, low in empathy, and easily angered. This description is very similar to the psychopathic personality arising from a weak superego described above. Yochelson and Samenow attempted to catalogue the traits or problematic thinking patterns that were present in criminals. This list included notions such as fear of injury and personal insult; a preference for concrete over abstract thinking; a mixture of responsibility and irresponsibility (i.e., an "inconsistent inconsistency"); a belief that they are special or unique; a susceptibility to suggestibility in group settings; lying; a lack of trust; and a super-optimistic outlook.

Some serious issues need to be raised with this research. First, the study sample that was the basis of the theory is highly questionable. It is unlikely that the patterns observed in the sample would be found in all or even most offenders, since most offenders are not criminal psychopaths. In other words, since this sample was drawn from a forensic psychiatric institution, it should come as no surprise that the sample of offenders exhibited serious psychiatric issues uncommon in other offenders. Second, these theorists seem to be proposing a theory with an internal logical contradiction: They suggest that criminality is inborn, while at the same time claiming criminals make rational choices to commit crimes (Lilly, Cullen, & Ball, 2007). The problem here is that the theorists seem to assume that criminals are *made* and not *created*, while still insisting that criminals have free will and choose to commit crimes.

Psychoanalytic theories remain influential in criminology today. For example, the impact of psychoanalytic approaches is still visible in some forms of control theory (for example, Gottfredson & Hirschi, 1990; Hirschi, 1969). However, other psychological approaches have gained popularity.

Psychological Learning Theories and Criminology

Psychological learning theories have contributed a great deal of insight to criminology. Specifically, classical and operant conditioning, the frustration–aggression hypothesis, and social learning theory have all informed criminological thinking, and, in some cases, have offered fully developed explanations of why people commit crime (see Figure 8.3).

Classical Conditioning

Most people are familiar with the story of Pavlov's dogs. Ivan Pavlov was a Russian physiologist who studied digestive reflexes in dogs. During his experiments, he discovered that he could induce salivation in dogs by simply ringing a bell. The dogs salivated because they had come to associate the ringing of the bell with receiving food. This process of learning is referred to as "classical conditioning." Pavlov's (1927/1960) work was the inspiration for a number of learning theories that later emerged in psychology.

Hans Eysenck's (1964) theory of the criminal personality was greatly influenced by classical conditioning theory. Eysenck argued that three key traits define one's personality. **Extraversion (E)** focuses on a person's activity level. People who are high in extraversion are called "extraverts" and tend to be more outgoing, sociable, and

extraversion (E)
A person's activity level; people high in extraversion enjoy social interaction and being around groups of people, while people low in extraversion generally prefer solitude and quiet conversations with those close to them.

action-oriented. "Introverts" are people on the other end of this continuum, and tend to be more withdrawn, isolated, and introspective. **Neuroticism (N)** refers to a person's level of excitability and emotional stability. People high in neuroticism tend to be emotionally unstable and overreact to minor situations. **Psychoticism (P)** includes attributes such as aggression, lack of empathy, and tough-mindedness. Although psychoticism has been compared to psychopathy, the connection between these two concepts is still unclear (Eysenck & Eysenck, 1978).

neuroticism (N)
A person's excitability level and emotional stability; highly neurotic people tend to be emotionally unstable and overreact to minor situations.

FIGURE 8.3   Psychological Learning Theories of Criminal Behaviour

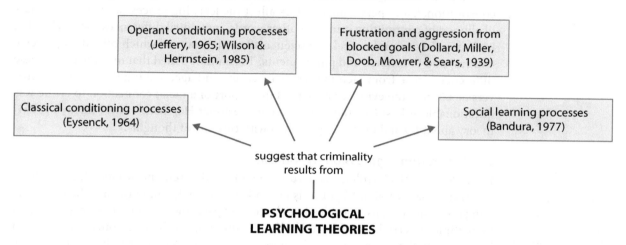

According to Eysenck (1964), **cortical arousal** (the level of activity in the reticular formation of the brain) is tied to one's level of extraversion. Extraverts tend to be cortically underaroused, and therefore seek out stimulation in their environment. They also condition (or respond to punishment and fear) less readily than introverts, which makes them prone to impulsive types of behaviour, including crime.

Eysenck's theory posits that people who are high in all three traits are at the greatest risk for committing crime because they condition poorly (high E), are very emotionally volatile (high N), and have little regard for others' feelings (high P). These traits lay the groundwork for a personality that is well suited to crime. Conversely, those low in all traits will condition most effectively, be much easier to socialize, and, therefore, be unlikely to commit crime.

psychoticism (P)
A measure of attributes such as aggression, empathy, and tough-mindedness; those who score high in psychoticism tend to be cold, callous, and manipulative.

cortical arousal
Activation of the reticular formation of the brain.

Operant Conditioning

B.F. Skinner's (1953) operant conditioning theory represents a major advancement in learning theory. Skinner's approach, known as **behaviourism**, suggests that all behaviour can be shaped by rewards and punishments. He supported his theory with a variety of experiments done on pigeons and rats. In these experiments, he demonstrated that he could make these animals do amazing things (for example, solve simple puzzles or play Ping-Pong) by motivating them with rewards in the form of food. Like Pavlov's (1927/1960) classical conditioning, Skinner's (1953) operant conditioning has also influenced the field of criminology, giving rise to several theories of criminal behaviour.

behaviourism
A learning theory that suggests all behaviour can be shaped by rewards and punishment.

C. Ray Jeffery (1965) proposed a theory based on Skinner's operant conditioning and Sutherland's differential association theory. The central proposition in Jeffery's theory was as follows: If the reward for crime is high and the likelihood of punishment is low, the chances of criminal behaviour increase. He also said that *non-social reinforcers* (for example, material goods, money, and instinctual drives) are more important than *social reinforcers* (for example, praise, status, and sense of belonging from one's intimate groups) when it comes to criminal behaviour.

James Q. Wilson and Richard Herrnstein (1985) also applied operant conditioning in their well-known book *Crime and Human Nature*, arguing that behaviour is determined by its consequences. They also argued that individual differences in biological, constitutional, and personality factors affect the learning process and an individual's likelihood of committing crime. In other words, individual differences such as low IQ, high impulsivity, and a weak conscience affect the ways in which offenders perceive and respond to rewards and punishments. The authors stated that in some cases, these differences arose from factors such as race, sex, and age, making their work controversial. Clearly, the evidence presented in support of a racial connection to crime was questionable at best (see the discussion above about Herrnstein and Murray's [1994] theory about IQ and race, and problems with this line of thought).

The Frustration–Aggression Hypothesis

John Dollard, Neal Miller, Leonard Doob, O.H. Mowrer, and Robert Sears's (1939) **frustration–aggression hypothesis** expanded on early learning theories by incorporating Freudian insights. Specifically, this group of psychologists and social psychologists (sometimes referred to as "the Yale School") fused the early behaviourist approach to learning with the pleasure principle offered in psychoanalytic approaches to personality to explain how frustration can lead to aggression.

frustration–aggression hypothesis
The view that crime is a natural byproduct of aggression and can be explained as a consequence of frustration.

goal responses
Behaviours meant to achieve particular goals that provide pleasurable outcomes.

These theorists argued that various stimuli (for example, desire for money and material goods) motivate behaviour and lead to different types of **goal responses**, or behaviours meant to achieve particular goals that provide pleasurable outcomes. Of course, crime is often committed in pursuit of these pleasurable outcomes. When a goal response (for example, stealing to get money) is rewarded or is accompanied by little or no punishment, the learning process that takes place leads to similar behaviour in the future. "Frustration" is thought to result when a goal is inaccessible or when the individual is punished in response to seeking a particular goal. Dollard and colleagues viewed "aggression" as a normal response to frustration. However, they point out that people do not always express that aggression because most learn to suppress their aggressive impulses when properly socialized.

According to this theory, crime is a natural byproduct of aggression, and most crime can be explained as a consequence of frustration (Andrews & Bonta, 2010). Crime is also thought to be a function of a high level of frustration and a low level of anticipated punishment. In other words, if one is very frustrated and perceives a low risk of being punished, the likelihood of criminal behaviour will increase (Dollard et al., 1939).

Social Cognitivism (aka Social Learning Theory)

Albert Bandura is a well-known psychologist and is the leading proponent of social learning theory in psychology. While most refer to Bandura's work as "social learning theory," he prefers to call it "social cognitive theory," or "social cognitivism." (For that reason, we will use that term in this chapter; it will also help avoid confusion between this theory and Ronald Akers's [1998] social learning theory, examined in more detail in Chapter 9.)

Bandura's (1959, 1965) early research focused on aggression, particularly in children and adolescents. His simple, well-known experiment involved young children observing adults physically assaulting a Bobo doll (a children's toy resembling a clown, designed to bounce back up when struck). Bandura found that children imitated aggressive, violent behaviour after observing it. Critics suggested that the doll was designed to be punched, and that the children would not have attacked an actual person after merely observing others do it. In later studies, researchers were able to demonstrate that children were also willing to attack people dressed as clowns, as long as the behaviour was modelled by adults.

Social cognitive theory includes several explanatory mechanisms, including modelling and self-efficacy, both of which are relevant to understanding criminality. According to Bandura (1963, 1977), **modelling** is an important form of learning:

> Learning would be exceedingly laborious, not to mention hazardous, if people had to rely solely on the effects of their own actions to inform them what to do. Fortunately, most human behavior is learned observationally through modeling: from observing others one forms an idea of how new behaviors are performed, and on later occasions this coded information serves as a guide for action. (Bandura, 1977, p. 22)

Modelling (also known as "observational learning" or "imitation") refers to learning that occurs through observation of others and **vicarious reinforcement** (Bartol & Bartol, 2011). In other words, if an impressionable person sees someone perform some behaviour that's rewarded, the person will be more likely to imitate that behaviour based on the anticipation of the reward.

Bandura (1977) also claims that models vary in their ability to influence observers, and observers vary in their susceptibility to be influenced. If observers lack confidence or self-esteem, they are generally more likely to copy the behaviour of more confident people. However, confident and well-adjusted observers will model behaviour that is demonstrated to be highly useful (for example, a clever student doing poorly in a course will figure out how to study more effectively by observing students who are doing well). A model is more likely to be imitated by the observer if the model is held in high esteem by or has high status for the observer. Further, if the model has a close relationship with the observer (for example, if the model is a parent, sibling, or close friend), modelling is more likely to occur.

On the basis of findings of research on modelling theory, social cognitive theorists question the effectiveness of overreliance on deterrence as crime control policy and practice (Bandura, 1977). While they do concede that observing punishment can have an inhibiting effect on criminal behaviour, they also point out that the vicarious reinforcement of crime is much more common and widespread. In other words, within one's own intimate groups it is much more common to see someone successfully commit a crime and be rewarded for it (either monetarily or with praise from one's peers) than it is to see someone apprehended and punished for a crime. This is simply because of all crime that is committed, very little is reported, let alone punished. Instead of focusing primarily on deterrence achieved through punitive tactics, social cognitive theorists suggest that crime control policies should also seek to help offenders develop pro-social alternatives to crime (Bandura, 1977).

modelling
A form of learning that occurs through observation of others and vicarious reinforcement; also known as observational learning or imitation.

vicarious reinforcement
Reinforcement that is experienced indirectly through observing another person's behaviour being rewarded.

Another key aspect of social cognitive theory is self-efficacy. Self-efficacy is an important self-regulatory mechanism and refers to one's belief in his or her own ability to accomplish difficult tasks and deal with threatening situations. According to Bandura (1997), positive modelling and social support are ways of raising levels of self-efficacy. While self-efficacy is only marginally relevant to criminology, in the sense that it determines one's likelihood to change and possibly desist from criminal behaviour, its macro-level counterpart, collective efficacy, has received much more attention from criminologists.

Collective efficacy theory in criminology is a modern incarnation of social disorganization theory that accounts for disparities in neighbourhood crime rates. Robert Sampson (2013), the founder and main proponent of collective efficacy theory, argues that neighbourhoods with higher levels of collective efficacy are able to more effectively control crime.

Sampson's work is discussed in greater detail in Chapter 9.

The psychological learning theories discussed above have offered a more rigorous account of criminality than did earlier psychoanalytic explanations. However, these more recent theories still seemed to overlook factors and processes that many thought were important to understanding criminal behaviour. For example, how do people develop morals? This question seems relevant to understanding why people commit crime. It is also the focus of the moral development theories that will be discussed in the following section.

Moral Development and Criminality

Moral development theory has provided a significant contribution to the understanding of criminal behaviour. This theory can be traced back to the work of Jean Piaget (1932), who studied cognitive development in children and adolescents. To summarize, Piaget argued that morality is not a natural state of humans, and it develops in a series of stages. According to Piaget, moral development takes place alongside cognitive development. In other words, the development of one's morals is linked to the ability to reason (Palmer, 2003).

Kohlberg's Six Stages of Moral Development

Inspired by Piaget's work, Lawrence Kohlberg (1958) set out to replicate his research and to extend the theory beyond adolescence. Kohlberg proposed that people progress through six stages of moral development, divided into three levels (see Figure 8.4).

The first level of moral development is the pre-conventional level, or the hedonic level. At this level, the individual makes no distinction between moral and selfish values. In stage one, known as "punishment and obedience," the individual follows rules to avoid punishment and obeys authority figures without question. Punishment is evidence that a behaviour is wrong and should be avoided. In stage two, "instrumental purpose and exchange," self-interest emerges, and the individual begins to justify behaviour based on his or her personal needs. Not surprisingly, this stage also involves an increased interest in rewards as a motivation for behaviour (Garz, 2009; Kohlberg, 1969).

The second level of moral development is the conventional level. At this level, the individual appreciates the importance of conformity and social expectations.

FIGURE 8.4   Moral Development

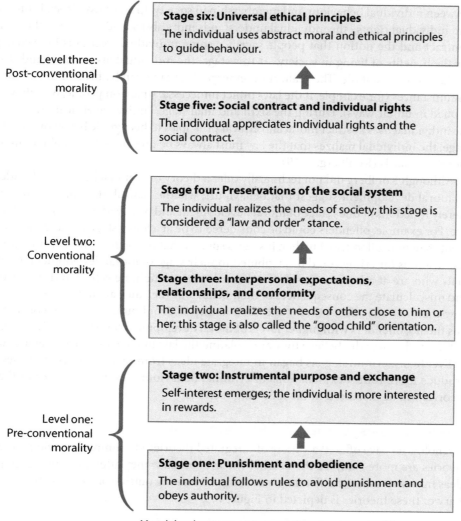

Moral development occurs over three levels, each with two stages.

Sources: Adapted from Garz (2009, p. 40) and Kohlbert (1969).

In stage three, "interpersonal expectations, relationships, and conformity," the individual becomes aware of the needs of others close to him or her. This stage is also called the "good child" orientation (Kohlberg, 1969). During this stage, the focus is on maintaining important relationships by demonstrating loyalty (Palmer, 2003). In stage four, "preservation of the social system," the individual's concerns branch out to society, and he or she understands the importance of obeying laws and performing one's duties. The view here is clearly a "law and order" stance that has its basis in a respect for authority and a consideration of wider social needs.

The third level of moral development is the post-conventional level, or the "principled," level. It involves developing a more nuanced understanding of the relationship between individual behaviour and membership in society. In stage five, "social contract and individual rights," the individual understands more abstract ideas such as the social contract and the notion that people sacrifice some individual freedoms in exchange for the benefits of living in society. At this stage, the individual also understands that the law is not infallible. The realization emerges that laws can be broken under some circumstances (for example, if the laws inflict unnecessary pain on people, or if they are applied in unfair ways). During the sixth and final stage, "universal ethical principles," the individual uses abstract moral and ethical principles to help guide behaviour. At this stage, the individual realizes that the law must always be questioned and held to higher moral standards (Kohlberg, 1969).

Although Kohlberg did not technically offer a theory of criminal behaviour, his ideas on moral development suggest that behaviours, whether law-abiding or criminal, are merely functions of one's stage of moral development and one's wider conception of justice. For example, offenders could be considered to be at a lower stage of moral development than non-offenders. Further, his ideas suggest that offenders' rationalizations and justifications for crime could be attributed to their stage of moral development. Criminals who are at a lower stage of moral development might be selfish and impulsive, and miscalculate the consequences of their behaviour (i.e., they are not concerned with how their actions affect others) and their ability to avoid punishment. According to this theory, offenders with higher levels of moral development tend to be activists, protesters, and those who believe they are violating the law in the name of a greater good.

Eventually, criminologists began to integrate ideas from many different theories to produce more robust explanations of criminal behaviour. Several examples of these theories will be discussed in the following sections.

Integrating Psychological Explanations

Psychologists have offered a variety of integrated theories of criminal behaviour. These theories are more complex than earlier theories because they attempt to fuse together ideas from a number of different areas, some originating outside of psychology. A summary of these theories is depicted in Figure 8.5.

Andrews and Bonta's Personal, Interpersonal, Community-Reinforcement Theory

D.A. Andrews and James Bonta's (2010) personal, interpersonal, community-reinforcement (PIC-R) theory is an attempt to integrate many of the psychological theories described above into one theory of criminal behaviour. According to Andrews and Bonta (2010), four key risk factors appear in almost every empirical study of criminality as the strongest predictors of criminal behaviour. They call these factors "the Big Four," which are as follows:

- anti-social attitudes;
- anti-social associates;
- a history of anti-social behaviour; and
- an anti-social personality pattern.

FIGURE 8.5   Integrated Psychological Theories

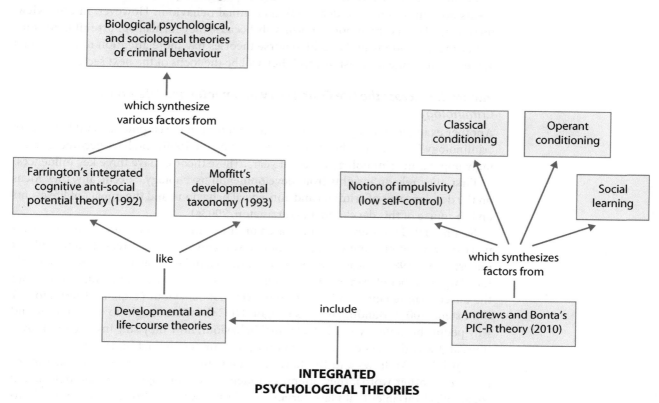

The key explanatory mechanisms in PIC-R theory are derived from various psychological theories, and Andrews and Bonta propose how these are connected to the Big Four factors. For example, they draw on psychodynamic theory, especially notions of self-control and impulsivity, to explain the development of anti-social personality patterns. They also consider cognitive processes associated with social learning theory, such as self-regulatory mechanisms (for example, self-efficacy) and criminal thinking patterns, to explain the development of anti-social personality patterns (Andrews & Bonta, 2010).

Aspects of modelling, as well as classical and operant conditioning, are also used to explain behavioural outcomes and are particularly useful to understanding why factors such as anti-social associates and anti-social attitudes consistently predict criminal behaviour. For example, if an individual is constantly around friends that are involved with crime, that individual will eventually either quit associating with them (out of fear of getting into trouble) or will adopt their anti-social attitudes. These attitudes are usually adopted because an individual sees his or her peers (i.e., models) being rewarded for their criminal behaviour in both social (for example, praise, belonging, and status) and non-social ways (for example, money, personal items). Further, the individual may come to feel close to these criminal models, which may further reinforce his or her law-breaking attitude.

Finally, Andrews and Bonta (2010) acknowledge that social systems and environments are important to understanding criminal behaviour. However, in their view, these social factors are important primarily they furnish opportunities to commit crime. Developmental and life-course theories pay more attention to these social and environmental dimensions, and they will be the focus of the next section.

Integration Across the Life Course: Developmental and Life-Course Criminology

Another example of integrated theory can be found in developmental and life-course criminology (DLC). DLC theories emerged during the 1990s and have become increasingly popular in criminology in recent years. These theories have three key influences.

First, they rely on insights from developmental psychology. Specifically, they focus on the development of criminal and anti-social behaviour, and the impact of life events on the course of this development (Farrington, 2003a).

Second, DLC theories rely on research on the criminal career paradigm. The criminal career paradigm emerged in a National Academy of Sciences report on the subject undertaken in 1986. Researchers found that a small number of offenders were responsible for a large number of crimes. Data obtained from this study also raised questions about the onset, maintenance, and cessation of criminal behaviour (Piquero, Farrington, & Blumstein, 2003). Building on this insight, DLC theorists sought to explain how and why people become involved in criminal behaviour, how they stay involved in it over time, and why they choose to stop committing crimes (Farrington, 1992).

Third, like Andrews and Bonta (2010), DLC theorists embrace a risk factor approach. In other words, they attempt to identify key biological, psychological, and sociological variables that place certain people at greater risk to commit crime. Common risk factors include impulsivity, low empathy, low intelligence, delinquent friends, weak social bonds, economic/financial strain, and presence of criminal opportunities (Farrington, 2003a).

While DLC theories incorporate a number of different factors, both David Farrington's (1992, 2003a) integrated cognitive anti-social potential (ICAP) theory and Terrie Moffitt's (1993) developmental taxonomy have their foundations in psychology.

Farrington's Integrated Cognitive Anti-Social Potential Theory

David Farrington's (1992) ICAP theory was proposed to explain the results of the *Cambridge Study in Delinquent Development [Great Britain], 1961–1981* (Farrington, 1999; see also Farrington, 2003b). The key underlying construct in this theory is anti-social potential. Farrington (1992) argues that anti-social potential has both short-term and long-term aspects. Long-term anti-social potential focuses on the various individual differences between people that might contribute to a criminal predisposition. Key factors that determine one's long-term anti-social potential include impulsivity, low IQ, lack of empathy, weak conscience, anti-social models, delinquent peers, weak social attachments, and economic problems. People who have these risk factors will have a higher risk of engaging in criminal activity (Farrington, 1992).

Short-term anti-social potential refers to environmental and/or immediate situational factors that might lead to offending. This element of the theory emphasizes the dynamics of the crime rather than individual factors that predispose some people to crime. For example, in order for crime to take place, opportunities must be present in one's environment, and this often depends on the everyday or routine activities of the offender. The offender must also assess the situation and determine whether the crime is worth committing (i.e., there must be some sort of cognitive process involving a cost–benefit analysis). Another important situational factor is the mental state of the offender (for example, intoxicated, angry, bored, or frustrated) that might make a person more prone to crime.

Moffitt's Developmental Taxonomy Theory

Terrie Moffitt's (1993) developmental taxonomy is another leading DLC theory. The theory has been tested by using data supplied by the Dunedin Multidisciplinary Health and Development Study, a 32-year-long longitudinal study of a birth cohort of over 1,000 New Zealanders (Moffitt, 2007). The developmental taxonomy is an attempt to further explain the relationship between age and crime, also known as the age–crime curve. The age–crime curve demonstrates that rates of offending peak sharply around the age of 17 and then decline rapidly in young adulthood, with about 85 percent of offenders completely desisting by the age of 28 (Moffitt, 1993). Moffitt (1993) argues that the age–crime curve obscures two distinct categories of offenders: Life-course-persistent (LCP) and adolescent-limited (AL) offenders.

LCP offenders represent a small percentage of all offenders, at about 5 percent. These people show evidence of anti-social behaviour early in childhood and offend frequently throughout adolescence and into adulthood. Their anti-social behaviour is thought to stem from neuropsychological deficits occurring very early in life, often during fetal development. These deficits may be caused by a number of factors, including maternal substance abuse, poor prenatal nutrition, and exposure to toxic agents (Moffitt, 1993).

Neuropsychological deficits manifest themselves in a variety of ways and affect both verbal and executive functions. Moffitt (1993) states that problems with verbal and executive functions are known to be associated with anti-social behaviour. Verbal deficits lead to problems in reading, writing, expressive speech, and memory, while deficits in executive functions involve impulsive behaviour and inattention. In addition to contributing to anti-social behaviour, these deficits also create problems when interacting with parents, school teachers, and other authority figures. These negative interactions promote more anti-social behaviour through attenuated social bonds and negative labelling effects. The result is a life-course trajectory that slowly limits options for pro-social change, leading the person to become entrenched in crime and other forms of anti-social behaviour. It is clear that this theory is attempting to specify how traits (i.e., neuropsychological deficits) and one's environment (i.e., negative social interactions and labelling) interact to produce criminality and anti-social behaviour.

AL offenders have little to no childhood history of anti-social behaviour and participate in crime during their adolescent years only. AL offenders represent the largest percentage of all offenders, at about 95 percent. According to Moffitt (1993), the onset of AL offending occurs in response to the maturity gap created by modernization. The maturity gap refers to societal changes that have occurred in the past century that have served to delay entry into adulthood and activities associated with being an independent adult (for example, drinking, sex, labour force participation, getting married, and having children). At the same time, improvements in nutrition and health care have also lowered the age of biological maturity. All of these factors serve to lengthen the amount of time spent in the stage of adolescence; teenagers are forced to delay adult activities, contrary to some of the biological urges they may be experiencing.

Moffitt (1993) claims that the longer time spent in adolescence creates a role vacuum that causes some adolescents to look for ways to assert their independence. For example, AL offenders mimic LCP offenders because the older offenders appear to be adept at gaining the freedom desired by AL offenders. In short, offending is a way of expressing individualism and personal independence for AL offenders. AL offenders naturally desist from criminal activity as they age because adult responsibilities (such as having a job and family) begin to limit opportunities and motivation for delinquency.

Practical Implications: Treatment, Risk, and Mental Illness

Psychological theories have had a considerable impact on the criminal justice system, especially in the areas of correctional treatment and risk assessment. In the 1920s, the medical model made its way into correctional systems in Canada and the United States. The medical model was introduced by the Positivist School of criminology and viewed criminals as "sick" and in need of help or rehabilitation (Griffiths & Murdoch, 2017).

Early correctional treatment approaches in prison were implemented by people with psychiatric training and were based primarily on a clinical approach heavily influenced by psychoanalytic thought (Cohen, 1983). In the 1950s and 1960s, the correctional treatment model shifted to a behavioural approach based on learning theories that were popular in psychology at the time (i.e., operant conditioning and social learning). Modern forms of correctional treatment focus on cognitive aspects of behaviour and criminal thinking patterns (Andrews & Bonta, 2010; Ross & Ross, 1995).

Risk assessment is another area that has been influenced by psychological theories. Correctional Service Canada and the National Parole Board use many scales and other instruments to predict the risk posed by offenders after release. Many of the characteristics included on these scales (for example, anti-social attitudes and associates, impulsivity, and lack of empathy) are derived from psychoanalytic and learning theories, and from factors identified on the Psychopathy Checklist-Revised (PCL-R) (Hare, 2003; see Box 8.1 for a discussion of psychopathy).

Research psychologists have developed three types of risk assessment: unstructured clinical judgment, mechanical prediction, and structured professional judgment. "Unstructured clinical judgment" tends to be quite subjective as it uses no real guidelines apart from the judgment of a mental health professional as a basis for assessment. Consequently, assessments of the same individual could vary greatly if the opinions of the assessors are different (Pozzulo, Bennell, & Forth, 2015). "Mechanical prediction" makes use of predefined rules and structured guidelines to assess risk. In one popular type of mechanical prediction, known as actuarial prediction, these rules and guidelines identify risk factors to look for in offenders that are derived from theories or are based on findings from research studies in the social sciences and mental health fields (Serin et al., 2011). While actuarial risk-assessment instruments have been proven to perform better empirically when compared to unstructured clinical judgment, they still have some shortcomings. For example, some critics contend that risk assessments are overly reliant on static risk factors that are assumed not to change over time. In response to these criticisms, a hybrid approach has emerged known as "structured professional judgment." This approach is guided by not only evaluations performed by mental health professionals, but also those administered by law enforcement officers, probation officers, and social workers. Further, it incorporates risk factors that account for change over time (i.e., dynamic risk factors) and risk factors associated with aspects of the immediate situation and/or environment (Pozzulo, Bennell, & Forth, 2015).

There are several prominent risk-assessment instruments that play a large role in the management of criminal offenders. The Violence Risk Appraisal Guide (VRAG) was designed in Ontario and is used to predict violent recidivism (Pozzulo, Bennell, & Forth, 2015). The VRAG uses 12 items based on different static risk factors found to be highly correlated with violence (Serin et al., 2011). Another prominent violence risk assessment, the Historical, Clinical, Risk Management-20 (HCR-20), was developed by a group of researchers based out of Simon Fraser University in British Columbia. This scale makes use of structured professional judgment and a mixture of items based on static risk factors to make predictions about violence. The HCR-20 is specifically geared to assess risk of violent behaviour in correctional and forensic psychiatric samples and was found to be quite effective at predicting institutional recidivism when compared to other instruments (Pozzulo, Bennell, & Forth, 2015). The Self-Appraisal Questionnaire (SAQ) is an actuarial risk-assessment tool used to estimate risk of recidivism for both violent and non-violent crime. This instrument is unique because it is based on self-report questions derived from 67 different items theoretically and empirically linked to recidivism that are grouped into different subscales. One major advantage of this tool is that it uses dynamic risk factors relating to criminogenic needs that can be useful in designing treatment and other interventions. Some have suggested that self-reports from offenders will produce problematic results; however, the SAQ fares well in empirical assessments (Serin et al., 2011).

A few caveats are in order when discussing risk-assessment devices and their trustworthiness. It should always be kept in mind that risk prediction is far from an exact science; these tools are perhaps most beneficial when being used to determine how to manage and treat serious offenders. Unfortunately, risk assessments are often used to make decisions about parole and probation in which a non-probabilistic decision is required (i.e., the offender will either reoffend or not reoffend). It's important to bear in mind that these instruments are based on probabilities and do not in any way make perfect predictions about human behaviour (see Harcourt, 2007). In other words, we must consider the fact that there will always be false positives in which an offender is predicted to reoffend but then does not. Given this limitation, it seems unfair and unjust to put too much weight on risk assessment scores when trying to determine whether an offender should be released on probation or parole.

Many believe that people with mental illness are violent and more prone to crime than other people. Some studies have found that people with certain forms of mental illness (for example, major depression and alcohol/drug dependence) are more likely to commit violent acts; however, this connection is not so straightforward, as other studies have found that prior violence and substance abuse are much stronger predictors of future violence when compared to being diagnosed with a mental illness. Further, people with mental illness are actually less likely to reoffend than those without mental disorders. This suggests that mentally disordered people are not a threat if they get help with their problems (Pozzulo, Bennell, & Forth, 2015). The research literature on serious mental illness and violence suggests that the majority of people with mental illness are not violent. It is also important to bear in mind that causal mechanisms associated with the link between mental illness and violence are not clearly understood. Some speculate that the connection between violence and mental illness may actually be spurious or misleading, and that other factors that tend to be present in the lives of those with mental disorders (for example, poverty, substance use, unemployment, and homelessness) may be more important to understanding why some behave violently (Serin et al., 2011).

While it is true that those with mental illness are not destined to be violent, one must also keep in mind that schizophrenia, major depression, and bipolar disorder are much more prevalent among inmates and others under the control of the criminal justice system (for example, those on probation and parole) when compared to the general population (Griffiths & Murdoch, 2017). There are three explanations as to why this disparity exists. First, it could be that people with mental illness are more likely to be arrested because their behaviour attracts more attention. Indeed, the Canadian Mental Health Association found that people with mental illness are more likely to be detected and arrested for nuisance offences (for example, trespassing or disorderly conduct) and are more likely to be held in custody for these offences. A second explanation suggests that people who are mentally ill often commit very poorly planned crimes that make them more likely to be detected, caught, and apprehended. Finally, people with mental illness are more likely to plead guilty; in some cases, this relates to their inability to secure a good lawyer or understand the consequences of their plea agreement. It is very likely that some or possibly all of these explanations might apply depending on the individual case; however, more research is needed in this area. (Pozzulo, Bennell, & Forth, 2015, pp. 235–236).

Over the past decade, there have been a variety of problems stemming from the inability of correctional institutions to properly manage inmates with mental issues. For example, in 2007 a correctional review panel noted that Correctional Service Canada was failing to meet the needs of inmates with mental conditions. In 2009, the Correctional Investigator argued that mental health services for inmates were inadequate and they were basically "warehousing" this population without addressing public safety issues posed by their needs (Crocker, 2012, pp. 33–34). When compared to other countries, federal correctional institutions in Canada tend to have a robust set of programs that focus on addressing mental health and addiction issues. However, most prisoners are in the provincial and territorial systems with limited access to correctional treatment and programming. The rehabilitation programs that are available take months to complete and have long wait lists; if one considers that sentences are under two years for all offenders (a month on average) the challenges to offering programs in provincial institutions become readily apparent (Griffiths & Murdoch, 2017). The case of Ashley Smith is a well-publicized example that illustrates the shortcomings of correctional systems when trying to deal with mentally ill inmates (see Box 8.2).

The Ashley Smith Case

Ashley Smith began to have school misconduct issues around the age of 12. These infractions started when she was a minor (for example, verbal disputes) and eventually grew much more serious (for example, bullying, stalking a teacher) (Reid & Bromwich, 2017). Starting at the age of 14, she was in and out of youth detention for a string of offences (for example, playing chicken with neighbourhood traffic, pulling fire alarms, making harassing phone calls, throwing crabapples at a postal worker, and stealing a CD while on probation). During her initial period of incarceration, assessments conducted by mental health professionals indicated that she suffered from several different mental issues, including a learning disorder, ADHD, and borderline personality disorder; she also exhibited traits suggesting narcissistic personality disorder (Reid & Bromwich, 2017).

Ashley turned 18 while in youth detention; however, because of frequent and serious behavioural issues she was eventually sent to an adult provincial facility under the *Youth Criminal Justice Act*. While in provincial custody, Smith engaged in self-harming behaviours and her various mental health issues made it extremely difficult for correctional staff to deal with her. As punishment for these incidents, she spent a great deal of time alone in segregation, often sleeping on the floor with no clothing and no mattress. Her sentence was ballooned to six years because of frequent conflicts with correctional staff that occurred because of her mental health issues; she was charged over 500 times while in custody (Zlomislic, 2011). In 2007, Smith died by suicide in her prison cell by wrapping a ligature around her neck while under the surveillance of correctional officers. Shortly before killing herself, she informed correctional staff of her intention to do so, and she was not provided with adequate or immediate medical care during the incident (Crocker, 2012). She was only 19 years old at the time.

It is readily apparent that Ashley was under extreme mental distress during much of the time that she was incarcerated and that the correctional system failed to provide adequate care given that it was aware of her condition. Further, while she was involved with the system as a youth, it was clear that her rights were violated based on the United Nations *Convention on the Rights of the Child*. Finally, the amount of time she spent in segregation also violated United Nations' rules relating to proper treatment of prisoners. A 2015 mandate letter from Prime Minister Justin Trudeau has called on the correctional system to rectify the problems that led to the outcome of the Ashley Smith case (Reid & Bromwich, 2017).

The Criminalization of Addiction

Gabor Maté, a medical doctor and expert in the field of addictions, makes an important observation about the criminalization of addiction in the passage below:

Drugs do not make the addict into a criminal; the law does. When alcohol was prohibited, drinkers were breaking the law. If cigarettes were illegal, there would be a huge underground market for tobacco products. Gangs would form, criminal business empires would flourish and smokers would be spending a large proportion of their income on nicotine-containing substances. Add health ravages and medical and economic costs of nicotine addiction, the hundreds of thousands of deaths it causes and the many family tragedies it already creates—and then factor in the enormous costs of waging the War on Drugs on yet another front. The result would be a monumentally costly and futile effort. (Mate, 2009, pp. 278–279)

The economic burden of the War on Drugs has been estimated at a minimum of US$100 billion per year; this approach has caused the courts to become overburdened, a steep rise in imprisonment, and a loss of respect for the law and police in many communities (Maté, 2009). Further, there is a great deal of evidence to suggest that throughout North America, attempts to criminalize addiction, while not only costly, have also failed and will continue to create problems in the future (Alexander, 2008; Boyd, Carter, & Macpherson, 2016; Robinson & Scherlan, 2014). If drug prohibition has failed, why do we continue the policies associated with it?

The reasons as to why we criminalize drugs are connected to assumptions that many hold about the nature of drug use and addiction. These assumptions form the basis for the theories that inform criminal justice practices. A core assumption that perpetuates drug prohibition is the notion that the addict is free to choose, at any moment, not to use drugs, and that society can control this behaviour through harsh punishment and stigmatization. However, much of the research on addiction and drug use does not support these assumptions; some claim that criminalization of drug use may actually increase harms. For example, Boyd, Carter, and Macpherson (2016) found that the research evidence on prohibition suggested that it increases violence, helps to create dangerous unregulated drug markets, prevents therapeutic uses of criminalized drugs (for example, cannabis), and can increase the negative effects of drug use (for example, stigma that make addicts reluctant to seek help; death from overdose). For these reasons, many experts have suggested that the tendency to view addiction as a criminal issue, or even a medical issue, is misguided (Lewis, 2015). Instead, the alternative approach asserts that addiction results from a lack of integration and connectedness to society and societal institutions (Alexander, 2008; Maté, 2009). The opioid drug overdose crises sweeping through North America at the time of writing suggest that this new point of view might be more accurate. In any case, it is unclear as to how punishment and other current criminal justice responses can make addicts feel connected to society and ease the opioid crisis.

Conclusion

Psychologists have offered numerous theories that have influenced criminology. Early approaches focused primarily on explaining the intelligence–crime connection, aggression, the psychopathic personality, and aspects of social learning and moral development (Aichhorn, 1925; Bandura, 1965, 1973; Dollard et al., 1939; Freud, 1920; Goddard, 1913; Kohlberg, 1969). Later, these insights were applied more directly and used to explain general forms of criminal behaviour (Burgess & Akers, 1966; Eysenck, 1964; Jeffery, 1965). Modern incarnations of psychological theories in criminology are often integrated in nature and include Andrews and Bonta's (2010) PIC-R theory and developmental theories such as Farrington's (1992) ICAP theory and Moffitt's (1993) developmental taxonomy. Psychological explanations of criminal behaviour have also influenced the criminal justice system in a variety of areas, such as correctional treatment and risk assessment.

SUMMARY OF KEY POINTS

- The discipline of psychology is composed of several different (and often competing) perspectives including psychoanalysis, behaviourism, social cognitivism (or social learning), and developmental psychology. These different approaches have produced numerous psychological theories that seek to explain aspects of criminal behaviour. They should not be lumped together as a single theory.

- IQ may be an important *correlate* of crime; however, the *causal connection* is not readily apparent. In many cases, IQ may be influenced by factors such as socio-economic status or prenatal care, which undermines theories that attempt to link crime, IQ, and race, for example.

- Psychiatrist Sigmund Freud, founder of psychoanalysis, influenced many criminologists. Freud claimed that personality has three components: the id, the ego, and the superego. Many basic human impulses and drives stem from the id, which functions according to the pleasure principle. Biological urges for aggression and sex can instigate criminal behaviour, but they are counterbalanced by the superego; both of these aspects are regulated by the ego.

- Not all psychopaths are criminals, and many are not even violent. Many are successful in politics, law, and business. Misconceptions about psychopathy abound. Psychopaths are not psychotic, mentally ill, or "sick" in the legal sense of the term; that is, the disorder does not "[render] the person incapable of appreciating the nature and quality of the act or omission or of knowing that it was wrong." In contrast, *psychotics* refers to people who are mentally ill in a legal sense and often have hallucinations and delusions that spur on their abnormal behaviours, and may suffer from schizophrenia. Furthermore, the terms "psychopathy," "anti-social personality disorder," and "sociopathy" are often used interchangeably, which is incorrect.

- Psychological learning theories have contributed a great deal to the field of criminological theory. The main theories in this area (and key names associated with each) are "classical and operant conditioning" (Eysenck and Skinner, respectively), the "frustration–aggression hypothesis" (Dollard, Miller, Doob, Mowrer, and Sears), and "social learning theory" (Bandura).

- Moral development theory has its origins in the work of Piaget, who studied cognitive development in children and adolescents. Piaget argued that morality is not a natural state of humans and develops in a series of stages. Kohlberg extended the theory beyond adolescence, proposing that people progress through six stages of moral development, divided into three levels.

- Psychologists (including Andrews and Bonta) have offered a variety of "integrated theories" of criminal behaviour. These theories are more complex than earlier theories because they attempt to combine ideas from a number of different areas, some originating outside of psychology.

- Psychological theories have had a considerable impact on the criminal justice system, especially in the areas of correctional treatment and risk assessment. Further, the ways in which the criminal justice system deals with mental illness and addiction are connected to implicit assumptions about human nature.

QUESTIONS FOR CRITICAL DISCUSSION

1. In what ways has the field of psychology influenced criminal justice processes? How has it influenced the study of criminology?
2. What are the key differences between a psychopathic person and a psychotic person?
3. How does one's level of moral development affect their interpretation of the law? How does it affect the likelihood that they will break it?
4. How is IQ connected to criminality? Is it reasonable to argue that less intelligent people will be more likely to break the law?
5. Is it possible to predict crime based solely on a person's psychological characteristics?
6. Are the integrated theories an improvement over the original theories?

SUGGESTED FURTHER READINGS

Appleby, T. (2011). *A new kind of monster: The secret life and chilling crimes of Colonel Russell Williams*. Toronto: Vintage Canada.

Fowles, D.C. (1987). Psychophysiology and psychopath: A motivational approach. *Psychophysiology, 25*(4), 373–391.

Haney, C. (2002). Making law modern: Toward a contextual model of justice. *Psychology, Public Policy and the Law, 8*(1), 3–63.

Robinson, M.B., & Beaver, K.M. (2008). *Why crime? An interdisciplinary approach to explaining criminal behavior*. Durham, NC: Carolina Academic Press.

Ross, R.R., & Ross, R.D. (1995). *Thinking straight: The reasoning and rehabilitation program for delinquency prevention and offender rehabilitation*. Ottawa: Air Training.

Websites

Association for Behavior Analysis International: http://www.abainternational.org

Society for the Scientific Study of Psychopathy: http://www.psychopathysociety.org/en

"Without Conscience": Robert Hare's website devoted to the study of psychopathy: http://www .hare.org

R v Prosper: Taking the Social Circumstances of the Offender into Account

The court's judgement in *R v Prosper* was influenced by the *Gladue* report and the hardships experienced by the offender as an Indigenous man.

Note to the reader: This case involves an offence that some readers may find disturbing. The study of such cases should be approached with sensitivity and respect.

In early August 2015, a young woman we will call K.J., at that time between the ages of 16 and 18, was at her home. A young man about four years older than her, Davis Prosper, who was visiting the house at the time, followed her to her bedroom. The graphic facts of their encounter are described in the 2017 judgment of Justice James Chipman of the Supreme Court of Nova Scotia.

To summarize, K.J. was lying on her bed while texting with her boyfriend when Mr. Prosper sat on her bed and proceeded to sexually assault her. K.J. was able to get away from him, at which point her boyfriend told Mr. Prosper, either by a telephone conversation or text message, to leave the house.

Justice Chipman had noted in his preliminary remarks that a jury trial was scheduled to hear this case of sexual assault in February 2017, but on the opening day of the trial Mr. Prosper changed his plea to guilty, and a sentencing hearing was then scheduled for June of the same year. Prior to the sentencing hearing, given Mr. Prosper's Indigenous status, the court had received a *Gladue* report, a pre-sentence report prepared by a probation officer, sentencing submissions from both Crown and defence counsel, and a victim impact statement prepared by K.J.

The Crown argued that the crime should be characterized as a major or serious sexual assault, warranting a sentence of two years' imprisonment, followed by a one-year period of probation. The defence counsel made the following submission, asking for a 90-day term of imprisonment, served intermittently with probation, and with the possibility of "restricted house arrest style curfews":

> The case before this Honourable Court does not involve a position of trust or a child victim. Mr. Prosper is approximately four years older than K.J. and for better or worse, was a friend ... . It appears to have been an impulsive, immature act. There were no threats, striking, choking, or sexual intercourse. His affidavit in the Section 276 application appears to be relatively candid as to his physical acts on that day. He did waive his Preliminary on the day of the hearing and changed his plea to guilty just before the trial commenced. While it is acknowledged that this was not an early resolution, K.J. did not have to testify at either hearing and he has accepted responsibility. (*R v Prosper*, 2017, at para. 9)

Justice Chipman then turned to the issue of the *Gladue* report, a report prepared for the court in accordance with section 718.2(e) of the *Criminal Code*:

(e) all available sanctions, other than imprisonment, that are reasonable in the circumstances and consistent with the harm done to victims or to the community should be considered for all offenders, with particular attention to the circumstances of Aboriginal offenders.

It is this specific reference to "Aboriginal offenders" that spurs the preparation of the *Gladue* report for sentencing purposes. The *Gladue* report notes that Mr. Prosper is of Aboriginal ancestry and notes:

- That he has experienced the adverse effects of the toxic social environment and poor socio-economic conditions that continue to impact the lives of Aboriginal people since the time of colonization, including:
  - Substance abuse; personally, immediate family, extended family and within the general community
  - Poverty: personally, family and community
  - Family (divorce, born out of wedlock) or community break down
  - Abuse: emotional, verbal, mental, emotional, physical and spiritual; domestic violence
  - Unemployed, low income, lack of employment opportunity
  - Lack of educational opportunities
  - Direct involvement with Family and Children's services
  - Family involvement with Criminal activities
  - Mental Health issues: Suicide & Depression (*R v Prosper*, 2017, at para. 16)

Justice Chipman concluded:

At the time, he was a friend ... to the teen. On the facts in context, I accept that Mr. Prospect's actions were impulsive. He acted for his own sexual gratification at great expense to the victim. Having said this, he made no threats and there was no striking, choking or sexual intercourse.

Given the circumstances of the crime, along with Mr. Prosper's status as outlined in the PSR and *Gladue* report, I am of the view that despite a difficult upbringing and poor socio-economic status, Mr. Prosper exhibits great potential. In these difficult circumstances, I have decided that a fit and proper sentence should not involve a lengthy period of incarceration as sought by the Crown. Having regard to all of the circumstances of the crime, all of the circumstances unique to Mr. Prosper and the authorities, I am satisfied that the following sentence is just:

1. A four month custodial sentence.
2. The four month period of custody shall be followed by 18 months of probation, with regular reporting and conditions as recommended by the Crown.
3. Ancillary orders with respect to DNA (s. 271) and a 10 year firearms prohibition (ss. 109(1)(a) and 109(2)), with an exception for Mr. Prosper to hunt for sustenance, as expressed by his counsel today and agreed to by the Crown. In this regard, he is clearly an aboriginal person. He has financial hardship and, no question, he hunts and fishes to bring food home to his family.
4. Mr. Prosper shall be subject to a SOIRA [Sex Offender Information Registration Order] for a period of 20 years, pursuant to s. 490.013(2)(b).
5. There shall be a $200 victim fine surcharge, payable within one year of today's date. (*R v Prosper*, 2017, at paras. 20, 21)

Before You Read Chapter 9

- Do you agree with the court's judgment in this case? Why or why not?
- To what extent should the person's Indigenous status be used as a relevant factor in sentencing. Does section 718.2(e) strike an appropriate balance?
- Imagine that you were to write a dissenting judgment in this case. Would you recommend a more lenient sentence or a harsher sentence? Why?
- After reading this chapter, return to this case study. Have your views of the appropriateness of the sentence changed after reading the chapter that follows this case study?
- Which sociological theories best explain the crime that was committed in this case?

Sociological Approaches

LEARNING OUTCOMES

After reading this chapter, students will be able to:

- Distinguish between sociological, psychological, and biological approaches to explaining criminal and deviant behaviour.

- Define the concept of social disorganization and explain how social disorganization can contribute to high crime rates.

- Discuss the "sociology of deviance," its contribution to labelling theory, and its position on social problems, moral entrepreneurship, and moral panics.

- Trace the development of anomie-strain theory through Émile Durkheim, Robert Merton, Robert Agnew, and Steven Messner and Richard Rosenfeld.

- Explain the relationship between differential association theory, techniques of neutralization, and social learning theory.

- Trace the development of social control theory, from Émile Durkheim to Travis Hirschi to the recent life-course-developmental theories.

CHAPTER OUTLINE

Introduction

Sociological approaches have been and continue to be the most prevalent and widely accepted of all criminological theories. Whether you take a larger sample of the 50 key thinkers in criminology or a smaller sample of 15 past and present pioneers in criminological thought (cf. Hayward, Maruna, & Mooney, 2010; Mutchnick, Martin, & Austin, 2009), between 60 and 75 percent of the theorizing can be attributed to the field of sociology alone. Even in areas of criminological theory covered in other chapters in this book, where the relationship might not be so readily apparent—such as feminist criminology and critical criminology—the majority of prominent thinkers come from a sociological background (Hayward, Maruna, & Mooney, 2010; Renzetti, 2013; Young, 2002).

The long-standing and durable relationship between sociology and criminology can be traced back to Émile Durkheim, the founder of academic sociology in France in the late 1800s, and to the sociology department at the University of Chicago (often referred to as the **Chicago School**). Durkheim was the originator of anomie theory and social control theory, both of which remain widely accepted today (Cullen, Wright, & Blevins, 2004). The Chicago School gave rise to social disorganization theory, differential

> See Chapters 10, Gender and Crime and 11, Critical Criminology for more on feminist and critical criminology.

Chicago School
The first school of sociology in the United States; contributed to social disorganization theory, cultural transmission theory, differential association theory, subcultural theory, the sociology of deviance, and symbolic interactionism.

association theory, the sociology of deviance, and labelling theory—all of which are very much a part of mainstream criminological thinking (Lilly, Cullen, & Ball, 2015; Williams & McShane, 2018).

Edwin Sutherland, a member of the Chicago School, and arguably the most prominent criminologist of the 20th century, played a key role in establishing sociology's dominance in the field of criminology (Laub & Sampson, 1991). The interrelationship between sociology and criminology can also be explained by the fact that, until recently, the discipline of criminology was often subsumed under the auspices of sociology departments (Sacco & Kennedy, 2011). It was not until about 50 years ago that independent criminology departments began to spring up around North America (Ratner, 2006).

Sociological explanations tend to view crime and deviance as normal, or at least semi-normal—as socially or culturally learned responses to social circumstances (Clinard & Meier, 2004; Cohen & Machalek, 1994). Rather than focusing on the biological or psychological deficiencies of individuals, sociological explanations emphasize the effects of social structure, social institutions, social organization, social class, social roles, social norms, and social learning in the shaping of criminal or deviant behaviour (Giddens, 1987). Biological explanations, on the other hand, investigate inherited biogenetic deficits or abnormalities that predispose certain individuals to engage in criminal or deviant activities (for example, Beaver, Ratchford, & Ferguson, 2010; Ellis & Walsh, 1997). Psychological explanations examine individual differences in personality, memory, perception, learning, and cognition and how such differences can lead to abnormal behaviour or character disorders (Andrews & Bonta, 2010; Gelles, 1993).

Sociologists might ask why some societies deem marijuana use, prostitution, or polygamy to be abnormal or criminal, whereas other societies do not, or why members of certain social classes seem more likely to be criminalized than members of other social classes. Biologists and psychologists, by contrast, might ask why certain individuals are more likely to behave in an abnormal or criminal manner, and then search for clues within that individual's genetic makeup or personality.

That said, considerable overlap exists between sociological, psychological, and biological explanations of crime and deviance. Ronald Akers's social learning theory (Akers, 2001; Burgess & Akers, 1966) combines Edwin Sutherland's differential association theory (a sociological theory) with B.F. Skinner's work on operant conditioning and Albert Bandura's work on imitation and modelling behaviour (both psychological approaches). Robert Agnew's general strain theory (1992) combines Robert Merton's anomie-strain theory (again, a sociological theory) with psychological and physiological variables, such as the "frustration–aggression hypothesis" and "pain-avoidance behaviour." Similarly, a number of recent psychological explanations have turned to a more integrative or "psychosocial" approach (involving sociological as well as individual variables) (Bartol, 1999; Wortley, 2011).

Durkheim's Influence

Émile Durkheim's influence on sociological approaches to crime and deviance cannot be overstated. Durkheim contributed to the "consensus perspective" in sociology and criminology, to what is now known as "structural functionalism" (the view that society is "natural" or "organic"), and to the notion that society requires both integration and regulation in order to be cohesive (Burtch, 2003; Williams & McShane, 2018). His work underpins Merton's anomie-strain theory, Agnew's general strain theory, Erikson's sociology of deviance, Messner and Rosenfeld's institutional-anomie theory, Hirschi's social bond theory, Thornberry's interactional theory, and Sampson and Laub's life-course-developmental theory (all discussed later in this chapter).

Durkheim was influenced by the French thinkers who preceded him: by Baron de Montesquieu, who is credited with laying the groundwork for what later became known as the "sociology of law" and the "sociology of knowledge"; by Henri de Saint-Simon, who called for a "human science" that would apply scientific principles to the study of society; and by August Comte, who first coined the terms "sociology" and "positivism" (Mutchnick, Martin, & Austin, 2009; Zeitlin, 2001). Durkheim's work was also affected by the political turmoil of the 17th and 18th centuries, marked by the English Revolution, where the British monarchy was replaced by parliamentary democracy; the American Revolution, which threw off the yoke of the British monarchy; and the French Revolution, which led to the guillotining of the French monarchy, the rise of Napoleon Bonaparte, and a century of political instability in France (Lilly et al., 2015; Zeitlin, 2001). In addition, Durkheim's writings were a reaction to the work of 19th-century German philosopher and economist Karl Marx, who advocated the overthrow of capitalism, and to the work of the Positivist School of criminology, which attempted to explain criminality in terms of inherited genetic defects such as "feeble-mindedness," and argued that criminals were degenerative, evolutionary throwbacks (Williams & McShane, 2018).

In "The Normal and the Pathological," Durkheim (1895/1970) rejected the "disease" analogy put forward by the Positivist School—the notion that criminality was an inherited trait, or that it was "abnormal" or "pathological" (Cohen & Machalek, 1994). Instead, he observed that crime had existed throughout history, and was present in all types of societies. He pointed out—applying the same scientific approach that early members of the Positivist School claimed to apply themselves—that abnormal, pathological, or morbid phenomena would not survive over time (i.e., they would be screened out through the evolutionary process of natural selection). Thus, Durkheim concluded that a certain amount of crime must be "normal," or at least, that crime must serve some sort of social function. He proposed that crime defined the moral boundaries of the community, and that crime contributed to the development of social cohesion or social solidarity (by creating a "them versus us" mentality or a "good guys" versus "bad guys" distinction) (Durkheim, 1964; Greenberg, 2010).

Unlike Marx, who saw society as rooted in social conflict and postulated that capitalism would eventually be overthrown and replaced with socialism, Durkheim argued that society was based on consensus (shared norms, values, and beliefs) and was comparable to a natural, functioning organism that does what it has to do to survive (Durkheim, 1965; Zeitlin, 2001). Durkheim talked about the "forces of integration" and the "forces of regulation," both necessary to the cohesiveness and smooth functioning of society. The forces of integration were the social bonds and shared (collective) beliefs that attracted people and held them together. The forces of regulation were the laws and the social institutions that helped ensure compliance with social norms, values, and beliefs (Lilly et al., 2015). We will see Durkheim's notion of social bonds and collective beliefs again when we come to Hirschi's social bond theory, Thornberry's interactional theory, and Sampson and Laub's life-course-developmental theory. We will also see the forces of integration and regulation again when we come to Merton's anomie-strain theory and Messner and Rosenfeld's institutional-anomie theory.

anomie
A term coined by Durkheim to describe periods of lawlessness, normlessness, and unrestrained choice, or a breakdown in social solidarity.

Durkheim is known for his work on **anomie**, which he described as a state of law-lessness, normlessness, or unrestrained ambition that if left unchecked could lead to a breakdown in social solidarity (Clinard, 1964; Durkheim, 1965). While Durkheim did not specifically relate anomie to crime, he saw periods of anomie as an impediment to the development of social relationships, and as a contributing factor to periodic increases in suicide rates (Cartwright, 2011; Clinard & Meier, 2004; Durkheim, 1951). Durkheim's anomie theory will be revisited when we discuss Merton's anomie-strain theory, Albert Cohen's work on "delinquent boys and the culture of the gang," Cloward and Ohlin's "illegitimate opportunity structures," and Messner and Rosenfeld's institutional-anomie theory.

The Chicago School

The Chicago School, established in 1892, was the first school of sociology in the United States (Lilly et al., 2015; Williams & McShane, 2018). Chicago School thinking was shaped by the rapid growth of the city of Chicago, the relatively new science of ecology, and a growing interest in the type of ethnographic work associated with cultural anthropology (Williams & McShane, 2018). The Chicago School is renowned for its urban sociology, its life histories, and its focus on community-level analysis (Sampson, 2002). Like Durkheim before them, members of the Chicago School rejected the social Darwinist notion that the poor were poor because of their degenerative evolutionary condition and challenged the then popular notion that most criminals were either criminal psychopaths or feeble-minded (of low intelligence) (Laub & Sampson, 1991; Lilly et al., 2015; Rafter, 1997). Rather, members of the Chicago School concluded that it was "the nature of the neighbourhood," not "the nature of the individual," that was the primary cause of criminality (Lilly et al., 2015). The Chicago School brought us many well-known criminological theories, including social disorganization theory, cultural transmission theory, cultural conflict theory, differential association theory, the sociology of deviance, and labelling theory.

Social Disorganization Theory

Between 1830 and 1930, Chicago increased in size from approximately 4,000 residents to 3 million residents (Lilly et al., 2015). Most of this population growth came through mass immigration from other countries (for example, Germans trying to escape the political instability and constant warring in Europe, Polish people leaving various countries in Europe just prior to the First World War, etc.), as well as waves of migrants from other parts of the United States (for example, African-Americans fleeing the American South after the Civil War, and farm workers and displaced farmers leaving the American countryside in hope of finding work in the recently industrialized urban centres) (Williams & McShane, 2018).

Park and Burgess's Concentric Zone Model

Robert Park and Ernest Burgess, two earlier Chicago School theorists, observed that Chicago had grown in a series of five concentric rings or zones, and each zone had its own distinctive land usage and population (Park & Burgess, 1967). Zone I, the Loop (or Central Business District), was situated on the waterfront on Lake Michigan and was the main rail and water transportation hub. Zone II, the Zone in Transition (or Interstitial Zone), was immediately adjacent to the Central Business District. Zone III, the Zone of Workingmen's Homes, was between the Zone in Transition and the Residential Zone (Zone IV). Zone V was the Commuters Zone, now commonly referred to as "the suburbs" (see Figure 9.1).

In keeping with the ecological and **functionalist** thinking that was prevalent in the early 20th century, Park and Burgess saw the city as a functioning organism, or natural human environment. They regarded the formation of these concentric zones as part of the natural evolutionary process of "invasion, dominance and succession" (Bernard, Snipes, & Gerould, 2010), much like what might happen in the animal kingdom when a new and more successful species invades a territory and gradually pushes the original—less successful or less adaptable—inhabitants to the periphery or to extinction (Traub & Little, 1985; Williams & McShane, 2018). As the Loop (Central Business District) grew and expanded outward, it put pressure on the Zone in Transition, which became a rundown urban slum, or ghetto. Those who had the ability to leave or avoid the Zone in Transition moved to the Zone of Workingmen's Homes, the Residential Zone, or the Commuters Zone.

functionalism

In sociology, the idea that society is comparable to a functioning organism with interrelated parts and structures to ensure that the parts work together; functionalists believe that society is based on consensus (shared values, beliefs), not conflict.

FIGURE 9.1   Park and Burgess's Concentric Zone Model

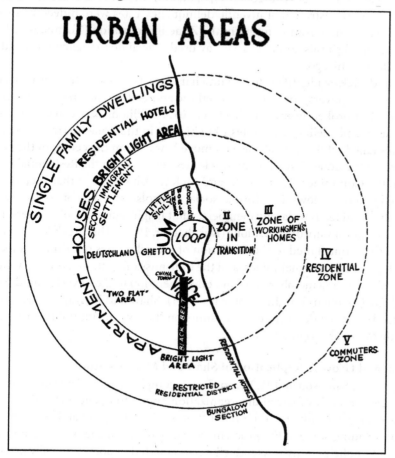

Source: Burgess (1925/1967, p. 55).

The socially disorganized Zone in Transition was populated primarily by recently arrived immigrants, transient workers, and others who could not afford to live in one of the more affluent zones of the city. The attraction for recently arrived immigrants or transient workers was that the rents were cheaper in the transitional zone because the buildings were old and rundown. Park and Burgess did not, however, attempt to explore the relationship between crime and the social disorganization found in the Zone in Transition. Rather, they regarded themselves as urban geographers, ethnographers, or ecologists, mapping out the city and trying to understand how the urban landscape had evolved over time (Lilly et al., 2015; Mutchnick, Martin, & Austin, 2009).

Shaw and McKay's Study of Social Disorganization in Chicago

social disorganization theory
The theory that a breakdown of the networks, norms, and trust that facilitate coordination and cooperation among residents of neighbourhoods can lead to greater crime and violence.

Although they did not invent the concentric zone model or come up with the concept of **social disorganization**, Clifford Shaw and Henry McKay's study of social disorganization remains a landmark in sociological explanations for why crime rates tend to be higher in urban centres. While they were not faculty members in the Chicago School, Shaw and McKay both did their graduate studies in sociology at the University of Chicago, and both were active in working with—and conducting research studies on—delinquents in the Chicago area (Snodgrass, 2011). Using the concentric zone model created by Park and Burgess (1925/1967), Shaw and McKay (1969) set out in the 1930s and 1940s to demonstrate that juvenile delinquency rates were indeed related to the type of social disorganization found in the Zone in Transition (Kornhauser, 1978). In order to accomplish this, Shaw and McKay used official delinquency rates and official census data for Chicago.

Shaw and McKay identified five main characteristics associated with socially disorganized areas: poverty, overcrowding, ethnic and cultural heterogeneity, residential instability, and broken homes (Lilly et al., 2015; Williams & McShane, 2018). They found that juvenile delinquency rates were highest in the Zone in Transition, and that those rates tailed off dramatically as you moved away from the centre of the city: They were lower in the Zone of Workingmen's Homes, lower still in the Residential Zone, and lowest in the Commuters Zone. Shaw and McKay also observed that social disorganization led to a breakdown in informal social controls—the type of controls exercised over children and teens by family members, adult neighbours, school teachers, religious leaders, and community organizations (Kornhauser, 1978). This breakdown in informal social controls contributed to the formation of juvenile gangs or criminal subcultures, the development of criminal values, and the transmission of those criminal values from gang member to gang member and from one generation to the next (Bernard, Snipes, & Gerould, 2010; Cullen, Wright, & Blevins, 2004). Shaw and McKay's observations can be regarded as a prelude to cultural transmission theory, subcultural theory, and social control theory (Cartwright, 2011).

Sampson and Groves's Replication of Shaw and McKay's Study

In 1989, Robert Sampson and W. Byron Groves completed their replication of Shaw and McKay's earlier study of social disorganization and delinquency. However, Sampson and Groves (1989) conducted their replication study in England and Wales rather than Chicago. Avoiding some of the problems associated with using official crime statistics (for example, policing activities tend to be concentrated in poorer, socially disorganized areas), Sampson and Groves used the results from the British Crime Survey, in which community members were asked to report their own victimization experiences. Moreover, data from the British Crime Survey—gathered at the community level rather than from aggregated census data—permitted them to drill down and examine what was happening within a particular community (or neighbourhood). Sampson and Groves also added three new intervening variables to their model—"sparse local friendship networks," "unsupervised teenage peer groups," and "low organizational participation" (see Figure 9.2)—which they said mediated between the five characteristics of social disorganization described by Shaw and McKay (residential density, poverty, ethnic and cultural heterogeneity, residential mobility, and family disruption) and the end product of "crime and delinquency" (Sampson & Groves, 1989).

FIGURE 9.2   Community Structure and Crime

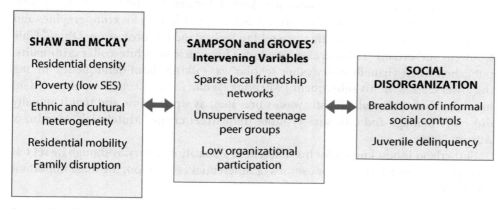

Source: Adapted from Sampson and Groves (1989, p. 783).

The Sampson and Groves study provides solid support for Shaw and McKay's earlier findings on social disorganization in Chicago. The results are compelling, given that the Sampson and Groves study was conducted in an entirely different country located on the other side of the Atlantic Ocean, using an entirely different data set, some 50 years after the Shaw and McKay study. Sampson and Groves found that one or more of the five main characteristics of socially disorganized areas identified by Shaw and McKay—in combination with one or more of the three intervening variables introduced by Sampson and Groves—predicted 61 percent of muggings and street robberies, 61 percent of burglaries, 42 percent of vandalism, and 42 percent of overall victimization (Sampson & Groves, 1989). The findings of the Sampson and Groves study were reconfirmed in a subsequent study by Christopher Lowenkamp, Francis Cullen, and Travis Pratt (2003) using more recent data from the British Crime Survey. The study by Lowenkamp and colleagues "revealed a high level of support for social disorganization theory" (p. 377).

The studies by Shaw and McKay, Sampson and Groves, and Lowenkamp, Cullen, and Pratt involved urbanized areas because social disorganization is generally considered to be a byproduct of urbanization and overcrowding. Nonetheless, Wayne Osgood and Jeff Chambers (2000)—using census data and official arrest rates, like earlier Chicago School researchers—found that one or more of the social disorganization variables of residential instability, ethnic heterogeneity, and broken homes (family disruption) had a strong effect on juvenile arrest rates for robbery, rape, and aggravated assault in rural counties in the United States. Clearly, social disorganization theory is a well-travelled, well-established sociological explanation of crime and delinquency.

Sutherland's Differential Association Theory

Edwin Sutherland has been described as "the most important criminologist of the 20th century" (Akers & Sellers, 2013, p. 85) and the individual most responsible for making sociology "the centerpiece ... of American criminology" (Akers & Matsueda, 1989, p. 24). Sutherland did his PhD at the University of Chicago and was a research professor there from 1929 until 1935 (Cullen & Messner, 2011). Apart from his **differential association theory**, he is known for his 1937 book, *The Professional Thief*, which—consistent with the Chicago School predilection for ethnographies and life histories—recounted the life story told to Sutherland by "professional thief" Chic Conwell. Sutherland (1940) is also known for his article on white-collar criminality, published when virtually every other scholar was talking about delinquency among the lower classes. In his subsequent 1949 book, *White Collar Crime*, he elaborated on his claim that white-collar crime was as prevalent as street crime and that it actually did more damage and cost society more than street crime (Mutchnick, Martin, & Austin, 2009).

Sutherland is best known for his differential association theory. Although he set out nine separate principles or propositions of differential association, the most important are as follows:

- "Criminal behaviour is learned."
- Criminal behaviour is "learned in a process of interaction with other persons" through communication (including words and gestures).
- Learning criminal behaviour "includes techniques of committing the crime" plus the "motives, drives, rationalizations and attitudes" that go along with being a criminal (Sutherland, 1947/1994, pp. 225–227).

In essence, Sutherland asserted that criminal behaviour is not the result of genetic defects, criminal psychopathy, or feeble-mindedness. Instead, he argued that people learn criminal behaviour, just like they learn other types of human behaviour, such as how to tie their shoes, or how to read and write (Lilly et al., 2015). Here, Sutherland was drawing upon the Chicago School concept of **symbolic interactionism**—the notion that meaning and reality are socially constructed through gestures used to show emotion or demonstrate how to do something, through symbols such as monetary instruments or university degrees, or through words, which are themselves socially created symbols that convey socially agreed-upon meanings (Bernard, Snipes, & Gerould, 2010). According to Sutherland (1947/1994), individuals will learn criminal behaviour to a different degree, depending on the frequency, duration, and intensity of their exposure to delinquent peers and delinquent values (Lilly et al., 2015).

differential association theory
Sutherland's theory that criminal behaviour is learned through the process of social interaction, and that the process includes the learning of criminal skills, motivations, attitudes, and rationalizations.

symbolic interactionism
The Chicago School notion that meaning and reality are socially constructed through the use or sharing of gestures, symbols, or words, which are themselves socially created symbols that convey socially agreed-upon meanings.

Sykes and Matza's Techniques of Neutralization

In 1957, Gresham Sykes and David Matza expanded on Sutherland's statement that criminal behaviour is learned, asserting that this learning includes the rationalizations, motivations, and attitudes that go along with being a criminal. According to Sykes and Matza (1957), criminals actually know that committing crime is wrong and experience feelings of guilt as a consequence. Thus, Sykes and Matza set out to enumerate the various rationalizations that criminals learn and use to neutralize their guilt and/or justify their criminal behaviour. They identified five techniques of **neutralization**:

1. denial of responsibility ("I didn't do it");
2. denial of injury ("Nobody was hurt");
3. denial of the victim ("He had it coming to him");
4. condemnation of the condemners ("The police and the politicians commit crimes themselves"); and
5. appeal to higher loyalties ("I did it to protect my gang's reputation") (Sykes & Matza, 1957).

Various research studies have provided support for Sykes and Matza's techniques of neutralization. For example, a study of 114 convicted rapists found that rapists excused or justified their behaviour by saying that their female victims were "seductresses," that "nice girls don't get raped," that the victims actually meant "yes" when they said "no," and that they (the rapists) were actually "nice guys" whose poor choice of behaviour was attributable to emotional problems or being under the influence of alcohol at the time of the offence (Scully & Marolla, 2003). Another study involving an online survey of 420 university students demonstrated that a number of students excused or justified academic dishonesty by saying that the teaching was of a poor quality, the class (or the test) was too difficult, they had no choice unless they wanted to fail the course, or they only cheated to help out a close friend or family member (Brent & Atkisson, 2011). A more recent study of online "booter" services (websites that sell access to illegal denial-of-service attacks) provided support for the tenets of differential association theory, in that the operators of these services learned about this opportunity through friends or other people who were already in the business. They acquired the necessary knowledge and skills from those who sold them the product in the first place, or from online support communities where skills and favourable definitions were shared. The study also demonstrated that operators of these booter services employed techniques of neutralization, claiming to be offering these services for the purposes of network testing, in order to provide their loyal customers with a secure network (appeal to higher loyalties), and claiming that any harm caused by the denial-of-service attacks was the responsibility of those who purchased the services, and not the providers of those services (denial of responsibility) (Hutchings & Clayton, 2016).

Burgess and Akers's Differential Association-Reinforcement Theory

Robert Burgess and Ronald Akers's (1966) differential association-reinforcement theory is another elaboration on Sutherland's differential association theory. Starting from Sutherland's contention that criminal behaviour is learned in the same manner that non-criminal behaviour is learned, Burgess and Akers set out to specify the

neutralization
An extension of Sutherland's differential association theory; the notion that criminals learn motivations and rationalizations to justify their criminal behaviour.

mechanisms that were involved in the learning process. To this end, they added elements of B.F. Skinner's behaviour modification (operant conditioning) plus Albert Bandura's observations on imitation and modelling behaviour. Rather than simply say, as Sutherland had, that "criminal behaviour is learned … in a process of interaction with other persons," Burgess and Akers stated that criminal behaviour is learned in accordance with the principles of operant conditioning (i.e., through reinforcement and punishment) and that it can also be learned in non-social situations (consistent with imitation and modelling). As behaviour modification and imitation and modelling behaviour both emerged from the field of psychology, it can be said that Burgess and Akers's differential association-reinforcement theory is a form of social psychology. Akers subsequently took ownership of differential association-reinforcement theory, which he went on to describe as "social learning theory" (Akers, 2011; Akers & Sellers, 2013). Social learning theory is a major theoretical perspective in its own right, and will be dealt with in greater detail, later in this chapter.

The Sociology of Deviance and Labelling Theory

Kai Erikson and Howard Becker are widely recognized as two of the most prominent thinkers in the sociology of deviance and labelling theory (Matsueda, 2001; Plummer, 1979). Erikson did his PhD in sociology at the University of Chicago, where he was influenced by a number of Chicago School symbolic interactionists, including George Mead, Charles Cooley, and Erving Goffman (cf. Erikson, 1962; Erikson, 1964). Becker did his PhD in sociology at the University of Chicago, and even taught at the famed Chicago School for several years (Mutchnick, Martin, & Austin, 2009; Snyder, 2010).

The sociology of deviance takes the position that deviance is "relative"—what is considered "normal" behaviour by some societies may be considered "abnormal" or even "criminal" behaviour by other societies (Clinard & Meier, 2004; Curra, 2011). To illustrate, polygamy is illegal in Canada, but legal in some countries. By contrast, adultery is legal (although frowned upon) in Canada, yet it is punishable by death in certain societies or cultures. A number of American states have now legalized marijuana, whereas other American states have not. To express it differently, deviance is "in the eye of the beholder" and thus is socially constructed. Those who are deemed by society to be deviant are often stigmatized or labelled as such and treated as social outcasts (Becker, 1963; Erikson, 1964; Erikson, 2005). Once an individual is labelled as deviant or criminal, that label becomes his or her new social identity (or master status), which then becomes a self-fulfilling prophecy (Lilly et al., 2015; Pfohl, 1985; Williams & McShane, 2018).

Erikson's Sociology of Deviance

sociology of deviance
Blends Chicago School symbolic interactionism with views on how crime and deviance are used to maintain social boundaries and/ or social control; it examines how certain groups or behaviours come to be viewed as "social problems."

At the beginning of this chapter, we explored Durkheim's work on "The Normal and the Pathological." Durkheim (1964) argued that even a "society of saints" would seek out some unusual behaviour within the community and declare it to be deviant to establish the moral boundaries of the community. Erikson's **sociology of deviance** is a blend of Chicago School symbolic interactionism and Durkheimian thinking about how crime and deviance function to maintain social cohesion. In *Wayward Puritans: A Study in the Sociology of Deviance*, Erikson described how the Puritans—a group of Christians who migrated to Massachusetts in the 1600s in search of religious freedom—suddenly discovered heretics and witches in the midst of their "society of saints" (Erikson, 2005). These "deviant" members of the religious community were banished, and in some cases (the Salem witch trials), they were even hung. According to Erikson, this persecution of imaginary witches was evidence of the need that all societies have for a certain amount of deviance, to draw a "symbolic set of parentheses" around what is believed to be *socially* acceptable behaviour (Erikson, 1962; Erikson, 2005).

Erikson also talked about the stigmatization (labelling) that takes place at "status degradation ceremonies" such as trials, insanity hearings, and courts martial, which are generally dramatic and staged to maximize public visibility. A stigma (or label) is affixed at the end of the ceremony (for example, guilty, mentally ill, etc.), and, once affixed, becomes difficult to remove, because there are no status restoration ceremonies. If individuals are stigmatized permanently, they may develop a deviant self-image, come to believe that they're no longer a part of the so-called normal community and thus feel compelled to continue with the disapproved behaviour.

Becker's Labelling Theory

Although Howard Becker never described himself as a labelling theorist, his name is most commonly associated with **labelling theory** (Deutschmann, 2002; Matsueda, 2001). Becker talked about how certain groups or behaviours come to be viewed as "social problems" not because they are necessarily deviant or criminal but because of the social reaction to these groups or behaviours (Matsueda, 2001; Mutchnick, Martin, & Austin, 2009). If these groups or behaviours were simply ignored by society, then they would not come to be regarded as deviant or criminal. According to Becker (1963), social groups actually create deviance by making up rules that turn other individuals—or entire groups—into outlaws or outsiders.

Becker also described the role of "moral entrepreneurs" or "moral crusaders" in rule making. Moral entrepreneurs generally come from the upper classes, have money and power, and feel that it is their duty to stomp out evil and impose their own moral standards on minority groups and/or the lower classes (Becker, 1963). Once their mission is accomplished (for example, a new law is implemented prohibiting public servants from wearing visible religious symbols at work), they move on to find other causes that seem worthy of their attention. The rule enforcers (the police, corrections officials, etc.) need to demonstrate that their enforcement activities are successful, yet at the same time, have to maintain the public perception that more work still needs to be done (Becker, 1963). Otherwise, they could soon find themselves out of a job.

It has been argued in some quarters that labelling theory is difficult to test, and that there is little evidence to support the notion that labelling (social reaction) actually contributes to further criminal involvement (Gove, 1980; Tittle, 1980). However, a large 1992 study found that, as predicted by labelling theory, parental appraisals did have a significant effect on the self-appraisals of "rule violators," and that those parental appraisals were in fact influenced by the prior behaviour of their offspring (Matsueda, 1992). A 2003 study found that being convicted and sentenced to imprisonment (extreme labelling) did indeed reduce occupational status, employment stability, and income (Davies & Tanner, 2003). Therefore, it can be said that labelling theory has enjoyed a reasonable amount of empirical support.

labelling theory
The theory that the stigma (or label) affixed through the criminalization process may lead individuals to develop a deviant self-image and feel separate from the "normal" community, and thus continue with deviant behaviour.

Social Problems, Moral Panics, and Critical Constructionism

moral panics

Phenomena—socially constructed by the media, politicians, and "moral entrepreneurs"—in which certain people or groups are labelled or stigmatized as the cause of a perceived social problem, resulting in widespread public alarm.

The sociology of deviance and the labelling perspective gave rise to critical constructionism, a field that examines how social problems and **moral panics** are socially constructed by the media, politicians, and special interest groups (Burns & Crawford, 1999; Cohen, 1987). Work in this area continues to this day, as evidenced by Timothy Brezina and Herbert Phipps's (2010) study on false news reports and the role of public officials in stirring up moral panic in the aftermath of Hurricane Katrina. Police and public officials—unprepared for the disaster and unable to organize rescue efforts—started blaming the powerless, low-status hurricane refugees, who (with vilification by the media) came to be viewed as the very personification of evil.

Critical criminology was in large part an outgrowth of the sociology of deviance, labelling theory, and critical constructionism. Critical criminologists subsequently criticized labelling theorists for what was seen as their "inadequate" analysis of the socio-economic inequalities of capitalism and the role of the rich and powerful in defining crime in their own interests (Taylor, Walton, & Young, 1973). That said, labelling theorists laid the groundwork for critical criminology by starting to examine the process through which certain individuals or groups came to be defined as deviant or criminal, and by asking who makes the rules and why. William Chambliss and Richard Quinney—two sociologists who eventually went on to become "critical criminologists"—began their careers as critical constructionists (or conflict theorists), talking about how laws and social reality were socially constructed (Lilly et al., 2015; Williams & McShane, 2018). Jock Young, co-author of *The New Criminology* (Taylor, Walton, & Young, 1973) and co-editor of *Critical Criminology* (Taylor, Walton, & Young, 1975) was also co-editor of *The Manufacture of News: Social Problems, Deviance and the Mass Media* (Cohen & Young, 1973), which focused on the role of the media in manufacturing deviance and social problems.

For further information on conflict and critical criminology, see Chapter 11.

Anomie-Strain Theory

anomie-strain theory

Merton's theory describing the state of anomie in American society caused by the disjunction (or dysfunction or strain) between the cultural goals of the "American dream" and the institutional means to achieve those goals.

Durkheim's work on anomie underpins Merton's **anomie-strain theory**, Agnew's general strain theory, and Messner and Rosenfeld's institutional-anomie theory. Recall that Durkheim described *anomie* as a state of lawlessness, normlessness, or unrestrained ambition, which if left unchecked could lead to a breakdown in social solidarity (Clinard, 1964; Durkheim, 1965). Durkheim said that a state of anomie would arise when the "forces of integration" (social bonds and collective beliefs) and the "forces of regulation" (laws and social institutions) were out of balance, and therefore not functioning properly (Lilly et al., 2015). While Durkheim discussed the function of crime and punishment in maintaining social solidarity, he did not specifically link anomie to crime. This task was left to American sociologist Robert Merton.

Merton's Anomie-Strain Theory

Robert Merton's 1938 article "Social Structure and Anomie" is one of the most widely cited works in the social sciences. In his article, Merton employed Durkheim's notion of anomie to explain high crime rates in American society. Using a functionalist approach, Merton argued that a dysfunction (a disjunction or imbalance) existed between the cultural goals of American society (for example, accumulation of wealth and social advancement) and access to the institutional means through which to achieve those cultural goals (for example, education and good employment opportunities). This dysfunction created a sense of strain or anomie—Americans believed that they were supposed to pursue the cultural goals but felt that their opportunity to do so was blocked (Bernard, 1995). In other words, social institutions—education, the economy, and the government—were unable to adequately integrate and regulate the cultural goals and the institutional means (Agnew, 1997).

TABLE 9.1   Robert Merton's Five Modes of Adaptation

Mode of adaptation	Cultural goals	Institutional means	Criminal?
Conformity	+ (Accepts)	+ (Accepts)	No
Innovation	+ (Accepts)	− (Rejects)	Yes
Ritualism	− (Rejects)	+ (Accepts)	No
Retreatism	− (Rejects)	− (Rejects)	Yes
Rebellion	± (Rejects—tries to replace)	± (Rejects—tries to replace)	Yes

Source: Adapted from Merton (1938, p. 676).

Merton (1938) observed that individuals in society dealt with this sense of anomie or strain through five possible modes of adaptation: conformity, innovation, ritualism, retreatism, and rebellion. The mode of adaptation would depend on whether individuals accepted or rejected the cultural goals of American (capitalist) society and the institutional means through which to achieve those goals (see Table 9.1, above). If individuals accepted the cultural goals and also accepted the institutional (legitimate) means through which to achieve those goals, as indicated by a "+" sign in Table 9.1, then they would be more likely to adapt through conformity. If individuals accepted the cultural goals (for example, accumulation of wealth and social advancement) but rejected the means, as indicated by a "−" sign in Table 9.1 (i.e., they did not feel that they had access to a good education or good job), then they would be more likely to adapt through innovation. Innovation refers to finding different or novel ways to attain the cultural goals of society, such as theft or fraud. Retreatists, who rejected the cultural goals and the institutionalized means through which to achieve them, might drop out of society and become alcoholics, drug addicts, or street people. Those who chose the rebellion mode would reject the cultural goals and institutionalized means of society, attempt to overthrow society, and try to replace the existing goals and means with new ones. While the behaviour of retreatists and rebels might be deviant, and even criminal, Merton argued that the innovators were most likely to typify criminals that came to the attention of the criminal justice system (Williams & McShane, 2018).

Subcultural Theories

Many of the subcultural theories that emerged in the 1950s and 1960s were premised upon a combination of Merton's anomie-strain theory and Sutherland's differential association theory. These theories were also grounded in **cultural transmission theory**,

cultural transmission theory
The Chicago School notion that criminal subcultures develop their own subcultural (criminal) values or norms, which are then transmitted from gang member to gang member and from generation to generation.

the Chicago School notion that criminal subcultures (usually found in socially disorganized areas) develop their own subcultural (criminal) values, which are transmitted from member to member within these subcultures (Williams & McShane, 2018).

The Culture of the Gang

In *Delinquent Boys: The Culture of the Gang*, Albert Cohen (1955/1964) set out to explain how delinquent subcultures formed, how they developed their new subcultural values, and how these values were transmitted within the subculture. Cohen stated that lower-class males had similar aspirations to middle- and upper-class males, but that they were unable to compete successfully for social status in the school environment. Therefore, lower-class males developed what Cohen (1955/1964) referred to as a sense of "status deprivation," which could be compared to a type of anomie-strain (Mutchnick, Martin, & Austin, 2009). They dropped out of school (a "reaction formation") and formed delinquent gangs (a "collective solution"), wherein they created a new set of "normative" values and proceeded to redefine the meaning of social status in terms of those new values. Members could achieve status within the gang by demonstrating their "toughness" or their willingness to violate conventional norms by committing acts of vandalism or theft (Cohen, 1955/1964). Thus, they rejected the unattainable goals of typical middle-class teens (for example, being popular, dressing fashionably, excelling at school) and replaced them with unconventional goals that they could attain.

Illegitimate Opportunity Structures

Richard Cloward and Lloyd Ohlin's (1960) *Delinquency and Opportunity* built on Merton's notion that lower-class individuals lacked access to legitimate opportunity structures (for example, a good education or a high-paying, high-prestige job). Drawing on life histories written by members of the Chicago School (such as Sutherland's *The Professional Thief*), Cloward and Ohlin elaborated on the notion that criminal skills were learned through cultural transmission (Lilly et al., 2015). Cloward and Ohlin also identified three types of illegitimate opportunity structures—the criminal subculture, the conflict subculture, and the retreatist subculture—through which lower-class youth could cope with their sense of strain, or "status frustration." However, they said that access to these subcultures would be differentially available, depending on where the individual lived and the degree of social organization (or disorganization) in that particular neighbourhood (Williams & McShane, 2018).

According to Cloward and Ohlin, criminal subcultures existed primarily in organized slums, where they already had networks of "professional" criminals who could take prospective gang members under their wing and teach them the tricks of the trade. Conflict subcultures existed in socially disorganized slums, where there was little organized criminal activity and, therefore, limited opportunity to learn criminal skills. Instead, conflict subcultures in disorganized slums emphasized toughness and a willingness to engage in physical violence (Cloward & Ohlin, 1960). Retreatist subcultures existed in both organized and disorganized slums but focused primarily on the buying and selling of illegal drugs, which individuals used to escape (or retreat) from status frustration, or anomie-strain (Williams & McShane, 2018).

Agnew's General Strain Theory

Earlier versions of anomie theory were criticized for placing too much emphasis on the strains supposedly experienced by the lower classes (Agnew, 1995). Critics said that anomie-strain theory failed to explain crime committed by the upper classes (for example, white-collar and corporate crime) and delinquent acts committed by teens from relatively affluent family backgrounds (Winfree & Abadinsky, 2010). Thus, Robert Agnew (1985) introduced **general strain theory**, which was intended to rectify some of the oversights of original anomie-strain theory.

Agnew (1985, 1992) stated that teens do not have the same concerns as adults: Teens are not worried about accumulation of wealth or social advancement, or even about getting a good job or a good education. Rather, teens have more immediate concerns or sources of strain, such as physical appearance, being popular (or unpopular) with peers, parental discipline, doing poorly at school, and pressure from peers to join gangs and participate in delinquent behaviour. Unlike adults, however, teens cannot escape their stressful circumstances by moving to a new neighbourhood or a different town, changing jobs, or quitting or changing schools because they are financially dependent and still subject to parental (and school) control (Hoffman, 2010). Agnew described the sources of strain experienced by teens as "the presentation of negative stimuli" (for example, parental punishment) and "the removal of positively valued stimuli" (for example, being kicked off the high school football team), arguing that these strains or stressors could lead to frustration, anger, and, in some cases, juvenile delinquency.

Agnew's general strain theory represents a combination of sociological theory (for example, Durkheim's anomie theory and Merton's anomie-strain theory) and psychological theory (for example, differences in personality, the frustration–aggression hypothesis, cognitive and behavioural coping mechanisms) (Agnew, 1995; Inderbitzen, Bates, & Gainey, 2013) and, as such, it is part of a newer trend toward theoretical integration. General strain theory has been highly researched and is one of the more well-supported theories in criminology (Cullen, Wright, & Blevins, 2004; Hoffman, 2010).

Messner and Rosenfeld's Institutional-Anomie Theory

In *Crime and the American Dream*, Steven Messner and Richard Rosenfeld (1994/2007) revisited Durkheim's forces of integration and regulation and Merton's anomie-strain theory, arguing that most criminological theories are overly focused on micro-level inquiry (the individual level), rather than on macro-level inquiry (the level of social structure or social organization) (Rosenfeld & Messner, 1995). Deploying Merton's 1938 notion about the relationship between social structure and anomie, Messner and Rosenfeld pointed to the cultural goals of capitalist society and the failure of social institutions—the political system, education, the family, and the economy—to properly integrate and regulate the pursuit of those goals (Messner & Rosenfeld, 1994/2007). If the social institutions were functioning properly, then the political system, educational system, and the family would act as restraints on the unfettered demands of the economy and on the unrestrained behaviour of individuals who were in hot pursuit of financial rewards. Essentially, they noted the existence of an institutional imbalance (institutional anomie) in which the economy dominates the political system,

general strain theory
Explains delinquent acts by teens from relatively affluent families; teens have more immediate strains than adults, such as physical appearance, popularity, parental discipline, academic performance, and peer pressure to join gangs and participate in delinquent behaviour.

the educational system, and the family, leading to an amoral "end justifies the means" attitude in society (Merton, 1938; Messner & Rosenfeld, 1994/2007).

We are surrounded by evidence of the explanatory power of **institutional-anomie theory**. We need look no further than the economic meltdown of 2007 and 2008, when the selling of "subprime mortgages" brought financial institutions, homeowners, and entire economies around the world to the brink of disaster. The public sector failed to provide adequate regulation and oversight, permitting financial institutions to issue mortgages to countless high-risk borrowers, and to borrow recklessly to back up those mortgages (Immergluck, 2011; Thompson, 2012). Rather than punishing bankers who had recklessly lent out vast amounts of money, secured by basically worthless "derivatives," governments around the world stepped in and bailed them out, using trillions of dollars of taxpayers' money. This is a clear-cut example of how the economy has come to dominate other social institutions, and how an "end justifies the means" attitude has come to permeate society.

Social Learning Theory

Social learning theory has its roots in the Chicago School's symbolic interactionism and Sutherland's differential association theory (Akers & Sellers, 2013). Starting with Sutherland's contention that criminal behaviour is learned, Burgess and Akers used their differential association-reinforcement theory to specify the mechanisms involved in the learning process, adding elements of B.F. Skinner's operant conditioning and Albert Bandura's observations on imitation and modelling behaviour (Burgess & Akers, 1966). Akers (1998) has continued to refine his earlier statements regarding social learning theory, clarifying the main concepts and propositions.

Similar to Sutherland's differential association theory, social learning theory posits that individuals learn definitions that are favourable or unfavourable to committing crime. According to Akers and Sellers (2013), individuals learn both positive and neutralizing definitions. Positive definitions might include the attitude held by certain subcultures that carrying a weapon and being prepared to use it are socially acceptable behaviours (cf. Wolfgang & Ferracuti, 1967). Neutralizing definitions—as described originally in Sykes and Matza's (1957) techniques of neutralization—include rationalizations or justifications for engaging in criminal behaviour (for example, being drunk at the time or being the victim of a poor upbringing). These definitions are learned through a process of differential reinforcement. Individuals are more or less likely to engage in criminal behaviour depending on whether their behaviour has previously been reinforced (rewarded) or punished, and the consequences they anticipate if they continue (Akers, 1998). Social rewards are largely symbolic and range from acquiring money or material goods to gaining social acceptance or prestige.

Akers's social learning theory is one of the most well established and well researched of all criminological theories (Cullen, Wright, & Blevins, 2004). A meta-analysis of studies conducted specifically on correctional treatment programs found that programs based on the principles of social learning theory had the greatest impact when it came to reducing recidivism (i.e., reducing the likelihood of offenders committing new crimes following their release from prison) (Cullen, Wright, Gendreau, & Andrews, 2003). A more recent meta-analysis indicated that stronger empirical support exists

institutional-anomie theory
Messner and Rosenfeld's theory that institutional anomie (institutional imbalance) is caused by the cultural goals of capitalist society and the failure of social institutions to properly integrate and regulate the pursuit of those goals.

social learning theory
Definitions (values about acceptable and unacceptable behaviour) favourable to criminal behaviour are learned through differential reinforcement; criminal behaviour depends on reward or punishment for past behaviour and anticipated consequences of persistence.

for social learning theory than for rational choice or deterrence theories (Pratt et al., 2010).

Social Control Theory

As is the case with many of the other sociological theories discussed in this chapter, the roots of **social control theory** can be traced back to Durkheim and to his view that individuals would behave immorally if left to their own devices. Durkheim stressed the role of social bonds and collective beliefs (forces of integration) and the law and social institutions (forces of regulation) in restraining individual wants and aspirations (Durkheim, 1951, 1964; Paternoster & Bachman, 2001).

The origins of social control theory can also be traced back to the Chicago School's notion that social disorganization contributes to the breakdown of informal social controls usually exercised by parents, adult neighbours, school teachers, and community leaders (Cullen, Wright, & Blevins, 2004; Sampson & Groves, 1989). Some of the earliest forays into social control theory were led by Chicago School theorists, such as Albert Reiss, who wrote in 1951 about "delinquency as a failure of personal and social controls," and Walter Reckless, whose 1967 containment theory included inner containments (a good self-concept, ability to tolerate frustration) and outer containments (institutional reinforcement, good family values) as sources of social control (Lilly et al., 2015; Williams & McShane, 2018).

Hirschi's Social Bond Theory

Travis Hirschi's 1969 **social bond theory** is the most well known of all the earlier social control theories (Winfree & Abadinsky, 2010). Social bond theory was rooted in Durkheimian notions about social bonds and collective beliefs, and Hirschi openly acknowledged as much. He also acknowledged the influence of Chicago School theorists Reiss and Reckless. Essentially, Hirschi's social bond theory can be broken down into four main elements or components:

1. attachment (to parents, school teachers, and significant others);
2. commitment (to doing well at school, keeping a good reputation);
3. involvement (in organized sports, doing homework); and
4. belief (in the law, in conventional norms and values) (Hirschi, 1969).

Hirschi argued that if the four components of the social bond were working as they should, then an individual would be disinclined to engage in criminal or deviant behaviour. Hirschi's social bond theory underpins a number of more recent social control theories, including Thornberry's interactional theory and Sampson and Laub's life-course-developmental theory.

In 1990, Gottfredson and Hirschi went on to co-author *A General Theory of Crime*. According to their general theory, all crime is caused by low self-control, which is itself caused by poor parenting, usually provided—or not provided, as the case may be—by parents who are themselves lacking in self-control (Gottfredson & Hirschi, 1990). Some observers have argued that the general theory of crime is a sociological (social process) theory, in that it talks about the socialization process, and what happens within the social institution of the family (Beaver, Ratchford, & Ferguson, 2010; Walsh, 2012). Others

See Chapter 12, Crime Choice Theory.

social control theory
Rooted in Durkheim's forces of integration, the Chicago School's concern with the breakdown in informal social controls holds that social bonds and informal social controls act as restraints on teen delinquency.

social bond theory
Social control theory by Hirschi (based on Durkheim's concept of the social bond); the four elements of the social bond include attachment, commitment, involvement, and belief.

have observed that Gottfredson and Hirschi's theory more closely resembles a bio-psychological (neo-Freudian) theory, in that it focuses on a number of characteristics—personality traits, temperament, impulsivity—that are thought to be inherited or, if not, then at least inculcated in very early childhood (Andrews & Bonta, 2010; Pratt & Cullen, 2000).

Gottfredson and Hirschi argued in their general theory of crime that low self-control offered a better explanation of criminality than social learning. However, a recent study of digital piracy found that individuals needed to associate with like-minded peers in order to learn how to engage in computer hacking and software piracy and acquire the values and attitudes supportive of such behaviours (Burruss, Bossler, & Holt, 2013). While low self-control might explain simple acts (like downloading and sharing illegally obtained software after being shown how to do so), the actual acts of hacking, cracking, and posting of such software on the Internet require a more sophisticated set of skills that could only be acquired by those with higher self-control. When the researchers included components of both theories in the same model, they found that the social learning components had a large and direct effect, whereas the low self-control components had a small, negative effect, suggesting that those with low self-control were actually less likely to engage in software piracy (Burruss et al., 2013).

Thornberry's Interactional Theory

interactional theory
Thornberry's theory that both social bond theory and social learning theory are needed to explain criminal behaviour, because weakening of the social bond and the social learning of criminal values is interactional or reciprocal (not unidirectional).

Terrence Thornberry's **interactional theory** is another type of social control theory, which combines elements of Hirschi's social bond theory with elements of Akers's social learning theory (Thornberry, 1987; Thornberry & Krohn, 2005). Thornberry observes that social bond theory and social learning theory are both unidirectional. Social bond theory assumes that if social bonds are weakened, individuals will be less constrained, and therefore more likely to engage in crime. Social learning theory assumes that if individuals learn definitions that are favourable to committing crime and have their deviant or criminal behaviour reinforced, then that may encourage involvement in crime (Cartwright, 2011). Thornberry argues that the interaction between social bonds and social learning is actually a two-way street, which can go in either direction, or even go back and forth (Akers & Sellers, 2013; Lilly et al., 2015). According to Thornberry, weakened social bonds can lead to exposure to delinquent peers and to the learning of delinquent values; at the same time, exposure to delinquent peers and the learning of delinquent values can lead to further weakening of social bonds. Therefore, he says that we need both theories in order to provide an adequate explanation of crime and delinquency.

Thornberry also points out in his interactional theory that social bonds change over the life course. Preschool children are primarily attached to their parents and close family members. Elementary school children are still attached to their parents and family members but may develop bonds with teachers and friends. Teenagers are more likely to be concerned with impressing their teen peers than they are about pleasing their parents or their schoolteachers. Adults develop social bonds with their spouses, employers, and fellow employees, and may forget entirely about any bonds they had with schoolteachers and teen peers (Thornberry, 1987; Thornberry & Krohn, 2005). In many respects, Thornberry's interactional theory is similar to Sampson and Laub's life-course-developmental theory.

Sampson and Laub's Life-Course-Developmental Theory

Robert Sampson and John Laub's **life-course-developmental theory** is a more recent extension of Hirschi's social bond theory. However, Sampson and Laub redefine the attachment and commitment elements of the social bond as "social capital," which they say is acquired as individuals reach adulthood and start to gain a stake in society by obtaining a high school or college diploma, finding a good job, getting married, and having children (Laub & Sampson, 1993; Laub, Sampson, & Allen, 2001; Sampson & Laub, 1992). While some individuals might appear to be on an inevitable "trajectory" (or pathway) toward a criminal career, they can still be deflected from this trajectory when they come to "turning points" through which they might transition out of and actually desist from committing crime (Laub, Nagin, & Sampson, 1998; Laub & Sampson, 1993). Indeed, they argue that desistance is by far the most common outcome of juvenile delinquency. Once individuals acquire social capital, or a stake in society, they are not willing to risk it because of the potential attachment and commitment costs (for example, loss of a job, loss of a spouse, loss of reputation). Considerable evidence supports Sampson and Laub's contention that the quality and quantity of social bonds vary over the life course, and that the propensity to engage in criminal activity varies over time, with most individuals aging out of crime when they reach adulthood (Akers & Sellers, 2013; Farrington et al., 2006; Lilly et al., 2015).

> **life-course-developmental theory**
> Sampson and Laub's theory that individuals can be deflected from the trajectory toward a criminal career by life events ("turning points") that can lead them to transition out of criminal behaviour.

Conclusion

This has been a brief tour of sociological approaches to crime and deviance. Out of necessity, a number of sociological theories or perspectives have been left out, including (but by no means limited to):

- Thorsten Sellin's (1938/1994) work on conflict theory and cultural conflict;
- Marvin Wolfgang and Franco Ferracuti's (1967) "subcultures of violence," premised on Sutherland's differential association theory and the notion that individuals in these subcultures learn norms that are favourable to carrying weapons and using them when provoked;
- Stanley Cohen's (1987) renowned work on folk devils and moral panics, which underpins many present-day endeavours in the field of critical constructionism;
- John Hagan's 1985 power-control theory, which seeks to explain why males commit more crimes than females, by examining the structure of the "patriarchal" family in capitalist society (Hagan, Gillis, & Simpson, 1985);
- James Messerschmidt's (1993, 2005) "sociology of masculinity," which examines how males construct masculinity differently, depending on their race and position in the class structure; and
- David Garland's (2001) sociological analysis of why control theories and rational choice theories have gained traction over the past 30 years, due to observable economic, social, and political changes.

Apart from comprising the lion's share of criminological theories, sociological approaches have been the driving force behind many past and present public policies aimed at reducing crime. Most public policies attempt to tackle criminogenic (crime-causing) social conditions, such as poverty, unemployment, lack of education, poor parenting, and poor housing (or homelessness) (Lilly et al., 2015). Urban renewal projects (including that of the Whalley-Newton community profiled in Box 9.1), social support centres, and parent-training programs aimed at improving social bonding with children are all examples of such initiatives (Agnew, 2010). In the Canadian criminal justice system, judges may impose a more lenient sentence on an offender who comes from a "disadvantaged background" (Schmalleger, MacAlister, & McKenna, 2004). Parole certificates may include a non-association condition, aimed at preventing a released offender from hanging out with and being influenced by delinquent peers. All of these actions come back to the Chicago School notion that "the nature of the neighbourhood" rather than "the nature of the individual" is the cause of crime (Lilly et al., 2015).

BOX 9.1

Transforming a Community

The rundown and socially disorganized Whalley-Newton neighbourhood is currently in the process of being transformed by large new redevelopments, such as the one in the renamed "Surrey City Centre."

While the Chicago School concept of social disorganization is not specifically mentioned in the City of Surrey's mission statement, there may be no better example of an official attempt to address the problem of social disorganization than the city's recent initiatives to transform the socially disorganized Whalley-Newton area into a socially organized or socially cohesive community (City of Surrey, 2010, 2012). The Whalley-Newton area of British Columbia has one of the highest crime rates in Canada (Munro, 1998; Skelton, 2004; Zytaruk, 2009). It also exhibits many of the characteristics of social disorganization and social disorder that were identified by the Chicago School, such as residential mobility (transience), poverty, broken homes, ethnic and cultural heterogeneity, and cheap and rundown rental accommodations (with landlords unwilling to maintain the properties because they're expecting the buildings to be knocked down as the land is purchased at a high price for real estate development/urban renewal projects) (Munro, 1998; O'Brian, 2003). The city renamed

Whalley as "Surrey City Centre" (Lamb, 1992) and built a new civic centre, community plaza, recreational centre, centre for the performing arts, and regional library, as well as many new residential developments. In essence, the City of Surrey is attempting to tackle criminogenic (crime-causing) social conditions such as poverty, unemployment, rundown housing, and general urban decay (social disorganization) by totally reorganizing the social environment and creating a sense of social cohesion and social identity.

Surrey, old and new: A rundown section of the city is contrasted with recent redevelopments in the new city centre, seen in the distance.

SUMMARY OF KEY POINTS

- While there are many theoretical approaches to studying crime, sociological approaches continue to be the most widely accepted.

- Rather than focusing on the biological or psychological deficiencies of individuals, sociological explanations of criminal or deviant behaviour place emphasis on the effects of social structures and institutions, social organization and class, and roles, norms, and social learning.

- Émile Durkheim contributed to the consensus perspective (which contrasts with conflict theories rooted in Marx) and to the notion that society is essentially organic (structural functionalism). His work underpins Merton's anomie-strain theory, Agnew's general strain theory, and several others.

- Durkheim observed that crime had existed throughout history and was present in all types of societies. He concluded that a certain amount of crime must be *normal*, or at least that crime must serve some sort of social function. He proposed that crime defined the moral boundaries of the community.

- Members of the Chicago School rejected social Darwinist notions and challenged the notion that most criminals were either criminal psychopaths or feeble-minded. Rather, members of the Chicago School concluded that it was "the nature of the neighbourhood," not "the nature of the individual," that was the primary cause of criminality. The Chicago School brought us many well-known criminological theories, including social disorganization theory, the sociology of deviance, and labelling theory.

- Edwin Sutherland, one of the leading criminologists of the 20th century, is best known for examining white-collar crime and for his differential association theory, which states that criminal behaviour is learned through the process of social interaction.

- The sociology of deviance takes the position that deviance is relative—what is considered *normal* behaviour by some societies may be considered *abnormal* or *criminal* by other societies. Those deemed by society to be deviant are often stigmatized or labelled.

- Robert Merton used Durkheim's notion of anomie to explain high crime rates. His anomie-strain theory argued that the distance between the cultural goals of American society and the means for most to achieve those goals created strain or anomie.

- Critics said that anomie-strain theory failed to offer an explanation for crime committed by the upper classes (for example, white-collar and corporate crime) or affluent teens. Robert Agnew introduced his general strain theory, which was intended to rectify this.

- Social learning theory holds that definitions favourable to criminal behaviour are learned through differential reinforcement; criminal behaviour depends on reward or punishment for past behaviour and anticipated consequences of persistence. Burgess and Akers's differential association-reinforcement theory aimed to specify the mechanisms involved in the learning process, adding elements of B.F. Skinner's operant conditioning and Albert Bandura's observations on imitation and modelling behaviour.

- Social control theory is rooted in Durkheim's forces of integration and the Chicago School concern with the breakdown in informal social controls. It holds that social bonds and informal social controls act as restraints on teen delinquency.
- Hirschi's social bond theory was based in Durkheimian notions about social bonds and collective beliefs. It can be broken down into four main elements: attachment, commitment, involvement, and belief.
- Sampson and Laub's life-course-developmental theory is a more recent extension of Hirschi's social bond theory. Sampson and Laub redefine the attachment and commitment elements of the social bond as "social capital," acquired as individuals reach adulthood and complete their education, find a job, get married, and have children.

QUESTIONS FOR CRITICAL DISCUSSION

1. How do sociological explanations of crime and deviance differ from psychological and biological explanations?
2. Why have sociological explanations tended to dominate the discipline of criminology?
3. What are the major criminological theories that can be traced back to the 19th-century French sociologist Émile Durkheim?
4. What major contributions did the Chicago School make to the study of criminology?
5. What (recent) evidence exists to validate earlier Chicago School notions of the relationship between social disorganization and crime rates?
6. What is the relationship (connection) between differential association theory, techniques of neutralization, and social learning theory?
7. What are the main principles of differential association theory?
8. What is the "sociology of deviance," and how is it related to labelling theory, to moral entrepreneurship, and to the concept of moral panics?
9. What are the four main components of Travis Hirschi's social bond theory?
10. Why would Terrence Thornberry's interactional theory and Robert Sampson and John Laub's life-course-developmental theory be considered contemporary extensions of (or elaborations on) Travis Hirschi's social bond theory?

SUGGESTED FURTHER READINGS

Agnew, R. (1985). A revised strain theory of delinquency. *Social Forces, 64*(1), 151–167.

Brezina, T., & Phipps, H.E. (2010). False news reports, folk devils, and the role of public officials: Notes on the social construction of law and order in the aftermath of Hurricane Katrina. *Deviant Behavior, 31*(1), 97–134. http://doi.org/10.1080/01639620902854803

Burgess, R.L., & Akers, R.L. (1966). A differential association-reinforcement theory of criminal behavior. *Social Problems, 14*(2), 128–147.

Erikson, K.T. (1962). Notes on the sociology of deviance. *Social Problems, 9*(4), 307–314.

Laub, J.H., & Sampson, R.J. (1993). Turning points in the life course: Why change matters to the study of crime. *Criminology, 31*(3), 301–325.

Merton, R.K. (1938). Social structure and anomie. *American Sociological Review, 3*(5), 672–682.

Sampson, R.J., & Groves, W.B. (1989). Community structure and crime: Testing social-disorganization theory. *American Journal of Sociology, 94*(4), 774–802.

Sutherland, E.H. (1940). White-collar criminality. *American Sociological Review, 5*(1), 1–12.

Sykes, G.M., & Matza, D. (1957). Techniques of neutralization: A theory of delinquency. *American Sociological Review, 22*(6), 664–670.

Case

R v Prosper, 2017 NSSC 173.

Legislation

Criminal Code, RSC 1985, c C-46.

Basil Borutski: A History of Violence Against Women

The case of Basil Borutski is an example of how gender is a powerful correlate of criminal violence.

In 2008, domestic assault charges were laid against Basil Borutski for the assault of his wife, Mary Ann Mask. The charges were eventually withdrawn, a peace bond was issued, and the marriage dissolved. As reported by the *Ottawa Citizen* (Helmer, 2017):

> Mask told a judge during 2011 divorce proceedings that Borutski 'destroyed her spirit by relentless threats and abuse.' One daughter told a judge the violence included hair-pulling, slapping and an attempt to push Mask out of a moving vehicle. Another daughter said Borutski repeatedly threatened to burn down the family home, which did burn to the ground, though no charges were laid.

In 2011, Basil Borutski met Nathalie Warmerdam, a hospice nurse who was caring for his ailing father, and he moved into her farmhouse. The relationship ended the following year; Borutski was arrested and charged with threatening to strangle Warmerdam's son, threatening to kill a family animal, and damaging property. He served a short time in jail and is released with a two-year term of probation and a 10-year weapons ban.

On September 22, 2015, 58-year-old Borutski killed three women in three separate incidents, all women that he had previous relationships with. One of those women was Nathalie Warmerdam. In November 2017, he was convicted of two counts of first-degree murder and one count of second-degree murder. In December 2017, Justice Maranger imposed a sentence of 70 years of consecutive imprisonment, without the possibility of parole. He wrote of the events of September 22, 2015:

> The 22nd day of September, 2015 will forever be remembered by the citizens of the Counties of Renfrew and Hastings. It will be remembered as a time of terror and of sorrow. It will always be considered one of the saddest, darkest days in the community's history.
>
> For on that day, Basil Borutski took it upon himself to exact vengeance, to act as judge, jury and executioner against three beloved innocent women. On that day, Basil Borutski committed three vicious cold-blooded murders.
>
> He first attended the cottage of Carol Culleton. The cottage door was locked. Basil Borutski broke into the cottage. He attacked her with a coaxial cable. He hit her with it. He then wrapped it six times very tightly around her head and neck suffocating her, murdering her.
>
> Then Basil Borutski drove to the residence of Anastasia Kuzyk. His attendance with a shotgun was witnessed by the victim's sister, Eva Kuzyk. He gained entry. Eva Kuzyk escaped when she saw him coming forward with a shotgun. She fled outside and then heard

the sound of a shot going off in the house. Basil Borutski shot Anastasia Kuzyk to death in the kitchen of her home. He murdered her in cold blood.

He then left the Kuzyk residence and drove to the farmhouse of Nathalie Warmerdam. Adrian Warmerdam witnessed him chasing his mother in their home with a 12-gauge shotgun. He escaped with his life. He heard a shot and he called the police. Basil Borutski shot Nathalie Warmerdam to death. He murdered her in cold blood.

These horrific events set into motion an unprecedented massive frightening manhunt for Basil Borutski in this part of eastern Ontario. It involved dozens of police officers, the locking down of a courthouse. There were fears that he had other victims in his sights.

At 2:30 in the afternoon in a field in Renfrew County, near Basil Borutski's family hunting cabin, he was arrested uneventfully.

On September 23rd, 2015, he gave a statement to Detective Sergeant Casey O'Neil. In that statement, he admitted to killing the three victims. He justified it by saying they were not innocent. That only killing something innocent was murder. (*R v Basil Borutski*, 2017, pp. 1–2)

And finally, in passing sentence, Justice Maranger made the following observations regarding Basil Borutski:

Basil Borutski has a history of violence against women. Two of the victims here were subjected to his abuse in the past. He has several criminal convictions supporting this fact. In his statement to Detective Sergeant O'Neil, Basil Borutski came across as someone who sees himself as a victim of basically everything. Of women, of society, of the police, of the justice system. He goes so far as to indirectly blame the police and the justice system for his murdering of these three women, all of which is outrageous. He seemed incapable of taking responsibility for his many wrongs. As *amicus* pointed out, there is perhaps some indication of an underlying mental health issue, but I conclude on the whole of the evidence, that the character of the accused is that he is a violent, vindictive, calculating abuser of women, who on September 22, 2015, took his hatred to its ultimate climax and committed the triple murders of Carol Culleton, Anastasia Kuzyk and Nathalie Warmerdam. (*R v Basil Borutski*, 2017, pp. 8–9)

Before You Read Chapter 10

- What can explain the crimes committed by Basil Borutski? How might he have become a vindictive and calculating abuser of women?
- Is male violence fundamentally different in character and form from female violence? Can you imagine the possibility of similar crimes committed by a female perpetrator?
- What might this case and others like it suggest to us about the gendered nature of violence?

Gender and Crime

LEARNING OUTCOMES

After reading this chapter, students will be able to:

- Identify key trends in the gender gap in criminal offending and victimization.
- Explain the gender gap in crime while drawing on criminological theories.
- Demonstrate a familiarity with contemporary research on gender and crime.

Introduction

Gender is a powerful correlate of criminal behaviour. A multitude of data sources, including police official arrest data, criminal court records, victimization surveys, and self-report surveys, reveal that men far exceed women in their rates of participation in an array of criminal behaviours. Yet, until recently, little research compared women and men in their motivations for and participation in crime; even less work directed attention to the nature and context of female criminality. The last 30 years has seen significant growth in the literature on gender and crime. This chapter explores this literature, addressing several key questions: How do women and men differ in terms of the types of crime they commit? Do women and men experience different motivations, prior victimizations, and social relationships that encourage their involvement in crime? What explanations have been offered to address the **gender gap** (the "gender ratio" problem) in crime? Is it possible to explain female criminality with theories of crime that were originally developed to explain male criminality (the **generalization problem**)?[1] Is gender central to understanding definitions of crime and victimization and responses to crime and victimization? Are gender and biological sex more complex than binary definitions might suggest in relation to criminal offending and victimization?

This chapter aims to achieve three goals: (1) to provide an overview of gender differences in criminal offending and victimization; (2) to offer an introduction to contemporary theories of the gender gap in crime; and (3) to highlight research studies that examine gender differences and similarities in criminal offending and victimization, including gangs and urban crime, intimate partner violence, and homicide and femicide.

gender gap
The difference between men and women in areas such as social, political, and economic attainment; a persistent finding in criminology is that men commit more crime than women.

generalization problem
The question of whether it is possible to explain female criminality with mainstream theories of crime that were originally developed to explain male criminality.

Trends in the Gender Gap in Criminal Offending

This section outlines some of the main gender differences in criminal offending in Canada. Where do we see the greatest contrast and similarity between men and women?

At first glance, official data suggest a high level of similarity between the criminal behaviour of women and men. In Canada, the Uniform Crime Reporting Survey (UCR) data, compiled by the Canadian Centre for Justice Statistics, demonstrate that males and females tend to engage in similar crimes. These data show that theft under $5,000 topped the list for females and was second for males. Assault level 1 (an offence that does not involve a weapon or serious bodily harm) ranked second for females and first for males (Mahony, Jacob, & Hobson, 2017, p. 25). The dramatic difference in male and female offending is not so much in the types of crime, but the volume of criminal offending.

Many more men are arrested each year than women. For example, approximately 993,000 individuals were accused of committing at least one *Criminal Code* offence in 2015. Females comprised just over 24 percent of the total number of individuals accused (Mahony et al., 2017, p. 28). The differences in arrest rates are particularly pronounced for serious violent offences. Males vastly outnumber females in the serious violent crimes of homicide (7.7 times the rate of females), attempted murder (5.8 times the rate of females), sexual assault, assault, robbery, arson, break and enter, motor vehicle theft, and forcible confinement, kidnapping, or abduction. The smallest gender gaps in offending are for relatively less serious property crimes such as theft under $5,000, fraud, and possession of stolen goods (Mahony et al., 2017, p. 25).[2]

In Canada, the Canadian Centre for Justice Statistics reports that the top arrest categories in 2015 for females (12 to 89 years of age, inclusive) were as follows:

1. assault level 1;
2. theft of $5,000 or under;
3. mischief;
4. assault level 2, weapon or bodily harm; and
5. fraud.

For males (12 to 89 years of age, inclusive), the top arrest categories in 2015 were as follows:

1. assault level 1;
2. theft of $5,000 or under;
3. mischief;
4. break and enter; and
5. assault level 2, weapon or bodily harm (Mahony et al., 2017, p. 25).

Although there are similarities in the rank order of criminal arrests for boys and girls, boys far outpace girls in their sheer volume of arrests. Male youths have twice the arrest rate of female youths (7,183.9 compared with 2,895.3 per 100,000) for all *Criminal Code* violations (Mahony et al., 2017, p. 20). The gender gap is most striking for violent *Criminal Code* violations, where the rate for male youths was 1,792.7 per 100,000 compared with 729.6 per 100,000 for female youths in 2015 (Mahony et al., 2017, p. 26). In sum, arrest data reveal similarities across gender (youths and adults) in the types of crime committed, with the most impressive difference in the sheer volume of male offending—a gender difference that is particularly pronounced for violent crimes.

A Narrowing of the Gender Gap in Crime over Time

The bigger question is whether this gender gap in crime has persisted or changed over time. Canadian crime data are displayed in Figure 10.1. This figure presents women as a percentage of adults charged with *Criminal Code* offences from 1998 to 2015. At first glance, it appears that women's involvement in violent crime has been on a steady rise since 2000, and certainly women's share of property crime appears to have increased after 2004 and more notably after 2008. However, the figures represent only women as a percentage of adults charged with *Criminal Code* offences. Perhaps men are committing fewer crimes and, therefore, a constant rate of female offending (or a less dramatic decline in female offending) might mean that women make up a greater share of total offending. Perhaps both men and women are participating more in crime, but women's crime rates are increasing at a faster rate, making up a greater share of the total. Focusing on percentage increases in women's offences is not particularly helpful either, because the very low base numbers lead us to see dramatic percentage increases. So, what do the rising percentages in Figure 10.1 tell us about women's rates of offending? Are women becoming more violent? Are women engaged in more property offences and crime generally? Is there more to this crime story?

FIGURE 10.1   Women as a Percentage of Adults Charged with Criminal Code Offences, 1998 to 2015

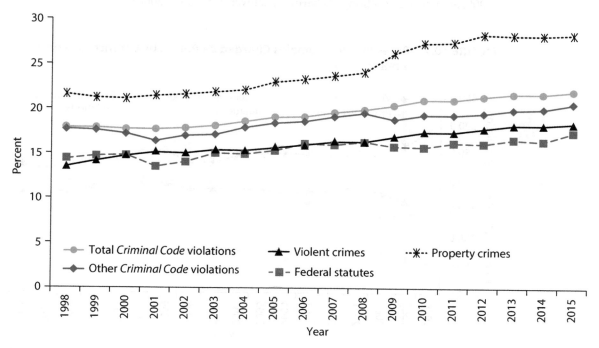

Note: Data exclude traffic violations.

Source: Mahony et al. (2017, Chart 12).

It is helpful to examine rates per 100,000 for each gender and to graph these rates across time. Data suggest that there has been a gradual increase in women's rates of violent crime from 1998 to 2015, while women's rates of property crime fell over this same period (see Figure 10.2). Meanwhile men's rates of violent offending fell over this same period and men's rate of property crime fell dramatically (see Figure 10.3). It appears that, in the Canadian context, the observed increase in women as a percentage of adults charged with property crime is the result of men's rates falling faster than the decline in women's rates. In contrast, there is some evidence for a narrowing in the gender gap in violent offending, with a gradual reduction in male offending and gradual increase in female offending. Examining these rates and graphs underscores the importance of comparing rates over time and exercising caution when interpreting either raw numbers or percentage figures.

Fluctuations in the rates of offending over time raise other questions. What causes crime rates to rise and fall? Why do women appear to represent a growing percentage of offenders? The background to these questions started in the mid-1970s with the publishing of two influential books: *Women and Crime* (Simon, 1975) and *Sisters in Crime: The Rise of the New Female Criminal* (Adler, 1975). Freda Adler and Rita Simon each reported that women's rates of crime and violence were increasing at a faster rate than those of men. The result was a narrowing of the gender gap in offending. These two books spurred research into the gender gap in crime across crimes, context, and time. Subsequent research, examining data on the gender gap in arrest rates from the 1960s to 2000, provided evidence that some significant narrowing occurred in the gender gap in arrests for property and violent crimes during this period (Heimer, Lauritsen, & Lynch, 2009; Steffensmeier, Zhong, Ackerman, Schwartz, & Agha, 2006).

FIGURE 10.2   Rates of Adult Females Charged by Police, by Offence Category, 1998 to 2015

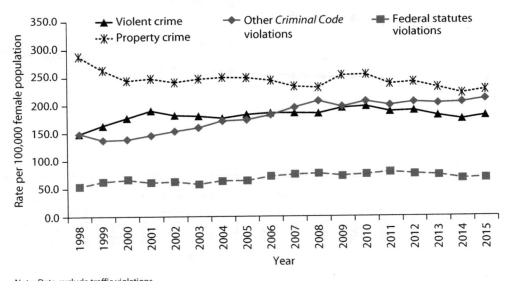

Note: Data exclude traffic violations.

Source: Mahony et al. (2017, Chart 13).

FIGURE 10.3 **Rates of Adult Males Charged by Police, by Offence Category, 1998 to 2015**

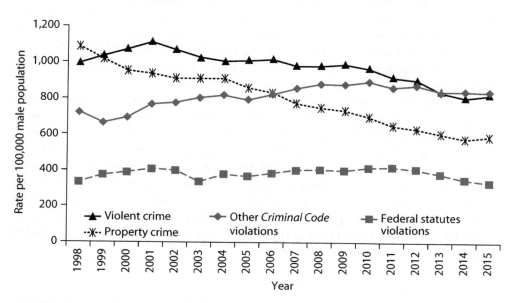

Note: Data exclude traffic violations.

Source: Mahony et al. (2017, Chart 14).

But what does it *mean* that the gender gap in arrests for violent crime is narrowing? One possibility is that a narrowing gap represents a real change in female behaviour in recent decades. The "liberation hypothesis" asserts that as women gain social power and freedoms, they are subject to fewer informal controls and should have more opportunities to commit crime and violence (Adler, 1975; Simon, 1975). The "economic marginalization hypothesis" contends that the economic circumstances of poor, uneducated women have worsened in comparison with those of male counterparts in recent decades (Heimer, Wittrock, & Ünal, 2006). The result is linked to greater increases in women's than in men's offending rates during periods of rising crime and smaller declines in women's rates during the recent crime bust (decline). A third hypothesis is that of "changing criminal justice practices." This hypothesis suggests that strides toward gender equality, combined with the public's reduced tolerance for violence, have led police to see female offending as a growing problem. Police are more inclined to charge women as accomplices to crime, and "charge up" offences that might have earlier been treated as lesser offences when committed by women. As well, domestic violence, once viewed as a private matter, increasingly receives intervention by police, leading to more arrests of women. Therefore, a narrowing of the gender gap in arrests could be the product of changing criminal justice practices (Steffensmeier et al., 2006).

These three explanations for changes in the gender gap in crime have been examined by Janet Lauritsen, Karen Heimer, and James Lynch (2009) using US UCR arrest data and victim reports from the US National Crime Victimization Survey (NCVS). These scholars refute the claim that a "new violent female offender" has emerged. Their study shows that female rates of violent offending have in fact declined over time. Lauritsen and colleagues (2009) also argue that the narrowing of the gender gap in violent crime is not simply the outcome of changing police practices; at least some of this narrowing of the gender gap reflects changes in the behaviours of male and female offenders. Most important, their analysis of victim reports suggests that the closing of the gender gap in violent offending was driven primarily by larger decreases in male offending and not by remarkable increases in female offending.

The patterns observed by Lauritsen, Heimer, and Lynch (2009) cast doubt on the liberation hypothesis. The liberation hypothesis would predict less substantial drops in female relative to male offending in the "crime drop" period of the 1990s and a more impressive and earlier impact of the feminist movement on women's opportunities for crime. The data are more consistent with the economic marginalization hypothesis. Lauritsen et al. (2009) argue that women did not gain as much income as men during the late 1990s, and consequently women's offending rates did not drop as much as those of men. It was during this period that the US government introduced substantial cutbacks to welfare assistance to marginalized women, which eroded an important buffer against poverty (Lauritsen et al., 2009).

Explaining the Gender Gap in Crime

Explaining the gender gap in crime raises important questions. Can existing criminological theories be applied or elaborated to encompass women's involvement in crime? Are the causes of women's crime better understood through gender-specific theories of crime? In response to these questions, three approaches have emerged. One approach is simply to add women to samples that examine criminal offending. Recall that many of the early studies of crime used samples of boys and men, excluding girls and women from analyses. The inclusion of girls and women in social survey samples is often termed the "add and stir" approach. A second approach is to explore how current theories may be developed further to help us understand differences in the types of crime women engage in, women's roles in collaborative offending, and the lesser volume of female offending. Finally, a third approach is to propose a new and gender-specific theory that treats female criminality as distinct from that of male criminality. In the next section, we explore several different theories, each born from one of these three approaches to the study of gender and crime.

Social Learning as the Catalyst of Crime

Early studies emphasized biological factors and sexual problems as the roots of gender differences in crime (see Lombroso & Ferrero, 1895/1958; Thomas, 1923/1969). A break from a biological emphasis came with social learning theories. For example, Edwin Sutherland (1947) argued that the higher rate of crime for boys can be explained by the differences in care and supervision of boys and girls. He maintained that girls are supervised more carefully and taught social codes with greater care and consistency than are boys. From infancy, girls are taught that they must be nice, while boys are taught that they must be tough. Furthermore, he argued that parents' fear that their daughters might become pregnant was a driving concern in the supervision of girls. Ruth Morris (1964) further developed the idea that female delinquency was deeply influenced by **socialization** patterns. Morris speculated that women experience both reduced access

socialization
The process through which children learn language, culture, roles, expectations, and beliefs. It is facilitated by parents, siblings, and relatives, and later by friends and within schools and community organizations.

to illegitimate means to reach success goals (for example, criminal opportunities) and greater social disapproval of delinquent acts than do their male counterparts. She also observed that girls are expected to abide by stricter moral standards, and deviant behaviour by girls is likely to result in greater guilt and disapproval by others. By contrast, more subcultural support exists for misbehaviour by boys (Morris, 1964).

More recent research has examined how gender roles are learned and influence youth delinquency and criminal offending. Darrell Steffensmeier and Emilie Allan (1996) argued that the adoption of masculine gender norms, which emphasize physicality, aggressiveness, and risk taking, is more conducive to delinquency. In contrast, stereotypes of femininity, including "weakness, submission, domestication, nurturance, and 'ladylike' behavior) are basically incompatible with qualities valued in the criminal world" (Steffensmeier & Allan, 1996, p. 476). Gender norms also result in greater supervision of girls and women in society, limited opportunities to engage in crime, and condemnation of women who engage in serious predatory crime (Steffensmeier & Allan, 1996). In addition to gender norms, this approach emphasizes the importance of gender-specific mechanisms such as differences in moral development, physical strength and aggression, social control, sexuality, and histories of physical and sexual abuse (Cutler, 2016). These differences in the organization of gender shape men and women's risk preferences and motivations for crime (Steffensmeier, Schwartz, & Roche, 2013). Recent studies have explored social learning and gender roles in the contexts of illicit drug use (Schulz, Murphy, & Verona, 2016) and non-medical prescription drug use (Cutler, 2016), and gangster subculture (Bengtsson, 2012). Contemporary work also argues that gender is a multidimensional, partly contextual-dependent factor, and heuristically not as meaningful to consider simply as a binary (Oldehinkel, 2018). Therefore, studies of gender roles have begun to examine trans women and trans men, genderqueer and cisgender men and women, and gender roles (Factor, 2017), and how gender role orientation influences gaming (Wilhelm, 2018) and risk-taking (Panno, Donati, Milioni, Chiesi, & Primi, 2018).

Control Perspectives on Gender and Crime

Another perspective focuses on dimensions of control in shaping gender differences in crime. Early work by Travis Hirschi, in his book *Causes of Delinquency* (1969), examined the importance of bonds to society and conformity that are taught through the family, schools, religious institutions, and the law. In a *General Theory of Crime* (1990), Michael Gottfredson and Travis Hirschi focused on the concept of "self-control" rather than societal control, emphasizing how some individuals may become crime-prone through individual behaviours and attitudes, such as an urge to gratify desires immediately; a lack of diligence and persistence in a course of action; a lack of skills and planning; a lack of commitment to a job, marriage, and children; and a tendency to drink excessively, use illegal drugs, or gamble. A core claim of this theory is that low self-control in association with situational opportunity is responsible for criminal behaviour (Gottfredson & Hirschi, 1990, p. 87). Another crucial assumption of the general theory of crime is that ineffective parenting is a major source of low self-control (Siegfried & Woessner, 2016). A further development in control research is a "life-course-developmental theory" of informal social control (Laub & Sampson, 2003). A life-course perspective stresses the importance of informal social ties at all ages, but differentiates the roles played by important institutions in informal social control on the bases of age or stage of the life span. Therefore, family, school, and peer groups are dominant forces of informal social control in childhood and adolescence; while in adulthood, dominant social control institutions are marriage, children, and employment (Massoglia & Uggen, 2010).

For theories of social control, including bonds, self-control, and life-course theories of informal control, a key issue is how people develop "control." One control theory that has focused special attention on gender differences is **power–control theory**. Originally formulated by John Hagan, A.R. Gillis, and John Simpson (1985), power–control theory explores how males and females differ in emotional reactions and behavioural responses, with close attention paid to the role of family socialization. According to this theory, parents with greater workplace authority and autonomy eschew rigid disciplinary practices at home to foster entrepreneurial, risk-taking orientations in their children. Freedom and control in the workplace are therefore reproduced in the family. Hagan and colleagues also contend that parental control of children is stratified by gender. They describe this as a fundamental instrument–object relationship (Hagan, Gillis, & Simpson, 1985). The two sides of this relationship are that mothers more than fathers are the instruments of familial controls, and daughters more than sons are the objects of familial controls. Female adolescents are taught to avoid risks generally and the risk of legal sanctions specifically. Power–control theory also has a class element. Power–control theory argues that in all classes males are freer to be delinquent than females. However, males are most free to be delinquent in the most powerful classes. Hagan and colleagues' early work examined common forms of youth delinquency, such as smoking cigarettes, drinking alcohol, fighting, stealing, illegal copying of software and music, and vandalism (Hagan et al., 1985).

A later formulation of the theory described **gendered** schemas embedded in parenting styles. These gendered schemas create behavioural disparities when mothers and fathers use different parenting styles for sons and daughters (Hagan, McCarthy, & Foster, 2002). In an interesting twist, Christopher Uggen (2000) uncovered a brighter side to power–control theory: Girls whose mothers hold workplace authority are likely to engage in a constellation of risk-taking activities that include pro-social and anti-social behaviours. He found these daughters were likely to pursue athletic competition, non-traditional employment, and entrepreneurial business and financial activity. Recent work, applying power–control theory, has revealed the importance of a close, affective bond between father and daughter for curbing adolescent substance use among females (Eitle & Eitle, 2015).

The control theories discussed so far include self-control, life-course theories of control, and power–control. These theories emphasize a quality of control that is both internal (one's ability to resist one's impulses) (Mamayek, Paternoster, & Loughran, 2017) and external (attachment to others, including job, family, spouse, and children) (Arocho & Kamp Dush, 2016). Some recent work suggests that control might be innate and not entirely developed through one's social context. Guang Guo, Michael Roettger and Tianji Cai (2008) found that genetic factors were significant predictors of serious and violent delinquency. The authors observed that the expression of genes depends heavily on environmental context. Specifically, they argued that the stronger social control influences of family, school, and friendship networks reduce the delinquency-increasing effects of a genetic variant, whereas weaker social control influences in these realms amplify the

---

power–control theory
A theory of crime that emphasizes the socialization by parents in the development of different levels of risk taking and the perceived sanctions among boys and girls.

gendered
The notion that processes (for example, learning roles) and behaviours (for example, participation in crime) are gender-based.

delinquency-increasing effect of a genetic variant (Guo, Roettger, & Cai, 2008, p. 561). Guo, Roettger, and Cai (2008) proposed that these effects likely differ by sex. Recent research suggests that genetic factors may play a greater role in behavioural outcomes among males (Beaver, Rowland, Schwartz, & Nedelec, 2011). However, research on gender differences with regard to genetics and crime remains in its infancy (Li & Guo, 2016).

> For a more detailed discussion of biological explanations of crime, see Chapter 7, Biological Approaches.

General Strain Theory Perspectives on Gender and Crime

General strain theory (GST) has been used to advance our understanding of gender differences in criminal offending. Robert Agnew (1985) proposed GST as a way of expanding on and generalizing the concept of strain, developed by Robert Merton (1938), at the social psychological level. The theory examines how individuals cope with strain emotionally and behaviourally. It broadens the concept of strain to include a variety of negative relations with others, and it assesses strain in terms of several criteria. When these criteria are elevated, crime is more likely (for detailed discussions of GST, see Agnew, 2006, 2013).

Lisa Broidy and Robert Agnew (1997) extended and applied GST to the study of gender differences in crime. Together, Broidy and Agnew addressed two questions: (1) How can we explain the higher rate of crime among males? and (2) How can we explain why females engage in crime? With respect to the first question, the authors suggested that gender differences in types of strain and the reaction to strain help explain the gender gap in criminal behaviour. With respect to the second question, they argued that several types of strain may lead to female crime under the right circumstances. Broidy and Agnew contended that GST cannot explain the higher rate of male crime by simply claiming that males experience more strain. They argued that males and females experience strain in qualitatively distinct ways. Broidy and Agnew outlined three important differences: (1) males and females experience different types of strain; (2) males and females differ in their emotional response to strain; and (3) males and females experience strain under different sorts of circumstances.

The first argument is that males and females experience different types of strain, with male strains being more conducive to serious violent and property crimes. For example, males more often report financial problems and are more upset when they experience financial or work-related problems. The greater emphasis on material considerations and greater financial stress may explain males' higher rates of property crimes. In addition, interpersonal conflicts and criminal victimization are more often experienced by males, which may explain their higher rates of violent crime. In contrast, females' strains, often connected to family violence, lead to escape behaviour such as running away and to more self-directed forms of control, such as drug use (Broidy & Agnew, 1997).

Second, Broidy and Agnew (1997) argued that males and females differ in their emotional response to strain. The anger females experience is more likely to be accompanied by depression, guilt, anxiety, and related states as a result of cultural socialization (Agnew, 2006). These emotional states reduce the likelihood of confrontational crimes and increase the likelihood of self-destructive offences. In comparison, males externalize their anger and react with "moral outrage." The angry male's moral righteousness may lead to serious violent and property offending. Nevertheless, Broidy and Agnew (1997) acknowledge that some females may react to strain with the same anger that males do, helping to explain the serious female offending that does take place.

Third, Broidy and Agnew (1997) maintained that males and females experience strain under different circumstances. Societal proscriptions against crime for females reduce the likelihood that females will respond to strain with crime. Moreover, females may have lower levels of self-esteem and self-efficacy, which may decrease the likelihood of their decision to commit a crime. Furthermore, gender differences in social support may affect how males and females respond to strain. Females tend to be more immersed in intimate networks, which lend them emotional social support that can reduce stress. Differences also exist in opportunities for crime and social control. Males may be granted more opportunities by others to join in criminal activities, and males may be less supervised and controlled by authority figures (Broidy & Agnew, 1997).

Recent research provides evidence that the experience of strain, both emotionally and behaviourally, is gendered (Jung et al., 2017). GST has also been extended through attention to the role of **conditioning factors**. For example, Wesley Jennings, Nicole Piquero, Angela Gover, and Deanna Pérez (2009) extend GST to explain interpersonal aggression and property offending among southwestern Mexican-American adolescents. Their study highlights the importance of peer social support, spiritual coping resources, and physical coping resources (for example, involvement in music) in crime prevention. Recent scholarship explores how strain theory works in conjunction with social learning and opportunity (Huck, Spraitz, Bowers, & Morris, 2017), offending and perpetration of intimate partner violence (Knight, Ellis, Roark, Henry, & Huizinga, 2017), and the relevance of polyvictimization (for example, experiences of multiple different types of victimization) on delinquency (Cudmore, Cuevas, & Sabina, 2017).

conditioning factors
Factors that shape the impact of a certain cause or correlate of crime.

A Break from Tradition: Feminist Explanations

Feminist critiques, embedded in conflict theory, argue that traditional theories of crime tend to overlook female offending. Many of the early studies of crime and delinquency used samples of males, and theories were developed with male youth and adult offenders in mind. Therefore, most of criminology has been a male-centred enterprise. The rationale for the focus on males is based on women's small numbers relative to men in criminal offending, particularly in violent crime. As a result, until recently, women were not of interest and deemed less relevant to the study of crime. Studies that began to include women and girls generally adopted an "add women and stir" approach, assuming that similar underlying processes generate male and female criminality. A further critique of these early works was that women lawbreakers were often portrayed as morally corrupt, hysterical, manipulative, and devious (Chesney-Lind, 2006). Contemporary theories, while not making such claims, still fall short in their efforts to account for the gender gap in violent offending (see Koon-Magnin, Bowers, Langhinrichsen-Rohling, & Arata, 2016). Feminist scholars argue that in attempting to understand criminality, researchers need to pay greater attention to female voices (as victims and offenders) and revise interpretations by the inclusion of women's experiences. Feminists claim that past work has failed to interrogate the nature of maleness and femaleness (masculinity and femininity) or the historically grounded relationship between them. Feminist criminology represents a radical break from traditional theories (Dunn, Clark, & Pearlman, 2017).

Common to feminist inquiries into crime is a focus on the forces that shape women's lives and experiences in order to explain female criminality (Maghsoudi, Anaraki, & Boostani, 2018). Some of this work emphasizes how physical and sexual victimization of girls and women can be underlying causes of women's criminal behaviour (Dunn et al., 2017). A considerable body of feminist scholarship has critiqued methodological strategies in criminology that rely on social surveys and statistical analyses, claiming that objectivist, value-neutral science overlooks the lived experiences of women and prevents more social activist and transformative research from taking place (Chesney-Lind, 2006). Therefore, the majority, although not all (see Simpson & Gibbs, 2006) of feminist criminology embraces qualitative methods of interviewing that seek to build theory inductively.

Within feminist criminology, various theories exist (for example, liberal, radical, and intersectional feminism), although the differences are generally a matter of emphasis rather than a paradigm shift. For example, "liberal feminists" emphasize comparisons of sameness and difference in criminal behaviour and treatment. This approach pays close attention to the impact of gender role socialization and women's reduced opportunities to engage in criminal networks in shaping women's lower offending rate (Burgess-Proctor, 2006). "Radical feminism" emphasizes dominance, or patriarchy, as the root cause of women's oppression. Radical feminist criminologists have examined male dominance and privilege through such crimes against women as domestic violence, sexual harassment, rape, and pornography. Radical feminists have also advanced law reform to improve the treatment of criminalized women (MacKinnon, 1991), revealed evidence of women's unequal treatment in sentencing (Gaarder & Belknap, 2002), and formulated a critique of women's prisons and parole (Hannah-Moffat & Yule, 2011). Recently, "intersectional feminism" recognizes that race, class, gender, sexuality, and other social positions of inequality influence one another (Kahle, 2018). These differences are grounded in historical contexts and operate at the level of individual day-to-day interactions and at the more macro level of law and governance (Burgess-Proctor, 2006). Contemporary feminist criminology has examined the intersection of gender and race with reference to drug treatment programs and imprisonment (McCorkel, 2013), women's victimization in partner violence (Sokoloff & Pearce, 2011) and intimate partner femicide (Messerschmidt, 2017), and women's violence on the street (Althoff, 2013).

In Sum: Contrasting Theories of Gender and Crime

Contemporary theories that seek to explain the relationship between gender and crime are diverse. Scholars build on past and current theoretical arguments, often importing research findings, concepts, and arguments from other theories. This dialogue of critique, infusion of ideas, and elaboration reminds us that each of these theories offers insight into different dimensions of gender and crime.

Contemporary Research on Gender and Crime

Three areas of contemporary research on gender and crime will be explored next: (1) gender, gangs, and urban crime; (2) domestic violence; and (3) femicide and homicide.

Gender, Gangs, and Urban Crime

Considerable research in the urban context has focused on gender and gang membership. Three common themes emerge in the literature on why youths join gangs: (1) neighbourhood disadvantage; (2) gang-involved family members or friends; and (3) problems within the family (for example, neglect, lack of supervision, and drug and alcohol addiction) (Tolle, 2017). But do females join gangs for the same reasons as do males?

> Several chapters in this book explore other areas of crime relevant to gender, including Chapter 5, Victims of Crime; Chapter 13, Violent Crime; Chapter 14, Sexual Offences and Problematic Sexual Interests; and Chapter 16, Crimes of Morality.

Jody Miller's (2008) research in St. Louis, Missouri found females' neighbourhood contexts provided exposure to gangs. Serious family problems of drug abuse and violence led girls to avoid home and join gangs to meet social and emotional needs. Finn-Aage Esbensen, Elizabeth Deschenes, and L. Thomas Winfree (1999) found similarities between males and females, who both reported joining gangs primarily for protection. Differences also exist. For example, Anne Campbell (1995) found that female gang members were more likely than male gang members to come from broken, unemployed homes with family violence, including parental drug abuse. Numerous studies argued that girls join gangs because they have few options in severely disadvantaged neighbourhoods and because they are in search of a "familial" peer group and emotional support that they do not find in their own families (Bell, 2009). Recent research provides insight into girls in gangs and their involvement in prostitution (Dorais & Corriveau, 2009), the abuse and violence girls are exposed to within gangs (Haymos & Gatti, 2010), and youth gang initiation rites (Descormiers & Corrado, 2016). Other work has examined group-based offences, although not necessarily gang-related (see Box 10.1).

BOX 10.1

Case Study: Gender and Burglary

In a fascinating study, Christopher Mullins and Richard Wright (2003) examined the ways in which gender affects participation in residential burglary, a quintessentially group-based offence. They explored how gender influences initiation into, participation in, and potential desistance from burglary. Their study revealed how men control both entry to burglary crews and access to networks for disposing of goods. In their study, men were initiated into burglary crews from a broad array of associates, including male relatives and friends. In contrast, women were most often drawn into male-dominated burglary crews by their boyfriends. Moreover, while men typically held marginal roles early in their careers (for example, lookout and get-away driver), men began undertaking more central and profitable roles as they gained experience. In contrast, women's roles were often limited to an accomplice role. Mullins and Wright (2003) also uncovered a striking gender difference in desistance from crime. When men were asked to explain why they had ceased burglaries, they cited the influence of a stable relationship with a woman as the main reason. For women, the situation was the opposite. Just as relationships with criminally involved men opened the door for women's initiation to burglary, the end of that romantic relationship also brought an end to women's offending.

Research has shown that women's motives for entering into criminal behaviour, such as burglary, and ceasing it can be quite different from those of men.

Although many studies highlight gender differences in urban crime, some work suggests the importance of underlying factors common to men's and women's involvement in crime. In a landmark study of urban crime, Darrell Steffensmeier and Dana Haynie (2000) analyzed data from 178 US cities using data from the Bureau of Census publications, the US UCR Survey, and FBI city arrest data. They found that despite an enormous difference in mean rates of offending between females and males, structural disadvantage variables (for example, poverty, income inequality, joblessness, female-headed single households) had significant effects on female rates of homicide and robbery, as well as moderate effects on female rates of aggravated assault, burglary, and larceny. Steffensmeier and Haynie (2000) uncovered other parallels: Structural variables of residential instability, structural density, and population size also had similar effects on rates of male and female offending. A key conclusion of this study was that macro-level causes of female crime are not fundamentally different from those of male crime. This finding suggests that the quest to identify gender differences in the causes of crime may focus too much on differences rather than on similarities. Building on this work, recent studies have documented the importance of structural disadvantage with reference to intimate partner violence (Copp, Kuhl, Giordano, Longmore, & Manning, 2015) and provided a deeper understanding of situational contexts of violence in disadvantaged urban communities (Cobbina, Like, & Miller, 2016) and the relevance of street codes for homeless youths as a population immersed in extremely impoverished situations (Baron, 2017).

Domestic Violence

One of the most significant contributions to the burgeoning body of literature on gender and crime has been the growth in research on criminal victimization. Violence against women has been identified as a major public health and human rights issue (Ellsberg, Jansen, Heise, Watts, & García-Moreno, 2008) and as a crime that has reached epidemic proportions in many societies (Asay, DeFrain, Metzger, & Mayer, 2016). Scholarship has shed light on previously understudied areas of violence against women, such as sexual assault, sexual harassment in the workplace, intimate partner violence, and **femicide** (the killing of women). We explore research on intimate partner violence next.

femicide
The act of killing a woman.

Numerous studies have examined the prevalence of different patterns of violent victimization among family members. Using the US NCVS, Wendi Goodlin and Christopher Dunn (2010) found that one-time victimization of a family member by others in the family occurred in about 80 percent of instances of family violence in households. Much lower rates of repeated victimization of the same victim took place—these occurred in close to 15 percent of the family violence in households. In addition, Goodlin and Dunn (2010) found that the co-occurrence of violence among different family members was about 5 percent of the family violence in households. The study also revealed that victims with less than a high school education had much higher odds of living in a co-occurrence household compared with a repeat victimization household.

Other research has focused on spousal violence, with the aim of understanding how socio-economic stresses impact families. Ross Macmillan and Rosemary Gartner (1999), for example, found that measures of socio-economic resources, such as personal and household income, had little impact on the risk of spousal abuse. However, the symbolic aspects of who has employment in the household are important: When women hold jobs and their male partners are unemployed, the risk of spousal violence is greater (Macmillan & Gartner, 1999). Further research suggests that employed women's risk of victimization appears partly contingent on the race of the victim. Ráchael Powers and Catherine Kaukinen (2012) found that for white women, employment heightens the risk of victimization, whereas for non-white women, the effects of employment are less clear, although regardless of employment status, non-white women are overall at greater risk of victimization. Recent studies identify additional risk factors of intimate partner violence, including: living in cohabitation (Castro, Cerellino, & Rivera, 2017), a history of parent–child physical aggression (Kaufman-Parks, DeMaris, Giordano, Manning, & Longmore, 2018), parental negativity and distrust (Giordano, Johnson, Manning, & Longmore, 2016), and communication difficulties (Elmquist et al., 2016).

BOX 10.2

"Enough Is Enough"

The following is an excerpt from an Ontario Court of Appeal decision in a case of homicide that took place after a woman had been subjected to long-term, non-violent spousal abuse.

In the early morning of March 31, 2006, the appellant, a middle-aged woman, who is by all accounts a decent person and a good mother, put a pillow over her husband's face as he was lying asleep in a drunken stupor on the couch. A few minutes later, the appellant took a large butcher knife from the kitchen and stabbed her husband four times in the chest. She then left the RV in which they were living and ran to a neighbour's house. The deceased was still alive when the appellant left, but died of blood loss a short time later.

The appellant went directly to her neighbour's house. She told them that she had killed her husband, and asked them to call 911. The appellant spoke to the 911 operator, again admitted killing her husband, and said, "I'm sick of my life ... everything is wrong."

After her arrest, the appellant gave lengthy videotaped statements to the police in which she acknowledged stabbing her husband to death. When asked by the officer to explain why she had done so, the appellant said, "enough is enough." The appellant's explanation that "enough is enough" can only be understood in the context of her relationship with the deceased. ...

On the evidence, the appellant fit the description of a battered wife. She was trapped in a relationship that belittled and dehumanized her to the point where she suffered a serious and ongoing mental disorder rendering her unable to perceive the obvious consequences of her actions. We are satisfied that the effect that the long-term

abuse had on this appellant should have been treated as a substantial mitigating factor on sentence. The trial judge erred in principle in diminishing that mitigating impact because the abuse did not involve serious physical abuse or sexual abuse. ...

Having regard to the entirety of the circumstances, and despite the powerful mitigating features, we are satisfied that incarceration was necessary in this case. This was a brutal homicide. As the trial judge observed, the sentence imposed must reflect the value that our society places on all human life. The appellant must bear responsibility for what she did, despite the mitigating features of this case.

The appellant has served about three years (two and a half years plus five months' pre-sentence custody). We are satisfied that a sentence of three years in custody certainly fully meets the needs of deterrence and denunciation in the circumstances. There is no need for any further incarceration.

As indicated at the end of oral argument, the conviction appeal is dismissed, the sentence appeal is allowed and the sentence is varied to time served.

Ontario Court of Appeal, case heard January 27, 2011, judgment released February 24, 2011.

What do you think should be considered as "mitigating factors" in homicide? In what ways does the appellant in this case fit (or not fit) the description of a "battered wife"? What are your thoughts on the court of appeal's decision to uphold the conviction while shortening the sentence (to time already served)?

Source: *R v Craig* (2011, paras. 4–6, 60, 64–66).

A sizable body of research on family violence assesses policing strategies and legal interventions. Since the 1980s, law enforcement, prosecution, and criminal and civil courts have developed a variety of new policies for responding to the victimization of women by intimate partners. Although considerable research has examined these new policies and practices, little consensus exists on which interventions are most effective. Results from a Minneapolis field experiment that involved a study of police responses to domestic violence from 1981 to 1982 were heralded as scientific evidence that arrest was the most appropriate and effective response to domestic violence (Sherman & Berk, 1984). However, a subsequent spousal abuse program that adopted this strategy and was implemented in six other US cities failed to reproduce results supporting the superiority of arrest in reducing domestic violence (Sherman et al., 1992). Other interventions have also been examined. For example, legal advocacy has been found to provide women with assistance in obtaining protection orders (called "restraining orders" in the United States and "no contact orders" in Canada). Moreover, as women seek legal remedies to domestic violence, they are less inclined to resort to lethal remedies (Dugan, Nagin, & Rosenfeld, 2003). The effectiveness of criminal justice responses to domestic violence also depends on local prosecutorial policy, including the willingness to grant protection orders (Muller, Desmarais, & Hamel, 2009) and to prosecute violators (Menjivar & Walsh, 2017). Specialized domestic violence courts and community services and networks have also been found to be effective in addressing domestic violence (Sullivan, 2018). A recent US study also demonstrates the importance of mandated gun restrictions as protection in partner abuse (Lynch & Logan, 2018).

Supporters chant during the release of a report by the Missing Women Commission of Inquiry in Vancouver in December 2012. The inquiry examined the years of inaction by police in investigating the disappearances of dozens of women, many of them poor Indigenous women working as prostitutes in Vancouver's Downtown Eastside. Many of the disappeared women were victims of mass murderer Robert Pickton.

Femicide and Homicide

The killing of women (femicide) appears to be very different from the killing of men (homicide). Among those who study homicide, it is well known that women and men are killed in different numbers, by different types of people, and in different circumstances. Women are less likely to be victims of homicide than men in virtually all societies. Women are also more likely than men to be killed by someone of the opposite sex. Women are more likely to be killed by persons with whom they are intimately involved. In contrast, men are more likely to be killed by acquaintances and strangers. Women are more likely to be killed in their own house than in any other place, while men are more likely to be killed in public places (Zorn, Wuerch, Faller, & Hampton, 2017).

In a study of intimate femicide (including spouses, ex-spouses, legal common law spouses, and current and former boyfriends) in Ontario, Rosemary Gartner, Myrna Dawson, and Maria Crawford (1999) identified several risk markers. They found that estrangement and common law status were associated with a higher risk of spousal killings of women. Compared with couples in registered marriages, common law partners were more likely to be poor, young, unemployed, and childless—all factors associated with higher homicide rates. Compared with co-residing couples, estranged couples were more likely to have a history of domestic violence. In addition, Gartner, Dawson, and Crawford (1999) found that Indigenous women's rates of spousal homicide were between five and ten times higher than those of non-Indigenous women. Furthermore, men's unemployment was a risk factor for wife assaults and was also associated with elevated risks of spousal homicide. They also found men who killed their intimate partners were more likely to be unemployed and to have a history of criminal violence. Perhaps the most disturbing element of Gartner, Dawson, and Crawford's study is that one of the distinguishing features of intimate femicide is the extent and nature of the violence done to the victim. Unlike killings by women of their intimate partners, intimate femicides often involve multiple methods or far more violence than is necessary to kill the victim (Gartner, Dawson, & Crawford, 1999). Recent studies have built on these risk markers, documenting how prior domestic violence and immigration status (Harper, 2017) and prior violence and mental health issues (Cullen et al., 2018) precipitate femicide.

Other research provides international comparisons on homicide. Gary LaFree and Gwen Hunnicutt (2006) documented female and male homicide victimization trends in 35 countries from 1950 to 2001. A widely held assumption in criminology is that homicide rates are higher for men than women. However, LaFree and Hunnicutt (2006) found that female rates exceeded male rates for at least part of the time period assessed in 11 countries (about one-third of their sample). The countries in which female rates were higher than male rates were clearly patterned. Female homicide victimization rates were greater than male rates in Western European democracies (Denmark, Switzerland, Sweden, Austria, Belgium, Norway, and Ireland) or countries with strong links to Western democracies (Israel, New Zealand, and Hong Kong). These patterns are consistent with research by Gartner (1990), suggesting that the gap in homicide victimization for women and men is smaller in nations with less **gender stratification**. In addition, LaFree and Hunnicutt (2006) found little evidence of convergence in the victimization rates of women and men during the second half of the 20th century (1950–2000). In fact, they found slightly more evidence of a female–male divergence in homicide victimization rates. For most countries in their sample, the gender gap in homicide victimization either remained constant or widened during the 50-year span (LaFree & Hunnicutt, 2006, p. 223).

gender stratification
A society's unequal distribution of wealth, power, and privilege between men and women.

Conclusion

This chapter set out to trace gender differences in criminal offending, to outline explanations for the involvement of men and women in crime, and to explore areas of research relevant to gender and crime. Available crime data show that the dramatic difference in male and female offending is in the quantity of criminal offending, rather than the types of crime committed. Research also suggests that in recent years a significant narrowing of the gender gap in crime has occurred, particularly for property and violent crimes. Theoretical explanations for women's and men's criminal offending are richly diverse. Some theories attempt to understand gender differences in crime through socialization processes and gendered roles. Some focus on control, including parental control, cultivation of self-control, and the role of genetic influences on self-control and crime. Another approach extends general strain theory to include gendered emotional responses and coping mechanisms that in turn shape deviance and criminal outcomes. Finally, feminist theories break from traditional theories by placing girls and women at the centre of inquiry and providing a critique of criminal justice system responses to the treatment of women. The final section of this chapter examined three areas of contemporary research on gender and crime, including gangs and urban crime, intimate partner violence, and homicide and femicide. This overview demonstrates how contemporary studies seek to document important differences and underlying similarities in male and female criminal involvement and to create effective intervention strategies.

SUMMARY OF KEY POINTS

- Available police arrest data reveal that men and women are arrested for similar crimes, including theft, assaults, and mischief.

- The dramatic difference between male and female offending relates to the quantity of criminal offending rather than the types of crime committed. In Canada, more than three times as many men as women are arrested for criminal violations. The differences are most pronounced for serious violent crimes, where men vastly outnumber women in homicide, sexual assault, assault, robbery, arson, break and enter, and motor vehicle theft.

- Research suggests that in recent years a significant narrowing of the gender gap in crime has occurred, particularly for property and violent crimes. In the United States, the most persuasive explanations lie with the economic marginalization hypothesis and changing criminal justice practices rather than the liberation hypothesis or an increase in violent female offenders. In Canada, recent data suggest that men's rates of property crimes have fallen more steeply over the past 20 years than the decline observed among women's rates of property crime. Thus, the narrowing of the gender gap does not suggest more women are becoming involved in crime.

- Scholars have attempted to explain gender differences in crime through conventional theories (social learning, control), by extending traditional theories (general strain theory), and with theories tailored to women's unique circumstances (feminist theories).

- Feminist theories break from traditional theories by placing girls and women at the centre of inquiry, challenging assumptions embedded in law, and calling for extensive reform of the criminal justice system's treatment of women.
- Research on gangs reveals that family problems with drug abuse and violence lead girls to avoid home and join gangs in an effort to meet social and emotional needs.
- Violence against women has been identified as a major public health and human rights issue and is a crime that has reached epidemic proportions in many countries.
- Women and men are killed in different contexts. Women are more likely to be killed by persons with whom they are intimately involved, while men are more likely to be killed by acquaintances and strangers. Women are more likely to be killed in their own home than in any other place, while men are more likely to be killed in public places.
- Studies identify risk factors for interpersonal violence escalating to killing, revealing that femicide is not an unpredictable crime of passion.

NOTES

1. These two problems, gender ratio and generalization of theories, have been central to inquiry on gender and crime (see Britton, Jacobsen, & Howard, 2018).
2. A notable reversal of this gender pattern exists in the United States, where women consistently outnumber men in prostitution and as runaways (a juvenile offence in the United States). For both these crimes, women and girls represent about 66 percent of those arrested (Britton et al., 2018, p. 24). In contrast, in Canada the *Criminal Code* does not criminalize prostitution but rather the procuring of persons for the purpose of prostitution and receiving a material benefit from the purchase of sexual service provided by individuals under 18 years of age (Mahony et al., 2017, p. 25), and as a result the number of arrests is low (26 females and 76 males in 2015) (Mahony et al., 2017, p. 25). The youth status-type offence of running away is absent from Canada's *Youth Criminal Justice Act* (Sprott, 2012).

QUESTIONS FOR CRITICAL DISCUSSION

1. What are the "gender ratio problem" and the "generalization problem"? How are these two problems different from each other?
2. Which approach to the study of gender and crime seems most persuasive (i.e., apply existing theories to samples of men and women, extend current theories to specify gender differences, or break from traditional theories to develop a separate theory of female criminality)? Why?
3. Which theories of male and female criminality do you find to be the most convincing? Are some theories better suited to particular types of deviance, delinquency, and crime?
4. How do men and women differ in terms of the types of crime in which they engage? Are there noteworthy differences between adult and youth offending and between Canadian and American crime statistics?

5. Are the rates of women's and men's offending converging, diverging, or remaining parallel? Are women becoming more violent? What are some of the possible reasons for the changing patterns observed in the criminal behaviour of male and females?

6. Studies of burglary, street gangs, intimate partner violence, and homicide/femicide reveal gendered processes in terms of motivations, entry to criminal networks, roles in co-offending crimes, levels of violence used, and reasons for ending criminal behaviour. Discuss any two of these crimes in terms of the gender differences and similarities that you find most intriguing.

7. Explore the economic marginalization hypothesis. What does it suggest are the causes of women's changing crime rates? For what types of crime would we expect to see more female participation? During which economic and political periods might we expect to see an increase in female crime?

8. Thinking about causes of crime, what factors best explain how male and female youths enter into crime and delinquency? Do similar processes generate male and female criminality? What differences exist? Do differences require a separate theory of crime for each gender? What are your thoughts?

SUGGESTED FURTHER READINGS

Baron, S.W. (2017). It's more than the code: Exploring the factors that moderate the street code's relationship with violence. *Justice Quarterly, 34*(3), 491–516.

Boyce, J. (2016). Victimization of Aboriginal people in Canada, 2014. Ottawa: Statistics Canada. Retrieved from https://www150.statcan.gc.ca/n1/pub/85-002-x/2016001/article/14631-eng.htm

Britton, D.M., Jacobsen, S.K., & Howard, G.E. (2018). *The gender of crime* (2nd ed.). Lanham, ML: Rowman and Littlefield.

Burczycka, M. (2016). Police-reported intimate partner violence. Ottawa: Statistics Canada. Retrieved from https://www150.statcan.gc.ca/n1/pub/85-002-x/2018001/article/54893/03-eng.htm

Chesney-Lind, M., & Shelden, R.G. (2014). *Girls, delinquency, and juvenile justice* (4th ed.). Chichester, UK: John Wiley and Sons.

Cullen, P., Vaughan, G., Li, Z., Price, J., Yu, D., & Sullivan, E. (2018). Counting dead women in Australia: An in-depth case review of femicide. *Journal of Family Violence* (April). https://doi.org/10.1007/s10896-018-9963-6

Gaudet, M. (2018). Police-reported hate crime in Canada, 2016. *Juristat.* Statistics Canada Catalogue no. 85-002-X. Retrieved from https://www150.statcan.gc.ca/n1/pub/85-002-x/2018001/article/54915-eng.htm

Harper, S.B. (2017). Out of the shadows: Shedding light on intimate partner homicide among Latina women. *Sociology Compass, 11*(11), 1–15. https://doi.org/10.1111/soc4.12534

Keighley, K. (2017). Police-reported crime statistics in Canada, 2016. *Juristat.* Statistics Canada Catalogue no. 85-002-X. Retrieved from https://www150.statcan.gc.ca/n1/pub/85-002-x/2017001/article/54842-eng.htm

Lynch, K.R., & Logan, T.K. (2018). "You better say your prayers and get ready": Guns within the context of partner abuse. *Journal of Interpersonal Violence, 33*(4), 686–711.

McCorkel, J.A. (2013) *Breaking women: Gender, race and the new politics of imprisonment.* New York: New York University Press.

Websites

FBI: Crime in the United States, 2017 report: https://ucr.fbi.gov/crime-in-the-u.s/2017

FBI: Uniform Crime Reports publications: https://ucr.fbi.gov/ucr

Statistics Canada, Crime and justice statistics: https://www150.statcan.gc.ca/n1/en/subjects/crime_and_justice

Cases

R v Basil Borutski, 2017 ONSC 7762.

R v Craig, 2011 ONCA 142.

Legislation

Criminal Code, RSC 1985, c C-46.

Youth Criminal Justice Act, SC 2002, c 1.

Racial Profiling: Mutaz Elmardy and the Toronto Police Services

Journalist and activist Desmond Cole questions Toronto Police Chief Mark Saunders about the force's street check policies at a public consultation meeting.

On a cold winter evening several years ago, Mutaz Elmardy was walking along a downtown street in Toronto when he was stopped by two police officers. They had pulled up alongside Mr. Elmardy and began to ask him questions, which he responded to with some verbal hostility. He had his hands in his pockets as he had no gloves. The officers got out of the car and asked Mr. Elmardy to take his hands out of his pockets. When he refused to do so, they subdued him and Constable Pak punched him twice in the face. They handcuffed his hands behind his back, searched his pockets, and for 20 to 25 minutes left him lying on wooden decking that was covered with ice, with his hands exposed to the ice.

In a 2015 judgment, Justice Myers of the Ontario Superior Court found that the two officers had no reason to suspect criminal conduct when they contacted Mr. Elmardy. He found further that Constable Pak had committed a battery, and that Mr. Elmardy's detention was unlawful and a breach of his Charter rights under section 9 (the right not to be arbitrarily detained or imprisoned). Further, he found that the search of Mr. Elmardy's pockets was a breach of section 8 (the right to be secure against unreasonable search or seizure), and that the failure to inform him why he was being detained or that he had a right to counsel was a breach of sections 10(a) and 10(b) (the right to be informed promptly and the right to retain and instruct counsel without delay).

Justice Myers awarded Mr. Elmardy $5,000 in damages for the battery that he experienced, $2,000 for the breach of his section 9 rights, and $1,000 each for the breach of his section 8 and 10 rights. He added $18,000 to this assessment as punitive damages, for a total of $27,000.

But Justice Myers declined to make a finding that Mr. Elmardy was a victim of racial profiling and, as a consequence, he appealed the judgment to a court of higher jurisdiction: the Ontario Supreme Court of Justice Divisional Court, with Sachs, Nordheimer, and Spies sitting as a three-person panel.

The decision of this panel was delivered in April 2017, with the unanimous conclusion that Mr. Elmardy had been subject to racial profiling. Justice Sachs, writing for the court, noted that racial profiling can rarely be proven by direct evidence, quoting from *R v Brown*, an earlier case from 2003: "if racial profiling is to be proven, it must be done by inference drawn from the circumstantial evidence."

Justice Sachs noted that the trial judge found that the officers had lied about their reasons for stopping Mr. Elmardy. She concluded that

> the conduct of Constable Pak was both high-handed and oppressive. The Appellant was not only touched; he was punched in the face twice. The interaction lasted half an hour, much of which time the Appellant spent on the ground, handcuffed, with his bare hands exposed to ice. The Appellant was an innocent man who had fled his country (Sudan) looking for a society in which his rights would be respected. Instead of finding the respect to which he is entitled, he was subjected to humiliating, violent and oppressive behaviour from one of this city's police officers, all because of the colour of his skin. Further, when questioned about their behaviour the police officers were found to have lied to the Court, conduct that can seriously undermine the administration of justice. (*Elmardy v Toronto Police Services Board*, 2017, para. 35)

The court then varied the award, having found that there was racial profiling in this case, setting the amount at $50,000 against the Toronto Police Services Board for their violations of the Charter, and $25,000 in punitive damages against both Constable Pak and the Toronto Police Services Board, in addition to the $5,000 that the trial judge had awarded for the battery of Mr. Elmardy.

Before You Read Chapter 11

- Does this case seem to be an isolated incident? Or is racial profiling a larger problem in at least parts of Canada?
- Does this case suggest that we need to be concerned about police attitudes toward visible minorities?
- Can you think of other instances, outside this very specific context of policing, in which racial profiling occurs?

Critical Criminology

Introduction

In 2015, about 1 in 37 adults—6,741,400 people—were living under some form of correctional supervision. That is roughly 2.7 percent of the adult population in the United States. And that total represents the lowest rate of incarceration in the United States since 1994 (Kable & Glaze, 2016).[1] In 2018, more than 2.3 million individuals were incarcerated in local jails or in state or federal prisons (Wagner & Sawyer, 2018). To place this figure in perspective, there are almost as many people incarcerated in the United States as the entire population of Canada's largest city, Toronto.

The US Bureau of Justice Statistics (BJS) announced in 2012 that the number of adults being supervised by local, state, or federal correctional systems had actually declined slightly over the previous two years (Glaze & Herberman, 2013). This decline is remarkable, given that in recent decades US incarceration rates have been rising steadily, largely as a result of a series of state and federal laws that promised to "get tough on crime." Many observers would take these declining custody rates as a welcome sign. Politicians, judges, and ordinary citizens have grown tired of policies that do little more than generate an ever-expanding prison system that increases social, economic, and other burdens. However, it might be premature to see this small reversal in a long-term trend as cause for optimism.

Various explanations have been put forward as to why so many people have been locked up in the United States, when crime rates have been consistently declining (Federal Bureau of Investigation, 2011). Although their views may differ in some

punitive turn

The move from criminal justice policies and programs aimed at rehabilitating offenders toward those that simply offer punishment for its own sake. This shift occurred despite declining crime rates and evidence that punishment is not always effective.

respects, as we will see shortly, one group of academic scholars—loosely known as "critical criminologists"—have generally attributed the rise in prison populations in the United States to a shift in public attitudes. This shift has been termed the **punitive turn**, in that it represents a move toward punishing people simply for the sake of punishment, rather than using lesser sanctions and rehabilitation efforts or decriminalization itself (Garland, 2001; Simon, 2007; Wacquant, 2009; Young, 1999). Some have suggested that this shift can be explained in part as a result of media coverage of horrendous crimes (Tonry, 2004), while others point to the formation of victims' rights groups and their increasing presence in the public debate on crime issues (Caplow & Simon, 1999). Still others point out that incarceration in the United States has become a private multi-billion dollar industry, with profitability tied to keeping prison beds full and costs low (Christie, 1993/2002). One thing most critical criminologists agree on, however, is that many American and Canadian politicians have seized on crime as a public policy issue that holds great appeal for voters (Simon, 2007). In recent decades, many elected officials have been trying to outdo one another on the question of who is "tougher on crime."

Beginning in the early 2000s, criminologists who had been studying the punitive turn in the United States started to look at other nations and their penal policies. Several researchers noted something unusual: Canada, right next door to the United States, had maintained adult imprisonment rates that were not only relatively stable but also relatively low (Christie, 2004; Meyer & O'Malley, 2005). This phenomenon caused noted criminologist Nils Christie (2004, p. 59) to ask: "What is so peculiar to Canada?" It also caused some Canadian criminologists to worry that perhaps we were not immune to the mass incarceration that had been happening in the United States and that, in time, it could also happen here (Meyer & O'Malley, 2005). Fast-forward to the current decade and, despite steadily declining crime rates over the past 20 years (Brennan, 2012), Canadians are experiencing their own version of the punitive turn. This change after a decades-long period of relatively cautious penal policies has come courtesy of a Conservative government that—seeing how popular "tough on crime" stances are in the United States—has adopted a similar agenda for Canada. With Stephen Harper's election in 2006 and subsequent re-elections, Canadians began to see many changes: an increase in mandatory minimum sentences for drug and other offences; restrictions on the use of conditional sentences; the creation of a new section of the *Criminal Code* that deals specifically with motor vehicle theft;[2] harsher sentences for sex offenders; a *Truth in Sentencing Act* (which prohibits judges from giving offenders a "2 for 1" credit for time served pretrial); the repeal of the "faint hope clause" that allowed individuals convicted of first-degree murder to apply for parole eligibility at 15 years instead of 25 years; and a *Tackling Violent Crime Act*, which, among other things, contains a "three strikes" provision that makes it easier for individuals to be labelled dangerous offenders and receive indeterminate sentences. The Harper government signalled its willingness to end statutory release for inmates and to give police new surveillance powers over Internet traffic and subscriber data. Critical infrastructure protection, for pipelines, for example, has spurred increased surveillance of environmentalists and Indigenous communities. This has continued since the election of Prime Minister Justin Trudeau's Liberal government.

The offender population in Canada has increased by 7.1 percent over the past five years, with much of this increase coming from marginalized groups such as

Indigenous people and Black people (Correctional Investigator Canada, 2013). In Canada, remand exceeds the sentenced population. In 2015–2016, adults in remand made up 60 percent of the population in custody. That year there were 14,899 people in remand in Canada compared with 10,091 in sentenced custody. The average number of adults in remand in 2015–2016 was 35 percent higher than in 2005–2006 (Reitano, 2016).

As critical criminologists have been at the forefront in exploring the rise of punitive policies in Canada and elsewhere, examining the punitive turn from various perspectives within the field will provide a better understanding of critical criminology. This chapter draws upon insights from the six main areas of the field of critical criminology in Canada today. In doing so, we also examine the work of several Canadian criminologists who focus on this area. First, however, it is useful to explain the nature and scope of critical criminology.

What Is Critical Criminology?

Critical criminology encompasses a broad range of criminological theories and perspectives that share one key element: a desire to challenge inequality, whether it is inequality linked to how crimes are created, defined, or applied to certain groups or individuals, or oppressive treatment or practices found within the criminal justice system. The starting point for critical criminology is the assumption that power is unequally distributed throughout society and that this is also true when it comes to crime and criminal justice. A critical criminologist's task is not simply to find and call attention to oppression, but to actively oppose it. Opposition can come in many forms: issuing calls for change, raising public awareness, participating in public debate and policy-making, and, for some practitioners, even engaging in protest.

There is a misconception that critical criminology started late, arising only in the turbulent 1960s, a time of significant social upheaval. In fact, there have been critical perspectives on crime, justice, and punishment and important critical engagements with criminology since the emergence of criminology as a field of academic research and writing. Many of the earliest critical criminologists were influenced by **anarchist** political movements and raised their criticisms of mainstream criminology as part of broader movements against state authority, discipline, and repression. Anarchists like Peter Kropotkin and Emma Goldman wrote and organized on issues of crime, punishment, and justice and offered criticisms for orthodox criminology at the turn of the 20th century. We can see critical criminology in the 1930s in the works of Thorsten Sellin and in the 1940s and 1950s in the works of critical sociologists like C. Wright Mills and Alex Comfort. That these histories have been marginalized or forgotten is itself an expression of power and dominant ideology.

The second wave of critical criminology emerged in the 1960s and 1970s. Criminologists were immersed in the radical politics of the day—civil rights, women's liberation, the anti-war movement, and, beginning in the early 1970s, LGBTQ+ rights issues. They also showed some of the anarchist influence, and critical criminologists like Jock Young and Stanley Cohen were involved in anarchist politics while students. They increasingly found that mainstream criminology, with its focus on the pathology of individual offenders, ran counter to their beliefs and practices. They rejected the idea of the so-called criminal mind, and instead turned their attention to how criminals are created, not by

critical criminology
A school of thought with multiple subfields but largely concerned with social justice and inequality, promoting active opposition to the status quo, and favouring larger-scale societal transformations rather than minor policy changes.

anarchism
A political and social perspective that rejects the necessity of imposed rule by external authorities such as the state. From the Greek *an archos*, it means the absence of rulers, though not the absence of rules. Anarchism has influenced critical criminology generally, and post-structural and peace-making criminology and restorative justice specifically.

birth, but through social processes. To better understand this process, critical criminologists use as their fundamental theoretical and empirical building blocks the concepts of class, race and ethnicity, gender and sexuality, and other social categories that have been employed to maintain oppressive relations between groups.

Many of the second wave of critical criminologists shared a world view based on **Marxism**—that is, they were interested primarily in class relations and how the structure of capitalism produces inequalities linked to crime and criminal justice. Over the years, however, critical criminology developed lines of academic research and thought, most of which are distinctly different from its early Marxist roots (for example, Quinney, 1977; Taylor, Walton, & Young, 1975). Neo-Marxist scholars continue to explore the intersection of capitalism and oppression, but they are now joined under the critical criminology umbrella by feminist scholars, who look at gender issues within criminal justice; critical race/post-colonial scholars, who explore the intersection of race and criminal justice; left realist scholars, who explore the deep social causes of crime in order to develop practical solutions; post-structuralist scholars, who seek to untangle the many ways in which power and inequality can manifest within and across social institutions; and peace-making scholars, who challenge conventional responses to crime that are considered not merely retributive but violent and counterproductive to the goal of community safety (Milovanovic, 2002).

Contemporary critical criminology is informed by new social movement struggles. Important contributions have been made by the Black Lives Matter and Idle No More movements.

Marxism
A school of thought developed by Karl Marx (1818–1883) arguing that society must be understood in terms of social conflict, class relations, and the inequalities caused by capitalism. Marxists promote revolution by the working class.

Montrealers protesting the shooting of Abdirahman Abdi by Ottawa police in 2016. Important contributions to contemporary critical criminology have been made by new social movement struggles such as Black Lives Matter.

Prominent Streams Within Critical Criminology

Neo-Marxism

Neo-Marxists take many of their cues from the work of 19th-century thinkers Karl Marx and Friedrich Engels, who condemned the social, political, and material inequalities produced within capitalist systems. Neo-Marxist criminologists focus on how the state uses the criminal justice system to legitimize unequal social arrangements through laws that cater to elite groups while oppressing the working class, the poor, and other marginalized groups. According to this perspective, crime is not a neutral, value-free concept, but a deeply political issue over which differently situated social groups struggle to maintain or overthrow oppression. Because of this view, neo-Marxists are typically referred to as **conflict theorists**[3]—they hold that society is not built on consensus, but, rather, on class conflict (Chambliss & Seidman, 1971).

You may wonder why this group is called "neo-Marxist" and not simply "Marxist." The name shift can be traced to Ian Taylor, Paul Walton, and Jock Young's book *The New Criminology* (1973), which included three key ideas derived from traditional Marxism:

1. In a capitalist system, the economy dictates the structure and functioning of society (including crime).
2. Capitalism is directly to blame for crime because it creates the conditions of inequality that lead to crime.
3. The only way to eliminate crime is to eliminate the conditions that create it—that is, eliminate capitalism.

conflict theories
Theories, originating primarily with Marx, that focus on the unequal distribution of power in society—for example, due to class, race, or gender. Conflicts between classes or groups are driven to a large extent by this unequal power and unequal access to resources.

interactionist perspective
A theoretical approach that focuses on relatively small-scale social interactions among individuals or small social groups, as well as the conscious acts of individuals and their interpretation of others' behaviour.

Private security guards patrol a public thoroughfare in Toronto's Chinatown, having been hired to deal with loiterers, beggars, and other people considered "undesirables" by local businesses. The increasing presence of private security in many public spheres can blur the lines between public and private spaces. It also alters one's concept of "policing" the public realm. This form of policing emphasizes the protection of certain privileged interests.

Taylor, Walton, and Young's modern (or "neo") approach differed from traditional Marxism because it also incorporated some aspects of the **interactionist perspective**, in particular the concept of "labelling" derived from labelling theory. An excellent example of how labelling theory helps flesh out Marxist ideas can be found in Hall, Critcher, Jefferson, Clarke, and Roberts's *Policing the Crisis* (1978). This book demonstrates how a **moral panic** over mugging incidents in the United Kingdom created new fears (the term "mugging" was reportedly not even a part of British vocabulary prior to the moral panic), demonized Black males, and united the public against this perceived threat. Notably, this *crisis* had the effect of diverting public attention away from the fact that the United Kingdom was in the midst of a serious economic decline.

A number of notable neo-Marxist criminologists are writing today. They include Colin Sumner in Ireland, Michael Welch in the United States, and George Rigakos in Canada. Rigakos draws on the Marxist tradition and infuses it with theoretical strands drawn from other perspectives. He has written extensively on the rise of private security and the role that this "commodity"[4] plays in facilitating social control of those seen as "dangerous." George Rigakos and Aysegul Ergul (2011) argue that policing—both public and now increasingly private—has historically served the interests of capital in a variety of ways, including supporting the retention and accumulation of private property (such as shopping malls and business complexes), cutting worker costs by replacing paid police officers with private security staff, and assisting in monitoring and regulating potential threats to capital from dissatisfied workers or citizens (for example, striking labourers or public protestors). Rigakos's overall objective is to create a "Marxist political economy of policing" (Rigakos & Ergul, 2011). His work often explores the ways in which public and private policing intersect in the service of capitalist enterprise.

The Creation of a Criminalized Class

A now classic text in neo-Marxist criminology is Jeffrey Reiman's *The Rich Get Richer and the Poor Get Prison* (1979/2004). An excerpt appears in Box 11.1. In it, Reiman argues that the goal of the US criminal justice system is not to fight crime, but to maintain existing class relations through the creation of a criminalized class among the poor. Those who might represent a potential challenge to the political, social, and economic elites are neutralized behind bars. The state does this by creating and policing crimes that are most typically associated with poverty and harshly sentencing offenders. If the goal of the criminal justice system is actually to fight crime, Reiman says, the state would attempt to address the root causes of street crime by eliminating the conditions that give rise to them and focus instead on the predatory crimes of the wealthy and powerful that affect everyone (such as white-collar and environmental crimes).

moral panic
Phenomena—socially constructed by the media, politicians, and "moral entrepreneurs"—in which certain people or groups are labelled or stigmatized as the cause of a perceived social problem, resulting in widespread public alarm.

For more on labelling theory, see Chapter 9, Sociological Approaches.

BOX 11.1

"The Rich Get Richer and the Poor Get Prison"

A key work in the field of critical criminology is Jeffrey Reiman's *The Rich Get Richer and the Poor Get Prison*. Reiman's approach is summarized in the following excerpt, which also touches on the theme of white-collar crime (discussed in more detail in Chapter 18, White-Collar Crime of this text).

Though crime rates have recently declined around the United States, the truth is that the criminal justice system is still failing. While politicians and police chiefs rush to claim credit for the declines, most independent observers credit most of the decline to factors such as the stabilization of the drug trade (which has led to reduced drug-gang violence) and the (until recently) improving economy, which offers idle young men better things to do than look for trouble. What's more, the decline is measured from the abnormally high crime rates of recent years. Crime and criminal violence are still extremely prevalent in the United States, as a look at any daily newspaper or TV news program will confirm. Now, instead of crime rates being *very, very* high, they have come down to only *very* high! Our crime rates are still higher by far than those of other modern nations, and we lead the world in the percentage of our children who are murdered.

So, the criminal justice system is still failing to protect us, even if the crime rates sometimes go down. But the failure is not random. It has a pattern. We have, over the last two decades, been on an imprisonment binge that has made us the country with the highest percentage of citizens behind bars. The vast majority of those locked up are poor inner-city men—many for drug dealing and non-violent offenses—insuring that there will be more children without fathers around, and more men with prison records unable to find decent jobs. On the other hand, still only a fraction of those responsible for Saving and Loan frauds are being made to face criminal prosecution, and, though there has been tough talk about the new crop of Enron and Enron-like corporate cheats, criminal prosecutions to date have been rare. So, while we throw more and more poor people into prison for non-violent offenses, high-class crooks continue to be treated leniently. But this is only the most visible bias against the poor. It applies to people found guilty of acts defined in law as crimes. The subtlest bias against the poor happens earlier, at the very point at which the powers that be decide which acts to define as crimes in the first place. Many of the ways in which the well-off harm their fellows (deadly pollution, unsafe working conditions, and the like) are not even defined as crimes *though they do more damage to life and limb than the acts that are treated as crimes.*

Source: Excerpted from © 2004, "The rich get richer and the poor get prison: Ideology, class, and criminal justice," by J. Reiman. Reproduced by permission of Taylor and Francis Group, LLC, a division of Informa plc.

Feminist Criminology

Spurred by the political struggles of the women's liberation movement in the 1960s and 1970s, feminist criminology emerged as a reaction to the biases that dominated the field of mainstream criminology. In the larger movement, feminists have been concerned with gender inequality, particularly within social institutions that create and/or sustain male privilege and female oppression. In surveying the landscape of mainstream criminology, feminist criminologists noted that much of this work was **patriarchal** in nature, which resulted in one of two significant problems:

1. androcentrism, with males routinely referenced as the de facto standard for criminological research (i.e., treating men and women the same despite their very different socialization, social problems, and social statuses) (Daly & Chesney-Lind, 1988; Griffin, 2010); and
2. disregard for women's issues altogether, particularly where they might represent a challenge to male dominance.

When women were represented in mainstream criminology works, they were depicted either as passive victims whom men sought to protect or, because they transgressed gender norms, as offenders who must be psychologically disturbed ("mad") or otherwise inherently pathological ("bad"). Feminist criminologists seek to challenge

For more in-depth discussion on these themes, see Chapter 10, Gender and Crime.

patriarchy
An elitist form of social structure, in which men dominate politics, economics, and other aspects of society and perpetuate that domination by limiting opportunities for women to exercise power.

gender norms and assumptions, as well as uncover systemic biases, in order to challenge treatment of women within law, the criminal justice system, and the larger society.

Feminists identify the violence against women perpetrated by the state, particularly in policing. Socialist feminists question the role of state institutions in perpetuating violence against women more broadly. This includes violence by police against street-involved women, the harassment of women within policing, and the high rates of domestic violence against women by police officers. They challenge the criminalization of sex work and other controls over women's bodies and labour by the state.

Although some overlap exists among them, the three major forms of critical feminist criminology are "Marxist," "socialist," and "radical" (Daly & Chesney-Lind, 1988):

- Marxist feminists focus on the unequal class and gender relations fostered by the capitalist mode of production.
- Socialist feminists apply a combination of Marxist and socialist ideas, locating the problem of inequality in class and gender conflict associated with the capitalist system, and advocating for sweeping (socialist) changes to the capitalist system, as well as an end to patriarchy.
- Radical feminists see patriarchy as present in all social relations, which requires nothing less than a radical overhaul of society and an equalizing of relations (Burgess-Proctor, 2006; Flavin, 2001).

BOX 11.2

Feminism and the War on Drugs

In recent decades, many North American governments and law enforcement agencies have pursued a "war on drugs," a multi-billion dollar effort to find, arrest, and severely punish offenders, but this has proven a failure in limiting the actual availability and consumption of drugs. However, the war on drugs has been cited as a principal contributor to harsher North American sentencing laws and increasing prison numbers. Meda Chesney-Lind (2009) examined the impact of the punitive turn on women when these policies began to be implemented. She noted that after 1980, female incarceration rates in the United States quintupled as a result of "gender blind, get tough policies on drugs." The "national zeal for imprisoning women," as she described it, had a particularly negative impact on women of colour: Between 1986 and 1991, rates of female Black American imprisonment for drug offences rose by 828 percent, followed by 328 percent among Hispanic women and 241 percent among white women. At the same time, state budgets experienced cuts to spending on education and social assistance programs. As Chesney-Lind observed:

> What we are seeing is a mindless and massive transfer away from education and welfare into prisons. This means that monies that once went to support low-income women and their children in the community, as well as the dollars to provide her with educational opportunities, are being cut back dramatically at the same time that monies to arrest, detain, and incarcerate women and men on the economic margins are being increased (2009).

More recently, similar phenomena have emerged in Canada, as female incarceration rates increased by 60 percent over the ten-year period between 2003 and 2013, and with marginalized Indigenous and Black females again being disproportionately represented in the Canadian prison population. The majority of Black women are incarcerated for drug offences, including trafficking, which many of them pursued, according to interviews with these inmates, in an effort to rise above poverty (Correctional Investigator Canada, 2013). Indigenous women are Canada's fastest growing prison population, with a rise of over 100 percent between 2001 and 2016 (Malone, 2016).

Feminist criminologists are well represented in the field of critical criminology. They include Meda Chesney-Lind, Nicole Rafter, and James Messerschmidt in the United States, and Pat Carlen, Loraine Gelsthorpe, and Frances Heidensohn in England. Notable Canadians working in this field include Karlene Faith, Gillian Balfour, and Elizabeth Comack. Since the 1990s, Comack has contributed substantially to our understanding of women's involvement with the criminal justice system. Much of her early work centred on women's imprisonment and the means by which women became "offenders." Through this research, which revealed significant patterns of physical and sexual abuse in the histories of female offenders, she became involved in projects aimed at understanding the "standpoint" of women in trouble with the law. That is, Comack was interested in representing how female study participants saw and understood the world and their experiences within it (Comack, 1996).

Critical Race Theory and Post-Colonial Theory

Although they share different beginnings, critical race theory and post-colonial theory overlap in their common goal: to fight racist oppression that is built into social structures and the very fabric of society. **Critical race theory** emerged in the 1970s, becoming in the 1990s an umbrella term for a variety of theories and practices developed by Black American, Latino, and Asian American scholars who were actively engaged in anti-racist scholarship and activism. Its roots are deeper, however, and can be found in the work of intellectuals such as 19th-century social reformer Frederick Douglass and early 20th-century sociologist and activist W.E.B. Du Bois. Critical race scholars have been instrumental in taking apart "essentialist" ideas of race that consider it as a biological category. Rather, for these scholars, race is a social category or "construct"—a meaning created by society that is placed on a person, significantly affecting his or her opportunities in life. Opportunities are open or closed to people not simply because other individuals carry prejudiced ideas around in their heads, but because racism exists within social relations, practices, and institutions. By contrast, **post-colonial theory** was developed largely from the struggles for political freedom among many former colonies of Britain, France, and other European powers. Frantz Fanon's *Black Skin, White Masks* (1952/2008) is a key anti-colonial text that documents the terrible effects of colonialism on the psyches of individuals. Post-colonial theory helps us understand how racialized relations play out across the globe and influence how we view and thus treat "the other."

Much of the work conducted by critical criminologists using these perspectives focuses on two important issues. One of these is the problem of **systemic racism** in the criminal justice system and its effects on people of colour. A significant early essay that tackled this issue was Robert Staples's *White Racism, Black Crime, and American Justice* (1975). Staples used Fanon's ideas on colonialism to explain "the American pattern of racial

critical race theory
A theory that examines the ways in which race and racial power are constructed by law and society, and that sees the law and criminal justice system not as solutions but as part of the problem.

post-colonial theory
The wide-ranging academic study of the social, political, and cultural legacy of colonial rule and its effects on individual and group identities and social power relations. It also examines the domination of other cultures through a discourse of "otherness."

systemic racism
The belief that racism does not occur only in isolated instances, but is entrenched in and perpetuated by our criminal justice system and other institutions.

dominance and subjugation" evidenced in the overpolicing of Black communities and the ill-treatment of Black citizens by police and the larger justice system (Staples, 1975, p. 14). Such maltreatment, he noted, is often justified by references to so-called "Black on Black" crime, a social fact that Staples acknowledges and explains. Violence within colonized groups, he argues, is not unusual in that the colonized have absorbed the aggressiveness of the dominant community that has attempted to impose its cultural values on them. The result is displaced aggression. A further significant contribution of critical criminologists in this area has been their critiques of the discipline of criminology itself and the means by which criminologists contribute to forms of oppression at home and abroad. One such example is the work of Tamari Kitossa (2012), who notes that critical race theory challenges mainstream criminology by uncovering its underlying racialized assumptions.

A number of criminologists draw inspiration from these theories, including Coretta Phillips in England and Elijah Anderson in the United States. In Canada, Renisa Mawani uses post-colonial theories to better understand how legal rules are used and applied in the social world. Using historical case studies, Mawani (2009) shows how racialized fears of "the other" by white Canadian colonists led to various forms of social control targeting Indigenous peoples and non-European migrants. What Mawani reveals is how the history of race relations—in particular white anxieties—led to the creation of racist forms of law, as in drug and alcohol prohibitions targeting specific racialized groups such as Indigenous people. Mawani argues that whenever we discuss multiculturalism and the pluralist society that Canada has supposedly become, we are always doing so within the context of a colonialist history that was far from benign.

Recently, the works of Black Lives Matter and public intellectuals like Desmond Cole and Robyn Maynard have focused public attention on police violence and lethal force against people of colour in Canada. Robyn Maynard's (2017) book *Policing Black Lives* shows that racialized criminal justice system violence is an ongoing feature of the Canadian state—it is not merely a recent development.

BOX 11.3

Racial Profiling

Although much of the discussion in this chapter has focused on incarceration rates (i.e., sentencing), policing policies also play a significant role in this phenomenon. Ben Bowling, for example, has explored how policing systems unfairly target Black and other minority communities. (The tendency for law enforcement officers to make assumptions about someone's potential involvement in criminal activity based on the colour of their skin or their ethnicity is known as **racial profiling**; see Case Study 11.1, which precedes this chapter.) Bowling's review of claims by the New York police that "zero tolerance" policing reduced that city's homicide rate reveals how aggressive crackdowns against people of colour (often for very minor offences, such as subway turnstile jumping) had little effect on the violent crime rate, which was already in decline. Looking at the British context, Bowling and Coretta Phillips (2002) have drawn attention to the overrepresentation of ethnic minorities among deaths in police custody and to the police practice of "stop and frisk," which entails conducting random spot searches of "suspect" minority youth, some as young as ten years old. A 2018 study in Vancouver found that street checks by police in that city disproportionately target Indigenous people (Canadian Press, 2018).

racial profiling
The act or tendency of law enforcement officers and others to consider people suspicious or more likely to commit crime because of the colour of their skin or their ethnicity.

Left Realism

Where neo-Marxist scholars had focused largely on white-collar crime and other crimes of the elite, the "left realist" branch of criminology, as it came to be known, explored crime and criminality more broadly. Left realist scholars started from the position that crime is a serious issue rooted in social conditions, the dynamics of which needed to be better understood and addressed in order to offer practical solutions. To help in this process, they expanded on the basic crime triangle—the offender, the victim, and the state—by introducing the "square of crime," which includes a fourth element: informal social controls within civil society.

Aside from widening the criminological lens, left realists have drawn attention to what are seen as three important and interrelated concepts for understanding the nature of crime within Western societies.

The first of these concepts is "relative deprivation." Building on Robert Merton's earlier work on anomie-strain theory, relative deprivation, and reference group theory, left realists have argued that crime is more likely in situations where members of a particular group experience discontent as a result of being deprived of things to which other groups have access, such as new technologies or designer clothes (Lea & Young, 1984; Young, 1999).

A second important concept for left realists is "subculture." A subculture is a segment of society that forms in response to a shared problem, and which possesses its own distinctive patterns of beliefs, values, mores, and expressions. Historically, much of the earlier Chicago School work on subculture formation focused on marginalized youth. Left realism has expanded this focus to include the formation of subcultures among middle-class youth and the forces that drive them to offend.

The third concept is "marginalization," which refers to the social and economic processes that lead some groups to be excluded from opportunities available to others. The result is that group members find themselves as social outcasts on the borders of society, looking in at those who are in the privileged position of being able to achieve the desired fame, fortune, and/or social standing.

Although originating in England with key thinkers such as Jock Young, John Lea, Richard Kinsey, and Roger Matthews, left realism has had a wide influence in North America and elsewhere. For example, in the United States, left realism is commonly associated with the work of Elliott Currie and Martin Schwartz. In Canada, the left realist perspective has been exemplified by the work of Walter DeKeseredy and colleagues who have explored the social, economic, and political forces that result in violence against women, notably exploring how the relationship between the North American masculine ideal—the economically successful male—and the reality of increasing economic disenfranchisement leads men within certain subcultures and communities to attempt to reassert masculinity through violence against women (DeKeseredy, Alvi, & Schwartz, 2006).

"The Exclusive Society"

In relation to the punitive turn, a key text is Jock Young's *The Exclusive Society* (1999). In his book, Young argues that the punitive turn is linked to economic changes that are making life increasingly precarious, not only for the poor and working class but also for middle-class families who fear poverty and overt symbols of poverty. As Young explains, relative deprivation is not just about the poor and working classes looking

For more on anomie-strain theory, see Chapter 9.

For more on the Chicago School, see Chapter 9.

upward; it is also about the middle classes looking down the social hierarchy to re-assure themselves that there *are* people below them. In a time of increasing economic and social instability, looking downward produces fear, because it reminds the middle classes of the often precarious state of their economic existence. This fear, Young suggests, underlies increased intolerance of marginalized groups and support for harsher treatment of offenders and other "deviant" groups.

BOX 11.4

A Case of "Affluenza"

In June 2013, news emerged of an affluent Texas teenager, Ethan Couch, who had killed four people while driving drunk. What made this all-too-common tragedy particularly newsworthy was the startling fact that he was able to avoid severe punishment because his defence team had successfully argued that he suffered from what has been dubbed "affluenza," an outgrowth of increasing social inequality, where someone suffers from a form of mental illness and acute social alienation due to their extreme wealth, which effectively renders them unable to properly understand the consequences of their actions.

Not surprisingly, the case generated extensive debate about sentencing practices, as well as whether this was even a legitimate psychological condition. Boyce Watkins drew on the title of Jeffrey Reiman's famous book (see Box 11.1) in writing his response to the case, entitled "Rich, White Kids Have 'Affluenza,' Poor, Black Kids Go to Prison":

> The very idea that this kid's wealth was turned into a convenient liability lies in contradiction to the fact that his wealth has always been a tremendous asset. It's allowed him to get whatever he wants, whenever he wants. But when the spoiled rich kid's actions finally catch up with him, the very thing that's given him an advantage is suddenly considered to be a huge disadvantage. …
>
> This case is even more sickening when one considers how often serious psychological problems are not taken into consideration when the cases involve poor, Black or brown people. How often do our kids commit crimes after being victims of years of abuse, neglect, hunger, miseducation and dire poverty? When my deceased uncle … was sent to prison, I never once heard a judge consider the fact that he suffered from severe mental illness all throughout his life. In fact, going to prison only served to worsen his mental illness, not make it better (Watkins, 2013).

In what ways might this case be considered an example of "the exclusive society" described by Jock Young?

---

post-structuralism
A theoretical perspective concerned with how power operates between and among individuals, groups, and social institutions (as opposed to belonging to the state or power elites alone). Post-structuralists look for differences in power in areas such as language use and social practices.

Post-Structuralism

Post-structuralist[5] criminology also developed as a reaction against prevailing ways of looking at crime: Marxism and structural functionalism. Despite their fundamental differences, Marxism (conflict theory) and structural functionalism (consensus theory) are perspectives that share a focus on the structure of societies and how the operation of the various parts of society support the state. Post-structuralists counter that power and prospects for oppression permeate all levels of society, as between a boss and worker, for example. Post-structuralism is influenced by earlier anarchist critiques of power in society (May, 1994).

Post-structuralists also argue that one can never stand outside a social system as an objective, neutral observer. They point out that our understanding of social and natural "realities" is dependent on language, and that the acts of naming, describing, and understanding phenomena will always be context, and status, specific. Drawing on the work of Michel Foucault, post-structuralists describe this phenomenon as **discourse**. As an example, groups within criminology and criminal justice use discourse to communicate shared meanings with other group members. Police talk about "bad guys," corrections officers might refer to someone as a "DO" (dangerous offender) or "con" (convict). These labels express power.

Foucault's work on historical changes in the nature of social control within a variety of social contexts provided a foundation for post-structuralism during the 1990s. Foucault (1979) described how different societies in different epochs dealt with punishment, sexuality, and the treatment of insanity and criminality. This has been supplemented by the writings of other prominent post-structuralist theorists (such as Jacques Derrida and Gilles Deleuze).

In the United Kingdom, a group of Foucauldian scholars emerged in the 1990s, including criminologist Nikolas Rose. Other key post-structuralist criminologists include Pat O'Malley in Australia and David Garland in the United States. Canadian criminologists have also drawn on post-structuralist theory and methodology to explain crime and criminal justice. Stéphane Leman-Langlois has conducted extensive research on human rights and post-conflict efforts in addressing human rights violations. Looking at the South African Truth and Reconciliation Commission (TRC), established in the mid-1990s after the fall of apartheid in that country, Leman-Langlois (2000) points to the creation of a language (or "discourse") that sought to legitimize the TRC in the eyes of victims and the larger society, while simultaneously excluding the possibility of offenders being punished or forced to provide compensation to victims.

discourses
Refers to forms of language, representation, and practices and how meaning is created and shared. Discourses take place within specific cultural and historical contexts.

BOX 11.5

A "Culture of Control"

Among notable post-structuralist scholars who have explored the punitive turn is David Garland. In his 2001 book, *Culture of Control*, Garland draws on his **Foucauldian** roots to argue that punishment and other forms of social control are tied to social forces that can often be understood only in hindsight. The turn to more punitive forms of social control, which Garland traces to the 1970s, is an example of this phenomenon. The 1960s were turbulent times, in which all levels of society underwent significant economic, social, and demographic changes. The resulting uncertainty led people to become increasingly anxious for themselves and their families, and their anxieties consequently began to centre on what were considered "criminal threats." In criminal justice circles, an influential study on offender rehabilitation argued that "nothing works" (Martinson, 1974). Politicians, the public, and some criminologists and criminal justice officials latched onto the idea that nothing works. The outcome was a shift in the discourse on how prisons and offenders were viewed, which resulted in major cutbacks to prison rehabilitation programs and lengthier offender sentences. As Garland notes, in the United States, little to no focus has been placed on rehabilitating the offender. Instead, "the prison is used today as a kind of reservation, a quarantine zone in which purportedly dangerous individuals are segregated in the name of public safety" (2001, p. 78).

Foucauldian
Relating to the works of influential French thinker Michel Foucault.

Peace-Making Criminology

social justice
Movement promoting the need for equality, tolerance, and fairness for all members of society, particularly with regard to different classes and the less privileged.

Peace-making criminology is a theoretical perspective that favours a **social justice** approach to preventing and responding to crime. The ultimate goal of peace-making criminologists is the eradication of crime through policies and programs that end the suffering they believe causes crime—poverty, racism, sexism, family violence, and social alienation. Adapting a slogan from the 1960s to help state their case ("make peace, not war"), peace-making criminologists oppose oppressive criminal justice measures such as the "war on drugs." Instead, they favour empathetic approaches to social problems, treating offenders as human beings who, despite their past behaviour, still need and deserve understanding, empathy, and kindness.

restorative justice
An approach to justice and sentencing, often influenced by Indigenous culture, that emphasizes the healing and reconciliation of victims, perpetrators, and their communities, and promotes positive social engagement instead of social control.

While peace-making criminologists express some interest in the causes of crime, their focus is more typically on the treatment of offenders by the state. In keeping with their adoption of **restorative justice** models that seek to foster understanding and reconciliation between the offender, victim, and community, they are opposed to any form of violence enacted against offenders by the state. This opposition can be seen in their attitudes toward capital punishment, which peace-making criminologists wish to see abolished wherever it is still practised. Peace-making criminologists differ somewhat in their attitudes toward imprisonment, however, and these differences say much about the diverse strands of thought—existentialism, Buddhism, Quakerism, Indigenous cultural beliefs, feminism, anarchism, and neo-Marxism, among others—that underlie "peace-making criminology" (Quinney, 1995). For example, some within this group seek to reduce the use of imprisonment through the use of social justice-oriented programs ("minimalists"), whereas others oppose the use of imprisonment altogether ("abolitionists").

Notable individuals working within the framework of the peace-making perspective include Australian restorative justice proponent John Braithwaite and Americans Hal Pepinsky, Richard Quinney, Anthony Nocella II, and Jeff Ferrell. A number of Canadian critical criminologists with very different theoretical approaches are also working within peace-making criminology, including Kevin Walby (who can be considered an "anarcho-abolitionist") and Heidi Rimke.

A prominent advocate of restorative justice is Andrew Woolford. In various books and articles, Woolford has examined both the politics of restorative justice and its potential to engender social transformation along class, gender, race, and other lines (2009). He argues that while restorative justice is still a tool of governance—meaning that it is used by the state to regulate individual and group behaviours—it is also a social movement that can transform the social and political landscape of societies by eradicating social injustices. Among other projects, Woolford has also been a strong proponent for a criminology of **genocide**, an approach that explores the phenomenon of genocide from a purely criminological standpoint in order to help minimize future group conflicts.

genocide
The deliberate and systematic attempt to exterminate an entire population or subpopulation that shares a racial, religious, national, or cultural identity.

Fostering a More Humane Society

One of the first critical criminologists to tackle the problem of rising incarceration rates across the Western world was Norwegian Nils Christie. In *Limits to Pain* (1981/2007), Christie took the radical position that our current practice of criminal justice is essentially a pain delivery system that is more about a given society's willingness to inflict pain on its citizens than a perceived need to respond to acts labelled as criminal. Christie expanded on this idea in *Crime Control as Industry* (1993/2002), wherein he demonstrated the extent to which criminal justice systems operate akin to private industries, which have continual growth as their ultimate objective. He further elaborated upon this theme in *A Suitable Amount of Crime* (2004). Long before anyone was discussing the "punitive turn," Christie drew on statistical and observational data to highlight the alarming extent to which the United States, Britain, and other Western states were expanding their penal systems through the creation of an increasing array of crimes, coupled with harsher penalties against offenders. For Christie, the **prison industrial complex** benefits only those who are employed by it or benefit from its profitability. Rather than treating individuals as "criminals" and punishing them with harsher sanctions that fail to prevent future criminal acts, he believes that we should treat the majority of offenders as individuals requiring therapeutic interventions aimed at helping them to reconcile with both their victims and the larger society. This would help foster a more humane society, one that would lessen the conditions that create and sustain anti-social behaviours.

prison industrial complex
Adapted from "military industrial complex"; a term used to attribute increases in incarceration rates to the efforts of private for-profit corporations that build and maintain prisons with the active legislative and financial support of their political allies.

BOX 11.6

Is There "A Suitable Amount of Crime"?

In his book *A Suitable Amount of Crime*, Norwegian criminologist Nils Christie poses many provocative questions about the role, and severity, of punishment in Western societies:

How large can we let the penal system grow, or conversely, how small can we have it, if we need it at all? Is it possible to establish upper, and eventually lower, limits to the amount of punishment that ought to be applied in a modern society? And lastly, for those of us working close to this field, is it possible to influence what happens? ... Is it possible to establish *some sort of criteria* for what might be seen as the suitable amount of punishment in a society? ... Turned into questions of the evaluation of the volume and of the life conditions of prisoners in modern times, when is enough, enough? And when is it more than enough? Where is the limit in modern societies? When has a prison population in a country reached a level when at least our intuition says that this is wrong, completely wrong, unacceptable! And when are life conditions below dignity? We have some intuitive answers. ... But is it possible to anchor views from the heart to some sort of reasoning? Let me attempt to do so by the discussion of three cases of *IF*.

1. *IF we believe in the values of kindness and forgiving—then we ought to keep the institution of penal law a small one ...*
2. *IF we believe in the values of keeping civil societies civil—then we have to keep the institution of penal law a small one ...*
3. *IF we believe in the value of living in cohesive, integrated societies—then we must retard the growth of the institution of penal law ...*

An essential question for us in the Nordic countries, and also in Western Europe and Canada, is whether the developments in the US are inevitable. Are they a consequence of their economic system? And will welfare states also gradually face consequences similar to the US model, consequences that will lead to increased class differentiation as well as to increased uncertainty among the population at large? We observe how the criminal policies of a number of industrial nations are becoming a central arena for presentation by politicians. ... Uncertainties are muffled by political promises about severe measures to be taken against *offenders*, a term that gradually has become a euphemism for *the lower-lower classes*, a term that may become a euphemism for *the dangerous classes* or, in certain countries, people of the wrong colour.

Source: "A Suitable Amount of Crime," N. Christie, © 2004, London, UK: Routledge, reproduced by permission of Taylor & Francis Books UK.

Conclusion

Although considerable overlap exists among the various branches of critical criminology, each branch has a distinct approach to theory and policy. Some critical criminologists call for a minimalist approach to state intervention, whereas others are outright abolitionists and call for the total abolition of imprisonment and capital punishment. Some come from a neo-Marxist perspective, while others come from anarchistic perspectives. Despite the diverse approaches, critical criminologists have by and large emerged from the conflict perspective in criminology. In other words, they consider that society and its laws are based on social conflict, not social consensus. Critical criminologists are united in challenging our basic assumptions about the existing social order and the purpose of law, arguing that the law primarily serves the interests of the power elite, not the interests of the marginalized, oppressed classes in society. They are typically unconcerned about "criminal motivation" (a preoccupation of most mainstream criminologists), because they start with the assumption that crime is the result of economic and political inequality. Putting people in prison or executing them does not resolve long-standing social problems like poverty, unemployment, and marginalization.

In many respects, critical criminology has acted as an alternative to mainstream (or orthodox) criminology, asking why criminologists traditionally spend so much of their time studying only those who are defined by the state as deviant, and/or obsessively measuring the criminalization of the lower classes. It also questions why "suite crime" (white-collar crime) is often regarded as a civil violation or simply as a shrewd business practice, whereas "street crime" is usually met with the full force of the criminal justice system. As Jock Young argues in "Critical Criminology in the Twenty-First Century: Critique, Irony, and the Always Unfinished" (2002), all criminology should be "critical." Criminologists should reflect on what they are doing, asking themselves who they are doing it for, and why.

SUMMARY OF KEY POINTS

- Critical criminology encompasses a broad range of criminological theories and perspectives, all of which share a desire to challenge inequality. This approach is applied not only to any oppressive treatment or practices found within the criminal justice system, but also to discussions about how crime is defined, and extends to discussions about the goals of criminology itself.

- The starting point for critical criminology is the assumption that *power* is unequally distributed throughout society and that this is also true when it comes to crime and criminal justice. A critical criminologist's task is not simply to find and call attention to oppression, but to actively oppose it.

- A shift in criminal justice policies and programs from those aimed at rehabilitating offenders toward those that simply offer punishment for its own sake is referred to by critical criminologists as "the punitive turn."

- Neo-Marxist criminologists focus on how the state uses the criminal justice system to legitimize unequal social arrangements through laws that cater to elite groups while oppressing the working class, the poor, and other marginalized groups. Neo-Marxists are typically referred to as conflict theorists because they hold that society is not built on consensus but, rather, on class conflict.

- Feminist criminologists—of which there are many streams—generally seek to challenge gender norms and assumptions, as well as uncover systemic biases, in order to equalize treatment of women within law, the criminal justice system, and the larger society.

- Critical race theory and post-colonial theory overlap in their goal to fight racist oppression that is built into social structures and the very fabric of society. A key area of focus is the view that criminal justice institutions—the police, the courts, and so on—are inherently racist; that is, they are an example of systemic racism.

- Left realist criminology explores crime and criminality more broadly, starting from the position that crime is a serious issue rooted in social conditions, the dynamics of which need to be better understood and addressed in order to offer practical solutions. They expand upon the basic crime triangle—the offender, the victim, and the state—by introducing the "square of crime," which includes a fourth element: informal social controls within civil society.

- Post-structuralism is a theoretical perspective that has been applied to criminology, which is concerned with how power operates between and among individuals, groups, and social institutions, as opposed to belonging to the state or power elites alone. Post-structuralists examine power in relation to, in particular, language and social practices.

- Peace-making criminology uproots and challenges the everyday violence reproduced and maintained by systems of statist criminal justice (police, courts, and corrections). Peace-making criminologists suggest that the absence of war is not the presence of peace in societies that are divided by class and status and regulated by institutions of state violence. They seek alternative forms of social mediation and transformation outside of state institutions like courts and prisons.

NOTES

Jeff Shantz thanks Eva Ureta for ongoing assistance and support. This chapter is adapted from an earlier version by Laura Huey.

1. Correctional supervision encompasses not only incarceration (local jails, and state and federal prisons) but also community corrections (probation and parole).
2. This offence was previously dealt with under general *Criminal Code* provisions for "theft," or "taking motor-vehicle ... without consent."
3. It should be noted that conflict theory is not necessarily the sole domain of critical criminology. Notable conflict theorists who came onto the scene prior to the advent of critical criminology include Thorsten Sellin and Austin Turk.
4. "Commodity" in this sense refers to the fact that private security is a contract service; thus, it represents something that can be bought and sold.
5. In critical criminology literature, "post-structuralism" is often confused or conflated with "postmodernism," likely because both of these relatively recent philosophies focus on language as a key component to understanding how we view the world.

QUESTIONS FOR CRITICAL DISCUSSION

1. Consider the ways in which critical criminologists examine the practice of criminal justice in Canada, and elsewhere. In what ways do their critiques raise

questions about economics or politics? To what extent do you think problems of crime are the result of economic factors?

2. How does the use of the term "critical" in "critical criminology" differ from its more common usage?

3. How can critical criminology be applied in concrete ways to the study of criminology and criminal justice? Provide examples.

4. Review the excerpt in Box 11.1. How applicable to Canada are Jeffrey Reiman's observations about the US criminal justice system?

5. Compare critical criminology to the other schools of criminological theory that are presented in the other chapters of Part Two. Where do you see overlaps or similarities? In which other school(s) of thought might you find thinkers who are most at odds with the tenets of critical criminology?

SUGGESTED FURTHER READINGS

Bowling, B., & Phillips, C. (2002). *Racism, crime and justice*. London, UK: Longman.

Christie, N. (2004). *A suitable amount of crime*. London, UK: Routledge.

Comack, E. (1996). *Women in trouble: Connecting women's law violations to their histories of abuse*. Halifax: Fernwood.

Fanon, F. (1952/2008). *Black skin, white masks*. New York: Grove.

Foucault, M. (1979). *Discipline and punish: The birth of the prison* (A. Sheridan, Trans.). New York: Vintage.

Reiman, J. (1979/2004). *The rich get richer and the poor get prison: Ideology, class, and criminal justice* (7th ed.). Boston: Allyn and Bacon/Pearson.

Websites

Critical Criminology: An International Journal: https://link.springer.com/journal/10612

Critical Criminology Information and Resources: http://www.critcrim.org

Critical Criminology Working Group (Kwantlen University) and *Radical Criminology: An Insurgent Journal* (an open journal): http://radicalcriminology.org

Michel Foucault, History Learning Site: Information on Foucault's views on crime and deviance: https://www.historylearningsite.co.uk/sociology/crime-and-deviance/michel-foucault

Ontario Human Rights Commission eLearning: Information on human rights issues, including racial profiling: http://www.ohrc.on.ca/en/learning/learning

Restorative Justice (Correctional Service Canada): http://www.csc-scc.gc.ca/restorative-justice/index-eng.shtml

Legislation

Tackling Violent Crime Act, SC 2008, c 6.

Truth in Sentencing Act, SC 2009, c 29.

Youth Criminal Justice Act, SC 2002, c 1.

Cases

Elmardy v Toronto Police Services Board, 2015 ONSC 2952.

Elmardy v Toronto Police Services Board, 2017 ONSC 2074.

Maynard v Toronto Police Services Board, 2012 HRTO 1220.

R v Brown, 2003 CanLII 52142 (Ont CA).

Rational Choice Theory in Action

In their 1986 work *The Reasoning Criminal*, Derek Cornish and Ronald Clarke set out a "rational choice theory" framework that, they argued, could be used to diminish the extent of crime within communities. Specifically, in relation to the example that follows, they urged policy-makers to increase the effort needed to commit crime, increase the risk of getting caught, reduce the rewards that might flow from crime, and remove the excuses that could justify crime.

A visible presence within a community and good communications with local stakeholders are just two strategies police use to prevent crime.

A recent study in the United Kingdom, led by criminologist Stuart Kirby, imposed a rational choice theory framework to counter the activities of an organized crime group (Kirby & Nailer, 2013). The study's researchers interviewed police officers about the group's actions within the village and surrounding area, asking about its impact on the community, the effectiveness of various policing interventions to date, the effectiveness of current preventive strategies, and the approach police were using to measure their successes in dealing with the group. The researchers also asked key community stakeholders about their knowledge of the organized crime group, what actions they might want to take to reduce crimes committed by this group, their evaluation of current police efforts, and the value of current communications between police and the community. Then, the researchers created profiles of the members of the organized crime group, noting their ages, the number of offences they were reported to have committed, and the number of criminal convictions attained.

What emerged from these consultations and research were a number of initiatives to tackle the group's criminal activities, all flowing from rational choice theory. Specifically, police took the following measures to increase the effort required to commit crime:

- traffic-calming activities to reduce speeding along the main street;
- increased police visibility in the area of the residences of those in the criminal network to challenge even low-level criminal behaviour; and
- communication with legitimate businesses to inform them that their products were being used to facilitate crime.

Furthermore, the police took the following measures to increase the risk to criminals of being caught:

- using automatic number plate recognition to identify all organized crime vehicles and their movement within the village;
- monitoring mobile phones, bank accounts, and travel documents of all members of the organized crime group;

- using closed circuit television throughout the village;
- implementing a zero-tolerance response to traffic violation by group members;
- gathering more intelligence on potential crimes committed by group members;
- having plain-clothed officers patrol specific areas; and
- supplying photos and information regarding members to partner agencies.

The police and prosecutors also took the following measures to reduce the potential rewards that might flow from crimes committed by those within the group:

- using the *Proceeds of Crime Act 2002* to seize and confiscate any moneys obtained from crime by group members;
- enforcing planning regulations to prevent group members from developing houses; and
- taking legal action (including demolition) against unlawfully built houses owned by group members.

Finally, police removed excuses that could justify crime with the following measures:

- instituting traffic-calming measures, as noted above;
- sending out notices to all residents of the village regarding anti-social conduct; and
- documenting the importance of noise by-laws and the need to take action against nuisance.

Two years after these initiatives were put in place, the police assessed their impact on the organized crime group. They found that the numbers within the group had declined, in part because some were now in prison, but also because some had simply ceased their involvement in criminal activity. The capacity of the group to commit crime had diminished, and, perhaps most noteworthy, all of those interviewed two years later—both community members and police—felt that the criminality of the organized crime group had significantly diminished.

This example demonstrates how the application of principles of choice can serve to reduce criminal activity, particularly with a group that has organized itself to commit crime as an occupation.

Before You Read Chapter 12

- Could you contemplate similar successes with responses to other crimes, such as domestic violence? Or is the principle of choice less applicable in such circumstances?
- How might one increase the effort needed to commit a crime such as, for instance, domestic violence, and increase the risk of getting caught, reduce potential rewards for the offender, and remove any excuses that might justify the crime?
- Do you think that the rational choice approach is more potent when applied to some kinds of crime and less potent when applied to others?

Crime Choice Theory

LEARNING OUTCOMES

After reading this chapter, students will be able to:

- Explain how choices are made, whether related to crime or not.
- Identify the range of costs and benefits involved in choices.
- Understand the key role of non-monetary (for example, psychological) costs and benefits in decisions.
- Understand the link between choice theory and policy efforts to design-out crime.
- Critically assess how plentiful crime opportunities, due to changed routine activities, make crime a rational choice.
- Specify how reduced crime opportunities are likely to have been a key driver of choices to reduce offending in recent years.

CHAPTER OUTLINE

Introduction

"Choose life. Choose a job. Choose a career. Choose a family ... But why would I want to do a thing like that? I chose *not* to choose life: I chose something else. And the reasons? There are no reasons. Who needs reasons when you've got heroin?" (*Trainspotting*, MacDonald & Boyle, 1996)

"A useful theory of criminal behavior can dispense with special theories of anomie, psychological inadequacies, or inheritance of special traits and simply extend the economist's usual analysis of choice." (Nobel Prize–winning economist Gary Becker, 1968, p. 170)

"We are our choices." (Jean-Paul Sartre, quoted in Atkins, n.d.)

One morning, you are running late. You skip breakfast and run for the bus. The next morning, you have more time. You choose oatmeal because it is tasty, good for you, and keeps you full longer.

Let's consider those early morning decisions again, but in terms of choices: When you were running late, you needed to save time. You placed a greater value on your time than on eating, so you chose to skip breakfast. On the day you chose oatmeal, you decided that the nutrition it provides (minus the "cost" of the time and effort to prepare it) was more valuable than the benefit from the alternatives (perhaps toast or sugary cereal). On this day you had already decided that time for breakfast was time well spent.

In both scenarios, you made a routine decision. Most of us are experts in such everyday choices, making them so easily and quickly that we rarely think twice about them. The consequences of a wrong decision in our daily lives are usually minor, though there are exceptions, such as choosing when to cross the road.

Yet, if we look more closely, we can see that our easy, everyday decisions often involve the implicit weighing of a variety of costs and benefits. In our breakfast scenario, the main costs of having oatmeal are the money to buy it; the travel time and expense of going to the store (even if you have done that beforehand); and the time, effort, and resources needed to cook it—a pot, a stove, some electricity or gas, a bowl, milk or water, and perhaps ten minutes or more. Then there is the time, effort, and materials needed for cleaning. Toast is cheaper, quicker, and requires fewer resources. The main benefits of having oatmeal are its nutritional value and the fact that it is satisfying. So, this simple everyday decision, made in a second or two, really involves weighing a lot of factors, even though we rarely spell them out.

We can take this further: You may want to spend your time checking your email rather than cooking oatmeal and scrubbing the pot. Or you may simply have different tastes in food from other people. Hence, your personal preferences also influence your decisions. Preferences vary between people for a lot of reasons, and they are important in explaining why two people make different decisions in circumstances that are otherwise the same. Other factors influencing our individual preferences are our abilities and experiences. For instance, a fitter person might be more likely to run for the bus than a less-fit person, and a health-conscious person might be more likely to choose a nutritious breakfast than a person who is less health-conscious.

Some other decisions are life changing. Deciding whether to go to university or college is one example. The "costs" may include not only tuition fees but also living expenses, relocating, and perhaps the emotional cost of leaving family and friends. Studying full-time also means missing out on the wages from a full-time job. But most students are prepared to accept these costs because of the potential benefits, and they expect to earn more in the long term with a degree. Students also benefit from the many life experiences of higher education, such as making new friends and enjoying new opportunities, new freedoms, and the personal gain of being better educated. Some uncertainties must also be considered: Students are not guaranteed that they will enjoy university or college, get the grades they want, or land the job they desire afterward.

Big decisions in life—buying a car or a home, deciding on marriage or children—involve a more explicit weighing of costs and benefits. We try to gather good information to make a more informed choice, reducing our risks of a poor decision. But even then we can make the wrong decision, particularly if we had incorrect information. This works both ways, though, and decisions can turn out to be better than expected.

In essence, criminal decisions are made through exactly the same process as any other decisions. This chapter will introduce this area of criminological theory and examine its links to real-world changes in crime and crime policy.

A Note About Terminology

Note that in this chapter we use the term **choice theory**, although a lot of the academic literature refers to **rational choice theory**. Choice theory is simpler and sidesteps common misunderstandings related to the term "rational" (the term is used differently in the theory as compared with everyday conversation). By definition, the term has to be used differently, of course, because most crimes do not appear rational to most people! Moreover, studies show that intuition is an important part of decisions alongside reason and rationality. Because criminology has developed its own set of frameworks and concepts relating to choice theory, we refer to the overall explanation as "crime choice theory."

Crime: Everybody Does It!

Let's begin by considering laws that nearly everyone breaks. Speeding while driving is an obvious one—virtually anyone who drives a car does it, at least sometimes. Particularly if one is running late, the perceived benefit from speeding is great, while the risk of being caught is small. Often, if you are not driving above the speed limit, other drivers are probably tailgating or honking. Or you may enjoy the thrill of speeding. And so, you drive a little over the limit. So what? Everybody does it. If you are unlucky enough to be stopped by the police, you will simply pay a fine and probably keep your licence. Weighing all of this, speeding appears to be a rational choice for most of us (and we tend to discount the relatively low risk of causing death or injury to others).

In his book *Everybody Does It!*, Thomas Gabor (1994) says committing crime is like the common cold: Nobody is immune, but we are not all equally susceptible. We differ mainly in the frequency, seriousness, and persistence with which we commit crime. Beyond speeding, consider petty crimes that many people commit, such as taking office supplies from the workplace (perhaps justified in one's mind as a "perk of the job") or avoiding paying taxes. Anyone can commit an assault if sufficiently provoked; for example, an otherwise mild-mannered mother who feels it necessary to protect her child may lash out.

The Costs and Benefits of Crime

> "People think it's all about misery and desperation and death and all that shite, which is not to be ignored. But what they forget is the pleasure of it. Otherwise we wouldn't do it." (*Trainspotting* [MacDonald & Boyle, 1996].)

An individual commits a crime when the perceived benefits of the crime outweigh its perceived costs, as in the case of the infamous bank robber presented in Box 12.1. This is the basic formula for crime choice theory, and its concepts can be shown to underlie all criminal decisions. That is, crime occurs when

$$\text{perceived benefits} > \text{perceived costs.}$$

This simple formula is very flexible and can easily apply to very complex decisions. The definitions of costs and benefits are broad and include the emotional aspects of crime as well as money. Likewise, the role of perceptions is important—note that the formula comprises *perceived* benefits and *perceived* costs—because it is how benefits and costs are perceived by the offender that is important. Those perceptions may be wrong, especially if the decision is skewed by factors such as emotion, alcohol, or drugs.

choice theory
The framework for understanding how decisions are made by individuals by weighing the perceived costs and benefits of an action.

rational choice theory
A modern version of Classical School thinking originating in economics; it assumes that humans are rational and have free will, and that offenders make conscious choices to commit crime based on a cost–benefit analysis.

A Very Rational Bank Robber

Willie Sutton, an infamous bank robber in the 1920s and 1930s, was asked why he robbed banks. He is said to have replied: "Because that's where the money is!"

This is a humorous anecdote, but it illustrates some relevant points:

1. Banks are tempting targets because they contain a lot of money.

2. Back when Sutton was robbing banks, they were not as secure as they are now.

3. Robbing banks seemed fairly easy and highly rewarding to Sutton because he got cash quickly and easily, and probably also "benefited" from the thrill of the experience.

Willie Sutton, photographed on the day he attempted to escape Eastern State Penitentiary in Philadelphia, April 3, 1945.

Even though most people do not consider robbing banks to be a rational choice, from Sutton's perspective it was. Of course, nowadays it is far more difficult to rob banks because of the vastly improved security (the important role of security in nudging offenders away from crime is discussed later in this chapter).

One of the most commonly misunderstood areas of crime choice theory is costs and benefits. It can be difficult to grasp that costs and benefits include emotions and other psychological aspects. Crime is not just about money. Other perceived benefits might be the thrill of committing crime or the psychological reward of the praise from peers (or kudos). While it is easy for us to think of the perceived benefits of a burglary or a theft in terms of money or valuables, it is not as easy (until you dig deeper) to think of the rewards of a sexual assault. The rewards to the offender from a sexual assault can include the "benefit" of the feeling of power and control gained from the crime as well as the sexual gratification. Beauregard, Proulx, Rossmo, Leclerc, and Allaire (2007) have produced excellent work on the application of choice theory to the decisions of serial sex offenders.

A summary of the different types of costs and benefits is shown in Table 12.1. Non-monetary costs and benefits are sometimes called "intangible" costs and benefits because emotions and other psychological aspects are not as easy to measure. That said, a lot of research now shows that we can, however crudely, develop estimates of the equivalent monetary costs of the impact of some crimes on victims. This area of research is still evolving, but it is important because otherwise a crime such as rape—which has a very high psychological impact on victims—appears to be less serious than a burglary if one considers only monetary aspects. In addition, the psychological aspects of committing crime—the thrill and kudos in particular—are important in understanding how the choice theory framework can be applied to all types of crime, not just property crime.

TABLE 12.1   The Costs and Benefits of Crime

	Monetary	Non-monetary
Benefits	• Cash from crime—from theft, robbery, etc. • Stolen consumer goods (e.g., jewellery, phones, cars) that can be resold for money. • Stolen goods that can be used by offenders—e.g., phones, cars. • Stolen information and personal data.	• Time and energy saved by cutting corners. • Excitement/thrill. • Feeling of power/control over others and over own acts. • Any boost to self-esteem. • Kudos—peers' and others' esteem. • Any other positive emotions or feelings.
Costs	• Expenditure on tools used to commit crime (e.g., crowbar). • Cost of travel to offence site. • Possible opportunity cost of time (including learning skills, search time, committing crime and escaping, selling stolen goods).	• Physical effort/energy. • Psychological and emotional effort/energy. • Shame, remorse, or guilt—peer, family, and other condemnation. • Worry/concern about punishment. • Any other negative emotions or feelings.

Source: Adapted from Farrell (2010).

Poor Decisions

Choice theorists use the terms **bounded rationality** and **limited rationality** to refer to decisions that are made in imperfect circumstances. In economics these terms usually refer to the decisions of companies and investors (Simon, 1957). But the work of Gary Becker (1968) changed all of this. Becker introduced the economic approach to the study of crime in a more formal way than had been done before. He argued that a theory of offending could be developed that was based on the concept of choice as it is used in economics. (Becker won the Nobel Prize in Economic Sciences mainly for this insight because he applied it to many areas of life, including crime.) He argued that our decisions relating to marriage and many other areas involve choices based on **utility maximization** (i.e., making a choice where the perceived benefits outweigh the perceived costs).

Many studies in recent years have examined how decisions—not just those relating to offending—are often not as rational as we believe them to be. Sometimes we make errors of judgment or have systematic biases in our decisions that arise, for example, from the immediate situation or recent experience. Other times, we make decisions based on imperfect information where we guess or use a rule of thumb (known as *heuristics*). Most of the studies on decision-making look at decisions that do not relate to crime, but it is clear that the issues are incorporated within the crime choice theory framework. Hence, while "the intuitive criminal" might be a useful term for studies that more closely examine the systematic way that offenders make mistakes, we view intuition as compatible with most of the literature on "rational" offending.

When it comes to crime, decisions often appear to be even less rational than they do in other walks of life. Here the concept of "limited rationality" is useful. It refers to decisions that are limited by a lack of information or decisions made in circumstances where the costs and benefits were not properly assessed. When it comes to crime, decision-making can be impulsive, made with a lack of information about the risks involved, or made when the person's judgment is impaired by alcohol or drugs. In fact,

bounded rationality (limited rationality)
Decisions are often made imperfectly as best guesses given available information and time constraints. Decisions are "bounded" by the limits of our knowledge and circumstances, and so our rationality is bounded.

utility maximization
Choices are made based on what one perceives will provide the greatest rewards for the lowest costs.

a large proportion of crime involves alcohol or drugs, as is clear by the rise in assaults and other street crimes that occur on weekends and during public holidays and celebrations. A summary of poor choices involving limited rationality is shown in Table 12.2.

TABLE 12.2   Poor Choices

Type	Description
Impulsive decisions	They are made too quickly, without thinking: "It seemed like a good idea at the time!" "I wasn't thinking." "I regret it now." "It was spur-of-the-moment."
Imperfect decisions	They are based on poor or wrong information: "I didn't know they had a dog/silent alarm/CCTV." "At the time, I didn't see the consequences."
Impaired decisions	They are impaired by emotion, alcohol, or drugs: "I wasn't thinking straight." "It was the alcohol/drugs, not me!" "It was my uncontrollable teenage angst/contempt for society." "She was chatting up my boyfriend."

Source: Adapted from Farrell (2010).

Box 12.2 shows how joyriding is a "rational" choice by offenders who want the benefit of the excitement and kudos. It also gives a preview of the connection between choice theory and crime control policy that is described later, because it is clear that joyriding has been largely eliminated in recent years by greatly improved vehicle security.

BOX 12.2

Making Joyriding a Harder Choice

"Joyriding" is the informal name given to car thefts committed for pleasure, usually by thrill-seeking teenagers. The "joy" in joyriding is the excitement of the car ride and breaking the law, and the prestige among peers and passengers—this "joy" is the perceived benefit in the choice to commit the crime. Hence, for some people, stealing a car is a fairly rational way of gaining prestige and satisfying a need for excitement.

It used to be very easy—and hence very rational—to steal most cars. Sometimes, only a coat hanger was required to break the lock, and a screwdriver could be used to start the engine, or thieves could "hotwire" the car by connecting wires in the steering column.

Recognizing joyriding as a choice is important because it then becomes easier to determine how to stop it; that is, by reducing the joy involved or by increasing the effort or skill needed to steal a car. For example, speed bumps and other traffic-calming measures make it less enjoyable to drive a car fast. Better door locks and central locking doors make it harder to break into a car. Electronic immobilizer systems may not block a thief from entering a car, but they make it very difficult to start the engine. In addition, parking lots can be designed and managed in many ways to make it harder to steal cars, for example, by improving barriers, having attendants, and installing closed-circuit television (CCTV).

As a result of better security, car theft in Canada (and most other industrialized countries) has fallen dramatically in the last decade (Hodgkinson, Andresen, & Farrell, 2016). It is now less easy to choose to steal a car and less rational to do so.

For further reading on the decline in joyriding, see Brown (2004); Farrell, Tseloni, and Tilley (2011); and Kriven and Ziersch (2007).

A Brief History of Choice Theory

Having examined the basic framework and concepts for understanding choice theory and its implications, let's step back and take stock of the origins of choice theory as it relates to crime.

Crime choice theory is said to have its origins in the 1764 essay "Of Crimes and Punishments" by Cesare Beccaria. This famous work was described by criminologist Marvin Wolfgang as "the most significant essay on crime and punishment in Western civilization" (1996, p. xi). Beccaria was Italian, but his work is said to have influenced Thomas Jefferson and others involved in writing the Constitution of the United States, along with a great many 18th- and 19th-century policy-makers across Europe and Asia, including areas not directly related to crime policy (Wolfgang, 1996). Box 12.3 presents leading scholars in choice theory. In choosing only six theorists, we offer only the starting lineup of our all-star ice hockey team, while acknowledging the many others who have done excellent work in this area.

The specifics of crime choice theory have evolved since Beccaria, but the theory has largely stood the test of time; in scientific terms, this means the theory is extremely robust, in a way comparable to Charles Darwin's theory of evolution through natural selection (Darwin, 1859). Like Darwin's work, Beccaria's theory continues to gather support and evidence, and is likely to continue to do so.

BOX 12.3

Leading Choice Theorists

The work of the following six scholars, past and present, has been tremendously influential on crime choice theory.

Cesare Beccaria (1738–1794): The 18th-century Italian scholar paved the way to study crimes as rational choices in his famous 1764 essay "On Crimes and Punishments." Beccaria realized that people made choices that involved calculating what was in their best interest. He termed this the "hedonistic calculus." It outlines the basic principles of choice theory that still apply today.

Jeremy Bentham (1748–1832): Bentham's theory of utilitarianism—the doctrine that one should choose to act in a way to maximize utility (i.e., the well-being, including happiness and pleasure, of individuals or the well-being of society as a goal of public policy)—is hugely influential in the world of philosophy and is also a cornerstone of choice theory. Crime, like all behaviour, is committed to maximize the perceived utility.

Gary Becker (1930–2014): This Nobel Prize–winning economist's landmark 1968 study examined crime using an economic approach. Becker said, "a useful theory of criminal behavior can dispense with special theories of anomie, psychological inadequacies, or inheritance of special traits and simply extend the economist's usual analysis of choice" (1968, p. 170).

Daniel Kahneman (1934–): Kahneman—a psychologist who won the Nobel Memorial Prize in Economics—has focused on intuitive choices: the errors, biases, and rules of thumb by which decisions are less than rational. While crime is not Kahneman's focus, his work is the basis for the "nudge theory" that is influential in public policy (Thaler & Sunstein, 2008) and closely related to situational crime prevention and designing-out crime.

Derek Cornish (1939–): Cornish is a greatly underrated criminologist who pioneered much of the rational choice way of thinking, from the study of gambling and crime displacement to the development of scripts that show the many stages and decisions involved in criminal events. He co-authored landmark studies on criminological choice theory with Ronald V. Clarke.

Ronald V. Clarke (1941–): Clarke is widely recognized as criminology's leading scholar on rational choice and situational crime prevention. His work has focused on these areas for over 40 years. He coined the term "situational crime prevention" and showed how choice theory directly informs crime control policy. He co-authored many key studies of choice with Derek Cornish.

In the study of human behaviour, choice theory has had widespread acceptance, influence, and longevity similar to Darwin's work in the natural sciences. Choice theory is tremendously influential, not only in criminology but also in economics, psychology, law, sociology, and elsewhere. Harvard University professors James Q. Wilson and Richard Herrnstein (1985) describe it as probably the most widely used theory in the behavioural sciences (the study of human behaviour).

Choosing a Criminal Career

The collaboration of Cornish and Clarke, mentioned in Box 12.3, has produced key theoretical advances. For example, they identified four broad stages of decisions in a criminal career, shown in Table 12.3.

Within each stage, key choices are made, and a variety of factors influence decisions. Many teenagers will commit a crime of some sort. Most of them do not decide to continue to commit more crimes for various reasons: Perhaps they did not enjoy it, or they were caught, or they realized their mistake when they were sober. Hence, while offending rates increase in the late teenage years, particularly as individuals gain their independence of movement, most people do not escalate to more serious crimes. The likelihood that a teenager will continue to offend or begin frequently offending is still relatively small. Even among the small proportion of people who go on to offend more frequently, most of them "age out" of offending over time. This is largely because, as we get older, our perceptions of the costs and benefits of committing crime change. We get a job, build relationships, and may start a family, which leaves much less time and energy to go out and break into cars (or we simply buy our own car). The potential personal cost (including to the family) of arrest and punishment also increases. Hence, only a very small proportion of the population, usually males, go on to an extended criminal career (Moffitt, 1993). And even then, as some studies have shown, drug dependency involves the choice to continue to take drugs. For example, Trevor Bennett's (1986) classic study of heroin users found that they often choose not to take drugs when they do not have the money or when they need to be able to do something where they prefer not to be under the influence.

TABLE 12.3   Key Decision Stages in a Criminal Career

Stage	Action	Decision
1	Initial involvement.	The initial decision to commit a crime.
2	The criminal event.	Decisions relating to the crime itself (see scripts, discussed in Box 12.4).
3	Continuing involvement.	The decision to continue and perhaps escalate to serious crime.
4	Desistence.	The decision to quit crime.

Source: Based on Clarke and Cornish's (1985) models.

Crime Event "Scripts"

Breaking down particular crime types into the sequence of actions involved, or a **script**, allows us to examine the many steps in decision-making and action. The concept of scripts, introduced to criminology by Cornish (1994), shows how many aspects of life can be viewed in terms of a script. Box 12.4 presents the scripts for a restaurant visit and two criminal events.

script
The steps in decision-making and the sequence of actions for a particular criminal event.

BOX 12.4

Examples of Scripts

Script 1: A Restaurant Visit

1. Enter the restaurant.
2. Wait to be seated.
3. Get the menu.
4. Order.
5. Be served.
6. Eat.
7. Get the bill.
8. Pay.
9. Exit the restaurant. (Tompson, 2011)

Script 2: A Snatch Theft or Robbery in a Subway System

1. Meet co-offenders and agree on hunting ground.
2. Enter the subway system.
3. Travel to hunting ground (the chosen station).
4. Wait/circulate at hunting ground.
5. Select victim and circumstance.
6. Close in/prepare.
7. **Press home attack.**
8. **Take money, jewellery, etc.**
9. Escape from the scene.
10. Exit from the system.
11. Fence the stolen goods. (Adapted from Ekblom, 1991; Leddo & Abelson, 1986)

Script 3: A Sexual Assault in a Residential Institution (For Example, Children's Home, Elderly Care Home)

1. Development of sexual fantasies, offending strategies, and inducements.
2. Selection of victim-rich setting.
3. Preconditions: legitimate role (job), absence of managers, disorganized setting.
4. Identification of suitable victims.
5. Initiation: non-threatening approach, initiation of interaction, preliminary grooming.
6. Actualization: isolation from others, removal to unsupervised area.
7. **Commission of sexual assault of the victim.**
8. Successful disengagement.
9. Disposal of evidence. (Adapted from Cornish, 1994; see also Beauregard et al., 2007)

Script 2 is a generic script for a snatch theft or robbery on the subway system. It involves 11 decision steps and actions. Many of these are the various stages of preparation—meeting co-offenders, travelling to the selected site, searching for a suitable victim, and closing in on the victim in suitable circumstances (where there is no "guardianship," or someone who watches over or protects). The criminal act itself (set off in bold type) may be relatively quick. To the victim, these crimes can appear opportunistic or spur-of-the-moment, but the script shows they are not. After the offence is committed, the offenders need to escape. But even after escaping, most offenders still need to go through further decision-making, including selling the stolen goods. Fencing goods is itself a multi-stage process and depends on whether the offenders know a good fence or choose to sell the goods via another route such as the Internet (which entails time, skill, computer resources, and some risks). It is clear that what seems to be an opportunistic snatch theft or robbery is, in fact, often a far more deliberately planned set of "rational" actions.

Script 3 shows a breakdown of decisions and actions for a sexual assault conducted in a residential institution, such as a children's home or an elderly care home. It is included here because sexual assault is often thought of as either impulsive or motivated by feelings beyond the control of the offender. The script shows how it is typically deliberate and often involves many decision stages and actions. When considered in this way, it clarifies how sexual offences often involve elements of rational decision making by offenders during the many stages of preparation for the crime, undertaking the crime, escaping, hiding the evidence, and making sure the victim does not report the crime. Note that the sexual assault itself takes place at step 7 of the script.

Scripts 2 and 3 are provided as fairly broad examples to show that all crime types can be broken down in this way, with some variation in the specifics for different types of crime. Though most sexual victimization is by families and known persons, the script above gives a clear indication of how even sexual assaults by strangers will involve many steps of planning and "rational" decisions.

Organized crime, terrorism, and gang activity may have so many different stages for planning and committing the crime that they have a long script that is embedded into a larger script of many crimes (Hancock & Laycock, 2010). Even bar fights have been shown to have a decision-making script, despite the fact that they may take place rapidly. The persons involved may have chosen to go to a particular bar where they know the chances of a fight are greater. The precise interaction that triggers a fight may be something relatively innocuous such as drinks spilled by bumping into another person. Even then, decisions are made that vary by a person's assessment of his or her opponent and whether the person will lose face with friends if he or she backs down. The presence of bouncers or the likelihood that someone may make a video of a fight on a smartphone may also influence the decision to commit a crime.

Scripts are increasingly used to inform crime prevention interventions. This is because the decision steps identified by script analysis are potential intervention points. This link to scripts should become clearer when we consider situational crime prevention (below).

Routine Activity Theory

While the emphasis in this chapter is on choice theory, it should be noted that choice theory and **routine activity theory** are complementary and interlocking rather than competing. Marcus Felson is the main routine activity theorist, and his primary focus is the development of theory, concepts, and evidence in this area. Felson and Rachel Boba (2010) are the co-authors of one of the seminal works in this area, *Crime and Everyday Life.*

For more on organized crime, terrorism, and gang activity, see Chapter 17, Organized Crime and Gangs

routine activity theory Felson's theory that everyday routines and legitimate activities are key determinants of crime opportunities.

Like the simple formula that underlies choice theory, routine activity theory can be stated very simply, as it was in the 1979 study that launched it: "Most criminal acts require convergence in space and time of *likely offenders, suitable targets*, and the *absence of capable guardians* against crime" (Cohen & Felson, 1979, p. 588).

Note that the theory lists three basic elements that are needed for a criminal event: a potential offender, a suitable target, and the *absence* of a capable guardian. While seemingly simple, this theory is also remarkably flexible and robust and can be applied to any criminal event. The three elements are defined broadly. We prefer the term "potential offender" to "likely offender" because it captures the notion described earlier: that everyone is a potential offender. When the situation is right, almost anyone can be tempted or provoked into choosing to commit crime (note that the word "choosing" is very important here, as it links routine activity theory to rational choice theory). Thus, the definition of "potential offender" could include all of us (if there is a wallet with cash left unattended) or certain individuals who might be more experienced and more actively searching for crime opportunities. A "suitable target" might be anything from a person in the street who could be robbed or have his or her bag snatched, to a house or car that could be broken into, to a computer terminal or network that could be hacked. Likewise, the term "capable guardian" is broad and can include any passerby who might intervene or call the police, a receptionist in an office who screens who comes and goes, or a bus driver who in addition to taking fares and driving also provides some implicit guardianship for the bus. Because many of them exist, these everyday types of guardianship are often far more important than the more formal types, such as police and security guards.

The three elements of a criminal event can be broken down further. A suitable target can be broken into "suitable" and "target" so that it refers to the number of potential targets (such as the number of cars on the road or the number of smartphones in the population) and their suitability. For example, although many target cars are on the road, more recent models are far less suitable to steal because of improvements in vehicle security.

The seemingly simple three-element framework of routine activity theory clarifies the importance of target suitability and capable guardianship. In fact, whole areas of theory have now developed relating to those concepts that are, at least in part, inspired by routine activity theory. "Target suitability" has led to studies of the characteristics of frequently stolen products, for example. Highly suitable targets are "CRAVED"—a useful mnemonic, or memory tool, developed by Ronald Clarke to identify desirable, frequently stolen objects such as smartphones and tablets (see Table 12.4).

TABLE 12.4   Frequently Stolen "Suitable Targets" Are CRAVED

Concealable	They are often small and easily hidden when stolen.
Removable	They are portable and not a permanent fixture.
Available	They are not locked away (unlike gold in Fort Knox) and can be accessed.
Valuable	They usually have a monetary value.
Enjoyable	They are enjoyed by offenders (e.g., smartphones) if not stolen for money.
Disposable	They can be disposed of—that is, easily fenced or sold.

Source: Clarke (1999).

The Connection Between Crime Choice Theory and Routine Activity Theory

These theories are connected via the fact that target suitability and the capability of guardians are huge influences on the decisions—the choices—of potential offenders. Simply put, if fewer or less suitable targets exist, offenders choose to commit less crime. Likewise, if more guardians exist because, say, sightlines across a residential area or office (or other place) are clearer, then offenders choose to commit less crime because it is not as easy.

Routine activity theory was originally proposed to explain why crime rates in most industrialized countries increased dramatically for much of the second half of the 20th century. Most criminological theory had tended to assert that crime would *decrease* as living standards improved, as people became wealthier and as education, health, and welfare improved. Yet—and this is the major paradox that routine activity theory addressed—while almost all social problems had lessened significantly as economies boomed in the second half of the 20th century, crime rates soared.

Routine activity theory showed how the tremendous increases in crime (Figure 12.2, later in the chapter, shows Canada's crime trends) were, in fact, caused by society being better off. The theory provided a two-pronged explanation for this phenomenon. First, because people were better off, more valuable consumer goods were available to steal—more cars on the road and more consumer goods in homes. As a result, more crime opportunities made it "rational" to choose to commit crime. Second, modern lifestyles had changed in ways that increased some crime opportunities. The fact that more women were going to work rather than staying at home meant that households were left unguarded during the daytime (which in turn meant that working women were also more routinely exposed to crimes such as theft and sexual victimization in the workplace). Routine activity theory is also closely linked to **crime pattern theory**, which offers a set of concepts for studying and understanding variations in crime patterns and trends (see Table 12.5).

crime pattern theory
A theory that helps explain how crime patterns arise; it asserts that crime is not random. Its concepts (for example, nodes, paths, and edges) describe how offenders move in the urban environment.

TABLE 12.5   Key Concepts of Crime Pattern Theory

Concept	Detail
Paths	The routes (roads, train routes, walkways) along which we, including potential offenders, travel between nodes.
Nodes	The main places we travel to and from—home, workplace, leisure and entertainment locations, and transportation hubs.
Edges	The area between land uses of different types where crime is more likely—for example, along the road where high- and low-income housing areas meet.
Ridges	The areas where crime often groups, along roads or transport routes, that form a pattern that appears as a crime "ridge."
Attractors	Places that attract offenders because they have a reputation as good places to commit crime.
Generators	Places such as train stations and entertainment districts where crime is generated by the interaction of high volumes of suitable targets and potential offenders in places with low guardianship.

Source: Brantingham and Brantingham (1993).

Long before routine activity theory had been proposed, Leslie Wilkins had made the connection between increased crime opportunities and increased crime. In 1964, Wilkins noted the direct relationship between increases in the number of cars and increases in the number of car crimes (see Figure 12.1). His work was ahead of its time, and his influence can be traced to the work of choice theorists such as Ronald Clarke (Gottfredson & Clarke, 1990).

Crime opportunity theory, based on the classic study "Crime as Opportunity" (Mayhew, Clarke, Sturman, & Hough, 1976), is not particularly hard to grasp, and perhaps that is why some criminologists did not take to it easily. It offers clear implications for crime control policy and suggests that convoluted social theories of crime and social inequality were largely incorrect. Bear in mind that Marxist and other "critical" theories were still influential in the 1960s.

Cars played a major role in the increase in crime from the 1960s and into the 1990s because of the multiple roles they played. They were excellent targets for different crime types (car theft, car vandalism, theft of items from cars), and they played a direct role in facilitating many other types of crime. Cars made it easier to drive to an illicit drug market, to reach destinations where crime could be committed (for example, suburban burglary became far easier), to transport stolen goods, and as getaway vehicles for store and bank robberies. So, before the 1990s, cars directly contributed to crime's more general increase. By contrast, more secure cars have likely influenced the decrease in crime over the last two decades. Figure 12.1 shows the relationship between the volume of crime opportunities (cars) and crime (car crimes), as found in one classic study.

crime opportunity theory
An umbrella term for the set of theories and concepts that are underpinned by the notion that the level of crime opportunities is the main cause of crime.

FIGURE 12.1   The Relationship Between Opportunities to Commit Crime and the Incidence of Crime (England and Wales)

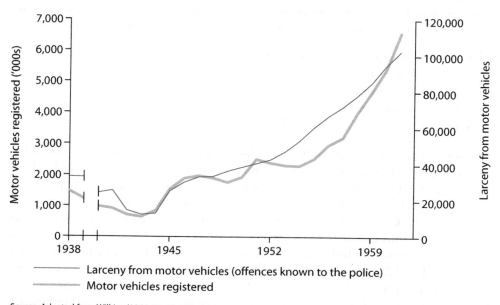

——— Larceny from motor vehicles (offences known to the police)
——— Motor vehicles registered

Source: Adapted from Wilkins (1964, pp. 54–55).

Crime Prevention Policy

"Unless a theory leads to clear and practical preventive policy, it should be regarded as suspect." (Clarke & Felson, 2011)

This section briefly introduces the link between choice theory and other key criminological theories as well as crime policy.

The notions of free will and rationality underpin the Canadian and many other legal systems. Adults are responsible for their own behaviour and decisions. That is why they are liable if they break the law.

dispositional theories
Theories that seek to explain variations between individuals in their tendency or disposition to commit crime. Explanations are usually biological or psychological.

The key connection between choice theory and **dispositional theories** of crime (those that look at individual "dispositions" or tendencies to commit crime) is the notion of individual tastes or preferences. Dispositional theories attempt to provide biological or psychological explanations of why particular people engage in crime. However, from a policy perspective, it is extremely difficult to influence the "hearts and minds" of offenders. The reason choice theory is particularly useful is because it offers many practical approaches to crime control policy. The most important of these approaches is situational crime prevention, which takes a variety of different forms that will be introduced here.

Choices are determined by the balance of perceived costs and benefits. Therefore, changes to those costs and benefits, or the way they are perceived, can alter the decision to commit crime. Some factors increase the perceived benefits of committing crime, and so crime increases. This is the case when new, valuable, easy-to-steal consumer goods such as smartphones and computer tablets become widely available. Yet it also means that efforts can be made to alter the balance of costs and benefits in ways that tip the scales away from offending. Those efforts fall within the realm of situational crime prevention.

Situational Crime Prevention

situational crime prevention (SCP)
Measures taken to reduce crime opportunities. SCP takes into account the nature of the crime, the environmental factors that allow for the crime, and the risks and rewards associated with crime.

Situational crime prevention (SCP) seeks to alter the costs and benefits involved in crime choices. It does so by **designing-out** crime from products, systems, and the built environment. SCP proposes five broad categories of actions to prevent crime:

1. Increase the effort needed to commit a crime.
2. Increase the risks of crime.
3. Reduce the rewards.
4. Reduce provocations.
5. Remove excuses. (Cornish & Clarke, 2003)

designing-out
The concept that crime prevention can start at the design process so that products and places are designed with potential criminal threats or opportunities in mind.

These same categories appear in Table 12.6 and offer options for tackling crime other than trying to influence the hearts and minds of offenders—a very difficult task at best. SCP has grown to become one of the more important areas of crime control policy.

SCP was first developed in the 1980s as a description of four broad categories of approach. Ronald Clarke, for whom SCP is a core focus, proposed a set of 12 techniques of situational crime prevention in 1992. Five years later, Clarke and Ross Homel (1997) extended the number of techniques to 16, and then six years later, Cornish and Clarke (2003) produced 25 techniques. The 25 techniques are a set of theoretical mechanisms for preventing crime. Note that the gradual building of SCP over time is characteristic of a robust theory and, as implied, SCP has become increasingly used and influential. For anyone studying crime prevention, it is particularly useful because it forces clarity of thinking about preventive mechanisms and illustrates the rich variety of ways in which crime can be designed-out of products, systems, and the environment.

TABLE 12.6   The 25 Techniques of Situational Crime Prevention

Increase the effort	Increase the risks	Reduce the rewards	Reduce provocations	Remove excuses
1. Target hardening: • Steering column locks. • Anti-robbery screens. • Tamper-proof packaging.	**6. Extend guardianship:** • Take routine precautions: Go out in groups at night, leave signs of occupancy, carry phone. • "Cocoon" neighbourhood watch.	**11. Conceal targets:** • Off-street parking. • Gender-neutral phone directories. • Unmarked bullion trucks.	**16. Reduce frustrations and stress:** • Efficient queues and polite service. • Expanded seating. • Soothing music/muted lights.	**21. Set rules:** • Rental agreements. • Harassment codes. • Hotel registration.
2. Control access to facilities: • Entry phones. • Electronic card access. • Baggage screening.	**7. Assist natural surveillance:** • Improved street lighting. • Defensible space design. • Support whistleblowers.	**12. Remove targets:** • Removable car radios. • Women's refuges. • Prepaid cards for pay phones.	**17. Avoid disputes:** • Separate enclosures for rival soccer fans. • Reduce crowding in pubs. • Fixed cab fares.	**22. Post instructions:** • "No parking." • "Private property." • "Extinguish camp fires."
3. Screen exits: • Ticket needed for exit. • Export documents. • Electronic merchandise tags.	**8. Reduce anonymity:** • Taxi driver IDs. • "How's my driving?" decals. • School uniforms.	**13. Identify property:** • Property marking. • Vehicle licensing and parts marking. • Cattle branding.	**18. Reduce emotional arousal:** • Controls on violent pornography. • Enforce good behaviour on soccer field. • Prohibit racial slurs.	**23. Alert conscience:** • Roadside speed display boards. • Signatures for customs declarations. • "Shoplifting is stealing."
4. Deflect offenders: • Street closures. • Separate bathrooms for women. • Disperse pubs.	**9. Utilize place managers:** • CCTV for double-deck buses. • Two clerks for convenience stores. • Reward vigilance.	**14. Disrupt markets:** • Monitor pawn shops. • Controls on classified ads. • License street vendors.	**19. Neutralize peer pressure:** • "Idiots drink and drive." • "It's OK to say no." • Disperse troublemakers at school.	**24. Assist compliance:** • Easy library checkout. • Public lavatories. • Litter bins.
5. Control tools/ weapons: • "Smart" guns. • Disabling stolen cellphones. • Restrict spray paint sales to juveniles.	**10. Strengthen formal surveillance:** • Red light cameras. • Burglar alarms. • Security guards.	**15. Deny benefits:** • Ink merchandise tags. • Graffiti cleaning. • Speed humps.	**20. Discourage imitation:** • Rapid repair of vandalism. • V-chips in TVs. • Censor details of modus operandi.	**25. Control drugs and alcohol:** • Breathalyzers in pubs. • Server intervention. • Alcohol-free events.

Source: Smith and Cornish (2003). From *Theory for Practice in Situational Crime Prevention*, edited by Martha J. Smith and Derek Cornish. Copyright ©2003 by Lynne Rienner Publishers, Inc. Used with permission of the publisher.

In your daily routine, take notice of how things around you (other than the obvious locks and bolts) may have been designed in order to prevent or sidestep crime, and try to identify the technique that has been employed.

Everyone routinely uses many of the techniques of SCP, even though they may not realize it. Consider the "routine precautions" that we all take every day to avoid, deter, or prevent crime. Locking the front door behind us, locking our car, and keeping our money in our pocket in certain places rather than waving it around are everyday routine precautions. Many such actions we take are so mundane that we do not even recognize them. Similarly, many aspects of everyday life are so common and accepted that we barely recognize their crime prevention role. A good example of this mundanity is same-sex washrooms in public places such as universities. The reason for same-sex washrooms is, to use the terminology of the 25 SCP techniques, to deflect offenders (technique 4) and to assist compliance (technique 24). In particular, same-sex washrooms are a simple way of reducing the sexual victimization of women by men. (There has been an increase in gender-neutral washrooms in many industrialized countries to show respect for and protect the chosen identities of non-binary or transgender individuals [Barnett, Nesbit, & Sorrentino, 2018], who are more likely to be victimized in same-sex washrooms [James, Herman, & Rankin, 2016]. However, to ensure the safety of all users, these washrooms should be designed as single-stall or have floor-to-ceiling stall doors.)

Public washrooms are so common that they are useful for illustrating other aspects of crime prevention. Some design changes are so ordinary that we take them for granted: Since illicit drug dealing and drug use can take place in public washrooms, cubicle doors are often designed to have a gap at the bottom so that it can be clearly seen whether multiple people are in a stall (the techniques of assisting natural surveillance and strengthening formal surveillance). In some public washrooms known to be sites of intravenous drug injection, blue lights have been fitted to reduce the ease with which veins can be identified by those involved.

Designing-out crime has been critical to the security advancements of the chip-and-pin credit and debit cards we use every day. Chip-and-pin cards were introduced to reduce credit card fraud. It was very easy to choose to commit fraud with a stolen card when only a signature was needed. The need for a four-digit personal identification number (PIN) has caused a dramatic decline in this crime. Some credit card fraud still occurs, and the PINs are now sometimes targeted by hackers who try to gain them from bank computer systems, but this is beyond the reach of most of us and can also be prevented by adequate computer software security and practices.

environmental criminology
A term coined by C. Ray Jeffery; it focuses on the environment (including targets, guardians, and places) as a key area of interest in understanding how and why crime occurs.

SCP is linked to a range of research and practice through the notion of designing-out crime. Influential thinkers include Jane Jacobs and C. Ray Jeffery, whose ideas launched the field of crime prevention through environmental design (CPTED). Influenced by C. Ray Jeffery (his colleague at the Florida State University), Paul Brantingham, with Patricia Brantingham, adopted Jeffery's term **environmental criminology** (Brantingham & Brantingham, 1980). The set of overlapping and conceptually related policy areas are shown in Box 12.5.

BOX 12.5

Crime Prevention Policy Areas Related to Crime Choice Theory

Many of the following policy areas are linked via the notion of designing-out crime or situational crime prevention (altering the situation). However, this is a large field; some would argue that it is a separate discipline (see "Crime Science," below) and that different topics require different theories and frameworks.

Crime Prevention Through Environmental Design (CPTED)

Much of the local environment—from road layout, to building layout, to the "furniture" of the environment, such as bushes and fences—can be designed or modified in ways that discourage crime. This may be achieved through denoting private property or trimming hedges in a way that increases natural and formal surveillance (Fennelly & Crowe, 2013; Jacobs, 1961; Jeffery, 1971).

Crime Prevention Through Housing Design (CPTHD)

Housing and residential areas can be designed in ways that discourage and prevent crime. Rachel Armitage examined the difference in crime rates between housing built to design-out crime and that which was not. In a pioneering study, she looked at them again ten years later and found that crime rates in the well-designed residential areas remained lower. Her book *Crime Prevention Through Housing Design: Policy and Practice* sets the standard (Armitage, 2013).

Crime Prevention Through Product Design (CPTPD)

Andrew Lester (2001) seems to have coined this term and identified the process by which products might be designed

to avoid crime. Paul Ekblom is a leading scholar in this area. His recent book *Crime Prevention, Security and Community Safety Using the 5Is Framework* (Ekblom, 2011) represents the state of the art. Many products, from cars to smartphones and computer tablets, can be designed in ways that reduce crime opportunities (see also Ekblom, 2012).

Problem-Oriented Policing (POP)

The term "problem-oriented policing" was coined by Herman Goldstein in a 1979 study and developed in his 1990 book of the same name. POP uses a problem-solving approach and situational prevention techniques to address crime and disorder problems (where problems are clusters of crime against certain people, places, at certain times, etc.).

Design Against Crime (and Designing-Out Crime)

This term is largely synonymous with situational crime prevention. In London, England, the Design Against Crime Centre is located at Central St. Martins College of Art and Design (www.designagainstcrime.com) and is one of the leaders in this field, having developed many projects and studies.

Crime Science

Crime science is pursued as a separate discipline to criminology, with its own academic journal and several dedicated university departments, institutes, and centres. Its relation to the sociology of deviance is analogous to how medicine is related to the sociology of medicine. Crime science focuses on crime prevention and incorporates the physical science disciplines as well as social science (for example, engineering-out crime).

Many studies show that SCP can be effective in reducing many different types of crime. In Canada, SCP gains little policy attention at the national level, and seems to be largely excluded from the National Crime Prevention Strategy led by Public Safety Canada. However, SCP is commonplace in several other countries, and the United Nations Office on Drugs and Crime (2002) includes SCP in its methods through which countries should prevent crime. In Australia, CPTED is now required in urban planning, and a crime reduction checklist exists for urban planners (Knepper, 2012). Denmark, Sweden, Finland, and Norway have all included SCP in their national strategies since the 1970s and 1980s (Knepper, 2012). SCP helps address specific crime issues, and while it offers no single "silver bullet" solution to crime, when done correctly it reduces opportunities for crime in general (Clarke, 1997).

One of the criticisms sometimes raised against SCP is that it may lead crime to "displace" or just move around the corner. In fact, many studies now show that displacement often does not occur. This finding makes sense. One target is chosen over another for a reason—perhaps because it is easier to access, easier to break into, or offers a larger reward that could be easily fenced. If this target becomes harder to victimize, it is not necessarily obvious where to find another target that is equally attractive (otherwise, that target would have been chosen in the first place). The possibility of displacement is now viewed very positively for a few reasons. First, if crime can be displaced, then it can be prevented, which means we need to strategically displace it to somewhere less damaging. Second, literature reviews that draw together the evidence of many studies show that often displacement does not occur. Third, when displacement does occur, it is usually less than 100 percent, so a net gain in terms of crime reduction is the outcome (see Guerette, 2009; Guerette & Bowers, 2009). See Box 12.6 for a classic case study on SCP and displacement.

BOX 12.6

Case Study: An Unexpected Drop in Suicides

A means of dying by suicide in Britain before the 1960s was to turn on the gas stove and put your head in the oven. The gas was poisonous carbon monoxide. American poet Sylvia Plath lived in Britain and died by suicide this way. When the source of the gas was changed for economic reasons, the new natural gas was not poisonous. As a result, the suicide rate fell unexpectedly. It was because people no longer had a simple, clean, and readily available way of dying by suicide. Many lives were saved, even though this was not a deliberate effort to tackle suicide.

Why did the rate of suicide decline? Two main explanations have been offered. The first is that other ways of committing suicide were not as easy, available, or attractive: They tended to be more difficult and often messier. People do not like to leave a mutilated or unrecognizable corpse for their relatives, friends, or others to find. The other explanation is that making it more difficult to die by suicide gave people more of a chance to pause and think about what they were doing and change their minds. The motivation to die by suicide appears to often be fleeting, and if the act can be stalled, then it may not be committed.

The gas suicide story provides three key lessons: First, even seemingly highly motivated acts such as suicide involve elements of rationality. Second, the rational element means that such acts can be blocked and prevented. Third, preventing one way of doing something does not just "displace" it to other means.

Sources and further reading: Clarke & Lester (1987); Clarke & Mayhew (1989).

The "diffusion of preventive benefits" is the term given to the fact that SCP can generate positive side effects. That is, studies now suggest that SCP can reduce crime beyond the scope of what was originally intended (Clarke & Weisburd, 1994; Weisburd & Telep, 2012).

The "Crime Drop" in Canada and Elsewhere

This section links crime choice theory to recent major trends in crime. Following nearly three decades of increasing crime, street crime in Canada has declined dramatically over the past two-and-a-half decades (although, since 2014, some crime types have begun to slowly increase). Figure 12.2, below, shows trends in recorded crime rates in Canada from 1886 to 2017. The data were compiled by Paul Brantingham from police-recorded crime and conviction data. Figure 12.3, below, shows the trends in police-recorded crime for a variety of crime types since 1991 based on the Uniform Crime Reports data collated annually by Statistics Canada.

FIGURE 12.2   Crime Trends in Canada: 1886–2017

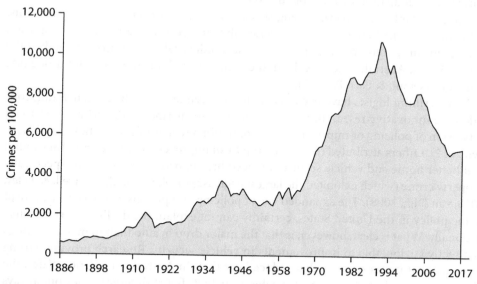

Source: Uniform Crime Reports from 1962; before 1962, estimates extrapolated from conviction date (personal communication by Paul Brantingham); with updates from Statistics Canada (2018): https://www150.statcan.gc.ca/n1/daily-quotidien/180723/dq180723b-eng.htm

FIGURE 12.3   Reported Crime Trends in Canada: 1991–2017

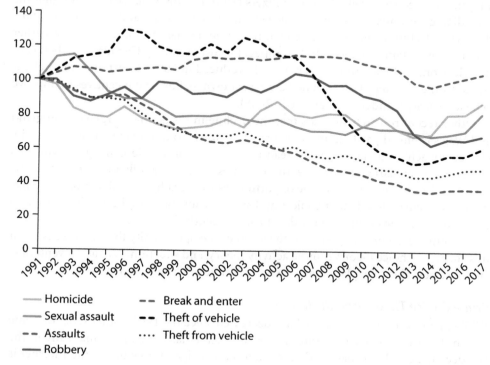

Source: Based on Allen (2018).

In this figure, all crime types start at 100 percent in 1991, and the relative change is indicated. So, between 1991 and 2014, break and enter in Canada declined by about 65 percent and homicide declined by 31 percent. Meanwhile, car theft continued at similar levels, then started to fall dramatically from around 2003.

An important question criminologists have sought to answer in recent years is this: Why did crime in Canada decrease so rapidly? In fact, Canada is not a special case. This "crime drop" has been experienced in most industrialized countries, including the United States, Australia, New Zealand, the United Kingdom, and most of Europe (see van Dijk, Tseloni, & Farrell, 2012).

Many criminologists have tried to explain why crime has declined, generating considerable innovative research. Some commentators attributed the crime drop to an expansion of policing or imprisonment or both (for a review of explanations, see Knepper, 2012). Others attributed the crime drop to an improvement in security. They found that better home and vehicle security reduced the opportunities for crime, specifically property crime (which exhibited the largest decrease) (Tseloni, Mailley, Farrell, & Tilley, 2010; van Dijk, 2008). The expanded use of policing and prisons, primarily a feature of crime policy in the United States, certainly cannot explain the decline in crime internationally. What is clear, however, is that the major drop in auto theft in many countries is directly attributable to improvements in vehicle security. Research provides strong evidence that it was security that reduced car theft in Australia, England, Wales, the Netherlands, and the United States, where car theft fell at different times but always consistently with the introduction of more and better security (Farrell, Tseloni, & Tilley, 2011; Fujita & Maxfield, 2012; van Ours & Vollaard, 2013).

In Canada, car theft has fallen dramatically since 2003, which seems to fit with the adoption of electronic vehicle immobilizers (Hodgkinson et al., 2016). Although the Canadian government made electronic vehicle immobilizers mandatory only in 2007, the earlier decline suggests a degree of anticipation by manufacturers as well as earlier adoption in certain provinces. In Winnipeg, for instance, long Canada's car-theft capital, electronic vehicle immobilizers were introduced in 2005 as part of a comprehensive auto-theft strategy that included giving car owners financial incentives to improve vehicle security (Linden & Chaturvedi, 2005).

Other recent research suggests that the decline in residential burglary in England and Wales is linked partly to more security but largely to improvements in the quality of security achieved via the widespread introduction of double-glazing for windows (Tilley & Farrell, 2013). In essence, these studies suggest that offenders *chose* to commit less crime because fewer crime opportunities were readily available. Box 12.7 links improved security to offender choices and suggests how bank robbery is likely to have declined for reasons similar to the decline in residential burglary.

Mounting evidence suggests that the set of crime opportunity theories discussed in this chapter—choice theory, routine activity theory, and situational crime prevention—are those best able to explain major trends in crime in Canada and elsewhere.

Crime Choice Theory and the Internet

While many types of street crime have decreased since the 1990s, other types of crime are on the rise. In particular, Internet-related crime has gone up dramatically in the last decade now that broadband access and knowledge of how to use the Internet is widespread. Yet this, too, fits well with crime choice theory. Simply put, new crime opportunities (such as fraud and cyberbullying) have arisen in relation to the Internet. Because those crime opportunities are relatively easy to commit, more offenders have chosen to pursue them. The same is true in relation to the theft of smartphones. Smartphones are highly valuable and easy to steal, so they are a "rational" choice as a target for would-be offenders. However, since the rise of the Internet (and social networking) occurred after the crime drop began, we can be fairly certain it was not the reason for the drop in other types of crime like homicide and car theft.

BOX 12.7

Changing Offender Choices Through Improved Security

Recall Box 12.1, about prolific bank robber Willie Sutton. Nowadays, with greatly improved security, it is far less rational to rob banks. Even in Sutton's time, banks had safes that were meant to be secure, and other forms of security. Nowadays the security is multi-layered and can include timed safes that are secured underground, bandit screens at the counter, CCTV, and security guards. All of these measures increase the effort required to commit a bank robbery. Banks are alarmed or have hidden alarms that can be activated by staff, all of which increase the risk for offenders. Even if the robbery and getaway are successful, cash can often be traced by serial numbers, or packs of money may contain exploding dye that make the money worthless. These many layers of security, working via different SCP techniques (for example, some making robbery more difficult, others lessening the rewards), all reduce the likelihood that any one of us will rob a bank.

Similar advances in security seem likely to have played an important role in explaining why many other types of crime have declined in recent years.

Conclusion

Choice theory provides an immensely flexible framework and set of concepts that can be applied to all types of human behaviour and decisions, including criminal decisions. The criminological version of choice theory focuses on immediate situations relating to crime and provides insights on how to design-out crime. When combined with routine activity theory as a broader set of crime opportunity theories, choice theory is vital to understanding the major trends and patterns in crime, both past and present. Since it informs efforts to design-out crime, it is also linked to some of the most practical crime control work undertaken by police and simultaneously promoted by government and the private sector. It is, in short, a tremendously important area of criminological theory.

The media's stereotypical distinction between "us" (non-criminals) and "them" (criminals) and their depiction of criminals (particularly the genius super-criminal and the heinous monster-criminal) is often misleading. Most offenders are teenage boys and most outgrow the desire to commit crime fairly quickly; most choose not to commit crime because they get caught, crime proves unattractive or difficult, or their circumstances and preferences change. The few that go on to criminal careers can choose not to, but their increasing expertise makes it easier to continue to choose crime. However, recent large-scale reductions in crime show that even the more hardened criminals can be prevented from committing crimes or deflected to less harmful activities.

SUMMARY OF KEY POINTS

- Criminal decisions are made by the same process as all other decisions.
- When the perceived benefits outweigh the perceived costs, a crime is more likely to be committed.
- Most people have the capacity to commit crime (for example, speeding) or can be tempted or provoked into committing a crime, depending on the circumstances.
- All crimes require an opportunity that can be taken. Fewer opportunities = fewer crimes.
- Designing-out crime opportunities is an attractive (non-punitive) way to nudge decisions away from crime.
- The large rise in crime from the 1960s to the 1990s in most industrialized countries occurred because easy crime opportunities became plentiful.
- The rapid decline in crime since the 1990s in many industrialized countries occurred because easy crime opportunities were removed, making crime less easy to choose.

QUESTIONS FOR CRITICAL DISCUSSION

1. Why would anyone choose to commit a bank robbery?
2. Why would two people make a different decision in the same circumstances?
3. If changes in the levels of crime opportunities (how easy it is to commit crime) make such a big difference to the crime rate, what does this say about offender motivation?
4. Do you think that crime opportunities or an offender's disposition to commit crime can be more easily addressed by crime policy?
5. Why has the crime rate in Canada and elsewhere fallen so much since the 1990s?
6. Based on choice theory, what policy options might be most efficient in addressing crime?

SUGGESTED FURTHER READINGS

Many good sources exist on choice theory and related areas. Almost everything written by Ronald V. Clarke is about rational choice theory and situational crime prevention—and his work is always clear, brilliant, and highly recommended. A good starting point:

Felson, M., & Clarke, R.V. (1998). *Opportunity makes the thief: Practical theory for crime prevention*. London, UK: Home Office.

The following textbook is a fine introduction for undergraduate students to many of the issues addressed in this chapter:

Felson, M., & Boba, R. (2010). *Crime and everyday life* (4th ed.). Thousand Oaks, CA: Sage.

For an excellent edited collection of academic scholarship, see the following:

Piquero, A.R., & Tibbetts, S.G. (Eds.). (2002). *Rational choice and criminal behavior*. New York: Routledge.

Websites

Center for Problem-Oriented Policing, or POP Center: http://www.popcenter.org

Legislation

Proceeds of Crime Act 2002 (UK), 2002, c 29.
Youth Criminal Justice Act, SC 2002, c 1.

PART THREE

Types of Crime

Violent Crimes in Canada: Two Recent Examples

On a cold February evening in 2011, after both men had been drinking excessively, Daniel Friday stabbed Stacy Steinhauer at Mr. Friday's apartment. Steinhauer received three stab wounds: one to his left cheek, one to his right thigh, and one in the middle of the right side of his back. After being stabbed, Mr. Steinhauer left the apartment and wandered outside before lying down in the snow; the temperature outdoors was about −30 degrees Celcius with the wind chill.

Nicholas Butcher was sentenced to life imprisonment for the murder of Kristin Johnston.

About six hours after the stabbing, Mr. Steinhauer was seen lying outside the apartment building by a person who assumed he was drunk and would soon come into the building. But some 15 minutes later, the same person went back outside and noticed that Mr. Steinhauer was bleeding and could not be roused.

Medical help arrived about an hour later, and Mr. Steinhauer was taken to hospital in critical condition. About 17 hours after the stabbing, he died in hospital. The medical examiner reported that his blood alcohol level at the time of admission to hospital (350mg per 100ml of blood) could be considered as the cause of death, irrespective of any other issues at autopsy, although death was likely due to the trilogy of stab wounds, exposure to the cold, and intoxication by alcohol.

Justice Brian Burrows described Mr. Friday as follows:

> Mr. Friday is 26 years old. He was 25 at the time of the stabbing. He was born on a First Nations reserve in Kamsack in east central Saskatchewan. He had no meaningful relationship with his father and has no contact with him now. His family consisted of his mother, older brother, younger sister, and himself. The First Nations community in which he lived was plagued by the social problems that feature largely in many First Nations communities: alcohol and other substance abuse, unemployment, and poverty. Mr. Friday does not recall any abuse when he was a child but his parents, like many in his community, suffered from chronic alcoholism. (*R v Friday*, 2012, para. 9)

Justice Burrows went on to describe Mr. Friday's past involvement with the criminal justice system:

> Mr. Friday also suffers from alcohol abuse. Indeed alcohol and drunkenness have featured in all of his previous convictions, which I am about to describe, as indeed it features in the present convictions.
>
> Mr. Friday has a significant criminal record. The record put in evidence indicates that this is the 14th occasion upon which he has been sentenced by a court since he became an adult 8 years ago. He has been convicted and sentenced for 25 offences on 13 previous occasions. His convictions have been for a wide variety of offences. (*R v Friday*, 2012, paras. 11–12)

Mr. Friday ultimately pleaded guilty to manslaughter and was sentenced to four years imprisonment.

Consider, alternatively, the plight of 32-year-old Kristin Johnston, a yoga instructor who lived in Halifax. After her yoga business failed in February 2016, she talked with friends about breaking up with her boyfriend, Nicholas Butcher, and moving closer to family in British Columbia. Ms. Johnston had been living with Butcher for about two months but had begun to feel trapped and stressed both by the relationship and the loss of her job. On March 25, 2016, Ms. Johnston had communicated with her friends on Facebook about her interest in ending the relationship. On that same day, Mr. Butcher accessed her Facebook page and read these messages. Later that evening, he managed to track her down, and ultimately found her in bed with another man. That man got out of his bed, got dressed, and left Ms. Johnston and Mr. Butcher alone. Mr. Butcher indicated to Ms. Johnston that he was not leaving without her. They drove back to the home that they had been sharing.

Justice Arnold, in the 2018 decision in which he sentenced Mr. Butcher on a conviction for second-degree murder, described the events that had occurred:

> Shortly after they arrived at 17 Oceanview Drive, Kristin Johnston changed her clothes and was lying in bed, at her most vulnerable. Mr. Butcher murdered Ms. Johnston. He put a pillow over her face and stabbed, slashed, and cut her in the neck ten times. The force used to cause the wounds was significant. Kristin Johnston died of sharp force injury. She had 10 sharp force injuries to her neck and throat and also had significant cuts on her hands that the forensic pathologist described as defensive wounds.
>
> After murdering Ms. Johnston, Mr. Butcher then attempted suicide by cutting his own arm with the knife and a razor lying next to Ms. Johnston in bed. When this did not work, he stabbed himself in the neck 13 times. When this did not work, Mr. Butcher retrieved a mitre saw from storage in the basement, brought it to the bedroom and then cut his own arm off. (*R v Butcher*, 2018, paras. 44–45)

As Justice Arnold noted in concluding this description, "When the police arrived Mr. Butcher said 'I'm sorry' to Sergeant MacGillivray. At the hospital, while awaiting surgery to repair the wounds to his neck and to re-attach his arm, he said, 'I really messed up' or 'I f**ked up' to the anaesthetist" (*R v Butcher*, 2018, para. 48).

At the sentencing hearing, Crown counsel had called two of Mr. Butcher's former girlfriends. One described Mr. Butcher as outgoing and fun at the outset, but moodier, less social, and more controlling as time went on. When she rejected him, he texted her, calling her a "slut" and a "bitch." The other girlfriend told the court that Mr. Butcher would prolong arguments for days and hold grudges over relatively minor conflicts. Justice Arnold sentenced Nicholas Butcher to life imprisonment for the murder of Kristin Johnston, with no possibility of parole for 15 years.

Before You Read Chapter 13

- Consider the nature of each of these two violent crimes in terms of the characteristics of the victims, the offenders, their relationships, and the violent incident itself. In what ways are they similar to one another? In what ways are they different?
- Can you say that one crime is worse than the other? If so, why, and for what reasons?
- What do you view as the primary causes of violent crime in our society?
- Violence has been at least some part of virtually every culture, both in the world today and historically. But are we gradually improving? Is our society becoming less violent?

LEARNING OUTCOMES

After reading this chapter, students will be able to:

- Describe the various definitions of "violence" and how they differ from one another.
- Understand how and why criminologists attempt to measure violent crime at a particular time and place.
- Describe trends in violent crime in Canada over time.
- Identify "risk markers" that increase the likelihood that someone will offend violently or be a victim of violence.
- Describe criminological theory and research on current issues related to urban violence, including the role masculinity plays in boys' and men's decisions to use violence to deal with conflict, "no snitching" codes, urban gun culture; and hot spots of violent crime.
- Identify the strategies used to respond to violent crime and which ones the research suggests may be most effective in preventing or reducing violent crime.

Introduction

- A teenage mother smothers her newborn child in an attempt to conceal the birth.
- A young male gang member is shot by a rival gang member in front of a neighbourhood community centre.
- A husband stabs his wife to death after she tells him she is leaving him because of a history of physical violence in the relationship.
- A gay man is attacked by two straight young men in a "gay-bashing" incident.
- A man is hit with a broken beer bottle in a bar fight with another patron.

The incidents described above are examples of various forms of **interpersonal violence**, violence that is most commonly inflicted by one individual against another or by a small group of individuals against another. One of the first questions that people tend to ask

interpersonal violence
Violence that is most commonly inflicted by one individual against another or by a small group of individuals against another.

when they hear of crimes such as these is *why*? Unfortunately, typically there is no easy answer because human behaviour, including the perpetration of violence, is complicated—and it is complicated because no single answer explains why people do what they do.

Someone who engages in violence does so for a variety of reasons. The weight of the available evidence suggests that no single factor causes violence; instead, it is the end result of multiple factors that converge to play important and interactive roles (Collins & Messerschmidt, 1993; White & Gorman, 2000). These factors include biology, psychology, personal history and experiences, socialization, community, and culture, which are discussed in detail in the various chapters in Part Two, Theories of Crime. To further complicate matters, the factors that converge to produce a violent act also vary from person to person. Given the "heterogeneous" and **multi-causal** nature of interpersonal violence, it should come as no surprise that no single theoretical perspective can explain all violence.

multi-causal
The notion that an event occurs as a result of more than one factor.

Defining Violence

A quick Internet search of the term "violence" produces a long list of different behaviours that occur in a wide range of contexts. Violence is indeed a multi-faceted phenomenon, and considerable disagreement exists over just how the term should be defined, prompting one scholar to describe violence as an "essentially contested concept" (de Haan, 2008). In the academic literature, definitions of "violence" range in scope from restrictive (narrow) to inclusive (broad). These definitions differ from one another in terms of the kinds of harm that qualify as violence. For example, some definitions restrict violence to behaviours that threaten or inflict physical harm, while other definitions include a host of other "injurious acts" (Jackman, 2002) such as psychological, emotional, verbal, and/or social harms. Still others argue that violence can not only be committed by an individual, but also by collectivities (for example, genocide committed by one ethnic group against another), by agents of the state (for example, violence perpetrated by the police and/or armed forces), and by corporate entities (for example, when corporations ignore health and safety measures, thereby putting employees at risk of harm). Despite these important differences, the definitions are bound by a common understanding that interpersonal violence is harmful, destructive behaviour. Examples of definitions of "violence" currently in use by those who study crime appear below.

Measuring Violence

Is gun violence increasing in Canadian cities? What are the risk markers for violent victimization and offending? Which city experiences the highest levels of gun violence, and why?

Answering these and other questions about the nature and extent of violent crime in Canada requires the collection and analysis of relevant data. These data are also important for gauging the effectiveness of public policy responses. As is the case with research on crime more generally, estimates of interpersonal violence are usually based on two key data sources: official reports, such as the Uniform Crime Reporting Survey (UCR), and surveys of the general population, such as the General Social Survey (GSS). While both surveys measure crime, important differences exist between them in terms of how they do so. As such, direct comparisons of the data findings from the two surveys are not recommended (Perreault, 2013). It is important to view data from the UCR survey and the GSS as complementary because, taken together, they enable researchers to gain a more complete picture of violent crime in Canada than could be gleaned from either source on its own.

The Uniform Crime Reporting Survey

The most common source of official data on violent crime in Canada is the UCR, compiled by the Canadian Centre for Justice Statistics (CCJS), a division of Statistics Canada. The UCR, as with most official sources of data on violent crime, relies on a narrow, restrictive definition of "violence" that emphasizes intended threatened or actual use of physical force against a person:

> **Violent crimes or offences/crimes against the person**
> Crimes against the person involve the use or threatened use of violence against a person, including homicide, attempted murder, assault, sexual assault and robbery. Robbery is considered a crime against the person because unlike other theft offences, it involves the use, or threat, of violence. (Statistics Canada, 2010)

Highlights of the findings of the 2017 UCR survey are presented in Box 13.1.

For more details on the UCR and GSS, see Chapter 4, Measuring Crime.

BOX 13.1

Highlights from the 2017 Uniform Crime Reporting Survey

- The police-reported violent crime rate increased in 2017, up 3 percent from 2016 to 1,098 violent incidents per 100,000 population. Canadian police services reported more than 403,000 violent incidents, almost 15,000 more than in 2016. Nevertheless, the police-reported violent crime rate was 19 percent lower than a decade earlier.
- Among the provinces and territories, the Northwest Territories had the highest violent crime rate in 2017, at 40,914 per 100,000, and Quebec the lowest, at 3,359 per 100,000 population.
- The homicide rate in Canada increased by 7 percent in 2017 compared to the previous year, moving from 1.69 to 1.80 per 100,000 population. Police reported 660 homicides in 2017, 48 more than in 2016.
- The increased homicide rate resulted from marked increases in British Columbia (+30 homicides) and Quebec (+26), counterbalanced by decreases in Saskatchewan (−17) and Ontario (−10). As is generally the case, in 2017, homicide rates were highest in the western provinces and the Territories, and lower in the central and eastern provinces. Every province east of Manitoba, except Nova

Scotia, recorded a homicide rate that was below the national average. Prince Edward Island reported no homicides in 2017.
- Almost 25,000 sexual assaults were reported to police in 2017, a 13 percent increase from 2016. However, the number of sexual assaults reported by police likely understates the actual number of sexual assaults that occurred in Canada in 2017. According to 2014 victimization data from the GSS, the vast majority of sexual assaults are never reported to police. Some criminologists speculate that the increase may not reflect a true increase in the actual incidence of sexual assault in Canada, but rather a growing tendency on the part of victims to report their victimization (for example, as a consequence of shifts in public opinion shaped by the #metoo movement), and a renewed commitment on the part of police to review their handling of sexual assault allegations, including a review of files previously classified as "unfounded" (meaning police had determined that no incident had taken place) (Canadian Centre for Justice Statistics, 2018; Doolittle, 2017; Greenland & Cotter, 2018).

- Physical assault was the most prevalent form of violent crime in Canada in 2017, accounting for 57 percent of violent offences reported by police. Of the 231,000 physical assaults reported in 2017, most (71 percent) were classified as common assault (level 1), an increase of 1 percent over the previous year.
- After decreasing steadily between 2007 and 2014, the national rate of major assault (levels 2 and 3)

increased in 2017 for the third consecutive year, due in large part to higher rates reported in Ontario (+4 percent) and Alberta (+7 percent).
- After an almost decade-long decline, robbery rates in Canada began to increase, starting in 2015. Police reported approximately 22,700 robberies in 2017, about 780 more than the year before.

Source: Allen (2018).

The General Social Survey

As discussed in Chapter 4, because official data sources reflect the number of violent crimes reported to the police, they *undercount* the true incidence of violence in any given time and place. As such, victimization surveys, such as the GSS, can help to uncover the **dark figure of crime**.

The GSS aims to estimate the amount of criminal victimization that exists in Canada among persons aged 15 and older; it seeks to measure victims' experiences, regardless of whether those experiences were reported to the police. The GSS includes three measures of violent victimization: **assault**, **sexual assault**, and **robbery**.

In addition to quantifying the amount of violent victimization in Canada, the GSS asks a series of questions to examine risk factors associated with victimization; to understand the reasons people do or do not report their victimization to the police; to evaluate fear of crime; and to gauge public perceptions of the criminal justice system. As such, and in addition to its value in uncovering the dark figure of violent crime, the GSS allows for a more nuanced understanding of violent crime and its effects than do official data sources.

Since 1999, the GSS has also included a separate set of questions about **spousal violence** in Canada. Like the UCR survey, GSS estimates of violent victimization in general are based on a narrow definition of violence that is limited to physical force and injury. However, GSS questions about spousal violence adopt a much broader understanding of violence that recognizes a variety of harms that victims (who are disproportionately women) typically suffer at the hands of violent spouses. Box 13.2 indicates how spousal violence is measured in the GSS and presents Figure 13.1, data from the GSS on self-reported financial and emotional abuse in 2009.

Trends over Time

Overall levels of violent crime in Canada had been declining for over a decade. Figure 13.2 shows the violent crime rate in Canada between 2007 and 2017. In this period, the national rate of violent crime declined from 1,354 incidents per 100,000 population in 2007 to 1,041 incidents per 100,000 population in 2014, then rose slightly between 2015 and 2017 (from 1,066 to 1,098 incidents per 100,000 population). Examining national rates, however, obscures important regional differences in rates of violent crime.

Figure 13.3 shows violent crime rates in Canada's provinces and territories in 2017. In this year, the rates were highest in the Northwest Territories (8,324 per 100,000 people),

dark figure of crime
Refers to the variation between the number of crimes that occur and the number of crimes that are actually reported to the police. This figure highlights the large number of unreported crimes.

assault
Applying force on a person, attempting to or threatening to apply force on a person, or using a weapon (or imitation of a weapon) to accost or impede a person.

sexual assault
Unwanted sexual activity, including sexual attacks and sexual touching.

robbery
Stealing property from someone, with or without using violence, threats of violence, or a weapon (or imitation of a weapon).

spousal violence
Acts including common assault, assault with a weapon, sexual assault, homicide, forcible confinement, uttering threats, criminal harassment, failure to provide the necessities of life, psychological abuse, and financial abuse.

Nunavut (8,230 incidents per 100,000 people), and Yukon (3,840 per 100,000 people). In the remaining regions, violent crime rates tend to be higher in the West and lower in the East. Only three regions experienced rates of violent crime that were lower than the national average of 1,098 incidents per 100,000 people: Ontario (841 incidents per 100,000 people), Prince Edward Island (892 per 100,000 people), and Quebec (1,037 per 100,000 people).

BOX 13.2

GSS Measurement of Spousal Violence and Data on Emotional and Financial Abuse

In the GSS, spousal violence is measured by a series of questions that indicate a broad understanding of violence:

The questions measure both physical and sexual violence, as defined by the *Criminal Code*, that could be acted upon by the police. This includes acts such as being threatened with violence, being pushed, grabbed, shoved, slapped, kicked, bit, hit, beaten, choked, threatened with a gun or knife or forced into sexual activity.

Respondents are also asked about emotional and financial abuse that they had experienced at the hands of a current or ex-partner within the previous five years. While incidents of emotional and financial abuse are not used to calculate the overall proportion of spousal violence victims, information about these other forms of abuse help to create a better understanding of the context in which physical or sexual violence may occur. (Statistics Canada, 2011, p. 8)

FIGURE 13.1   Victims of Self-Reported Emotional and Financial Abuse, by Sex and Type of Abuse, 2009

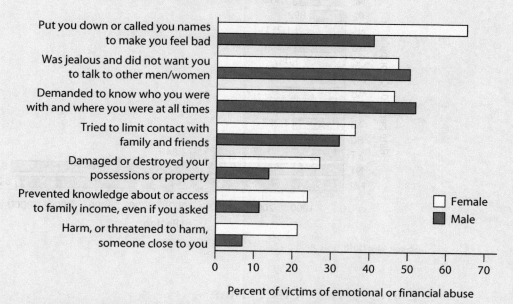

Percent of victims of emotional or financial abuse

Note: Includes legally married, common law, same-sex, separated and divorced spouses. Figures do not add to 100 percent due to multiple responses. Excludes data from the Northwest Territories, Yukon, and Nunavut.

Source: Statistics Canada (2011, Chart 1.5).

FIGURE 13.2   Violent Crimes, Canada, 2007–2017 (per 100,000 People)

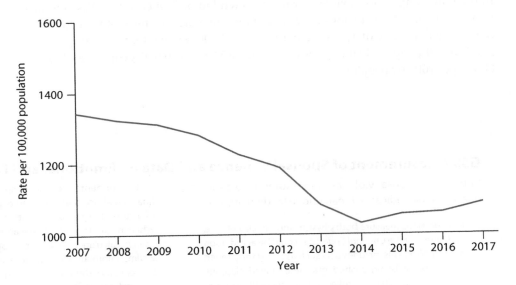

Source: Allen (2018, Table 1b).

FIGURE 13.3   Violent Crimes by Region, 2017 (per 100,000 People)

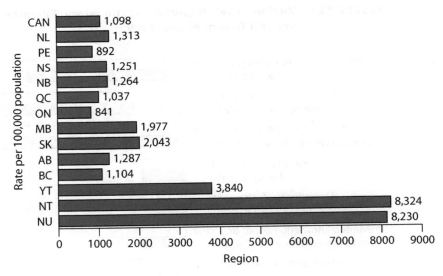

Source: Allen (2018, Table 2b).

Correlates of Violent Crime

correlates
In criminology, factors that are associated with or related to crime.

As social scientists, criminologists that study violence look to identify social factors that increase the likelihood, or the risk, of violent victimization and offending. A large body of criminological research has identified a consistent set of **correlates**, or factors that are associated with or related to violent crime. These risk factors cannot be said to be *causes* of violence; rather, they are factors that can help identify the context within which violence occurs. Identifying risk factors is important, not only to recognize those most vulnerable to violence, but also to develop crime prevention initiatives and interventions to help reduce violent victimization and offending.

Geography: Is There a "Frontier Phenomenon"?

Later in this chapter, we will examine the differences in the risk of violence across urban neighbourhoods, which are relatively small units of geography. However, research also consistently demonstrates that there is variation in the risk of violence across larger geographies, such as at the provincial/territorial level. For example, rates of homicide, and of violent crime in general, rise as one moves northward and westward from central Canada (see Figure 13.3). The reasons for this variation are not yet well understood, though some have suggested that it may be due to variations in criminal justice policies, policing practices, or the legacy of a historical "culture of violence" that may have existed during the settlement of Canada's northern and western frontiers.

The rest of this section provides an overview of some of the most consistent "individual-level correlates" of violent victimization and offending that have been identified in the criminological literature. Although these correlates are examined separately, it is important to understand that they never exist in isolation. When we look at the relationship between sex and violence, for example, we do so with the understanding that "men" and "women" are not homogeneous groups that share common experiences with violence on the basis of their sex. Instead, the experience of being male or female varies depending on age, race/ethnicity, social class, etc. And these characteristics intersect and interact with one another to produce a particular context within which violent victimization and offending occur.

Age and Violence

In the criminological literature, the relationship between age and violence has robust empirical findings. Studies indicate that a disproportionately large share of violent offending involves those in the age range between mid-adolescence and young adulthood (Farrington, 1986; Farrington, Piquero, & Jennings, 2013; Piquero, Farrington, & Blumstein, 2007).

Why does the likelihood of violent offending accelerate in adolescence and peak in early adulthood? Many theories have been offered to account for this pattern. Some explanations point to biological and psychological factors, such as fluctuating hormones and lower levels of maturity (Cruise et al., 2008). Others highlight socialization processes, such as conformity to peer group behavioural norms and expectations, risk-taking behaviours, and attitudes that defy authority—all of which may promote violent behaviour (Henry, Tolan, & Gorman-Smith, 2001). Other explanations point to lifestyles that may expose young adults to situations where violence is possible, particularly if alcohol use is also involved (such as drinking in bars and clubs). Adolescence and early adulthood are also periods that typically have fewer work- and family-related responsibilities that tend to make people consider the potential consequences of their actions.

Why does the likelihood of violent offending decline with age? Explanations in the literature are many and remain open to continuous debate among scholars.

For example, some research on deceleration points to a variety of "co-occurring developmental changes" that take place in early adulthood and are thought to drive declines in violent offending (Sweeten, Piquero, & Steinberg, 2013). These include "salient life events" (Loeber & LeBlanc, 1990; Sampson & Laub, 1990, 1993) such as completing one's education, entering the labour market, getting married, and becoming a parent—all of which could be jeopardized by continuing to engage in criminal behaviour.

Sex and Violence

Sex also very strongly correlates with violent victimization and offending, and while some similarities exist in the levels of certain types of violence experienced by males and females, important differences appear when it comes to more serious forms of violent victimization. Further, marked differences exist in the nature of violence that is typically experienced by males and females. The following discussion provides an overview of key trends in this area.

Sex and Violent Victimization

sub-lethal violent victimization
Violent victimization that does not cause death.

Overall, the levels of **sub-lethal violent victimization** (i.e., violent victimization that does not cause death) show relative symmetry/parity between men and women, meaning that men and women experience similar rates of this type of violence. For example, as Table 13.1 shows, in 2016, police-reported data show that 162,245 incidents involving male victims were reported to police, compared with 177,579 incidents for female victims (Allen & McCarthy, 2018). Self-reported violent victimization data from the GSS provide similar estimates; in 2014, approximately 1.23 million violent crimes (most of which were property-related crimes) were reported by female victims, compared with approximately 1 million by male victims (Perreault, 2015).

Despite similarities in the *quantity*, or amount, of sub-lethal violent victimization experienced by males and females, important differences exist in the *quality*, or the nature, of this victimization. For example, as Table 13.1 shows, men were more likely to be victims of attempted murder, aggravated and other physical assault, and robbery, whereas women were more likely to be victims of common assault and sexual assault (Allen & McCarthy, 2018). Other police-reported offences that disproportionately involved female victims include forcible confinement, kidnapping or abduction, and criminal harassment.

situational characteristics
Factors associated with an incident; in the case of a violent act, the location, weapon type, motive, and the victim–offender relationship are situational characteristics.

The **situational characteristics** of men's and women's violent victimization also differ in important respects. Situational characteristics refer to factors associated with the violent incident such as location, weapon type, motive, and the victim–offender relationship. Both police and self-reported victimization data show that men's victimization is more likely to involve a weapon, occur in public spaces (streets, parks, parking lots, places of leisure, etc.), and involve offenders who are acquaintances or strangers (Mahony, 2011; Perreault & Brennan, 2010). Female victimization, on the other hand, is more likely to occur in the home and be perpetrated by a former or current intimate partner (for example, legally married, separated, divorced, common law, dating [current and previous], or other intimate partner).

lethal violence
Violent victimization that causes death.

In contrast to relative parity across the sexes in the quantity of sub-lethal violent victimization, research consistently shows marked sex differences in the amount of **lethal violence** experienced by males and females. For example, in 2016, 75 percent of homicide victims and 86 percent of homicide accused in Canada were male

(David, 2017). Homicide victimization in Canada, as elsewhere, is therefore a male-dominated phenomenon. As we will see below, so, too, is homicide offending.

Table 13.1 Victims of Police-Reported Violent Crimes, by Type of Crime, 2016

Type of violent crime	Female victims		Male victims	
	Number	%[1]	Number	%[1]
Violations Causing Death and Attempted Murder				
Homicide and other offences causing death[2]	199	28	504	72
Attempted murder	187	24	581	76
Sexual Offences				
Sexual assault	18,638	89	2,267	11
Sexual violations against children[3]	5,118	83	1,053	17
Assaults				
Assault—level 3—aggravated	952	28	2,411	72
Assault—level 2—weapon or causing bodily harm	18,609	39	29,712	61
Assault—level 1	84,837	55	70,292	45
Other[4]	2,752	22	9,858	78
Other Violent Offences				
Robbery	5,757	30	13,676	70
Criminal harassment	9,902	76	3,117	24
Indecent/harassing communications	3,753	72	1,483	28
Uttering threats	20,078	46	23,656	54
Kidnapping, forcible confinement, abduction, or hostage taking	3,295	80	824	20
Trafficking in persons and prostitution	354	96	15	4
Other[5]	3,138	53	2,796	47
TOTAL	**177,569**		**162,245**	

1. Total victims includes victims where the sex was unknown. Percentage calculations exclude victims where the sex was unknown.

2. Excludes *Criminal Code* traffic violations causing death such as impaired driving.

3. Sexual violations against children are a set of *Criminal Code* offences that specifically concern offences involving child and youth victims. These include offences such as sexual interference, invitation to sexual touching and sexual exploitation, but exclude sexual assault and other sexual offences not specific to children. See the "Definitions" section for a full list of offences in this category.

4. Includes assaults against police and other peace officers, as well as other types of assaults such as criminal negligence causing bodily harm.

5. Includes violent firearm offences, extortion, and other violent violations.

Note: Victims refer to those aged 89 years and younger. Victims aged 90 years and older are excluded from analyses due to possible instances of miscoding of unknown age within this age category. Percentages may not add up to 100 due to rounding. For police-reported incidents that involve violations against the person, a victim record is collected for each victim involved in the incident. If an individual is a victim in multiple incidents in the same reference year, that individual will be counted as one victim for each separate incident.

Source: Adapted from Allen & McCarthy (2018, Table 1.2).

As with sub-lethal violent victimization, key sex differences exist in the nature of homicide. For example, female homicide victims are most often killed by a current or former intimate partner as a result of anger, despair, jealousy, or sexual violence (Vaillancourt, 2010). Male homicide victims, on the other hand, are more likely to be killed by friends/acquaintances or strangers, in public places (streets, parking lots, stores, bars, common areas of buildings), and with a firearm (Vaillancourt, 2010). Gang-related homicides are also more prevalent among male victims.

Sex and Violence: Offending

When compared with men, women commit a much smaller amount of violent crime; women are charged with violent offences generally about one-fifth of the rate for men (Kong & AuCoin, 2008).

Despite these differences in levels of violent offending by sex, women and men have some commonalities in the types of *Criminal Code* violent offences they are most likely to commit. Table 13.2 shows the number and rate of males and females accused of violent crime in 2009. Common assault (level 1) is the most prevalent violent offence committed by both men and women. For both sexes, level 2 assaults (assault with a weapon or causing bodily harm) and uttering threats were the next most prevalent violent offences, although the rate at which women were accused of each of these offences was approximately one-quarter of the rate for men accused (Mahony, 2011). Overall, however, as the severity of violence increases, female participation declines. The greatest sex differences emerge when it comes to sexual offences (all levels); in 2009, females were charged with a tiny proportion of these offences.

Although the gap between males and females in criminal offending is substantial, evidence suggests that it is becoming smaller, or converging, over time. For example, the last several decades have seen an increase in the number of women charged with violent offences; since 1991, the rate of females charged with violent crime has increased 34 percent. It is important to note that official crime data on trends in female offending over time may reflect changes in the criminal justice response to female offending as much as or more than to actual changes in offending rates. Indeed, some scholars have suggested that in the past, agents of the criminal justice system demonstrated "chivalry" or "paternalism" toward female offenders—and that these tendencies meant that women were not viewed as fully responsible/culpable for their offending, resulting in a lesser likelihood of charges. More recently, however, girls and women have been more likely to be viewed as responsible actors and, as such, may be held increasingly responsible for their violent offending.

Poverty and Violence

Socio-economic disadvantage, typically measured using indicators of poverty or income inequality, has generally been found to be highly correlated with violent crime (Blau & Blau, 1982; Fajnzylber, Lederman, & Loayza, 2002; Hannon, 2005). However, considerable debate exists among researchers with respect to the mechanisms through which economic disadvantage may lead to violence, which has prompted the development of a number of theoretical perspectives that aim to explain this relationship. For example, the concepts of strain, absolute deprivation, and relative deprivation suggest that as poverty and income inequality rise, so too does the risk of violent interpersonal conduct. According to classical **strain theories**, the contradiction between culturally ascribed goals of achieving status and wealth and the unequal distribution of opportunities to achieve those goals can lead to feelings of frustration, resentment, and injustice among those who perceive themselves to be unfairly disadvantaged over others in a purportedly egalitarian society (Merton, 1938). As feelings of resentment grow, so too does the potential for crime and violence.

For the ways in which scholars have hypothesized men's and women's violent offending, along with women's lesser involvement in violent offending, see Chapter 10, Gender and Crime.

These and other possible explanations for the convergence in men's and women's rates are reviewed in depth in Chapter 10.

strain theories
Theories that state certain societal stressors (for example, unequal opportunities to achieve success) increase the likelihood of crime.

Strain theories are discussed in Chapter 9, Sociological Approaches.

Table 13.2   Number and Rate of Youth and Adults Accused of Violent Crime by Police, by Sex and Type of Crime, 2009

Criminal Code violations	Total accused number	Female accused				Male accused			
		Total number	Total	Youth	Adult	Total number	Total	Youth	Adult
			rate per 100,000				rate per 100,000		
Total Criminal Code violations (including traffic)	1,008,615	233,074	1,580.3	4,010.8	1,360.3	775,541	5,403.1	9,700.4	4,981.4
Violent Criminal Code violations	287,362	63,314	429.3	1,065.7	371.7	224,048	1,560.9	2,581.6	1,460.8
Homicide	530	55	0.4	0.4	0.4	475	3.3	5.6	3.1
Attempted murder	564	79	0.5	1.2	0.5	485	3.4	4.1	3.3
Other violations causing death	65	11	0.1	0.0	0.1	54	0.4	0.2	0.4
Sexual assaults—all levels	10,695	253	1.7	5.4	1.4	10,442	72.7	146.7	65.5
Other sexual violations[a]	1,729	72	0.5	2.5	0.3	1,657	11.5	24.2	10.3
Assault—level 3—aggravated	3,132	496	3.4	5.1	3.2	2,636	18.4	28.7	17.4
Assault—level 2—weapon or bodily harm	37,301	8,140	55.2	107.7	50.4	29,161	203.2	391.4	184.7
Assault—level 1—common assault	131,144	32,788	222.3	579.3	190.0	98,356	685.2	996.3	654.7
Other assaults[b]	11,852	2,956	20.0	45.3	17.8	8,896	62.0	74.8	60.7
Forcible confinement, kidnapping, or abduction[c]	4,446	403	2.7	3.9	2.6	4,043	28.2	20.7	28.9
Robbery	14,500	1,742	11.8	49.5	8.4	12,758	88.9	305.4	67.6
Extortion	869	130	0.9	1.3	0.8	739	5.1	11.3	4.5
Criminal harassment	13,414	2,965	20.1	38.8	18.4	10,449	72.8	64.7	73.6
Threatening or harassing phone calls	9,125	3,650	24.7	31.8	24.1	5,475	38.1	50.0	37.0
Uttering threats	45,474	9,195	62.3	185.5	51.2	36,279	252.7	417.1	236.6
Other violent Criminal Code violations[d]	2,522	379	2.6	8.0	2.1	2,143	14.9	40.3	12.4

Note: One incident may involve multiple violations. Counts are based upon the most serious violation in the incident. Incidents where the age or sex of the victim is unknown were excluded.

a Other sexual violations primarily include sexual offences against children as well as other sexual offences involving adults.

b Includes assaults against peace officers, unlawfully causing bodily harm, criminal negligence causing bodily harm, and other assaults.

c Includes forcible confinement, kidnapping; abduction under 14, not parent/guardian; abduction under 16; removal of children from Canada; abduction under 14 contravening a custody order; abduction under 14, by parent/guardian.

d Includes firearm violations. Excludes other sexual violations involving adults.

Source: Mahony (2011, Table 7).

absolute deprivation
Low income or poverty in and of itself.

Some studies suggest that **absolute deprivation** (low income or poverty in and of itself) increases the risk of violence (Huff-Corzine, Corzine, & Moore, 1986; Williams & Flewelling, 1988). Under conditions of absolute deprivation, violence may be perceived as one of the few options available to those of limited economic means. That is, criminal activities designed to fulfill instrumental goals, such as the acquisition of money or other forms of calculable personal gain, may require or result in violence. Yet absolute deprivation may also give rise to expressive forms of violence, which may be the consequence of the dehumanizing effects of extreme poverty along with the "brutal and demoralizing" treatment suffered by the poor (Lynch & Groves, 1989, p. 63; Parker, 1989). The likeliest victims of this violence are those in close proximity to the absolutely deprived.

relative deprivation
The perception of unfair disparity between one's situation and that of others.

Other scholars argue that the concept of **relative deprivation** (the perception of unfair disparity between one's situation and that of others) is more relevant to an explanation of the poverty/violence relationship (Bailey, 1984; Messner, 1989). Relative deprivation may encourage violent crime because it generates a sense of injustice; perceived deprivation relative to others may create such feelings due to the disjunction between widely held cultural success goals and the distribution of opportunities to achieve them. People who experience relative deprivation may evaluate their socio-economic position relative to others (in their neighbourhoods and in the larger population) by the cultural success goals disseminated by the mass media. Robert Merton (1938) argued that inequality of opportunity creates situations in which some individuals engage in crime in order to achieve the social and economic goods that others possess. As with the conditions of absolute deprivation, the resulting frustration could manifest as expressive violence (acts that release anger or rage) or instrumental violence (attempts to acquire material goods that some individuals are unable to attain by legitimate means).

A variety of indicators of economic distress have also been linked to the risk of intimate partner violence. For example, financial problems can lead to feelings of stress and frustration that may find violent expression, most notably against female intimate partners (Macmillan & Gartner, 1999). Further, unemployed men or men earning low wages may be particularly likely to become violent during confrontations with their female partners. The reasons for this reaction may be twofold. First, violence may serve as a substitute for "socio-economic leverage" (Benson, Fox, DeMaris, & Van Wyk, 2003, p. 212), which can be a means for men to establish their dominance and authority in the home (Macmillan & Gartner, 1999). The second reason has to do with opportunity: Compared with their employed counterparts, unemployed men may commit more violence in the home as a function of the amount of time they spend there (Cohen & Felson, 1979).

Race and Violence

US-based criminological research has shown that race is highly correlated with violence (Tonry, 1995). However, less is known about the relationship between race and crime in the Canadian context. Although Canadian criminal justice agencies routinely collect information about the race of offenders that are processed through the system, they do not make this information public. There is, however, one exception: Indigenous peoples' identity data are collected and disseminated by many criminal justice agencies in Canada (Roberts & Doob, 1997; Thompson, 2013).

Indigenous peoples' identity data show that in 2014, Indigenous people experienced violent victimization at a rate that was more than double that of non-Indigenous Canadians (Perreault, 2015). Violent victimization rates are especially high among Indigenous women. For example, according to the 2014 GSS, Indigenous women reported a sexual assault rate of 115 per 100,000 population, a much higher rate than the 35 per 100,000 population reported by non-Indigenous women. These figures highlight the intersecting nature of race and sex when it comes to violent victimization.

Levels of spousal violence are also higher among Indigenous than non-Indigenous people. For example, the 2009 GSS found that 15 percent of Indigenous people reported having experienced physical or sexual violence at the hands of a spouse over the past five years, a figure 2.5 times greater than the proportion of non-Indigenous people (6 percent) who experienced spousal violence over the same period. Indigenous victims—particularly Indigenous women—were also much more likely to suffer the most serious forms of spousal violence, such as being beaten, choked, threatened or assaulted with a weapon, and sexually assaulted (Brennan, 2011).

Figure 13.4 shows that Indigenous victimization rates are especially pronounced compared with non-Indigenous people when it comes to lethal violence. In 2016, Indigenous people experienced homicide victimization rates that were six times the rate for non-Indigenous people (8.19 versus 1.34 per 100,000 population). The risk of this violence also shows sex differences; Indigenous males were killed at more than four times the rate of their female counterparts (13.2 versus 3.30 per 100,000).

FIGURE 13.4   Rates of Homicide Much Higher for Indigenous Victims in Canada, 2016

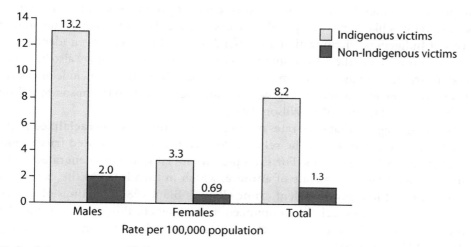

Note: Population counts were provided by Statistics Canada's Demography Division. The counts for Indigenous and non-Indigenous populations are based on Indigenous identity; for the years 2001 to 2011, they are derived from an interpolation between the censuses of population and the National Household Survey adjusted for net under coverage, partially enumerated reserves, and populations living in collective dwellings; the population counts from 2012 to 2016 are based on custom population projections.

Source: Adapted from David (2017, Table 7).

The rate at which Indigenous people are accused of homicide is also disproportionately high, particularly among Indigenous males, who were charged with murder at over eleven times the rate for non-Indigenous males (9.75 versus 0.88 per 100,000 population). This finding is not surprising given the large body of research that demonstrates that homicide tends to be an **intra-racial** phenomenon (Silverman & Kennedy, 2004). That is, if Indigenous people are at a greater risk of homicide victimization, given the intra-racial nature of homicide more generally, they are also more likely to perpetrate homicides involving Indigenous victims.

What might account for these higher levels of violent victimization and offending among Indigenous people in Canada? Many explanations point to the role of colonialism, racial discrimination (past and present), sexism, social and economic inequality, and the material conditions within which many Indigenous people live (La Prairie, 2002; Zimmerman, 1992).

Some evidence also suggests that Black Canadians are vulnerable to high levels of homicide. Using unofficial data to examine homicide in Toronto over the last several decades, Rosemary Gartner and Sara Thompson (2004) and Thompson (2009, 2013) found that Black people and, in particular, young Black men, have been disproportionately represented as homicide victims and offenders since at least the late 1980s. For example, since at least 1991, the risk of homicide victimization for Toronto's Black population has been substantially higher than the overall risk of homicide in Toronto. Even when excluding 1991, which had an unusually high number of Black homicides, the homicide rate per 100,000 Black people in Toronto averaged 10.1 between 1992 and 2003. This figure was almost five times greater than the average overall homicide rate of 2.4 per 100,000 population (Gartner & Thompson, 2004).

The issue of Black disproportionality in violent victimization and offending has received considerable research attention in the United States, but comparatively little academic consideration in Canada. This limited research is due, in large part, to the suppression of race-based criminal justice data for groups other than Indigenous people. Yet it is likely that many of the factors that are thought to contribute to high levels of Indigenous victimization and offending—and that have been identified in American research in the relationship between race and violence—may also be at play for some segments of the Black community in Canada. These factors include high levels of poverty, economic inequality, segregation, and social isolation (Sampson & Wilson, 1995; Stewart & Simons, 2006; Wilson, 1987).

Research suggests that high rates of violent crime among some **racialized** populations may be the result of the relative deprivation and associated frustrations experienced by these groups. For example, the social injustices generated by income inequality lead to a state of **anomie**, which in turn leads to the expression of hostility in the form of violent crime (Blau & Blau, 1982). Feelings of relative deprivation may be especially pronounced in members of those racial groups that experience the highest levels of social and economic disadvantage (Stolzenberg, Eitle, & D'Alessio, 2006).

Studies show that Indigenous peoples and Black Canadians are disproportionately likely to experience chronic and acute levels of poverty (Fong & Shibuya, 2000). This issue has been called the "racialization of poverty," and it may go some way toward understanding the high levels of violent victimization and offending discussed

---

intra-racial
Within the same race of people.

racialized
The process of marginalizing a group of people based on perceived physical and socio-cultural differences.

anomie
A term coined by Durkheim to describe periods of lawlessness, normlessness, and unrestrained choice, or a breakdown in social solidarity.

above. That is, Black Canadians may experience higher levels of violence because they are also more likely to experience high levels of poverty and income inequality (Messner & Tardiff, 1985; Sampson, 1995), which, as we saw in the discussion of poverty and violence, are themselves associated with high levels of violent victimization and offending.

Current Issues in Criminological Research on Violence
Masculinity and Violence

Thus far we have seen that men, particularly young, economically disadvantaged, and racialized men, are more likely to be the victims and perpetrators of violent crime, and that although females experience high levels of victimization, they are, overall, underrepresented as perpetrators of violent crime. In addition to the theoretical perspectives on criminal and violent offending discussed above and elsewhere in this text, the concept of gender may be useful in making sense of these consistent sex differences in trends and patterns of violent victimization and offending. Indeed, since at least the early 1990s, interest in research that examines the relationship between masculinity and violence has grown.

The concept of **hegemonic masculinity** refers to the idealized form of masculinity at a particular time and in a particular place. Connell (1987, 2002) points out that in contemporary North American society, mainstream hegemonic masculinity emphasizes normative heterosexuality, autonomy, and success (Connell, 1987; Mullins & Cardwell-Mullins, 2006). For middle- and upper-class men, hegemonic masculinity is typically demonstrated through workplace success, which generates "masculine capital"—such as social and political clout, and various material accoutrements (designer clothing, a large home, a high-end car, and other forms of "bling") that communicate their power to others (Mullins & Cardwell-Mullins, 2006). But such resources and material displays are only available as symbols of masculinity for a small proportion of men. As such, less affluent men strive to enact some version of hegemonic masculinity in varying ways and using whatever resources are at their disposal to demonstrate their masculinity to others (Mullins & Cardwell-Mullins, 2006). For some men, a violent presentation of self is a key way of performing masculinity and generating masculine capital.

hegemonic masculinity
A culturally idealized form of masculinity; in contemporary Western societies, for example, hegemonic masculinity involves displays of autonomy, aggressive individualism, a lack of emotion, normative heterosexuality, and the capacity for violence.

The work of Elijah Anderson (1999) highlights the link between social inequality, economic disadvantage, and the construction of violent masculinities among some men. Anderson argues that in some disadvantaged neighbourhoods and among some residents, a set of informal rules emerges that governs interpersonal public behaviour and defines masculine identity for those who abide by them. Toughness, dominance, and the willingness to resort to violence to resolve interpersonal conflicts are central dictates of this "street code."

When navigating the streets, many residents, whether or not they have internalized the dictates of the street code, feel compelled to "go for bad"—adopting a "tough guy" pose that is intended to prevent violent attacks against them. Ironically, however, this posturing may invite violence rather than deter it. Adhering to the street code may actually increase the likelihood of a violent encounter due to the perception that others (who are also abiding by the dictates of the code) will use violence against them. In this sense, the use of violence becomes a pre-emptive strike of sorts, in that "it's either him or me."

The street code also provides a means by which to acquire respect, or "juice," and avoid humiliating situations of status degradation or disrespect. For example, if one young man is assaulted by another, the code dictates that he must salvage his self-respect and the respect of his "running buddies" by avenging himself, or else risk being labelled "soft" and targeted for violent attack by others. Further, the proliferation of guns on the streets of some urban neighbourhoods has implications for the degree of violence that is ultimately meted out: Guns provide a quick and sometimes final resolution to a dispute, transforming a minor dispute over a "diss" into a deadly act.

Another key aspect of the street code and the particular form of masculinity it generates involves "no-snitch codes," or the vilification of those who cooperate with formal authorities. Snitching is viewed as a violation of masculinity because a real man is expected to "act hard" and resolve interpersonal conflicts without the help of outsiders (Woldoff & Weiss, 2010). In the end, however, no-snitch codes may actually lead to additional violence, via the meting out of "street justice" to deal with interpersonal disputes. See Box 13.3.

In sum, then, Anderson's work highlights the ways in which some young men in poor urban neighbourhoods prove their manhood by conforming to a code that prescribes norms of minding one's own business and taking care of matters without outside assistance. Respect based on one's reputation as a tough guy and for keeping one's mouth shut is a form of masculine capital in such environments—which may lead to the amplification of violence in affected communities.

BOX 13.3

"Stop Snitching": From Street Code to Slogan

The code of the street has long stressed that there is something dishonourable—not to mention highly risky—about informing on another person to law enforcement. *Omertà,* the Mafia's blood oath of silence, is but one example of this type of honour code, which is also common in gang culture. Gang members learn very early that to "rat" on someone is likely to lead to the informant being targeted for retaliation, as suggested by the old saying, "snitches get stitches."

Informants have always been a vital element of law enforcement, and their testimony is often critical in ensuring that a criminal is successfully prosecuted. But there has also emerged a movement—grounded in profound distrust of police in communities that are "over-policed but underserved"—to discourage potential informants from cooperating with law enforcement. The "Stop Snitching" campaign began to appear in several US cities around 2004. Supporters wore the red, stop sign-shaped "Stop Snitching" logo on t-shirts, sometimes even while in court rooms during trials. The clear message to anyone who might stand up and testify: You will face consequences if you identify someone for a crime. This message has also been amplified by

Rapper Lil' Kim arriving at court during her trial. She was convicted for lying to prosecutors about what she knew about a shooting incident involving rival hip-hop groups.

many high-profile hip-hop artists and rappers, such as Lil Wayne, Ice Cube, and Lil' Kim, who have used their songs to push the message that snitching is unacceptable. Other artists, such as Chuck D of Public Enemy, have strongly criticized the movement, saying that it promotes the continuation and rewarding of crime.

But an aversion to snitching is not solely found in criminal gangs and the hip hop and rap scenes. Scholars have long pointed out the parallels between the "no snitch" codes described above and the "blue wall of silence" that often exists among police officers, a term used to denote informal rules that forbid reporting on fellow officers' errors, misconduct, or crime. More recently, in August 2017, US President Donald Trump promoted a "Stop Snitching" campaign aimed at former members of his administration and inner circle, such as personal lawyer Michael Cohen, who had begun making plea deals with Special Counsel Robert Mueller as part of his investigation into Trump's many alleged crimes.

Some people have taken the anti-snitching sentiment to extremes: Adam Louie of Toronto launched the website Golden Snitches, on which he posts the images, names, and alleged crimes of people whom he has deemed to be police informants. While he maintains that these informants are by and large criminals themselves looking to avoid the consequences of their own misdeeds, critics suggest that Louie is engaging in a dangerous form of vigilantism that could seriously undermine the legal rights of the people implicated.

Sources: Based on Krishnan, M. (2017, August 22). This man is hell bent on publicly outing "snitches." *Vice*. Retrieved from https://www.vice.com/en_ca/article/a3373e/this-man-is-hell-bent-on-publicly-outing-snitches; Hampson, R. (2009, March 29). Anti-snitch campaign riles police, prosecutors. *USA Today*. Retrieved from http://usatoday30.usatoday.com/news/nation/2006-03-28-stop-snitching_x.htm; Mathis-Lilley, B. (2018, August 23). President launches stop snitching campaign. *Slate*. Retrieved from https://slate.com/news-and-politics/2018/08/trump-stop-snitching.html.

Gun Violence

In 2016, 36 percent (223 of 611 killings) of homicides in Canada were committed with a firearm, and handguns accounted for 58 percent of all firearms used to commit homicide that year (David, 2017). The risk of gun violence is higher in urban areas, and research shows that, in Toronto, guns have figured more prominently in the city's homicides over time (Gartner & Thompson, 2004). During the 1970s and 1980s, for example, 25 percent of homicides in Toronto were committed with guns, a figure that increased to 32 percent by the 1990s. And since 2000, at least half of all homicides in Toronto were committed with guns. The trend for Canada as a whole is quite different, with gun homicide rates declining over time.

Thompson's (2009) research on gun homicide in Toronto between 1988 and 2003 shows that the "social distribution of gun homicide" (or the segments of the population most vulnerable to this violence) is heavily influenced by age, sex, and race. Over this period, the majority of victims of gun homicide were young (38 percent were under the age of 24, and 39 percent were in the 25 to 34 age range), male (87 percent), and Black (54 percent). Further, just as the risk of gun violence is not evenly distributed across social groups, it is also not evenly distributed across the cityscape. Instead, and consistent with the research on the geography of violence, discussed below, high levels of gun homicide tend to cluster in a small number of disadvantaged neighbourhoods. This begs the question why.

The concept of a "local gun culture" may help to understand why high levels of gun homicide are concentrated in particular urban neighbourhoods. Building on Anderson's (1999) concept of "the code of the streets," Jeffrey Fagan and Deanna Wilkinson (1998) argued that guns are part of the "ecology," or the social environment, of inner-city neighbourhoods, and have become the ultimate social tool used to attain status and respect. One of the young men they interviewed for this research explains the role of guns in creating the right "rep" on the streets: "If you got a gun you the man (laughing). Ain't no more manhood, it's gunhood" (p. 81). Fagan and Wilkinson also identify self-defence as the primary reason for carrying a firearm; all of their subjects spoke of either the "protection" or "defence" of self, family, and/or friends, and felt that safety in their neighbourhoods was uncertain, at best. One subject even deemed his gun "my visa" for navigating the streets of his neighbourhood in safety (p. 83).

Gun possession was also common among young men involved in the drug trade, burglaries, and hustling, but firearms' instrumental value existed in concert with their value as symbols of social status, self-worth, and personal power. Fagan and Wilkinson concluded that gun use has become a central part of status and identity formation within the "street-oriented" world of some inner-city US neighbourhoods. Further, the presence of firearms has changed the "scripts" for how interpersonal conflict is handled on the street. Boys in particular learn that guns are part of day-to-day life in some inner-city neighbourhoods, and that gun violence is one of the few options available for resolving interpersonal disputes.

In sum, then, gun possession, which is often associated with high levels of drug- and gang-related activity (Cohen, Cork, Engberg, & Tita, 1998), increases the risk of violent death in some inner-city neighbourhoods. However, these risks are not limited to drug dealers and gang-involved individuals; for reasons of status and personal protection, gun-related violence has also spread to other residents—namely young men—in affected communities (Blumstein, 1995; Grogger & Willis, 1998).

The Geography of Urban Violence

Thus far, we have seen that the risk of violent victimization and offending is not randomly distributed across the population. Rather, the "social distribution of risk," or the segments of the population at greatest risk of violent victimization and offending, is heavily influenced by age, sex, race, and socio-economic status.

Research on the "geography of violence" shows that violence is also not evenly distributed across urban neighbourhoods. Instead, a disproportionate amount of violent crime is concentrated in a small number of neighbourhoods that are characterized by multiple forms of social and economic disadvantage (Messner & Zimmerman, 2012; Sampson, 1995). These patterns of **spatial inequality** were first identified by researchers in Chicago in the 1940s, and since then, a large amount of research in the United States, and an emerging body of related work in Canada, has examined violence hot spots in some urban neighbourhoods. This research consistently shows that neighbourhoods that experience the highest levels of violent crime are also characterized by high and concentrated levels of poverty, racial segregation, population turnover, joblessness, low educational attainment, and large numbers of young people and single-parent families (Charron, 2009; Messner & Zimmerman, 2012; Thompson & Gartner, 2014). Data maps, such as the one shown in Figure 13.5, are used to track crime.

To some extent, the concentration of violence in poor neighbourhoods is to be expected, given that, as discussed above, the risk of violence is disproportionately high for socially and economically disadvantaged people. This effect is called a **compositional effect**—meaning that larger numbers of poor people living in

spatial inequality
The unequal distribution of resources and services from one area to another.

compositional effect
The combination of parts that make up something. In neighbourhoods, a compositional effect refers to the aggregate characteristics of individual residents.

certain neighbourhoods would necessarily mean that these neighbourhoods would also experience higher levels of violent crime.

FIGURE 13.5   2018 Homicide Crime Map, City of Winnipeg

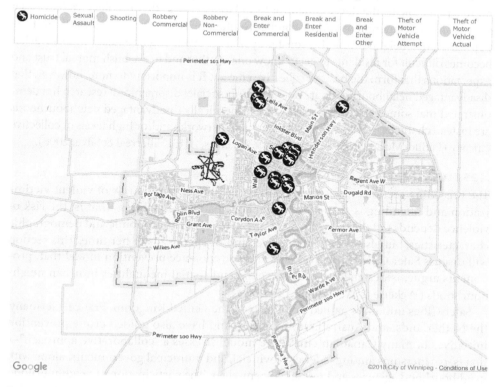

Source: © Winnipeg Police Service (2018).

Yet neighbourhoods also experience **contextual effects**—meaning that levels of violent crime stem from neighbourhood social context. For example, **social disorganization theory** views the geography of violence as a function of the differing degrees to which neighbourhoods can informally control the nature and amount of local illegal activity. According to this view, the prevalence and density of social networks and the level of participation in community-based organizations generate solidarity and mutual trust, or "social cohesion," among neighbourhood residents. In turn, social cohesion promotes the neighbourhood's capacity to monitor and manage criminogenic situations. Cohesive neighbourhoods that can effectively mobilize to regulate the behaviour within their boundaries are said to have high levels of **collective efficacy** (Sampson, Raudenbush, & Earls, 1997). So-called disorganized neighbourhoods, on the other hand, are theorized to lack the networks, norms, and trust that facilitate coordination and cooperation for mutual benefit among residents. The end results, according to this perspective, are higher levels of crime and violence in the neighbourhood.

Research has identified a series of neighbourhood characteristics that are thought to be indicative of social disorganization. These include poverty, high population turnover, the concentration and segregation of racialized groups, and large numbers of young men

contextual effect
The influence of environmental factors on human behaviours.

social disorganization theory
The theory that a breakdown of the networks, norms, and trust that facilitate coordination and cooperation among residents of neighbourhoods can lead to greater crime and violence.

collective efficacy
A group's shared belief that it can come together and achieve desired goals.

and single-parent families (Sampson, 1995). These characteristics are thought to impede the formation and maintenance of social networks, cohesion, and collective efficacy in varying ways. For example, large numbers of young male residents in neighbourhoods characterized by various forms of structural disadvantage may render that neighbourhood more susceptible to the development of local "street codes" that privilege violence as a means of status attainment and/or conflict resolution (Anderson, 1999). Further, if the population of a neighbourhood is constantly in flux (due to high population turnover), it becomes difficult for residents to get to know one another and to establish mutual trust and expectations that form the basis of collective efficacy. It is important to note, however, that disadvantaged neighbourhoods are not *necessarily* socially disorganized; research has demonstrated that some extremely socially and economically disadvantaged neighbourhoods are instead characterized by strong social ties and networks and/or high levels of collective efficacy (Patillo-McCoy, 1999; Thompson & Bucerius, 2013; Villarreal & Silva, 2006).

Responding to Urban Violence

The preceding sections discussed research that shows that the risk of violent victimization and offending is shaped by social and spatial inequalities. That is, the risk of violence depends not only on who one is, in terms of socio-economic and demographic characteristics, but also on where one lives and/or spends his or her time. This section will discuss Safer Cities initiatives, a crime-and-violence prevention model that, proponents argue, is designed to address social and spatial inequalities in urban neighbourhoods (Wekerle & Whitzman, 1995).

Safer Cities initiatives gained popularity in the United Kingdom, France, Germany, the Netherlands, and Australia in the 1980s, and have also guided crime prevention initiatives in many Canadian cities. The model stresses a "collaborative approach"— that is, partnerships among federal, provincial, and municipal governments, along with neighbourhood agencies and residents themselves. The participation of neighbourhood agencies and residents is seen as key to the model's success because both are viewed as "experts" in the issues that affect their neighbourhoods.

Using this collaborative, or partnership, approach, the Safer Cities model aims to address crime by both attending to the root causes of crime and violence, and addressing issues with the neighbourhood's built environment that may be facilitating crime and violence. As such, the model rests on the "twin pillars" of crime prevention through social development (CPSD) and crime prevention through environmental design (CPTED). These approaches are discussed in Box 13.4.

BOX 13.4

Crime Prevention Approaches

Crime Prevention Through Social Development

CPSD involves long-term, integrated actions that deal with the root causes of crime. Its aim is to reduce risk factors that start people, particularly children and youth, on the road to crime, and to build protective factors that may mitigate those risks. The risk factors associated with criminal involvement are also related to many other social problems, such as child abuse and neglect, drug and alcohol misuse, school failure, teenage pregnancy, and unemployment. So, when people and organizations work to prevent crime, they are also working to make our communities healthy, safe and sustainable in many respects. ...

CPTED principles focus on the spaces in which people move, observe each other, and interact.

CPSD works at making people healthy, responsible, and resilient. In a free society, there will always be opportunities and temptations to do wrong—to take advantage of another person or a situation for our own benefit. CPSD promotes community values about non-violence and respect for other people and their property, and helps young people resist peer pressure and make good decisions.

CPSD programming can occur at three levels:

1. At the primary level, crime prevention refers to universal, population-based programs such as public education and health care.

2. At the secondary level, crime prevention refers to programs that target those at higher risk for criminal activity. This level would include programs for youth at risk of leaving school and parenting programs for high-risk parents.

3. At the tertiary level, crime prevention refers to rehabilitative and supervision programs for offenders to reduce re-offending.

Crime Prevention Through Environmental Design

CPTED is about the places and things, the "built environment," which can be either targets of criminal activity or the location where crime takes place. The proper design, effective use, and maintenance of the built environment can lead to a reduction in the incidence and fear of crime, and an improvement in quality of life.

CPTED is complementary to, and inter-related with, CPSD strategies as people live in the built environment and the built environment influences how people behave.

CPTED is based on the premise that much crime is opportunistic and contextual. Inadvertently, nuisance and criminal behaviour can be facilitated by poorly planned and designed space, leading to actual opportunities for crime, as well as increased levels of fear.

Through the effective use of CPTED principles, crime, nuisance behaviour and the fear of crime can be reduced. Application of CPTED principles to new developments prevents future problems; and using CPTED enhances problem-solving capability for existing developments.

There are four key CPTED design principles:

1. Natural access control—design that directs and influences the flow of people to naturally maximize control and surveillance (for example, exterior and interior design of a building, landscaping, lighting, and traffic calming).

2. Natural surveillance—design to maximize visibility and ensure legitimate users can observe and monitor activities around them in a formal or casual manner (for example, office or apartment windows with unimpeded sightlines to parking areas or other areas where crime is likely to occur).

3. Territoriality—design of the physical environment to extend a perceived sense of influence or territory. People taking ownership of their surroundings makes it more difficult for offenders to carry out crimes or disorder.

4. Maintenance—enhancement, maintenance, and management of the built environment encourages the users of the area to respect their surroundings (for example, removing graffiti and litter, avoiding overgrowth of hedges, fixing inoperative lighting, installing good locks).

Source: Excerpted from Law Courts Education Society (n.d.). Community crime prevention guide. Retrieved from https://www2.gov.bc.ca/assets/gov/public-safety-and-emergency-services/crime-prevention/community-crime-prevention/publications/crime-prevention.pdf

In addition to CPSD and CPTED, a role also exists for law enforcement in crime prevention, although the Safer Cities model downplays the importance of so-called law-and-order approaches. Nevertheless, it appears that law enforcement often has a significant role in applying the Safer Cities model, so much so that some scholars have suggested the model really ought to be described as a three-pronged model that includes CPSD, CPTED, *and* enforcement-based initiatives (Thompson & Gartner, 2007).

What is known about the *efficacy* of the twin pillars of crime prevention? Research shows that CPTED strategies may be effective in reducing crime and fear of crime in urban neighbourhoods (Casteel & Peek-Asa, 2000; Cozens, Saville, & Hillier, 2005), particularly if the strategies are implemented in tandem with psycho-social initiatives, such as those that fall under the umbrella of CPSD (Saville, 1998). Indeed, a large body of research demonstrates that programs and initiatives that address the root causes of crime and violence hold the greatest promise for reducing crime and violence in urban neighbourhoods (Doob, 2004; Howell & Hawkins, 1998; Smith, Lizotte, & Thornberry, 1995; Tremblay & Japel, 2003).

Finally, as discussed above, a common intervention in high-crime neighbourhoods involves intensive, *targeted* law enforcement strategies. Research, however, suggests that while these interventions may sometimes have positive short-term effects, they generally do not reduce crime and violence in the long term (Cohen, Gorr, & Singh, 2003; Ludwig, 2005; Rosenfeld, Fornango, & Baumer, 2005). Given that police crackdowns and related tactics are unlikely to have beneficial long-term effects, it appears that these activities take a back seat to the twin pillars of CPTED and CPSD, as the Safer Cities model indicates.

Conclusion

As this chapter has demonstrated, violence is a multi-faceted phenomenon that occurs in a wide range of contexts and for a variety of reasons. Moreover, the likelihood that a person will commit a violent crime is associated with a number of factors, including age, sex, poverty, race, and where one lives and spends time. Criminological theory and research make important contributions to our understanding of patterns, trends, correlates, and consequences of different forms of violence. They are also fundamental to the development of crime prevention through social development (CPSD), crime prevention through environmental design (CPTED), and collective efficacy—initiatives that seek to reduce and prevent violent victimization and offending more generally.

SUMMARY OF KEY POINTS

- The weight of the available evidence suggests that no single factor causes violence; instead, it is the end result of multiple factors that converge to play important and interactive roles.
- Criminological research has identified a consistent set of individual-level correlates of violent victimization and offending. These include age, sex, socio-economic

class, and race. A variety of theoretical perspectives seek to account for these relationships.

- The concept of masculinity may be helpful in explaining the overrepresentation of males as victims and offenders of violent crime. Research highlights the ways in which some young men in poor urban neighbourhoods prove their manhood by conforming to a code that prescribes norms of minding one's own business and taking care of matters without outside assistance. Respect based on one's reputation as a tough guy and keeping one's mouth shut is a form of masculine capital in such environments—which may lead to the amplification of violence in affected communities.

- Gun violence is an increasingly urban problem in Canada, and some segments of the population—in particular, young, racialized males—are especially vulnerable to this violence. The concept of a local gun culture may be helpful in understanding the social and geographic distribution of gun violence. According to this perspective, guns are part of day-to-day life in some urban neighbourhoods, and gun violence is viewed by some to be one of the few options available for resolving interpersonal disputes.

- Research on the geography of violence shows that violence is also not evenly distributed across urban neighbourhoods. Instead, a disproportionate amount of violent crime is concentrated in a small number of neighbourhoods (sometimes referred to as violence hot spots) that are characterized by multiple forms of social and economic disadvantage. The concepts of compositional and contextual effects can assist in understanding the ways in which violent crime maps across urban neighbourhoods.

- High levels of violent crime in urban neighbourhoods are usually addressed using one or a combination of the following approaches: CPSD, CPTED, and law enforcement-based strategies and initiatives. Research consistently demonstrates that CPSD approaches, which aim to address the root causes of violent crime, hold the greatest promise for reducing violent crime in urban neighbourhoods over the long term.

QUESTIONS FOR CRITICAL DISCUSSION

1. Consider the different sides of the debate over the use of police informants, or "snitching." Whose argument do you believe is most valid? Should the communities described in Box 13.3 be more cooperative with police in the name of reducing crime, or do they have reason to be wary of police tactics?
2. How might boys and men challenge and reconstruct the notion of a violent masculinity? Is it possible to develop alternative ways of demonstrating that one is "a real man"?
3. Why are law enforcement approaches commonly used to tackle high levels of violence when research consistently demonstrates that they generally do not work and come with serious consequences for police–community relationships?
4. In Canada, criminal justice agencies routinely collect race-based data (i.e., information on the racial/ethnic background of people who come into contact with the system as victims, offenders, etc.), but they do not publicly release these data.

Why do you think that is? If these data were released to the public, what positive consequences might there be? What negative consequences might there be?

5. Residents of urban neighbourhoods that are identified as hot spots for violent crime sometimes argue that mapping the geography of violence in this way stigmatizes the neighbourhood and its residents in the public imagination. Why might they feel this way?

6. In what ways is the "blue code of silence" (the equivalent of "no snitch" codes in police culture, wherein officers are expected to be loyal to one another above all else) among police officers similar to or different from the "no snitch codes" that exist in some poor, urban neighbourhoods?

SUGGESTED FURTHER READINGS

Anderson, E. (1999). *The code of the street: Decency, violence and the moral life of the inner city.* New York: W.W. Norton.

Fagan, J., & Wilkinson, D. (1998). Guns, youth violence, and social identity in inner cities. In M. Tonry & M. Moore (Eds.), *Crime and justice: Vol. 24* (pp. 105–188). Chicago: University of Chicago Press.

Pinker, S. (2011). *The better angels of our nature: Why violence has declined.* New York: Viking.

Thompson, S.K. (2013). Case study: Black homicide victimization in Toronto, Ontario, Canada. In S. Bucerius & M. Tonry (Eds.), *The Oxford handbook of ethnicity, crime and immigration* (pp. 450–453). New York: Oxford University Press.

Websites

Canadian Council on Social Development, Nation building through evidence, collaboration and design: http://www.ccsd.ca

CPTED Ontario: http://www.cptedontario.ca

Toronto crime by neighbourhood, 2004–2011: http://www.cbc.ca/toronto/features/crimemap

Legislation

Criminal Code, RSC 1985, c C-46.

Cases

R v Butcher, 2018 NSSC 194.

R v Friday, 2012 ABQB 371.

Luka Magnotta: Sexualized Crime and the Role of the Internet

The Berlin café where Luka Magnotta was apprehended.

In July 1910, when Dr. Hawley Crippen arrived by ocean liner in Quebec City, he was arrested for the murder of his wife.[1] The emerging technology of the wireless telegraph was responsible for his capture. The good doctor was the first person to be caught in such a manner: He had fled the United Kingdom with his lover, but the wireless telegraph (precursor to the telephone) allowed British authorities to send a message to police in Canada.

Much has changed since 1910. Today we have communication technologies that would have seemed unthinkable even 20 years ago. The arrest of Luka Magnotta is a telling illustration of the power of the Internet, which has, in a relatively short period of time, become closely intertwined with sexualized crime.

As the sordid saga of Magnotta reveals, the Internet can be both lauded and reviled. The global release of photos, videos, and stories about the "Canadian psycho" who gruesomely murdered and dismembered Jun Lin in Montreal in May 2012 left Magnotta with no place to hide; he was detected, appropriately enough, in an Internet café in Berlin a few weeks later, surfing for both pornography and news about himself.

But it was also the Internet that provided a platform for Magnotta, giving him the opportunity to broadcast repulsive videos of sadistic cruelty. And videos, once released into cyberspace, are almost impossible to remove, despite the efforts of authorities. (In 2013, Edmonton police charged website owner Mark Marek with the rare obscenity charge of "corrupting morals" for posting Magnotta's horrific video of the crime. For his part, Marek claims he posted the video as "a public service," in order to help track down the perpetrator [Parrish, 2013].)

And so we can see that while the Internet makes possible the wide distribution of such materials, it is that very same online visibility that served to facilitate Magnotta's capture. Put differently, every critique of the Internet's porous lack of accountability can be met with the observation that online exposure also shines a light into the darkest recesses of human behaviour, most particularly the realm of sexual deviance.

Journalism plays an important role in shining that light; however, in the digital age—when website "hits" are the main goal—sensational stories take precedence, and facts often get lost amid online gossip and opinion. We now know of the horrific murder and dismemberment of Jun Lin; Luka Magnotta was convicted of first-degree murder by a jury in December 2014.[2] The sensational nature of his case is also a depressingly familiar reminder of how most of us come to understand the reality of crime. Only the most horrific and sexualized allegations of homicide are reported with any detail in the mainstream press or online. The barbaric sex crimes of notorious Canadian criminals Robert Pickton, Paul Bernardo, and Clifford Olson are well known. But much more typical forms of sexual crime—such as incest or inappropriate groping by a friend or an acquaintance—receive little or no attention. We learn of the rarest and most predatory of criminal acts in the media, not of the staples of crime that occupy our police officers, courts, and correctional centres.

The problem with this selective reporting ("if it bleeds, it leads"), based on the understandable journalistic principle that the most horrific acts make for more readers, is that extensive coverage of these crimes skews our perceptions of sex crimes and criminals. The media tend to overemphasize the predatory offender, relative to the norm of sexual offences. We rarely hear, for example, of the reality that 35 percent of the 13,300 inmates in federal penitentiaries have significant mental health impairments and are in need of treatment (Makin, 2011).

The case of Luka Magnotta is a reminder of our collective myopia with regard to this issue, and of the media's imperatives. News organizations are selling a product, one that often verges on entertainment and spectacle; education of the public is neither critical nor necessary for this task. And so we have another riveting tale of horror: the haunting and disturbing face of Luka Magnotta on the front pages of almost every major newspaper. Unfortunately, this reliance on sexualized sensationalism is a feature of crime reporting that seems unlikely to disappear.

Before You Read Chapter 14

- What is your impression of the prevalence of sexual crime in Canada, or in your own community, based on the media coverage you have seen? What might explain the media (and the public) interest in sensational sexual crime stories?
- How has media reporting affected the public's perception of sexual offences—from high-profile sex cases (such as Magnotta's) to the more common forms of sexual offences (such as sex assault and inappropriate touching)?
- How realistic is it to expect authorities to be able to track down and prosecute a significant percentage of Internet-facilitated sexual offences?
- How could media coverage affect the trial of an alleged sex offender?

Sexual Offences and Problematic Sexual Interests

LEARNING OUTCOMES

After reading this chapter, students will be able to:

- Understand the difference between risk and dangerousness in sex offenders.

- Describe how sexual offenders have been dealt with by the criminal justice system over time.

- Understand the difference between sexual offences and deviant sexual interests.

- Define forms of deviant sexual interests and behaviours.

- Know factors associated with increased risk of sexual recidivism.

- Understand Canadian criminal justice approaches used in managing the risk of sex offenders.

Introduction

Sexual behaviours in societies throughout the world are influenced by varying moral codes, cultural and social expectations, myths, religious principles, and often unscientific beliefs. Historically, criminal sexual offences and other problematic sexual behaviours have been a concern (Bartol & Bartol, 2016). However, within the past 35 years, criminological issues involving sexual offending have risen to prominence in academic, social, political, and clinical realms. Sexual offending, especially against children, is universally viewed as a serious problem, but what is considered "deviant" and/or criminal, the reasons why, and the appropriate responses vary by perspective, location, and time period.

In North America, the goal of the criminal justice system is to deter, punish, rehabilitate, and manage the risk posed by sex offenders. While doing so, the justice system must maintain a balance between public safety and protection of the individual rights of the accused. Attempts to maintain this balance can be especially difficult when dealing with sex offenders; a subgroup of offenders who are viewed by society as highly dangerous and "morally tainted." Even within the prison population, sex offenders, especially those whose crimes were against children, are stigmatized.

Despite widespread coverage of sexual crimes in the media that often leads the general public to believe that sexual offending is at an all-time high, sexual offences against both adults and children have been steadily decreasing on a global scale since the 1980s (Bartol & Bartol, 2016; Morgan & Kena, 2016; Perreault, 2013). The only exceptions to this trend are child pornography offences, which have been on the rise (Seto, 2013).

Highly publicized incidents of a relatively small number of child abductions and sexual assaults throughout Canada and the United States during the 1980s and early 1990s elicited widespread shock and anger. These cases acted as a catalyst for new criminal justice attempts to manage sex offenders both during incarceration and upon their release into the community (Murphy et al., 2009a; Petrunik, Murphy, & Fedoroff, 2008).

Individuals who have committed a sexual offence are often classified as a homogeneous group. However, wide variation exists in offender characteristics (such as gender, age, socio-economic background, personality, intelligence, attitude, and social skills). Offence characteristics and subsequent risk of recidivism vary widely. Victim characteristics can vary in terms of the age, gender, number of victims, offence history, relationship history, medical history, psychiatric history, offender–victim relationship, and many other significant variables. Offences also differ in terms of degree of planning, motivation, and the level of violence.

Perpetrators of sexual offences are typically characterized as "all the same": extremely dangerous, anonymous, unstable, and mobile (McAlinden, 2007; Murphy et al., 2009a; Robbers, 2009). Although this singular conceptualization is not supported by research, it has been perpetuated by media portrayals that claim society needs to defend itself from "predatory pedophiles" and "rapists" who are categorized as all men, strangers, and increasingly prevalent, thereby creating an imminent high risk to the safety of all women and children. In fact, reports have found that as many as 80 to 98 percent of known sexual acts against children are committed by someone well known to the victim. Rates are similar for adult victims (Doerner & Lab, 2014; Freeman-Longo, 1996; Greenfield, 1997). These facts highlight the inaccurate portrayal by the media that facilitates the concept of "stranger danger."

This chapter provides an overview of how sexual offences and responses to sex crimes have been conceptualized by criminal justice officials over time; the characteristics of sex offenders and associated levels of recidivism; the difference between clinical mental health and legal understandings of and responses to problematic sexual interests and behaviours; and approaches to treating and managing sex offenders once they are released into the community.

The Concepts of Dangerousness and Risk

dangerousness
The capacity of a person to physically, psychologically, or morally harm oneself or others. It includes an estimation of both the severity and likelihood of harm.

risk
The probability that a person will commit future harmful acts.

When referring to sex offenders from criminal justice perspectives over time, two concepts are important to understand. The concepts of dangerousness and risk have a long history in civil and criminal legislation, as well as correctional and psychiatric practice. **Dangerousness** refers to the capacity of a person to harm oneself or others. It includes an estimation of the severity, imminence, predictability, and likelihood of harm. The term **risk** typically refers only to the probability that a person will commit future harmful acts (Petrunik, 2003, 2005; Thomas, 2005).

One assumption about the dangerousness of high-risk sex offenders is that the motivation behind their crimes is due to overly strong sexual desires and uncontrolled sexual impulses. The belief that people who commit sexual offences cannot be changed has led to a focus on incapacitation (preventing an offender from being able to commit another offence through incarceration or other means of management) to enhance public safety. An offender's past criminal behaviour is often used to appraise the risk of recidivism, but it is not the only significant variable. **Recidivism** refers to reoffending or committing another crime. General recidivism refers to any new offence, and sexual recidivism refers to another sexual offence (Bartol & Bartol, 2016; Perreault, 2013).

An individual who has a **paraphilia** or a personality disorder may commit a number of non-violent sexual offences against children (for example, exposing him/herself to children in a park or asking a child to sexually touch him/her). From a criminal justice perspective, this individual may be viewed as more dangerous than an individual who commits a non-sexual murder. The murderer typically receives a sentence designed to incapacitate and punish. The sex offender not only receives a sentence aimed at incapacitation and punishment, but also typically faces conditions intended to continue surveillance once the person has been released back into the community.

Criminal Justice Responses to Sexual Offences over Time

Throughout North America in the early 1800s, criminality, including sexual offending, was considered to be endemic within the "dangerous classes," where crime was associated with immoral populations (groups of people who were economically marginalized and socially stigmatized, and seemed to live by a different set of moral standards than the rest of society). Such individuals included prostitutes, vagrants, the mentally ill, and, sometimes, predatory criminals. During this time it was believed that immorality and criminality were closely intertwined, with "immorality" often acting as a precursor to criminal acts. Offenders were held accountable for their crimes within a system that emphasized "proportionate sentencing" and "due process" (Petrunik, 2003, 2005; Thomas, 2005).

Forensic-Clinical Model

Beginning in the late 19th century, proponents of a "forensic-clinical model" of dangerousness were less concerned with concepts of due process and proportionate sentencing, and instead lobbied for indeterminate confinement. This model developed in response to the perceived shortcomings of classical criminology. Supporters of the forensic-clinical model considered requirements for due process and proportionate sentencing to be a hindrance to the process of effective treatment. These proponents contended that offenders could not be sufficiently deterred by a fixed term of punishment because of mental or personality disorders that made them prone to criminal activity. Sentences needed to be indeterminate, since it could not be specified in advance how long it would take for treatment to decrease the offender's level of dangerousness (Connelly & Williamson, 2000; Gudjonsson & Young, 2007; Petrunik, 1982).

Justice Model

The "justice model" became popular during the 1970s and was based on the principles of due process and proportionate sentencing. Themes seen during the classical period of criminology began to resurface, with a penal shift back to determinate sentences

recidivism
Also referred to as "reoffending," when an offender goes on to commit another crime; general recidivism refers to any new offence, and sexual recidivism refers to another sexual offence.

paraphilia
Mental health term for sexual interest in an activity other than masturbation that does not include mutual consent with another person.

For more on classical criminology, see Chapter 6, Theories of Crime: A Brief Introduction.

that were proportionate to the gravity of the offence. Societal challenges emerged from a revolution in mental health legislation and criminal law reform in which due process was extended to include individuals suffering from mental illness. Some social scientists questioned the ability of forensic mental health workers to assess the risk posed by offenders, and to diagnose and treat disorders effectively (Petrunik, 2003). Greater safeguards were put in place against commitment to asylums for indeterminate periods of time, and against involuntary treatment. With few exceptions, offenders with mental illness also retained the right to refuse treatment.

Community Protection Approach

The emergence of a "community protection approach" during the late 1980s and early 1990s resulted from concerns that previous models had not given enough attention to overall public safety and the rights of victims. The primary focus of this new approach was not on the treatment or rehabilitation of the individual offender but on the overall safety of the community. This approach was guided by the concerns of victims' rights groups, crime prevention advocates, and the general public (Murphy et al., 2009a; Petrunik, 2003; Petrunik et al., 2008). Proponents called for governments to actively address perceived increases in society's fears resulting from a series of highly publicized sex crimes, and to give increased attention to the rights of victims and their families (Kemshall & Wood, 2007; Petrunik, 2003; Petrunik et al., 2008).

For more on victims' rights, see Chapter 5, Victims of Crime.

One factor that contributed to the shift toward the community protection approach was the media's inaccurate construction of "stranger danger," and stereotyping sex offenders as "predators lurking in the bushes" who were driven by an uncontrollable impulse to victimize unsuspecting children. This sensational portrayal of the typical sex offender is false. The majority of sexual offences are committed by someone who is well known to the victim (Murphy et al., 2009a). In fact, most child abductions are committed by a parent estranged from his or her spouse and involved in a custody dispute.

The community protection approach justifies the preventive restriction of liberty of the offender based on the perceived risk of that person committing offences in the future, rather than solely on retribution for acts committed in the past. This approach suggests that the best way to deal with the dangerousness of high-risk sex offenders is through a combination of social controls (surveillance, monitoring, and restriction of liberties) both during incarceration and after release into the community (Petrunik et al., 2008). These mechanisms of risk management for sex offenders include the following: longer and full sentences; intensive community supervision with orders restricting freedom of movement and association; notification of release into the community; sex offender registries (SORs); and, last, civil and/or criminal incarceration, allowing for indeterminate confinement based on a designation of extreme dangerousness and severe mental illness (Kemshall & Wood, 2007; Murphy et al., 2009a; Petrunik, 2003; Petrunik, et al., 2008; Worley & Worley, 2013). The intended goal is to manage the risk posed by this population in order to prevent the recurrence of crime and to reduce the probability or magnitude of the predicted harm.

Community Protection Approach in American and Canadian Legislation

The crucial event that sparked the emergence of the community protection approach within the United States was the 1989 abduction and sexual assault of a seven-year-old boy in Washington state by Earl Shriner. This incident became a catalyst for rapid legislative reform throughout the United States. Washington state passed the 1990 *Community Protection Act* (CPA) that called for a state-wide **sex offender registry (SOR)**, a system of community notification of release of sex offenders and post-sentence completion of **civil commitment** of offenders who meet the criteria of a sexually violent predator (SVP). In response to political pressure by victims' rights organizations across the country, the *Jacob Wetterling Crimes Against Children and Sexually Violent Offender Registration Act* (JWA) of 1994 required all states to establish a functioning SOR (Murphy et al., 2009a; Petrunik, 2002, 2003; Petrunik et al., 2008; Worley & Worley, 2013). All states in the United States now have their own SOR as well as a national SOR.

The sexual assault and murder of Megan Kanka by her neighbour, who had been convicted for sexual offences twice before, led to the 1994 creation of New Jersey's *Megan's Law*. *Megan's Law* permits the public release of specific information (such as the offender's name, photo, and address). The potential for widespread notification increased when the state of Indiana introduced *Zachary's Law* in 1994. This legislation mandated the creation of a publicly accessible state website that listed pertinent information about known sex offenders (Jenkins, 2001). In the years to follow, public notification under *Megan's Law*, including databases publicly accessible via the Internet, became federal legislation. More recently, the 2006 *Adam Walsh Child Protection and Safety Act* replaced the JWA and resulted in amendments to mechanisms of community-based sex offender management, notably changes in registration and notification requirements (Murphy et al., 2009a; Petrunik, 2002, 2003; Petrunik et al., 2008).

Compared with the rapid development of policies for the management of sex offenders within the United States, legislation by the Canadian government developed in a significantly slower and more cautious manner. In 1988, one year before Shriner's crime in Washington, Joseph Fredericks abducted, sexually assaulted, and murdered Christopher Stephenson in Ontario. Fredericks had spent his life in and out of high-security psychiatric hospitals and had left federal prison only a few months before the murder. Canadian citizens responded to the sensational media coverage of Christopher's murder with shock and outrage. Despite the clear parallels between the Shriner and Fredericks cases, it took the Ontario government 12 years to create a provincial SOR under *Christopher's Law* (Murphy & Fedoroff, 2013; Murphy, Fedoroff, & Martineau, 2009b; Petrunik et al., 2008).

After the creation of the Ontario SOR, community members and victims' rights advocates demanded the creation of a national SOR (NSOR). Even then, plans for an NSOR were not announced until after the provincial governments threatened to create an independent system of interlinking SORs across Canada. The *Sex Offender Information Registration Act* (SOIRA) of 2004 was finally implemented to manage registrants throughout the country. Both registries are still functioning and have undergone reviews and amendments to improve their effectiveness and functionality (Murphy & Fedoroff, 2013; Murphy et al., 2009b). Fortunately, to date, routine public notification has not been implemented in Canada. The fact that convicted sex offenders are not publicly disclosed means they can obtain housing, employment, and attend treatment more easily.

Base Rates and Survival Curves in Sex Offender Recidivism

Before estimating the risk posed by any population, it is critical to examine the recidivism base rate for the population in question. The base rate is the proportion of offenders who will recidivate (go on to commit another offence) over a given period of time, known as

sex offender registry (SOR)
A searchable database with information on convicted sexual offenders.

civil commitment
Also known as "involuntary commitment," the legal process by which a person is detained after serving a sentence due to concerns that he or she will commit further crimes.

the "follow-up period." Base rates have been established by recidivism studies completed around the world on a variety of samples of sex offenders. Rates of sexual recidivism can be plotted on "survival curves." A survival curve measures the time at which released sex offenders commit a reoffence. The survival curve begins at 100 percent, which indicates that no released sex offenders in the study population have recidivated. As time goes on, if a sex offender recidivates, the curve begins to form. At the end of the follow-up period, the number left is the number not known to have recidivated, meaning those who have "survived" (Webster & Hucker, 2003). For example, if 25 out of 100 sex offenders were reconvicted for new sexual offences over a given time period, the recidivism base rate for that time period would be 25 percent and the rate of survival would be 75 percent. Survival rates are sometimes used to estimate recidivism rates over time (Faust, Bickart, Renaud, & Camp, 2015; Hanson, Morton, & Harris, 2003; Wormith & Hogg, 2011). While the overall survival rate decreases with time, it has now been established that the longer a sex offender does not recidivate while living in the community, the less likely it is that he or she ever will (Hanson, Harris, Helmus, & Thornton, 2014).

The outcome of risk prediction falls into one of four categories: true positive, true negative, false positive, and false negative. See Table 14.1 for a breakdown of the possible risk prediction outcomes.

TABLE 14.1   Outcomes of Risk Prediction

	Predict reoffence	Predict no reoffence
Do reoffend	True positive	False negative
Do not reoffend	False positive	True negative

Accurate risk prediction maximizes "true positives" (correctly identifying people who are truly high risk) and minimizes "false negatives" (miscategorizing high-risk people as low risk) while simultaneously minimizing "false positives" (incorrectly labelling innocent individuals) and maximizing "true negatives" (correctly identifying innocent individuals). The ideal outcome for risk prediction is a true negative whenever an offender is correctly predicted to not recidivate. The problematic nature of a false negative is heightened when the political and social climate becomes intensely preoccupied with issues surrounding sexual offending, as seen during the community protection approach outlined earlier. False positives, on the other hand, raise ethical concerns because inaccurate predictions unjustly impinge on the rights and liberty of the former offender (Craissati, 2004). They can be due to the inadequacy of the risk-assessment instrument, but they are more often due to a misunderstanding of risk assessment. Actuarial risk-assessment estimates compare the individual being assessed with others who have similar characteristics, but they can never provide specific estimates for the individual, especially if treatment and other interventions are not taken into account.

Data sources on the prevalence of sexual offending (both first-time offences and recidivism) include official statistics (such as police-reported numbers of charges or convictions), victim surveys, clinical reports, and research studies. Since sexual offences can be unreported, the use of official statistics can be problematic because they may underestimate the prevalence of sexual offending. Of the sexual offences reported to the

Chapter 14

police, a small number lead to arrest, and an even smaller number result in official convictions. Therefore, victimization surveys and clinical reports help to provide a more comprehensive estimate. However, even these sources do not represent all instances of sexual offending. The remaining unknown rates are referred to as the **dark figure of crime**. One reasonable estimate of the true rate of sexual offending is about 10 to 15 percent higher than the official rate (Delisi et al., 2016; Hanson et al., 2003; Huey, 2016). Despite this "dark figure," the number of reported sexual assaults has actually been decreasing since the early 1980s (Bartol & Bartol, 2016; Bureau of Justice Statistics, 2016; Perreault, 2013).

dark figure of crime
Refers to the variation between the number of crimes that occur and the number of crimes that are actually reported to the police. This figure highlights the large number of unreported crimes.

Predictors of Sex Offender Recidivism

A common misconception is that all sex offenders have a high frequency of recidivism. Official statistics and research studies do not support this assumption. Most sex offenders recidivate significantly less often than other types of violent and non-violent offenders. However, study results can vary greatly depending on how recidivism is defined. For example, rates vary depending on whether the authors include arrests, charges, and/or convictions as a measure of recidivism. Another important variable to consider is the length of the follow-up period. As demonstrated in the earlier discussion on the survival curve, the longer a person lives within the community, the more opportunity the study group has to recidivate. Commonly, follow-up periods in recidivism studies range from 5 to 15 years.

The common assumption is that sex offenders in the community are "ticking time bombs" who become increasingly dangerous the longer they are in the community. However, Harris and Hanson (2004) conducted a meta-analysis on relative recidivism rates among categories of sex offenders, and the survival curves for follow-up periods of 5 years, 10 years, and 15 years. This meta-analysis measured recidivism by a combination of charges and convictions. Results showed that recidivism rates among sex offenders decreased in frequency over time. The authors stated that

> without exception, the longer offenders remain offence-free in the community the less likely they are to sexually recidivate. ... The highest risk period is in the first few years after release. (p. 7)

See Table 14.2 for recidivism rates over time broken down by offender type. No peer-reviewed papers refute this claim. More recent meta-analytic data provides strong support for these findings. The authors suggest that offence history can be viewed as a valid but time-dependent indicator of a person's propensity to sexually recidivate (Hanson et al., 2014).

TABLE 14.2   Sexual Recidivism Rates by Offender Type and Time

	5 years	10 years	15 years
Rapists	14%	21%	24%
Homosexual extrafamilial offenders	23%	28%	35%
Heterosexual extrafamilial offenders	9%	13%	16%
Heterosexual incest offenders	6%	9%	13%

Source: Harris and Hanson (2004, p. 23).

static factors
Individual characteristics associated with the risk of reoffending that are immutable to external influences (for example, age at first offence and offence history). They can be used to determine an overall risk level but are not targets for change.

dynamic factors
Individual characteristics associated with the risk of reoffending that are amenable to change and are targets for treatment (for example, attitudes tolerant to criminal behaviour and criminal associates). A reduction in dynamic factors is associated with a decreased risk for recidivism.

acute dynamic factors
Individual characteristics associated with the risk of reoffending that are rapidly changing and include factors such as intoxication and mood.

Three types of risk factors have been associated with reoffences. **Static factors** are characteristics that cannot change (such as age at first offence and offence history). These factors can be used to determine an overall risk level but are not targets for change in therapy. **Dynamic factors** are amenable to change and are, therefore, targets for treatment. These are often referred to as criminogenic needs and include characteristics such as attitudes tolerant of criminal behaviour and criminal associates. A reduction in dynamic factors is associated with a decreased risk for recidivism and subsequently plays a larger role in identifying targets for assessment and intervention. **Acute dynamic factors**, on the other hand, are ones that change rapidly, such as intoxication and mood (Hanson & Harris, 1998; Hanson et al., 2003; Mann, Hanson, & Thornton, 2010).

Certain variables have been found to be associated with an increased risk of sexual recidivism; for example deviant sexual interest, prior sexual offences, having committed offences against male victims, and having committed offences against extrafamilial victims. Among the population of child molesters, heterosexual intrafamilial (incest) offenders with no other victim types exhibit the lowest rates of recidivism. Same-sex extrafamilial child molesters have the highest rate of recidivism, especially when they have more than one victim (Mann et al., 2010; Quinsey, Harris, Rice, & Cormier, 1998).

Results from a comprehensive meta-analysis by Mann et al. (2010) reviewing three meta-analytic, longitudinal studies identified several variables associated with an increased risk of sexual recidivism. Developmental variables included lack of emotionally intimate relationships with adults, childhood behaviour problems, and poor cognitive problem-solving. Demographic variables included job instability and being unmarried. Concerning general criminality, offence history, the victim type and relationship, and negative social influences also played significant roles. No one variable alone predicts recidivism; however, a deviant sexual preference for children as measured by penile tumescence was found to have the highest correlation with sexual recidivism. This finding did not hold for deviant preference profiles for the sexual assault of adult women (Quinsey et al., 1998). It is important to note that the identified factors were associations and not proven causes of the sexual offences or paraphilias.

Risk-Need-Responsivity Model

risk-need-responsivity (RNR) model
An assessment and rehabilitation theory that suggests it is possible to accurately predict the likelihood that someone will reoffend and provides principles on how to effectively intervene to reduce the risk.

The **risk-need-responsivity (RNR) model** has been used to assess and manage the risk factors for recidivism, and is based on three principles. The "risk principle" states that in the context of limited resources, it is best to turn maximum attention to offenders with the greatest risk of reoffending. Therefore, it suggests that the likelihood of recidivism decreases when the intensity of the treatment provided to the offender is proportional to the offender's risk to reoffend. The "need principle" calls for an individualized approach to matching the needs of the person being treated to the proposed treatment. The "responsivity principle" requires that intervention be tailored to the learning style, motivation, abilities, and strengths of the offender. These principles have been associated with more positive treatment outcomes for sex offenders treated in custody (Bonta & Andrews, 2007).

Clinical Interpretation of Deviant Sexual Behaviours

The clinical term "paraphilia" is a mental health classification defined in the *Diagnostic and Statistical Manual of Mental Disorders* (DSM-5) as "any intense and persistent sexual interest other than sexual interest in genital stimulation and preparatory fondling with phenotypically normal, physiologically mature, consenting human partners" (APA, 2013, p. 685). The DSM-5 is a handbook used by health-care professionals in many parts of the world as a guide to diagnosis of mental disorders. The current definition of paraphilia has been criticized (Fedoroff, Di Gioacchino, & Murphy, 2013a).

"Sex offender" is a legal term denoting someone who has committed a sexual offence as determined by the *Criminal Code*, whether or not that person has been convicted. Most sex offenders would not meet the clinical criteria for a paraphilic disorder. However, some paraphilias, if acted upon, could be considered sexual offences due to the non-consenting nature of the sexual interests. Many more paraphilias than are listed in the DSM-5 have been described (see Fedoroff, 2010; Murphy, Bradford, & Fedoroff, 2014a).

Paraphilias Associated with Criminal Activity
Pedophilia

The true prevalence of "pedophilia" is unknown, since estimates are based mainly on law enforcement statistics or clinical records. Estimates from law enforcement likely do not provide an accurate estimate, since not all individuals who commit sexual offences against a child are pedophilic and not everyone with pedophilia commits sexual offences. Furthermore, of those that do act on their sexual interests, not all are arrested (Aggrawal, 2009). Nevertheless, pedophilia is the most common paraphilia leading to arrest (Murphy et al., 2014a). The DSM-5 (APA, 2013) diagnostic criteria for pedophilia are based on persistent sexual fantasies or desires involving sex with a prepubescent child, typically under the age of 13.

Most studies on pedophilia have involved people with pedophilia who have acted on their interests and were arrested. That focus has led to confusion over the distinction between persons with pedophilia and persons that commit a sexual crime against a child for non-sexually-motivated reasons. Not all individuals who sexually abuse a child meet the DSM-5 criteria for pedophilia. Conversely, not all individuals with a sexual interest in children go on to commit child sexual abuse (Bradford & Meston, 2014; Fedoroff, 2008, 2010). Some individuals with pedophilia control their urges and never commit a hands-on offence against a child, whereas some child molesters may sexually abuse a child out of convenience and do not have a greater interest in children than consenting adults. Many child molesters commit a single, situational sexual offence that is not part of any broader pattern of offending. Individuals with pedophilia who have never committed a contact sexual offence against a child highlight the important difference between paraphilic sexual interests and acting on those sexual interests. An individual should not be charged for problematic sexual interests or thoughts alone.

The persistent rise in child pornography offences that began with the creation of the Internet has led some criminologists and law enforcement officers to question whether it represents a new type of offence for people with the same problematic interests in children or the emergence of a truly new type of offender. In effect, child pornography existed long before the Internet. However, with the increased popularity of personal computers and online communications, clinicians and criminal justice officials have seen a rise in the creation of, access to, and trade of child pornography that is difficult to police (see Box 14.1). In Canada, the legal age of consent for sexual activity is 16. However, the age of consent to participate in the production of pornography is 18.

Policing Online Child Pornography

The Internet has been a versatile medium for individuals to create, possess, and distribute child pornography (CP) from the comfort of their own homes. While the Internet provides access to illegal materials such as CP, it also provides a method for police to identify and arrest people who access such materials, and arrests related to these offences have thus increased (Ly, Murphy, & Fedoroff, 2016; Wolak, Finkelhor, & Mitchell, 2011).

Given the international scope of the Internet, criminal justice officials around the world are faced with a number of challenges in policing CP offences. These challenges are based on the nature of the materials and actions depicted, and variation in legislation from one international jurisdiction to the next (Ly et al., 2016). Despite universal social condemnation of material depicting child sexual abuse, legislative responses vary significantly.

One area of dispute is the definition of a "child." In some cultures, the differentiation between child and adult is not marked by chronological age but by rituals that signify a "rite of passage." For some, these rituals may be marked by puberty, marriage, or death of the head of the family. Other cultures rely on a legal concept of adulthood as determined in jurisdictional legislature, usually on the basis of age (Murphy, Ranger, & Fedoroff, 2014b; Sinclair & Sugar, 2005).

Since it is not always known how old a person in a pornographic image is, and, more important, because it is possible to make an adult model look younger, most jurisdictions use legislation that is based on the "apparent age" of the child depicted in images as opposed to the actual age.

Even when the age cut-off for CP is clearly defined, issues arise in accurately determining the age of the individual depicted in confiscated material, since many victims in CP are never identified. Within the material itself, it is easier for investigators to identify prepubescent children compared with postpubescent children due to their physical maturity. Accurate age estimation is further aggravated by the fact that children of different ethnic backgrounds develop at different rates (Murphy et al., 2014b; Sinclair & Sugar, 2005).

Another area of dispute between jurisdictions and countries is the threshold for determining what constitutes CP. Given the cross-jurisdictional variation in defining CP, policing issues arise when an offender is found possessing CP in one country and the images were created by an unknown offender in another country with a different legal definition of CP. A common variation in legislation relates to the legal status of the type of behaviour being depicted. Some jurisdictions have broad definitions of illegality (for example, any erotic material depicting children) and others have more narrow definitions of illegality (for example, material depicting children engaged in explicit sexual acts). Another variation in legislation relates to the depiction of real or pseudo children engaged in explicit sexual acts. Some jurisdictions consider the following material illegal: computer-simulated children, animated children, or real children that have been digitally altered to be nude or in sexual scenarios (Murphy et al., 2014b). Despite these challenges to law enforcement, online CP arrests have resulted in people receiving treatment, whereas if CP offenders are never detected, the likelihood that they will seek or receive treatment is lower.

Sexual Sadism

Clinically, the diagnosis of "sexual sadism disorder" applies to individuals who derive sexual pleasure from non-consensual domination and infliction of harm on another person. For people with sexual sadism disorder, the infliction of pain is a means to elicit submission, obedience, fear, and/or humiliation. The key DSM-5 features of sexual sadism are that the individual experiences sexual arousal from the physical or psychological suffering of another person. The literature tends to separate sexual sadism into two distinct categories. The first category is criminal sadists who are interested in non-consenting partners. The other category includes individuals who are interested in the consensual culture of BDSM (bondage-discipline, dominance-submission, and sado-masochism). For this group, the sadistic sexual activities do not cause distress to their partner, nor are they personally distressed by their interests and behaviours (Knack, Murphy, & Fedoroff, in press).

It is important to highlight that the diagnosis of sexual sadism does not include general sexual assault of adult women. There is no psychiatric diagnosis for sexual assault (less commonly referred to as "rape"), as this is a legal term and not a clinical term. Some individuals who sexually assault women, however, may meet the clinical criteria for sexual sadism (Fedoroff, 2008; Murphy et al., 2014a).

Although the age of onset for non-consensual sexual sadism can vary, it typically occurs in early adulthood and is usually chronic. In a small sample of women referred to treatment for paraphilic disorders, 29 percent met the criteria for sexual sadism. While these findings cannot be generalized to the general population, they do illustrate that females also have sexually sadistic interests and associated paraphilias (Fedoroff, Fishell, & Fedoroff, 1999).

Exhibitionism

The motivation behind the offence of exposing oneself in public can be divided into three categories. "DSM-5–defined exhibitionists" include people who derive sexual arousal from exposing their genitals to unsuspecting victims in public. They are sexually aroused by the shock and surprise of the victim. This subcategory of offender is typically not aroused by going to a nude beach, where consensual nudity is the norm. "Public masturbators" masturbate in public while attempting to remain hidden from an unsuspecting victim or group of victims. These individuals do not step out of their hiding place because they are aroused by the risk of sexual pleasure in public without actually being detected. "Exhibitionists for sex" expose themselves in public with the hope that an unsuspecting stranger will see them and become so aroused that sexual relations with that person will result (Murphy et al., 2014a).

Exhibitionism is one of the most commonly reported paraphilias and comprises about one-third of reported sexual offences, although many incidents of exhibitionism are never reported to the police. Exhibitionists, along with voyeurs, have the highest rates of sexual recidivism. However, unless they have coexisting paraphilias, exhibitionists rarely deteriorate to more serious sexual offences (Murphy et al., 2014a). Studies have identified a bimodal pattern for the age of onset, ranging from 11 to 15 and then 21 to 25, with a mean age of first arrest at 25 (Aggrawal, 2009). Few official reports are made of women exposing themselves, although they do exist (Fedoroff et al., 1999).

Exhibitionism is reported to co-occur with voyeurism and frotteurism approximately 80 percent and 70 percent of the time, respectively (Murphy et al., 2014a). The prevalence of these disorders occurring together, in addition to a preference for non-consensual intercourse, have been coined "courtship disorder" based on the apparent absence of the typical progression of sexual relationships from sight, to touch, to disrobing, and finally to sexual intercourse (Freund & Blanchard, 1986). Courtship disorder is not a DSM diagnosis and is not universally accepted. Some have argued that all paraphilias are courtship disorders.

Voyeurism

"Voyeurism" is characterized by sexual urges or fantasies of observing unsuspecting and non-consenting persons in various stages of undress or sexual activity. It is important to distinguish between true voyeurism and normal arousal from observing nudity or sexual activity. In interviews with adult heterosexual men, 54.3 percent reported sexual fantasies of secretly witnessing sexual intercourse of others, while 40.4 percent also reported a sexual interest in being unknowingly watched during intercourse. In most instances, these men would not meet the clinical criteria for voyeurism (or exhibitionism) (Aggrawal, 2009).

People with voyeurism are typically aroused as soon as they leave their home in search of strangers to spy on. In contrast, people without voyeurism might become aroused if by accident they saw a naked person through a window; their arousal is due to the nudity and not from the non-consensual nature of the situation (Murphy et al., 2014a). True voyeurs typically are not sexually aroused by attending a strip bar or a "peep-show" because they know the dancers are aware that they are being watched. While women can be diagnosed with voyeurism, almost all arrests for voyeurism involve male offenders. Some research has indicated that at the time of arrest, the typical voyeur is a married man in his late twenties with a long history of offending (generally and sexually), beginning in adolescence (Aggrawal, 2009).

Frotteurism

Also referred to as toucherism, "frotteurism" is characterized by sexual urges or fantasies of touching or rubbing one's genitals against an unsuspecting person. The intention is to become more sexually aroused. Typically, people with frotteurism seek out crowded places, such as subways or concerts (Murphy et al., 2014a).

Some claim that approximately 85 percent of people diagnosed with frotteurism also have another courtship disorder paraphilia (Aggrawal, 2009). Most frotteurs are between the ages of 15 and 25; but there is also a subgroup of older men, often with social inhibitions, who engage in frotteuristic activities. Many incidents of frotteurism have been reported in Japan. Overcrowding on mass transit and public awareness of the problem in Japan may account for this. One survey found that 58.4 percent of adult women in Japan disclosed being touched sexually by an unknown person in public (Aggrawal, 2009).

Management of Sex Offenders Within the Community
Criminal Justice Approaches

After a sex offender is convicted and serves his or her sentence, that person is released into the community. In Canada, the majority of people charged with sexual offences are also subject to a range of other community supervision orders while on bail, during pre-trial, and after release from prison (for example, a conditional sentence, probation, parole, or long-term supervision orders). When offenders are released at their statutory release date (two-thirds of their sentence), probation and parole supervision occurs.

For sex offenders who are deemed to be a high risk for committing another sexual offence or serious personal injury crime, the option exists to keep such individuals incarcerated until the very end of their sentence, known as the **warrant expiry date (WED)**. The rationale for using this option is to keep the offender incapacitated for as long as possible, due to the elevated risk of recidivating. One significant drawback of holding offenders until their WED is that they are released into the community without any criminal justice control because they have served their full sentence (Rice, Murphy, & Fedoroff, 2011). This lack of criminal justice follow-up is perplexing since these high-risk individuals are the ones most in need of criminal justice sanctions to help them successfully reintegrate into the community.

In response to this shortcoming, a community policing peace bond known as the **810.1 order** was created. This is a prohibition order for sex offenders who are deemed to be a high risk to commit another sexual offence or a serious personal injury crime. This recognizance order, as well as probation or parole orders, includes a list of conditions designed to help monitor and limit the person's movement, accommodations, and social interactions. The order also includes specific requirements of the person under supervision, such as frequent meetings with a supervising officer (a probation, parole, or bail officer), and attendance in specific treatment programs. The intended objectives of the order are to provide a structured release of the offender that results in maximum public protection and management of risk for sexual recidivism. Other stated objectives of this order include monitoring a former offender's whereabouts and limiting behaviours associated with the person's previous offence (such as consuming alcohol or using the Internet). An 810.1 order expires automatically after two years, but it can be renewed (*Criminal Code*, 1985; Rice et al., 2011).

Under provincial community safety legislation, public notification about the release of high-risk sex offenders and other violent offenders is permitted. The rationale is to improve public protection through the release of information on high-risk offenders. Public notification occurs on a three-tier system that can take the form of (1) notification of local law enforcement only; (2) notification of local law enforcement and relevant community organizations, such as schools and recreational facilities; or (3) broad notification within a certain radius through the use of media and/or flyers. Decisions on whether to undertake public notification and the appropriate level of notification are made by the police and a high-risk offender committee. However, public notification is rarely used, and when it is, it is supposed to happen only after all available alternatives have been considered (Murphy et al., 2009b).

When an offender who has been convicted of a designated sexual offence is released into the community, he or she is required to report to a local law enforcement agency to register on the Ontario and/or National SOR. The registrant is required to report for a designated period of time (for example, 10 years, 20 years, or life). This database contains information such as the registrant's name, address, date of birth, photo, and sexual offence history. Unlike SORs in the United States, which are publicly accessible via the Internet, Canada's SORs are private and are not linked to the system of public notification. Critics of SORs in the United States have suggested that a system of open registries goes beyond public protection and focuses more on public shaming and branding (Murphy et al., 2009a; Worley & Worley, 2013). See Box 14.2 for a discussion of the ethical issues surrounding the use of SORs and public notification.

warrant expiry date (WED)
A correctional option to detain a sexual offender until the very end of his or her sentence. Those who are detained under a WED have been deemed to be a high risk for committing another sexual offence or serious personal injury offence until the very end of their sentence.

810.1 order
A community prohibition order for sexual offenders deemed to be a high risk that includes conditions designed to monitor and limit the person's movement, accommodations, and social interactions.

BOX 14.2

Ethical Issues with Public Notification and the Registration of Sex Offenders

Sex offender registration and public notification are controversial issues that have been subject to considerable ethical criticism and litigation throughout North America. Opponents of these mechanisms of management have drawn attention to a number of fundamental human rights issues, such as imposing additional measures on sex offenders that do not apply to non–sex offenders. This argument suggests that since those with higher recidivism rates (for example, break-and-enter offenders, drunk drivers) or those causing serious personal injury (for example, murderers) are not subject to such scrutiny, sex offenders should not be either (Worley & Worley; 2013). Another argument against SORs is the fact that registries and public notification may create a false sense of security, since the majority of sex offenders are not repeat offenders (Murphy, 2013).

Similarly, critics argue that it is unfair to impose additional measures on sex offenders because they have already paid their debt to society upon completing their sentence. From a research perspective, the rationale for public notification and registration is not to add punishment but to manage risk of recidivism. This perspective can be challenged on several grounds because sex offenders as a group do not pose a higher risk of recidivism than many other offender types. Even within the sex offender population, great variation in risk exists between different sex offender types. However, this variation is not identified in public SORs, such as those found in the United States. As a result, a man convicted of sexual assault for slapping the buttocks of an unknown woman after a night of drinking would appear on the registry alongside someone with a long history of violent sexual assaults against strangers. When the public accesses this registry in the United States, they will see no differentiation between these offender types.

Giving the public unrestricted access to SORs without educating them on how to deal with this information has been found to heighten general community fear. Although open SORs are intended to provide a sense of awareness for the public while the former offender reintegrates into the community, they often elicit feelings of anger and increase the danger of vigilante actions. Numerous incidents of unintended consequences and **vigilantism** have been cited across the United States, leading to ostracism of registrants by family, loss of stable jobs or housing, dropping out of therapy, destruction of personal property, and, in some cases, violence so severe that it resulted in death (Murphy, 2013; Murphy, et al., 2009a).

Research has shown that when SORs are open to the public (as is the case in the United States), the result is significantly lower rates of registrant compliance as compared with SORs that are accessible to law enforcement only (as is the case in Canada). In Canada, rates of SOR compliance are typically around 95 percent, whereas in some American states, compliance rates range between 40 percent and 60 percent (Murphy et al., 2009a; Murphy et al., 2009b; Murphy & Fedoroff, 2013). These findings are problematic because offenders who choose to become non-compliant and "go underground" lose access to a more stable lifestyle with social support and treatment options. Registrants who become non-compliant are at a much higher risk for recidivism (Murphy, 2013; Murphy & Fedoroff, 2013). SORs might be justified if the effectiveness of public notification and registration was supported by research. However, to date that has not been the case because research findings have not been consistent.

vigilantism
When a person or group of people take the law into their own hands, typically in a violent manner, in an attempt to effect justice according to their understanding of what is right and wrong.

From a policing perspective, SORs are meant to be used as an investigative tool. This perspective is based on the rationale that having current and reliable information on convicted sex offenders will be useful in the investigation of new child abductions or sexual crimes, enabling police to identify or rule out suspects more efficiently. Criminologists have also suggested that SORs may provide a deterrent effect, because it is assumed that being on the registry may make offenders more reluctant to commit a new sexual offence. Additionally, SORs may be a general deterrent for potential first-time offenders. However, to date, research has yet to conclusively support such a rationale (Murphy et al., 2009b).

Some high-risk sex offenders and other violent offenders in Canada can be considered for a dangerous offender (DO) or long-term offender (LTO) designation. These designations are the result of a sentencing hearing and only occur following the offence that the offender was most recently convicted for (known as the "predicate offence"). In Canada, DOs are designated as such at the time of their criminal sentence and are not civilly committed at the end of their criminal sentence, as is the case for SVPs in the United States. The following criteria must be met for the Crown attorney (prosecution) to raise the question of a DO or LTO designation:

- commission of a serious personal injury offence;
- a pattern of persistent, aggressive, and repetitive behaviour;
- failure of the offender to restrain his or her actions;
- indifference to consequences of his or her behaviour;
- index offence so brutal it is unlikely inhibited by normal standards; and
- when there is a history of sexual offences, failure to control his or her sexual impulses (Fedoroff, Ranger, & Murphy, 2013b; Petrunik et al., 2008).

The primary difference between a DO and an LTO is that the DO is deemed to be such a high risk that he or she cannot reasonably be managed within the community. A DO can be given either an indeterminate or determinate sentence. With an LTO, although the offender meets all of the aforementioned requirements, it is determined that with appropriate interventions that are currently available, a reasonable prospect exists that the person can be managed within the community. The LTO is given a determinate sentence with up to ten years of community supervision. Judges must consider the LTO designation before they consider a DO designation (Fedoroff et al., 2013b; Petrunik et al., 2008).

Mental Health Treatment and Prevention

Contemporary treatments for sex offenders and people with problematic sexual interests typically combine different psychological and psychopharmacological approaches. Three psychological therapeutic treatments commonly used during the past three decades target cognitions and behaviour. Cognitive behavioural therapy (CBT) gained popularity during the 1980s and remains one of the most frequently cited approaches for the treatment of paraphilias and sexual offending. The goal of CBT in this population is to increase control over problematic sexual interests and behaviours, and to also equip patients with the skills and attitudes necessary to achieve their goals in healthy and prosocial ways. CBT is commonly used in combination with other treatment approaches.

Relapse prevention (RP) techniques, commonly used with CBT, work to identify behavioural chains and triggers that increase the likelihood of relapse or recidivism. The intention of RP is to assist the patient with identifying, anticipating, and coping with triggers that may lead to a potential relapse or reoffence. In addition to cognitive and behavioural measures, RP uses educational and skill-developing approaches. RP therapy for sex offenders received a setback when a large randomized controlled study failed to show that it significantly improved outcomes. Explanations for this unexpected result are discussed in Fedoroff and Marshall (2010).

Emerging from criticisms of RP, which focuses on avoidance, the Good Lives Model (GLM) has risen in prominence to become the most commonly used psychological treatment approach in Canadian prisons and community-based treatment programs. The GLM focuses on ways to maximize human potential and individual strengths rather than focusing on psychological deficits (as is often the case in CBT and RP). This model is founded upon a strength-based framework and uses an individualized rehabilitative approach to interests, abilities, and aspirations. Concerning paraphilias and sexual offending, the model suggests that people exhibit deviant sexual interests or behaviours because they lack the internal and external resources necessary to satisfy sexual needs in less harmful ways. The attainment of happiness and well-being includes healthy living through physical satisfaction, inner peace through emotional regulation, and relatedness through intimacy. The GLM seeks to help individuals identify any obstacles that prevent them from living a "good life." GLM therapy not only identifies the resources the patient is missing but also provides the patient with tools useful to living life in a more fulfilling, pro-social, and law-abiding manner (Murphy et al., 2014a).

Several psychopharmacological approaches can also be used to treat sex offenders and people with paraphilias. Common medications include those that target neurotransmitters in the brain (such as selective serotonin reuptake inhibitors [SSRIs]) and hormones (such as anti-androgens that decrease circulating testosterone levels). Modulation of SSRIs has been found to decrease problematic sexual interests and behaviours. For some, a re-emergence of healthy sexual interests and behaviours occurs as a result. When the desired goal of treatment is the reduction of overall sex drive, the use of anti-androgens (sometimes called "chemical castration") has been identified as the gold standard. The suppression of sexual arousal can help patients focus on aspects of treatment designed to correct previous social skills deficits (Murphy et al., 2014a). That is, the use of anti-androgens can eliminate the persistent sexual thoughts that are reported by many individuals with paraphilias. This medication allows them to focus on treatment of the underlying issues that led to the development of their deviant sexual interest or behaviours in the first place. Once their lives are normalized, it is possible in many cases to taper or stop the medication, which results in the return of their sex drive, but this time within a pro-social, adult-consenting relationship. This approach makes the idea of trying medication much more acceptable to patients, who should always be allowed to provide informed, revocable consent to treatment.

Effectiveness of Treatment

From 1993 to 2007, Marshall and colleagues (2008) reviewed the effectiveness of the sex offender treatment program used in a Canadian federal prison system. The program uses elements of CBT, the GLM, and RNR. The sample included 534 sex offenders

(352 child molesters and 182 rapists) who had been living in the community for an average of 5.42 years. Based on the averaged risk levels, the expected recidivism rate for the group was 40 percent for general recidivism and 16.8 percent for sexual recidivism. The reported sexual recidivism rate after treatment was significantly below the rate expected: 3.2 percent for sexual recidivism (1.6 percent for rapists and 4.0 percent for child molesters) and 13.6 percent for general recidivism.

Although the majority of studies on sex offender treatment focuses on recidivism, interest has increased toward preventive approaches that seek to provide treatment for individuals with problematic sexual interests before they go on to commit an offence. For example, the German initiative Prevention Project Dunkelfeld treats people who have a sexual interest in children but have never been identified by law enforcement. The initiative's media campaign has included advertisements on local buses that ask the question "Do you like kids too much?" and provides a number to call for assessment and treatment. The treatment program is located in Berlin, and the project has seen a self-referral rate of 15 to 20 individuals monthly from all over Europe. Approximately half of the self-referrals are people who have committed an offence in the past but remained undetected, and the rest are people who have never acted on their interests. Such proactive and preventive approaches not only get pedophilic men and women involved in treatment before they create a victim but also provide treatment to sex offenders who have never been detected by the criminal justice system. The positive effects of such programs are immeasurable. The authors of this article and their team have recently launched a similar type of program. The program focuses on primary prevention of child sexual abuse in Ottawa. See sexualbehavioursclinic.ca for more information.

Circles of Support and Accountability (CoSA) is another initiative that has been receiving increased attention for its positive work with sex offenders who have been released to the community. CoSA is an innovative, non-profit, community reintegration program designed to address the unique needs of convicted sex offenders in the process of reintegrating into the community. Sex offenders assisted by the program are at a high risk to recidivate and, as a result, have been detained by the criminal justice system until their WED. Since these offenders are detained until their WED, they are released into the community without any criminal justice supports to assist with the reintegration process. The CoSA program aims to prevent future sexual victimization by introducing offenders to trained volunteers who support the reintegration of released sex offenders into the community (Clarke, Brown, & Völlm, 2017; Hanvey, Philpot, & Wilson, 2011). The unique goals of this program are underlined by its twin mottos: "no more victims" and "no one is disposable."

A study on the recidivism rates of former sex offenders involved with CoSA in Canada showed very encouraging results. In the study, recidivism was defined as any new charges or convictions. A group of 44 former offenders in CoSA were matched with a group of similar offenders not involved in the program. Results over a three-year follow-up period found that the CoSA group had significantly lower levels of all types of recidivism. Sexual recidivism for the CoSA group was 2.27 percent as compared with 13.67 percent in the control group. Violent recidivism was 9.09 percent for the CoSA group and 34.09 percent for the control group. Any type of recidivism at all, including breaches of correctional conditions, occurred at a rate of 11.36 percent for the CoSA group and 38.64 percent for the control group (Wilson, Cortoni, & McWhinnie, 2009).

Conclusion

Sexual offending, especially against children, is a serious problem. Many factors can impact the nature of criminal sexual behaviours over time and place. The goals of the criminal justice system in Canada and the United States are to provide general deterrence, incapacitation, punishment, rehabilitation, and management of the risk posed by sex offenders. It is crucial for the justice system to maintain a balance between public safety and protection of the individual rights of victims and the accused. Sexual offences against both adults and children have been steadily decreasing on a global scale since the 1980s.

Large variations exist within sex offender populations, and it is important to examine the characteristics, risk levels, and recidivism rates of each subgroup separately. A number of developmental, demographic, and offence-related characteristics are associated with increased risk of sexual recidivism. Although Canada's sex offender legislation has developed at a much slower pace than that of the United States, there is no evidence indicating that recidivism rates are lower in the United States.

It is important to distinguish between clinical and legal conceptualizations of sexual offences and unconventional sexual interests. Various treatment approaches and community-based initiatives have shown promise in reducing sexual recidivism. More research needs to be conducted on ways to manage the limited risk posed by sex offenders and on treatment options to prevent sexual crimes and further reduce sexual recidivism.

SUMMARY OF KEY POINTS

- While working to deter, punish, rehabilitate, and manage the risk posed by sex offenders, the justice system must also maintain a balance between public safety and protection of the individual rights of the accused. Attempts to maintain this balance can be especially difficult when dealing with sex offenders, a subgroup of offenders who are viewed by society as highly dangerous and "morally tainted."

- Individuals who have committed a sexual offence are often classified as a homogeneous group. However, there are wide variations in offender characteristics (such as gender, age, socio-economic background, personality, intelligence, attitude, and social skills). Offence characteristics and subsequent risk of recidivism vary widely.

- Two important concepts in this area are "dangerousness" and "risk." They have a long history in civil and criminal legislation and correctional and psychiatric practice. Dangerousness refers to the capacity of a person to harm oneself or others. It includes an estimation of the severity, imminence, predictability, and likelihood of harm. Risk typically refers only to the probability that a person will commit future harmful acts.

- The emergence of a community protection approach during the late 1980s and early 1990s resulted from concerns that previous models had not given enough attention to overall public safety and the rights of victims. The primary focus of this new approach was not on the treatment or rehabilitation of the individual offender but on the overall safety of the community.

- A common misconception is that all sex offenders have a high frequency of recidivism. Official statistics and research studies do not support this assumption.

- Large variations exist within sex offender populations, and it is important to examine the characteristics, risk levels, and recidivism rates of each subgroup separately.
- It is important to distinguish clinical and legal conceptualizations of sexual offences from unconventional sexual interests.
- Various treatment approaches and community-based initiatives have shown promise in reducing sexual recidivism.

NOTES

1. This case study is adapted from Boyd (2012).
2. For updates on this and other cases and issues, go to the Updates tab on the book's website at http://emond.ca/crim2.

QUESTIONS FOR CRITICAL DISCUSSION

1. In what ways have the media perpetuated the myth of "stranger danger"?
2. When looking at studies on recidivism, what factors are important to take into account?
3. Why is it important to examine sex offenders by their offence type instead of as a singular type of offender?
4. Why is it important to differentiate between paraphilias and sexual offences?
5. What are the pros and cons of public sex offender registries and private sex offender registries?

SUGGESTED FURTHER READINGS

Aggrawal, A. (2009). *Forensic and medico-legal aspects of sexual crimes and unusual sexual practices*. Boca Raton, FL: CRC Press.

Bartol, C., & Bartol, A. (2016). *Criminal behaviour: A psychological approach* (11th ed.). Englewood Cliffs, NJ: Prentice Hall.

McAlinden, A.M. (2007). *The shaming of sex offenders: Risk, retribution and reintegration*. Portland, OR: Hart.

Petrunik, M. (2003). The hare and the tortoise: Dangerous and sex offender policy in the United States and Canada. *The Canadian Journal of Criminology and Criminal Justice, 45*(4), 43–72.

Saleh, F.M., Grudzinskas, A.J., Bradford, J.M., & Brodsky, D.J. (2009). *Sex offenders: Identification, risk assessment treatment, and legal issues*. New York: Oxford University Press.

Websites

American Psychiatric Association DSM-5 Development: https://www.psychiatry.org/psychiatrists/practice/dsm

Circles of Support and Accountability (CoSA): http://www.cosacanada.com

Prevention Project Dunkelfeld (PPD): https://www.dont-offend.org

Legislation

Christopher's Law (Sex Offender Registry), 2000, SO 2000, c 1.

Criminal Code, RSC 1985, c C-46.

Sex Offender Information Registration Act, SC 2004, c 10.

CASE STUDY 15.1

Wayne Jackson: A Profile of a Person Convicted of Property Crime

The motivations for committing property crime can be complex.

In February 2016, Wayne Jackson appeared before Judge Cozens in the Territorial Court of Yukon to be sentenced for committing the offence of theft under $5,000, contrary to section 334 of the *Criminal Code*, and the offence of obstructing justice by giving a false name, contrary to section 129(a) of the *Criminal Code*.

In September 2015, the RCMP had received a report of theft from Canadian Tire, with a man being detained by staff. Wayne Jackson falsely identified himself as Phillip McLeod. He was arrested, informed of his Charter rights, and searched. That search revealed his actual identity, along with a DVD remote control, some socks, and a few other small items. The total value of the stolen goods was $154. Mr. Jackson had been released on parole from Matsqui Federal Institution five days before these offences took place.

At the time sentence was imposed, Mr. Jackson was 49 years old and had an extensive criminal record dating back to 1983. He had 68 convictions for theft, nine for possession of stolen property, four for forgery, five for possession of a stolen credit card, six for possession of restricted and illegal drugs, and a host of other convictions for similar kinds of crime.

Crown counsel suggested a sentence of one year in custody, while defence counsel argued that Mr. Jackson should receive a three-month sentence, allowing him to attend a treatment camp upon his release.

Judge Cozens described the personal circumstances of Mr. Jackson in the following terms:

A formalized Gladue Report (the "Report") was prepared for Mr. Jackson's sentencing. This report provided background information regarding First Nations peoples of the Yukon and, in particular, First Nations peoples in the Champagne and Aishihik First Nations and the impact of the construction of the Alaska Highway and the residential school system. With respect to Mr. Jackson's personal circumstances, he is a 49-year-old member of the Champagne and Aishihik First Nations. His father is Caucasian. He is the youngest of 11 children. Both his parents are deceased. (*R v Jackson*, 2016, paras. 33–34)

Judge Cozens went on to note,

Mr. Jackson provided the author of the Report with a lengthy recollection of his memories of his life, which was unusual. The Report's author incorporated in full, with editing changes only, these memories into the Report. I find this recollection to be very helpful and informative.

Certainly there was much in the way of trauma and dysfunction in Mr. Jackson's childhood. This included him being subjected to physical abuse and the deprivation of the necessities of life at times.

He lived in places that he felt safe and then, without explanation, would be moved to places where he did not feel safe. He had no sense that he belonged to any family,

333

first meeting his sister when he was 10. He lived in group homes and was seriously sexually abused while in the care of one group home. When he finally told the supervisor about the abuse, he was not believed:

> Instead I was yelled at, strapped, grounded, told I was lying and given extra chores. I was told that I should be grateful that Jacques, [the abuser] cared enough about me to take me to his house. (paras. 35–37)

Judge Cozens concluded, "He was subjected to racism and bullying. He stated that he learned to 'numb out the pain and emotions.'" Mr. Jackson further stated that he felt shame and said:

> I thought I was ugly, useless, weak and helpless. I began to believe that I was just a dumb stupid Indian that my mom and dad didn't want. I had no self-esteem, trouble concentrating, poor sleep, feelings of confusion and anger. The heaviest one to carry was shame. I was ashamed of who I was. I bottled up my emotions and feelings and started to distrust people in authority. ... (para. 38)

As Judge Cozens noted, Mr. Jackson ended up using alcohol and drugs, and he became HIV positive. In passing sentence on Mr. Jackson, he made the following comments:

> A recognition of the over-representation of Aboriginal offenders incarcerated in prisons, and a recognition of the harm governmental policies such as the residential school system have caused to Aboriginal peoples, requires action to be taken to attempt to redress that harm. Where there are reasonable sentencing options available that offer hope to breaking the cycle of destruction and criminality in an offender's life, those options should be given fair consideration and chosen where possible. (para. 66)

Judge Cozens continued,

> In Mr. Jackson's case, I find that the risk of serious and significant harm is not great and there is enough merit in the plan put forward and the commitment of Mr. Jackson's support team as well as sufficient motivation on his part to seek to pursue treatment or programming to take that risk.
>
> I am not saying that I am confident that Mr. Jackson will be successful in trying to live a pro-social and non-criminal life. I am not. I am, however, equally not confident in saying that he has no hope of rehabilitation. As long as there remains that hope and the risk remains as it is, I am satisfied that sentences that either avoid incarceration or limit it should, where possible, be imposed. Every case will depend on its own circumstances, however. (paras. 68–69)

In response to consideration of all relevant information, Judge Cozens sentenced Mr. Jackson to a further 85 days imprisonment for the theft from Canadian Tire, beyond the 15 days he had spent in pre-trial custody. He noted that this would mean that Mr. Jackson would be out of custody in time to prepare for and attend a treatment program at Jackson Lake.

Before Reading Chapter 15

- This case study notes a background of abuse and neglect and long-standing use of alcohol and drugs. What other sorts of motivations or backdrop come to mind when you think of someone committing "property crime"?
- Have you ever been the victim of property crime? Had your home broken into or your vehicle either stolen or stolen from? What did you learn from this experience?

After reading this chapter, return to this case study. How many of the factors described in the chapter as relevant to property crime can you identify in this profile of Wayne Jackson?

Property Crime

Introduction: A Brief History of Property Crime Laws

As we saw in Chapter 3, Criminal Law in Canada, Canadian criminal laws, including laws governing property, came directly from English common law. Jerome Hall (1952), a scholar who is internationally recognized for his research on criminal law and jurisprudence, traced the growth of property and theft laws to the rise of commerce and industrialization in 18th-century England. He noted that, with the beginning of business and trade, a new economic class of traders and industrialists emerged who needed protection for their property and other business interests. These laws included what today would be called **embezzlement** laws and laws governing stolen property and **obtaining goods under false pretenses** (Vago, 1997, p. 56).

Generally, two theoretical perspectives are used to understand the emergence of such laws and their enforcement: **structural functionalism** and **conflict theory**. According to structural functionalists, crime, including property crime, is inevitable in all societies. Moreover, they consider property crime laws to be based on a shared belief system in which customs, over time, become codified into legal statutes believed to promote solidarity and stability in society. This sociological perspective was originally proposed by Émile Durkheim (1933) in France in the late 19th century and was prominent until the 1960s.

In the 1970s and early 1980s, however, Marxist-inspired scholars (for example, Chambliss & Seidman, 1982; Quinney, 1975; Reasons & Rich, 1978) began to interpret research such as Hall's by arguing that theft laws were created to primarily protect the interests of the capitalist class. As such, since law-making and enforcement were put into place by the state to protect the interests of the propertied class, the working class was viewed

embezzlement
To take money or misappropriate funds that belong to someone else.

obtaining goods under false pretenses
Misrepresenting the truth to obtain goods that belong to someone else.

structural functionalism
A sociological theory that explains how society functions according to the structure of a system of interrelated parts.

conflict theories
Theories, originating primarily with Marx, that focus on the unequal distribution of power in society—for example, due to class, race, or gender.

For more on Durkheim's sociological approaches to crime, see Chapter 9, Sociological Approaches.

Marxism
A school of thought developed by Karl Marx (1818–1883) arguing that society must be understood in terms of social conflict, class relations, and the inequalities caused by capitalism. Marxists promote revolution by the working class.

to bear the brunt of this one-sided legal system. For **Marxist** conflict theorists, property crimes committed by those from the working class are subject to criminalization, while the illegal activities of the elites are considered to be largely immune from legal censure.

In more recent years, the conflict viewpoint has been judged to be a rather simplistic and instrumental interpretation of the origins of property law. Law-making, including the making and amending of property laws, is now considered to be a more complex and dynamic process than what the conflict interpretation would suggest. For instance, if property laws existed simply as a means to protect the property of the rich from the thieving poor, why is it that a great deal of property crime victims are from the working class? Research has shown that a majority of street crime, including that related to property, is **intra-class crime**. That is, it takes place between people with similar social class backgrounds (Tunnell, 2006). Also, in recent years, particularly in the United States, a number of high-profile property crime cases have involved offenders from privileged backgrounds who have been sentenced to lengthy prison terms. For example, in 2009, Bernie Madoff, a New York millionaire, was given a 150-year prison sentence for defrauding investors of over $60 billion. And in Canada, in 2009, Garth Drabinsky and Myron Gottlieb, founders and executives of Livent (an entertainment company), were found guilty of defrauding investors of $500 million and were sent to prison for seven and six years, respectively (Canadian Press, 2012; O'Grady, 2011).

intra-class crime
Crime in which the victim and offender are from the same social group (for example, an ethnic or racial group); by contrast, inter-class crime takes place between different social groups.

Regardless of the various interpretations of the origins of property laws and whose interests they may or may not support in society, what is clear is that the vast majority of property offenders who come before the courts, unlike Drabinsky and Gottlieb, are people who do not have a great amount of power and prestige in society. Many are young, have relatively low levels of formal education, and are poor. Indeed, this profile will be returned to later in the chapter when the analysis shifts to an empirical study of a group of socially excluded property crime offenders.

Defining, Measuring, and Penalizing Property Crime in Canada

Property crime involves the taking of money or property and, unlike robbery, does not involve force or threat of force against a victim. The main types of property crime listed in the Canadian *Criminal Code* are as follows:

- theft (theft under and theft over $5,000),
- break and enter,
- mischief (vandalism),
- possession of stolen property,
- arson,
- motor vehicle theft, and
- fraud.

According to Figure 15.1, since 1962, rates of police-reported property crimes have consistently been greater than rates of all other forms of police-reported crimes in Canada, including violent crime. In 2016, property and other *Criminal Code* non-violent offences accounted for about four-fifths of police-reported *Criminal Code* incidents in Canada (excluding traffic offences). The trend lines in Figure 15.1 clearly show that rates of police-reported property offences have been declining since the early 1990s. In 2017, the rate of property offences was about half what it was in the early 1990s.

FIGURE 15.1   Police-Reported Crime Rates, Canada, 1962–2017

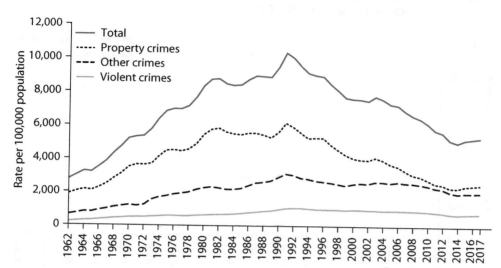

Note: Information presented in this chart represents data from the Uniform Crime Reporting (UCR1) Aggregate Survey, and permits historical comparisons back to 1962. New definitions of crime categories were introduced in 2009 and are only available in the new format back to 1998. As a result, numbers in this chart will not match data released in the new UCR2 format. Specifically, the definition of violent crime has been expanded. In addition, UCR1 includes some different offences in the "Other Crimes" category. Populations are based upon July 1st estimates from Statistics Canada, Demography Division.

Source: Allen (2018, Chart 2).

Break and enter and **motor vehicle theft** are two of the most common police-reported property crime offences. In Canada, on average, about one break-in happens every three minutes and one motor vehicle theft happens every seven minutes (Perreault, 2013). A key reason these property crimes are most often reported to the police is that insurance companies require police reports before home or vehicle owner claims can be processed. For this reason, criminologists tend to treat these crimes as reasonably reliable measures of property crime compared with property crimes that do not normally involve insurance companies, such as the possession of stolen property.

However, as Figure 15.2 illustrates, with the exception of a slight increase in the year 2015, the number of motor vehicle theft and break and enter crimes have generally been declining. This trend continued in 2016, with rates of breaking and entering and motor vehicle theft declining by 2 percent and 1 percent respectively. From 2006 to 2016, the rates of breaking and entering and motor vehicle theft were 43 percent and 55 percent lower than a decade ago.

Why have the rates of break and enter and motor vehicle theft been declining in Canada since the early 1990s? While criminologists are not in agreement in terms of what accounts for these particular shifts in property crime, there is good reason to believe that advances in home security systems and technological advances in motor vehicle anti-theft systems account, at least to some degree, for these decreases. However, as Figure 15.1 indicates, most other types of crime (including violent crime) in Canada have also been falling over this same time period. So, it is possible that what accounts for the drop in property crime may also explain the decline in violent crime.

break and enter
A type of property crime where the accused trespasses on private property with intent to commit a crime.

motor vehicle theft
The act of stealing or attempting to steal a motor vehicle.

FIGURE 15.2 Breaking and Entering and Motor Vehicle Theft, Police-Reported Rates, Canada, 1986–2017

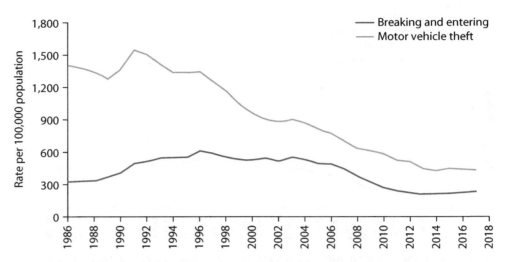

Note: Populations are based upon July 1st estimates from Statistics Canada, Demography Division.

Source: Allen (2018, Chart 13).

Even though aggregate rates of property crime have declined in Canada in recent years (particularly break and enter and motor vehicle theft), one form of property crime increased: fraudulent e-commerce (including telephone and mail purchases) (Keighley, 2017). According to data reported in the Card Fraud Report 2015 (Forster, 2015), losses due to credit card fraud increased on a year-by-year basis from 2009 to 2013. A detailed breakdown of these losses appears in Table 15.1.

In relation to credit card fraud, **counterfeiting** involves using computer devices to read and copy data encoded on a credit card's magnetic stripe, and then transfer that

counterfeiting
Producing imitation currency without legal sanction of the government; it is a form of fraud.

TABLE 15.1 Credit Card Fraud Statistics for Canadian-Issued Cards, 2009–2013

Category of credit card fraud	2009 Loss in Cdn$	2010 Loss in Cdn$	2011 Loss in Cdn$	2012 Loss in Cdn$	2013 Loss in Cdn$
Lost	$13,599,382	$12,957,262	$10,757,451	$8,663,910	$8,773,052
Stolen	$27,208,823	$22,823,193	$21,692,185	$18,322,777	$16,457,871
Non-receipt	$6,088,948	$5,635,525	$4,736,900	$3,628,009	$4,968,221
Fraudulent applications	$4,707,088	$4,262,498	$6,075,704	$8,552,715	$11,803,264
Counterfeit	$158,809,947	$135,725,233	$120,166,543	$118,109,538	$111,538,212
Card not present (fraudulent e-commerce, telephone, and mail purchases)	$140,443,893	$176,115,080	$259,498,535	$268,573,473	$299,374,609
Account takeovers/other	$140,443,893	$8,198,153	$13,661,440	$13,543,195	$12,219,780
Total	$358,361,292	$365,916,944	$436,588,757	$439,363,617	$465,135,009

Sources: Forster (2015); RCMP (2011).

data to a counterfeit or blank card. The enhanced security of chip and pin technology has forced those engaged in this type of fraud to change their methods of operation. This could explain the recent increase in **card not present fraud**, which refers to fraud committed online, by phone, or by mail in a transaction for which the presence of a credit card is not necessary.

card not present fraud
A form of fraud usually carried out over the telephone or the Internet when a stolen or forged credit card is used to purchase a good or to acquire a service.

Unlike other property crimes (such as break and enter and motor vehicle theft), the police typically are not involved in investigating credit (or debit) card fraud. The major banks and financial institutions in Canada have their own security divisions that monitor and try to control this form of fraud. However, they also often work in conjunction with fraud specialists (for example, forensic accountants from the RCMP) for credit card fraud that is committed against them. While Canadian data exist on most property crimes that could be described as "street crimes," data are lacking on the number of

cases of credit card fraud that are solved as well as the nature of the penalties issued by the courts for those found guilty of this type of fraud.

The penalties for property crime vary considerably, according to the *Criminal Code*. The information in Table 15.2 displays this variation. Interestingly, maximum penalties for arson and break and enter are life in prison—the same maximum for first-degree murder.

TABLE 15.2   Penalties for Property Crime in Canada

Theft-related offences			
Offence	**Code section**	**Maximum (summary)**	**Maximum (indictable)**
Theft over $5,000	334(a)	N/A	10 years of jail
Theft under $5,000	334(b)	6 months of jail or $5,000 fine	2 years of jail
Possession of stolen property over $5,000	355(a)	N/A	10 years of jail
Possession of stolen property under $5,000	335(b)	6 months of jail or $5,000 fine	2 years of jail
Fraud over $5,000	380(1)(a)	N/A	14 years of jail
Fraud under $5,000	380(1)(b)	6 months of jail or $5,000 fine	2 years of jail
Property damage offences			
Offence	**Code section**	**Maximum (summary)**	**Maximum (indictable)**
Mischief over $5,000	430(3)	6 months of jail or $5,000 fine	10 years of jail
Mischief under $5,000	430(4)	6 months of jail or $5,000 fine	2 years of jail
Arson (disregard for human life)	433	N/A	Life
Arson (damage to property)	434/434.1	N/A	14 years of jail
Arson (fraudulent purpose)	435	N/A	10 years of jail
Arson (negligence)	436(1)	N/A	5 years of jail
Possession of incendiary materials	436.1	N/A	5 years of jail
Breaking and entering			
Offence	**Code section**	**Maximum (summary)**	**Maximum (indictable)**
Breaking and entering with intent (dwelling)	348	N/A	Life
Breaking and entering with intent (not dwelling)	348	6 months of jail or $5,000 fine	10 years of jail
Being unlawfully in a dwelling-house	349	6 months of jail or $5,000 fine	10 years of jail
Possession of break-in instruments	351	N/A	10 years of jail

Source: *Criminal Code* (1985).

Why Do People Commit Property Crime?

Conventional explanations of property crime tend to be based on a logic rooted in the **Classical School of criminology**. And most explanations normally deal with property crime that can be defined as "street crime," such as theft and breaking and entering into businesses and residences, and do not apply so easily to Internet crimes such as e-commerce fraud.

The origins of the Classical School can be found in the writing of Jeremy Bentham (1780/1973) and Cesare Beccaria (1764/1995) in the 18th century, which is based on the **utilitarian** belief that society is comprised of rational, free-willed decision-makers. Based on this proposition, people engage in property crime if they feel the benefits of stealing something outweigh the costs of getting caught. Conversely, based on a similar rational calculation, if people believe that the costs associated with stealing outweigh the benefits, then the crime will not be committed. In fact, Canada's sentencing laws are in keeping with deterrence-based logic because what are deemed to be more serious forms of property crime are associated with more severe penalties.

Punishment is supposed to have a deterrent effect, both on the lawbreaker (individual deterrence) and on potential criminals (general deterrence). Delving into **deterrence theory** a bit further, the effectiveness of punishment is considered to be conditioned by three factors:

1. the severity of the punishment for committing the crime;
2. the certainty that the punishment will be applied—in addition to the certainty of being apprehended in the first place; and
3. the swiftness with which the punishment will be applied.

Supporters of deterrence theory (which typically include conservative political parties) endorse policies such as longer prison sentences, increased penalty severity (for example, a mandatory minimum sentence), and the hiring of more police officers. Together, these policies are considered to control and reduce the reoffending of convicted offenders and curb potential lawbreakers from becoming involved in crime in the future. However, little evidence confirms the effectiveness of this approach. Since the late 1960s, criminologists have been putting the deterrence hypothesis to the empirical test. In 1969, for example, Charles Tittle's often-cited study on deterrence found some support for deterrence theory and concluded that the *certainty* of imprisonment deters some crime, but that *severity* can only deter crime when the certainty of punishment is reasonably guaranteed. Little research has shown that the rapidity of punishment deters crime, and some research has shown that increasing penalty severity may actually increase the possibility of reoffending by released offenders (Tonry, 2011).

Because of the limitations of deterrence theory–based explanations of crime, including property crime, criminologists have developed other theories to explain offending. While it is beyond the scope of this chapter to provide a detailed review of these explanations (for example, strain theory, control theory, differential association theory, routine activity theory, and the general theory of crime, which are explored in Part Two, Theories of Crime), the analysis that follows will demonstrate that property crime needs to be understood within the social context in which it takes place. Although stealing a loaf of bread from a supermarket may be considered to be a simple matter of free-willed decision

Classical School of criminology
A body of work that emerged in Europe in the 17th and 18th centuries that argued people have the capacity to think rationally; contemporary deterrence theory is rooted in this school of thought.

utilitarianism
A philosophy that suggests reasoned decisions will produce the greatest good for the greatest number.

deterrence theory
A theory based on the idea that for punishment to be effective, it must be swift, sure, and certain.

For more on this line of reasoning, see Chapter 12, Crime Choice Theory.

making, criminologists consider crimes (including property crimes) not so much as *individual events* but as *social events* (Kennedy & Sacco, 1996). This distinction suggests that the backgrounds and current situational adversity of offenders need to be taken into account in addition to the actions of lawmakers, the police, the courts, the correctional system, the public, victims, and the mass media. We must not lose sight of the social character of crime. Indeed, more advanced courses in criminology and criminal justice typically go well beyond studying the simple act of crime commission and focus on the broader social context in which crime and crime control take place.

Before you begin reading the following case study, you may find it useful to refer to the overview of crime statistics that appeared in Chapter 4, Measuring Crime. Note also that some of the tables in this case study include "p values": $p < 0.05$ means that the relationship is statistically significant and that we are 95 percent confident that the findings are not due to chance; $p < 0.01$ means that the relationship is statistically significant and that we are 99 percent confident that the findings are not due to chance; and $p < 0.001$ means that the relationship is statistically significant and that we are 99.9 percent confident that the findings are not due to chance.

Case Study: An Analysis of Property Crime Among Homeless Youth in Toronto

Informed by a line of thinking that incorporates the social context of crime, what follows is a case study analysis of self-reported property crime based on original research carried out with a group of homeless youth in Toronto. For the purposes of this chapter, this analysis will only focus on the background and situational adversity of property crime offenders to show that decisions that people make to commit property crimes are predominantly shaped by **social forces**. While there is no denying that some degree of decision-making is involved during the commission of a property crime, this analysis will point out that levels of property crime within the sample are related to the backgrounds of these youth and the situational adversity they face.

Before we turn to an analysis of data collected from 360 street-involved youth in Toronto, we will briefly review the nature of youth **homelessness** in Canada. Approximately 150,000 youth in Canada are homeless on any given night. The number of youth using Toronto shelter services where this study was undertaken increased by 16.2 percent between 2006 and 2009 (Lem, Coe, Haley, Stone, & O'Grady, 2013). Accurate homeless counts are difficult to achieve, as youth commonly "couch surf" (move from place to place), squat (stay in abandoned or unoccupied buildings), sleep rough (i.e., outdoors), engage in prostitution or other activities in exchange for shelter, or use other forms of transient or marginal housing. Research also shows that compared with Canadian youth who have stable housing, homeless youth partake in more illegal activity (Baron, 2013; Hagan & McCarthy, 1997).

Canadian youth become street involved for a number of reasons. While each youth has his or her own specific story and set of circumstances, the main causes of youth homelessness are as follows:

- *Individual/relational factors*: Between 60 and 70 percent of homeless youth left family environments where they experienced interpersonal violence, including physical, sexual, and/or emotional abuse.

social forces
In sociology, the perspective that elements of society have the capability of causing cultural change or influencing human behaviour.

homelessness
A range of physical living conditions that can include living on the streets or in the open, staying in emergency shelters, or being provisionally housed (couch surfing with friends or relatives).

- *Structural factors*: Broader systemic factors, including poverty, lack of food, inadequate housing, and discrimination, can lead to homelessness.
- *Institutional and system factors*: The failure of systems of care and support, including child protection, health, mental health care, and corrections, can lead to homelessness (Gaetz, O'Grady, Buccieri, Karabanow, & Marsolais, 2013).

As Table 15.3 shows, approximately two-thirds of the sample is male and one-third is female. This gender ratio is consistent with other Canadian research that has studied street youth (for example, Hagan & McCarthy, 1997). The average age of the sample is 21, also in keeping with other research that has focused on this population. It is important to note that the age range that researchers normally use in Canadian research on homeless youth is 16 to 24. The reason why 16 tends to be the floor of this age range is that youth who are under the age of 16 are not legally permitted to stay in youth shelters, because young people under the age of 16 in Canada must be in the care of an adult guardian. Twenty-four years of age is the ceiling, since individuals 25 years of age and older who are in need of emergency shelter must use the adult system. In terms of the sexual orientation of the sample, 30 percent self-reported that they did not self-identify as being heterosexual. Many LGBT (lesbian, gay, bisexual, transgender) youth in Canada have experiences with street involvement, as do youth who have spent time in foster homes and/or have experiences with children's aid societies. Slightly more than one-half of the sample grew up in Toronto, and just under one-half did not finish high school, with the average level of schooling being grade 11. Many of the youth who were interviewed for the study reported that they have been street-involved for prolonged periods of time. For example, 37 percent said that they have been on the streets for seven years or longer.

TABLE 15.3   Characteristics of the Toronto Homeless Youth Sample

Characteristic	Percentage
Gender	Male: 64% Female: 36%
Mean age	21
Sexual orientation	Straight: 70% Lesbian: 2% Gay: 5% Bisexual: 14% Other: 9%
Grew up in Toronto	Yes: 53% No: 47%
Completed high school	Yes: 43% No: 57%
Length of time street-involved	< 1 year: 9% 2–3 years: 18% 4–6 years: 36% 7+ years: 37%
Lived in foster/group home	43%
Current housing status	Own place: 22% Shelter: 62% Street: 15% Squat: 1%

$n = 360$.

Source: Gaetz, O'Grady, & Vaillancourt (1999).

The Effects of a Selected Number of Variables on Property Crime

Through statistical analysis, we will now explore the effects that a selected number of variables have on three forms of property crime: break and enter/theft, scamming, and selling stolen goods. The case study sample was asked to self-report whether (within the past year) they had stolen something or committed a break and enter; been involved in scamming or conning (a common "short con" involves asking someone to change an amount of money and exchanging coins or bills back and forth to confuse and ultimately shortchange the person); or sold stolen goods.

The data collected demonstrate that gender, housing status, and level of drug use are all strong predictors of engaging in property crime for this sample of Toronto homeless youth. After describing these predictors and their association with property crime, we will then discuss why a solid understanding of the nature of property crime requires that we look beyond explanations that focus merely on rational actors who weigh the costs and benefits of whether it is in their interest to commit crime.

In the field of criminology, gender is widely recognized as a key predictor of crime, including property crime, and research shows that crime is highly correlated with gender (Messerschmidt, 2006). With the exception of fraud (for example, writing bad cheques) and shoplifting, males generally commit more property crime than females. It is beyond the scope of this chapter to review the wide range of explanations on why males outnumber females in the commission of crime. The literature on gender and crime provide scant evidence that would suggest females operate with a different mindset than males when it comes to weighing the costs and benefits of crimes such as stealing. Instead, gender differences have mainly been linked to unequal gender relations in society and differences in socialization patterns and opportunity structures. Not surprisingly, the data in Table 15.4 show that male homeless youth are more likely than female homeless youth to steal, scam, and sell stolen goods.

A second factor that links homeless youth to property crime is housing status. Three levels of housing quality were measured in the study. The first category, "own place," refers to youth who reported having a place of their own, which generally meant that they were provisionally housed. This category includes people who have temporary rental arrangements, such as staying in a motel, a hostel, or a rooming house. It also includes those who are couch surfers, or the hidden homeless. The "hidden homeless" are people who stay with friends, extended family, or even strangers. The second category, "shelter," refers to youth who reported sleeping in the emergency shelter system. These shelters typically have minimal eligibility criteria, offer shared sleeping facilities and amenities, and often expect clients to leave in the morning. They may or may not offer food, clothing, or other services. Some emergency shelters allow people to stay on an ongoing basis, while others are short term and are set up to respond to special circumstances, such as extreme weather (Canadian Homelessness Research Network, 2012). The final category, "street/squat," refers to youth who reported living on the street or staying in a squat. This category includes public spaces such as sidewalks, squares, parks, transit shelters, wooded areas, and spots under bridges, as well as rooftops and vacant/abandoned buildings.

For more on why males outnumber females in the commission of crimes, see Chapter 10, Gender and Crime.

TABLE 15.4   Property Crime of Homeless Youth in the Past Year, by Gender

	Break and enter/theft[a]	Scamming[b]	Selling stolen goods[c]
Males	Yes: 45% No: 55%	Yes: 42% No: 58%	Yes: 41% No: 59%
Females	Yes: 33% No: 67%	Yes: 33% No: 67%	Yes: 22% No: 78%

[a] $n = 284, p < 0.05$.
[b] $n = 279, p < 0.01$.
[c] $n = 278, p < 0.001$.

Source: O'Grady (n.d.).

TABLE 15.5   Property Crime of Homeless Youth in the Past Year, by Housing Status

	Break and enter/theft[a]	Scamming[b]	Selling stolen goods[c]
Own place	23.1%	28.8%	21.6%
Shelter	42.1%	37.0%	34.4%
Street/squat	75.0%	70.4%	61.5%

[a] $n = 258, p < 0.001.$
[b] $n = 255, p < 0.001.$
[c] $n = 251, p < 0.01.$

Source: O'Grady (n.d.).

According the data in Table 15.5, above, housing status is clearly related to property crime. Youth in the most precarious housing situations were most likely to engage in all three forms of property crime. For example, 23.1 percent of youth who were staying in their own place were involved in theft/breaking and entering, compared with 42.1 percent who were staying in shelters and 75.0 percent who were unsheltered. These statistics clearly illustrate the strong relationship between the quality of housing and the commission of property crime. This finding shows that situational adversity is linked to criminal behaviour among street youth, which echoes earlier research on the topic by John Hagan and Bill McCarthy (1997). In their study of homeless youth, they argued that the presence of strain and the absence of social controls lead to street crime, particularly theft of food. The **absolute deprivation** that leads to living in places that are not intended for human habitation causes stress and makes daily survival extremely difficult. The idea that theft is significantly influenced by people's immediate desperate circumstances has a long pedigree in criminology. For example, early European criminologists such as Willem Bonger (1916) argued that the poor commit crime out of need or out of a sense of injustice. It would not be a stretch to apply this logic to youth who are desperate and sleep under bridges or in abandoned, derelict buildings and steal in order to survive.

absolute deprivation
Low income or poverty in and of itself.

While not all homeless youth use drugs and alcohol, research has consistently shown that a substantial number do, at least on occasion (Buccieri, 2013). The Public Health Agency of Canada (PHAC) (2006) found that in 2003, 26.9 percent of the Canadian street youth surveyed reported drinking alcohol more than once per week, and 36 percent reported alcohol intoxication in the previous three months. Additionally, more than 95 percent reported injection and/or non-injection drug use in their lifetime (PHAC, 2006).

According to a research report from the British Home Office, a statistically significant relationship exists between opiate and cocaine use and the amount of reported annual illegal income. Almost half (46 percent) of a sample of arrestees in England who reported using drugs in the last 12 months believed that their drug use and property crime were linked. Not surprisingly, the most common connection cited was the need for money to buy drugs (Bennet & Holloway, 2004).

The data from the Toronto street youth study show that involvement in property crime is also closely linked to levels of illegal drug use. In Table 15.6, we see that engaging in break and enter/theft, scamming, and selling stolen goods is associated with elevated levels of drug use. Specifically, for those who used drugs more than once a week, 53 percent committed break and enter/theft, 51 percent scammed, and 47 percent sold stolen goods. For those who used drugs less than once a week, 18 percent committed break and enter/theft, 17 percent scammed, and 11 percent sold stolen goods. Interestingly, when levels of these three forms of property crime are measured only for males who live on the streets/in squats and are regular drug users, the percentages rise to 78 percent for break and enter/theft, 77 percent for scamming, and 82 percent for selling stolen goods.

TABLE 15.6   Property Crime of Homeless Youth in the Past Year, by Level of Drug Use

	Break and enter/theft[b]	Scamming[c]	Selling stolen goods[d]
Drug use > 1 week[a]	Yes: 53% No: 47%	Yes: 51% No: 49%	Yes: 47% No: 53%
Drug use < 1 week	Yes: 18% No: 82%	Yes: 17% No: 83%	Yes: 11% No: 89%

[a] Those in category "Drug use > 1 week" (drugs = crack/cocaine/crystal meth/marijuana) use more than once a week. Those in "Drug use < 1 week" (drugs = crack/cocaine/crystal meth/marijuana) use less than once a week.

[b] $n = 274$, $p < 0.001$.

[c] $n = 268$, $p < 0.001$.

[d] $n = 267$, $p < 0.001$.

Source: O'Grady (n.d.).

Overall, these data show that youth, particularly boys, who live in the most precarious living conditions and use drugs more than once a week are the most likely to engage in property crime. Thus, while all street youth ultimately make decisions to steal, scam, or try to sell stolen property, it is clear from these data that such decision-making takes place within different contexts and constraints.

Conclusion

This chapter began with a discussion on the emergence of property crime laws. The origins of such laws were traced to the rise of capitalism in England, and Canadian criminal laws are largely based on English common law. We examined how property crime is defined in Canada and how property crime statistics have been changing over time. While some forms of property crime (for example, break and enter and motor vehicle theft) have been declining in recent years, other types of property crime (for example, credit card fraud) appear to be on the increase. One of the main reasons for the increase in credit card fraud is the growth in online e-commerce. Although different criminological explanations of property crime exist, criminologists consider property crimes not so much as *individual events* but as *social events*. The original case study analysis of self-reported property crime by a group of homeless youth (the demographic group most commonly involved in committing property crime offences) in Toronto showed that the commission of property crimes is very much socially patterned, and that the situational adversity that these youth face needs to be considered in an attempt to explain why street youth steal, scam, and sell stolen property.

SUMMARY OF KEY POINTS

- According to "structural functionalists," crime, including property crime, is inevitable in all societies. Moreover, they consider property crime laws to be based on a shared belief system in which customs, over time, become codified into legal statutes believed to promote solidarity and stability in society. For Marxist "conflict theorists," property crimes committed by those from the working class are subject to criminalization, while the illegal activities of the elites are considered to be largely immune from legal censure.

- Regarding conflict theories, however, it should be noted that research has shown that a majority of street crime, including that related to property, is intra-class crime.

- The vast majority of property offenders who come before the courts are young, have relatively low levels of formal education, and are poor.

- Property crime involves the taking of money or property and, unlike robbery, does not involve force or threat of force against a victim. The main types of property crime listed in the *Criminal Code* are theft, break and enter, mischief (vandalism), possession of stolen property, arson, motor vehicle theft, and fraud.

- Most (Classical School) explanations deal with property crime that can be defined as "street crime," such as theft and breaking and entering into businesses and residences, and do not apply so easily to Internet crimes, such as e-commerce fraud.

- Supporters of "deterrence theory" endorse policies such as longer prison sentences, increased penalty severity, and the hiring of more police officers. However, little evidence confirms the effectiveness of this approach.

- Research, such as that done on Toronto homeless youth, demonstrates that gender, housing status, and level of drug use are all strong predictors of engaging in property crime.

- Gender is widely recognized as a key predictor of crime, including property crime. With the exception of fraud and shoplifting, males generally commit more property crime than females.

- While some forms of property crime have been declining in recent years, other types of property crime (for example, credit card fraud) appear to be on the increase.

- Although there are different criminological explanations of property crime, criminologists consider property crimes not so much as *individual* events but as *social* events.

QUESTIONS FOR CRITICAL DISCUSSION

1. Discuss how structural functionalist and conflict explanations account for the emergence of property crime laws.
2. How have levels of police-reported property crime changed in Canada from 1962 to 2016?
3. How does deterrence theory explain property crime?
4. Why do gender, housing status, and levels of drug use predict differing levels of property crime for homeless youth?

SUGGESTED FURTHER READINGS

Brand, R. (2007). *My booky wook*. London, UK: Hodder and Stoughton.

Gibson, K. (2011). *Street kids: Homeless youth, outreach, and policing New York's streets*. New York: New York University Press.

Reynolds, B. (2000). *An autobiography of a thief: The man behind the great train robbery* (2nd ed.). London, UK: Virgin Books.

Websites

Security Magazine, E-commerce fraud: https://www.securitymagazine.com/articles/88451-e-commerce-fraud-loss-reaches-578-billion

The Homeless Hub: http://www.homelesshub.ca

Legislation

Criminal Code, RSC 1985, c C-46.

Case

R v Jackson, 2016 YKTC 9.

CASE STUDY 16.1

Rethinking Canada's Prostitution Laws: The Bedford Case

Dominatrix Terri-Jean Bedford speaking to the media, flanked by lawyer Alan Young and prostitutes' rights activist Valerie Scott.

In June 2013, the Supreme Court of Canada listened to arguments about the circumstances in which men and women might be allowed to legally buy and sell sex. The justices of the Supreme Court were considering the arguments made by the lawyer for dominatrix Terri-Jean Bedford, former prostitute Valerie Scott (both from Ontario), and Vancouver sex worker Amy Lebovitch.

The heart of the argument made by counsel Alan Young was that the law, as it is written, has the practical consequence of endangering the lives of women in the sex trade, particularly those women who work the street—women who might best be described as "survival sex workers," often drug addicted and frequently subjected to violence at the hands of some of their customers. Women who work in massage parlours or for escort agencies also experience risks, but these risks are significantly diminished by the protections offered by each of these businesses—the tracking of clients through credit cards and other means, and an agreed-upon location for the sexual transaction, known to those operating the business.

The trial court in *Canada (AG) v Bedford* (2013) had heard from 12 women who worked in the sex trade; they all told the court that street prostitution is less safe than indoor work, and the conclusions of these 12 women were based on interviews they themselves had conducted with approximately 800 sex trade workers. They also heard evidence from academics who have studied the safety of work in the sex trade; street-level prostitutes were, in all of these studies, found to be much more likely to be assaulted, kidnapped, or killed than those working indoors.

The two *Criminal Code* provisions that directly affect prostitution are the prohibition against anyone who "keeps a common bawdy-house" (s. 210) and the prohibition against communication for the purpose of soliciting "illicit sexual intercourse with another person" (s. 212). But, as the court heard in *Bedford*, the bawdy-house provisions are rarely enforced; they are not generally the subject of public complaints, and, more important, police investigations of suspected bawdy houses are time-consuming and expensive. In contrast, the prosecution of street prostitutes is much less difficult, and these prosecutions now form the bulk of all cases that are heard in Canadian courts.

The federal government's response to these claims and concerns noted that even indoor sex work in bawdy houses has not eliminated violence against prostitutes. Crown lawyer Michael H. Morris argued that criminal prohibition exists to prevent the harmful effects of prostitution, and the personal interests and choices of those who engage in this economy should not trump the goal of preventing harm.

349

In December 2013, the Supreme Court, in a unanimous decision, declared the laws governing prostitution in Canada to be invalid for one year. The judgment of the court was delivered by then Chief Justice Beverley McLachlin, who wrote in the final paragraphs in *Bedford*:

> How prostitution is regulated is a matter of great public concern, and few countries leave it entirely unregulated. Whether immediate invalidity would pose a danger to the public or imperil the rule of law (the factors for suspension referred to in *Schachter v. Canada*, [1992] 2 S.C.R. 679) may be subject to debate. However, it is clear that moving abruptly from a situation where prostitution is regulated to a situation where it is entirely unregulated would be a matter of great concern to many Canadians.
>
> On the other hand, leaving the prohibitions against bawdy-houses, living on the avails of prostitution and public communication for purposes of prostitution in place in their present form leaves prostitutes at increased risk for the time of the suspension—risks which violate their constitutional right to security of the person.
>
> The choice between suspending the declaration of invalidity and allowing it to take immediate effect is not an easy one. Neither alternative is without difficulty. However, considering all the interests at stake, I conclude that the declaration of invalidity should be suspended for one year. (paras. 167–169)

How might prostitution be regulated? To what extent *should* it be regulated? The debates continue over the role of the criminal law in relation to current provisions against bawdy houses, living on the avails of prostitution, and soliciting. Some would like to see the law amended to target only the male customers of prostitutes. Others believe that this approach would not be a step forward, and that it would only serve to entrench the harms that street prostitutes currently experience by ensuring that such transactions would increasingly take place away from public view and further reduce any potential protection for these vulnerable women.

Before You Read Chapter 16

- Should the work of those in the sex trade be considered, in law, to be any different from work in other morally contested realms—serving drinks in a bar, selling cannabis (marijuana) to willing consumers, or operating a casino that includes slot machines and roulette wheels?
- Do critical differences exist across morally contested activities, and, if so, what are they?

Crimes of Morality

LEARNING OUTCOMES

After reading this chapter, students will be able to:

- Explain the characteristics of crimes of morality and how they differ from consensus crimes.
- Identify the classical arguments concerning the proper role of law in regulating moral conduct.
- Explain the tenets of the harm principle and opposing arguments on the role of government and law.
- Understand opposing views on prostitution and their implications for its treatment under law.
- Understand the history of existing drug laws and identify competing policy perspectives.

CHAPTER OUTLINE

Introduction

Universal agreement exists in society that crimes such as murder, rape, and assault deserve strict punishment. The seriousness of these crimes is beyond dispute. In other words, the consensus is that committing these crimes is wrongful in itself. "Consensus crimes" (such as murder, rape, and assault) inflict real harm on persons and society, and thus require a matching societal response. However, certain crimes are more ambiguous, divisive, or subject to dispute—these crimes are the focus of this chapter.

Unlike consensus crimes, **crimes of morality** are subject to widespread disagreement and considerable debate. Laws that prohibit gambling, certain types of drug use, and the exchange of sex for money are all relevant examples. Sometimes known as "victimless" or "vice-related" crimes, crimes of morality are not crimes because they cause direct harm to society or persons but because they are seen as threatening to societal **morals**.

Crimes of morality do not necessarily cause harm or have a victim. Commonly, such crime involves an offender who has "offended" in the sense of having broken an existing norm. Crimes of morality reflect the current moral standards of a society. As moral standards change, the laws that define them are also subject to change. The move to legalize and regulate the sale of cannabis in Canada in October 2018 is a prominent example. Whether laws evolve in step with moral standards or stay stagnant and reflect standards and opinions of an earlier era, crimes of morality are subject to debate.

crimes of morality
Illegal activities that are against the law because they are regarded as threatening to values.

morals
The normative standards, codes, and beliefs governing judgments and values concerning right and wrong action, justice, and fairness.

Customers line up to buy lottery tickets at a mall kiosk. In recent decades, gambling has gone from a socially unacceptable and closely policed "vice" to a government-sanctioned activity that funnels huge amounts of money into public coffers through casinos, lotteries, and sports betting. Other than the financial rewards to governments, what other reasons might account for this change in attitude toward gambling and lotteries?

Considerable disagreement exists among policy observers and lay people about the role of government in legislating morals. Canadian experience in this area offers ample illustrations of both the flexibility of law and societal resistance. Gambling has evolved in recent decades into a regulated industry and a legitimate source of revenue for governments (and charities), which reap enormous profits from casinos and Canadians who try their luck in lotteries each week. At the same time, federal government–sponsored advertisements cautioning those who gamble of the risks involved in playing games of chance have become commonplace.

The laws that govern prostitution represent moral legislation that has shifted toward a more pragmatic stance. Canada's drug laws, by comparison, have proven more resistant. With few exceptions, drug laws continue to reflect a moral standpoint that has more to do with history and dominant group interests than concern for persons who use substances per se. These observations are supported by discrepancies between the treatment of accepted substances (such as alcohol and cannabis) and others (such as heroin and cocaine) whose users are deemed criminal. To further illustrate, this chapter takes a closer look at drug use and prostitution as examples of crimes against morality. We begin with an overview of classic arguments presented by philosophers and legal scholars before examining these topics further.

What Is the Role of Law in Regulating Moral Conduct?

We are social animals whose very existence depends on those around us to fulfill our basic needs. Moreover, our survival as a species and our quality of life are dependent on the social interactions that maintain them. The benefits acquired from interaction and dependence on others in our social group, however, have a price. The cost of the fulfillment of human beings' social nature is our agreement to abide by certain rules and regulations that serve to limit freedom and immediate gratification.

Whereas we are presumably free to do as we desire in our "natural state", as social beings we put limits on these freedoms to ensure the survival of the group. As philosophers and legal scholars (including Sigmund Freud) have long argued, the rule of law is an instrument that ensures our happiness and is our greatest source of unhappiness as well (Fisher, 1982; Freud, 1930/2002; Gay, 1989).

The civilizing process and development of law demands conformity and can sometimes infringe on our desire for freedom from constraint. Society's demands for conformity, however, are far from absolute. Within the realm of regulation, some room for individual freedom, and even deviance, exists. Not all deviant behaviour is universally condemned. Some varieties of deviance, even criminal behaviours, are recognized as tolerable differences that pose little risk of harm to society or to persons that commit the crime and those around them (Stebbins, 1996).

Tolerable deviance includes legitimate, non-criminal, and criminal activities. In North American society, for example, considerable scope exists for freedom of religion, speech, and thought. In addition to these legally protected activities, other practices or lifestyles may violate standard norms of conduct in the general population but not legal statutes or the "letter of the law."

Of particular concern are those varieties of tolerable deviance that are technically illegal but recognized as neither particularly threatening nor harmful to society. Prostitution and the use of certain drugs are examples of criminal tolerable deviance that are often debated among scholars and others who are critical of **overcriminalization** (Richards, 1982).

The legislation and enforcement of morality through law, without either a victim or a complainant, is not only difficult but also a waste of resources. It is also arguably a threat to social order and to the legitimacy of the rule of law. In democratic, multicultural societies such as Canada and other Western nations, the legislation of morality raises important questions about the proper role of government and whose morality or justice ought to be enforced. Before continuing, this chapter will revisit some classic philosophical positions and debates on the question of morality enforcement by the state.

overcriminalization
The intrusion of the law into consensual activities that are relatively harmless to the actor(s) and society.

The Pursuit of Happiness and Law

According to the classic utilitarian perspective, the purpose of law is to make people happy. This philosophical position was developed by Jeremy Bentham (1748–1832), who built on the ideas of highly influential Enlightenment-era philosopher Immanuel Kant. Bentham sought to ascertain the nature of morality. While Kant believed that morality is determined by intentions, which lead to actions that are *inherently* good or bad, Bentham believed that the morality of an action is determined by its *consequences* (Rosen, 2003).

Thus, for Bentham, an action was deemed morally justified, or good, if the action produced a desirable result. This "consequentialist" perspective on morality is generally consistent with the modern view of law, which holds that its function is to maximize "the good" for the majority (Bentham, 1781/2007). This utilitarian approach to law is hedonistic in that it seeks to increase happiness, or pleasure, while reducing pain for the greatest number—that is, it serves the common good.

Some of the early philosophical influences on the development of criminology, and some related terminology, are discussed in more detail in Chapter 6, Theories of Crime: A Brief Introduction.

Bentham sought to quantify the benefits and costs that determine the utility of any given law. His calculus, based on the pleasure principle, consisted of a formula for calculating the morality of actions through the measurement of their circumstances. His equation for determining morality included the elements of intensity, duration, certainty, and the extent of influence of an action's costs and benefits in relation to the law.

Bentham's student, renowned 19th-century thinker John Stuart Mill, was more pragmatic in his recognition that the principles of law cannot be so easily reduced to mathematical equations that determine the utility of actions. Mill's primary concern was the problem of preserving individual freedoms and the rights of the minority in a democratic system of government concerned with seeking to maximize the common good.

Mill's (1859/2002) utilitarian perspective on the proper function of the state enacted through the rule of law emphasized the value of protecting individuals from the imposition of the will of the majority. The "tyranny of the majority," he argued, must be countered by limiting the authority of governments. In particular, he rejected the legislation or enforcement of morality. The only purpose for which power should be exercised, Mill asserted, is to prevent harm to other persons.

Since all persons are deemed sovereign over their minds and bodies, Mill argued, the state is never justified to interfere with actions of an individual for his or her "own good." Put otherwise, we have the right to do as we please, as long as our actions do no harm to others. Mill's utilitarian perspective was concerned with the realization of the common good through the cultivation of personal autonomy. His view of human nature likened us to trees that should be free to flourish and develop on all sides—rather than machines built from some preordained design.

The Harm Principle

Mill's (1859/2002) view suggests that legal sanctions must be limited to actions that inflict real harm on assignable persons as opposed to actions to which others take offence. Those who are merely offended by an action or opinion have ready access to the remedy of seeking other company. Thus, formal intervention by the state in such situations is unnecessary.

Mill maintained a liberal position on morality. He viewed morality as a trait to be acquired through education, whose business it was to cultivate the propensity to act in the best interests of society. He believed that although the state is justified in seeking to prevent harm, legislators must be mindful of the circumstances of the action justifying enforcement of the law. While excessive drinking may be harmful, for example, moderate use of alcohol is not. Therefore, an outright ban is not permissible. However, restrictions may be warranted to regulate consumption and help consumers mitigate known risks.

harm principle
A central tenet in the writing of John Stuart Mill, who is often regarded as the father of moral liberalism. The harm principle holds that the actions of individuals should only be limited to prevent harm to other individuals.

Mill's articulation of the **harm principle** is well known for its elegant simplicity. His point of view was unequivocal. He made very few exceptions, other than for children and the mentally disabled, who arguably are lacking the capacity to exercise their right to full autonomy—thereby allowing greater scope for protection by parental figures and/or the state.

He also believed that extending the coercive power of government to limiting the personal autonomy of adults was both unnecessary and a travesty of justice impeding the realization of the common good. In Mill's own words:

> A state which dwarfs its men, in order that they may be more docile instruments in its hand, even for beneficial purposes will find that with small men no great thing can really be accomplished; and that the perfection of machinery to which it has sacrificed everything will in the end avail it nothing. (1859/2002, p. 161)

Opposing Arguments

The classic Millsian perspective on the function of the state has been challenged by observers with less liberal positions on the propriety of enforcing morality through law. The most well-known propositions in the literature adopt a more conservative or moderate perspective that, in practice, tends to be reflected in legal policy provisions in Canada and many other jurisdictions around the world.

The case for the legislation of morality, in direct contradiction of Mill's position on the matter, was famously made by Lord Devlin in 1950s Britain. According to Devlin, legislating morals was precisely what the role of the government should be. Devlin (1965) firmly believed in **moral absolutism**, based on the consensus of reasonable people, that ought to be safeguarded through law enforcement. Homosexuality and prostitution are examples of activities that Devlin saw as threatening to conventional standards of morality, thereby justifying interference by the state to preserve the common good. (In contrast, **moral relativism** holds that what is considered moral behaviour can and does change over time and from culture to culture.)

A more moderate or middle-ground position between Devlin's (conservative) and Mill's (liberal) view of the function of law was taken up by legal scholar Herbert Lionel Adolphus Hart (1963). According to Hart, government is obligated to fulfill the role of parent for its citizens in order to protect them from the harm that they are liable to inflict on themselves when lacking proper guidance and moral regulation. Although his position is less punitive than Devlin's, it is also less liberal than Mill's—who would no doubt be offended by the notion that some freedom must be sacrificed by adults to protect us from ourselves "for our own good."

As an evolving system of rules and regulations, criminal law in Canada is probably best characterized as a tool reflecting all of these concerns. The principles put forward by Mill are clearly evident in section 1 of the *Canadian Charter of Rights and Freedoms*. The limitations clause states that our rights and freedoms are "subject only to such reasonable limits prescribed by law as can be demonstrably justified in a free and democratic society." This clause puts the onus on government to justify prohibiting an action. It also further establishes that the prohibition must be minimally intrusive, rational, and proportionate to the harm inflicted by the action. This clause is, of course, subject to interpretation that, necessarily, can never be conclusive. The debates and legal challenges surrounding this clause are meant to be ongoing.

The foregoing discussion was provided as a background to considering the appropriate role of law in democratic constitutional societies such as Canada. We now turn to a discussion of prominent areas of contention and continual debate in the legislation of morality: prostitution and drug use.

moral absolutism
A philosophical perspective that holds that certain actions are absolutely right or wrong, regardless of other circumstances such as their consequences or the intentions behind them.

moral relativism
A perspective on the nature of morality asserting that norms or standards of behaviour are not fixed or absolute.

Gloria Taylor, who suffered from ALS, was the first Canadian to win the right to a physician-assisted suicide (from the BC Supreme Court, but which the federal government appealed), but died of natural causes. What should the state's role be in such cases? What is the "crime" and who is harmed if a person chooses to end his or her own suffering?

Prostitution

In Canada, the average number of arrests for prostitution-related offences has been steadily declining for the past 15 years. The act of prostitution, or exchanging sex for money, was not technically illegal in this country until recently. However, under section 213 of the *Criminal Code*, "communication for the purposes of prostitution" was regarded as a criminal offence.

In 2014, new legislation was enacted in response to the Supreme Court of Canada's 2013 decision in *Bedford*. The *Protection of Communities and Exploited Persons Act* (PCEPA) made it a criminal offence to purchase sexual services. Treating prostitution as exploitive of sex workers, who are primarily women and girls, the aim of PCEPA is to penalize the purchasers instead, as well as those who benefit from prostituting others.

In many Canadian cities, thinly veiled ads for prostitution can be found in newspapers and online, using terms such as "massage" or "escort services." This tacit acceptance of prostitution, particularly when it is less "open" and not on highly visible street corners, suggests that Canadians' attitudes on this issue are changing.

Opinion polls suggest that a majority of Canadians believe that prostitution should be legal for sex workers and their clients (Forum Research, 2015). Criticism of the new law and support for further changes will lead to future challenges and legislative action. To put ongoing policy discussions in perspective, we will review the academic literature on sex work with particular attention to theoretical debates.

Types of Prostitution

Although policy discussions tend to refer to prostitution as a singular activity, it comprises different types of sex work with distinctive characteristics. The stereotypical depiction of prostitutes is probably closest to those known as "hookers" or "street walkers." The women fitting this description often come from lower-class backgrounds, use heavily addicting drugs, and are typically most visible in run-down areas of inner cities. Of all sex workers, they are often the most vulnerable and victimized, the most frequently arrested, and the most abused by clients—with many working for a "pimp" who controls their activities (Lowman, 2000).

Less visible to most people are those who work in bars or hotel lounges waiting to be propositioned (Prus & Irini, 1980). Although often freelance workers who are not controlled by pimps, "bar girls" sometimes have arrangements with a bartender, who may be compensated for compliance by having clients buy them "drinks" (which are often just coloured water, thus providing generous tips).

Other kinds of sex workers set up shop in brothels, where a portion of the money earned goes to the proprietor. Although brothels are legal in some jurisdictions in other parts of the world, in Canada sex services of this kind have been limited—until recently—to those provided in "massage parlours," which disguise their services for those not "in the know."

Sex workers receive clear advantages from working in secure environments where clients are controlled and monitored by others who administrate the service in exchange for rent or a cut of their profits. While this model has existed in a variety of forms throughout human history and throughout the world, its benefits are particularly evident where regulations ensure protections for sex workers and their clients in a setting that is legitimate, hygienic, and secure.

A hierarchy exists in sex work in which the most well-paid prostitutes are known as "escorts" or "call girls." Catering to wealthy clients, these women occupy the other end of the continuum of sex work from "street walkers," sometimes earning thousands of dollars a night. Often well-educated, from the middle and upper classes, call girls work independently or for an escort agency, meeting clients in hotel rooms or their own or clients' homes. Typically, they provide more than sex to clients; they are often hired for companionship as well.

Although escorts are well paid for their services and often have regular clients they come to know well, they face risks similar to those faced by other sex workers and must take precautions to protect themselves. These safeguards include travelling with a personal driver (or trusted cab driver) who knows their whereabouts while on the job. Other precautions include taking business cards and requiring contact information from new clients (for those not working through an agency that can collect this information).

In summary, it seems that stereotypical portrayals of prostitution represent an oversimplification of the nature of the business of sex work. It is ordinarily assumed that women enter prostitution out of desperation—due to poverty, addiction, lack of self-esteem, abuse, or other circumstances—as victims who are forced into a lifestyle that degrades them. Undoubtedly, depictions of this nature are an accurate characterization of a segment of the population of sex workers.

More generally, however, research shows that many prostitutes do not see themselves as victims. On the contrary, sex workers often view their occupation as fulfilling a valued function in society, in terms similar to those employed throughout the service industry. These opposing points of view on prostitution largely coincide with contradictory arguments presented in academic literature and policy perspectives. Oversimplifying these discussions is not conducive to the development of well-informed opinions and debates. Accordingly, our next task is to consider important theoretical contributions that inform discussions on the role of law in the regulation of sex work.

A Subcultural Perspective

Although financial need is an important motivation for many women who enter into prostitution, it is rarely a sufficient explanation in itself. Social learning is required to obtain the special knowledge that is ordinarily needed to succeed. Since prostitution is a highly stigmatized profession, existing on the fringes of conventional society, introduction and acceptance in the subculture of sex work is often necessary to become a prostitute.

Since ancient times, sex workers have regarded the profession as a way of gaining independence as women in societies where men have dominated wealth and power. Indeed, historically financially independent women were often prostitutes who were, by definition, women not beholden to or possessed by men. This traditional perspective on the roles of men and women is still dominant within the subculture of sex work (Dalla, 2000; Roberts, 1992).

Many prostitutes perceive themselves as equal or superior to women who marry for financial security. Sex work is often viewed as a superior alternative to low-paying jobs where women are exploited and commonly subjected to sexual harassment. In particular, female escorts who work independently see real advantages in working for themselves with no interference from male managers or bosses (Perkins, 1991).

Social learning in the prostitution subculture, moreover, promotes a view of sex work as a service that fulfills an important function in society. This outlook has been echoed and developed systematically in what is widely known as the "functionalist" approach.

Social Functions of Sex Work

A functionalist interpretation of "deviant behaviour" rejects the pathological perspective, wherein deviance is likened to a disease of the body or an activity that is necessarily harmful to society. Instead, deviance is understood as having positive functions for society, which may not be intended but nonetheless fulfill a beneficial role (Merton, 1957; Parsons, 1951).

Famous sociologist Émile Durkheim (1933, 1938) once observed that deviance and crime are universal, having always existed in society in one form or another. He argued that one could even find them in a society of saints. Even the purest of the pure of human groups, in other words, require examples of wrongdoing to maintain their moral boundaries. To understand what God is, we also need the Devil. Without the Dark, one cannot truly see the Light. Deviant behaviour serves to designate an out-group, or common enemy, whose very existence serves to strengthen social solidarity among the law-abiding. Among its other functions, social deviance facilitates greater harmony and clarifies existing moral standards in society (Erikson, 1966). It provides a scapegoat for the problems of society, enabling the righteous to feel good about themselves.

In addition to providing jobs in law and law enforcement, social work, and corrections (and other jobs sought after by criminology graduates), deviant behaviour sometimes offers an example of a society's capacity for change. Just like the first women who dared to dream of voting in Canada a century ago, prostitutes are outlaws whose behaviour may be deviant but need not necessarily be considered as such (Cohen, 1966).

Apart from its potential to initiate reform by challenging social attitudes about the role of women, prostitution arguably serves two specific functions. Historically, sex work has enabled a small segment of the female population to meet the sexual needs of men (Davis, 1937). Accordingly, it functions as a "safety valve" for men seeking sex outside the bonds of marriage or those who might otherwise resort to raping women. By enabling an exchange of sex for money, prostitution reduces the sex act to an impersonal transaction that avoids the kind of emotional entanglements that threaten the stability of domestic family life (Davis, 1980). This functionalist perspective on the role of prostitution, however, has been challenged by observers who dispute the chauvinistic assumptions underlying this approach (Matza, 1969; Polsky, 1985).

Feminist Perspectives

Whereas the "safety valve" interpretation may suit men, feminists argue that it also represents a double standard based on gender inequality that needs to be addressed. Male promiscuity is often celebrated. Bedding women is depicted as a mark of manhood and virility in our culture. While men with many notches in their bedposts are celebrated as successful "players," studs, and modern-day Don Juans, the same behaviour among women typically gets one labelled as a slut.

While it is reasonable to argue that social attitudes are changing, it is also fair to say they have not changed that much. The age-old double standard (known as the "Madonna/whore" complex) holds that men want a mate who has saintly virtue *and* the ability to meet their sexual desires. As reasonable as this idea may seem from a male perspective, it points to contradictions in our culture on the role and expectations of women, which historically have been defined in terms of men's needs.

Classic and contemporary feminist perspectives are generally consistent in their emphasis on seeking gender equality by promoting women's rights. Interestingly, however, there is considerable disagreement regarding prostitution and the nature of sex work within feminism. Nineteenth-century feminists, such as Elizabeth Cady Stanton and Susan B. Anthony, viewed prostitution as a threat to social order and stability. Sexual promiscuity, they argued, was the cause of all kinds of social ills, including prostitution. Eradicating prostitution was their primary objective as a means to reclaim the purity and virtue of these wayward women and society at large (Jenness, 1993).

By contrast, other feminists viewed prostitution as a legitimate expression of female sexuality outside the bonds of marriage. Repression of sexuality by criminalizing prostitution, argued Victoria Woodhall, is a goal exceeding the limits of state power. She rejected criminalizing prostitution on the grounds that such measures deny women control over their sexuality. From her perspective, sexuality is an empowering tool for women (Rosen, 1982). Woodhall contended that unlike married women at the time, who lacked the legal power to deny sex to their husbands, prostitutes were free to choose the men who used their bodies. Whereas the prostitute may be forced to sell her body "on piecework as a wageworker," said Engels (1884/1942), the married woman "sells it once and for all into slavery" to one man. From this standpoint, prostitution represented the potential for female liberation from sexual domination by men and the male desire to control a woman's body (Meil-Hobson, 1987; Tong, 1984).

Contemporary Feminism

While early feminist perspectives put emphasis on moral purity and chastity as female characteristics, over time that emphasis shifted toward sexual liberation as a tool for challenging gender inequality. The last century has seen important social changes, which have helped facilitate these aims. Marriage laws have changed to the extent that women can legally divorce and are no longer legally defined as property belonging to their husbands (or their fathers).

Female participation in the workforce has expanded over recent decades, which has meant that women have greater independence and are not dependent on marriage for financial security. Gender inequality is still apparent in the workplace, and women tend to occupy positions of less status in many occupations as compared with men. There are signs, however, that the "gender gap" is narrowing, and that social attitudes are changing. Female representation in higher education has dramatically expanded. Moreover, the opportunities for gaining both financial and sexual independence are greater for many women than they once were.

While modern feminists agree that these changes are no cause for complacency and that important work remains to be done, the role of prostitution is especially contentious and divisive in the feminist movement. For many feminists, prostitution is a symbol of women's continued exploitation and subordination in a society that is still controlled by men. They assert that prostitution represents the socio-economic disempowerment of women, and thus threatens the security and well-being of every girl and woman. From this perspective, "prostitution thrives in a society which values women more for their sexuality than for their skilled labour, and which puts women, particularly young, poorly educated women who have limited employment records, at a disadvantage" (Johnson & Rogers, 1993, p. 101).

Feminists remain divided on the role of prostitution with respect to gender inequality and choice. Without free choice, some argue, there cannot be true equality. Others note that without gender equality, choice is nothing more than an illusion for sex workers (Bell, 1987; Jenness, 1993).

Equality First

From an equality first standpoint, women's liberation can never be fully realized in a society where men view women as sexual objects. Those who subscribe to this point of view see prostitutes as victims of male domination over women in society. From a radical perspective, heterosexual sex itself is viewed as a form of sexual slavery in which women are subjected to male power and exploitation. Although not all radical feminists believe that heterosexual sex is necessarily oppressive and demeaning, it is generally agreed that prostitution (and pornography) are obvious representations of female subordination that must be done away with for women to be free (Dworkin, 1989; Miller, 1991; Overall, 1992).

Free Choice First

Some feminists take a more liberal perspective on the role of prostitution. They see prostitutes as workers who should have the freedom to choose what they do for a living. The basis of women's liberation, from this standpoint, is empowering women to exercise free choice. Controlling the activities of women is regarded as degrading to their status as free members of society. For example, this view considers that attempts by well-intentioned individuals to deter women from sex work "for their own good" only disempowers them (Chapkis, 1997; Schur, 1984; Walkowitz, 1982).

Criminalizing prostitution is seen as a form of interference that only perpetuates gender inequality. From this perspective, prostitutes are free agents who resist oppressive moral and social norms. Arguably, they also hold the dominant position and power to choose to whom they sell their bodies. It is the man paying for sex who occupies the subordinate position in the sex-for-money interaction. Male promiscuity is thus seen as a form of weakness to be exploited by a woman, whose service must be paid for and cannot be had for free. The sex worker's promiscuity, from this point of view, is neither good nor bad, but rather an expression of individual freedom to employ her body for financial gain. Each sexual encounter between consenting adults, whether money changes hands or not, should be understood on its own terms—as opposed to the manifestation of gender inequality or other social problems (Alexander, 1987; Beran, 2012; Phoenix, 2001).

In summary, feminist perspectives lead to different versions of the nature of the sex trade and different policy perspectives on regulating prostitution. The free choice first perspective favours legalizing sex work and reflects a Millsian point of view. It is also evident in the recent changes to Canada's official response to prostitution. Prostitution laws in Canada are changing in response to legal claims about the rights of workers and the role of government to ensure their health and safety, rather than enforcing moral norms.

BOX 16.1

Supreme Court Strikes Down Canada's Prostitution Laws

The sections of the *Criminal Code* that criminalize sex work were struck down by the Supreme Court of Canada in 2013 in *Bedford*. The ruling overturned provisions against keeping a common bawdy house (s. 210), living on the avails of prostitution (ss. 211 and 212), and communication for the purpose of prostitution (s. 213). These sections of the *Criminal Code* were ruled as violating the *Canadian Charter of Rights and Freedom*'s rights to freedom of expression and security of the person. In particular, the law was criticized for forcing prostitutes to work in dangerous circumstances:

The Supreme Court of Canada has struck down the country's major prostitution laws, saying that bans on street soliciting, brothels and people living off the avails of prostitution create severe dangers for vulnerable women and therefore violate Canadians' basic values.

Chief Justice Beverley McLachlin, writing for a unanimous court, stressed that the ruling is not about whether prostitution should be legal or not, but about whether Parliament's means of controlling it infringe the constitutional rights of prostitutes.

"Parliament has the power to regulate against nuisances, but not at the cost of the health, safety and lives of prostitutes," she wrote. "The prohibitions ... do not merely impose conditions on how prostitutes operate. They go a

critical step further, by imposing dangerous conditions on prostitution; they prevent people engaged in a risky—but legal—activity from taking steps to protect themselves from the risks."

[The Conservative government's Justice Minister Peter] MacKay suggested in a statement that the government will continue to look at prohibiting prostitution in some fashion. The government is "exploring all possible options to ensure the criminal law continues to address the significant harms that flow from prostitution to communities, those engaged in prostitution, and vulnerable persons," he said.

The court suggested Parliament has wide options for continuing to criminalize prostitution-related activities, even perhaps maintaining aspects of the existing laws. It said the prohibitions on street soliciting, brothels and living off the avails are all intertwined and have an impact on one another.

"Greater latitude in one measure—for example, permitting prostitutes to obtain the assistance of security personnel—might impact on the constitutionality of another measure—for example, forbidding the nuisances associated with keeping a bawdy-house. The regulation of prostitution is a complex and delicate matter. It will be for Parliament, should it choose to do so, to devise a new approach, reflecting different elements of the existing regime."

Source: Fine (2013). *Globe and Mail*, December 20, 2013. © Douglas Tripp. Reprinted by permission.

Illegal Drugs

The long history of substance use and the various efforts by the state to control it are probably best described as an ambivalent relationship in the sense that drugs are both sought after and condemned. Psychoactive drugs have been taken by people for millennia to alter consciousness or mental states, to cope with hardship, and to bring people closer to their gods. Since ancient times as well, cultural and religious taboos have existed against the use of certain drugs. Much like the ban on prostitution, the prohibition of psychoactive substances has typically been justified on the grounds that drug use is immoral and laws against it are necessary measures to protect the common good.

Whereas the use of drugs such as alcohol, tobacco and, more recently, cannabis are subject to control through regulation, the use of other drugs has been outlawed altogether. Our social history suggests that the legal status of a substance is connected more to the characteristics of the user and less to chemical properties or evidence of harm. In other words, it is apparent that morality is closely related to perceptions about the drugs that "bad" people use. The drugs used by bad people, social outcasts, or outsiders have often been outlawed as a method of controlling people or putting undesirable people "in their place."

The history of drug laws in Canada date back about a century, when smoking opium was banned (see Boyd, 1991; Giffen, Endicott, & Lambert, 1991). Soon after, cocaine and then cannabis were outlawed. In each instance, the outlawed drug was linked, as will be explored below, to certain ethnic groups and argued to cause insanity, indecency, and sexual promiscuity on the part of ethnic men who victimized white women. Outlandish and exaggerated claims—such as the claim that using cannabis causes heroin addiction, or using LSD causes genetic abnormalities—have been a fixture of many commentaries regarding Canadian drug laws ever since.

The last half-century has seen increasing efforts to incorporate medical and scientific knowledge into policy perspectives that determine the response to use of drugs. These efforts include classifying drug addiction, for example, as a "disease" for which the addict requires treatment rather than a jail term or other form of punishment. While this point of view appears increasingly accepted, and has expanded the jurisdiction of the medical profession, the punitive response to substance use is ever present.

People who use certain types of drugs are still considered by some to be morally deficient and deserving of punishment, in accordance with existing moral norms and legal codes. Evidence that rates of substance use are on the rise is considered proof of yet another "epidemic" to be met with calls for stricter laws, police activity, and measures to protect our kids from drugs.

In reality, the greatest harm from substance use is caused by alcohol, tobacco, and prescription medications—including OxyContin, tranquilizers, sleeping pills, and other addictive narcotics that have become a scourge in many Canadian communities—which are regulated to reduce their harm. By comparison, illegal drugs are used by a small fraction of the Canadian population. The only exception is cannabis, which partially explains the recent changes in the law.

Canada has among the highest rates of past-year use of cannabis (UNODC, 2017). The prevalence of past-year use in 2015 was 12 percent (or 3.6 million) of Canadians age 15 or older. The majority of past-year users had used it in the past three months (72 percent), and a third of this group (or 840,000) reported that they use it every day or almost daily (CTADS, 2015).

Despite the great disparity in prevalence of use, policy discussions of the "drug problem" are typically focused on the topic of illicit substance use. Accordingly, this section is devoted to examining social factors that explain why people use illicit drugs and why these drugs have been criminalized. We will conclude with a discussion of social policy positions on illicit substance use in relation to the classic debates on use of law in the enforcement of morality.

Social Learning and Subcultural Perspectives

Social learning and subcultural perspectives on the use of illicit drugs rely on the assumption that drug users learn the behaviour from peers and role models within their social group. The social learning model is supported by research evidence suggesting that the use of drugs is higher among youth whose parents, older siblings, and peers use drugs as well (Bahr, Hoffmann, & Yang, 2005). Social learning typically refers to early childhood (or primary) socialization. Subcultural perspectives prioritize learning processes (or secondary socialization) occurring later among youth.

The higher rates of drug use among disadvantaged groups is also understood as a result of learning processes that take place within a deviant subculture of peers. Frustration due to lack of opportunity among social groups with lower socio-economic status provides a structural explanation for the prevalence of crime involvement and illicit drug use among the lower classes. Another observation is that neighbourhoods with a higher prevalence of substance use are socially disorganized, resulting in the absence of parental and community controls that serve to prevent criminal behaviour.

Despite the compelling logic of the subcultural perspective and the support provided by official crime statistics, the association between social class and drug use is partly a reflection of policing practices. Illegal drug use is more visible in certain disadvantaged communities, which has led police to focus more on and gather more evidence of drug use in those communities. However, greater focus by police on certain communities rather than others does not necessarily reflect the actual prevalence of substance use behaviour.

It is increasingly observed that substance use is no less common among youth and young adults in the middle and upper classes (Aldridge, Measham, & Williams, 2011). This population of drug users, rather than reacting to social deprivation or frustration stemming from a lack of opportunity, considers that some experimentation with illicit drugs is "normal." Many users view drug use as a rational response to the demands of daily life. Their use is justified as being motivated by desire for relaxation, stimulation, altered consciousness, or merely socializing with one's peers.

Clearly, substance use can be harmful. Any drug can be abused. Substance use is rewarding and addictive for the user, and can result in adverse consequences for families, health, relationships, and careers; it can even result in death. On the other hand, drug laws do nothing to address these problems and, many would argue, only contribute to the harms of substance use.

Prohibition creates the very conditions that make using outlawed substances more dangerous than substance use itself. This conclusion was drawn indisputably nearly a century ago when alcohol was banned in the United States (from 1920 to 1933, a time known as "the prohibition era"). The result was an unregulated product of unknown potency and content—among other dangerous practices by drinkers and suppliers that included violent criminals who were willing to take risks to keep up with demand. The

prohibition
A law forbidding a specific act.

lessons learned were soon forgotten, or never thought to be applicable, to other out-lawed substances in North America and elsewhere.

In Canada, the notion that drug laws present a problem more serious than substance use emerged in the 1960s—an era marked by an increase in youth experimentation with illicit drugs. A new class of criminal had been created, to whom the anti-drug laws had not applied before. Before proceeding to discuss opposing policy positions arising from debates about the problems with these laws, we examine functional and critical perspectives on the ban on certain kinds of drugs.

Drug Law Functions

Like the laws that target prostitution, prohibitions against possessing psychoactive drugs support an underground economy involving persons willing to risk arrest and punishment to provide this service. In addition to the jobs created for those willing to break the law to reap black market profits, prohibitions create opportunities for legitimate employment in the criminal justice system and beyond.

A large segment of the law enforcement budget is devoted to enforcing prohibition laws. Charges for the possession and supply of outlawed drugs account for a significant proportion of public spending for police, corrections, prosecution, and rehabilitation (for those sentenced to mandatory treatment).

Other vested interests in the prohibition industry include those who deal in legal drugs such as alcohol, tobacco, prescription medications—and now cannabis. They include the corporations that directly profit from the sale of regulated drugs and a wide variety of peripheral parties—such as pharmacists, physicians, and the proprietors of bars, restaurants, and others in the hospitality industry.

Notwithstanding recent changes in the marijuana laws, there has been little indication of political commitment to more far-reaching Canadian drug policy reform. The system has distinguished "good" drugs from "bad" drugs, and those who deal in bad drugs go to jail. Despite declining rates of crime prior to 2015, federal spending on prisons nearly doubled between 2006 and 2012—from $1.6 billion to $2.98 billion (Davis, 2011). A decrease in federal expenditures more recently has been offset by increased provincial spending on corrections. In 2015–2016, federal spending on prisons was $2.4 billion, with one in five inmates serving sentences for drug-related offences (Reitano, 2017). Considering the investment, it is unlikely that the government is planning to reduce the pool of eligible inmates by legalizing other outlawed drugs.

A Critical Perspective

The origin of drug laws in Canada and elsewhere can be traced to class and racial conflict. Drug use by the powerful is seldom subject to the same scrutiny or legislative action as that by the non-powerful. Consider the social history of Canadian laws related to opium: In the *Opium Act, 1908*, the manufacture of opium for smoking (an activity engaged in mainly by Chinese immigrants) was banned, while its use in medications that were widely used by white Canadians at the time was not.

The same pattern of discriminatory legislation and enforcement was repeated with cocaine, then marijuana, and (decades later) synthetic drugs such as LSD and ecstasy. In all instances, the common theme over the last century has been the prohibition of a substance used (primarily) originally by persons perceived to be a threat to moral standards.

Long known simply as "cannabis," the Spanish term *marijuana* (or *marihuana*) became widely used by US legal authorities beginning in the 1920s and 1930s. By closely tying the term to the increasing Mexican immigrant populations in the US south who often used the drug, it became easier for lawmakers to target "outsiders" and implement bans on "the devil's weed." Hollywood films, whose content was closely regulated by the US government, played a major role in stigmatizing cannabis, as this 1940s movie poster attests.

The *Opium Act, 1908*, the first drug law in Canada, served to target Chinese immigrants who presumably preferred smoking opium to drinking alcohol. This preference per se was not a problem. However, it became a problem with the emerging tide of racist sentiment in Canada. When industrious immigrants became prosperous, their presence was resented and perceived as threatening to white Canadian values.

Canada's early narcotics laws reflected a complex blend of moral–racial and financial interests. Once this formula had been established, it became a simpler legislative matter to add foreign drugs to the growing schedule of banned substances. Cocaine and cannabis, like opium, were not widely used or even known to most Canadians. This mattered little. Enough was known by citizens exposed to anti-drug hysteria to understand that these drugs presented a grave threat.

It was believed that cocaine was being used by Black men to lure white women into sinful interracial unions. Once under the drug's intoxicating spell, the female addict was enslaved and helpless to resist. Like the imagery associated with opium smoking, that of cocaine use was wickedness, contagion, and the invasion of a foreign substance used by outsiders who were unwelcome guests.

The ban on cannabis in Canada in 1923 (through the *Opium and Drug Act*) played on much the same themes. No debate took place in Parliament to refute the wildly exaggerated claims of its use and effects. Moreover, it became clear, despite the ease with which the ban passed, that it served a function more symbolic than instrumental in responding to a manufactured threat. The first arrests and seizures of the drug did not occur for more than a decade after the law was passed. This delay suggests that no one in the country at the time the ban was instituted was using marijuana. Important questions come to mind about the function served by the introduction of "a law without a problem" (Giffen, Endicott, & Lambert, 1991). The symbolic function of the war on certain drugs is arguably to criminalize rather than protect those who use them. The main criteria for banning drugs are devised on the basis of the characteristics of their primary consumers, as opposed to evidence of harm.

Those perceived as threatening to the established social order are ordinarily the primary targets of the law. Since targeting social groups or persons is widely recognized as a discriminatory practice in constitutional democracies, the government's focus is on substances. Enforcement of the law against those who use banned substances is thus considered equally applicable to all. The groups targeted by default via the substances they use include cultural outsiders (especially non-whites), members of the lower classes, youth, and others who use drugs for reasons other than improving productivity—that is, reasons considered to threaten the moral order.

The disparity in sentencing for cocaine users based on class and racial characteristics is a prominent example of the symbolic function of the war on drugs. In the United States, for example, prison terms for crack cocaine users are disproportionately higher than those for powder cocaine users (Tonry, 1995).

The crack scare in America in 1986 resulted in the passing of the US *Anti-Drug Abuse Act*. The Act imposed a mandatory minimum sentence of five years' imprisonment for possessing 5 grams of crack cocaine. The same prison term was mandated for possessing 500 grams of cocaine powder at the time. Although the addictive properties of "rock," or crack cocaine, presumably would justify discrepancies in sentencing, it was widely recognized that the large disparity had more to do with where, and by whom, the drug was used. While the primary consumers of crack were known to be poor and Black, residing in inner-city slums, the primary consumers of powder cocaine were associated more with white, well-to-do professionals who used the drug to party. The disparity resulting from this legislation stood for a quarter-century. In 2010, the sentencing disparity between offences for crack and powder cocaine were reduced under the *Fair Sentencing Act* from 100:1 to 18:1 (Office of Research and Data, 2011).

The discrepancy in the regulatory measures used to control drugs based on race and class distinctions indicates that a hierarchy of social disapproval and punishment exists for those who use illicit drugs. This discrepancy also appears in the regulatory measures for controlling legal psychoactive drugs with properties or chemical effects similar to illegal drugs. The regulation applied to legal drugs does not guarantee no harm to users and society. But neither does the ban on outlawed drugs. Put otherwise:

> By far the most direct harms ... occur in high-risk populations such as injectors, street youth, the inner-city poor and Natives. ... **The indirect harms and costs of illicit drugs by far outweigh direct harms and are completely disproportionate to their level of use; these indirect harms and costs are the result of drug policy and legislation, not the drugs per se.** [Emphasis added.] (Riley, 1998, p. 2)

Alternatives to Criminalizing Drugs

In light of the indirect harms and questionable cost-effectiveness of drug laws, the alternatives of **legalization** and **decriminalization** have been seriously discussed among drug policy observers. The legalization option has parallels with regulated

legalization
The removal of an existing prohibition against something that is currently unlawful. In the case of drugs and prostitution, the term often implies a regulated system of supply or licensing of services provided.

decriminalization
The removal of criminal penalties, though fines may still apply.

substances such as alcohol, tobacco, and now cannabis, as well as prescription medications and over-the-counter drugs. While some restrictions—such as age, point of sale, and driving after using—may apply, these different regulatory models generally allow for legal use of a product licensed by the government for sale.

Cannabis has been legalized in Canada for those who qualify for access due to chronic health conditions since 2001. New legislation has responded to support for the creation of a regulated system for non-medical consumption. Such changes in the law, which now allows for wider access, are reforms long called for by well-qualified observers (see Senate Special Committee on Illegal Drugs, 2002). The prospect of legalizing other outlawed drugs remains highly controversial and unlikely in Canada (for the time being at least). Shifting boundaries of morally acceptable behaviour, allowing the sale of legalized drugs to adults for recreational consumption, are also evident in law reform in the United States. Starting in 2012 with Washington and Colorado, a number of marijuana legislation initiatives have been passed at the state level. By the end of 2018, eight more US states—Alaska, California, Maine, Massachusetts, Michigan, Nevada, Oregon, and Vermont—had adopted laws legalizing marijuana for recreational use. Yet despite the recent shift toward less punitive approaches to the use of cannabis in North America and elsewhere, the prospect of legalizing other outlawed drugs remains highly controversial and unlikely (for the time being at least).

Many policy observers who acknowledge the shortcomings of drug prohibition favour decriminalization. In the 1970s, this more moderate reform option was adopted in some states, such as New York and California, for cases of simple marijuana possession. Indeed, prior to legalization this model was already followed to a certain extent in Canadian jurisdictions where arrests for small amounts of marijuana resulted in fines instead of jail terms. The decriminalization of all drugs in Portugal in 2001 has been shown to have reduced drug-related harm and problem use (Hughes & Stevens, 2010). This pragmatic option is preferred by those who argue that decriminalizing drug possession will alleviate the harm to users of acquiring a permanent criminal record—while maintaining the deterrent impact of the law and the message that the state does not condone the use of drugs.

Among other policy options, this strategy is more oriented to the aims of public health. The harm-reduction model more explicitly endeavours to reduce the harm to people who use illicit drugs. The function of the state, from this perspective, is not to moralize or punish substance users.

In spite of stringent efforts to prevent it, there have always been (and will always be) people who use drugs. Recognizing this reality, the most pragmatic policy is to provide the services and information needed to help them use these substances more safely.

Examples of harm-reduction measures are numerous—from distributing free needles to injection drug users to using shatterproof glass in bars to prevent bloodshed. Despite the cost-effectiveness and logic of such measures, from a public health perspective on the use of state resources, the case of InSite in Vancouver is a prominent example of the controversy surrounding **harm reduction** (see Box 16.2).

harm reduction
A public health–oriented policy or program designed to reduce the harmful consequences of behaviours with known risks, which are often illegal, such as prostitution and recreational drug use.

Vancouver's InSite Drug Injection Clinic Will Stay Open: Top Court Rules on Clinic's Exemption from Federal Drug Laws

In 2011, the Supreme Court of Canada ruled that a Vancouver safe injection facility could remain open. In a unanimous decision, the court argued that its services improved the health and safety of drug addicts, thereby warranting an exemption from the federal drug laws.

Vancouver's controversial InSite clinic can stay open, the Supreme Court said ... in a landmark ruling.

In a unanimous decision, the court ruled that not allowing the clinic to operate under an exemption from drug laws would be a violation of the Charter of Rights and Freedoms.

The court ordered the federal minister of health to grant an immediate exemption to allow InSite to operate.

"InSite saves lives. Its benefits have been proven. There has been no discernible negative impact on the public safety and health objectives of Canada during its eight years of operation," the ruling said, written by Chief Justice Beverley McLachlin.

If InSite wasn't allowed to operate it would prevent injection drug users from accessing the health services offered at the facility, threatening their health and their lives, the ruling said. Withdrawing the exemption would even undermine the purpose of the federal drug law, which includes public health and safety, the court said.

The Supreme Court said that if the health minister, currently Leona Aglukkaq, receives applications for more exemptions, she must continue to exercise her discretion and aim to strike a balance between Charter rights and protecting public health and safety.

Where there is no evidence that a supervised injection site would have a negative impact on public safety, the minister "should generally grant an exemption," the court said.

The Conservative government is opposed to the InSite operation, and when it came to power it dropped harm reduction from the national anti-drug strategy. Aglukkaq said Friday the government's investments are targeted at prevention and treatment.

"Although we are disappointed with the Supreme Court of Canada's decision today, we will comply," Aglukkaq said in question period. "We believe that the system should be focused on preventing people from becoming drug addicts."

Aglukkaq said the government planned on reviewing the decision.

Conclusion

Notwithstanding opposition from the former federal government, initiatives like InSite lend support to trying other policy alternatives to criminalizing drugs. Increasing pressure on the government to initiate reform is arguably more consistent with the spirit of the Charter—which puts the onus on the state to justify intrusion into the affairs of individuals. Drug policy reforms need not be mutually exclusive. A multi-layered perspective on the function of the state recognizes the complexity of mitigating harm from a behaviour through criminal law. Decriminalizing the possession of small amounts of drugs, for example, need not preclude stepped-up enforcement of laws that target organized crime and large-scale trafficking. Similarly, "red light districts" that allow prostitution facilitate containment of the trade and redirect criminal justice resources to enforcing laws that target sexual slavery and prostituting children.

As noted in Box 16.1, in its unanimous decision, Canada's Supreme Court supports the role of government to "regulate against nuisances, but not at the cost of the health, safety and lives of prostitutes" (Fine, 2013). In so doing, it struck down the prohibition against earning a living on the avails of prostitution. To ensure the safety of sex workers, the Supreme Court recognized the role of drivers, managers, and bodyguards, whose services do not necessarily amount to exploitation. It was also ruled that the provision in the law prohibiting communication prevented prostitutes "from screening potential clients for intoxication and propensity to violence." The provision was accordingly deemed "grossly disproportionate ... to the possibility of nuisance caused by street prostitution" (*Bedford*, 2013). The Supreme Court's ruling makes it increasingly apparent that the spirit of the Charter's constitutional protections are functioning to shape interpretation of the law.

Similarly, our drug laws are presently in limbo, and continuously in flux. Whatever the perspective of the reader, it is hoped that this chapter has provided some direction to continue to develop your position on the appropriate role of the law in these and other social policy debates.

SUMMARY OF KEY POINTS

- Unlike consensus crimes (such as murder, rape, and assault), crimes of morality are subject to widespread disagreement and considerable debate.

- In democratic, multicultural societies such as Canada and other Western nations, the legislation of morality raises important questions about the proper role of government and whose morality or justice ought to be enforced.

- Section 1 of the Charter puts the onus on government to justify prohibiting an action. It also further establishes that the prohibition must be minimally intrusive, rational, and proportionate to the harm inflicted by the action.

- Historically, sex work has enabled a small segment of the female population to meet the sexual needs of men and provide a "safety valve" for men seeking sex. Earlier and contemporary feminist perspectives (for example, the equality first and free choice first perspectives) lead to different versions of the nature of the sex trade and different policy perspectives on regulating prostitution.

- The long history of substance use and the various efforts by the state to control it are probably best described as an ambivalent relationship in the sense that drugs are both sought after and condemned. Our social history suggests that the legal status of a substance is connected more to the characteristics of the user and less to chemical properties or evidence of harm. The origin of drug laws in Canada and elsewhere can be traced to class and racial conflict. Changing demographic profiles and depictions of the user—as white, middle-class, and otherwise conforming—are explanations for legalizing cannabis that go beyond descriptions of the prevalence of use. Drug use by the powerful is seldom subject to the same scrutiny or legislative action as that by the non-powerful. Decriminalization and harm-reduction measures, however cost-effective and logical, remain sources of controversy.

QUESTIONS FOR CRITICAL DISCUSSION

1. What is your perspective on the enforcement of morality? Do you agree with Mill, Hart, or Devlin? Do you have a different point of view?
2. Can you think of other crimes of morality that might be argued to represent examples of overcriminalization?

3. Do you think that prostitution should be legalized, decriminalized, or remain illegal? Which of the feminist perspectives on sex work makes sense to you?

4. Should illegal drugs be legalized, decriminalized, or neither? If you support changes in the law, does your perspective apply to all illegal drugs or only some—and why?

5. Can you think of other examples of harm reduction as applied to drugs or prostitution, or any other activities involving certain risks?

SUGGESTED FURTHER READINGS

Hathaway, A.D. (2015). *Drugs and society*. Don Mills, ON: Oxford University Press.

Richards, D.A.J. (1982). *Sex, drugs, death and the law: An essay on human rights and overcriminalization*. Totawa, NJ: Rowman & Littlefield.

Sanders, T., O'Neill, M., and Pitcher, J. (2018). *Prostitution: Sex work, policy and politics* (2nd ed.). Thousand Oaks, CA: Sage.

Websites

Drugs—Canadian Drug Policy Coalition: http://drugpolicy.ca

Drugs—EROWID: Documenting the Complex Relationship Between Humans and Psychoactives: http://www.erowid.org

Gambling—Alberta Gambling Research Institute (which researches various aspects of gambling): https://abgamblinginstitute.ca/library-resources

Prostitution—Sextrade Public Awareness and Education: http://www.sextrade101.com

Prostitution (The Canadian Encyclopedia, Historica Canada): http://www.thecanadianencyclopedia.com/en/article/prostitution

Legislation

Canadian Charter of Rights and Freedoms, Part I of the *Constitution Act, 1982*, being Schedule B to the *Canada Act 1982* (UK), 1982, c 11.

Criminal Code, RSC 1985, c C-46.

Protection of Communities and Exploited Persons Act, SC 2014, c 25.

Cases

Canada (AG) v Bedford, 2013 SCC 72.

Carter v Canada (AG), 2012 BCSC 886 (the Gloria Taylor "death with dignity" case).

CASE STUDY 17.1

Gang Life: Often Nasty, Brutish, and Short

How can we distinguish street gangs from other types of criminal organization?

On a November evening in 2013, Reshane Hayles-Wilson was carrying a loaded handgun to a basketball tournament at the North Kipling Community Centre in Toronto. When he was just outside the front doors of the centre, Mr. Hayles-Wilson drew his handgun and fired eight shots at Neeko Mitchell from very close range, causing Mr. Mitchell's death. The killing was captured on the centre's video surveillance cameras. Mr. Hayles-Wilson immediately fled from the scene of the crime with the help of a number of his associates, remaining at large for 10 months and successfully disposing of the murder weapon. In January 2014, a Canada-wide warrant was issued for his arrest, and he was ultimately found and taken into custody in late September of that year.

Justice Code of the Ontario Superior Court of Justice concluded that there was a plan to murder Mr. Mitchell, which was carried out by Mr. Hayles-Wilson. Because events unfolded very quickly outside the centre, Justice Code concluded that there was insufficient time for deliberation, and hence insufficient evidence to establish that this was first-degree murder, rather than second-degree murder. Mr. Hayles-Wilson was, accordingly, convicted of second-degree murder.

Justice Code said of the circumstances surrounding the homicide:

There was some kind of grievance between Mr. Hayles-Wilson and his associates, on the one hand, and the deceased Neeko Mitchell on the other hand. This grievance provided the motive for the murder. The exact nature of the grievance was not proved at this trial but there was evidence that a leader of a neighbourhood criminal gang known as "Monstarz," Jermaine Dunkley, was in close contact with Mr. Hayles-Wilson at the Centre that evening and was talking to him and to Kashana Duncan immediately prior to the shooting. In addition, Mr. Dunkley's gang was heavily involved in drug trafficking and Neeko Mitchell also appears to have been involved in drug trafficking to some extent. Mr. Hayles-Wilson admits that he was a drug trafficker. Finally, Mr. Dunkley's brother had been murdered a few months previously and both Mr. Dunkley and Mr. Hayles-Wilson were upset by this prior murder of a close friend and family member. Whether Neeko Mitchell had any connection to that prior murder, or was believed to be connected to the prior murder, is unclear on the evidence at this trial. As I stated, the exact nature of the motive was not proved at this trial but I am satisfied that some kind of grudge or grievance, related in some fashion to the above circumstances, explains why a plan was formed to murder Neeko Mitchell. That plan was then executed quickly by Mr. Hayles-Wilson. (*R v Hayles-Wilson*, 2018, para. 7)

371

Mr. Hayles-Wilson was sentenced for this crime in June 2018, after spending almost four years in custody while awaiting trial. In describing the aggravating characteristics of this case, Justice Code noted that the crime had been planned and that the accused was carrying a loaded and hidden handgun in a public place. Justice Code quoted approvingly from a 2005 decision of the Ontario Court of Appeal: "The use of handguns in public places cries out for lengthy increased periods of parole eligibility. Society must be protected from criminals armed with deadly handguns" (*R v Danvers*, 2005, para. 77). Justice Code also made reference to the fact that there had been 199 shootings in Toronto in the first six months of 2018.

Justice Code also cited four mitigating factors before sentencing Mr. Hayles-Wilson. First, he was only 23 years old at the time of his offence, and second, he had no criminal record. Third, he had the continued support of his family and engaged in a constructive program at the Toronto South Detention Centre while awaiting trial. And finally, fourth, he apologized to Neeko Mitchell's family and asked for forgiveness in his statement to the court at the end of the sentencing hearing.

After reviewing a range of cases, and imposing a sentence of life imprisonment, Justice Code concluded:

> The last case in this mid-range group of cases is *Stewart*. The murder took place in a crowded downtown square in Toronto, after the annual Caribana parade. The accused and the deceased were both gang members involved in drug dealing. There was some kind of "confrontation" between them, the accused pulled out a loaded handgun, and he shot the deceased who was unarmed. The 23-year-old accused habitually carried a loaded gun and was a "committed gangster" with a prior criminal record. The jury rejected his account of self-defence. The trial judge imposed a 16-year period of parole ineligibility. As in the previous three cases—*Danvers*, *Monney*, and *John*—Mr. Hayles-Wilson is a better situated offender than the accused in *Stewart*, but the offence in the present case is more serious because it was a targeted planned murder. (*R v Hayles-Wilson*, 2018, para. 29)

Justice Code continued:

> Based on the above analysis of the case law and applying the principle of parity set out in s. 718.2(b) of the *Criminal Code*, I am satisfied that 14 to 16 years of parole ineligibility is appropriate for this offence and this offender. Given that the mitigating and aggravating circumstances in this case, already set out above, are relatively equally balanced, I would situate the present case in the middle of the applicable range. Accordingly, a 15-year period of parole ineligibility is appropriate in this case. (para. 30)

Before Reading Chapter 17

- What effects do you think a crime such as this has on the surrounding community?
- What specific measures do you think could be taken by police, the community at large, or even the federal government to quell this kind of crime? Could the regulation of illegal drugs undermine the profits of these gangs and thereby reduce violence on the streets and elsewhere?

After reading Chapter 17, return to this case study. Which of the four levels of gangs, described in this chapter, might fit best with the crime that is described here?

CHAPTER 17 / SCOT WORTLEY AND ADAM ELLIS

Organized Crime and Gangs

LEARNING OUTCOMES

After reading this chapter, students will be able to:

- Identify various ways in which gangs and organized crime groups have been defined.
- Understand the reasons why it has been difficult to identify a uniform definition of gangs.
- Describe the four levels of gangs and provide examples of each.
- Identify six types of gang violence.
- Discuss the ways in which key criminological theories can be applied to examinations of organized crime and gang behaviour.
- Describe the impact of gang suppression strategies.
- Identify some promising prevention strategies, as well as those that have proven ineffective in reducing gang membership.

Introduction

In recent decades, Canadians have been bombarded with a variety of terms used to identify various forms of organized criminal activity. These terms have been used to capture such phenomena as the Mafia, outlaw motorcycle clubs, Chinese triads, youth gangs, girl gangs, **drug cartels**, hate groups, and even terrorist cells. Canadians have also been confronted with the idea that street gangs are an increasing threat to our society. Indeed, one study found that over 80 percent of Toronto residents feel that street gangs and gang-related violence are on the increase in Canada (Wortley & Tanner, 2007). The question is, how can the general public believe that street gangs are on the rise when no uniform definition of what constitutes a gang or organized crime group exists? (See Ball and Curry, 1995; Esbensen, Winfree, He, and Taylor, 2001; and Ezeonu, 2014.) As Finn-Aage Esbensen, Thomas Winfree, Ni He, and Terrance Taylor (2001) indicate, "there is little, if any, consensus as to what constitutes a gang and who is a gang member, let alone what gangs do either inside or outside of the law" (p. 106).

Thus, before we can even begin to understand the "gang" or "organized crime" issue, we must first address some fundamental questions: What constitutes "organized

drug cartel
A criminal organization, often highly organized and with many partnerships, involved primarily in the trafficking of illegal drugs.

crime"? What is a "gang"? How do gangs differ from other social groups? How can we identify gang members and gang-related crime? How can we distinguish street gangs from other types of criminal organization?

Defining Gangs and Organized Crime

Frederick Thrasher (1927/1963) was one of the first criminological researchers to provide a detailed "gang" definition. He argued that gangs were part of normal peer group activity for adolescents and involved behaviours that ranged from the conventional to the deviant. He proposed that gangs can be identified by six characteristics:

1. a spontaneous and unplanned origin;
2. intimate face-to-face relations;
3. a sense of organization, solidarity, and morale that is superior to that exhibited by the mob;
4. a tendency to move through space and meet a hostile element, which can precipitate cooperative, planned conflict, a morale-boosting activity in itself;
5. the creation of a shared *esprit de corps* and a common tradition or "heritage of memories"; and
6. a propensity for some geographic area or territory, which they will defend through force if necessary. (pp. 36–46)

It is interesting to note that the characteristics identified by Thrasher are neither intrinsically "good" nor "bad" and do not include acts of crime, violence, or delinquency. Thus, at least according to this scholar, we must differentiate between "law-abiding" and "criminal" gangs.

Since Thrasher's (1927/1963) groundbreaking work, the number of distinct gang definitions—within both academia and the criminal justice system—has soared, and these definitions often seem to mirror the needs of the academics or criminal justice organizations that propose them. For youth gangs alone, hundreds of definitions exist within the literature, including the following:

- "A gang is an organized group of three or more individuals, who rely on group intimidation, violence and criminal acts to gain power and recognition and/or control certain areas of unlawful activity" (Halifax Police Service; as cited in Hemmati, 2006, p. 25).
- "A criminal street gang is an ongoing group, club, organization or association of five or more persons formed for the purpose of committing a violent crime or drug offence, with members that have engaged, within the past five years, in a continuing series of violent crimes or drug law violations that affect interstate or foreign commerce" (US Code Title 18—Crimes and Criminal Procedure; as cited in Wheatley, 2008, p. 86).
- "A group must be involved in a pattern of criminal acts to be considered a youth gang. These groups are typically composed only of juveniles but may include young adults in their membership. Prison gangs, ideological gangs, hate groups and motorcycle gangs are not included. Likewise gangs whose membership is restricted to adults and do not have the characteristics of youth gangs are excluded" (Curry & Decker, 1998, p. 6).

In addition to those definitions for street and youth gangs, we can also list some common broader definitions of gangs and organized crime groups:

- "A criminal street gang is a group of people following a common code of conduct, having common beliefs and identifiers, existing in a semi-structured organization or **hierarchy**, and attempting to accomplish their goals through criminal activity" (Howell 1998, p. 1).
- "The gang is a spontaneous, semi-secret, interstitial, integrated but mutable social system whose members share common interests and that functions with relatively little regard for legality but regulates interaction among its members and features a leadership structure with processes of organizational maintenance and membership services and adaptive mechanisms for dealing with other significant social systems in its environment" (Ball & Curry, 1995, p. 240).
- "A group or gang that, in the past twelve months, has done reprehensible acts" (Gatti, Tremblay, Vitaro, & McDuff, 2005, p. 1180).

These definitions range from the simplistic to the theoretically complex. They also clearly illustrate that considerable disagreement exists in the literature about exactly what constitutes a gang (see Langston, 2003; Petersen, 2000; Short, 2009; and Wood & Alleyne, 2010).

Definitions in the Criminal Code

As stated in the *Criminal Code*, section 467.1(1), a "criminal organization" is a group, however organized, that

a) is composed of three or more persons in or outside Canada; and
b) has as one of its main purposes or main activities the facilitation or commission of one or more serious offences that, if committed, would likely result in the direct or indirect receipt of a material benefit, including a financial benefit, by the group or by any of the persons who constitute the group.

The *Criminal Code* definition does not include a group of persons that forms randomly for the immediate commission of a single offence, nor does it mention how long a group must exist before it can be considered a criminal organization (although it has typically applied to groups that have been in existence for at least one month). The *Criminal Code* also explicitly states that one of the main purposes of a criminal organization must be the commission of crime *for material benefit*. This definition could potentially exclude gangs that are involved in crime or violence for status, honour, or excitement. By contrast, the United Nations' definition of an organized criminal group (outlined in article 2 of the United Nations *Convention against Transnational Organized Crime and the Protocols Thereto*, 2004) refers to a group committing a serious crime "for the purpose of obtaining a financial or other benefit." The use of the term "other benefit" could be used to include gangs that are involved in crimes that do not have a material or financial motive.

The strength of the *Criminal Code* definition is that it is flexible enough to be applied to a variety of criminal groups. Although it was originally developed to deal with such traditional organized crime groups as the Italian Mafia and the Hells Angels motorcycle gang, it has since been used to target the activities of newer, less organized entities, such as street gangs. A similar situation has been documented in the United States where the **Racketeer**

hierarchy
Group structure built around easily identified leaders and followers; in gangs, the hierarchy often determines the roles, obligations, and rewards of members.

racketeering
Criminal activity commonly related to gangs that typically involves obtaining money through acts such as extortion, bribery, illegal gambling, and loan sharking.

Influenced and Corrupt Organization Act (RICO), originally enacted to dismantle the Mafia, has since been used to successfully prosecute the members of street gangs (see Carr, Slothower, & Parkinson, 2017; Wheatley, 2008). Today, the broadening of the legal definitions on gangs correlated with the merging of organized crime and gang legislation/laws has led to an increase in the policing, arrest, and detention of gang members and their associates (see Carr et al., 2017). A number of gang scholars highlight that these enhanced gang laws have led to the overpolicing and hyperincarceration of predominantly young, disadvantaged minority males. While gang injunctions are an American phenomenon, Canadian scholars have noted similar trends in the way law enforcement has used intelligence-led policing or "carding" to identify and target gangs and gang members. Moreover, scholars such as Ezeonu (2014) are concerned that similar trajectories toward gang injunctions/enhancements may also be a Canadian reality in the near future.

Classifying the Various Types of Organized Crime and Gangs

Several scholars have attempted to develop a classification system for different types of criminal organization. Robert Gordon's (2000) work in British Columbia, for example, distinguished between criminal business organizations, street gangs, and "wannabe" groups. Similarly, Mercer Sullivan (2005) developed a gang typology that differentiates between action-sets, cliques, and named gangs. Finally, Cheryl Maxson and Malcolm Klein (1995) identify five different types of gang: (1) the classical or traditional gang; (2) the neo-classical gang; (3) the compressed gang; (4) the collective group; and (5) the specialty group. All of these typologies reflect the specific focus of the individual researcher. However, at a basic level, all of these scholars classified gangs according to their size, permanence, level of organization, and level of involvement in criminal activity.

A Gang Classification System

The following represents one of the many possible ways of classifying gangs. It generally moves from the least to the most organized and stable criminal groups.

Level One Gangs

Level one gangs are characterized by fluid friendship groups, usually based on a common neighbourhood and/or cultural identity. Their criminal activity is periodic, opportunistic, unorganized, and unplanned. Gang members often engage in crime for immediate gratification (including fun and excitement) rather than long-term economic interests. Members make no attempt to specialize or control a particular type of illicit activity. They are rarely involved in serious violence. Level one gangs have no leadership or hierarchical organizational structure. These gangs generally do not have a formal gang name or related gang symbols. Gang membership is often temporary. These gangs often form and disband quickly and are similar to what Gordon (2000) termed "wannabe" groups, or what other scholars have called "delinquent youth groups." Few level one gangs remain in existence for more than a year.

Example: A nameless group of teenagers who hang out in a mall or on the street corner during summer vacation. These youth may engage in shoplifting, bullying, drug use, and other minor forms of criminality, but they never develop a permanent identity and disband once the school year begins.

Level Two Gangs

Level two gangs exist for a significant period of time (i.e., one year or longer). Their criminal activity is often planned and deliberate. Although gang members engage in a variety of criminal activities, they show little criminal specialization. These gangs may or may not have a name and may have group symbols, colours, or a unique language. Activities may or may not be based in a particular neighbourhood or territory. Level two gangs are often egalitarian and typically do not have a formal leadership structure. Individual gang members often engage in crime to further their own personal interests rather than the objectives of the group. Gang activity often involves violence. Disputes over honour or reputation are common.

Example: A group of delinquent youth who maintain ties beyond the summer vacation period. Gang members give themselves a name and begin to engage in more serious crimes, including the extortion and robbery of other neighbourhood youth. This type of gang may even begin to sell drugs on the street for more established criminal organizations.

Level Three Gangs

Level three gangs are characterized by a hierarchical organizational structure with easily identified leaders and followers. These gangs exist for a significant period of time (i.e., one year or longer). Gang-based criminal activities are almost always planned and deliberate. These gangs usually have a name and may have group symbols, colours, or a unique language. Level three gangs typically try to control a particular type of illicit activity (for example, drug trafficking) or all illicit activities within a defined geographical area. Gang activity often involves serious violence—including the use of firearms. Gang violence can occur for both economic reasons and to settle disputes over honour or respect. Gang members are often influenced by an informal or formal gang code. An enforced code of silence means that level three gang members rarely testify against other members. Witness intimidation is common.

Example: Gang sets—sometimes with names such as the Bloods or Crips—traffic in drugs and operate within specific public housing communities.

Level Four Gangs

Level four gangs have a long, stable history (i.e., they have been in existence for at least five years). These gangs have a sophisticated organizational structure with easily identified leaders and followers. Gang-based activities are almost always planned and deliberate. These gangs are commonly involved in both the illicit and the licit economy and often engage in international business transactions (often funding legal enterprises with the proceeds of crime). Individual gang members often have specialized skills or tasks. Level four gangs sometimes work with lower-level gangs in order to meet their economic goals. Level four gangs will use violence to protect their economic interests. However, lower-level gangs or gang members are often used to perform risky criminal acts as a means of protecting the gang leadership. Violence is used for strategic purposes and rarely involves issues of honour or respect.

Example: Level four gangs include such established criminal organizations as the Italian and Russian Mafia, Asian Triads, Jamaican posses, Mexican and South American drug cartels, and outlaw motorcycle gangs.

Members of the Hells Angels motorcycle club attend a funeral for one of their own. They and other outlaw biker gangs have often been the source of the sort of "moral panics" described in Chapter 2, The Media: Shaping Our Understanding of Crime.

Having a distinct gang definition or gang classification system does not, of course, eliminate the problem of gang member identification or questions about how to best identify gang-related crime. For example, how does one distinguish real gang members from other civilians who reside in high-risk, gang-dominated neighbourhoods? A possible solution would be to define a gang member as "any individual who admits gang membership or who is identified as a gang member through expert investigation." However, the specific criteria for "expert" identification still needs to be established.

Criminality as a Gang Criterion

criminality
The state of being criminal; criminal acts or practices.

A significant debate that has emerged within the gang literature is whether **criminality** should be considered a necessary criterion for gang membership. Thrasher (1927/1963), the godfather of gang research, did not include criminality in his gang definition and subsequently argued that we must distinguish between criminal and non-criminal gangs. This stance has also been put forward by a number of contemporary scholars (see Bennett & Holloway, 2004; Ezeonu, 2014). Others, however, maintain that the absence of criminality makes the definition of a gang too broad. Indeed, without the criminality criterion, the study of gangs, in practice, would become the study of all organized group behaviour—including sports teams, church groups, and youth clubs. Overall, Wood, and Alleyne (2010) captured the sentiments of most gang scholars and criminal justice officials when they stated the following:

> The argument that criminality should be a measure criterion for defining a gang is compelling. One of the defining features of an entity is who is interested in it. Those interested in gangs include the police, criminologists, task force agents and more recently forensic psychologists. Thus, it is the criminal activity of gangs that triggers the interest of these parties. As such it makes sense that criminal behaviour should be included as a necessary criterion for defining a gang. (p. 102)

Meanwhile, a growing number of academics have argued that it would be more productive for both scholars and criminal justice officials to focus on all forms of individual and collective violence, and not focus on "gangs" at all (see Sullivan, 2005, 2006).

Yet another perspective holds that violent crime—not crime itself—distinguishes street gangs from other social groups. Should violence be a gang criterion? Or should we consider all groups that engage in a regular pattern of criminal activity? For example, college fraternities often meet the standard of most gang definitions:

1. They involve three or more members.
2. They usually have a name, group symbols, and initiation rituals.
3. They have a clear organizational structure.
4. Research suggests that fraternities are often involved in various criminal activities including illegal drug use, drug trafficking, under-age drinking, illegal alcohol sales, and illegal gambling (see Hickson & Roebuck, 2009; McCabe et al., 2005; Sanday, 1990; Shaefer, 2004).

However, fraternities may have been able to escape the gang label because they rarely engage in serious violence (with the possible exception of some extreme examples of hazing) and typically do not have a "street orientation." The same might be said of corporate crime groups. For example, groups of executives who conspire to defraud investors are almost never identified as criminal gangs—even though they often meet the numerical and organizational criteria of most gang definitions. They also engage in serious economic crimes that often have profound consequences for both individual victims and national economies. When defining gangs, therefore, we must be clear about what types of crime to include as gang criteria and provide a clear justification for why some types of criminality are excluded. This is particularly important when developing gang-based sentencing enhancements.

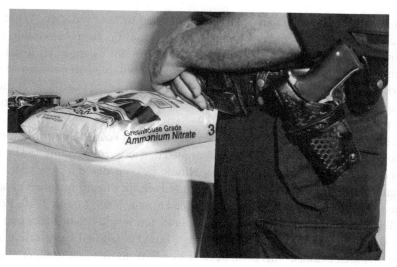

Police display a bag of ammonium nitrate, evidence in the case against the Toronto 18, who had been accused of plotting bomb attacks in Toronto and Ottawa in 2006. Several of the politically motivated young Muslim men pleaded guilty to participating in a terrorist group. Although a very rare phenomenon, the existence of such groups within Canada, the United Kingdom, and other Western nations in the years after the September 11, 2001 attacks and the wars that followed adds yet another variation to the many definitions of what constitutes a "gang" or "organized crime."

Identifying Gang Members and Gang-Related Crime

Among criminologists and criminal justice authorities, no standard methodology exists for identifying gang members or gang-related crime. For example, Fudge (2014) found very little consensus with respect to how social scientists, law enforcement, and legislative authorities come to define gangs. Barrows and Huff's (2009) study of American gang member databases, for example, found that only 15 states have a formal gang member definition, many of them quite vague. For example, Wisconsin simply defines a gang member as an individual who participates in criminal gang activity (p. 685). Barrows and Huff argue that such definitions are fundamentally inadequate and could lead to a significant problem with gang member over-identification.

Following the lead of local police services, the Canadian Centre for Justice Statistics (2008) attempted to develop a national strategy for identifying gang members. According to the Uniform Crime Reporting Survey (UCR), the following conditions confirm street gang membership. First and foremost, a person must be "directly or indirectly" involved in a gang crime. In addition, the person must meet at least two of the following five criteria:

1. Display gang identification marks, engage in initiation rituals or possess gang paraphernalia (for example, tattoos, weapons, etc.).
2. Be identified as a gang associate by a reliable source (i.e., inside gang member or rival gang member, community resource, school authority, member of the business community, citizen, etc.).
3. Be identified as a gang associate by a police surveillance report.
4. Self-report gang membership.
5. Be identified as a gang member by a judicial finding (Canadian Centre of Justice Statistics, 2008, pp. 143–144).

Most of the listed criteria are imprecise and open to manipulation. What, for example, constitutes "gang paraphernalia" and information from "a reliable source"? According to the Canadian Centre for Justice Statistics, for example, almost anyone—including average citizens, business owners, and criminals—can confirm to a police service that someone associates with a gang. Without knowing exactly what these concepts mean and how they are measured, it is impossible to determine how gang members are to be identified.

Law enforcement officials have found it equally difficult to come up with a common definition for "gang-related crime." Some have argued that any crime committed by a known gang member—or former gang member—should be considered a gang crime. Others have argued that gang crimes must be committed within the group context and clearly promote the goals or interests of the gang (see Howell, 1999; Mares, 2010; Rosenfeld, Bray, & Egley, 1999; Weerman et al., 2009). Overall, few would debate that a gun battle or drive-by shooting between two competing gangs should be labelled a gang crime. But what if a gang member, acting on his own, decides to sell drugs or rob a stranger at gunpoint for his own personal gain? Similarly, what if a known gang member, acting on his own, assaults or kills a relative during a family dispute? Should these incidents also be classified as gang-related? Clearly, how gang-related crimes are defined and measured will dramatically influence the amount of gang-related crime recorded within specific jurisdictions.

BOX 17.1

Gang Membership, Criminal Offending, and Victimization: A Canadian Example

The Toronto Youth Crime and Victimization Survey illustrates the strong relationship between gang membership and both criminal offending and criminal victimization. This survey, conducted in 2000, involves a random sample of 3,394 high school students from the Toronto region. All respondents were asked if they had ever been a member of a gang. Those who responded in the affirmative were classified as the members of either social gangs (those who did not engage in crime with fellow gang members) or criminal gangs (those who engaged in criminal activity within the gang context). The survey further distinguished between current and former gang members. Overall, 88.8 percent of the sample indicated that they had never been a member of a gang, 2.0 percent are former social gang members, 1.5 percent are current social gang members, 3.4 percent are former criminal gang members, and 4.3 percent identified themselves as current criminal gang members (Tanner & Wortley, 2002, p. 143).

No matter the type of criminal activity—from marijuana use to aggravated assault—current criminal gang members reported much higher rates of criminal involvement than all other groups (see Table 17.1). For example, Craig, Vitaro, Gagnon, and Trembly (2002) note that "compared to youth who do not become gang members, those who become involved in gangs generally engage in more delinquent behaviour, with the highest involvement in fighting, stealing, vandalism, and drug use" (cited in Hemmati, 2006, p. 14). The potential seriousness of gang involvement is demonstrated by the fact that almost 70 percent of current criminal gang members report that they carried a knife or gun with them during the past year. The need to carry and use weapons within the gang context is highlighted by Linden (2010), who reports that the increase in gang-related homicides in Canada may be directly related to an increase in the number of gangs across the nation.

TABLE 17.1 Percentage of Toronto High School Students Who Have Engaged in Various Criminal Activities in the Past 12 Months, by Type of Gang Affiliation

Type of criminal behaviour	Never in a gang	Former social gang member	Current social gang member	Former criminal gang member	Current criminal gang member
Theft from motor vehicles	2.8	4.5	5.8	13.8	45.5
Motor vehicle theft	0.9	6.0	1.9	11.2	37.3
Broke into a home or business	2.0	7.5	2.0	13.8	35.2
Sold drugs 10 or more times	2.1	0.0	0.0	21.6	51.4
Vandalism	18.0	28.4	28.8	44.8	62.0
Minor theft (less than $50)	17.8	15.9	25.0	40.5	69.5
Major theft ($50 or more)	6.6	11.9	5.8	31.0	60.0
Carried a gun or knife	11.2	20.9	11.8	48.2	68.3
Extortion/robbery	5.6	4.5	5.9	21.1	43.0
Aggravated assault	7.4	6.0	5.9	45.6	57.7
Physical fight	26.5	32.8	27.5	58.8	90.8
Gang (group) fight	12.7	19.7	23.5	47.4	79.6
Sexual assault	0.3	3.0	0.0	3.5	11.3
Used marijuana	26.3	31.8	19.6	65.5	84.6
Used cocaine/crack	1.6	4.5	2.0	11.2	17.5
Used other illicit drugs	5.3	7.6	2.0	26.7	25.2

Source: Tanner and Wortley (2002).

For example, St. Louis typically records a much higher rate of gang homicide than Chicago. However, the St. Louis Police Department considers any murder that involves a known gang member (as either a victim or an offender) to be gang-related. By contrast, the Chicago police only classify a murder as a gang homicide if clear evidence shows that the incident "grew out of a street gang function" (Mares, 2010, p. 44).

Characteristics of Youth Gangs

An adequate definition of a gang must not only identify core (essential, universal) elements of the gang, but also distinguish it from other social groups that young people might involve themselves in. The various characteristics used to describe and define youth gangs have included the following:

1. age restrictions (the age criteria for inclusion in a "youth gang" ranges from eight to thirty years, depending on the study and/or organization);
2. a group name or identity;
3. the wearing of colours, distinctive group symbols, or defining insignia (for example, tattoos);
4. the control of or claim to a specific neighbourhood, territory, or turf;
5. evidence of group organization, including a hierarchical structure (i.e., leaders and followers);
6. number of members (most definitions require at least three members);
7. durability or stability (must exist as a social entity for a specified period of time);
8. a gang code (a set of rules or regulations that must be followed by gang members);
9. initiation rituals for new gang members;
10. street orientation (gang activities are conducted away from the home, work, or school);
11. regular and/or continuous group involvement in crime, violence, or delinquency; and
12. common ethnic or racial background.

However, disagreement exists on the relative importance of these and other factors. American studies strongly suggest that how youth gangs are defined will have a major practical impact on how many gangs are identified in a particular community (Bjerregaard, 2002; Ezeonu, 2014; Kennedy, 2009; Spergel, 2009). For example, if gangs must have a name, display specific colours, engage in criminal activity, and so on, then fewer of them are going to be found than if one concludes that all groups of young people that hang out together are involved in gang activity. In other words, the larger the number of criteria that have to be met, the smaller the gang count is going to be.

The research literature clearly demonstrates that when it comes to violent offending, gang membership matters: Gang membership increases violent behaviour, even among those individuals who demonstrate violent traits prior to their gang involvement (see Delaney, 2014). Gang members are also much more likely to become the victim of serious violence—including homicide—than youth who are not involved in gangs. As Linden (2010) reports, gangs "are characterized by a high propensity for violence. ... Street gangs are responsible for many of the gang-related homicides in Canada" (p. 5). **Longitudinal studies** suggest that rates of violent victimization rise significantly during

longitudinal studies
Research that involves long-term observation of specific variables, often across decades (for example, cohort studies).

periods of gang membership and decline once gang involvement ends (see Decker & Curry, 2002; Melde, Taylor, & Esbensen, 2009; Spano, Freilich, & Bolland, 2008). This finding is particularly interesting since many youth report that they join gangs for protection (Wortley & Tanner, 2008).

Typologies of Gang Violence
Recent Trends

On December 26, 2005, Jane Creba, a 15-year-old student out exploring Boxing Day sales with her mother, was shot to death in the middle of Toronto's busiest shopping district. Six other innocent bystanders were wounded. Creba and the other victims had apparently been caught in the crossfire of a shootout between two rival youth gangs. In June 2012, a young man opened fire in one of Toronto's busiest shopping malls. The shooting was allegedly retribution against fellow gang members for their part in his kidnapping and attempt on his life. In July 2012, Toronto experienced its worst-ever mass shooting when gang-related violence erupted at an afternoon picnic on Danzig Street in Scarborough, leaving two dead and dozens wounded. Later, in July 2018, two girls, aged 5 and 9, were shot in a playground in what police identified as a gang-related shooting. One month later, a popular Toronto rap artist was gunned down in broad daylight at a busy intersection in the city. However, these were not isolated incidents. Over the past decade, gang violence has claimed the lives of many other young people in Canada, and a number of disturbing trends have emerged. Although rates of violent crime have dropped over the past two decades, violent crime has become much more concentrated among Canada's youth population (12 to 24 years of age). Violent offending and victimization has also become more concentrated among young male minorities who reside in Canada's poorest communities. Research also suggests that firearms are becoming more and more prevalent in violent incidents involving young people (Hayden, 2004) and that an increasing proportion of violent events are taking place in public rather than private settings (see Gartner & Thompson, 2004; Wortley, 2008). These trends are consistent with the rise in gang activity reported by police services across Canada (see Chettleburgh, 2007). Many of these homicides of young minority men—which often go unsolved—have been directly attributed to gang activity (David, 2017). Speaking on the increase in gang-related crime, Public Safety Canada (2018) notes that

> in 2016 alone, police reported 141 gang-related homicides, 45 more than in 2015. The largest increases in the number of gang-related homicides committed with a firearm were reported in Ontario (+22) and British Columbia (+12), with the majority of these occurring in Toronto and Vancouver. Since 2013, firearms murders in Canada's largest cities have almost doubled from 134 to 223.

In most Canadian cities, gang-related homicides typically account for one-quarter to one-third of the annual total (Boyce & Cotter, 2013, p. 35). In 2005—still infamously referred to in Toronto as "the Year of the Gun"—it was estimated that over 50 percent of all Toronto-area homicides were gang-related. Comparatively, in a 2018 news article, Mayor of Toronto John Tory reported that 75 percent of the city's gun crimes were attributed to gang-related violence (The Canadian Press, 2018, p. 1). Thus, understanding the reasons behind gang-related violence and other criminal activity has become an extremely important issue for both law enforcement officials and policy-makers.

Police speak to a young woman in the aftermath of a gang-related mass shooting at a neighbourhood street party on Danzig Street in Scarborough in July 2012. Two people died and many more were wounded in the crossfire.

The Toronto Street Gang Pilot Project

The Toronto Street Gang Pilot Project took place in November 2004.[1] It involved detailed qualitative interviews with a large sample of "known gang members" from a variety of backgrounds and neighbourhoods. The term "known gang member" was used to describe individuals who were identified as gang members by police officers, social workers, probation officers, and youth counsellors. The research team completed 209 face-to-face interviews. The vast majority of gang respondents were male (83.3 percent). Almost all came from disruptive family backgrounds: 63.1 percent were raised in a single-parent household, and 13.8 percent grew up within the child-protection system. The majority of respondents were born in Canada (76.1 percent)—a finding that challenges the myth of the alleged link between immigration and gang activity. Nonetheless, the sample was racially diverse: 43.1 percent of respondents self-identified as Black, 24.8 percent as white, 12.4 percent as Hispanic, 4.3 percent as Aboriginal, 2.9 percent as Asian, 2.4 percent as of South Asian descent, and 10.0 percent as a mixed-race identity. Interestingly, minority respondents were more likely to be born in Canada (79.6 percent) than white respondents (65.4 percent). A large number of white respondents were immigrants from Eastern Europe. Finally, consistent with previous research, most respondents grew up under circumstances of poverty and social disadvantage (Wortley & Tanner, 2007).

The typical respondent belonged to a gang or "crew" with between 10 and 30 members, and virtually every respondent (98.1 percent) indicated they had been involved in some form of gang violence at some point in their life. That violence generally took one of six forms: (1) economically motivated crime; (2) disputes over territory or turf; (3) involvement in the illicit economy; (4) retaliation for attacks on fellow gang members; (5) conflicts over reputation or honour; and (6) witness intimidation.

1. Economically Motivated Crime

extortion
The crime of demanding money from someone using force or threats.

Many respondents indicated that they engaged in economically motivated crimes, including robbery and **extortion**. This finding is consistent with previous research, which suggests that many youth join gangs for the assumed economic benefits. These crimes may take the form of opportunistic robberies or muggings (Wortley & Tanner, 2008):

> Sometimes we would just be hangin' out, see some kid with something we wanted and we would jump them, give them a couple of shots, threaten the shit out of them and take what we wanted. Like an iPod or some kicks (sneakers). When we did that we usually take their cash too … and tell them that we would fuck them up more if they call the cops. That type of s**t we did all the time. Just take what we wanted. (Case number 126, Black male, 17 years old)

In other cases, the gang youth planned more complex robberies—usually against rival gang members or individuals within their community who were involved in illegal gun sales or drug trafficking. Gang youth often refer to these types of crimes as "missions":

> We would just go on missions against other, weaker crews. We would find out where they were at and rob them. Sometimes I would play that I wanted to get with one of them so that I could find out what they had. It was easy 'cause those guys like to show off. (Case number 18, white female, 22 years old)

2. Disputes over Territory or Turf

The gang literature often makes direct reference to the issue of gang violence based on territorial disputes. Some contemporary gang activity is linked to the symbolic control of, or emotional attachment to, a particular neighbourhood—often a specific housing project, school, or block. At other times, however, turf disputes were less about neighbourhood control than market control. Having control of the drug trade within a specific area makes good business sense. The buying and selling of drugs is a very lucrative business but also a very dangerous one:

> Oh yeah we would defend our territory. Yeah, to the fullest. Say somebody was messin' around with my friends, we go there and defend it, you know. Stuff like that. Or, like, if someone came and stole out of our pockets we'd go and retaliate, y'know, defend it. Basically, territory fights too, that happens a lot. So like them wanting to sell drugs where you sell drugs? Yeah. So like, we'd have some out-of-towners, or outsiders we like to call them, come in and try to sell drugs to our people that we sell drugs to already. We didn't like that much, so we'd get into a lot of fights because of that, y'know. (Case number 34, Hispanic male, 23 years old)

3. Involvement in the Illicit Economy

Almost 90 percent of respondents were or had been involved in the illicit drug trade. Many claimed that in order to survive in the drug trade, they had to be ready and willing to use violence. Many respondents stated that they were often the target of predatory criminals, including rival gangs, because (1) they often had large quantities of both cash and drugs in their possession, and (2) the illegal nature of their activities made it impossible for them to rely on the police for protection:

> Like sometimes you had to beat people cause they owed you money man. Like you had spotted them some drugs and they promised to pay you later. Then they like conveniently forget. They say like, "What are you talkin' about? I don't owe you f**kin' anything." Well guys like that you gotta beat their ass and beat them good. Leave some marks, you know what I'm sayin'? If you don't, well, people know you're soft and they'll just keep ripping you off. (Case number 77, white male, 20 years old)

4. Retaliation for Attacks on Fellow Gang Members

From the interviews, it was clear that a great deal of gang violence is retaliatory—typically against other gangs or crews. Retaliation seems to result when either a robbery has taken place or when a member of the gang has been attacked by another crew.

As with failed business transactions, respondents often feel that you need to retaliate in order to prevent future victimizations:

> This guy from our crew named Sticks got the s**t kicked out of him by these bouncers at a club. So he just called us and we came with bats. We just waited to the club was closing and then we jumped them and knocked them out. We broke some ribs and s**t. Nobody does that s**t to one of us and gets away with it. Everybody at the club saw what we did to those guys. We sent all of them a message. Don't f**k with us. Don't show no disrespect. (Case number 122, Asian male, 20 years old)

5. Conflicts over Reputation or Honour

Although some "beefs" (a term used by our respondents to denote individual or group conflict) were motivated by entrepreneurial ambitions and revenge, most were not. Indeed, many violent incidents occurred because a cardinal rule of street life—the need for respect—had been broken. Even relatively minor insults were likely to be met with violence, including the use of weapons:

> On the streets it about reputation, man. You gotta be tough and not take shit from anybody, no matter how big they is or how tough they seem. If somebody dis you, you gotta fight them and show them you don't take that s**t. If somebody insult your gang you gotta represent. You can't let anybody punk your crew. If I find out somebody in my crew let our name be disrespected, if I find out that they like did nothin' about it, man I'll beat their ass myself. (Case number 88, Black male, 19 years old)

As with business-related violence, several respondents believed that standing up for your honour, and establishing a reputation for using violence, could actually prevent future victimization.

6. Witness Intimidation

Another form of instrumental gang violence involved the intimidation of potential witnesses. Gang members routinely engage in criminal activities that take place in public spaces—including drug trafficking, robbery, and extortion. Community members are often very aware of the gangs in their neighbourhood and the criminal activities they engage in. Gang members often try to create a culture of fear within their community and will use violence against witnesses or former gang members to minimize the risk of them cooperating with the police:

> At school we had to beat this kid who did not come up with the money he owed us. This new kid who transferred from another school saw us do it and told the principal who called the cops. Two of us got arrested. The rest of us waited a while then followed that little snitch home from school one day and beat him till he lost some teeth. We told him that the cops may get one or two of us at one time but never all of us at one time. We told him that the ones on the street always deal with snitches. He won't never snitch again. He also was like an example to other kids 'bout how we deal with snitches. Got to make people afraid so you can go on with your business. (Case number 110, Aboriginal male, 19 years old)

Although the typology of gang violence described above was developed using interviews with street gang members, it could easily be applied to more sophisticated criminal organizations. For example, it is common knowledge that the Italian Mafia, outlaw motorcycle groups, and South American drug cartels all use violence to develop a reputation for ruthlessness, control illicit markets, settle business disputes, and intimidate or eliminate witnesses.

Causes of Gang Crime and Violence

As the interviews above indicate, gang violence can reflect either utilitarian economic motives or more expressive, subcultural values. However, theories explaining the deeper roots of gang formation and gang violence are as varied as the field of criminology. They range from micro-level explanations that focus on individual psychology (Delaney, 2014; Ellis, 2017; Kerig, Wainryb, Twali, & Chaplo, 2013) to macro-level theories that focus on the impact of historical oppression and contemporary structural inequalities (Klein & Maxson, 2006; Wood & Alleyne, 2010). Several of the most relevant theories, as seen in the theory chapters of this book, can be applied to gangs and organized crime.

> Chapters on theories appear in Part Two, Theories of Crime.

Social Disorganization and the Cultural Transmission of Gang Values

One of the earliest—and most influential—explanations for gang behaviour is provided by social disorganization theory (Thrasher, 1927/1963). Social disorganization theory links crime rates and gang activity to neighbourhood characteristics. Gangs and gang violence, it is argued, are most likely to emerge in highly disadvantaged communities that are unable to provide essential services, such as quality education, health care, and housing. Such communities are usually marked by poverty, high levels of unemployment, low family incomes, a high proportion of the population on social welfare, a high number of single-parent families, and a high concentration of public housing units. Within such communities, traditional sources of social control (the family, church, school, social service agencies, etc.) are weak. This, in turn, damages community unity, increases fear, and hinders attempts to solve community problems. It is under these circumstances—when conventional controls are weak and the needs of local youth are unfulfilled—that gangs are most likely to emerge (Thrasher, 1927/1963).

Shaw and McKay (1942) further developed Thrasher's ideas by arguing that when conventional institutions have little functional authority, youth are likely to succumb to deviant norms and values and will sometimes form gangs to meet their needs for excitement, social support, material goods, and social status. A key component of Shaw and McKay's analysis is that criminal traditions can be *culturally transmitted*, and once firmly established within disorganized communities, pro-gang values can be passed down from generation to generation via normal socialization processes. The idea that criminal behaviour—including gang involvement—is learned through one's social environment has also been proposed by differential association theory (Sutherland & Cressey, 1974), social learning theory (Akers, 1997), and subcultural theory (Anderson, 1999). All of these theories propose that exposure to gang members and pro-gang values greatly increases the likelihood that youth will become gang-involved themselves.

Both social disorganization theory and social learning theory have greatly influenced subsequent gang research (see Lane & Meeker, 2004; Papachristos & Kirk, 2006;

Spergel, 1995). These perspectives are supported by contemporary research results that suggest the following:

1. gangs and serious gang violence are more likely to emerge in economically disadvantaged communities than in middle-class or upper-class neighbourhoods;
2. youth from poor, single-parent families are at the highest risk of gang involvement;
3. peer delinquency and peer pressure are strong predictors of both gang membership and gang violence;
4. youth are often introduced to gangs by close friends or family members;
5. new gang members are commonly socialized into gang culture by peers who teach them the rules and requisite skills of gang life; and
6. compared with non-gang youth, gang members tend to share a belief system that condones violence as a means of dealing with interpersonal conflict (see Brownfield, 2006; Hagedorn, 2008; Mares, 2010).

Critics argue that social disorganization theory does not adequately explain why most poor youth fail to become involved in gangs and why some middle-class youth become active gang members. Such anomalies, however, can be explained by the social learning perspective (i.e., some poor youth are exposed to positive role models while some middle-class youth are exposed to deviant peers).

Strain Theory

The central argument of early strain theory is that society sets specific cultural goals—including wealth and status—that are widely accepted by the general population. However, not everyone in society has equal access to legitimate means of attaining these goals. This situation produces anomie or status frustration. Some scholars argue that gangs are formed among young people—especially the poor and disenfranchised—because they do not have access to legitimate means of attaining culturally prescribed goals. Deprived of legitimate economic opportunities, the gang is an "adaption" or "innovation" that provides members with an "illegitimate" strategy for attaining their economic objectives (Merton, 1938).

Subsequent strain theorists (Cohen, 1955) have argued that status frustration sometimes causes lower-class youth to completely reject mainstream norms and establish their own subcultural goals and beliefs. These new goals are attainable for youth from lower-class backgrounds and thus provide an alternative avenue for status achievement. Within this new subculture, gangs often put an emphasis on toughness, courage, criminality, and instant gratification.

The strain perspective is supported by research suggesting that many youth initially join gangs because of the perceived economic benefits (Klein & Maxson, 2006; Wortley & Tanner, 2008). Research further suggests that some gang members believe that they would not be able to make the same amount of money in the legitimate economy because of problems with the education system and bias in the employment sector (Kemp-North, 2007). Gang members often perceive mainstream institutions, particularly the criminal justice system, as unjust, and engage in crime and violence as acts of defiance (Brownfield, 2006; Wortley & Tanner, 2008).

Impulsivity, Empathy, and Self-Control

Social disorganization, cultural transmission, social learning, and strain theories all argue that gang involvement facilitates or enhances criminal activity and violence. By contrast, control theorists maintain that gangs do not cause violence. Rather, violent individuals are drawn to or selected into gangs because of their violent propensities and their lack of alternative friendship choices. In other words, violent individuals create gangs—gangs do not create violent individuals.

Michael Gottfredson and Travis Hirschi's (1990) general theory of crime is arguably the most influential theory within this theoretical camp. These authors maintain that the cause of all criminality—including gang-related violence—is low self-control. Low self-control, they argue, is caused by poor parenting and neglect during the first five years of life. Individuals who do not develop self-control by late childhood will never develop it. Gottfredson and Hirschi argue further that people with low self-control

1. are impulsive and desire immediate gratification,
2. have little empathy for others, and
3. cannot anticipate the long-term consequences of their actions.

Crime is attractive to people with low self-control because it is relatively easy and provides immediate gratification. As Gottfredson and Hirschi (1990) state: "Crime provides money without work, sex without courtship and revenge without court delays" (p. 46).

Alternative Explanations

There is a growing body of research that highlights the relationship between trauma, post-traumatic stress, and gang violence (see Ellis, 2017; Kerig et al., 2013). While most of the theoretical scholarship on gangs has focused on the broader macro socio-economic forces that elicit membership and subsequent violence (i.e., strain, social disorganization, social bond, etc.), other scholars are now recognizing a strong relationship between the root causes of violence (for example, systemic racism, poverty, marginalization, lack of access to education, masculinity/honour, etc.) and long-term psychological distress. Scholarship in this area suggests that children, youth, and adults living in gang-dominant areas may experience similar levels and types of violence to those found in global conflicts, and, because of this, gang-involved youth may develop negative internal coping strategies that affect their biopsychological functioning and subsequent development across the life-course (Denny & Brownell, 2010). As a result, researchers suggest that exposure to interpersonal/community violence may lead to post-traumatic reactions that are subsequently conducive to further risk-taking behaviours, aggression, and violence ("hurt people hurt people"). Within this model, scholars argue that current suppression efforts by law enforcement may in fact cause more trauma and, as a result, contribute further psychological stress that is conducive to reinforcing the cycle of violence that exists within gang-dominant communities.

Suppression and Prevention

Suppression Strategies

In their thorough analysis of the gang phenomenon in the United States, Judith Greene and Kevin Pranis (2007) argued that once a gang problem has been acknowledged by local politicians, the conversation usually turns to how the police can resolve the problem. As a result, the policy responses that usually follow the emergence of a gang problem include the following:

1. the formation of a special "gang" or "organized crime" unit within the police service;
2. the creation of a "gang member database" to document gang members and their associates;
3. police crackdowns in "high-crime" neighbourhoods, which includes the addition of special police patrols that aggressively enforce public ordinances; and
4. efforts that target gang "leaders" and "hardcore" gang members through heightened surveillance and harsh sentencing practices (including sentencing enhancements for gang-related crime). (pp. 67–68)

Considerable evidence suggests that a similar model has been adopted within many Canadian jurisdictions. For example, following a rash of gun-related homicides, the Toronto Police Service received additional public funds to develop its own gang unit (the Integrated Gun & Gang Task Force). The federal government is also supporting new legislation that will produce tougher sentences for gang and gun-related crimes.

suppression strategies
Efforts to eliminate gangs or significantly reduce gang-related crime through a process of deterrence and incapacitation.

The basic objective of most gang **suppression strategies** is to eliminate gangs or significantly reduce gang-related crime through a process of deterrence and incapacitation. Tough enforcement practices, it is argued, will deter people from joining gangs and cause current gang members to reduce or cease their criminal activity. However, the bulk of empirical evidence suggests that despite years of operation, police gang suppression efforts have not produced significant reductions in overall gang activity or gang-related violence (Greene & Pranis, 2007; Hagedorn, 2008; Katz & Webb, 2006; Klein & Maxson, 2006). Indeed, although public spending on police gang suppression strategies is at an all-time high in the United States, research suggests that the number of gangs and gang members has actually increased over recent years (see Egley, Howell, & Moore, 2010). Terrence Thornberry, David Huizinga, and Rolf Loeber (2004) effectively summarize these research results:

The findings from these studies are quite consistent. In general, arrest has little impact on subsequent delinquent behavior, and when it does have an impact, it is most likely an increase in future delinquent behavior. … In addition, those who are arrested and incarcerated as juveniles are subsequently more likely to be incarcerated as adults. (p. 12)

This is not to say that the police have no impact on gangs. Police anti-gang strategies can be very effective at dismantling specific criminal organizations and arresting specific gang members. The evidence, however, suggests that such intervention strategies have little overall impact on reducing gang formation or overall levels of gang-related violence. As Huff (2002) observes, "suppression is a necessary but not sufficient strategy for dealing with gang-related crime" (p. 292). Although effective suppression strategies may temporarily remove violent gang members from a community, gangs and gang violence will ultimately return if we do not address the social factors (poverty, inequality, social disorganization, etc.) that produce gangs in the first place. As a result, many experts believe that we must engage in a coordinated **weed and seed** strategy to reduce gangs (see Bridenhall & Jesilow, 2005; Waller, 2006; Wortley et al., 2008).

weed and seed
A strategy combining the removal of violent gang members from a community with long-term community development.

Police must first remove violent gangs and gang members from our communities (the weed side of the equation). Following the removal of criminal elements, however, the government must also engage in concentrated and long-term community development efforts in order to ensure that gangs do not return (the seed side of the equation). Unfortunately, when it comes to fighting gangs, governments have been much more enthusiastic about funding law enforcement suppression strategies than in-depth community development programs (Bridenhall & Jesilow, 2005).

Prevention Strategies

An increasing number of policy-makers and police officials have recognized the limitations of traditional police gang suppression strategies. As a result, several jurisdictions have sought to develop more community-based enforcement initiatives. These programs tend to share similar characteristics:

1. a focus on reducing gang-related violence rather than efforts to completely eradicate gangs;
2. an attempt to balance gang suppression activities with the provision of social services and other employment/educational opportunities for youth from highly disadvantaged communities;
3. efforts to engage a broader range of stakeholders—including schools, social workers, and grassroots community groups—in the development of gang prevention policies; and
4. efforts to collaborate with researchers on the design and implementation of robust evaluation strategies.

Operation Ceasefire

The Operation Ceasefire model provides a problem-oriented framework for preventing gang-related violence. The approach consists of six basic elements:

1. the selection of a specific crime problem, such as youth homicide;
2. the creation of an interagency working group—including police officials and community leaders—to plan and coordinate an intervention strategy;
3. research to identify key offenders, groups, and behaviour patterns;
4. the development of a deterrence-based response to offenders and groups of offenders that uses various sanctions (known as "pulling levers") to reduce violent behaviour;
5. a coordinated effort to provide social services and opportunities to targeted offenders and groups; and
6. an effort to directly and repeatedly communicate with offenders to make them understand why they are receiving special attention (Kennedy, 2006).

The Operation Ceasefire model was pioneered in Boston and has since been replicated in several other American cities. During the early 1990s, gun-related homicides in Boston increased dramatically. An investigation revealed that this violence was being perpetrated by loosely organized youth gangs. Operation Ceasefire was implemented by the Boston Police Department's Youth Violence Strike Force on May 15, 1996 to address this problem. The assumption behind Operation Ceasefire was that youth violence had resulted in a self-perpetuating cycle where youth resorted to guns and violent behaviour to settle disputes. Fear of reprisals was also causing youth to carry guns to protect themselves (Braga, Kennedy, & Tita, 2002).

The program's primary targets were high-risk youth and serious and violent juvenile offenders, as well as illicit firearms traffickers who supplied youth with guns. The prevention strategy depended on regular meetings between the police and both community groups and gang members. During these meetings the consequences of gang violence were clearly communicated. The program's suppression component used every legal recourse against violent offenders and gun traffickers. Concrete actions included an increase in the number of search and arrest warrants issued, the rigorous enforcement of all probation and parole conditions, and an effort to work more closely with prosecutors to ensure long sentences for chronic offenders (Braga et al., 2002). In Boston, "pulling levers" also meant communicating a direct message to all youth that "articulated explicit cause-and-effect connections between the behavior of the target population and that of the authorities. Knowledge of what happened to others in the target population was intended to prevent further acts of violence by gangs in Boston" (p. 280). This tactic is known as "marketing deterrence." The authorities also attempted to break the cycle of violence by immediately contacting gang members following violent incidents, thus reducing the risk of retaliation. Importantly, the enforcement effort was complemented by an increase in social services and opportunities available to gang youth and other young people residing in high-risk communities.

Even without the support of a formal evaluation, Boston's Operation Ceasefire was hailed by the media as a great success. However, a US Department of Justice evaluation eventually revealed that at least some of this praise was warranted. Using a quasi-experimental longitudinal design to analyze trends in serious violence between 1991 and 1998, this study found that Operation Ceasefire was associated with a 63 percent decline in the monthly number of homicides in Boston, a 32 percent decrease in gun calls, and a 25 percent decline in gun assault incidents. Analysis suggests that program effects remained after statistically controlling for other explanatory variables (Kennedy, 2006).

In the late 1990s, Operation Ceasefire was successfully replicated in several other US cities. For example, it was associated with a 34 percent reduction in monthly homicides in Indianapolis (National Institute of Justice, 2011). Similarly, in Chicago, an evaluation of the Ceasefire program found greater reductions in homicides and gun-related violence within treatment communities than control neighbourhoods (Papachristos, Meares, & Fagan, 2007). Finally, an impact evaluation of an Operation Ceasefire program in Lowell, Massachusetts found that the pulling levers strategy significantly decreased both gun-related homicides and aggravated assaults (Braga, Pierce, McDevitt, Bond, & Cronin, 2008).

In sum, the Operation Ceasefire model has shown at least some positive results with respect to reducing gang violence. Supporters argue that the model is successful for a variety of reasons:

1. It focuses on gang violence rather than gang formation.
2. It allows local police and community workers to develop unique, local approaches to gang problems.

3. It provides rewards or incentives to youth who refrain from violence (including access to social services and reduced police attention).
4. It focuses suppression efforts on serious offenders and not on all youth who are gang-involved.

However, critics argue that the program has not worked in all communities. They also maintain that the Operation Ceasefire model subjugates community interests to those of the police, which can create tension within program committees and ultimately prevent the development of even more effective violence prevention strategies (see Greene & Pranis, 2007; Welford, Pepper, & Petrie, 2005). Nonetheless, compared with traditional suppression strategies, the Operation Ceasefire model has shown promise and may eventually pave the way for greater police–community cooperation.

The Comprehensive Gang Prevention Model

The comprehensive gang prevention model, also known as the Spergel model, is designed to provide both social controls and social supports to gang members and other "at-risk" youth from disadvantaged neighbourhoods. The model was first implemented in the Little Village neighbourhood of Chicago during the mid-1990s (Spergel, 2007).

The Spergel model calls for the development of an integrated program team consisting of law enforcement officials, probation officers, youth workers, school officials, and social workers. This committee shares information about individual youth and gang activities and develops specific program strategies. Front-line workers focus on individual youth and family counselling, educational support, job training, and the provision of social services. Besides their traditional law enforcement duties, police and probation officers refer youth to the program and monitor the behaviour of program participants in the community. Youth workers also gather and clarify information about gang crime and help the police identify youth involved in serious gang violence. Information sharing between law enforcement and community workers is thought to improve both suppression and rehabilitation objectives as well as increase opportunities for social development (Spergel, 2007).

An extensive evaluation of the Chicago program produced positive results. At the individual level, participation in the program was associated with a statistically significant reduction in serious violence, fewer arrests for violent crime, fewer arrests for drug offences, and decreased association with known gang members. The greater the level of contact with program workers, the greater the overall reduction in criminal behaviour. Program effects were particularly strong for youth who found employment or re-enrolled in school. At the community level, the program also contributed to a significant drop in gang-motivated crime. Despite these successes, the Chicago police failed to institutionalize this program. The police justification for this decision was that their primary mission was crime suppression—not community development or social work (Spergel, 2007).

Gang Resistance, Education, and Training

Gang Resistance, Education, and Training (GREAT) is another promising gang intervention program. GREAT provides preteen youth from gang-infested communities with a school-based education program that focuses on crime, victimization, prejudice, cultural sensitivity, conflict resolution skills, drugs, and personal responsibility. The program is delivered by police officers working within the school system. The program has been evaluated numerous times. The most ambitious evaluation effort was a study conducted over a four-year period and involving almost 6,000 grade 8 students from 11 different cities. The study found that compared with the control group, GREAT participants had more negative attitudes toward gangs and gang membership, fewer delinquent friends, a greater commitment to pro-social activities, lower levels of impulsivity, better attitudes toward the police, and greater attachment to parents. According to the researchers, program participants also had statistically reduced levels of delinquency and gang affiliation. Overall, the results of the study suggest that, four years after program completion, program participants demonstrated more positive social attitudes and behaviours on 25 of 29 outcome measures (see Esbensen, Osgood, Taylor, Peterson, & Freng, 2001).

The Philadelphia Model

The Philadelphia Youth Violence Reduction Partnership (YVRP) is another multi-agency, wrap-around program that includes various youth-serving organizations and criminal justice agencies. Its aim is to reduce gang activity and violent victimization among young people—14 to 24 years of age—who are currently under court supervision. The program's staff consist of members of more than ten public and private organizations as well as more than 50 police officers, probation officers, and street workers. Staff members are in close contact with program youth and their families through frequent visits. The police and the probation officers also work closely with one another to ensure strict enforcement of probation and parole conditions. The YVRP tries to help participants develop a more productive lifestyle by providing them with increased supervision, vocational counselling, access to job skills and employment training, mentoring, health care, and drug treatment. Street workers play a major role in this program. They are responsible for mentoring participants and helping them with their health care and educational needs. YVRP staff also help the parents of program youth with their employment, health care, and housing needs. They do so to ensure a more stable family life for youth in the program. Preliminary results suggest that the program is working. An evaluation of the YVRP, conducted one year after the program commenced, found that program youth had significantly lower rates of violent victimization than control group subjects and that the homicide rate declined significantly in those areas of Philadelphia in which the initiative was operating (McClanahan, 2004).

The examples above indicate that some targeted gang prevention strategies may be effective. However, most gang prevention programs—especially those in Canada—have yet to be properly evaluated (see Chatterjee, 2006). Furthermore, a growing number of scholars have argued that governments should be paying less attention to programs that focus exclusively on gangs and gang members and more attention to programs that focus on youth violence in general (see Greene & Pranis, 2007; Sullivan, 2005, 2006). After all, gang violence represents only a small proportion of all youth violence. Research also suggests that the risk factors associated with gang violence are very similar to the risk factors associated with other types of youth crime and violence. Indeed, studies reveal that youth often have violent histories long before they become involved in gangs. Finally, while few gang prevention programs have been properly evaluated, a large number of evidence-based practices have been proven to work with violent, delinquent youth (see the review in Wortley et al., 2008).

Ineffective Programs

Along with programs proven to significantly reduce youth and gang-related violence, it is equally important to highlight programs that have been shown to be ineffective and a potential waste of resources. Some high-profile crime prevention programs either have no impact on gang violence or actually have a negative impact. These include the following:

- **Scared Straight programs**,
- gun buyback programs,
- curfews for adolescents,
- instructional programs that do not incorporate cognitive-behavioural techniques,
- peer mentoring programs,
- correctional boot camps using traditional military training,
- harsh sentences for young offenders,
- zero-tolerance programs in school systems, and
- heightened security (including the use of metal detectors) within schools (Farrington & Welsh, 2007; Greenwood, 2006; Leschied, 2007; Waller, 2006).

Scared Straight programs
Programs that expose at-risk youth to examples of prison life and other consequences of criminal behaviour, along with testimonials from convicts.

Conclusion

The research literature suggests that gangs, gang members, and gang-related violence are difficult concepts to define. The literature also suggests that gangs are not homogeneous—they vary dramatically with respect to size, organization, durability, and type and level of criminal activity. Nonetheless, the literature suggests that gang-related violence has some common attributes: It often involves disputes over honour, territory, and control over illicit markets. Furthermore, the roots of gang activity seem to stem from common criminological risk factors, including social disorganization, social strain, peer deviance, and low self-control. Finally, research suggests that the solution to gangs and gang violence are complex. As such, programs that focus on enforcement alone are bound to be less successful than programs that combine police efforts with community investment and youth development initiatives. The solution will involve all segments of society, not only those charged with enforcing the law.

SUMMARY OF KEY POINTS

- Many urban-dwelling Canadians feel that street gangs and gang-related violence are on the increase, but clear trends can be difficult to determine due to the lack of widely agreed-upon definitions of street gangs.
- Frederick Thrasher, one of the first criminological researchers to examine gangs, argued that gangs were part of normal peer group activity for adolescents and involved behaviours that ranged from the conventional to the deviant.

■ Following Thrasher's groundbreaking work, the number of distinct gang definitions—within both academia and the criminal justice system—has soared. There are also numerous ways in which types of gangs have been broadly categorized (in this chapter, four levels or types of gangs are identified).

■ As stated in the *Criminal Code*, section 467.1(1), a "criminal organization" is a group that (a) is composed of three or more persons in or outside Canada; and (b) has as one of its main purposes or activities the facilitation or commission of one or more serious offences, that, if committed, would likely result in the direct or indirect receipt of a material benefit by the group.

■ A significant debate that has emerged within the literature concerning gangs is whether criminality should be considered a necessary criterion for gang membership.

■ An adequate definition of a gang must not only identify essential elements of the gang, but also distinguish it from other social groups that young people might involve themselves in.

■ Research of gang members shows that violence generally takes one of six forms: (1) economically motivated crime; (2) disputes over territory or turf; (3) involvement in the illicit economy; (4) retaliation; (5) conflicts over reputation; and (6) witness intimidation.

■ An increasing number of policy-makers and police officials have recognized the limitations of traditional police gang-suppression strategies. As a result, several jurisdictions have sought to develop more community-based enforcement initiatives, such as Operation Ceasefire.

■ Some high-profile crime prevention programs tend to have little or no impact. These include Scared Straight programs, gun buyback programs, and military-style "boot camps."

NOTE

1. The Toronto Street Gang Pilot Project was funded by a research grant from the Solicitor General of Canada through the Drug and Crime Prevention Strategies Unit.

QUESTIONS FOR CRITICAL DISCUSSION

1. What is a gang? What is an organized crime group? How do gangs differ from other types of social groups?
2. What are the causes of gang activity? Do the causes of gang activity differ from the causes of individual criminal behaviour?
3. Are all gangs or criminal organizations the same? How do gangs differ?
4. Can the police prevent gang activity? Why or why not? Besides policing and punishment, are there any other ways to reduce gangs?
5. Research the Toronto 18 to find out their motivations, how they came together, and what they were accused of plotting. Of the four levels of gangs described in this chapter, which best describes them, and why?

SUGGESTED FURTHER READINGS

Katz, K. (2011). The enemy within: The outlaw motorcycle gang moral panic. *American Journal of Criminal—Humanities, Social Sciences and Law Justice, 36*(3), 231–249.

Marsden, W., & Sher, J. (2006). *Angels of death: Inside the bikers' global crime empire.* Toronto: Knopf Canada.

Wortley, S., Dorion, J., Levinsky, Z., Owusu-Bempah, A., Marshall, L., Adhopia, R., … Boyce, A. (2008). Preventing youth crime and violence: A review of the literature. In R. McMurtry & A. Curling (Eds.), *The review of the roots of youth violence: Vol. 5. Literature reviews* (pp. 229–561). Toronto: Queen's Printer for Ontario. Retrieved from http://www.children .gov.on.ca/htdocs/English/professionals/oyap/roots/volume5/preventing01_introduction.aspx

Legislation

Criminal Code, RSC 1985, c C-46.

Cases

R v Danvers, 2005 CanLII 30044, 201 OAC 138 (CA).

R v Hayles-Wilson, 2018 ONSC 4337.

The Eron Mortgage Fraud: Lessons from a Ponzi Scheme

In the summer of 1920, Charles Ponzi was the talk of Boston. His seven-month-old business, The Security Exchange Company, was taking in more than a million dollars a week from investors. He had guaranteed them 50 percent interest on their principal in 45 days—an astonishing rate of return. The mechanism for generating this wealth was an international reply postal coupon, a device for facilitating international business. Ponzi told his prospective purchasers that he could buy a postal coupon in Spain for about one cent, and when he cashed it in America, he could buy six one-cent stamps. His plan was to convert on a grand scale—buy millions of dollars of coupons in foreign countries and convert them into five and ten times their value in America. It was all legal, and it was lauded by some commentators as a brilliant plan.

Frank Biller of Eron Mortgage served a short jail term for fraud. His parole board described him as "a prototypical white-collar offender with no previous criminal history who was reportedly motivated by greed and power associated with wealth and a luxurious lifestyle."

The scheme appeared to work. Early investors did see 50 percent returns on their money and, as a consequence, investments grew exponentially through the spring and summer of 1920. But Ponzi was simply using the money from new investors to enrich himself and pay off earlier obligations; he had created a new variation on the long-standing pyramid deception—a variation that is now termed a "Ponzi scheme." The *Boston Post* questioned the legitimacy of Ponzi's approach in July 1920: Who, after all, would buy the millions of dollars' worth of stamps that Ponzi was said to be collecting? In response to increasing media criticism, Ponzi allowed an auditor to examine his books, and his abrupt decline began. The newspaper learned that Ponzi had previous convictions for forgery and smuggling and had spent time in prison in both Canada and the United States; his books quickly revealed his latest deception. He was convicted of fraud and sent to jail for 14 years, leaving thousands of Americans in financial ruin.

Eron Mortgage of British Columbia was a contemporary, albeit more sophisticated, version of Charles Ponzi's scheme. Like the postal reply coupon, the high returns on investments promoted by Eron Mortgage—real estate developments in Canada and the United States—seemed plausible to investors at the time. Like Charles Ponzi, the principals of Eron Mortgage did not actually carry out the plans that they enthusiastically described to their willing contributors, although their businesses were widely praised by many media commentators. And in both cases, after questions were raised about their businesses, their books were examined and their frauds discovered. But for both Ponzi's investors and the investors of Eron Mortgage, it was too late; the businesses had crashed, their money was gone, and little could be done to retrieve it.

A few years after the 1999 conviction of Eron Mortgage's top officials, a research team based at Simon Fraser University conducted a post mortem of the Eron Mortgage fraud. It focused on more than 550 responses from the 2,200 men and women who invested in Eron Mortgage. The team found that about 60 percent of Eron investors were male and older than the average Canadian investor; most were in their mid-50s or older at the time of their initial investment. The Eron investors were no better educated and no more affluent than the average British Columbian of a similar age. They were not particularly wealthy; approximately two-thirds reported total annual incomes of less than $75,000, and with an average age of 55, their net worth was approximately $200,000.

The purpose of the Eron investment was, for the overwhelming majority of these investors, to fund retirement. These men and women were approaching that time of life without adequate resources, and the post mortem learned that the majority of the investors took their existing retirement funds, borrowed money, and mortgaged their homes to invest in Eron. Additionally, those who described themselves as "highly knowledgeable" investors—typically affluent middle-aged men—lost more than twice as much as the other Eron investors.

The effects of the Eron mortgage losses were devastating to hundreds of investors. More than half of those who lost more than $50,000 reported extreme or major harm to their emotional well-being, their current financial situation, and their retirement security. Between 20 and 30 percent of these investors also reported extreme or major harm to their marital relations, friendships, and physical health.

The story of Eron Mortgage resonates with this chapter: The public, our courts, and our law and policy-makers must better understand the very considerable consequences of investment fraud. In both civil and criminal contexts, the penalties imposed do not adequately reflect the harms created by such activity. The deliberateness of the conduct of the principals and the devastating consequences for hundreds of individuals stand in stark contrast to so much violent crime—the sort of criminal activity that receives considerably more attention and attracts much more substantial penalties.

Before You Read Chapter 18

- Why do you believe "street crime" tends to get relatively more attention and receive harsher sentencing than "white-collar crime" such as that of Eron Mortgage?
- Consider the media's role in dealing with white-collar crime. How are the perpetrators typically portrayed?
- Compare the Ponzi and Eron Mortgage cases described above. How are they similar? In what ways has white-collar crime changed in the century between Ponzi's time and today?

White-Collar Crime

LEARNING OBJECTIVES

After reading this chapter, students will be able to:

- Understand the origins of the term "white-collar crime" and contemporary debates about the concept's scope and content.
- Recognize the principal distinctions between traditional or "street" crime and white-collar crime, including issues concerning criminal liability for corporations.
- Identify the legal frameworks relevant to prominent cases of white-collar criminality across the criminal, regulatory, and civil domains.
- Explain the impact of a number of prominent white-collar cases in Canada and the United States in recent years.
- Appreciate the regulatory, legal, and social-scientific aspects of white-collar investigations and prosecutions.
- Understand the ways in which corporations are reacting to white-collar crime under corporate governance, including whistle-blowing protocols and corporate social responsibility.

Introduction

Polished floors, cubicle rows, leather-clad boardrooms—these are usually not the first images that spring to mind when we think of the word *crime*. Yet both the incidence of and damage associated with **white-collar crime** today far outstrips that of traditional forms of crime. The first decade of the new millennium began and ended with unprecedented white-collar scandals that shook the public's faith in business: the meteoric fall of Texas-based energy giant Enron in an infamous accounting fraud in 2001 and the unravelling of Bernie Madoff's record-breaking US$65 billion **Ponzi scheme** in 2009. More recently, Volkswagen's "Dieselgate" scandal raised cross-Atlantic concerns about the integrity of business. These and other scandals have fuelled demand for stiffer white-collar penalties and tougher quasi-criminal and civil regulation to keep a watchful eye on markets. Far more troubling than the dramatic, economy-wide impact of its worst cases, however, is the extent to which so much white-collar misconduct could lurk behind the veil of legitimate business

white-collar crime
A crime committed by a person, usually of high social status, in the course of his or her occupation.

Ponzi scheme
An investing scam where a fraudster pays returns to existing investors with new investors' funds under the false pretense that returns are being made, sustained by the constant recruitment of new contributors.

activities—in Madoff's case, for as many as four decades before prosecutors knocked on his door.

Canada, despite its reputation for politeness and conservative regulation, has never been immune to the patterns of white-collar crime observed in the United States. For example, there were the accounting misdeeds at Livent, a theatre production company, that proved to be Canada's own Enron; the larger-than-life former Canadian newspaper magnate Conrad Black who notoriously served out a US prison term for fraud; and more recently, in late 2017, national grocer Loblaws admitted to having criminally fixed the price of Canadians' bread for 15 years. Indeed, a historically softer enforcement culture may have made Canada a haven for white-collar offenders. A 2009 *Economist* article refers to Canada's "shockingly slow" approach to white-collar crime and corruption compared with its US neighbour, noting how not only weaker legal tools but also Canada's deference-to-authority culture may be to blame ("White-collar crime," 2009).

In this chapter, we explore the perplexing phenomenon of white-collar crime in a Canadian context. The chapter begins by tracing the term's origins to the work of sociologist Edwin Sutherland and explores how white-collar criminality encompasses conduct broader than the strictly "criminal." The chapter also presents an overview of several of the most prominent white-collar laws in Canada, including those on fraud, money laundering, bribery, embezzlement, tax evasion, insider trading, market manipulation, price fixing, workplace safety, and cybercrime. It also explores the enforcement process for white-collar offences from the investigation process through to sentencing. Finally, the chapter discusses the many roles of the corporation in relation to white-collar crime, including criminal defendant, in-house investigator, and "good corporate citizen."

What Is White-Collar Crime?

The Origins of the Label

The pioneer in the study of white-collar crime was American sociologist Edwin Sutherland. Sutherland first conceived of the term in an influential 1939 address to the American Sociological Society titled "White-Collar Criminality" (Sutherland, 1940). He defined "white-collar crime" as "crime committed by a person of respectability and high social status in the course of his occupation" (Sutherland, 1949/1983, p. 7). So jealously guarded was that "respectability" that the companies named in Sutherland's landmark 1949 book on the topic, *White Collar Crime*, used legal threats to successfully keep their references out of its text for 34 years (Beare, 2003).

Edwin Sutherland's work is discussed in Chapter 6, Theories of Crime: A Brief Introduction and Chapter 9, Sociological Approaches.

Sutherland questioned the then-prevailing wisdom that crime was a lower-class phenomenon reducible to low intelligence, mental illness, slum neighbourhoods, and broken homes. Instead, he entertained the notion that samples of criminality might be class-biased (Sutherland, 1940, p. 2). In one paper, Sutherland analyzed 547 legal findings against 70 large US companies under competition law, false advertising, labour, and intellectual property statutes. He found that while only 49 (9 percent) were prosecuted criminally, 473 (87 percent) involved conduct designated as socially injurious for which a penalty was attached—revealing what he saw to be a marked legal double standard in favour of white-collar actors (Sutherland, 1945). Sutherland also speculated that white-collar crime's financial cost was "several times as great" as traditional crime, combined with a reduction in social trust that produced "social disorganization on a large scale" (Sutherland, 1940, p. 5). Sutherland concluded that dominant definitions of criminal conduct were underinclusive, and that "convictability rather than actual conviction should be the criterion of criminality" (Sutherland, 1940, p. 6).

BOX 18.1

Edwin Sutherland: The Problem of White-Collar Crime

Pioneering American sociologist Edwin Sutherland's influential 1949 book, *White Collar Crime,* called for criminology to widen its scope beyond "street crime," or crime in the lower socio-economic classes. The following excerpt is from the opening chapter, "The Problem of White Collar Crime," in which he points out the inherent bias in the ways crime was defined and prosecuted.

> Social and personal pathologies are not an adequate explanation of criminal behavior. The general theories of criminal behavior which take their data from poverty and the conditions related to it are inadequate and invalid, first, because the theories do not consistently fit the data of criminal behavior; and second, because the cases on which these theories are based are a biased sample of all criminal acts. ...
>
> And much more important is the bias involved in administration of criminal justice under laws which apply exclusively to business and the professions and which therefore involve only the upper socioeconomic class. Persons who violate laws regarding restraint of trade, advertising, pure food and drugs, and similar business practices are not arrested by uniformed policemen, are not tried in criminal courts, and are not committed to prisons; their illegal behavior receives the attention of administrative commissions and of courts operating under civil or equity jurisdiction. For this reason such violations of law are not included in the criminal statistics nor are individual cases brought to the attention of the scholars who write the theories of criminal behavior. The sample of criminal behavior on which the theories are founded is biased as to socioeconomic status, since it excludes these business and professional men. The bias is quite as certain as it

> would be if the scholars selected only red-haired criminals for study and reached the conclusion that redness of hair was the cause of crime.
>
> The thesis of this book, stated positively, is that persons of the upper socioeconomic class engage in much criminal behavior; that this criminal behavior differs from the criminal behavior of the lower socioeconomic class principally in the administrative procedures which are used in dealing with the offenders; and that variations in administrative procedures are not significant from the point of view of causation of crime. The causes of tuberculosis were not different when it was treated by poultices and bloodletting than when treated by streptomycin.
>
> These violations of law by persons in the upper socioeconomic class are, for convenience, called "white collar crimes." This concept is not intended to be definitive, but merely to call attention to crimes which are not ordinarily included within the scope of criminology. White collar crime may be defined approximately as a crime committed by a person of respectability and high social status in the course of his occupation. ...
>
> The significant thing about white collar crime is that it is not associated with poverty or with social and personal pathologies which accompany poverty. If it can be shown that white collar crimes are frequent, a general theory that crime is due to poverty and its related pathologies is shown to be invalid. Furthermore, the study of white collar crime may assist in locating those factors which, being common to the crimes of the rich and the poor, are most significant for a general theory of criminal behavior.

Source: Excerpted from "White-Collar Criminality" by Edwin H. Sutherland, *American Sociological Review,* Vol. 5, No. 1 (Feb., 1940), pp. 1–12. American Sociological Association.

Subsequent scholars have taken up Sutherland's proposal in full, extending the definition of "crime" to not only civil and regulatory law violations but also "harmful acts for which no legal remedy yet exists" (Brown & Chiang, 1995, p. 32)—a virtually bottomless definition that would confound most lawyers. Others have approached Sutherland more critically, making note of his often transparent anti-corporate bias and deficient methodologies (Clinard & Quinney, 1978). In one departure from Sutherland, Susan Shapiro (1990) calls for "collaring the crime, not the criminal," or for a definition of "white-collar crime" that focuses on the nature of crimes rather than the privileged identity of their perpetrators. Sutherland's suspicion of white-collar crime's low public visibility and significant financial and human cost, however, has been broadly and consistently sustained through the years.

What Makes White-Collar Crime Distinct?

While white-collar crime can easily be distinguished from street crime—comprising such offences as murder, assault, sexual assault, and robbery—the term's lack of precise boundaries otherwise belies its ubiquity in popular and academic usage. What is it about white-collar criminality that makes it such an enduring concept? The factors below, in our view, provide a useful starting point.

Material Privilege

Class is the fundamental ingredient of Sutherland's definition of white-collar crime, and one that appears to have continuing validity. For example, to use education as a proxy for class, one US study found that only 21.2 percent of defendants convicted of murder, manslaughter, assault, robbery, burglary, and auto theft ("street offenders") had been to university, while that number rose to 49.7 percent among defendants convicted of fraud, embezzlement, bribery, tax offences, competition offences, and food and drug violations ("white-collar offenders"). Likewise, 78.3 percent of street offenders had a high school education or less, while only 45.8 percent of white-collar offenders had that educational profile (Shover & Hochstetler, 2006, p. 53).

Influence on the System

Related to the privileged status of white-collar offenders is their immensely greater influence on both "the law in the books" and "the law in action." Corporations and professional associations have long invested resources to mould legislation, regulation, and judicial precedents to their interests, including through direct lobbying, advertising, and court or regulatory interventions. Street criminals, in contrast, often lack the means to engage in advocacy in their own court cases. White-collar offenders are also far more likely to share the middle-class or upper-middle-class backgrounds of those doing the enforcing or judging relevant to their conduct—a "class bias" well grasped by Sutherland (1940, p. 7).

Occupational Context

Most observers share Sutherland's starting point that white-collar crime occurs in workplace environments—hence, of course, the term's reference to office apparel. The offence of impaired driving, for example, tends not to be regarded as white-collar crime despite the fact that middle-class people frequently show up as offenders (as do elites such as celebrities, business leaders, and politicians).

Complexity

The dissection of white-collar conduct often engages bodies of complex economic and scientific knowledge, especially in regulated domains such as securities, energy, environmental law, and competition law. As a result, a "battle of the experts" can take place at trial between equally credentialed prosecution and defence witnesses, each producing an account, for example, of the mechanics of a given industry or market; of the scientific or technological details relevant to an offence; or of the policy implications of enforcement. Given this complexity, governments often delegate the adjudication of white-collar conduct to administrative bodies headed by officials with relevant education and experience that the judiciary may not possess (and whose decisions are typically afforded respect when appealed to courts).

Public Ignorance

White-collar crime's complexity can lead the public to "tune out," as the evidence overwhelmingly suggests it does (Cullen, Hartman, & Jonson, 2008; Holtfreter, Van Slyke, Bratton, & Gertz, 2008). Topics such as derivatives trading, for example, hardly lend themselves to attention-grabbing headlines for lay newsreaders. In contrast, the human drama of a local murder case can easily capture front-page coverage for weeks. Yet the abuse of derivatives can entail incredible, even economy-wide risks and repercussions, while "mass panics" about isolated street crime betray decades-long data about its diminishing prevalence.

Wide Impact

While some white-collar crimes impact only a small number of people, others can harm hundreds or thousands in a way that no street crime can. For example, a global price-fixing scheme in the market for now-ubiquitous LCD televisions affected almost all early adopters from 2001 to 2006 by artificially raising sets' prices (FBI, 2012). While few deny that the economic effect of white-collar crime far exceeds street crime, the indirect and diffuse nature of that harm can also make its quantification difficult (Gustafson, 2007).

Corporate Context

White-collar crime's corporate context also makes it a distinct animal in criminology. A far broader range of stakeholders is harmed by corporate misconduct than a traditional offence, including employees, creditors, customers, shareholders, community partners, and even tax-collecting governments. As discussed below, the corporation's separate legal personality also allows it to be sued or charged separately from its managers or employees, giving the corporate investigation or prosecution unique legal and ethical characteristics.

Use of Technology

The modern-day explosion of information technology has produced a concomitant rise in white-collar crime that abuses the Internet's facilitation of long-distance, anonymous commerce. While some forms of cybercrime are relatively simple (such as email scams), others are very sophisticated, such as cyberterrorism aimed at undermining government computer networks. Such conduct often reflects a more educated and resourceful offender base.

Physical Integrity

While white-collar crime tends to be associated with guile and the abuse of trust rather than the confrontation and violence seen in street crime, the concept can arguably encompass a range of conduct implicating individuals' physical integrity. Most notably, in 2017, the #metoo movement generated a sea change in the public and employer attitudes toward workplace sexual assault and harassment after more than a dozen women approached the press with accusations against film producer Harvey Weinstein, who was eventually criminally charged in May 2018. The ensuing "Weinstein effect" saw accusations brought against men in positions of power spanning the entertainment, literature, journalism, political, and sports realms, among others, and generated a broader public debate—and calls for legal reform—in relation to issues of workplace culture and inclusivity in many countries, including Canada. The conduct implicated by the #metoo movement notably features many of the classic markers of white-collar conduct—including offender status, low detectability, and a workplace nexus—and has been linked to the economic prejudice faced by women in traditionally male-dominated industries.

BOX 18.2

Green Criminology

green criminology
The analysis of environmental harms from a criminological perspective.

One relatively new area of study that is commonly included within the imprecise boundaries of the term "white-collar crime," and the related field of corporate crime, is **green criminology**. As the name suggests, it is concerned with bringing the tools of criminology to the study of environmental issues. Gary Potter notes:

> As elsewhere in criminology, this means thinking about offences (what crimes or harms are inflicted on the environment, and how), offenders (who commits crime against the environment, and why) and victims (who suffers as a result of environmental damage, and how), and also about responses to environmental crimes: policing, punishment and crime prevention. (2010)

Recent environmental disasters and scandals have increased interest in this topic. For example, the explosion and massive oil spill at BP's Deepwater Horizon rig in the Gulf of Mexico in 2010 has resulted in BP absorbing over US$60 billion in liability to date, and led to a marked increase in public scrutiny and protest in relation to oil and gas projects, including two Canadian pipeline projects that would enable increased crude-by-tanker shipments off Canada's West Coast. More perniciously, Volkswagen's "Dieselgate" scandal—which has led to over $30 billion in penalties for the company globally to date— saw the company preside over the creation of "defeat devices" that enabled its cars to cheat emissions tests and understate the noxious impacts of its diesel-powered cars. One key consideration in examining such issues through a criminological lens is that, in the case of long-term environmental degradation, or climate change effects, the specific harms may be impossible to quantify with any precision and, in many cases, the victims may not have been born yet. Additionally, for many green criminologists, the "victims" of environmental abuses may not be human beings; consider, for example, the illegal trade in ivory, which threatens the existence of the African elephant.

According to Potter, in 2008, the UK government department responsible for generating the most legislation for "new crimes" (852 of them) was the Department of the Environment, Food, and Rural Affairs. The "message seems clear: If sociologists and criminologists are concerned with crime, then this statistic alone is reason enough to become interested in the environment" (Potter, 2010).

An Overview of White-Collar Offences in Canada

Canada's criminal law presently covers a range of white-collar crime, both in the *Criminal Code* and in other federal, provincial, and territorial statutes. We survey some of the most prominent categories below. While we largely confine ourselves to conventional, legal definitions of crime, we also survey some of the conduct Sutherland would have described as "white-collar criminality" more broadly. In particular, a universe of administrative and civil penalties exist in Canada and elsewhere for socially injurious white-collar conduct akin, in many respects, to criminal conduct.

Fraud

The most typical case of white-collar crime is **fraud**—a social wrong as ancient as commerce itself. The Roman poet Phaedrus (15 BCE–50 CE) captured the anti-social connotations of the act when he wrote that "whoever is detected in a shameful fraud is as ever after not believed if even they speak the truth." In modern-day Canada, fraud is addressed in section 380(1) of the *Criminal Code* and applies broadly to

> every one who, by deceit, falsehood or other fraudulent means … defrauds the public or any person … of any property, money or valuable security or any service.

The Supreme Court of Canada has interpreted "other fraudulent means" to refer to an act that would be "dishonest" in the eyes of a reasonable person. When such an act fuses with a "deprivation" or even a *risk* of deprivation to a person, a fraud exists (*R v Théroux*, 1993).

A "mandatory minimum" two-year term of imprisonment is in place for frauds over $1 million. This minimum was introduced in 2011 as part of the prior Conservative government's Bill C-21, the *Standing Up for Victims of White-Collar Crime Act*. While mandatory minimums for certain minor firearms and drug offences were overturned at the Supreme Court of Canada in 2015 as a "grossly disproportionate" punishment in violation of the *Canadian Charter of Rights and Freedoms* (*R v Nur*), the fraud minimum has not been challenged, and appears likelier to survive judicial scrutiny.

Fraud has also long been a civil wrong, or tort, that can support a lawsuit between two private parties. In civil form, fraud is known as the tort of "deceit" or "negligent misrepresentation," depending on whether the defendant intentionally or negligently misled the plaintiff, respectively. Torts are not found in legislation but in the common law (i.e., the body of law found in judicial precedents from past court decisions); they lead to monetary **liability** for damages caused rather than a conviction; and they are proven to the court on a "balance of probabilities" rather than the criminal level of "beyond a reasonable doubt."

Money Laundering

Money laundering is the process of making "dirty" money obtained from crime (formally referred to as "the proceeds of crime") appear "clean" or legitimately sourced to escape legal scrutiny. Money laundering is specifically prohibited in section 462.31(1) of the *Criminal Code*. While the International Monetary Fund's estimate of the global volume of laundered funds is a staggering US$2 to US$4 trillion, estimates of the inherently concealed practice's prevalence remain unreliable. Money laundering is an indispensable

fraud
A dishonest act that deprives, or risks depriving, another person of something.

liability
Legal responsibility for an act or omission.

money laundering
The process of concealing the transformation of illegitimately obtained money into ostensibly legitimate assets.

part of large-scale organized crime, and the first laundering operations on record tracked the vast underground liquor economy of the prohibition era (Beare & Schneider, 2007).

The recommendations of a task force at the 1989 Paris G7 Economic Summit gave momentum to Canada's first money-laundering statute in 1991 and a voluntary protocol between the RCMP and the Canadian Bankers Association in 1993. These initiatives established private sector systems for transaction monitoring, usually based on monetary thresholds or circumstantial triggers of suspicion. In 2000, Canada adopted a mandatory monitoring regime in the *Proceeds of Crime (Money Laundering) Act* of 2000. The Act also establishes the Financial Transactions and Reports Analysis Centre of Canada (FINTRAC), an independent agency that receives and analyzes transaction reports for potential links to criminal behaviour.

The September 11, 2001 terrorist attacks in the United States spurred legislatures to devise laws to thwart "terrorist financing"—a mirror image of money laundering that looks to funds' destinations rather than their origins. In the United States, the controversial "war on terror"–era *PATRIOT Act* dedicated a full section to "anti-money laundering to prevent terrorism." Canada's money-laundering statute was likewise amended into the *Proceeds of Crime (Money Laundering) and Terrorist Financing Act* in December 2001, with FINTRAC's responsibilities enlarged in turn.

Bribery

bribery
The practice of illegally inducing a person, company, or government to act in one's favour, usually by transferring money or property.

Another white-collar crime of international scope targets Canadian nationals who bribe foreign officials. For much of the 20th century, **bribery** was the "unspoken rule" of corporate multinationals when operating in developing countries. The US Securities and Exchange Commission (SEC) launched a voluntary disclosure program in 1975 to encourage companies to admit to bribery in exchange for lenient prosecutorial treatment. The results were striking: Over 400 companies responded, accounting for bribes of over US$300 million. Before a congressional hearing, for example, the Lockheed Corporation admitted to spending US$24 million on bribes worldwide, claiming the amounts to be legal and merely a part of its business (Kochan & Goodyear, 2011). On the tail of such revelations, the United States enacted the *Foreign Corrupt Officials Act* in 1977.

In 1999, Canada passed its own *Corruption of Foreign Public Officials Act* to ratify the anti-bribery convention of the Organisation for Economic Co-operation and Development (OECD), signed that year. However, the country's anti-bribery efforts have come under fire since Transparency International recently called out the "little or no enforcement" of the statute (Sher, 2011). In 2013, amendments increased the Act's penalties and extraterritorial reach and removed a prior exemption for facilitation or so-called "grease" payments to officials to expedite or secure the performance by officials of their assigned responsibilities.

Embezzlement

embezzlement
To take money or misappropriate funds that belong to someone else.

Embezzlement involves a person's misappropriation of funds entrusted to him or her. An investment adviser, for example, might be found guilty of embezzling client funds transferred to purchase stocks or bonds.

Beyond attracting criminal sanction, embezzlement may also be a "fiduciary duty" violation when engaged in by a professional with a civil duty to act in the best interests of a "principal" he or she serves. A lawyer, for example, has a common law fiduciary duty to his or her client. Likewise, section 122 of the *Canada Business Corporations Act* sets out the fiduciary duty of corporate board members and officers to "act honestly and in good faith with a view to the best interests of the corporation."

BOX 18.3

Conrad Black

Conrad Black was involved in a notable case of corporate embezzlement. As a director of newspaper conglomerate Hollinger International Inc., he personally received "non-competition" side payments in sale agreements between Hollinger and buyers of its newspaper subsidiaries. Theoretically, these payments would have protected the buyers from Black or his co-directors *personally* setting up competing newspapers in small towns in the United States—a scenario a Chicago court found implausible. The buyers themselves never requested this protection, and Hollinger itself was unaware of this bargain until it was a *fait accompli*. While part of Black's conviction was overturned on extraneous legal grounds before the Supreme Court of the United States, the Chicago court, in reconsidering the case, affirmed Black's convictions for both obstructing justice and fraudulently appropriating money to which Hollinger was legally entitled (*United States v Black*, 2010).

Media baron Conrad Black is perhaps Canada's best-known white-collar felon. He served 42 months in prison in the United States for fraud and obstruction of justice and was released in 2012. He has since returned to public life in Canada and has also become an outspoken advocate for prison reform.

Tax Evasion

Taxes are the lifeblood of Canadian government: Approximately 80 percent of federal revenues, for example, were forecast to come from taxes in the 2018–2019 fiscal year (Government of Canada, 2018). Accordingly, tax evasion criminalizes the illegal circumvention of taxes. Tax evasion can be contrasted with the legal practice of tax *avoidance*: The law generally allows people to strategize to reduce their taxes by legally approved means. While income earners at all levels can commit tax evasion, the average offender has a markedly white-collar profile: "male, under age 50 in a high tax bracket with a complex return" (Sabatini, 2007).

History's most infamous tax evader remains Al Capone, who, despite escaping prosecution for his organized-crime activities, was caught evading taxes amounting to US$2.8 million in today's dollars. Capone was sentenced to 11 years in prison—at the time, the longest tax evasion sentence in US history. Canada's *Income Tax Act* is less punitive: Tax evaders can be liable for a fine of between 50 and 200 percent of the amount of the tax sought to be evaded and a prison term of up to two years (s. 239(1)).

Starting in 1988, Canadian tax authorities began narrowing their view of tax avoidance's legality in line with the enactment of the general anti-avoidance rule (GAAR) in section 245 of the *Income Tax Act*. The non-criminal rule allows the Canada Revenue Agency to target otherwise legal activities incompatible with the spirit of the law, or what it has recently characterized as "aggressive" or "abusive" tax planning (Fleury, 2010). The GAAR requires taxpayers to include wrongly claimed amounts in their taxes rather than pay a penalty. While not extensively used, the GAAR reflects the trend in favour of non-criminal enforcement paths by regulators.

Insider Trading

One of the most notorious and difficult to detect white-collar crimes is the securities law offence of **insider trading**. Insider trading is the purchase or sale of stocks or other securities by individuals with access to non-public information about a company. The criminalization of insider trading relates to a core policy aim of securities markets: the maintenance of a level playing field between investors in relation to market information. Separate disclosure rules also serve that end by requiring companies to issue press releases of material events affecting their operations, thus preventing insiders (such as directors, officers, employees, and advisers to the company) from reaping windfalls from large, strategically timed stock purchases or sales. While a number of academics, including the late Nobel Prize–winning economist Milton Friedman, have argued that insider trading should be legalized on the basis that it facilitates the flow of information in markets, concerns about distributional fairness to ordinary investors continue to underpin support for prohibition.

> **insider trading**
> The practice of trading in a stock, bond, or other security while possessing material, non-public information about the company in question.

Market Manipulation

Market manipulation is another key securities prohibition, and it can be understood as a specialized branch of fraud aimed at protecting the fair and transparent operation of securities markets. Market misconduct affects not only upper-middle-class investors who hire professional money managers but, for example, working-class pension plan members whose ability to retire comfortably is equally tied to the market. Ontario's *Securities Act* prohibits a person or company from

> **market manipulation**
> The practice of interfering with the proper operation of a market, usually by employing or creating misleading or artificial information.

> any act, practice or course of conduct relating to securities ... that the person or company knows or reasonably ought to know ... (a) results or contributes to a misleading appearance of trading activity in, or an artificial price for, a security ... or (b) perpetuates a fraud on any person or company. (s. 126.1(1))

A classic market manipulation device is a "pump-and-dump" scheme, whereby a significant shareholder makes false positive statements about a stock—thereby pumping up its value—before selling his or her holdings at a large profit (dumping) to investors who suffer the inevitable fall in the security's value.

Price Fixing

Direct and indirect forms of consumer predation are also a preoccupation of the enforcement authorities overseeing competition law (known as "antitrust law" in the United States). The quintessential competition law offence is **price fixing**, which refers to the practice by which groups of competing buyers or sellers (together, a "cartel") agree to collude to set prices in a market. The "conspiracy" provision in section 45 of the *Competition Act* criminalizes the act in Canada. Price fixing, like

> **price fixing**
> An agreement between competitors to fix the price for a good or service by buying or selling at an agreed-to price or by manipulating supply or demand.

insider trading, is challenging to detect. At the same time, modern developments—including anonymous tipping from employees and competitors, wiretapping, and the development of immunity guarantees for price-fixing cartel "defectors" that assist in the prosecution of others—have resulted in enforcement victories. Wiretap techniques, for example, enabled the Competition Bureau's recent string of price-fixing guilty pleas in gasoline cartels in Quebec and eastern Ontario between 2008 and 2017 (Competition Bureau, 2018). Likewise, the Bureau's immunity program provided national grocer Loblaws with the incentive to disclose its participation in a 15-year-old scheme to fix bread prices in late 2017. While many criticized Loblaws' ability to escape prosecution, the disclosure enabled a broad, cross-sector Bureau investigation that may never have materialized otherwise, as stressed by the Bureau itself (Pecman, 2018).

Convictions or settlements in price-fixing cases often leave a trail of class action lawsuits that can boost the deterrent effect of a conviction. Class actions are civil lawsuits where a "representative plaintiff" sues a company on behalf of a larger group of persons with closely associated claims. The procedure assists a group of plaintiffs to recover small individual losses that, aggregated together, often scale into the millions. For example, following a guilty plea by Hershey Canada in June 2013 concerning price fixing in the chocolate industry, the company and competitors Cadbury Adams Canada, Nestlé Canada, and Mars Canada settled a class action suit that made $23.2 million available for payouts to purchasers who bought at least $1,000 in chocolate in the period of alleged price fixing, which was between October 1, 2005 and September 30, 2007 (CBC News, 2013).

Health and Safety Breaches

Prior to the advent of modern health and safety legislation, the British common law had evolved to recognize the duty of employers in physically dangerous workplaces "to take all reasonable precautions for the workman's safety" rather than deem employees to have "voluntarily assumed" risks to their safety under their employment contracts (*Smith v Baker*, 1891). Workplace deaths also spurred on legislation that empowered inspectors to ensure that workplaces adhered to minimum standards, especially in inherently dangerous locations such as mines (Edmonds & Edmonds, 1963). In Canada, the provinces administer the modern successors to these regimes under statutes such as Ontario's *Occupational Health and Safety Act*, with federal workplaces falling under the *Canada Labour Code*.

The governing philosophy of modern health and safety laws, however, is a compliance-oriented concept of shared employer–employee responsibility for workplace safety, including through initiatives such as joint health and safety committees led by worker and employer representatives.

Nevertheless, corporations continue to come under scrutiny for a perceived indifference to workplace safety. A particularly tragic safety incident occurred in the case of an explosion at the Westray Mine in Plymouth, Nova Scotia on May 9, 1992, which killed 26 miners. Subsequent legal proceedings failed to yield convictions of two mine managers and a corporation. A public inquiry led to a recommendation that the federal government study how to make corporate managers properly accountable for their company's wrongful or **negligent** treatment of workplace safety (Richard, 1997). Part of

negligence
A legal intent standard that considers whether a person, regardless of actual intent or knowledge, failed to take reasonable care in doing or failing to do something.

A mourner visits the Westray Miners' Memorial in Nova Scotia. The explosion at the Westray Mine on May 9, 1992 was one of the worst industrial accidents in Canadian history. The tragedy led to a public inquiry that examined the owners' management of the mine and workplace safety, as well as the lack of proper government oversight.

the federal government's response in Bill C-45 (discussed in greater detail below) included new section 217.1 of the *Criminal Code*, placing supervisors under a direct legal duty to "take reasonable steps to prevent bodily harm" to those performing tasks under their direction. While conceptually similar to the common law duty set out above, this change effectively exposes supervisors to conviction under the criminal negligence provisions of the Criminal Code, which provides in section 219(1) that "every one is criminally negligent who ... in omitting to do anything that it is his duty to do, shows wanton or reckless disregard for ... other persons." Such penalties should, at a minimum, provide a personal incentive for directors and officers to invest resources in proper health and safety procedures in the workplace.

Cybercrime

The newest white-collar crimes fall into a nebulous category of conduct known as **cybercrime** (sometimes called "technological crime" or "technocrime"), and capture the growing information-age impact of computers and the Internet on crime. As one scholar puts it, "crooks can con better with technology; pedophiles can lure their victims better; and anyone can harass, defame, threaten or blackmail better with technology" (Leman-Langlois, 2008, p. 2). Cybercrime also includes new forms of criminal activity that cannot be committed without modern technology, such as computer-systems penetration, data alteration, and hacking. While many cybercrimes can be prosecuted using "classical" criminal law (such as fraud), specific computer-related prohibitions can also be found within the *Criminal Code*, such as unauthorized use of computer (s. 342.1), mischief in relation to data (s. 430(1.1)), and interception of communications (s. 184).

Technology has escalated concerns about **identity theft** in particular, where a person uses another's credentials to access information, siphon funds, or even commit fraud. In recognition of impersonation's new "faceless" form, Canada's federal government introduced Bill S-4 in 2010 to create new *Criminal Code* offences prohibiting, among other things, a person from knowingly obtaining or possessing another's identity information in circumstances giving rise to a reasonable inference that that information will be used to commit an offence (*Criminal Code*, s. 402.2(1)).

Criminal law's increasing attention to identity-theft issues is consistent with a heightened emphasis on privacy law by both federal and provincial governments. Privacy legislation restricts the extent to which public institutions—a prime target of cybercrime—can collect, use, and disclose "personal information" obtained in the course of government business.

cybercrime
The use of cyberspace or computer technology to facilitate acts of crime and deviance.

identity theft
The theft and use of a person's identifying information, usually for monetary gain.

Cybercrime is discussed extensively in Chapter 19, 21st-Century Crimes: Cybercrime and Terrorism.

White-Collar Crime Enforcement in Canada

A vast regulatory apparatus surrounds the investigation and prosecution of laws relating to white-collar crimes such as those outlined above. The following sections provide an overview of the actors, processes, and challenges involved in the battle against white-collar crime in Canada.

Responsible Agencies

The detection and enforcement of conventional crime in Canada overwhelmingly takes place within the jurisdiction of police departments operating at the municipal, provincial, and federal levels. These agencies also play a role in white-collar matters. In particular, the RCMP's ten Integrated Market Enforcement Teams (IMETs) operating in Toronto, Vancouver, Montreal, and Calgary target capital markets fraud offences and include specialized investigators from the RCMP, local police, provincial securities regulators, and other federal and provincial agencies, as well as in-house forensic accountants (Public Safety Canada, 2015). However, an account of the enforcement landscape would be incomplete without mention of other governmental and non-governmental oversight authorities associated with particular regulatory regimes and the thousands of officers under them. Federally, these authorities include agencies and departments such as the Competition Bureau, the Canada Revenue Agency, Environment Canada, Fisheries and Oceans Canada, Health Canada, the National Energy Board, the Security Investigations Service of Canada Post, and the Canadian Food Inspection Agency. In the provinces and territories, they include regulators or government departments overseeing the securities, financial services, health and safety, environmental, transportation, and energy domains. At the provincial and territorial level, the enforcement apparatus also includes the "colleges" and licensing bodies of self-regulated professions such as medicine, nursing, dentistry, and law.

Enforcement staff are frequently drawn from the ranks of industry or its advisers and consultants. For example, securities commissions regularly recruit attorneys from private sector law firms that advise companies selling stocks, bonds, or other securities to the public. While such an approach ensures that the body has sufficient expertise to regulate effectively, it also introduces the risk of **regulatory capture**: a phenomenon, first identified by Nobel Prize–winning economist George Stigler, where public-interest bodies begin to serve the commercial or other interests of those they regulate (Stigler, 1971). An interesting alternative theory, however, is that the prospect of subsequent private sector job opportunities encourages current enforcers to pursue conduct more—not less—aggressively to showcase their expertise (Kedia, 2012).

regulatory capture
A theory of corruption whereby regulatory bodies in a sector advance the private interests of the actors they regulate over the public interest.

The Investigative Process

Most enforcement bodies adopt a relatively structured investigative process to reduce legal risks associated with officer discretion and error—including potential constitutional attack under the Charter—that can unravel enforcement efforts and deprive the public of the regulatory regime's benefits.

The investigative process begins with monitoring for compliance, which is accomplished by varying means. Some agencies are data-heavy, relying on the expertise of economists, accountants, and others to detect anomalies in a market or in documents submitted pursuant to legal reporting or disclosure requirements. Securities and energy

414 Part Three   Types of Crime

market regulators exemplify this style of "behind-the-desk" monitoring. Others, such as health and safety and environmental regulators, rely more heavily on actual "field" visits to workplaces or on obligating companies to inspect and self-report issues themselves.

A conceptual separation exists between "inspections" and "investigations" by enforcement personnel who attend offices and other workplaces. Inspections—common among regulatory agencies—can be scheduled or carried out at random and are targeted at monitoring regulated actors' overall compliance with the regulatory regime's requirements. Investigations, in contrast, follow the discovery of specific misconduct or risks, often have prosecution as their end-point, and nearly always involve the gathering of evidence. By law, investigations almost always require a search warrant authorized by a judge. That warrant is another requirement of the Charter, which protects both individuals and companies against "unreasonable search and seizure." Courts have generally given leeway to investigators to assess the line between a "reasonable" and "unreasonable" search. In so doing, they have drawn a distinction between the invasiveness of searching a home versus an office, where individuals have a lower expectation of privacy (*British Columbia Securities Commission v Branch*, 1995). A poorly executed search, however, can still derail a case: Critically important yet unconstitutionally obtained evidence can be excluded under section 24(2) of the Charter.

The volume of evidence produced in white-collar cases can be daunting for the regulator and the regulated alike. Investigators will often request companies to provide all records relating to the topics under investigation. In the information age, such a search will often require thousands of documents (especially emails) to be reviewed in a costly and lengthy "regulatory due diligence" process typically led by legal teams and their contractors. One reason lawyers conduct the review is that responsive records may be subject to attorney–client privilege, a legal doctrine intended to allow clients to speak freely with lawyers. Unless waived by the client, the doctrine makes communications for the purposes of legal advice permanently inadmissible in a hearing. The amount and complexity of evidence are just two factors behind why it takes so long for white-collar cases to result in convictions. A particularly lengthy example of a white-collar prosecution was a case involving the fraudulent misstatement of financial statements by Canadian entertainment moguls Garth Drabinsky and Myron Gottlieb at Livent, the theatre production company they co-founded. While the conduct at issue took place between 1993 and 1998, it took until 2009 for the duo to be convicted (*R v Drabinsky*, 2009). A landmark 2016 Supreme Court ruling has had important implications in this regard. The court interpreted a Charter guarantee to trial "within a reasonable time" to require an accused to move between charges to trial in 18 or 30 months, depending on whether the accused is being tried in a provincial or superior court, or a case will be thrown out (*R v Jordan*, 2016).

Once the police or relevant enforcement body possesses enough evidence to support a criminal charge against the person or company in question, the matter proceeds according to ordinary criminal procedure. A document (called an "information" or an "indictment") is sworn in court outlining the allegations against an accused. While police can arrest a white-collar criminal like any other, more common in the case of less serious offences is the issuance of an "appearance notice," which involves a promise to appear in court. Since corporations, plainly, cannot be arrested, a summons or notice pursuant to section 703.2 of the *Criminal Code* is sufficient. The Crown must provide "disclosure" to the accused of the relevant case-related information it possesses—another Charter-protected right (*R v Stinchcombe*, 1991).

With respect to less serious forms of white-collar conduct, regulatory authorities may opt against criminal enforcement in favour of a more informal and educational response, with the ultimate goal being rehabilitation rather than punishment. Especially where corporations are concerned, avoiding an adversarial, sanctions-based approach can be a more effective method of securing compliance and other public-interest outcomes. This is especially true where personnel respond to the regulator's feedback, as John Braithwaite has argued in his model of "Responsive Regulation" (Braithwaite, 2011). Cooperative models of regulation involving closer government–industry relations, however, can also invite concerns of regulatory capture as officials begin to personally relate to those on the other side (Snider, 1993).

Another regulatory "half-way house" is civil or administrative enforcement. The British Columbia Securities Commission, for example, can elect to proceed on a criminal or civil track for many violations of the BC *Securities Act*. The former route, set out in section 155 of the Act, allows for jail time up to three years and fines up to $3 million or more, depending on profits earned. The latter, set out in sections 161 and 162, forfeits a "hard time" sanction but allows for a range of orders "in the public interest." These include an order to resign or refrain from assuming a director or officer position; to pay back profits earned from non-compliance; and to account for a financial penalty of up to $1 million per contravention—a so-called **administrative monetary penalty (AMP)**. The increasing use of AMPs has been controversial. While many Charter challenges have been brought over the years against AMPs alleged to be so high that they amount to a disguised criminal fine levied without accompanying criminal law due process standards, the Supreme Court of Canada settled the matter in a 2015 case upholding the *Income Tax Act*'s AMP regime (*R v Guindon*, 2015).

> **administrative monetary penalty (AMP)**
> A non-criminal penalty issued by a regulatory body, without court approval, for the violation of a law it administers.

White-Collar Prosecutions and Hearings

Prosecutions in any white-collar case differ according to forum. Criminal-track prosecutions are heard in court and face the scrutiny of the both the criminal law's traditional "beyond a reasonable doubt" burden of proof and the strict rules of evidence applicable in court settings. The ordinary criminal process applies. Accused persons are entitled to a bail hearing and will generally be able to elect to hear their case by a judge alone or, alternatively, by a judge and jury, which includes a preliminary inquiry. The preliminary inquiry determines whether enough evidence exists to stand the accused for trial, and also has the advantage of giving the defence a preview of the Crown's case prior to trial. Corporations "appear in court" through agents or their counsel, as set out in sections 538 and 556 of the *Criminal Code*.

Administrative cases, in contrast, are heard before specialized tribunals or boards. Hundreds of these administrative avenues exist in Canada. To provide for a more speedy and accessible process relative to a court setting, legislation often provides that these venues are not subject to the strict laws of evidence. For example, "hearsay" evidence—second-hand evidence not tendered through a witness in court—can be accepted without resort to the complex rules governing its admission in court. Moreover, applicants before administrative bodies need to prove their case only on a "balance of probabilities," which is a far cry from the criminal "beyond a reasonable doubt" standard.

However, administrative hearings in other respects resemble a court process: the adversarial setting; the presence of lawyers; the hearing of evidence; and the procedural formalities involved (such as rules of procedure).

Class actions and civil cases in respect of white-collar cases are heard in court. While the civil court process, similar to the criminal court process, requires that various evidentiary and procedural formalities be followed, the burden of proof remains a "balance of probabilities." Owing to this standard, civil and administrative hearings can result in liability even if a parallel criminal proceeding renders a "not guilty" finding. For example, in the infamous O.J. Simpson–Nicole Brown murder saga, the former NFL football player was held criminally "not guilty" for murder, but civilly liable for "wrongful death."

Sanctions in White-Collar Cases

At the end of a criminal trial, the accused is either "not guilty" or "guilty" (and thus an "offender"). At the end of a civil trial or administrative process, "liability," and not "guilt" in the strict sense, is assessed. Many, including Sutherland, were bothered by the ability of white-collar offenders to escape the stigma of the criminal system. However, civil and administrative tracks also enable white-collar accountability in cases where the prosecution cannot secure a watertight "beyond a reasonable doubt" case. In such cases, filling the gap with AMPs and public-interest orders, or in lesser cases with warnings and education, may arguably be a better result for the public interest than the elusive trophy of conviction.

Just as the overwhelming majority of civil lawsuits are settled prior to trial, plea bargaining and settlement pervade criminal and administrative disputes between enforcers and those accused of white-collar crime. One tool used by prosecutors is the "deferred prosecution agreement" (DPA). A DPA involves a promise by an enforcer not to prosecute a criminal charge against a company on the condition that the company complies with specified, contract-like terms. These terms usually commit the company to substantial internal compliance reforms as well as requirements that personnel cooperate with the government, often to build a criminal case against individual employees (Spivack & Raman, 2008). The result, in one commentator's view, is a brave new world where the corporation becomes, in effect, "the branch office of the prosecutor" (First, 2010). In 2018, the Trudeau government introduced legislative amendments within Bill C-74 that enable DPAs (styled as "remediation agreements") in Canada, which aligned its practice with that in other jurisdictions.

When an individual or corporate accused pleads guilty or is convicted of a crime at trial, a separate hearing follows whereby a sentence is determined on the basis of factors such as the nature of the offence, the offender's circumstances, and the offence's community or victim impact. The sentence must be guided by the sentencing objectives in section 718 of the *Criminal Code*:

> (a) to denounce unlawful conduct and the harm done to victims or to the community that is caused by unlawful conduct;
> (b) to deter the offender and other persons from committing offences;
> (c) to separate offenders from society, where necessary;
> (d) to assist in rehabilitating offenders;

(e) to provide reparations for harm done to victims or to the community; and

(f) to promote a sense of responsibility in offenders, and acknowledgment of the harm done to victims and to the community.

The "fundamental principle" of sentencing is specified in section 718.1 of the *Criminal Code*: "A sentence must be proportionate to the gravity of the offence and the degree of responsibility of the offender." White-collar crimes present competing considerations in light of these criteria. On one hand, white-collar conduct often (but not always) results in predominantly *economic* harm rather than physical harm, which can pose more lasting (including psychological) consequences for victims and immediate risks to society at large. On the other hand, individual white-collar offenders frequently abuse positions of high social and economic privilege and commit carefully planned acts more likely to be motivated by greed than passion or desperation.

In the Westray Bill, or Bill C-45, additional sentencing factors were enacted into section 718.21 of the *Criminal Code* specific to corporate and other organizational offenders. These include consideration of, among other things, any advantage realized by the organization through the offence, impacts on the organization's economic viability and employees, and any internal measures adopted by the company since the offence.

Corporate Criminal Liability and Governance

Corporations are a focal point of any discussion around white-collar crime, especially with respect to sanction: How, exactly, does it make sense to attach culpability to organizations that have "no soul to damn" and "no body to kick" (Coffee, 1981)?

The Criminal Liability Debate

Whether the criminal law should seek to punish corporations is a hotly debated topic among criminologists, lawyers, and economists. In Canadian law, however, the matter has been settled: Canada's experience with treating corporations as capable of being convicted dates back to a case that is well over a century old (*Union Colliery Co v The Queen*, 1900).

One puzzle is how the requirement of *mens rea*, or intent, attached to most criminal offences sits with purely legal persons that lack a "mind." In a landmark competition law case, *R v Canadian Dredge & Dock Co* (1985), the Supreme Court of Canada elaborated on the logic behind its approach to this matter. The court accepted identification theory as the basis for criminal liability. According to this theory, guilt can be assigned to a corporation when a crime is committed by senior personnel (the "directing mind"), including "the board of directors, the managing director, the superintendent, the manager or anyone else delegated by the board of directors to whom is delegated the governing executive authority of the corporation" (para. 32). Guilt can extend from such a person to the corporation where the person takes an action that "(a) was within the field of operation assigned to him; (b) was not totally in fraud of the corporation; and (c) was by design or result partly for the benefit of the company" (para. 66).

Largely in response to Nova Scotia's Westray Mine disaster and the scathing recommendations of Justice Peter Richard in its inquiry, Parliament enacted significant reforms to this liability framework in 2004 by enacting Bill C-45. In cases where the prosecution must prove the company's negligence, section 22.1 of the *Criminal Code* provides that "an organization is a party to the offence" if a "representative" is a party to the offence—defined to include a director, partner, employee, member, or even an agent or a contractor of the organization. For offences requiring proof of more than negligence (i.e., an intentional or reckless act), a higher standard is set out in section 22.2: Only the actions of a "representative" directed or overseen by senior officers can be attributed to the company. Together, these provisions represent a significant expansion of the Supreme Court's model of liability.

Even if one accepts the logic of corporate criminality as declared by the Supreme Court and Parliament, the concept has other difficult implications. For one, convicting a corporation financially impacts a wide body of innocent bystanders. Shareholders stand to lose from a decline in the value of their securities. Innocent rank-and-file employees, too, may suffer if the conviction has a lasting impact on the firm's fortunes in the market. For example, the collapse of Enron auditor Arthur Andersen led 27,000 people to lose their jobs—a massive unintended consequence of the prosecution of the company (Meeks, 2007). Another critique of corporate criminal liability is that it breeds an antagonism between government oversight bodies and regulated entities that is incompatible with regulatory law's core goal of promoting compliance rather than punishing actors for anti-social behaviour (Snider, 1993, p. 135). As Shapiro (1985, p. 199) puts it, "criminal prosecution is associated with regulatory failure. It is a response to offences that are discovered too late to prevent substantial harm." Finally, criminal prosecution is inefficient and unduly involved: "It is too slow, too expensive, and there are too many legal protections for powerful corporations to exploit to circumvent compliance" (Snider, 1993, p. 136).

Still, a compelling case can be made that no AMP can compensate for the sheer moral condemnation of a criminal conviction. While fines or penalties themselves seldom make a lasting dent on a large company's balance sheet, the stigma associated with culpability can have a grave impact on the "reputational capital" required to keep an enterprise afloat—a good reason for high-level personnel to abide by the law. Without parallel prosecutions of individual decision-makers, however, both deterrence and punishment are arguably diminished. DPAs present an attractive way around the problem, allowing regulators to pursue individual employee responsibility through the criminal law while leaving corporate responsibility to be dealt with by enforceable DPA conditions (such as employee education and cooperation with investigations).

Internal Investigations

The progressive expansion of criminal, administrative, and civil liability for corporations has led to a sea change in internal corporate practice. Multinational companies in particular now administer substantial internal compliance programs that represent a multi-million-dollar business (Green & Podgor, 2013). Companies hire not only consultants but also specialized, full-time personnel, such as internal investigation attorneys, to manage such processes (Murphy & Dervan, 2005). Having robust procedures around misconduct allows companies to demonstrate due diligence at the corporate and management levels. A lack of due diligence is a minimum legal requirement for criminal culpability in Canada, according to the Supreme Court of Canada (*R v Sault Ste Marie*, 1978), but also for many forms of civil and administrative liability. Compliance procedures also allow companies to be proactive in putting out fires, rather than reacting to regulatory sanctions.

Companies have increasingly embraced "whistle-blowing" protocols in particular. The term **whistle-blower** refers to a person who exposes actual or potential misconduct at an organization. By the Association of Certified Fraud Examiners' (2018) count, 40 percent of occupational fraud is detected by these "tipsters," and that is over twice as much as by the next-most-common source (detection by internal audit). However, stories of retaliation against whistle-blowers—who may be perceived as disloyal "snitches" within the company culture—have prompted legislators to enact protective legislation. The US *Sarbanes-Oxley Act* of 2002 made retaliation itself a criminal offence punishable by seven to ten years of jail time. In the *Dodd-Frank Wall Street Reform and Consumer Protection Act* of 2010, this regime was bolstered by provisions awarding whistle-blowers 10 to 30 percent of the value of any judicial award or monetary settlement obtained by the SEC. These reforms reflect a growing prosecutorial realism about the extent to which white-collar crime can be effectively detected from the outside. Since 2015, Ontario and Quebec securities regulators have adopted whistle-blower programs to encourage reporting of securities law breaches in those jurisdictions (although only Ontario's system offers compensation).

Company investigations that follow misconduct reports typically feature the formation of a "special committee" of the board of directors with its own legal counsel. This institutional device insulates the investigation, at least in part, from pressures to cover up misconduct and allows conflicts of interest between the company and implicated employees (including, potentially, the executive team) to be managed more effectively.

Corporate Social Responsibility

The rise of in-house attention to such compliance matters can also be tracked to the growing **corporate social responsibility (CSR)** movement. CSR has been described as "a concept whereby companies integrate social and environmental concerns in their business operations and in their interaction with stakeholders on a voluntary basis" (European Commission, 2001, p. 6). CSR takes matters a step beyond the mere *avoidance* of misconduct by firms: Rather, it envisions them voluntarily pursuing higher standards. Companies have increasingly adopted CSR language—such as "sustainability," the "triple-bottom-line" ("profit, people, planet"), "corporate citizenship," and so forth—in their disclosure documents, suggesting a discrete awareness of shareholder and customer concern over such issues.

Some critics, however, have charged that companies' CSR initiatives are mere window dressing. To mediate between industry and activist concerns about "greenwashing"—the term used to describe a company's deceptive promotion of an environmentally friendly image or products—the Competition Bureau and the Canadian Standards Association jointly developed a guidance document in 2008 to delineate between legitimate and illegitimate green marketing (Competition Bureau, 2008).

Judges are also taking note of the CSR concept. In its landmark corporate law decision in *BCE Inc v 1976 Debentureholders* (2008), the Supreme Court of Canada—albeit without much elaboration—described a corporate director's duty "to act in the best interests of the corporation viewed as a good corporate citizen" (para. 66). Such language serves as a marked departure from past shareholder-focused conceptions of the corporation's mission. It envisions corporate managers as considering a broad range of stakeholders in making important decisions, including "shareholders, employees,

whistle-blower
A person who reports misconduct within an organization.

corporate social responsibility (CSR)
A theory of corporate self-regulation whereby companies actively pursue compliance with the law and ethical norms as a part of doing business.

suppliers, creditors, consumers, governments and the environment" (para. 39). While CSR claims will continue to require a probing eye, the concept carries some promise as a normative vision of corporate governance—one in which corporate boards are bound more by the "social sanction" of an ethical corporate culture than by legal deterrents.

Conclusion

While blunt in their conclusions and liberal with their facts, Edwin Sutherland's early studies on white-collar crime's prevalence and social impact remain as true today as they were in the 1940s. But what has changed? For one, a series of high-profile scandals—from Enron to the financial crisis to "Dieselgate" and beyond—has made the scourge of white-collar crime more visible, prompting a more sustained legislative focus on the problem from both the business-skeptical left and the tough-on-crime right. The result, in turn, has been a stepping-up of North American white-collar enforcement, using both the traditional tools of criminal law and an array of administrative powers. Private enforcement, too, has played a role, with victims better able to assert multi-million-dollar class-action claims against at-fault companies to recover their losses. Investors recovered $7.2 billion, for example, in a 2008 class-action settlement with banks alleged to be complicit in Enron's accounting fraud (Lozano, 2008). Technology has also changed the landscape of white-collar crime by allowing for more anonymous, high-speed, and cross-border forms of criminality, and by forcing police and regulators to adapt in step. Finally, large corporations are voluntarily joining the battle against white-collar crime, either to limit their liability risks or to fulfill self-imposed CSR commitments. Sutherland saw a "lack of social organization" against white-collar crime as its greatest enabler (Sutherland, 1940). In the first two decades of the 20th century, white-collar crime appears to be firmly on the public agenda amidst a generational peak in skepticism toward business in light of the financial crisis, repeated corporate scandals, and a rise in anti-elite political sentiments. Whether public concern can support current resource investments into the longer term will have lasting consequences for the fairness and competiveness of Canada's economy for years to come.

SUMMARY OF KEY POINTS

- The term "white-collar crime" was coined by sociologist Edwin Sutherland in 1939, and it generally describes a category of misconduct defined by either the privileged identity of the offender or the occupational context of the act.
- White-collar criminality is captured in criminal, regulatory, and civil laws, sometimes all at once. Purely criminal offences make up only a fraction of the legal response to white-collar misconduct in Canada.
- Technology is changing the nature of white-collar crime and creating new opportunities for computer-based exploitation. It has also made investigations and prosecutions more complex and document heavy.
- Regulators are increasingly turning to administrative monetary penalties (AMPs) and compliance-oriented regulation—including the use of deferred prosecution agreements (DPAs)—to overcome the criminal law's limitations in prosecuting white-collar conduct, especially that of corporations.

- Companies are increasingly taking a proactive approach to preventing employee misconduct—both to avoid penalties and protect their reputation—by developing rigorous internal compliance processes. "Corporate social responsibility" envisions a concept of "corporate citizenship" whereby companies serve not only their shareholders, but the broader community.
- Eron Mortgage, Bernie Madoff, and other high-profile business scandals will continue to be the primary impetus for tougher white-collar enforcement by shifting public attitudes away from a "default" complacency. The scandal-plagued 2000s tracked a sustained legislative interest in white-collar criminality.

QUESTIONS FOR CRITICAL DISCUSSION

1. Is Canada unduly "soft" on white-collar crime? If so, why do you think that is?
2. Is the criminal law an effective sanction against corporations?
3. Should white-collar crime be defined by the privileged status of its perpetrators, or the nature of the offences themselves? Does it matter?
4. Is white-collar crime more or less blameworthy than traditional "street" crime?
5. Do you believe Sutherland was right in describing the criminal law's underinclusiveness with respect to white-collar misconduct? Have things changed? What conduct should—or should not—be criminal, and why?

SUGGESTED FURTHER READINGS

Byttle, S. (2012). *Still dying for a living: Corporate criminal liability after the Westray Mine disaster*. Vancouver: UBC Press.

McLean, B., & Elkind, P. (2004). *The smartest guys in the room: The amazing rise and scandalous fall of Enron*. New York: Portfolio Trade.

Puri, P. (2001). Sentencing the criminal corporation. *Osgoode Hall Law Journal, 39*, 611–653.

Sutherland, E.H. (1940). White-collar criminality. *American Sociological Review, 5*, 1–12.

Websites

Competition Bureau. Legal Actions and Opinions: http://www.competitionbureau.gc.ca/eic/site/cb-bc.nsf/eng/h_00020.html

FBI. White-Collar Crime: http://www.fbi.gov/about-us/investigate/white_collar/whitecollarcrime

KPMG. Global profiles of the fraudster: An illustrative look at the findings: https://home.kpmg.com/xx/en/home/insights/2016/05/global-profiles-of-the-fraudster.html

Legislation

Canada Business Corporations Act, RSC 1985, c C-44.

Canada Labour Code, RSC 1985, c L-2.

Canadian Charter of Rights and Freedoms, Part I of the *Constitution Act, 1982*, being Schedule B to the *Canada Act 1982* (UK), 1982, c 11.

Competition Act, RSC 1985, c C-34.

Corruption of Foreign Public Officials Act, SC 1998, c 34.

Criminal Code, RSC 1985, c C-46.
Income Tax Act, RSC 1985, c 1 (5th Supp).
Occupational Health and Safety Act, RSO 1900, c O.1.
Proceeds of Crime (Money Laundering) and Terrorist Financing Act, SC 2000, c 17.
Securities Act, RSBC 1996, c 418.
Securities Act, RSO 1990, c S.5.
Standing Up for Victims of White-Collar Crime Act, SC 2011, c 6.

Cases

BCE Inc v 1976 Debentureholders, 2008 SCC 69.
British Columbia Securities Commission v Branch, [1995] 2 SCR 3, 1995 CanLII 142.
R v Canadian Dredge & Dock Co, [1985] 1 SCR 662, 1985 CanLII 32.
R v Drabinsky 2009 CanLII 12802, 242 CCC (3d) 449 (Ont Sup Ct J).
R v Guindon, 2015 SCC 41.
R v Jordan, 2016 SCC 27.
R v Nur, 2015 SCC 15.
R v Sault Ste Marie, [1978] 2 SCR 1299, 1978 CanLII 11.
R v Stinchcombe, [1991] 3 SCR 326.
R v Théroux, [1993] 2 SCR 5, 1991 CanLII 45.
Smith v Baker, [1891] UKHL 2 (BAILII).
Union Colliery Co v The Queen, 31 SCR 81, 1900 CanLII 31.
United States v Black, 625 F 3d 386 (7th Cir 2010).

R v Dobson: The Emerging Crime of Internet Luring

It can be difficult to monitor an accused's actions on the Internet.

In June of 2013, Scott Dobson was sentenced after conviction on two counts of Internet luring, contrary to section 172.1(2) of the *Criminal Code*. Mr. Dobson had pled guilty to these crimes in 2012. Justice Perkins-McVey made the following statement before providing her reasons for judgment, placing this kind of crime in historical context:

> The offence of internet luring came in force on July 23, 2002. Section 172.1 prohibits electronic communication with a person under the age of 14 when such communication is for the purpose of facilitating the commission of one of the enumerated offences. In this case, the enumerated offences are the offence of sexual assault under section 271 of the *Criminal Code* and the offence of Invitation to Sexual Touching contrary to s. 155 of the *Criminal Code*. The harm sought to be avoided by the offence is that of communication which renders children at risk to the offences. The Crown does not have to establish that the offender would have actually committed one of the offences. (*R v Dobson*, para. 2)

Justice Perkins-McVey goes on to note:

> The offence of internet luring is an offence of the modern age—born of the modern reality of the internet, where an accused can counsel and entice children to engage in the prohibited activity within the sanctity of his or her own home. (para. 3)

What Mr. Dobson did between January 20, 2012 and March 14, 2012 was to engage in Internet chats with someone he believed was a girl under the age of 14; he was 45 years of age at the time. During these Internet chats, he asked a number of explicit sexual questions, indicated that he would pay her for sexual acts, and ultimately arranged to meet her at a prearranged location. In fact, Mr. Dobson was not corresponding in this chat room with a 14-year-old girl, but with Detective Michael Pelletier of the Ottawa Police Service, who had logged into the chat room in an undercover capacity. When Mr. Dobson went to the location where he was to meet the 14-year-old girl, Detective Pelletier engaged him in conversation and uniformed officers arrested him.

Prior to sentence, a psychiatric report was prepared by Dr. Fedoroff of the Royal Ottawa Mental Health Centre. Although Mr. Dobson indicated that he was only interested in adult females rather than children, phallometric testing revealed a positive response to children, contradicting his denial of this interest. Dr. Fedoroff also noted that Mr. Dobson appeared to have no interest in assaulting either adults or children, and suggested that he receive counselling for this behaviour; he concluded that the prognosis for Mr. Dobson was "excellent."

Mr. Dobson had no previous criminal record prior to this offence and, once arrested, sought a referral to treatment. The court noted that he does not have any issues with substance abuse nor any mental health or psychiatric conditions. He has been gainfully employed for most of his adult life, although he lost his job as a custodian with the federal government after these charges were laid against him.

Justice Perkins-McVey set out the position of the defence:

> The defence asks the Court to impose a conditional jail sentence of 15 to 18 months plus probation with strict conditions including curfew. The defence argues his prospects for rehabilitation are good; he pled guilty and accepts responsibility. The defendant argues he has also sought help and argues in mitigation, no explicit photos were transmitted over the Internet. The defence urges that such a sentence would adequately address the need for general deterrence and denunciation given his pre-sentence custody, given his release on strict bail conditions and given that since these offences, the accused has not breached the conditions of his release. The defence argues that if a real jail sentence is required, that a sentence of 90 days should be imposed. (para. 39)

Alternatively, as Justice Perkins-McVey wrote:

> The Crown asks for a jail sentence of 18 to 24 months followed by 3 years' probation. The Crown argues that despite having no prior record that this offence is serious, and that there are 26 separate chats documented to have occurred between January 2012 and March 2012, wherein sexualized conversations took place. In addition, having learned the "girl" came from an impoverished background, the accused offered money for sex. He argues that the accused knows how young the girl is because he asks, and yet he still engages in these sexualized conversations and suggesting sexual activity to the girl over the Internet. The Crown also raised concerns regarding the degree of Mr. Dobson's insight into the degree and extent of his sexual disorders as identified in the Sexual Behaviours Assessment. The Crown argues that this is <u>not</u> one of those rarest one of cases that would warrant consideration of a conditional sentence. Further the facts are aggravating in that the accused offers and arranges to meet the "girl" on more than one occasion and does in fact show up on another occasion, at the designated location where he is arrested. Further the chat logs filed in the sentencing hearing show that during the February 27th conversation, he sought to add another young girl to the chat. I agree with the Crown that this is another aggravating factor. (para. 40)

Finally, Justice Perkins-McVey imposed a sentence of 18 months imprisonment, noting:

> In my view, given the aggravating factors, the imposition [of] a conditional sentence would be inconsistent with the fundamental purpose and principles of sentencing. As indicated in *R. v. Folino*, and subsequent case law, a conditional sentence is to be imposed only in the rarest of cases. This is not one of those cases. There is nothing exceptional in Mr. Dobson's background or the facts of this case that would put this case in the category of the rarest cases. I accept he has a supportive family, and pled guilty, sought treatment, but this is not enough to be "the rarest of cases." The aggravating facts, particularly his arranging to meet on two or more occasions and actually attending at the meeting with the 14 year old for a sexual purpose and further, given that these offences occurred over the Internet where it is so difficult to monitor an accused's actions, I cannot be satisfied that service of the sentence in the community would not endanger the safety of the community. (para. 47)

Before You Read Chapter 19

- Do you agree with the sentence imposed by Justice Perkins-McVey in this case? If so, why, and if not, why not?
- A broad range of computer crimes is discussed in this chapter. Where does this crime fall, within this range?
- What kinds of challenges exist with respect to enforcement of a crime such as this, or in relation to other computer-facilitated crimes?

21st-Century Crimes: Cybercrime and Terrorism

LEARNING OUTCOMES

After reading this chapter, students will be able to:

- Understand how technology is being used to commit crime in the 21st century.
- Differentiate between a broad range of cybercrimes and their impacts.
- Unpack the complexities associated with the causes of terrorism and radicalization when they change from non-violent to violent.
- Describe the various ideological beliefs and motives associated with terrorist groups.
- Explain the primary targets and tactics of terrorist campaigns.
- List ways that terrorists use the Internet to promote their activities.
- Draw distinctions between the approaches to countering violent extremism and terrorism.

CHAPTER OUTLINE

Introduction

The ways in which people connect, communicate, and interact with each other have evolved at a rapid pace in the last two decades, largely thanks to advances in computer technology and globalization. So too have the ways in which people engage in criminal activity in the 21st century. Nowadays, computers and the Internet provide countless opportunities for people to misuse such technological advances and facilitate acts of deviance and crime online, cutting across national boundaries and targeting victims on a global scale (Holt & Bossler, 2014). And with international institutions weakening and law enforcement agencies struggling to police international borders, we are seeing a rise in cybercrimes in general, and transnational crimes in particular, ranging from environmental crimes (UNEP-Interpol, 2016) and counterfeiting crimes (Interpol, 2018c) to drug trafficking (Europol, 2018) and human smuggling (Interpol, 2018b). In the 21st century, terrorism, although its roots can be traced back thousands of years, has also been understood as crime, because terrorist organizations have developed into transnational networks as a result of modern information and communication technologies (Hoffman 2006). The Internet, for example, has provided terrorist groups with a centralized space in which they can connect, recruit, and mobilize, as well as disseminate propaganda and plan attacks, both within and beyond domestic borders (Conway, 2006).

This chapter explores some key concepts and ideas associated with cybercrime and terrorism in the 21st century. In the first half of the chapter, we provide an overview of the scale and scope of cybercrime, followed by an overview of the various classes and prominent types of cybercrimes, as well as their impacts and how governments are responding. In the second half of the chapter, we highlight the challenges of defining terrorism and radicalization in the 21st century, followed by a look at the ideologies, tactics, and targets of various international terrorist groups, as well as an overview of how terrorists use the Internet. We conclude with a discussion of some of the types of initiatives that have been developed to combat terrorism and violent extremism in the 21st century.

Definition and Explanation of Cybercrime

People around the world are increasingly using computer technologies and computer-mediated communications to connect with each other. The Internet's seamless accessibility and user-friendly platform have revolutionized the sharing of information and communications (Newman & Clarke, 2003). Criminals have embraced this changing digital landscape, and the extent to which they engage in **cybercrime**—the use of cyberspace or computer technology to facilitate acts of crime and deviance—has grown rapidly around the globe (Clough, 2015). Juniper Research (2015), for example, estimated that the global cost of cybercrime will increase threefold from an estimated $500 billion in 2015 to $2 trillion by 2019. Worth noting, however, is that the scale and scope of cybercrime is difficult to estimate for a number of important reasons.

First, there is no universally accepted definition of cybercrime that law enforcement agencies refer to (Interpol, 2018a). In fact, there are as many terms to describe cybercrime as there are cybercrimes themselves (Clough, 2015). One law enforcement agency, for example, may collect official crime statistics on cybercrimes by referring to one definition, while another agency may collect statistics on cybercrime using another definition. These inconsistencies in data collection make it challenging to draw conclusions about the extent of the problem.

Second, many cybercrimes are existing offences in the *Criminal Code* that are facilitated by technology. Yet, official crime statistics do not draw distinctions between the online and offline components of a crime (McGuire & Dowling, 2013b). As an example, a man plants a tracking device in his ex-girlfriend's cellphone and stalks her for weeks before she reports it to police, but the responding officer decides to record the crime as "stalking" and not "the use of technology in stalking."

Third, the rate at which cybercrimes are being committed may not be accurately reflected in crime statistics because of underreporting (Australian Cyber Security Centre, 2016). Reasons for underreporting vary, but the most common include that the victim felt the crime was not serious enough to report or saw no benefit in reporting (Australian Cyber Security Centre, 2016). Also, ordinary computer users may not be aware that they were victims of a cybercrime (McGuire & Dowling, 2013a), and law enforcement agencies may lack the expertise and/or resources to identify and respond to cybercrime (Clough, 2015).

Lastly, many of those who compile data on cybercrime may overestimate its prevalence (Anderson et al., 2012). Some of these compilers, for example, may have an agenda, such as security software vendors who want to upsell their product. There may also be methodological errors with the data collection; for example, a survey may be given to

cybercrime
The use of cyberspace or computer technology to facilitate acts of crime and deviance.

a self-selected sample of participants (McGuire and Dowling, 2013b). In addition, the number of cybercrimes may be distorted by the media, as the media tend to focus on and even sensationalize new forms of crime (for example, cybercrime), offering uncritical accounts of a particular story (Clough, 2015). When these aspects come into play, it is difficult—nearly impossible, really—to gauge the extent and degree of cybercrime.

Nonetheless, it is becoming increasingly apparent that the number of cybercrime incidents is on the rise around the globe, and while there is no general consensus as to why cybercrimes are increasing, some answers have been found by cybercrime scholars, especially those relying on Cohen and Felson's (1979) "routine activity theory" (RAT). RAT has been used to explain why people commit cybercrimes in general (Williams, 2016) and how key features of digital technology have facilitated crime and inhibited law enforcement efforts in responding to it (Clough, 2015). In short, RAT posits that crimes are committed when an offender has a large selection of victims, motivated offenders, and an absence of capable guardians.

To further illustrate, first, with roughly 84 percent of households having Internet access in the developed world (International Telecommunication Union, 2017), the Internet allows users to communicate with countless people, both easily and cheaply, and on a global scale. In turn, the rate with which offenders can commit crimes online, compared to offline, is much higher because they have a much richer pool of victims to select from (Clough, 2015). And because of the scale and accessibility of digital technology, cybercriminals can also connect and communicate with other like-minded individuals and form virtual communities to further their offending (Westlake & Bouchard, 2016).

Second, the anonymous nature of digital technology facilitates cybercrime because offenders can operate while concealing their identities online using proxy servers, spoofed email or Internet protocol (IP) addresses, anonymous emails, or encryption software (Clough, 2015).

Lastly, digital technology presents an array of challenges for law enforcement officials. Aside from the sheer volume of users and the interconnected nature of modern communications, both of which make surveillance a difficult undertaking, law enforcement agencies must work with various entities during an investigation because infrastructure is privately owned and communications are oftentimes routed through multiple jurisdictions. Law enforcement will therefore require the assistance of local law enforcement agencies (Clough, 2015). Law enforcement, too, must use sophisticated forensic techniques to retrieve, preserve, and validate evidence for use in criminal trials, which is indeed a difficult task given the volatile nature of electronic data (Clough, 2015). Taken together, these factors complicate the investigate process and cybercriminals use this to their advantage.

Types of Cybercrimes

Although there is no universally accepted definition of cybercrime, the general consensus among experts is that there are three principal categories of cybercrime: (1) **computer-supported crimes**, (2) **computer-facilitated crimes**, and (3) **computer crimes**. Each type requires some element of a computer being used during the commission of a criminal offence, and some crimes may cut across categories. The following is an explanation of the crimes that fit within each category, with the greatest emphasis on the most prevalent—and impactful—computer-facilitated crimes and, to a lesser extent, computer crimes.

computer-supported crime
Crime in which computers do not play a central role, but may contain evidence.

computer-facilitated crime
Crime in which computers are used as a tool.

computer crime
Crime in which a computer or computer network is the target.

Levels of the Internet

Whether it's shopping for the latest tech gadget or booking that last-minute flight to London, the vast majority of people will do so by searching Google or a similarly popular search engine, or by visiting sites that are indexed by a search engine. But what about sites that are not indexed to a search engine? These unknown, sometimes deep or dark digital spaces can be best explained by highlighting the three levels of the Internet:

- *Surface web*: This is the portion of the Internet that we spend our time on and that is indexed by search engines (for example, Google, Yahoo, and so on).
- *Deep web*: Deep web sites are publicly available but are not indexed by traditional search engines because of the way that the URL is configured. The deep web runs below the surface web on the Internet and includes non-indexed content such as databases, web archives, and password-protected sites.
- *Dark web*: This is the portion of the Internet that requires encrypted access through a Darknet program (for example, Tor, 12P, or Freenet). The dark web takes active measures to hide the identity of visitors, sellers, buyers, and payments (Chertoff, 2017).

Tor (The Onion Router) is a program used to gain access to the dark web that actively hides a user's location and identity. Instead of a user travelling through one path to reach the recipient's computer (node) and revealing the

user's location through their IP address, as is the case with Internet browsers on the surface web, Tor travels through a series of nodes, each of which are random and rebuilt every 10 minutes, wherein each path is encrypted with a different key at each node in the path (Figure 19.1). Each node only knows the location of the previous node and the next node in the path, so the sender of the message and the recipient will not know each other's location (Guitton, 2013). Programs such as Tor are used for:

1. *Communications*: A chat application that runs on Tor hides all identities and IP addresses.
2. *Visiting Internet websites*: A user can access a site without the site knowing the user's location, or a user can visit a site that blocks their access (for example, the government of China restricts the content that its residents can access online, but Tor enables access); and
3. *Visiting hidden services websites*: A user can access hidden/anonymous sites inside the Tor network without the sites knowing the user's location.

Content found on the dark web includes drugs, weapons, hit-man-for-hire services, black markets, child exploitation material, fake identification cards, credit card numbers, and carding products such as magnetic skimmers (Guitton, 2013).

FIGURE 19.1   Tor (The Onion Router)

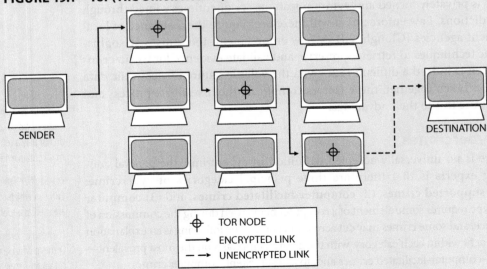

SENDER · DESTINATION

⊕ TOR NODE
→ ENCRYPTED LINK
- -> UNENCRYPTED LINK

Computer-Supported Crimes

Computer-supported crimes are those in which computers are not central to the crime but may contain evidence of the crime. For example, computer-supported crimes could involve a police officer finding a victim's home address on the suspect's computer (or phone) or in online communications between the victim and the offender that took place before the offence, or a photograph that the offender took of the victim at the crime scene before the crime took place. In instances like these, technology merely serves as a repository for evidence rather than being implicated in the commission of the offence itself.

Computer-Facilitated Crimes

Computer-facilitated crimes are those in which computers are a tool used to commit crime. Online crimes of this nature are wide-ranging, and include theft, organized crime, harassment, abuse, and exploitation.

Online Theft

Various forms of online theft, including fraud, identity fraud, and identity theft, are a growing concern around the globe. In 2004, for example, the Aberdeen Group estimated that $221 billion dollars was lost every year by businesses as a result of identity theft. From 2004 to 2005, Canada's largest credit bureaus received over 1,800 identity theft complaints every month (BC Freedom of Information and Privacy Association, 2005). Most recently, identity theft has only grown in scope, with a massive data breach at Equifax Canada as a key example of this. In 2017, approximately 19,000 Canadian Equifax customers were affected by a massive data breach when hackers accessed their credit card records—which included names, addresses, credit or debit card numbers, and Social Insurance Numbers (Stewart, 2017). Delta Air Lines was also the victim of one of the latest cyberattacks, when cyber criminals accessed the credit card information of approximately 100,000 of its customers without their authority (Sasso, 2018). Money losses notwithstanding, the time that victims must spend to get their lives back to normal as a result of identity theft is troublesome. The Identity Theft Resource Center (2005), for example, reported that it took victims of identity theft an average of 330 hours to recover assets or repair damages from identity theft. The Identity Theft Resource Center (2017) has also shed light on the fallout from identity theft, which includes significant negative financial impact on victims and high levels of psychological and emotional distress.

Online Organized Crime

Other crimes that fall within the computer-facilitated cybercrimes class include organized crime, transnational organized crime, and money laundering. Historically, cybercrime has been committed at an individual or small-group level (Interpol, 2018a), wherein an individual was self-sufficient and had the necessary skills that were required to complete all aspects of a crime (Brenner, 2002). Often, these offenders did not target a specific group of individuals or entities because they had only a small pool of resources but wanted results quickly. Today, however, crimes are being committed worldwide by organized groups, especially in cyberspace, and these international syndicates are seeking profit by targeting intellectual property, source code, blueprints, and credit cards, to name but a few (Goldman, 2011). These groups also have more resources, money, and time and, as a result, the means by which organized cybercriminals gain access to an assigned target is systematic and well planned; offenders are targeting specific entities, both in a stealth-like manner and on a persistent basis, over long periods of time (Goldman, 2011). To illustrate this process, once a hacker in an organized group gains access to a targeted system and reaches the furthest point that their expertise will take them, they will pass the hack "up the chain" to a more expert hacker. This process is repeated until it reaches the top hacker in the organization, at which point they will steal the information they are searching for and then cover the tracks of all the hackers.

Organized cybercrime groups operate covertly because they do not want their victims to know that their system was breached (Goldman, 2011). Organized cybercrime groups are also formed on the basis of skill; one member, for example, may specialize in malware development, while another is responsible for malware quality assurance, and yet another for malware distribution. The purpose of this arrangement and structure is to create a multi-faceted virtual network that draws from a number of skillsets, wherein members rarely meet others in the network. Only trusted associates have access to core operations, and this prevents law enforcement from infiltrating the group (Tropina, 2010).

In light of this development, the extent to which international syndicates are involved in organized crime remains unclear, as it is easy to confuse schemes that are highly organized with "organized crime" in the traditional sense (see Lusthaus, 2013). Nonetheless, what is much clearer is that some organized crime groups, whether in Canada (see Criminal Intelligence Service Canada, 2014) or internationally (see Levi & Reuter, 2006), use money laundering tactics in cyberspace to hide the proceeds of their crime. Typically, this involves the funnelling of money out of the country in what the United Nations Office on Drugs and Crime (2018) describes as a three-step process (see Figure 19.2).

FIGURE 19.2   Money Laundering Process

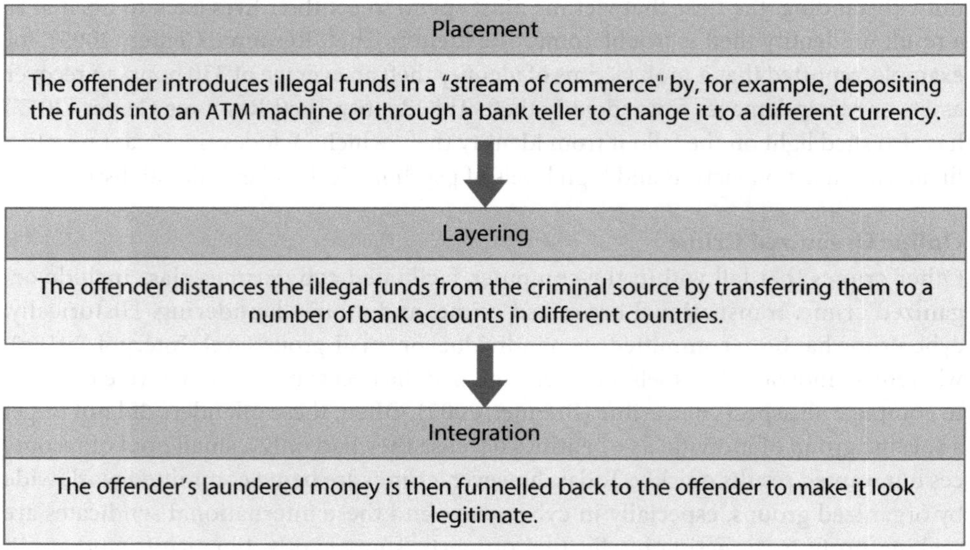

Placement
The offender introduces illegal funds in a "stream of commerce" by, for example, depositing the funds into an ATM machine or through a bank teller to change it to a different currency.

Layering
The offender distances the illegal funds from the criminal source by transferring them to a number of bank accounts in different countries.

Integration
The offender's laundered money is then funnelled back to the offender to make it look legitimate.

Source: Levi and Reuter (2006).

Because offenders must distance themselves from their illegal funds, organized crime groups tend to transfer the money through **money mules** who are located in different countries from the victim and offender. If an offender is trying to launder money through merchandise, the offender will likely purchase products online with the illegal funds and ship the products to a mule who will later reship them back to the offender in exchange for funds (Hao et al., 2015). In addition, offenders may launder their money with **crypto-currencies**, such as through Bitcoin, because they can make anonymous payments and/or international money transfers, which are hard to track, and then transfer the stolen money to Bitcoin, move the currency to a new Bitcoin address so that the original source of the funds is obscured, and then swap the Bitcoin back to hard currency (Meiklejohn et al., 2013).

BOX 19.2

Bitcoin

Bitcoin was the first form of crypto-currency. It was released to the public in 2009 as a set of rules—in the form of computer programs—that created and managed a supply of money and processed payments as well. Bitcoin is open source and is implemented by volunteers (known as Bitcoin miners) who validate and maintain the **blockchain**. Bitcoin was modelled after gold and behaves like cash online, but it is designed for the Internet (see Bitcoin, 2018). This form of currency facilitates money laundering (Moore & Rid, 2016).

Online Harassment, Abuse, and Exploitation

The final group of offences that fits within the definition of computer-facilitated cyber-crimes includes **cyberbullying** and **cyberstalking**, **child exploitation** and child luring, and **human trafficking**. Bullying, whether committed in cyberspace or in the physical world, involves an imbalance of power wherein bullies take advantage of and hurt their victims—whether it is physical (for example, hitting, punching), verbal (for example, name-calling, threats), or on a social level (for example, spreading rumours, excluding a person from a group) (Royal Canadian Mounted Police, 2017a). Cyberbullying, however, is committed through communication technologies, from text messages to posts on social media sites. Forms of cyberbullying range in scope, from posting embarrassing photos of someone to setting up fake websites to make fun of someone, but unlike bullying in the physical world, bullying in cyberspace has no boundaries (Royal Canadian Mounted Police, 2017a). Bullies can reach victims anywhere, and not just in the schoolyard. Cyberbullying can also be much harsher than offline bullying because the bully can say things online, in relative anonymity, that they would not say in person and the messages can also be forwarded ad infinitum (Senate of Canada, 2012). While anyone can be cyberbullied, cyberbullying tends to involve classmates, "friends," or peers. The victims of cyberbullying are most often girls, while the offenders are most often boys (Lenhart, 2010).

Like cyberbullying, cyberstalking can have a significant impact on victims, including anxiety, sleep disturbances, post-traumatic stress disorder, and suicidal thoughts (Clough, 2015). Similar to cyberbullying, cyberstalking offenders have a desire to exert control over their victims, with the majority of cyberstalkers being males and

money mules
A person who relays the received money or merchandise from a victim to an offender and keeps a portion of the proceeds.

crypto-currency
A digital currency in which encryption techniques are used to secure and make the virtual asset and transaction anonymous.

blockchain
A continuously growing list of records (blocks) or a chain of transactions on a public transaction system that functions as a distributed ledger that is linked and secured using cryptography.

cyberbullying
Bullying through the use of communication technologies.

cyberstalking
The use of the Internet or other electronic communication devices to stalk another person, which includes harassing or threatening behaviour that an individual engages in repeatedly.

child exploitation
A photographic, film, video, or other visual representation, whether or not it was made by electronic or mechanical means, that shows a person under the age of 18 engaged in explicit sexual activity or the dominant characteristic of a sexual organ or the anal region of a person under the age of 18.

human trafficking
The act of recruiting, transporting, transferring, harbouring, or receiving a person through a use of force, or other means, for the purpose of exploiting them.

the majority of victims being females who shared some prior relationship with their cyberstalker. Cyberstalking, as with offline stalking, often takes place when a female attempts to break off a relationship with her male partner (Bureau of Justice Statistics, 2017), and the Internet—which can be impersonal and easy to use, and sometimes anonymous—is the medium of choice for some men to "get back" at their former partners. Online harassment and threats may escalate to more serious crime. Law enforcement agencies, to some extent, have taken swift action to respond to cyberstalking. In Canada, for example, there are specialized police units available to investigate and prosecute cases of cyberstalking (Department of Justice Canada, 2017). Yet these cases are difficult to investigate because law enforcement at all levels must be properly trained to use the network investigative techniques and legal processes required to respond to such cases, and must do so while protecting the privacy of legitimate users of the Internet. In light of this, it is important for law enforcement to become more sensitive to cyberstalking complaints and devote the necessary training and resources to allow for proper investigations and subsequent prosecutions (Department of Justice Canada, 2017).

In many respects, technological developments and the introduction of the Internet has helped to re-victimize children, essentially driving the child exploitation market—from the production to the distribution and viewing side of it. In the pre-Internet era, child exploitation—more commonly referred to as child pornography—consisted of small networks in which the content was expensive and of poor quality, and consumers were at high risk of being apprehended (Beech, Elliot, Birgden, & Findlater, 2008). Nowadays, given that the Internet is semi-anonymous and offenders can hide from victims, law enforcement, and even distance themselves from co-offenders, perpetrators are in a much better position to consume, develop, and sell illegal content. Moreover, the global reach of the Internet further puts children at a disadvantage because perpetrators have a larger pool of children that they can lure, recruit, and exploit, and they can do so at an international level (Beech et al., 2008). The existence of the Internet has increased the rate of offending because it offers quick and effective communications between co-offenders (Holt, Blevins, & Burkert, 2010). Yet—for similar reasons that were previously described for cybercrime in general—the scope of the problem is unknown. In 2005, a Royal Canadian Mounted Police (RCMP) officer who was heading an initiative that dealt with online child exploitation estimated that such material could be found on more than 100,000 websites (Butters, 2005). In response, law enforcement has taken active steps to combat online child sexual abuse. For example, the RCMP created a National Child Exploitation Coordination Centre to investigate sexual exploitation of children on the Internet through various services, including coordination of investigative files, management of multi-jurisdictional cases, and expertise in victim identification techniques (Royal Canadian Mounted Police, 2013).

Lastly, intertwined in this digital world of crime are human traffickers. Unlike "classic trafficking" in which people are hidden in cargo containers, shipped across the sea in small boats, and smuggled across borders, "Internet-based trafficking" has made the human trafficking process much easier: Social media sites can be used to recruit victims, and these victims and their services can be advertised on classified websites and elsewhere online. As a result, the number of these victims is staggering. Although the extent of human trafficking is difficult to assess, in 2012 the International Labour Organization estimated that the total number of victims of forced labour, including forced sexual exploitation, was 20.9 million people around the globe. Of that number, 18.7 million people (90 percent) were forced into the private economy either by individuals or enterprises, and 4.5 million (22 percent) of these people were victims of forced sexual exploitation, while 14.2 million (68 percent) of them were victims of forced labour exploitation. A total of 55 percent of these victims were women and girls, compared to 45 percent men and boys. And an estimated 5.5 million of these victims were children (International Labour Organization, 2012). Canada, according to RCMP assistant commissioner Todd Sean, is not known to be a significant country of origin for human trafficking victims, but instead is primarily a destination country. In response, the Government of Canada launched a National Plan to Combat Human Trafficking, which introduced aggressive new initiatives to prevent human trafficking in all its forms by providing assistance to victims and building on their current responses (Public Safety Canada, 2018).

Computer Crimes

Computer crimes are those that target a computer or network and other information specifically, which involves some element of **hacking**. Hackers require a much higher level of technical proficiency than the offenders discussed above, all of whom can be categorized into three central types of hackers, based on their skill:

hacking
Unauthorized access to computers and computer systems.

- *Novice hackers*: Oftentimes referred to as "script kiddies," they comprise the largest subpopulation of hackers and have limited computing skills.
- *Intermediate hackers*: Unlike novice hackers, intermediate hackers are much fewer in number, are highly motivated hackers, are competent, and have a strong understanding of computer concepts.
- *Elite hackers*: This small group, who are very difficult to detect, identify, and capture, have an in-depth understanding of the inner workings of most commercial systems and are capable of breaking into most systems.

BOX 19.3

Cyberwarfare

Traditional types of war have been fought in four domains: land, sea, air, and space. In these domains the equipment includes bullets, landmines, tanks, bombs, battleships, and aircraft fighters, which are expensive and designed to be classified. Warfare participants include state combatants and the military, all of whom are easily attributed to warfare, and the targets of such warfare, under the Geneva Convention, include the "legitimate military targets" attribution. But with the advent of the Internet, a fifth domain—cyberspace—has changed the dynamics of how war can be fought (Lucas, 2017).

Cyberwarfare is relatively cheap compared to traditional warfare. The targets of cyberattacks are communication networks and critical infrastructure, which are privately owned and carry civilian data. Cyberweapons used during war include code exploits that can bring servers down using zero-day exploits, as well as distributed denial-of-service (DDoS) attacks using botnets to knock websites offline or attacks on supervisory control and data acquisition (SCADA) systems that control critical infrastructures. Actors in these

cyberwarfare
Computer- or network-based conflict that involves a politically motivated attack by a nation-state or international organization.

attacks are not only the state, but groups and individuals, thus making it difficult and near impossible to attribute the attack to a particular entity (Lucas, 2017). Questions are also raised about (1) whether it was an "armed" attack, according to how a particular nation defines war, and in turn whether allies will help; and (2) disproportional retaliation, particularly whether a state, for example, will retaliate using cyberwarfare, or with kinetic or nuclear weapons. Neutral territory also becomes a concern because the target of the attack, critical infrastructure, is used to carry Internet traffic. Most important, perhaps, is that questions are raised about who the attacker was, given that it is easy for the attacker to hide—even obfuscate—the trail of attack. It may, in fact, not be a nation-state attacker but, instead, a group such as Anonymous.

Aside from their skillsets, what differentiates hackers is their motivation (Clough, 2015). Novice hackers, for example, tend to be motivated by reputation, wherein they will find exploits, study and learn from them, and trade them with other hackers for the purpose of gaining a reputation and communicating with other hackers, especially elite hackers. Intermediate hackers, on the other hand, are more competent than novice hackers but less experienced than elite hackers and, as a result, they too want to gain a reputation—by acquiring a valuable piece of information or pulling off a noteworthy attack, for example—in order to communicate with the most elite hackers. Conversely, elite hackers are financially driven, so they will create new system exploits and either hoard or trade them with small groups of peers, simply for financial gain. Regardless of their skillset, though, hackers tend to wear one of the following hats:

- *White hat hackers*: Also referred to as "ethical hackers," this group will hack into a computer system or break computer security for non-malicious reasons, such as testing their own security system or making a penetration and vulnerability assessment within a contractual agreement.
- *Black hat hackers*: This group will hack into a computer system or break computer security without authorization, using technology for malicious reasons such as vandalism, credit card fraud, identity theft, piracy, or other types of illegal activity.
- *Gray hat hackers*: This group will hack into a computer system or break computer security without authorization, notify the system administrator about the hack, and then may offer to repair the system for a small fee (Zetter, 2016).

Other types of hackers, such as hacktivists, may be motivated by human rights, free speech, or freedom of information, while those who are driven by political or religious motivation are referred to as cyberterrorists.

Hackers will most often draw from a number of tools and techniques to gain access to or infect a computer or computer system. For example, hackers may develop and/ or use various types of **malware** (also known as "computer viruses"). Malware can be a small piece of software that piggybacks on another file, moving from one host to another, and when a host unknowingly launches the infected software, it spreads and infects computer files (Clough, 2015). "Computer worms," another type of malware, are

malware
Malicious software intended to damage or disable computers and computer systems.

small pieces of software that use computer networks and security holes to self-replicate without needing to infect files to survive. Hackers also use Trojan Horse programs that hide malware in what appears to be a harmless program, damaging a user's computer by, for example, erasing the hard drive when the computer is used. Trojans, unlike worms, do not replicate automatically unless they are bundled with a worm (Clough, 2015). But perhaps most popular among hackers is the implementation of a type of malware that takes advantage of a computer system's vulnerabilities, holding a user's computer hostage and preventing or limiting the user from accessing his or her system until a "ransom" fee has been paid: **ransomware**. In 2015, for example, Canadians were affected by 1,600 ransomware attacks each and every day, and the Canadian Cyber Incident Response Centre's investigation into ransomware had nearly doubled by September 2016 (Royal Canadian Mounted Police, 2017b). An Osterman Research survey report (2016) showed that of the 125 anonymous Canadian organizations participating in the global survey, a staggering 72 percent experienced a ransomware attack in the previous 12 months and 35 percent reported being the victim of a ransomware attack. The vast majority of these victims paid ransoms between $1,000 and $50,000, which is much higher than the cost of ransomware attacks in United States. A total of 11 organizations had to shut down while they dealt with an attack, and five were health-care organizations. This put lives at risk (Osterman Research, 2016).

In response to this growing concern, law enforcement and security agencies have developed ways to combat ransomware. A number of agencies, including McAfee, Europol, the Dutch National Police, and Kaspersky Lab, have created a web portal to help users remove ransomware without paying their attackers. At the portal, users can upload the encrypted files to a website, and the site checks its known 160,000 decryption keys for the correct key (Europol, 2016).

Nonetheless, one of the most difficult types of malware to find and remove is a **rootkit**. Once installed, the rootkit uses stealth technologies to hide its presence and prevent users from receiving accurate information about what is taking place in their system or network (Clough, 2015). This malicious software is frequently used to eavesdrop on someone's computer by exploiting a known vulnerability or cracking a password through the use of a **keylogger**. Although there are numerous types of keyloggers, cybercriminals use them as spyware tools to steal users' data (for example, personally identifiable information, sensitive enterprise data, or login credentials) for fraudulent purposes. This is the method most commonly used by cybercriminals when they steal confidential information, and they often combine keyloggers with viruses or worms, infecting the computer first, logging the keystrokes, and then sending the keystroke data back to the offender (Clough, 2015).

Malware today tends to consist of a combination of the previously described types of malware, wherein cybercriminals can combine worms with keyloggers, or viruses with worms, for example, to gain some important piece of information. For instance, a Trojan Horse program can be used to gain access to an organization's computer system and, from there, a cybercriminal can then install a worm in the system. That worm then moves around and infects other computers with a virus or ransomware. Malware can also be used to attack mobile devices (Clough, 2015). In 2014, for example, iPhone's iOS operating system was secure, and only four "malware families" were able to attack jailbroken iOS mobile devices (jailbroken mobile devices are those that are stripped

ransomware
Malicious software that locks a user out of their files or devices until a payment is made.

rootkit
A collection of tools or computer software programs, most often malicious software programs, that grants cybercriminals root privilege to computers or computer networks and provides them with both administrator and basic access to those systems.

keylogger
A type of malicious software that is used in surveillance technology to monitor and record each keystroke typed on someone's computer keyboard.

of manufacturer or carrier restrictions so that users are provided with access to their entire file system). In 2015, however, iOS became vulnerable, with a number of malware families available that all had the ability to attack non-jailbroken mobile devices (Vanian, 2016).

While a broad range of computer-facilitated crimes and computer crimes have been described above, a common attribute that can be found in most, if not all, of these crimes is some element of "social engineering," a term defined by Mitnick and Simon (2002) in this way:

> Social engineering uses influence and persuasion to deceive people by convincing them that the social engineer is someone he [or she] is not, or by manipulation. As a result, the social engineer is able to take advantage of people to obtain information with or without the use of technology. (p. iv)

Fraudsters, con artists, and even magicians use this technique to deceive and, in some cases, manipulate people into either believing something or taking information from them without them knowing. Social engineering attacks are set out here in four stages:

1. *Research the victim*: An attacker will learn about a potential victim in order to be able to gain the person's trust, as well as decide whether they are the best target.
2. *Develop rapport and trust*: An attacker will establish contact with the potential victim, often by telephone or email or through face-to-face communication, to obtain information about them directly.
3. *Exploit the trust*: To exploit the trust that has been gained, an attacker will rely on psychological techniques such as authority, linking and similarities, and being helpful and reciprocal.
4. *Use the information*: The attacker will get the information desired and, in some cases, the information gained from the attack will be used toward a new social engineering attack (Mitnick & Simon, 2002).

Defining Terrorism

terrorism
The use of violence or the threat of violence to advance political objectives.

While the act of **terrorism** has existed since the dawn of recorded history, it has only been in the last 20 years that it has gained widespread attention, particularly in the West. The 9/11 attacks on the World Trade Center in New York City and two other locations in the United States, for example, marked a point after which national security would never be the same—especially with regard to combatting those inspired by radical Islam. The terrorist activities of far-right extremist Anders Breivik, who killed 77 people in Norway (69 in Oslo and eight on Utøya Island), were a sad reminder that **lone actor terrorism**, also known as "lone wolf" terrorism, was on the rise around the world (Hamm & Spaaji, 2017). And more recent terrorist attacks in the United Kingdom, France, and Sweden, inspired by the so-called Islamic State (IS), highlight the extent to which radical ideologies can fuel such senseless violence. Canada, too, has been a target of terrorism, with the cases in 2017 and 2018 including a man, inspired by IS, running down four pedestrians with his vehicle on a busy street in Edmonton and later stabbing a police officer while he was being apprehended (CBC News, 2017), as well as the Quebec City mosque shooting, which resulted in the death of six worshippers (Roach, 2018). Both cases involved **homegrown terrorism**. Canada, like other

lone actor terrorism
The use of violence or the threat of violence by a single perpetrator—or a small cell—without direct support in the planning, preparation, or execution of attack, and whose decision to act is not directed by a terrorist group or other individuals.

homegrown terrorism
Terrorism that targets victims within a country in which the perpetrator shares the same citizenship as the victims.

Western nations, is also faced with the challenge of dealing with **foreign fighters** who, after leaving to fight in Syria and Iraq for IS and other less known jihadist groups, want to return home (Dawson, 2017). And with these terrorism-related events transpiring around the world, many are left wondering, "What is terrorism, anyway?"

The question of what constitutes "terrorism" remains one of the most significant challenges faced by academics and practitioners around the globe, as one individual, for example, may be perceived as a terrorist in one setting but deemed a freedom fighter in another. Debates continue to flare up around the controversial nature of the term, with stark disagreements arising about its meaning (Cooper, 2001). As a result, no single definition has yet to receive universal acceptance by experts. In an exhaustive search by authors Easson and Schmid (2011), for example, they identified over 250 definitions of terrorism that had been developed by scholars, governmental organizations, and intergovernmental agencies. In part, these inconsistencies are a symptom of how international judicial systems govern terrorism (Young, 2006). In the United States, for example, terrorism is understood as activities that

> involve violent acts or acts dangerous to human life that are a violation of the criminal laws of the United States or of any State [that] appear to be intended to intimidate or coerce a civilian population; to influence the policy of a government by intimidation or coercion; or to affect the conduct of a government by mass destruction, assassination, or kidnapping. (Office of the Law Revision Counsel of the United States House of Representatives, 2018, p. 2)

In contrast, the United Kingdom recognizes and governs terrorist violence as the

> use or threat [of action] designed to influence the government or an international governmental organisation or to intimidate the public or a section of the public, and the use or threat is made for the purpose of advancing a political, religious, racial or ideological cause. (*Terrorism Act 2000* (UK), 2000, s. 1(1)(a)–(c))

foreign fighter
Anyone who, motived by ideology, religion, and/or kinship, travels to a country other than their own for the purpose of joining a non-state, armed group in an armed conflict abroad.

Mourners gathered in Quebec City to remember victims of the January 2017 mosque shooting. Similar public memorials were held across Canada, with communities coming together and standing against hate.

A crime relating to terrorism in Canada, on the other hand, is defined as an act committed

> in whole or in part for a political, religious, or ideological purpose, objective or cause" with the intention of intimidating the public "with regard to its security, including its economic security, or compelling a person, a government or a domestic or international organization to do or to refrain from doing any act. (Department of Justice Canada, 2015, p. 1)

This summarizes parts of section 83.01 of the Canadian *Criminal Code*. The *Criminal Code* also identifies terrorism as activities that cause death and bodily harm through the use of violence; endanger a person's life; pose risks to the health and safety of the public; cause significant property damage; and interfere or disrupt essential systems, facilities, or services (Department of Justice Canada, 2015).

While there is a clear discrepancy between how terrorism is characterized and subsequently enforced in the Western nations mentioned here, the common thread that characterizes the activities and behaviour of terrorist entities is their political motivation and the use of threats of violence. To this end, then, terrorism,

> in the most widely accepted contemporary usage of the term, is fundamentally and inherently political. It is also ineluctably about power: the pursuit of power, the acquisition of power, and the use of power to achieve political change. Terrorism is thus violence—or, equally important, the threat of violence—used and directed in pursuit of, or in service of, a political aim. (Hoffman, 2006, pp. 2–3)

But why does terrorism happen? Criminological theories, in recent times, have attempted to answer this crucial question. Some leading theories include Robert Agnew's general strain theory, which posits that collective strains increase the likelihood of terrorism, simply because strains increase negative emotions, as well as reduce social control and self-control and the ability to cope through both legal and military channels, thus fostering the social learning of terrorism by strengthening group ties and the formation of terrorist groups (Agnew, 2010). Ron Akers's social learning theory has also been applied to how individuals learn to be terrorists and the process by which they engage in terrorist actions, from recruitment and building kinships, to suicide attacks (Akins & Winfree, 2017). Per-Olof Wikström's situational action theory, which draws from the social and behavioural sciences to explain human action and crime causation through person–environment interaction, has been applied to explain why people commit acts of terrorism (see Wikström & Bouhana, 2017). Although these theories approach the phenomenon of terrorism from various frameworks, consistently raised within these theories—as well as discussed by the general public more broadly—are questions about how someone "becomes" a terrorist. A term that is oftentimes injected into these discussions is **radicalization**.

The highly contested and contentious term "radicalization" has received considerable attention in the past ten years and has raised a number of theoretical and pragmatic questions: Why do some individuals transition from non-violent to violent ideology? This complex and often unknowable pathway has been attributed to a number of influences, including intergroup conflict (McCauley & Moskalenko, 2008), religious and political leaders (Moghaddam, 2005), social networks and personal connections (Bouchard, 2015), family (Asal, Fair, & Shellman, 2008), prison (Hamm, 2013), and the

For more on general strain theory, see Chapter 9, Sociological Approaches and Chapter 10, Gender and Crime.

radicalization
The process of developing extremist ideologies and beliefs and subsequent behaviour in line with those beliefs.

Internet (Conway, 2012). What is increasingly apparent, though, is that radicalization is multi-dimensional and cannot be explained by a single factor—there is no silver bullet justification for it. It should come as no surprise, then, that the term "radicalization" is surrounded by a cloud of confusion and remains difficult to define. As Bubolz and Simi (2015) correctly pointed out, radicalization

> has been a source of confusion for scholars because radicalization alone does not necessarily imply action, just as those who act in an extreme manner may not necessarily be radicalized. (p. 2)

Those who become far-right Christians or convert to fundamental Islam, for example, do not necessarily become radicalized, and those who engage in a fanatical or profound activity may not be radicalized. While this raises the critical question of whether radicalization is about *belief* or about *action*, most experts agree that it is the combination of the two, wherein a key component of "becoming radicalized" involves one's willingness to engage in action to maintain a high level of commitment to a radical cause. It is also theorized as a non-linear process—or pathway—of developing radical views, principles, and ideas, and changing subsequent behaviour in line with those beliefs (Borum, 2011).

Ideological Beliefs and Motivations of Terrorists

Terrorists are motivated by an array of radical beliefs. The following are the primary categories of radical beliefs that have motivated individuals to radicalize to violent and non-violent extremism, as well as associate with violent extremist groups and join terrorist organizations.

Jihadists

Jihadists are religious terrorists who are inspired by Sunni Islamist-Salafists and seek to maintain an Islamist society by employing violent militant strategies to defeat incumbent regimes and non-Muslim forces. A number of ideological principles exist within this framework, including the creation of an expansionist Islamic state or caliphate; the imposition of sharia law with violent jihad as a central component; and the use of local, national, and international grievances affecting Muslims (Moghadam, 2008). Some of the most active international terrorist groups who subscribe to these tenets include IS, Al-Qaeda, Al-Shabaab, and Boko Haram.

Right-Wing Terrorists

Right-wing terrorists may also subscribe to a radical interpretation of religion, ranging from national socialism to Christian Identity, but unlike Islamist-inspired terrorists, many extreme right adherents are not inspired by religious beliefs—the actors are more broad ranging and their ideologies overlap. Militant gun rights advocates, for example, may be motivated by far-right, anti-government ideologies, while the Alternative Right, more commonly known as the "alt-right," may adhere to a range of different ideologies, including identitarianism, anarcho-capitalism, and/or radical traditionalism. Nonetheless, what binds these ideologies and actors is a racially, ethnically, and sexually defined nationalism, which is typically framed in terms of white power and grounded in xenophobic and exclusionary understandings of the perceived threats posed by such groups as non-whites, Jews, immigrants, homosexuals, and feminists.

Here the state is perceived as an illegitimate power serving the interests of all but the white man and, as such, extremists are willing to assume both an offensive and defensive stance in the interests of "preserving" their heritage and their "homeland" (Perry & Scrivens, 2016). Adherents' ideological principles, though wide in scope, include Christian Identity, neo-Nazi, racist skinhead, Holocaust denial, anti-immigrant, and white nationalist. Some of the most recognizable right-wing terrorist groups include the Ku Klux Klan (KKK), Blood & Honour/Combat 18, Aryan Nations, and The Order.

Left-Wing Terrorists

On the other end of the ideological spectrum are left-wing terrorists who consist of individuals and groups that subscribe to some form of Marxism-Leninism/Communism (Hoffman, 2006). The primary goal of these groups is to overthrow the capitalist system, including governments, in an effort to substitute it with an anti-imperialist economic order that empowers the working class (Smith, 1994). Unlike those who subscribe to radical right-wing ideologies, for example, left-wing extremist identity is not grounded in race-based issues, but instead in economic-based issues, and includes the Red Army Faction, Red Brigades, and Revolutionary Armed Forces of Colombia (FARC). Note, however, that other left-wing terrorist groups identify with eco-rights and animal rights from a leftist political position; for example, the Earth Liberation Front and Animal Liberation Front.

Single-Issue Terrorists

Last, single-issue terrorists, as opposed to the above-mentioned groups, are motivated in large part by a single issue rather than a broad ideology, and recent examples include anti-abortion movements (for example, Army of God), Jewish extremist movements (for example, Jewish Defense League), and independence movements (for example, Puerto Rican independence movement). Single-issue terrorists may also be motivated by idiosyncratic ideologies. Ted Kaczynski, more commonly known as the "Unabomber," is a primary example of a single-issue terrorist in the United States. Fiercely opposed to industrialization, Kaczynski terrorized an entire nation over a span of 17 years, mailing and delivering a series of increasingly sophisticated bombs and targeting people who were involved in technical fields, including those in computing and genetics. In total, he killed three people and injured 23 others (Chase, 2000).

Terrorist Campaigns: Tactics and Targets

Terrorist groups, despite media claims and popular belief, are—in most cases—neither crazed nor capricious, and they tend to execute carefully planned and premeditated attacks. Both the tactics and targets of terrorism, however, vary in scope and largely depend on the group's aims, motives, and ideology (Hoffman, 2006). Although there is no clearcut "brand" of terror for a particular group or ideology, there are indeed trends that suggest that some groups are more likely to engage in one tactic versus another.

Right-Wing Terrorist Tactics and Targets

One of the oldest right-wing terrorist groups in the United States, the KKK, engaged in a number of premeditated terrorist campaigns following the American Civil War, up until the mid 20th century, including political assassinations against members of the Civil Rights Movement, Black lynchings, and Baptist Church bombings (Newton

& Newton, 1991). In the 1980s, new right-wing terrorism groups emerged, including a number of white supremacist terrorist organizations who were responsible for multiple murders, bombings, and assassinations (Smith, 1994). And by the 1990s, in addition to the tragic Oklahoma City bombing by right-wing terrorist Timothy McVeigh, over 35 terrorist plots were planned or carried out by the extreme right, including bombing and burning government buildings, banks, synagogues and mosques, as well as assassinating police officers, judges, politicians, and Civil Rights Movement figures (Blejwas, Griggs, & Potok, 2005). Most recently, lone actor terrorism, a tactic first popularized by KKK and Aryan Nations representative Louis Beam, has become the strategy of choice for the extreme right, with Anders Breivik, who killed 77 people in Norway, and Dylann Roof, who killed nine people in the June 17, 2015 church shooting in Charleston, South Carolina as but two examples of the devastating impact that such attacks can have. Worth noting, however, is that contemporary right-wing terrorists are the least likely to carry out sophisticated attacks and are the least selective about who they target (Hoffman, 2006). This, too, is the case in Canada, where contemporary right-wing terrorist groups tend to engage in unsophisticated, opportunistic "street" violence, arbitrarily targeting individuals or property associated with particular groups according to race, religion, ethnicity, or sexual identity (see Perry & Scrivens, 2016).

Left-Wing Terrorist Tactics and Targets

Traditional left-wing terrorists, on the other hand, have been much more calculated and selective about their use of violence. Their tactic of choice in the United States, for example, has been bombing campaigns, with businesses—banks in particular—as the principal targets (National Consortium for the Study of Terrorism and Responses to Terrorism, 2017). Similar tactics have been employed by left-wing groups in Canada, starting as early as the 1960s with the bombing campaigns of the Front de Libération du Québec (Amirault & Bouchard, 2015). And more recently, for example, anarchist group Black Bloc targeted what they described as "symbols of capitalism" in Toronto during a G20 protest in 2010 by setting police cars on fire and smashing storefront windows (White, 2010). Symbolically, businesses and government buildings represent capitalist exploitation and repression; the target, then, represents the repressive state and its actors, and the target is therefore "justified." It should be noted that most left-wing adherents, unlike right-wing terrorist groups, for example, observe it as counterproductive, even hypocritical, to produce innocent casualties, and so, in turn, their use of violence has been heavily constrained (Hoffman, 2006). Regardless of their "morals," an assessment of the casualties and damages associated with left-wing terrorist attacks in the United States has demonstrated that their attacks have in fact, over time, involved fatalities and injuries (National Consortium for the Study of Terrorism and Responses to Terrorism, 2017).

Religious Terrorist Tactics and Targets

Finally, religious terrorists engage in the most indiscriminate acts of violence, executing carefully planned attacks and targeting a wide audience of "enemies" who do not share their religious faith. Violence, to them, is seen as a sacred duty, carried out in an effort to serve God and, as a result, their target list is much more open, because to them, "infidels are all the same" (Hoffman, 2006). Al-Qaeda, for example, have called for unimpeded attacks on Americans and all other non-believers, which reveals the extent of their list of enemies. In turn, their tactics have been those that can cause the most wide-spread damage. For example, in their attacks, religious terrorists employ improvised explosive devices (IEDs), suicide bombings, and targeted assassinations using machetes or knives (Zelin, 2017). Recently, terrorist groups such as IS have called for the execution of all "infidels" and, in order to obtain their goals, they have promoted do-it-yourself (DIY) terrorism, encouraging supporters to use vehicle-ramming as a deadly weapon by running "infidels" over with a car or truck, or encouraging them to slaughter their enemies with a knife if they do not have access to IEDs or bullets. These violent calls for action are often communicated online (Gartenstein-Ross & Blackman, 2017).

Terrorists' Use of the Internet

Terrorists, like the general population, are tech-oriented and computer-savvy, and they have increased their presence in a variety of online settings, including websites, forums, and blogs, as well as on various social media outlets, including Twitter, Facebook, and YouTube (Conway, 2016). Terrorists have exploited the Internet's easy-to-use, quick and cheap, unregulated, and relatively secure platforms, and have in turn created an online environment that promotes terrorist activities (Davies, Bouchard, Wu, Joffres, & Frank, 2015). A number of explanations have been developed about how terrorists make use of the Internet (for example, Sageman, 2004; Tsfati & Weimann, 2002). Conway (2006), however, developed what many experts would describe as the most well-rounded understanding of how terrorists take advantage of the Internet by focusing on five core uses:

- *Information provision*: The dissemination of unimpeded rhetoric through any combination of online communication outlets, ranging from spreading hate propaganda on extremist sites to engaging opponents in online "psychological warfare."
- *Financing*: In an effort to expose others to their ideologies, as well as recruit a broader audience and support and sustain their cause, terrorist groups attempt to raise funds online, from donation pages to online stores that showcase an array of merchandise, including books, magazines, videos, clothing, flags, and music.
- *Networking*: Using a decentralized, "all-channel" manner to communicate and coordinate both quickly and efficiently and at a low cost by linking subgroups and external organizations from around the world to central online spaces, such as web-forums, blogs, and social media sites.
- *Recruitment*: In an effort to raise awareness and convince people to join them, terrorists use the Internet to increase the possibility of interacting with potential recruits, as well as roam online spaces looking for like-minded individuals (usually young people). They make it easy for potential recruits to gather information from their online material, which contains a high level of appeal and persuasion, by (1) masking their use of violence and instead reconstruct a less hostile and less violent image of their campaign, while discussing mainstream social issues and world events in a bid to garner sympathy from an international audience; and (2) luring followers in through the use of eye-catching and visually appealing websites, often presented in a multimedia format that features audio files, digital videos, interactive chat rooms, bulletin boards, cybercafés, and

webpages that feature caricatures and children's stories, as well as video games, music, technology, art, dating advice, and humour/jokes pages.

- *Information gathering*: Given that the Internet contains an overwhelming amount of information, among many other aspects of planning, terrorists can collect information on specific targets that will help them develop opportunities, learn about anti-terrorism measures, share online training manuals about how to make homemade bombs, plan assassinations, and get information on how to avoid surveillance.

Within this context, a number of critical questions have been raised about how terrorists use the Internet, but arguably the most pressing in recent times has been whether the Internet plays a significant or even a central role in an individual's process of becoming radicalized to violent extremism (Ducol, Bouchard, Davies, Ouellet, & Neudecker, 2015). Although there has been a lot of speculation—particularly from practitioners and policy-makers—as to whether exposure to the Internet causes change in violent extremist behaviour, only a few researchers have managed to unpack this complex question. Gill and colleagues (2017), for example, uncovered that while the Internet affords greater opportunities for violent radicalization and attack planning, both online and offline interactions are interconnected and the Internet cannot be treated as a singular causal mechanism for violent radicalization. In other words, face-to-face interaction is also a key component to an individual's pathway to violent radicalization, and this is a finding that may assist with the development of counter-terrorism strategies.

Counter-Terrorism Strategies

An entire industry has sprung up around the enterprise of challenging violent extremism on the ground and online. Known in academic and government circles as **countering violent extremism (CVE)**, this non-coercive strategy is largely designed to divert individuals from radicalization to violence (Harris-Hogan, Barrelle, & Zammit, 2015). The emphasis on these "soft" approaches springs from critical resistance to purely securitized and/or criminal justice responses to extremism largely because, while neutral on their surface, CVE initiatives have mostly been focused on countering violent Islamists (Ahmed, 2015). Instead, scholars such as Bjørgo and Horgan (2009) draw our attention to factors that account for radicalization to violent extremism and, by extension, are ripe for targeting for counter-radicalization. Across the Western world, government and non-government organizations (NGOs), agencies, and centres have likewise emerged with an eye to developing and implementing novel strategies around counter- and de-radicalization, including the Institute for Strategic Dialogue (ISD) based in London in the United Kingdom, the International Centre for Counter-Terrorism (ICCT) in the Hague, the National Consortium for the Study of Terrorism and Responses to Terrorism (START) in Maryland in the United States, and the Centre for the Prevention of Radicalization Leading to Violence (CPRLV) based in Montreal.

CVE is, however, an umbrella term that encapsulates an array of approaches to responding to radicalization to violent extremism and terrorism; proactive approaches seek to stop or slow an individual at risk of being radicalized to violence and/or at risk of joining a violent extremist or terrorist organization, while reactive approaches seek

countering violent extremism (CVE)
Non-coercive strategies to reduce violent extremism and terrorism.

to reverse someone's radical thought process once they have been radicalized (Koehler, 2016). CVE programs are guided by a specific set of goals, all of which can be used to separate CVE programs into the following types (note that each of these types can be used in coordination with the other):

- *Prevention*: Similar to the public health model, prevention programs seek to stop or decrease the spread of individuals becoming radicalized to violence, often by targeting a segment of the population rather than a specific individual, and through large-scale educational or counter-narrative campaigns to the public.
- *Intervention*: These programs seek to interrupt an individual's journey into violent extremism, either by targeted intervention at the early stages of radicalization or after radicalization has occurred, with two sub-branches of programming. **Disengagement** programs—often the first step in an intervention program—seek to stop someone from partaking in terrorist or violent extremist activities, and **deradicalization** programs attempt to transform an individual's radical thought processes in an effort to change that person's behaviour.
- *Repression*: Programs or initiatives that seek to disrupt violent extremism and terrorism through official government sanctioning, such as enforcing laws, prison sentences, and community policing.
- *Rehabilitation*: These programs are an extension of repression programs and are either mandated or voluntarily pursued by an individual in prison, where a rehabilitation plan is developed after assessing the person's general needs and risk of reoffending.

disengagement
The process of leaving terrorist or violent extremist involvement.

deradicalization
The process of change in an individual's radical belief system in which the person rejects extremist ideology and adopts more moderate and non-violent views.

While CVE initiatives can be conducted both online and offline, or in a combination of the two (Davies, Neudecker, Ouellet, Bouchard, & Ducol, 2016), the purpose of these programs is to have an impact on society on a number of levels, including on a micro-level (for example, one-on-one counselling), a meso-level (for example, schools and community campaigns and programs), and a macro-level (for example, city or nation-wide programming or national counter-terrorism laws) (Koehler, 2016). It must be noted that, in light of these unique and motivational programs, concerns have been raised about their impact and effectiveness (see Koehler, 2016). However, approaches to responding to violent extremism—a complex and multi-faceted phenomenon, grounded in both individual and social conditions—have increasingly promoted a multi-sectoral approach, wherein counter-extremist initiatives must be multi-dimensional, building on the strengths and expertise of diverse sectors, including but not limited to community organizations, police officers, and policy-makers. In other words, efforts to counter violent extremism cannot be seen as only a law enforcement or intelligence issue. These efforts must be seen as a social issue, and, as a result, law enforcement officials should partner with various community organizations, human rights activists, and academics so that they can share knowledge and ideas for enhancing and/or developing CVE initiatives (Scrivens & Perry, 2017).

Conclusion

In our increasingly digitalized world, technology is interwoven with nearly every aspect of our daily lives, thus making people much more vulnerable to criminal activity. Before the advent of the Internet, criminals were largely restricted to targets at a local level. Nowadays, people, companies, and governments from around the globe are free to interact on a global level, which has influenced offending behaviours (Holt & Bossler, 2014). Cybercriminals have exploited the development of information and communication technologies to reach a larger pool of targets (Clough, 2015), while terrorists, at the same time, have exploited these technologies to connect with a larger group of like-minded individuals (Conway, 2016).

Both cybercriminals and terrorists use technology in ways similar to those that everyday people use it, whether it's to gather information on the latest news story or perhaps communicate with a co-worker in another country. As a result, we ought to be aware of the ways in which advances in technology can affect offending and victimization patterns, and, for example, take active steps to protect ourselves from cybercriminals, as well as develop effective strategies to counter violent extremism. We hope that this chapter has not only provided you with insight into some of the most prevalent and pressing crimes taking place in the 21st century, but has sparked your interest to explore cybercrime and terrorism in more detail.

SUMMARY OF KEY POINTS

- Cybercrimes are broad ranging and have a significant social impact, but the scale and scope of cybercrime remains largely unknown because of inconsistent legal definitions and data collection efforts on the part of law enforcement, as well as underreporting by victims.

- Cybercrimes are a significant challenge for law enforcement officials to investigate because of the sheer volume of data to monitor, the forensic skills needed to investigate such crimes, and jurisdictional issues.

- Most cybercrimes include some element of social engineering, which involves researching the potential victim, developing trust with the person, and exploiting that trust to obtain information to commit the crime.

- "Terrorism" and "radicalization" are highly contested terms because of the varying social, cultural, and political context in which these terms are defined, and the complex and multi-dimensional nature of each phenomenon.

- Terrorist groups and sympathizers have their own distinct ideologies, but they share similarities in their motives and violent tactics, such as the need to preserve their heritage from a perceived threat, and calls for violence that are symbolic.

- Effective counter-terrorism and CVE initiatives require that an array of key stakeholders—including law enforcement officials, community groups, and academics—be involved in the process, because the causes of terrorism and violent extremism are multi-faceted and require a multi-faceted response.

QUESTIONS FOR CRITICAL DISCUSSION

1. How can law enforcement officials better record and track cybercrimes?
2. What are the best ways to protect yourself from cyberattacks?
3. Most cybercrimes can be classified as falling into one of three categories. What are these categories? Which of the categories includes the most types of cybercrimes?

4. What leads someone to go down a path toward violent extremism?
5. How can communities prevent or counter violent extremism?

SUGGESTED FURTHER READINGS

Grabosky, P. (2006). *Electronic crime.* Upper Saddle River, NJ: Prentice Hall.
Royal Canadian Mounted Police. (2015). *Royal Canadian Mounted Police Cybercrime Strategy.* Retrieved from http://www.rcmp-grc.gc.ca/en/royal-canadian-mounted-police-cybercrime-strategy
Wall, S. & Williams, M. (Eds.) (2014). *Policing cybercrime: Networked and social media technologies and the challenges for policing.* New York: Routledge.

Websites

Canadian Centre for Cyber Security. Cyber incidents: Reporting a cyber incident: https://cyber.gc.ca/en/cyber-incidents
Government of Canada. Cybercrime: https://www.canada.ca/en/services/policing/police/crime-and-crime-prevention/cybercrime.html
International Journal of Cyber Criminology: http://www.cybercrimejournal.com
Law Enforcement Cyber Center: http://www.iacpcybercenter.org/resource-center/cyber-crime-community-resources
National Consortium for the Study of Terrorism and Responses to Terrorism (START): http://www.start.umd.edu
Perspectives on Terrorism: http://www.terrorismanalysts.com/pt/index.php/pot
VOX-Pol Network of Excellence: http://www.voxpol.eu

Legislation

Criminal Code, RSC 1985, c C-46.
Terrorism Act 2000 (UK), 2000, c 11.

Case

R v Dobson, 2013 ONCJ 150.

Glossary

810.1 order A community prohibition order for sexual offenders deemed to be a high risk that includes conditions designed to monitor and limit the person's movement, accommodations, and social interactions.

absolute deprivation Low income or poverty in and of itself.

active audiences The concept that audiences are not passive recipients of information or meanings but are instead active in the process of creating meaning.

actual victim A person who is the direct target of victimization.

actus reus The criminal act or personal conduct relating to a crime; it may include a failure to act but does not include the mental element of a criminal offence.

acute dynamic factors Individual characteristics associated with the risk of reoffending that are rapidly changing and include factors such as intoxication and mood.

administrative monetary penalty (AMP) A non-criminal penalty issued by a regulatory body, without court approval, for the violation of a law it administers.

anarchism A political and social perspective that rejects the necessity of imposed rule by external authorities such as the state. From the Greek *an archos*, it means the absence of rulers, though not the absence of rules. Anarchism has influenced critical criminology generally, and post-structural and peace-making criminology and restorative justice specifically.

anomie A term coined by Durkheim to describe periods of lawlessness, normlessness, and unrestrained choice, or a breakdown in social solidarity.

anomie-strain theory Merton's theory describing the state of anomie in American society caused by the disjunction (or dysfunction or strain) between the cultural goals of the "American dream" and the institutional means to achieve those goals.

anti-social personality disorder (APD) A personality disorder characterized by a lack of morality, impulsivity, and aggressive behaviour; individuals with APD often have a history of criminal behaviour.

assault Applying force on a person, attempting to or threatening to apply force on a person, or using a weapon (or imitation of a weapon) to accost or impede a person.

atavism A term associated with Cesare Lombroso and the Positivist School of thought; the notion that criminals are less evolved than "normal" humans.

attention deficit hyperactivity disorder (ADHD) A condition that includes a combination of behaviours, such as difficulty sustaining attention, hyperactivity, and impulsive behaviour.

behaviourism A learning theory that suggests all behaviour can be shaped by rewards and punishment.

blame continuum The range of blaming possibilities, from total guilt to total innocence, of both the victim and the victimizer.

blockchain A continuously growing list of records (blocks) or a chain of transactions on a public transaction system that functions as a distributed ledger that is linked and secured using cryptography.

bounded rationality (limited rationality) Decisions are often made imperfectly as best guesses given available information and time constraints. Decisions are "bounded" by the limits of our knowledge and circumstances, and so our rationality is bounded.

break and enter A type of property crime where the accused trespasses on private property with intent to commit a crime.

bribery The practice of illegally inducing a person, company, or government to act in one's favour, usually by transferring money or property.

card not present fraud A form of fraud usually carried out over the telephone or the Internet when a stolen or forged credit card is used to purchase a good or to acquire a service.

Chicago School The first school of sociology in the United States; contributed to social disorganization theory, cultural transmission theory, differential association theory, subcultural theory, the sociology of deviance, and symbolic interactionism.

child exploitation A photographic, film, video, or other visual representation, whether or not it was made by electronic or mechanical means, that shows a person under the age of 18 engaged in explicit sexual activity or the dominant characteristic of a sexual organ or the anal region of a person under the age of 18.

choice theory The framework for understanding how decisions are made by individuals by weighing the perceived costs and benefits of an action.

civil commitment Also known as "involuntary commitment," the legal process by which a person is detained after serving a sentence due to concerns that he or she will commit further crimes.

civil law A system in which the law is primarily set out in legislation, and judges' discretion is limited to interpretation and application of those written provisions.

Classical School of criminology A body of work that emerged in Europe in the 17th and 18th centuries that argued people have the capacity to think rationally; contemporary deterrence theory is rooted in this school of thought.

clearance rates The proportion of criminal incidents solved by the police. A crime is cleared when the police believe they have found its perpetrator.

collective efficacy A group's shared belief that it can come together and achieve desired goals.

common law A body of law defined primarily through successive decisions of judges, as opposed to through legislation.

community and social support factors The people and resources that support the individual experiencing traumatic stress; that is, community members, family, and friends that serve to insulate the community and its members from traumatizing events through prevention and/or by fostering resilience.

compositional effect The combination of parts that make up something. In neighbourhoods, a compositional effect refers to the aggregate characteristics of individual residents.

CompStat COMPuter STATistics; the name given to the New York City Police Department's accountability process that was introduced in the 1990s to facilitate a reduction in crime.

computer crime Crime in which a computer or computer network is the target.

computer-facilitated crime Crime in which computers are used as a tool.

computer-supported crime Crime in which computers do not play a central role but may contain evidence.

computer tomography A medical technique combining X-rays taken at many different angles and computer technology.

concordance rate In a random sample of pairs, the proportion of pairs that share a certain characteristic.

conditioning factors Factors that shape the impact of a certain cause or correlate of crime.

conflict theories Theories, originating primarily with Marx, that focus on the unequal distribution of power in society—for example, due to class, race, or gender. Conflicts between classes or groups are driven to a large extent by this unequal power and unequal access to resources.

consensus theories In opposition to conflict theories, consensus theories, which originate with Durkheim, hold that society functions through social bonds and collective beliefs, and is characterized by widespread acceptance of values, norms, and laws.

constructionist Constructionist perspectives emphasize the idea that life does not come with categories and labels, and that we understand and define the world on the basis of our socialization and interactions with others.

contextual effect The influence of environmental factors on human behaviours.

corporate social responsibility (CSR) A theory of corporate self-regulation whereby companies actively pursue compliance with the law and ethical norms as a part of doing business.

correlates In criminology, factors that are associated with or related to crime.

correlation The finding that two measurable phenomena occur together, suggesting a relationship but not necessarily one of direct cause and effect.

cortical arousal Activation of the reticular formation of the brain.

counterfeiting Producing imitation currency without legal sanction of the government; it is a form of fraud.

countering violent extremism (CVE) Non-coercive strategies to reduce violent extremism and terrorism.

crime funnel A model indicating that the actual total quantity of crime is much higher than the decreasing proportion that is detected, reported, prosecuted, and punished.

crime opportunity theory An umbrella term for the set of theories and concepts that are underpinned by the notion that the level of crime opportunities is the main cause of crime.

crime pattern theory A theory that helps explain how crime patterns arise; it asserts that crime is not random. Its concepts (for example, nodes, paths, and edges) describe how offenders move in the urban environment.

crimes of morality Illegal activities that are against the law because they are regarded as threatening to values.

criminal justice system The various institutions and processes through which an offender passes, such as the police, the courts, and correctional facilities and programs.

criminal law The entire set of principles, procedures, and rules established by governments through the courts and criminal legislation in order to ensure public safety. It includes definitions of crimes, criminal responsibility, punishments, and defences to a criminal charge.

criminality The state of being criminal; criminal acts or practices.

criminalization To define an act as a crime and thereby subject that act to formal punishment.

criminology The study of crime and criminal behaviour, which are defined by reference to criminal law.

critical criminology A school of thought with multiple subfields but largely concerned with social justice and inequality, promoting active opposition to the status quo, and favouring larger-scale societal transformations rather than minor policy changes.

critical race theory A theory that examines the ways in which race and racial power are constructed by law and society, and that sees the law and criminal justice system not as solutions but as part of the problem.

critical thinking The process of evaluating information, claims, or arguments through careful questioning and the application of reason.

crypto-currency A digital currency in which encryption techniques are used to secure and make the virtual asset and transaction anonymous.

culpable Deserving of blame; guilty of wrongdoing.

cultural transmission theory The Chicago School notion that criminal subcultures develop their own subcultural (criminal) values or norms, which are then transmitted from gang member to gang member and from generation to generation.

cyberbullying Bullying through the use of communication technologies.

cybercrime The use of cyberspace or computer technology to facilitate acts of crime and deviance.

cyberstalking The use of the Internet or other electronic communication devices to stalk another person, which includes harassing or threatening behaviour that an individual engages in repeatedly.

cyberwarfare Computer- or network-based conflict that involves a politically motivated attack by a nation-state or international organization.

dangerousness The capacity of a person to physically, psychologically, or morally harm oneself or others. It includes an estimation of both the severity and likelihood of harm.

dark figure of crime Refers to the variation between the number of crimes that occur and the number of crimes that are actually reported to the police. This figure highlights the large number of unreported crimes.

decriminalization The removal of criminal penalties, though fines may still apply.

demographics Statistical data relating to characteristics of a population, such as relative size of age groups, gender balance, or any other measurable information.

denunciation A formal expression that conduct is unacceptable.

deradicalization The process of change in an individual's radical belief system in which the person rejects extremist ideology and adopts more moderate and non-violent views.

designing-out The concept that crime prevention can start at the design process so that products and places are designed with potential criminal threats or opportunities in mind.

determinism The doctrine that one's will is not the sole cause of choices, but that those choices are conditioned or determined by factors external to one's will.

deterrence A principle of sentencing or punishment intended to discourage citizens from offending or reoffending.

deterrence theory A theory based on the idea that for punishment to be effective, it must be swift, sure, and certain.

deviance Behaviour that differs from accepted social norms; it may include acts that violate specific rules (crime), sexual behaviours, or non-criminal acts that challenge accepted values.

differential association theory Sutherland's theory that criminal behaviour is learned through the process of social interaction and that the process includes the learning of criminal skills, motivations, attitudes, and rationalizations.

direct victim A person who is present at the time of victimization and experiences harm.

discourses Refers to forms of language, representation, and practices and how meaning is created and shared. Discourses take place within specific cultural and historical contexts.

disengagement The process of leaving terrorist or violent extremist involvement.

dispositional theories Theories that seek to explain variations between individuals in their tendency or disposition to commit crime. Explanations are usually biological or psychological.

dopamine A neurotransmitter that controls the reward and pleasure centres of the brain.

drug cartel A criminal organization, often highly organized and with many partnerships, involved primarily in the trafficking of illegal drugs.

duress An unlawful threat or coercion used by one person to induce another to perform some act against his or her will.

dynamic factors Individual characteristics associated with the risk of reoffending that are amenable to change and are targets for treatment (for example, attitudes tolerant to criminal behaviour and criminal associates). A reduction in dynamic factors is associated with a decreased risk for recidivism.

ego An aspect of Freud's theory of personality; the aspect of personality that helps negotiate the demands of the real world.

embezzlement To take money or misappropriate funds that belong to someone else.

empirical That which is understood or verified through experiment, measurement, or direct observation; as opposed to theoretical.

environment The external conditions, resources, and stimuli a person interacts with.

environmental criminology A term coined by C. Ray Jeffery; it focuses on the environment (including targets, guardians, and places) as a key area of interest in understanding how and why crime occurs.

eugenics Methods to improve populations by controlling breeding to increase the occurrence of desirable heritable characteristics.

extortion The crime of demanding money from someone using force or threats.

extraversion (E) A person's activity level; people high in extraversion enjoy social interaction and being around groups of people, while people low in extraversion generally prefer solitude and quiet conversations with those close to them.

feeble-mindedness A term used in the 19th century to describe individuals with low intelligence or low IQ.

femicide The act of killing a woman.

fetal alcohol spectrum disorder (FASD) The range of disorders that can arise in a child if the child's mother drank alcohol while pregnant. It is a leading cause of preventable developmental disability in Canada.

folk devils Originating in images from folklore, this term refers to people or groups presented in media as deviant outsiders and the cause of social problems.

foreign fighter Anyone who, motived by ideology, religion, and/or kinship, travels to a country other than their own for the purpose of joining a non-state, armed group in an armed conflict abroad.

forensic entomology The study of insects to assist in legal investigations; insects found on a corpse can help identify facts about the time and place of the victim's death.

Foucauldian Relating to the works of influential French thinker Michel Foucault.

fraud A dishonest act that deprives, or risks depriving, another person of something.

free will A will whose choices are not conditioned or determined by factors external to itself; also, the doctrine that free will exists.

frustration–aggression hypothesis The view that crime is a natural byproduct of aggression and can be explained as a consequence of frustration.

functionalism In sociology, the idea that society is comparable to a functioning organism with interrelated parts and structures to ensure that the parts work together; functionalists believe that society is based on consensus (shared values, beliefs), not conflict.

gender gap The difference between men and women in areas such as social, political, and economic attainment; a persistent finding in criminology is that men commit more crime than women.

gender stratification A society's unequal distribution of wealth, power, and privilege between men and women.

gendered The notion that processes (e.g., learning roles) and behaviours (e.g., participation in crime) are gender-based.

general strain theory Explains delinquent acts by teens from relatively affluent families; teens have more immediate strains than adults, such as physical appearance, popularity, parental discipline, academic performance, and peer pressure to join gangs and participate in delinquent behaviour.

generalization problem The question of whether it is possible to explain female criminality with mainstream theories of crime that were originally developed to explain male criminality.

genocide The deliberate and systematic attempt to exterminate an entire population or subpopulation that shares a racial, religious, national, or cultural identity.

geographic profiling A tool that permits police officers to focus on the likely residence of offenders in cases of serial crimes.

goal responses Behaviours meant to achieve particular goals that provide pleasurable outcomes.

green criminology The analysis of environmental harms from a criminological perspective.

habeas corpus The right of an accused (in the form of a "writ") to appear before a court and not be detained without just cause.

hacking Unauthorized access to computers and computer systems.

harm principle A central tenet in the writing of John Stuart Mill, who is often regarded as the father of moral liberalism. The harm principle holds that the actions of individuals should only be limited to prevent harm to other individuals.

harm reduction A public health–oriented policy or program designed to reduce the harmful consequences of behaviours with known risks, which are often illegal, such as prostitution and recreational drug use.

hedonism The view that pleasure is the primary good; the pursuit of pleasure.

hegemonic masculinity A culturally idealized form of masculinity; in contemporary Western societies, for example, hegemonic masculinity involves displays of autonomy, aggressive individualism, a lack of emotion, normative heterosexuality, and the capacity for violence.

heritability The statistical estimate of the amount of variance in a trait that is due to genetics.

hierarchy Group structure built around easily identified leaders and followers; in gangs, the hierarchy often determines the roles, obligations, and rewards of members.

homegrown terrorism Terrorism that targets victims within a country in which the perpetrator shares the same citizenship as the victims.

homelessness A range of physical living conditions that can include living on the streets or in the open, staying in emergency shelters, or being provisionally housed (couch surfing with friends or relatives).

human trafficking The act of recruiting, transporting, transferring, harbouring, or receiving a person through a use of force, or other means, for the purpose of exploiting them.

id An aspect of Freud's theory of personality; the impulsive part of one's personality.

identity theft The theft and use of a person's identifying information, usually for monetary gain.

indictable offence A serious offence, such as murder or rape, which carries a severe penalty. An *indictment* is the formal process of setting out a criminal charge in a document for serious, "indictable" offences.

indictment A formal written accusation, usually reserved for more serious crimes.

indirect victim A person who is not immediately affected by victimization, but nonetheless suffers in some way as a result of it.

insider trading The practice of trading in a stock, bond, or other security while possessing material, non-public information about the company in question.

institutional-anomie theory Messner and Rosenfeld's theory that institutional anomie (institutional imbalance) is caused by the cultural goals of capitalist society and the failure of social institutions to properly integrate and regulate the pursuit of those goals.

insulators Social and psychological factors that protect an individual from being harmed.

integrationist A combination of structuralist, positivist, and constructionist approaches in criminology facilitating the inclusion of philosophy and sociology of law, the empirical study of crime, and its interpretation by those who control and implement the law.

interactional theory Thornberry's theory that both social bond theory and social learning theory are needed to explain criminal behaviour, because weakening of the social bond and the social learning of criminal values is interactional or reciprocal (not unidirectional).

interactionist perspective A theoretical approach that focuses on relatively small-scale social interactions among individuals or small social groups, as well as the conscious acts of individuals and their interpretation of others' behaviour.

interjurisdictional Relating to crimes, legislation, or other legal issues that cross the boundaries of nations, provinces, or other jurisdictions.

interpersonal violence Violence that is most commonly inflicted by one individual against another or by a small group of individuals against another.

interventions Strategies intended to shape the physical environment to mitigate crime; also various programs targeting individual offenders, offering alternatives to criminal behaviour.

intoxication A potential defence in which drugs or alcohol may prevent an accused from forming the necessary intent to commit a particular crime.

intra-class crime Crime in which the victim and offender are from the same social group (for example, an ethnic or racial group); by contrast, inter-class crime takes place between different social groups.

intra-racial Within the same race of people.

IQ (intelligence quotient) A standardized measure of intelligence used by psychologists.

keylogger A type of malicious software that is used in surveillance technology to monitor and record each keystroke typed on someone's computer keyboard.

labelling theory The theory that the stigma (or label) affixed through the criminalization process may lead individuals to develop a deviant self-image and feel separate from the "normal" community, and thus continue with deviant behaviour.

legalization The removal of an existing prohibition against something that is currently unlawful. In the case of drugs and prostitution, the term often implies a regulated system of supply or licensing of services provided.

lethal violence Violent victimization that causes death.

liability Legal responsibility for an act or omission.

life-course-developmental theory Sampson and Laub's theory that individuals can be deflected from the trajectory toward a criminal career by life events ("turning points") that can lead them to transition out of criminal behaviour.

lone actor terrorism The use of violence or the threat of violence by a single perpetrator—or a small cell—without direct support in the planning, preparation, or execution of attack, and whose decision to act is not directed by a terrorist group or other individuals.

longitudinal studies Research that involves long-term observation of specific variables, often across decades (for example, cohort studies).

magnetic resonance imaging A medical diagnostic technique that uses a powerful magnet, radiofrequency waves, and computer imaging to produce images of tissues.

malware Malicious software intended to damage or disable computers and computer systems.

market manipulation The practice of interfering with the proper operation of a market, usually by employing or creating misleading or artificial information.

Marxism A school of thought developed by Karl Marx (1818–1883) arguing that society must be understood in terms of social conflict, class relations, and the inequalities caused by capitalism. Marxists promote revolution by the working class.

media effects The concept that exposure to media has an effect on behaviour. For example, young people exposed to violent media will behave aggressively.

memory fade The phenomenon whereby a survey participant forgets about a victimization that has taken place.

mens rea The mental element of a criminal offence or the state(s) of mind of the offender; it is the intent to commit a criminal act.

meta-analysis A quantitative statistical analysis of several similar experiments or studies to test for statistical significance.

modelling A form of learning that occurs through observation of others and vicarious reinforcement; also known as observational learning or imitation.

money laundering The process of concealing the transformation of illegitimately obtained money into ostensibly legitimate assets.

money mules A person who relays the received money or merchandise from a victim to an offender and keeps a portion of the proceeds.

moral absolutism A philosophical perspective that holds that certain actions are absolutely right or wrong, regardless of other circumstances such as their consequences or the intentions behind them.

moral entrepreneur A person, group, or organization that takes the lead in identifying certain behaviour as deviant and in need of legal sanctions.

moral panics Phenomena—socially constructed by the media, politicians, and "moral entrepreneurs"—in which certain people or groups are labelled or stigmatized as the cause of a perceived social problem, resulting in widespread public alarm.

moral relativism A perspective on the nature of morality asserting that norms or standards of behaviour are not fixed or absolute.

morals The normative standards, codes, and beliefs governing judgments and values concerning right and wrong action, justice, and fairness.

motor vehicle theft The act of stealing or attempting to steal a motor vehicle.

multi-causal The notion that an event occurs as a result of more than one factor.

negligence A legal intent standard that considers whether a person, regardless of actual intent or knowledge, failed to take reasonable care in doing or failing to do something.

net widening Imposing a form of control on individuals who might otherwise not be subject to such control.

neurotic According to psychoanalytic theory, a condition that results from an overactive superego.

neuroticism (N) A person's excitability level and emotional stability; highly neurotic people tend to be emotionally unstable and overreact to minor situations.

neurotransmitter A substance that carries signals from cell to cell.

neutralization An extension of Sutherland's differential association theory; the notion that criminals learn motivations and rationalizations to justify their criminal behaviour.

obtaining goods under false pretenses Misrepresenting the truth to obtain goods that belong to someone else.

other A person or group of people defined as fundamentally different, or even deviant, by the dominant culture, often through stereotyping.

overcriminalization The intrusion of the law into consensual activities that are relatively harmless to the actor(s) and society.

paraphilia Mental health term for sexual interest in an activity other than masturbation that does not include mutual consent with another person.

parliamentary supremacy The concept that the legislative body is superior to other institutions, including the executive and the courts.

patriarchy An elitist form of social structure, in which men dominate politics, economics, and other aspects of society and perpetuate that domination by limiting opportunities for women to exercise power.

penal law A law that imposes punishment, as opposed to (for instance) a law that provides only the right of a victim to compensation.

personal protective factors The characteristics an individual possesses to help deal with stress, including coping skills, the ability to handle new situations, and social skills.

phrenology The study of the shape and size of the skull as a supposed indication of character and mental abilities. This theory has been discredited.

pleasure principle The notion that one should maximize pleasure and minimize pain.

Ponzi scheme An investing scam where a fraudster pays returns to existing investors with new investors' funds under the false pretense that returns are being made, sustained by the constant recruitment of new contributors.

positivism The application of the scientific method to the study of society, including the study of crime and criminals.

Positivist School A school of thought that attributed criminal behaviour to biological or psychological factors; often referred to as the "Italian School."

positron emission tomography A recording of body images via a radioactive isotope injected into the blood that can be followed in the body during activities. It is commonly used to study the functioning of parts of the brain.

post-colonial theory The wide-ranging academic study of the social, political, and cultural legacy of colonial rule and its effects on individual and group identities and social power relations. It also examines the domination of other cultures through a discourse of "otherness."

post-structuralism A theoretical perspective concerned with how power operates between and among individuals, groups, and social institutions (as opposed to belonging to the state or power elites alone). Post-structuralists look for differences in power in areas such as language use and social practices.

post-traumatic stress disorder (PTSD) A set of symptoms that emerge as a result of the stress of experiencing severe trauma. Symptoms may include recurring nightmares, jumpiness, agitation, trouble sleeping, trouble concentrating, and social isolation.

power–control theory A theory of crime that emphasizes the socialization by parents in the development of different levels of risk taking and the perceived sanctions among boys and girls.

price fixing An agreement between competitors to fix the price for a good or service by buying or selling at an agreed-to price or by manipulating supply or demand.

primary victim A person who is directly harmed as a result of a victimizing experience.

prison industrial complex Adapted from "military industrial complex"; a term used to attribute increases in incarceration rates to the efforts of private for-profit corporations that build and maintain prisons with the active legislative and financial support of their political allies.

problem frame A narrative that is easily understood because it focuses on the existence of something extraordinary and "bad" that affects many people, and identifies unambiguous solutions that can be implemented in the future.

prohibition A law forbidding a specific act.

psychoanalysis A therapeutic technique in psychiatry and philosophy pioneered by Sigmund Freud.

psychopathy A personality disorder characterized by a lack of empathy, egocentrism, manipulation of others, and a tendency toward anti-social and criminal behaviour.

psychoticism (P) A measure of attributes such as aggression, empathy, and tough-mindedness; those who score high in psychoticism tend to be cold, callous, and manipulative.

punitive turn The move from criminal justice policies and programs aimed at rehabilitating offenders toward those that simply offer punishment for its own sake. This shift occurred despite declining crime rates and evidence that punishment is not always effective.

qualitative The study of phenomena based not on measurement but an exploration of the reasons for human behaviour and the qualities of subjective experience.

quantitative Relating to the measurement of something—its quantity—rather than its qualities.

racial profiling The act or tendency of law enforcement officers and others to consider people suspicious or more likely to commit crime because of the colour of their skin or their ethnicity.

racialized The process of marginalizing a group of people based on perceived physical and socio-cultural differences.

racketeering Criminal activity commonly related to gangs that typically involves obtaining money through acts such as extortion, bribery, illegal gambling, and loan sharking.

radicalization The process of developing extremist ideologies and beliefs and subsequent behaviour in line with those beliefs.

ransomware Malicious software that locks a user out of their files or devices until a payment is made.

rape myths Stories that reflect belief systems that reveal incorrect assumptions about the causes of sexual assault.

rape trauma syndrome (RTS) A set of PTSD symptoms that have been linked specifically to those who have experienced severe violence in the form of sexual assault.

rational choice theory A modern version of Classical School thinking originating in economics; it assumes that humans are rational and have free will, and that offenders make conscious choices to commit crime based on a cost-benefit analysis.

reality principle The notion that one should assess the demands of the real world and act accordingly.

recidivism Also referred to as "reoffending," when an offender goes on to commit another crime; general recidivism refers to any new offence, and sexual recidivism refers to another sexual offence.

regulatory capture A theory of corruption whereby regulatory bodies in a sector advance the private interests of the actors they regulate over the public interest.

relative deprivation The perception of unfair disparity between one's situation and that of others.

resilience The ability to successfully recover from trauma.

restorative justice An approach to justice and sentencing, often influenced by Indigenous culture, that emphasizes the healing and reconciliation of victims, perpetrators, and their communities, and promotes positive social engagement instead of social control.

retribution Punishment for transgressions.

risk The probability that a person will commit future harmful acts.

risk-need-responsivity (RNR) model An assessment and rehabilitation theory that suggests it is possible to accurately predict the likelihood that someone will reoffend and provides principles on how to effectively intervene to reduce the risk.

robbery Stealing property from someone, with or without using violence, threats of violence, or a weapon (or imitation of a weapon).

rootkit A collection of tools or computer software programs, most often malicious software programs, that grants cybercriminals root privilege to computers or computer networks and provides them with both administrator and basic access to those systems.

routine activity theory Felson's theory that everyday routines and legitimate activities are key determinants of crime opportunities.

rule of law The principle that governments, individuals, and corporations must follow the law; governments may take actions that limit the activities or rights of citizens only in accordance with substantive and procedural requirements prescribed by law.

sampling In statistics, the selection of a subset of the population in such a way that will allow the results of one's research to be generalizable to the population as a whole.

Scared Straight programs Programs that expose at-risk youth to examples of prison life and other consequences of criminal behaviour, along with testimonials from convicts.

script The steps in decision-making and the sequence of actions for a particular criminal event.

secondary victim A person who is not directly impacted by the harmful effects of a victimizing event but may witness the event or have to deal with the after-effects of a victimizing event, such as supporting a victim in recovery.

serotonin A neurochemical that plays an important role in depression, anxiety, and bipolar disorder. Also involved in brain development, serotonin dysfunction could lead to an increase in impulsiveness.

sex offender registry (SOR) A searchable database with information on convicted sexual offenders.

sexual assault Unwanted sexual activity, including sexual attacks and sexual touching.

single-photon emission computed tomography A recording of body images via a radioactive isotope injected into the blood that provides a 3D image of tissues. It is commonly used to measure brain blood flow.

situational characteristics Factors associated with an incident; in the case of a violent act, the location, weapon type, motive, and the victim–offender relationship are situational characteristics.

situational crime prevention (SCP) Measures taken to reduce crime opportunities. SCP takes into account the nature of the crime, the environmental factors that allow for the crime, and the risks and rewards associated with crime.

social bond theory Social control theory by Hirschi (based on Durkheim's concept of the social bond); the four elements of the social bond include attachment, commitment, involvement, and belief.

social control theory Rooted in Durkheim's forces of integration, the Chicago School's concern with the breakdown in informal social controls holds that social bonds and informal social controls act as restraints on teen delinquency.

social disorganization theory The theory that a breakdown of the networks, norms, and trust that facilitate coordination and cooperation among residents of neighbourhoods can lead to greater crime and violence.

social forces In sociology, the perspective that elements of society have the capability of causing cultural change or influencing human behaviour.

social justice Movement promoting the need for equality, tolerance, and fairness for all members of society, particularly with regard to different classes and the less privileged.

social learning theory Definitions (values about acceptable and unacceptable behaviour) favourable to criminal behaviour are learned through differential reinforcement; criminal behaviour depends on reward or punishment for past behaviour and anticipated consequences of persistence.

socialization The process through which children learn language, culture, roles, expectations, and beliefs. It is facilitated by parents, siblings, and relatives, and later by friends and within schools and community organizations.

sociology of deviance Blends Chicago School symbolic interactionism with views on how crime and deviance are used to maintain social boundaries and/or social control; it examines how certain groups or behaviours come to be viewed as "social problems."

somatotyping A research technique that links behavioural characteristics to body types, such as mesomorphy.

sousveillance The recording, by a citizen participant or witness, of an incident or activity, to hold a bureaucratic organization to account. It can be used to record incidents in which police may be seen abusing their power.

spatial inequality The unequal distribution of resources and services from one area to another.

spousal violence Acts including common assault, assault with a weapon, sexual assault, homicide, forcible confinement, uttering threats, criminal harassment, failure to provide the necessities of life, psychological abuse, and financial abuse.

static factors Individual characteristics associated with the risk of reoffending that are immutable to external influences (for example, age at first offence and offence history). They can be used to determine an overall risk level but are not targets for change.

stereotyping The simplistic and often belittling representation of a person or group, using exaggerations of traits that the larger group supposedly possesses.

stigmatize To strongly disapprove of a person or behaviour; to find disgraceful.

strain theories Theories that state certain societal stressors (for example, unequal opportunities to achieve success) increase the likelihood of crime.

structural functionalism A sociological theory that explains how society functions according to the structure of a system of interrelated parts.

sub-lethal violent victimization Violent victimization that does not cause death.

summary offence A relatively minor offence, punishable by a fine or a maximum jail sentence of six months.

superego An aspect of Freud's theory of personality; one's moral compass, conscience, and ethical principles.

suppression strategies Efforts to eliminate gangs or significantly reduce gang-related crime through a process of deterrence and incapacitation.

surveillance The monitoring of individuals or populations for the purposes of control and/or care (Lyon, 2001).

symbolic interactionism The Chicago School notion that meaning and reality are socially constructed through the use or sharing of gestures, symbols, or words, which are themselves socially created symbols that convey socially agreed-upon meanings.

systemic racism The belief that racism does not occur only in isolated instances, but is entrenched in and perpetuated by our criminal justice system and other institutions.

telescoping The phenomenon whereby a survey participant recalls events as having occurred more recently than is actually the case.

terrorism The use of violence or the threat of violence to advance political objectives.

tertiary victim A person who may suffer repercussions of victimization even though they are not directly involved in or witness to the harmful event.

traits Those attributes or features that distinguish or characterize an individual.

utilitarianism A philosophy that suggests reasoned decisions will produce the greatest good for the greatest number.

utility maximization Choices are made based on what one perceives will provide the greatest rewards for the lowest costs.

vicarious reinforcement Reinforcement that is experienced indirectly through observing another person's behaviour being rewarded.

vicarious victim A person who does not experience direct victimization but nonetheless responds as if they had been victimized directly after learning of the event.

victim A person harmed, injured, or killed as a result of a crime, accident, or other event or action.

victim blaming A process whereby a victim is found at fault for his or her own victimization, in whole or in part.

victim impact statement (VIS) A written document describing the harm done to the victim as a result of victimization that may include statements about physical, emotional, or financial impact(s).

victim precipitation The problematic assumption that victims can somehow influence or bring about their own victimization by exhibiting behaviours that provoke a victimizer.

victimless crimes Actions (often perpetrated consensually) that are ruled illegal but do not directly violate or threaten the rights of other individuals.

victimology The study of victims.

vigilantism When a person or group of people take the law into their own hands, typically in a violent manner, in an attempt to effect justice according to their understanding of what is right and wrong.

warrant expiry date (WED) A correctional option to detain a sexual offender until the very end of his or her sentence. Those who are detained under a WED have been deemed to be a high risk for committing another sexual offence or serious personal injury offence until the very end of their sentence.

weed and seed A strategy combining the removal of violent gang members from a community with long-term community development.

whistle-blower A person who reports misconduct within an organization.

white-collar crime A crime committed by a person, usually of high social status, in the course of his or her occupation.

References

Chapter 1

Blumstein, A., & Wallman, J. (Eds.). (2000). *The crime drop in America*. New York: Cambridge University Press.

Bonnar-Kidd, K. (2010). Sexual offender laws and the prevention of sexual violence or recidivism. *American Journal of Public Health, 100*(3), 412–419.

Bonnycastle, K. (2012). *Stranger rape: Rapists, masculinity, and penal governance*. Toronto: University of Toronto Press.

Boyd, N. (1988). *The last dance: Murder in Canada*. Toronto: Prentice-Hall.

Brantingham, P.J., & Brantingham, P.L. (1984). *Patterns in crime*. New York: Macmillan.

Brantingham, P.L., & Brantingham, P.J. (1993). Environment, routine and situation: Toward a pattern theory of crime. *Advances in Criminological Theory, 5*, 259–294.

Brower, M.C., & Price, B.H. (2001). Neuropsychiatry of frontal lobe dysfunction in violent and criminal behaviour: A critical review. *Journal of Neurology, Neurosurgery and Psychiatry, 71*, 720–726.

Casteel, C., & Peek-Asa, C. (2000). Effectiveness of crime prevention through environmental design in reducing robberies. *American Journal of Preventive Medicine, 18*, 99–115.

Cozens, P., Saville, G., & Hillier, D. (2005). Crime prevention through environmental design: A review and modern bibliography. *Journal of Property Management, 23*(5), 328–356.

Farrell, G., Tilley, N., Tseloni, A., & Mailley, J. (2011). The crime drop and the security hypothesis. *Journal of Research in Crime and Delinquency, 48*(2), 147–175.

Felson, M. (1987). Routine activities and crime prevention in the developing metropolis. *Criminology, 25*, 911–931.

Fox, J.A. (2000). Demographics and U.S. homicide: Trends by age, sex and race for 1976–1998 and beyond. In A. Blumstein & J. Wallman (Eds.), *The crime drop in America* (pp. 288–318). New York: Cambridge University Press.

Hanson, R.K., & Bussière, M.T. (1998). Predicting relapse: A meta-analysis of sexual offender recidivism studies. *Journal of Consulting and Clinical Psychology, 66*(2), 348–362.

Jeffery, C.R. (1971). *Crime prevention through environmental design*. Beverly Hills, CA: Sage Publications.

Kriven, S., & Ziersch, E. (2007). New car security and shifting vehicle theft patterns in Australia. *Security Journal, 20*(2), 111–122.

Laub, J.H. (2004). The life course of criminology in the United States: The American Society of Criminology 2003 presidential address. *Criminology, 42*(1), 1–26.

Levine, N., & Block, R. (2011). Bayesian journey-to-crime estimation: An improvement in geographic profiling methodology. *The Professional Geographer, 63*(2), 213–229.

Lussier, P., Tzoumakis, S., Cale, J., & Amirault, J. (2010). Criminal trajectories of adult sex offenders and the age effect: Examining the dynamic aspect of offending in adulthood. *International Criminal Justice Review, 20*(2), 147–168.

Marvell, T., & Moody, C. (1991). Age structure and crime rates: The conflicting evidence. *Journal of Quantitative Criminology, 7*, 237–273.

Maxwell, A. (2017). Cases completed in adult criminal court, by age group and sex of the accused, Canada, 2014/2015. *Juristat, 37*(1). Statistics Canada Catalogue no. 85-002-X. Retrieved from https://www150.statcan.gc.ca/n1/pub/85-002-x/2017001/article/14699-eng.htm

Mednick, S.A., Gabrielli, W.F., & Hutchings, B. (1984). Genetic influences in criminal convictions: Evidence from an adoption cohort. *Science, 224*(4651), 891–894.

Moffitt, T.E. (1993). Adolescence-limited and life-course-persistent antisocial behavior: A developmental taxonomy. *Psychological Review, 100*, 674–701.

Murphy, E. (1922). *The black candle*. Toronto: Thomas Allen.

Padgett, K., Bales, W., & Blomberg, T. (2006). Under surveillance: An empirical test of the effectiveness and consequences of electronic monitoring. *Criminology and Public Policy, 5*(1), 61–91.

Parkinson, G. (2008). Recovering the early history of Canadian criminology: Criminology at the University of British Columbia, 1951–1959. *Canadian Journal of Criminology and Criminal Justice, 50*(5), 589–620.

Parnaby, P. (2007). Crime prevention through environmental design: Financial hardship, the dynamics of power, and the prospects of governance. *Crime, Law and Social Change, 48*(1), 73–85.

Pinker, S. (2011). *The better angels of our nature: Why violence has declined*. New York: Viking.

Rafter, N. (2009). *The origins of criminology: A reader*. London UK: Taylor and Francis.

Raine, A. (2013). *The anatomy of violence: The biological roots of crime*. New York: Pantheon.

Rossmo, D.K. (1999). *Geographic profiling*. Boca Raton, FL: CRC Press.

Statistics Canada. (2013). General social survey: An overview, 2013. Retrieved from https://www150.statcan.gc.ca/n1/pub/89f0115x/89f0115x2013001-eng.htm

Taylor, I., Walton, P., & Young, J. (1973). *The new criminology: For a social theory of deviance*. London: Routledge.

Tewksbury, R. (2009). Qualitative versus quantitative methods: Understanding why qualitative methods are superior for criminology and criminal justice. *Journal of Theoretical and Philosophical Criminology, 1*(1), 38–58.

Trahan, A., & Stewart, D. (2013). Toward a pragmatic framework for mixed-methods research in criminal justice and criminology. *Applied Psychology in Criminal Justice, 9*(1), 59–74.

United Nations Office on Drugs and Crime. (2013, February). Comprehensive study on cybercrime. Retrieved from https://www.unodc.org/documents/organized-crime/UNODC_CCPCJ_EG.4_2013/CYBERCRIME_STUDY_210213.pdf

Weisburd, D., & Piquero, A. (2008). How well do criminologists explain crime? Statistical modeling in published studies. *Crime and Justice: A Review of Research, 37*, 453–502.

Zimring, F. (2006). *The great American crime decline.* New York: Oxford University Press.

Chapter 2

Altheide, D. (1997). The news media, the problem frame, and the production of fear. *Sociological Quarterly, 38*(4), 647–668.

AndrewScheer. (2018, July 28). Canadians expect our immigration system to be safe, orderly, and compassionate. … [Twitter Post]. Retrieved from https://twitter.com/andrewscheer/status/1023298547184107520?lang=en

Becker, H. (1963). *Outsiders: Studies in the sociology of deviance.* New York: Free Press of Glencoe.

Beckett, L. (2018, March 31). Florida school shooting survivors march on unfazed by personal attacks. *The Guardian.* Retrieved from https://www.theguardian.com/us-news/2018/mar/31/florida-school-shooting-survivors-march-personal-attacks

Brezina, T., & Phipps, H.E. (2010). False news reports, folk devils, and the role of public officials: Notes on the social construction of law and order in the aftermath of Hurricane Katrina. *Deviant Behavior, 31*, 97–134.

Bucerius, S.M., & Tonry, M. (2014). *The Oxford Handbook of Ethnicity, Crime and Immigration.* New York: Oxford University Press.

Carnagey, N., Anderson, C., & Bartholow, B. (2007). Media violence and social neuroscience: New questions and new opportunities. *Current Directions in Psychological Science, 16*(4), 178–182.

Carter, S. (1988). When victims happen to be black. *Yale Law Journal, 97*, 420–447.

Chesney-Lind, M., & Eliason, M. (2006). From invisible to incorrigible: The demonization of marginalized women and girls. *Crime Media Culture, 2*(1), 29–47.

Christie, N. (1986). The ideal victim. In E. Fattah (Ed.), *From crime policy to victim policy* (pp. 17–30). London, UK: Macmillan.

Cohen, S. (1972/1980). *Folk devils and moral panics: The creation of the mods and rockers.* Oxford, UK: Basil Blackwood.

Cohen, S., & Young, J. (1973). *The manufacture of news: Social problems, deviance and mass media.* London, UK: Constable.

Common Sense Media. (2015). *The common sense census: Media use by tweens and teens.* San Francisco: Common Sense Media.

Coogan, D. (2012). Race and crime in sports media: Content analysis on the Michael Vick and Ben Roethlisberger cases. *Journal of Sports Media, 7*(2), 129–151.

DeLisi, M., Vaughn, M., Gentile, D., Anderson, C., & Shook, J. (2012). Violent video games, delinquency and youth violence: New evidence. *Youth Violence and Juvenile Justice, 11*(2), 132–142.

Dickerman, C., Christensen J., Beatriz, S., & McClain, K. (2008). Big breasts and bad guys: Depictions of gender and race in video games. *Journal of Creativity in Mental Health, 3*(1), 20–29.

Dowler, K., Fleming, T., & Muzzatti, S.L. (2006). Constructing crime: Media, crime and popular culture. *Canadian Journal of Criminology and Criminal Justice, 48*(6), 837–850.

Doyle, A. (2003). *Arresting images: Crime and policing in front of the television camera.* Toronto: University of Toronto Press.

Federman, J. (1998). *National television study: Vol. 3.* Thousand Oaks, CA: Sage.

Ferrell, J. (1999). Cultural criminology. *Annual Review of Sociology, 25*(1), 395–418.

Gentile, D.A., & Bushman, B.J. (2012). Reassessing media violence effects using a risk and resilience approach to understanding aggression. *Psychology of Popular Media Culture, 1*(3), 138–151.

Goldstein, J., & Schweber, N. (2014, July 18). Man's death after chokehold raises old issues for the police. *New York Times.* Retrieved from https://www.nytimes.com/2014/07/19/nyregion/staten-island-man-dies-after-he-is-put-in-chokehold-during-arrest.html

Goode, E., & Ben-Yehuda, N. (1994). Moral panics: Culture, politics and social construction. *Annual Review of Sociology, 20*(1), 149–171.

Grant, T. (2016, September 28/2018, May 16). 320,000 newcomers came to Canada in past year, highest number since 1971. Retrieved from https://www.theglobeandmail.com/news/national/canada-welcomed-320000-immigrants-in-past-year-highest-number-since-1971/article32102991

Hall, S., Critcher, C., Jefferson, T., Clarke, J.N., & Roberts, B. (1978). *Policing the crisis: Mugging, the state and law and order.* London, UK: Macmillan Press.

Hickman, M., Thomas, L., Silvestri, S., & Nickels, H. (2011). *Suspect communities?: Counter-terrorism policy, the press, and the impact on Irish and Muslim communities in Britain.* London: London Metropolitan University, 1–39.

Immigration Watch Canada. (2018). Say no to Vancouver apology: Mainland Chinese rape of Vancouver dwarfs alleged discrimination against Chinese. Retrieved from http://immigrationwatchcanada.org/2018/04/06/12809

Inciardi, J.A., & Dee, J.L. (1987). From the Keystone Cops to Miami Vice: Images of policing in American popular culture. *Journal of Popular Culture, 21*(2), 84–102.

Jefferson County Sheriff's Department. (n.d.). The media response [report on Columbine High School incident]. Retrieved from http://www.cnn.com/SPECIALS/2000/columbine.cd/Pages/MEDIA_TEXT.htm

Leary, M., Kowalski, R., Smith, L., & Phillips, S. (2003). Teasing, rejection and violence: Case studies of the school shootings. *Aggressive Behavior, 29*(3), 202–214.

Lemert, E. (1951). *Social pathology: A systematic approach to the theory of sociopathic behaviour.* New York: McGraw-Hill.

Lyon, D. (2001). *Surveillance society: Monitoring everyday life.* Buckingham, UK: Open University Press.

Mahari, J., & Conner, R. (2003). Black violence has a bad rap. *Journal of Social Issues, 59*(1), 121–140.

Malcolm, C. (2018, November 8). Canadians leery of mass immigration. *Toronto Sun.* Retrieved from http://torontosun.com/opinion/columnists/malcolm-canadians-leery-of-mass-immigration

Mann, S., Nolan, J., & Wellman, B. (2003). Sousveillance: Inventing and using wearable computing devices for data collection in surveillance environments. *Surveillance & Society, 1*(3), 331–355.

Martin, B. (2018, May 20). "Overwhelming grief": 8 students, 2 teachers killed in Texas high school shooting. *Washington Post.* Retrieved from https://www.washingtonpost.com/news/post-nation/wp/2018/05/19/ten-killed-in-texas-high-school-shooting-were-mostly-students-police-say-suspect-confessed

MediaSmarts. (2018). Digital and media literacy fundamentals. Retrieved from http://mediasmarts.ca/digital-media-literacy/general-information/digital-media-literacy-fundamentals/media-literacy-fundamentals

Muschert, G.W. (2009). Frame-changing in the media coverage of a school shooting: The rise of Columbine as a national concern. *The Social Science Journal, 46,* 164–170.

Muschert, G.W., Henry, S., Bracy, N.L., & Peguero, A.A. (Eds.). (2014). *Responding to school violence: Confronting the Columbine effect.* London, UK: Lynne Rienner Publishers.

Perrault, S., Sauvé, J., & Burns, M. (2009). Multiple victimization in Canada, 2004. Statistics Canada Catalogue no. 85F0033M. Retrieved from http://publications.gc.ca/collections/collection_2010/statcan/85F0033M/85f0033m2010022-eng.pdf

Puar, J., & Rai, A. (2002). Monster, terrorist, fag: The war on terrorism and the production of docile patriots. *Social Text 72, 20*(3), 117–148.

Ringrose, J. (2006). A new universal mean girl: Examining the discursive construction and social regulation of a new feminine pathology. *Feminism & Psychology, 16*(4), 405–424.

Rochlin, N. (2017). Fake news: Belief in post-truth. *Library Hi Tech, 35*(3), 386–392.

Spohr, D. (2017). Fake news and ideological polarization: Filter bubbles and selective exposure on social media. *Business Information Review, 34*(3), 150–160.

Surette, R. (2013). Cause or catalyst: The interaction of real world and media crime models. *American Journal of Criminal Justice, 38,* 392–409.

Taylor, I.R., Walton, P., & Young, J. (1973). *The new criminology: For a social theory of deviance.* London, UK: Routledge.

Tierney, K., Bevc, C., & Kuligowski, E. (2006). Metaphors matter: Disaster myths, media frames, and their consequences in Hurricane Katrina. *Annals of the American Academy of Political and Social Science, 604,* 57–81.

Tzanelli, R., Yar, M., & O'Brien, M. (2005). "Con me if you can": Exploring crime in the American cinematic imagination. *Theoretical Criminology, 9*(1), 97–117.

VoiceOfFranky. (2018, August 24). So let's put aside the issue of how many immigrants are coming. … [Twitter Post]. Retrieved from https://twitter.com/VoiceOfFranky/status/1032806326940983297

Witt, E. (2018, February 19). How the survivors of Parkland began the Never Again movement. *The New Yorker.* Retrieved from https://www.newyorker.com/news/news-desk/how-the-survivors-of-parkland-began-the-never-again-movement

Zhang, H. (2014, April). *Immigration and crime: Evidence from Canada.* Canadian Labour Market and Skills Researcher Network (CLSRN), Working Paper No. 135. Retrieved from http://www.clsrn.econ.ubc.ca/workingpapers/CLSRN Working Paper no. 135 - Zhang.pdf

Chapter 3

Paternoster, R. (2010). How much do we really know about criminal deterrence? *Journal of Criminal Law and Criminology, 100*(3), 765.

Roach, K. (2008). A Charter reality check: How relevant is the Charter to the justness of our criminal justice system? *Supreme Court Law Review, 40*(2), 717–759.

Chapter 4

Allen, M. (2018). Police-reported crime statistics in Canada, 2017. Juristat, 38(1). Statistics Canada Catalogue no. 85-002-X. Retrieved from https://www150.statcan.gc.ca/n1/pub/85-002-x/2018001/article/54974-eng.htm

Barrett, D. (2015, March 19). Frauds worth £12bn go unreported, says report. *London Telegraph.* Retrieved from https://www.telegraph.co.uk/news/uknews/crime/11480715/Frauds-worth-12bn-go-unreported-says-report.html

Black, D.J. (1970). Production of crime rates. *American Sociological Review, 35,* 733–748.

Black, D.J., & Reiss, A.J. (1970). Police control of juveniles. *American Sociological Review, 35,* 63–77.

Brantingham, P.J., & Brantingham, P.L. (1984). *Patterns in crime.* New York: Macmillan.

Cohen, S. (2002). *Folk devils and moral panics* (3rd ed.). New York: Routledge.

ComScore. (2011). It's a social world: Top 10 need-to-knows about social networking and where it's headed. *ComScore.* Retrieved from http://www.comscore.com/Press_Events/Presentations_Whitepapers/2011/it_is_a_social_world_top_10_need-to-knows_about_social_networking

Conroy, S., & Cotter, A. (2017). Self-reported sexual assault in Canada, 2014. Juristat, 37(1). Statistics Canada Catalogue no. 85-002-X. Retrieved from https://www150.statcan.gc.ca/n1/pub/85-002-x/2017001/article/14842-eng.htm

Dauvergne, M., & Turner, J. (2010). Police-reported crime statistics in Canada, 2009. Juristat, 30(2). Statistics Canada Catalogue no. 85-002-X. Ottawa: Statistics Canada.

Denzin, N.K. (2017). *The research act: A theoretical introduction to sociological methods*. New York: Routledge.

Ditton, J. (1979). *Controlology: Beyond the new criminology*. London, UK: Macmillan.

Doolittle, R. (2017, February 3). Why police dismiss 1 in 5 sexual assault claims as baseless. *Globe and Mail*. Retrieved from https://www.theglobeandmail.com/news/investigations/unfounded-sexual-assault-canada-main/article33891309

Dutton, D.G., Boyanowsky, E.O., Palys, T.S., & Heywood, R. (1982). *Community policing: Preliminary results from a national study of the RCMP*. Research report prepared for the Research Division of the Solicitor General Canada.

Eterno, J.A., & Silverman, E.B. (2010). The NYPD's CompStat: Compare statistics or compose statistics? *International Journal of Police Science & Management*, *12*(3), 426–449. Retrieved from http://nylawyer.nylj.com/adgifs/decisions/011311eterno_silverman.pdf

Farrell, G., Tilley, N., Tseloni, A., & Mailley, J. (2011). The crime drop and the security hypothesis. *Journal of Research in Crime and Delinquency*, *48*(2), 147–175. https://doi.org/10.1177/0022427810391539

Farrington, D.P., & Dowds, E.A. (1985). Disentangling criminal behaviour and police reaction. In D.P. Farrington & J. Gunn (Eds.), *Reactions to crime: The public, the police, courts and prisons* (pp. 41–72). Chichester, UK: Wiley.

FBI. (2012). Crime in the United States: By volume and rate per 100,000 inhabitants, 1992–2011. Retrieved from http://www.fbi.gov/about-us/cjis/ucr/crime-in-the-u.s/2011/crime-in-the-u.s.-2011/tables/table-1

Fetter, B. (2009). Collecting crime data in Canada. Statistics Canada's International Symposium Series, Catalogue no. 11-522-X. Retrieved from https://www150.statcan.gc.ca/n1/en/pub/11-522-x/2008000/article/11012-eng.pdf

Government of British Columbia. (2015). Overview of crime data collection in British Columbia, 2014. Retrieved from https://www2.gov.bc.ca/assets/gov/law-crime-and-justice/criminal-justice/police/publications/statistics/crime-data-collection.pdf

Griffiths, C.T. (2019). *Canadian criminal justice: A primer* (6th ed.). Toronto: Nelson.

Gruszczyńska, B.Z., & Heiskanen, M. (2012). Trends in police-recorded offences. *European Journal of Criminal Policy Research*, *18*(1), 18–83. https://doi.org/10.1007/s10610-011-9160-0

Home Office, United Kingdom. (2013). A summary of recorded crime data from 1898 to 2001/02 (Microsoft Excel file). Statistics: Historical crime data. Retrieved from https://data.gov.uk/dataset/f79c8194-93b0-41eb-bba5-56a83fd32f10/historical-crime-data

Jick, T.D. (1979). Mixing qualitative and quantitative methods: Triangulation in action. *Administrative Science Quarterly*, *24*(4), 602–611. Retrieved from http://www.jstor.org/stable/2392366

Kaspersky Labs. (2014). Consumer security risks survey 2014: Multi-device threats in a multi-device world. Retrieved from: https://media.kaspersky.com/en/Kaspersky_Lab_Consumer_Security_Risks_Survey_2014_ENG.pdf

Levens, B.P., & Dutton, D.G. (1980). *The social service role of the police: Domestic crisis intervention*. Ottawa: Solicitor General of Canada.

Lowman, J. (1982). Crime, criminal justice policy and the urban environment. In D.T. Herbert & R.J. Johnston (Eds.), *Geography and the urban environment: Vol. 5* (pp. 307–341). Chichester, UK: Wiley.

Lowman, J., & Palys, T.S. (1991). Interpreting criminal justice system records of crime. In M.A. Jackson & C.T. Griffiths (Eds.), *Canadian criminology: Perspectives on crime and criminality* (pp. 349–369). Toronto: Harcourt Brace Jovanovich.

MacDonald, Z. (2002). Official crime statistics: Their use and interpretation. *The Economic Journal*, *112*(477), F85–F106. https://doi.org/10.1111/1468-0297.00685

Mishra, S., & Lalumière, M. (2009). Is the crime drop of the 1990s in Canada and the USA associated with a general decline in risky and health-related behavior? *Social Science & Medicine*, *68*(1), 39–48. https://doi.org/doi:10.1016/j.socscimed.2008.09.060

Muncie, J. (2001). The construction and deconstruction of crime. In J. Muncie & E. McLaughlin (Eds.), *The problem of crime* (2nd ed., pp. 7–70). London, UK: Sage.

Palys, T., & Atchison, C. (2008). *Research decisions: Quantitative and qualitative perspectives* (4th ed.). Toronto: Thomson Nelson.

Palys, T., & Atchison, C. (2014). *Research decisions: Quantitative, qualitative and mixed methods approaches* (5th ed.). Toronto: Thomson Nelson.

Palys, T., Isaac, R., & Nuszdorfer, J. (2012). *Taking Indigenous justice seriously: Fostering a mutually respectful coexistence of Aboriginal and Canadian justice*. Research report prepared for Vancouver's Downtown Community Court and Vancouver Aboriginal Transformative Justice Services. Retrieved from http://www.sfu.ca/~palys/PalysEtAl-2012-Aboriginal&CanadianJustice-final.pdf

Perreault, S. (2012). Homicide in Canada, 2011. *Juristat*, *32*(1). Statistics Canada Catalogue no. 85-002-X. Retrieved from http://www.statcan.gc.ca/pub/85-002-x/2012001/article/11738-eng.pdf

Perreault, S. (2015). Criminal victimization in Canada, 2014. *Juristat*, *35*(1). Statistics Canada Catalogue no. 85-002-X. Retrieved from https://www150.statcan.gc.ca/n1/pub/85-002-x/2015001/article/14241-eng.htm

Pinker, S. (2011). *The better angels of our nature: Why violence has declined*. New York: Viking Penguin.

RCMP. (2016). Internet safety resources. Retrieved from http://www.rcmp-grc.gc.ca/is-si/index-eng.htm

Rood, D. (2011, May 27). Police will outsource crime stats. *The Age*. Retrieved from http://www.theage.com.au/victoria/police-will-outsource-crime-stats-20110526-1f6b7.html

Sacks, H. (1972). Notes on police assessment of moral character. In D. Sudnow (Ed.), *Studies in social interaction* (pp. 280–293). New York: Free Press.

Skogan, W.G. (1975). Measurement problems in official and survey crime rates. *Journal of Criminal Justice, 3,* 17–32.

Skogan, W.G. (1982). Methodological issues in the measurement of crime. In H.J. Schneider (Ed.), *The victim in international perspective* (pp. 203–208). Berlin: DeGruyter.

Smyth, S. (2010). *Cybercrime in Canadian criminal law.* Toronto: Thomson Reuters Canada.

Statistics Canada. (2014). General Social Survey—Victimization (GSS): Definitions, data sources and methods. Retrieved from http://www23.statcan.gc.ca/imdb/p2SV.pl?Function=getSurvey&SDDS=4504

Wallace, M., Turner, J., Matarazzo, A., & Babyak, C. (2009). *Measuring crime in Canada: Introducing the Crime Severity Index and improvements to the Uniform Crime Reporting Survey* (Catalogue no. 85-004-X). Ottawa: Statistics Canada.

Chapter 5

American Psychiatric Association. (2013). *Diagnostic and statistical manual of mental disorders* (5th ed.). Washington, DC: Author.

Amir, M. (1971). *Patterns in forcible rape.* Chicago: University of Chicago Press.

Ashworth, A. (1993). Victim impact statements and sentencing. *Criminal Law Review, 7,* 498–509.

Bergeman, C.S., & Wallace, K.A. (1999). Resiliency in later life. In T.L. Whitman, T.V. Merluzzi, & R.D. White (Eds.), *Life-span perspectives on health and illness* (pp. 207–225). Mahwah, NJ: Erlbaum.

Bonanno, G.A. (2004). Loss, trauma, and human resilience: Have we underestimated the human capacity to thrive after extremely adverse events? *American Psychologist, 59*(1), 20–28. https://doi.org/10.1037/0003-066X.59.1.20

Canadian Mental Health Association. (n.d.). Post-traumatic stress disorder (PTSD). Retrieved from http://www.cmha.ca/mental_health/post-traumatic-stress-disorder

Davis, R.C., Lurigio, A.J., & Skogan, W.G. (1999). Services for victims: A market research study. *International Journal of Victimology, 6,* 101–115.

Eigenberg, H. (2003). Victim blaming. In L. Moriarty (Ed.), *Controversies in victimology* (pp. 15–24). Cincinnati, OH: Anderson.

Erez, E., & Rogers, L. (1999). Victim impact statements and sentencing outcomes and processes: The perspectives of the legal professionals. *British Journal of Criminology, 39*(2), 216–239.

Ferraro, K.F. (1996). Women's fear of victimization: Shadow of sexual assault? *Social Forces, 75*(2), 667–690. https://doi.org/10.1093/sf/75.2.667

Frazier, P.A., & Borgida, E. (1992). Rape trauma syndrome: A review of case law and psychological research. *Law and Human Behavior, 16,* 293–311.

Garmezy, N. (1991). Resilience in children's adaptation to negative life events and stressed environments. *Pediatric Annals, 20,* 459–466.

Giannelli, P. (1997). Rape trauma syndrome. *Criminal Law Bulletin, 33,* 270–279.

Hinch, R. (1985). Canada's new sexual assault laws: A step forward for women? *Contemporary Crises, 9*(1), pp. 33–44.

Lauritsen, J.L., & Laub, J.H. (2007). Understanding the link between victimization and offending: New reflections on an old idea. In M. Hough & M. Maxfield (Eds.), *Surveying crime in the 21st century* (pp. 55–75). Monsey, NY: Criminal Justice Press/Willow Tree Press.

Masten, A.S., & Powell, J.L. (2003). A resilience framework for research, policy, and practice. In S.S. Luthar (Ed.), *Resilience and vulnerability: Adaptation in the context of childhood adversities* (pp. 1–25). New York: Cambridge University Press.

Naffine, N. (1987). *Female crime: The construction of women in criminology.* London, UK: Allen and Unwin.

Ong, A.D., Bergeman, C.S., Bisconti, T.L., & Wallace, K.A. (2006). Psychological resilience, positive emotions, and successful adaptation to stress in later life. *Journal of Personality and Social Psychology, 91*(4), 730–749. https://doi.org/10.1037/0022-3514.91.4.730

Oxford Dictionaries (n.d.). Victim. Retrieved from http://www.oxforddictionaries.com/definition/english/victim

Perreault, S. (2015). Criminal victimization in Canada, 2014. *Juristat.* Statistics Canada Catalogue no. 85-002-X. Retrieved from https://www150.statcan.gc.ca/n1/pub/85-002-x/2015001/article/14241-eng.pdf

Perreault, S. (2017). Canadians' perception of personal safety and crime, 2014. *Juristat.* Statistics Canada Catalogue no. 85-002-X. Retrieved from https://www150.statcan.gc.ca/n1/en/pub/85-002-x/2017001/article/54889-eng.pdf?st=z0lHYtxZ

Perreault, S., & Brennan, S. (2010). Criminal victimization in Canada, 2009. *Juristat, 30*(2). Statistics Canada Catalogue no. 85-002-X. Retrieved from http://www.statcan.gc.ca/pub/85-002-x/2010002/article/11340-eng.htm

Quinney, R. (1972). Who is the victim? *Criminology, 10*(3), pp. 314–323. https://doi.org/10.1111/j.1745-9125.1972.tb00564.x

Rienick, C., Mulmat, D.H., & Pennell S. (1997). *Meeting the needs of victims.* San Diego, CA: San Diego Association of Governments.

Scott, H. (2003). Stranger danger: Explaining women's fear of crime. *Western Journal of Criminology, 4,* 203–214.

Statistics Canada. (2014). General social survey—victimization. Ottawa: Statistics Canada. Retrieved from http://www23.statcan.gc.ca/imdb/p2SV.pl?Function=getSurvey&SDDS=4504&lang=en&db=imdb&adm=8&dis=2

Strobl, R. (2010). Becoming a victim. In S.G. Shoham, P. Knepper, & M. Kett (Eds.), *International handbook of victimology* (pp. 3–26). Boca Raton, FL: CRC Press.

Summer, C.J. (1987). Victim participation in the criminal justice system. *Australian and New Zealand Journal of Criminology, 20,* 195–217.

Wolfgang, M.E. (1958). *Patterns of criminal homicide.* Philadelphia: University of Pennsylvania Press.

Chapter 6

Agnew, R. (2005). *Why do criminals offend? A general theory of crime and delinquency.* New York: New York University Press.

Agnew, R. (2011). *Toward a unified criminology: Integrated assumptions about crime, people and society.* New York: New York University Press.

Akers, R.L. (1989). A social behaviorist's perspective on integration of theories of crime and deviance. In S.F. Messner, M.D. Krohn, & A.E. Liska (Eds.), *Theoretical integration in the study of deviance and crime: Problems and prospects* (pp. 179–195). Albany, NY: State University of New York Press.

Akers, R.L., & Jensen, G.F. (2003). *Social learning theory and the explanation of crime: A guide for the new century.* New Brunswick, NJ: Transaction.

Akers, R.L., & Jensen, G.F. (2006). The empirical status of social learning theory of crime and deviance: The past, present and future. In F.T. Cullen, J.P. Wright, & K.R. Blevins (Eds.), *Taking stock: The status of criminological theory* (pp. 37–76). New Brunswick, NJ: Transaction.

Akers, R.L., & Sellers, C.S. (2009). *Criminological theories: Introduction, evaluation, and application* (5th ed.). New York: Oxford University Press.

Alpert, J., & Hajaj, N. (2010, July 25). We knew the web was big ... [Blog post]. Retrieved from http://googleblog.blog spot.com/2008/07/we-knew-web-was-big.html

Anderson, G. (2007). *Biological influences on criminal behavior.* Boca Raton, FL: CRC Press.

Andrews, D.A., & Bonta, J. (2010). *The psychology of criminal conduct* (5th ed.). Cincinnati, OH: Anderson.

Bartol, C.W. (1999). *Criminal behaviour: A psychosocial approach.* Upper Saddle River, NJ: Prentice Hall.

Beaver, K.M., Ratchford, M., & Ferguson, C.J. (2009). Evidence of genetic and environmental effects on the development of low self-control. *Criminal Justice and Behavior, 36*(11), 1158–1172. https://doi .org/10.1177/0093854809342859

Benson, M.L., & Simpson, S.S. (2009). *White-collar crime: An opportunity perspective.* New York: Routledge.

Bernard, T.J., & Snipes, J.B. (1996). Theoretical integration in criminology. *Crime and Justice, 20,* 301–348.

Bernard, T.J., Snipes, J.B., & Gerould, A.L. (2010). *Vold's theoretical criminology* (6th ed.). New York: Oxford University Press.

Bradley, K. (2010). Cesare Lombroso (1835–1909). In K. Hayward, S. Maruna, & J. Mooney (Eds.), *Fifty key thinkers in criminology* (pp. 25–30). London: Routledge.

Broadhurst, R. (2006). Developments in the global law enforcement of cyber-crime. *Policing: An International Journal of Police Strategies and Management, 29*(3), 408–433. https://doi.org/10.1108/13639510610684674

Bruinsma, G. (2016). Proliferation of crime causation theories in an era of fragmentation: Reflections on the current state of criminological theory. *European Journal of Criminology, 13*(6), 659–676. https://doi.org/10.1177/1477370816667884

Burtch, B.E. (2003). *The sociology of law: Critical approaches to social control* (2nd ed.). Toronto: Nelson Thomson.

Clarke, R.V. (2009). Situational crime prevention. In B.R.E. Wright & R.B. McNeal, Jr. (Eds.), *Boundaries: Readings in deviance, crime and criminal justice* (pp. 145–193). Boston: Pearson Custom.

Clarke, R.V., & Cornish, D.B. (2001). Rational choice. In R. Paternoster & R. Bachman (Eds.), *Explaining criminals and crime: Essays in contemporary criminological theory* (pp. 23–42). Los Angeles: Roxbury.

Cohen, L.E., & Felson, M. (1979). Social change and crime rate trends: A routine activity approach. *American Sociological Review, 44*(4), 588–608.

Cohen, S. (1985). *Visions of social control: Crime, punishment, and classification.* New York: Polity Press.

Colvin, M., Cullen, F.T., & Vander Ven, T. (2002). Coercion, social support, and crime: An emerging theoretical consensus. *Criminology, 40*(1), 19–42.

Cullen, F.T. (1994). Social support as an organizing concept for criminology: Presidential address to the Academy of Criminal Justice Sciences. *Justice Quarterly, 11*(4), 527–559.

Cullen, F.T., Jonson, C.L., Myer, A.J., & Adler, F. (2011). Introduction: Preserving the origins of American criminology. In F.T. Cullen, C.L. Jonson, A.J. Myer, & F. Adler (Eds.), *The origins of American criminology: Advances in criminological theory: Vol. 16* (pp. 1–14). New Brunswick, NJ: Transaction.

Cullen, F.T., Wright, J.P., Gendreau, P., & Andrews, D.A. (2003). What correctional treatment can tell us about criminological theory: Implications for social learning theory. In R.L. Akers & G.F. Jensen (Eds.), *Social learning theory and the explanation of crime: A guide for the new century* (pp. 339–362). New Brunswick, NJ: Transaction.

Deutschmann, L.B. (2002). *Deviance and social control* (3rd ed.). Toronto: Nelson Thomson Learning.

DiCristina, B. (2012a). The emergence of the classical school. In B. DiCristina (Ed.), *The birth of criminology: Readings from the eighteenth and nineteenth centuries* (pp. 12–21). New York: Wolters Kluwer Law & Business.

DiCristina, B. (2012b). Jeremy Bentham. In B. DiCristina (Ed.), *The birth of criminology: Readings from the eighteenth and nineteenth centuries* (pp. 55–56). New York: Wolters Kluwer Law & Business.

DiCristina, B. (2012c). Physiognomy, phrenology and the Italian school. In B. DiCristina (Ed.), *The birth of criminology: Readings from the eighteenth and nineteenth centuries* (pp. 69–82). New York: Wolters Kluwer Law & Business.

Donohue, J.J., & Wolfers, J. (2009). Estimating the impact of the death penalty on murder. *American Law and Economics Review, 7*(2), 249–309. https://doi.org/10.1093/aler/ahp024

Durkheim, É. (1964). In G.E.G. Catlin (Ed.), *The rules of sociological method* (J.H. Mueller & S.A. Solovay, Trans.) (8th ed.). New York: The Free Press of Glencoe.

Duster, T. (2006). Comparative perspectives and competing explanations: Taking on the newly configured reductionist challenge to sociology. *American Sociological Review, 71*(1), 1–15. Retrieved from http://www.jstor.org/stable/30038973

Einstadter, W.J., & Henry, S. (2006). *Criminological theory: An analysis of its underlying assumptions* (2nd ed.). Lanham, MD: Rowman & Littlefield.

Elliott, D.S., Ageton, S.S., & Canter, R.J. (1979). An integrated theoretical perspective on criminal behavior. *Journal of Research in Crime and Delinquency, 16*(1), 3–27.

Ellis, L., & Walsh, A. (1997). Gene-based evolutionary theories in criminology. *Criminology, 35*(2), 229. https://doi .org/10.1111/j.1745-9125.1997.tb00876.x

Erikson, K.T. (1962). Notes on the sociology of deviance. *Social Problems, 9*(4), 307–314.

Farrell, G. (2010). Situational crime prevention and its discontents: Rational choice and harm reduction versus "cultural criminology." *Social Policy & Administration, 44*(1), 40–66. https://doi .org/10.1111/j.1467-9515.2009.00699.x

Farrington, D.P. (2004). Criminological psychology in the twenty-first century. *Criminal Behavior and Mental Health, 14*(3), 152–166. https://doi.org/10.1002/ cbm.583

Farrington, D.P., Coid, J.W., Harnett, L.M., Jolliffe, D., Soteriou, N., Turner, R.E., & West, D.J. (2006). *Criminal careers up to age 50 and life success up to age 48: New findings from the Cambridge Study in Delinquent Development.* London, UK: Home Office Research, Development and Statistics Directorate.

Felson, M., & Clarke, R.V. (2010). Routine precautions, criminology and crime prevention. In H.D. Barlow & S.H. Decker (Eds.), *Criminology and public policy: Putting theory to work* (pp. 106–127). Philadelphia: Temple University Press.

Fishbein, D.H. (1990). Biological perspectives in criminology. *Criminology, 28*(1), 27–72.

Foucault, M. (1979). *Discipline and punish: The birth of the prison* (A. Sheridan, Trans.). New York: Vintage Books.

Garland, D. (2001). *The culture of control: Crime and social order in contemporary society.* Chicago: University of Chicago Press.

Glueck, S., & Glueck, E. (1950/1994). Unraveling juvenile delinquency. In J.E. Jacoby (Ed.), *Classics of criminology* (2nd ed., pp. 241–246). Prospect Heights, IL: Waveland Press.

Hirschi, T. (1979). Separate and unequal is better. *Journal of Research in Crime and Delinquency, 16*(1), 34–38.

Hirschi, T. (1989). Exploring alternatives to integrated theory. In S.F. Messner, M.D. Krohn, and A.E. Liska, (Eds.), *Theoretical integration in the study of deviance and crime: Problems and perspectives.* Albany, NY: State University of New York Press.

Jeffery, C.R. (1978). Criminology as an interdisciplinary behavioral science. *Criminology, 16*(2), 149–169.

Laub, J.H., & Sampson, R.J. (1991). The Sutherland-Glueck debate: On the sociology of criminological knowledge. *American Journal of Sociology, 96*(6), 1402–1440.

Lemert, C.C. (1993). *Social theory: The multicultural and classic readings.* Boulder, CO: Westview Press.

Lilly, J.R., Cullen, F.T., & Ball, R.A. (2015). *Criminological theory: Context and consequences* (6th ed.). Thousand Oaks, CA: Sage.

Meier, R. (1985). *Theoretical methods in criminology.* Beverly Hills, CA: Sage Publications.

Messner, S.F, Krohn, M.D., & Liska, A.E. (1989). Strategies and requisites for theoretical integration in the study of crime and deviance. In S.F. Messner, M.D. Krohn, and A.E. Liska (Eds.), *Theoretical integration in the study of deviance and crime: Problems and perspectives.* Albany, NY: State University of New York Press.

Moffitt, T.E. (1993). Adolescence-limited and life-course-persistent antisocial behavior: A developmental taxonomy. *Psychological Review, 100*(4), 674–701.

Mutchnick, R.J., Martin, R., & Austin, T.W. (2009). *Criminological thought: Pioneers past and present.* Upper Saddle River, NJ: Prentice Hall.

Netcraft. (2010). April 2010 web server survey. Retrieved from http://news .netcraft.com/archives/2010/04/15/ april_2010_web_server_survey.html

O'Malley, P. (2010). Jeremy Bentham (1748–1832). In K. Hayward, S. Maruna, & J. Mooney (Eds.), *Fifty key thinkers in criminology* (pp. 7–12). London, UK: Routledge.

Passas, N. (1995). Continuities in the anomie tradition. In F. Adler, W.S. Laufer, & R.K. Merton (Eds.), *The legacy of anomie theory* (pp. 91–112). New Brunswick, NJ: Transaction.

Paternoster, R., & Bachman, R. (2001). The positive school of criminology: Biological theories of crime. In R. Paternoster & R. Bachman (Eds.), *Explaining criminals and crime: Essays in contemporary criminological theory* (pp. 47–56). Los Angeles: Roxbury.

Pfohl, S.J. (1985). *Images of deviance and social control: A sociological history.* New York: McGraw-Hill.

Piquero, A.R., & Blumstein, A. (2007). Does incapacitation reduce crime? *Journal of Quantitative Criminology, 23*(4), 267–285. https://doi.org/10.1007/ s10940-007-9030-6

Rafter, N.H. (1997). Psychopathology and the evolution of criminological knowledge. *Theoretical Criminology, 1*(2), 235–259. https://doi.org/ 10.1177/1362480697001002004

Rafter, N.H. (2009a). Criminal anthropology. In N.H. Rafter (Ed.), *The origins of criminology: A reader* (pp. 161–162). Oxon, UK: Routledge.

Rafter, N.H. (2009b). Introduction. In N.H. Rafter (Ed.), *The origins of criminology: A reader* (pp. xiii–xxvi). Oxon, UK: Routledge.

Raine, A. (2013). *The anatomy of violence: The biological roots of crime.* New York: Pantheon.

Raine, A., & Yaralian, P.S. (2001). Biological approaches to crime: Psychophysiology and brain dysfunction. In R. Paternoster & R. Bachman (Eds.), *Explaining criminals and crime: Essays in contemporary criminological theory* (pp. 57–72). Los Angeles: Roxbury.

Reiman, J. (2003). The Marxian critique of criminal justice. In C.M. Renzetti, D.J. Curran, & P.J. Carr (Eds.), *Theories of crime: A reader* (pp. 179–189). Boston: Allyn and Bacon.

Renzetti, C.M., Curran, D.J., & Carr, P.J. (Eds.). (2003). *Theories of crime: A reader.* Boston: Allyn and Bacon.

Robinson, M.B., & Beaver, K.M. (2008). *Why crime? An interdisciplinary approach to explaining criminal behavior.* Durham, NC: Carolina Academic Press.

Sacco, V.F., & Kennedy, L.W. (2011). *The criminal event: An introduction to criminology in Canada* (5th ed.). Toronto: Nelson Education.

Sampson, R.J., & Laub, J.H. (1992). Crime and deviance in the life course. *Annual Review of Sociology, 18*(1), 63–84.

Sutherland, E.H. (1940). White-collar criminality. *American Sociological Review, 5*(1), 1–12.

Sutherland, E.H. (1950). The diffusion of sexual psychopath laws. *American Journal of Sociology, 56*(2), 142–148.

Sutherland, E.H. (1994). Differential association. In J.E. Jacoby (Ed.), *Classics of criminology* (2nd ed., pp. 226–227). Prospect Heights, IL: Waveland Press.

Tremblay, R.E. (2012). Developmental origins of aggression: From social learning to epigenetics. In R. Loeber & B.C. Welsh (Eds.), *The future of criminology* (pp. 20–29). New York: Oxford University Press.

Walsh, A. (2002). *Biosocial criminology: Introduction and integration.* Cincinnati, OH: Anderson.

Walsh, A. (2012). *Criminology: The essentials.* Thousand Oaks, CA: Sage.

Walsh, W.A., & Wolak, J. (2005). Nonforcible Internet-related sex crimes with adolescent victims: Prosecution issues and outcomes. *Child Maltreatment, 10*(3), 260–271. https://doi.org/10.1177/1077559505276505

Williams, F.P., & McShane, M.D. (2018). *Criminological theory* (7th ed.). Upper Saddle River, NJ: Pearson.

Wortley, R. (2011). *Psychological criminology: An integrative approach.* London, UK: Routledge.

Yar, M. (2010). Cesare Beccaria (1738–94). In K. Hayward, S. Maruna, & J. Mooney (Eds.), *Fifty key thinkers in criminology* (pp. 3–7). London, UK: Routledge.

Young, J. (2002). Critical criminology in the twenty-first century: Critique, irony and the always unfinished. In K. Carrington & R. Hogg (Eds.), *Critical criminology: Issues, debates and challenges* (pp. 251–274). Cullompton, UK: Willan.

Zeitlin, I.M. (2001). *Ideology and the development of sociological theory* (7th ed.). Upper Saddle River, NJ: Prentice Hall.

Chapter 7

Amato, M.S., Magzamen, S., Imm, P., Havlena, J.A., Anderson, H.A., Kanarek, M.S., & Moore, C.F. (2013). Early lead exposure (<3 years old) prospectively predicts fourth grade school suspension in Milwaukee, Wisconsin (USA). *Environmental Research, 126*, 60–65. https://doi.org/10.1016/j.envres.2013.07.008

Andersen, S.L., & Teicher, M.H. (2004). Delayed effects of early childhood stress on hippocampal development. *Neuropsychopharmacology, 29*(11), 1988–1993.

Anderson, G.S. (2007). *Biological influences on criminal behavior.* Boca Raton, FL: CRC Press.

Archer, J. (1991). The influence of testosterone on human aggression. *British Journal of Psychology, 82*, 1–28.

Arseneault, L., Moffitt, T.E., Caspi, A., Taylor, A., Rijsdijk, F.V., Jaffee, S.R., … Measelle, J.R. (2003). Strong genetic effects on cross-situational antisocial behaviour among 5-year-old children according to mothers, teachers, examiner-observers, and twins' self-reports. *Journal of Child Psychology and Psychiatry, and Allied Disciplines, 44*(6), 832–848.

Barzman, D.H., Mossman, D., Appel, K., Blom, T.J., Strawn, J.R., Ekhator, N.N., … Geracioti Jr., T.D. (2013). The association between salivary hormone levels and children's inpatient aggression: A pilot study. *Psychiatric Quarterly, 84*(4), 475–484. https://doi.org/10.1007/s11126-013-9260-8

Beaver, K.M. (2011). Genetic influences on being processed through the criminal justice system: Results from a sample of adoptees. *Biological Psychiatry, 69*(3), 282–287. https://doi.org/10.1016/j.biopsych.2010.09.007

Beckley, A.L., Caspi, A., Broadbent, J., Harrington, H., Houts, R.M., Poulton, R., … Moffitt, T.E. (2018). Association of childhood blood lead levels with criminal offending. *JAMA Pediatrics, 172*(2), 166–173. https://doi.org/10.1001/jamapediatrics.2017.4005

Begleiter, H. (1995). The collaborative study on the genetics of alcoholism. *Alcohol, Health and Research, 19*(3), 228–236.

Bennett, P. (2018). The heterogeneous effects of education on crime: Evidence from Danish administrative twin data. *Labour Economics, 52*(C), 160–177.

Bernet, W., Vnencak-Jones, C.L., Farahany, N., & Montgomery, S.A. (2007). Bad nature, bad nurture, and testimony regarding MAOA and SLC6A4 genotyping at murder trials. *Journal of Forensic Science, 52*(6), 1362–1371. https://doi.org/10.1111/j.1556-4029.2007.00562.x

Bernhardt, P.C., Dabbs, J.M., Fielden, J.A., & Lutter, C.D. (1998). Testosterone changes during vicarious experiences of winning and losing among fans at sporting events. *Physiology & Behavior, 65*(1), 59–62.

Billings, S.B., & Schnepel, K.T. (2018). Life after lead: Effects of early interventions for children exposed to lead. *American Economic Journal: Applied Economics, 10*(3), 1–31. https://doi.org/10.1257/app.20160056

Bo, S., Abu-Akel, A., Kongerslev, M., Haahr, U.H., & Simonsen, E. (2011). Risk factors for violence among patients with schizophrenia. *Clinical Psychology Review, 31*(5), 711–726. https://doi.org/10.1016/j.cpr.2011.03.002

Bohman, M. (1996). Predisposition to criminality: Swedish adoption studies in retrospect. *Ciba Foundation Symposium, 194*, 99–109.

Book, A.S., Starzyk, K.B., & Quinsey, V.L. (2001). The relationship between testosterone and aggression: A meta-analysis. *Aggression and Violent Behavior, 6*, 579–599.

Bozanich, E. (2013). *The potential impact of the "warrior" gene on the Canadian criminal justice system* (Honours thesis). Simon Fraser University, Burnaby, BC.

Brunner, H.G., Nelen, M., Breakefield, X.O., Ropers, H.H., & van Oost, B.A. (1993). Abnormal behavior associated with a point mutation in the structural gene for monoamine oxidase A. *Science, 262*(5133), 578–580.

Caspi, A., McClay, J., Moffitt, T.E., Mill, J., Martin, J., Craig, I.W., … Poulton, R. (2002). Role of genotype in the cycle of violence in maltreated children. *Science, 297*(5582), 851–854. https://doi.org/10.1126/science.1072290

Caspi, A., Sugden, K., Moffitt, T.E., Taylor, A., Craig, I.W., Harrington, H., … Poulton, R. (2003). Influence of life stress on depression: Moderation by a polymorphism in the 5-HTT gene.

Science, 301(5631), 386–389. https://doi.org/10.1126/science.1083968

Cook, E.H., Stein, M.A., Krasowski, M.D., Cox, N.J., Olkon, D.M., Kieffer, J.E., & Leventhal, B.L. (1995). Association of attention-deficit disorder and the dopamine transporter gene. *The American Journal of Human Genetics, 56*(4), 993–998.

Coolidge, F.L., Thede, L.L., & Jang, K.L. (2001). Heritability of personality disorders in childhood. *Journal of Personality Disorders, 15*, 33–40.

da Cunha-Bang, S., Hjordt, L.V., Perfalk, E., Beliveau, V., Bock, C., Lehel, S., … Knudsen, G.M. (2017). Serotonin 1B receptor binding is associated with trait anger and level of psychopathy in violent offenders. *Biological Psychiatry, 82*(4), 267–274. https://doi.org/10.1016/j.biopsych.2016.02.030

Dabbs, J.M., Frady, R.L., Carr, T.S., & Besch, N.F. (1987). Saliva testosterone and criminal violence in young adult prison inmates. *Psychosomatic Medicine, 49*, 174–182.

Dabbs, J.M., & Hargrove, M.F. (1997). Age, testosterone and behavior among female prison inmates. *Psychosomatic Medicine, 59*(5), 477–480.

Damasio, H., Grabowski, T., Frank, R., Galaburda, A., & Damasio, A. (1994). The return of Phineas Gage: Clues about the brain from the skull of a famous patient. *Science, 264*(5162), 1102–1105.

Darwin, C. (1859). *On the origin of species.* London, UK: John Murray.

Dormer, D. (2018, September 7). Victims' families say killer Matthew de Grood should never be released. *CBC News.* Retrieved from https://www.cbc.ca/news/canada/calgary/matthew-degrood-stabbing-3rd-ncr-hearing-perras-hunter-rathwell-hong-segura-1.4813615

Dos Santos, M., Cahill, E.N., Bo, G.D., Vanhoutte, P., Caboche, J., Giros, B., & Heck, N. (2018). Cocaine increases dopaminergic connectivity in the nucleus accumbens. *Brain Structure & Function, 223*(2), 913–923. https://doi.org/10.1007/s00429-017-1532-x

Eley, T.C., Lichtenstein, P., & Stevenson, J. (1999). Sex differences in the etiology of aggressive and non-aggressive antisocial behavior: Results from two twin studies. *Child Development, 70*(1), 155–168.

Farrer, T.J., Frost, R.B., & Hedges, D.W. (2012). Prevalence of traumatic brain injury in intimate partner violence offenders compared to the general population: A meta-analysis. *Trauma, Violence, & Abuse, 13*(2), 77–82. https://doi.org/10.1177/1524838012440338

Fast, D.K., & Conry, J. (2009). Fetal alcohol spectrum disorders and the criminal justice system. *Developmental Disabilities Research Reviews, 15*(3), 250–257. https://doi.org/10.1002/ddrr.66

Fast, D.K., Conry, J., & Loock, C.A. (1999). Identifying fetal alcohol syndrome among youth in the criminal justice system. *Journal of Developmental and Behavioral Pediatrics, 20*(5), 370–372.

Fazel, S., Langstrom, N., Hjern, A., Grann, M., & Lichtenstein, P. (2009). Schizophrenia, substance abuse, and violent crime. *The Journal of the American Medical Association, 301*(19), 2016–2023.

Foley, C., Corvin, A., & Nakagome, S. (2017). Genetics of schizophrenia: Ready to translate? *Current Psychiatry Reports, 19*(9), 61. https://doi.org/10.1007/s11920-017-0807-5

Foley, D.L., Eaves, L.J., Wormley, B., Silberg, J.L., Maes, H.H., Kuhn, J., & Riley, B. (2004). Childhood adversity, monoamine oxidase A genotype and risk for conduct disorder. *Archives of Genetic Psychiatry, 61*, 738–744.

Gavaghan, C., & Bastani, A. (2014). Genes, blame and loss of control: Is there a place in criminal law for a "genetic defense"? *Recent Advances in DNA & Gene Sequences, 8*, 119–125.

Gordon, N., & Greene, E. (2018). Nature, nurture, and capital punishment: How evidence of a genetic-environment interaction, future dangerousness, and deliberation affect sentencing decisions. *Behavioral Sciences & the Law, 36*(1), 65–83. https://doi.org/10.1002/bsl.2306

Graveland, B. (2018, September 7). Review Board hears man found not criminally responsible for killing five, says he is a model patient. *The Toronto Star.* Retrieved from https://www.thestar.com/calgary/2018/09/07/killer-found-not-criminally-responsible-appears-before-review-board-four-years-later.html

Grigorenko, E.L., De Young, C.G., Eastman, M., Getchell, M., Haeffel,

G.J., Klinteberg, B., … Yrigollen, C.M. (2010). Aggressive behavior, related conduct problems, and variation in genes affecting dopamine turnover. *Aggressive Behavior, 36*(3), 158–176. https://doi.org/10.1002/ab.20339

Hixt, N., & Tucker, E. (2016, May 19). Matthew de Grood trial: Expert witnesses support not criminally responsible defence. Retrieved from https://globalnews.ca/news/2709507/edmonton-psychologist-to-testify-in-day-4-of-matthew-de-grood-murder-trial

Howes, O.D., McCutcheon, R., Owen, M.J., & Murray, R.M. (2017). The role of genes, stress, and dopamine in the development of schizophrenia. *Biological Psychiatry, 81*(1), 9–20. https://doi.org/10.1016/j.biopsych.2016.07.014

Kendler, K.S., Morris, N.A., Ohlsson, H., Lonn, S.L., Sundquist, J., & Sundquist, K. (2016a). Criminal offending and the family environment: Swedish national high-risk home-reared and adopted-away co-sibling control study. *The British Journal of Psychiatry, 209*(4), 294–299. https://doi.org/10.1192/bjp.bp.114.159558

Kendler, K.S., Ohlsson, H., Sundquist, K., & Sundquist, J. (2016b). The rearing environment and risk for drug abuse: A Swedish national high-risk adopted and not adopted co-sibling control study. *Psychological Medicine, 46*(7), 1359–1366. https://doi.org/10.1017/S0033291715002858

Kim, S.S. (2016). *Recognizing the difference and rethinking fatalism in the criminal justice system.* (Honours thesis). Simon Fraser University, Burnaby, BC.

Kim-Cohen, J., Caspi, A., Taylor, A., Williams, B., Newcombe, R., Craig, I.W., & Moffitt, T.E. (2006). MAOA, maltreatment, and gene–environment interaction predicting children's mental health: New evidence and a meta-analysis. *Molecular Psychiatry, 11*(10), 903–913. https://doi.org/10.1038/sj.mp.4001851

Kingston, D.A., Seto, M.C., Ahmed, A.G., Fedoroff, P., Firestone, P., & Bradford, J.M. (2012). The role of central and peripheral hormones in sexual and violent recidivism in sex offenders. *Journal of the American Academy of Psychiatry and the Law, 40*, 476–485.

Kirkpatrick, R.M., Legrand, L.N., Iacono, W.G., & McGue, M. (2011). A twin and adoption study of reading achievement: Exploration of shared-environmental and gene-environment-interaction effects. *Learning and Individual Differences, 21*(4), 368–375. https://doi.org/10.1016/j.lindif.2011.04.008

Lahlah, E., Lens, K.M., Bogaerts, S., & van der Knaap, L.M. (2013). When love hurts: Assessing the intersectionality of ethnicity, socio-economic status, parental connectedness, child abuse, and gender attitudes in juvenile violent delinquency. *Child Abuse & Neglect, 37*(11), 1034–1049. https://doi.org/10.1016/j.chiabu.2013.07.001

Laucht, M., Brandeis, D., & Zohsel, K. (2014). Gene-environment interactions in the etiology of human violence. *Current Topics in Behavioral Neurosciences, 17*, 267–295. https://doi.org/10.1007/7854_2013_260

Lencz, T., Knowles, E., Davies, G., Guha, S., Liewald, D.C., Starr, J.M., … Malhotra, A.K. (2014). Molecular genetic evidence for overlap between general cognitive ability and risk for schizophrenia: A report from the Cognitive Genomics consorTium (COGENT). *Molecular Psychiatry, 19*(2), 168–174. https://doi.org/10.1038/mp.2013.166

Lewis, D.O., Pincus, J.H., Bard, B., Richardson, E., Prichep, L.S., Feldman, M., & Yeager, C. (1986). Psychiatric, neurological and psycho-educational of 15 death row inmates in the United States. *American Journal of Psychiatry, 143*(5), 838–845.

Lewis, D.O., Pincus, J.H., Bard, B., Richardson, E., Prichep, L.S., Feldman, M., & Yeager, C. (1988). Neuropsychiatric, psychoeducational, and family characteristics of 14 juveniles condemned to death in the United States. *American Journal of Psychiatry, 145*(5), 584–589.

Loo, S.K., Fisher, S.E., Francks, C., Ogdie, M.N., MacPhie, I.L., Yang, M., … Monaco, A.P. (2004). Genome-wide scan of reading ability in affected sibling pairs with attention-deficit/hyperactivity disorder: Unique and shared genetic effects. *Molecular Psychology, 9*(5), 485–493.

Maestripieri, D. (2003). Similarities in affiliation and aggression between cross-fostered rhesus macaque females and their biological mothers. *Developmental Psychobiology, 43*(4), 321–327.

McCabe, B. (2017, May 11). My friend killed five people in my home but I won't call him a monster. *Vice.* Retrieved from https://www.vice.com/en_ca/article/bmwd8w/my-friend-killed-five-people-in-my-home-but-i-wont-call-him-a-monster

McSwiggan, S., Elger, B., & Appelbaum, P.S. (2017). The forensic use of behavioral genetics in criminal proceedings: Case of the MAOA-L genotype. *International Journal of Law and Psychiatry, 50*, 17–23. https://doi.org/10.1016/j.ijlp.2016.09.005

Mednick, S.A., Gabrielli, W.F.J., & Hutchings, B. (1984). Genetic influences in criminal convictions: Evidence from an adoption cohort. *Science, 224*(4651), 891–894.

Mednick, S.A., Gabrielli, W.F.J., & Hutchings, B. (1987). Genetic factors in the etiology of criminal behavior. In S.A. Mednick, T.E. Moffitt, & S.A. Stack (Eds.), *The causes of crime: New biological approaches* (pp. 74–91). Cambridge, UK: Cambridge University Press.

Mehta, P.H., & Josephs, R.A. (2010). Testosterone and cortisol jointly regulate dominance: Evidence for a dual-hormone hypothesis. *Hormones and Behavior, 58*(5), 898–906. https://doi.org/10.1016/j.yhbeh.2010.08.020

Meynen, G. (2016). Neurolaw: Recognizing opportunities and challenges for psychiatry. *Journal of Psychiatry and Neuroscience, 41*(1), 3–5.

Newsome, J., Boisvert, D., & Wright, J.P. (2014). Genetic and environmental influences on the co-occurrence of early academic achievement and externalizing behavior. *Journal of Criminal Justice, 42*(1), 45–53. https://doi.org/10.1016/j.jcrimjus.2013.12.002

Niehoff, D. (1999). Seeds of controversy. In D. Niehoff (Ed.), *The biology of violence: How understanding the brain, behavior and environment can break the vicious circle of aggression* (pp. 1–30). New York: Free Press.

Ouellet-Morin, I., Cote, S.M., Vitaro, F., Hebert, M., Carbonneau, R., Lacourse, E., … Tremblay, R.E. (2016). Effects of the MAOA gene and levels of exposure to violence on antisocial outcomes. *British Journal of Psychiatry, 208*(1), 42–48. https://doi.org/10.1192/bjp.bp.114.162081

Rees, E., O'Donovan, M.C., & Owen, M.J. (2015). Genetics of schizophrenia. *Current Opinion in Behavioral Sciences, 2*, 8–14. https://doi.org/10.1016/j.cobeha.2014.07.001

Rocque, M., & Posick, C. (2017). Paradigm shift or normal science? The future of (biosocial) criminology. *Theoretical Criminology, 21*(3), 288–303. https://doi.org/10.1177/1362480617707949

Rocque, M., Welsh, B.C., & Raine, A. (2012). Biosocial criminology and modern crime prevention. *Journal of Criminal Justice, 40*(4), 306–312. https://doi.org/10.1016/j.jcrimjus.2012.05.003

Salvador, A., Suay, F., Martinez-Sanchis, S., Simon, V.M., & Brain, P.F. (1999). Correlating testosterone and fighting in male participants in judo contests. *Physiology & Behavior, 68*(1-2), 205–209.

Schofield, P.W., Butler, T.G., Hollis, S.J., Smith, N.E., Lee, S.J., & Kelso, W.M. (2006). Traumatic brain injury among Australian prisoners: Rates, recurrence and sequelae. *Brain Injury, 20*(5), 499–506. https://doi.org/10.1080/02699050600664749

Schwartz, J.A., & Beaver, K.M. (2014). Exploring whether genetic differences between siblings explain sibling differences in criminal justice outcomes. *Comprehensive Psychiatry, 55*(1), 93–103. https://doi.org/10.1016/j.comppsych.2013.06.002

Shorter, K.R., & Miller, B.H. (2015). Epigenetic mechanisms in schizophrenia. *Progress in Biophysics & Molecular Biology, 118*(1–2), 1–7. https://doi.org/10.1016/j.pbiomolbio.2015.04.008

Snyder, S.M., & Smith, R.E. (2015). The influence of school engagement on counts of delinquent behaviors among maltreated youths. *Children & Schools, 37*(4), 199–206. https://doi.org/10.1093/cs/cdv015

Soler, H., Vinayak, P., & Quadagno, D. (2000). Biosocial aspects of domestic violence. *Psychoneuroendocrinology, 25*(7), 721–739.

St Pierre, M.E., & Parente, R. (2016). Efficacy of legal judgments for defendants with traumatic brain injury. *NeuroRehabilitation, 39*(1), 125–134. https://doi.org/10.3233/NRE-161344

Stergiakouli, E., & Thapar, A. (2010). Fitting the pieces together: Current research on the genetic basis of attention-deficit/hyperactivity disorder (ADHD). *Neuropsychiatric Disease and Treatment, 6,* 551–560. https://doi.org/10.2147/NDT.S11322

Sugden, K., Arseneault, L., Harrington, H., Moffitt, T.E., Williams, B., & Caspi, A. (2010). Serotonin transporter gene moderates the development of emotional problems among children following bullying victimization. *Journal of the American Academy of Child Adolescent Psychiatry, 49*(8), 830–840.

Teicher, M.H., Dumont, N.L., Ito, Y., Vaituzis, C., Giedd, J.N., & Andersen, S.L. (2004). Childhood neglect is associated with reduced corpus callosum area. *Biological Psychiatry, 56*(2), 80–85. https://doi.org/10.1016/j.biopsych.2004.03.016

Van Honk, J., Terburg, D., & Bos, P.A. (2011). Further notes on testosterone as a social hormone. *Trends in Cognitive Sciences, 15*(7), 291–292. https://doi.org/10.1016/j.tics.2011.05.003

Weder, N., Yang, B.Z., Douglas-Palumberi, H., Massey, J., Krystal, J.H., Gelernter, J., & Kaufman, J. (2009). MAOA genotype, maltreatment, and aggressive behavior: The changing impact of genotype at varying levels of trauma. *Biological Psychiatry, 65*(5), 417–424. https://doi.org/10.1016/j.biopsych.2008.09.013

Wertz, J., Caspi, A., Belsky, D. W., Beckley, A.L., Arseneault, L., Barnes, J.C., ... Moffitt, T.E. (2018). Genetics and crime: Integrating new genomic discoveries into psychological research about antisocial behavior. *Psychological Science, 29*(5), 791–803. https://doi.org/10.1177/0956797617744542

Wiberg, A. (2015). Rehabilitation of MAOA deficient criminals could lead to a decrease in violent crime. *Jurimetrics, 55,* 509–526.

Wille, R., & Beier, K.M. (1989). Castration in Germany. *Annals of Sex Research, 2,* 103–134.

Zhu, E.C., Hu, Y., & Soundy, T.J. (2017). Genetics of alcoholism. *The Journal of the South Dakota State Medical Association, 70*(5), 225–227.

Chapter 8

Aichhorn, A. (1925). *Wayward youth.* New York: Viking Press.

Akers, R.L. (1998). *Social structure and social learning: A general theory of crime and deviance.* Boston: Northeastern University Press.

Alexander, B. (2008). *The globalization of addiction: A study in the poverty of the spirit.* New York: Oxford University Press.

Alexander, F., & Healy, W. (1935). *Roots of crime.* Montclair, NJ: Patterson Smith.

Andrews, D.A., & Bonta, J. (2010). *The psychology of criminal conduct.* Cincinnati, OH: Anderson.

Appleby, T. (2011). *A new kind of monster: The secret life and chilling crimes of Colonel Russell Williams.* Toronto: Vintage Canada.

Babiak, P., & Hare, R.D. (2006). *Snakes in suits: When psychopaths go to work.* New York: Regan.

Bandura, A. (1959). *Adolescent aggression: A study of the influence of child-training practices and family interrelationships.* New York: Ronald Press.

Bandura, A. (1963). *Social learning and personality development.* New York: Holt, Rinehart, and Winston.

Bandura, A. (1965). Influence of models' reinforcement contingencies on the acquisition of imitative responses. *Journal of Personality and Social Psychology, 1*(6), 589–595.

Bandura, A. (1973). *Aggression: A social learning analysis.* Englewood Cliffs, NJ: Prentice Hall.

Bandura, A. (1977). *Social learning theory.* Englewood Cliffs, NJ: Prentice Hall.

Bandura, A. (1997). *Self-efficacy: The exercise of control.* New York: W.H. Freeman.

Bartol, C., & Bartol, A.M. (2011). *Criminal behavior: A psychosocial approach* (9th ed.). Boston: Prentice Hall.

Bernard, T.J., Snipes, J.B., & Gerould, A. (2010). *Vold's theoretical criminology.* New York: Oxford University Press.

Blackburn, R. (1990). *The psychology of criminal conduct: Theory, research, and practice.* New York: John Wiley and Sons.

Blair, R.J.R., Mitchell, D., & Blair, K. (2005). *The psychopath: Emotion and the brain.* Malden, MA: Blackwell.

Boyd, S., Carter, C.I., & Macpherson, D. (2016). *More harm than good: Drug policy in Canada.* Halifax: Fernwood Publishing.

Burgess, R.L., & Akers, R.L. (1966). A differential association-reinforcement theory of criminal behavior. *Social Problems, 14,* 128–146.

Cleckley, H. (1964). *The mask of sanity.* Augusta, GA: Emily S. Cleckley.

Cohen, S. (1983). Social control talk: Telling stories about correctional change. In D. Garland & P. Young (Eds.), *The power to punish: Contemporary penality and social analysis* (pp. 101–129). London, UK: Heinemann Educational.

Crocker, D. (2012). Imprisonment. In *Crime in Canada* (pp. 27–45). Don Mills, ON: Oxford University Press.

Dollard, J., Miller, N.E., Doob, L.W., Mowrer, O.H., & Sears, R. (1939). *Frustration and aggression.* New Haven, CT: Yale University Press.

Dutton, K. (2012). *The wisdom of psychopaths: What saints, spies and serial killers can teach us about success.* Toronto: Doubleday.

Einstadter, W., & Henry, S. (2006). *Theoretical criminology: An analysis of its underlying assumptions.* Lanham, MD: Rowman and Littlefield.

Eysenck, H.J. (1964). *Crime and personality.* London, UK: Methuen.

Eysenck, S.B.G., & Eysenck, H.J. (1978). Impulsiveness and venturesomeness: Their position in a dimensional system of personality description. *Psychological Reports, 43*(3), 1247–1255.

Farrington, D.P. (1992). Explaining the beginning, progress, and ending of antisocial behavior from birth to adulthood. In J. McCord (Ed.), *Facts, frameworks, and forecasts: Advances in criminological theory: Vol. 3* (pp. 253–286). New Brunswick, NJ: Transaction.

Farrington, D.P. (1999). *Cambridge study in delinquent development [Great Britain], 1961–1981,* ICPSR 8488. Ann Arbor, MI: Inter-university Consortium for Political and Social Research. https://doi.org/10.3886/ICPSR08488.v2

Farrington, D.P. (2003a). Developmental and life course criminology: Key theoretical and empirical issues—The 2002 Sutherland award address. *Criminology, 41*(2), 221–255.

Farrington, D.P. (2003b). Key results from the first forty years of the Cambridge Study. In T. Thornberry & M.D. Krohn (Eds.), *Taking stock of delinquency: An overview of findings from contemporary longitudinal studies* (pp. 137–174). New York: Kluwer Academic/Plenum.

Freud, S. (1920). *A general introduction to psychoanalysis*. New York: Boney and Liveright.

Freud, S. (1923). *The ego and the id*. New York: W.W. Norton.

Garz, D. (2009). *Lawrence Kohlberg: An introduction*. Leverkusen Opladen, Germany: Barbara Budrich.

Goddard, H.H. (1913). *The Kallikak family*. New York: Macmillan.

Gottfredson, M.R., & Hirschi, T. (1990). *A general theory of crime*. Stanford, CA: Stanford University Press.

Griffiths, C., & Murdoch, D. (2017). *Canadian Corrections* (5th ed.) Toronto: Nelson College Indigenous.

Harcourt, B.E. (2007). *Against prediction: Profiling, policing, and punishing in an actuarial age*. Chicago: University of Chicago Press

Hare, R.D. (1970). *Psychopathy: Theory and practice*. New York: Wiley.

Hare, R.D. (1993). *Without conscience: The disturbing world of the psychopaths among us*. New York: Pocket Books.

Hare, R.D. (1996). Psychopathy: A clinical construct whose time has come. *Criminal Justice and Behavior, 23*, 25–54.

Hare, R.D. (2003). *Manual for psychopathy checklist—revised* (2nd ed.). Toronto: Multi-Health Systems.

Hare R.D., & Cox, D.N. (1978). Clinical and empirical conceptions of psychopathy, and the selection of subjects for research. In R.D. Hare & D. Schalling (Eds.), *Psychopathic behavior: Approaches to research* (pp. 107–144). Chichester, UK: Wiley.

Herrnstein, W., & Murray, C. (1994). *The bell curve*. New York: Free Press.

Hirschi, T. (1969). *Causes of delinquency*. Berkeley, CA: University of California Press.

Hirschi, T., & Hindelang, M. (1977). Intelligence and delinquency: A revisionist review. *American Sociological Review, 42*, 571–587.

Jeffery, C.R. (1965). Criminal behavior and learning theory. *The Journal of Criminal Law, Criminology and Police Science, 56*, 294–300.

Johns, J.H., & Quay, H.C. (1962). The effect of social reward on verbal conditioning in psychopathic and neurotic military offenders. *Journal of Consulting and Clinical Psychology, 26*, 217–220.

Kohlberg, L. (1958). *The development of modes of thinking and choices in years 10 to 16* (Doctoral dissertation). Chicago: University of Chicago.

Kohlberg, L. (1969). Stage and sequence: The cognitive-developmental approach. In D.A. Goslin (Ed.), *Handbook of socialization theory and research* (pp. 347–480). Chicago: Rand McNally.

Lewis, M. (2015). *The biology of desire*. New York: Public Affairs Publishing.

Lilly, R.J., Cullen, F.T., & Ball, R.A. (2007). *Criminological theory: Context and consequences* (4th ed.). Thousand Oaks, CA: Sage.

Maté, G. (2009). *In the realm of hungry ghosts: Close encounters with addiction*. Toronto: Vintage Canada.

McIlroy, A., & Anderssen, E. (2010, October 22). How a psychopath is made. *Globe and Mail*. Retrieved from http://www.theglobeandmail.com/life/health-and-fitness/health/conditions/how-a-psychopath-is-made/article4268124

Moffitt, T. (1993). Adolescence-limited and life-course-persistent antisocial behaviour: A developmental taxonomy. *Psychological Review, 100*, 674–701.

Moffitt, T.E. (2007). A review of the research on the taxonomy of life-course persistent versus adolescence-limited antisocial behavior. In F.T. Cullen, J.P. Wright, & K.R. Blevins (Eds.), *Taking stock: The status of criminological theory* (pp. 277–312). New Brunswick, NJ: Transaction.

Mulholland, A. (2012, May 19). Col. Williams' double life not uncommon: Experts. *CTV News*. Retrieved from https://www.ctvnews.ca/col-williams-double-life-not-uncommon-experts-1.564807

Palmer, E.J. (2003). *Offending behavior: Moral reasoning, criminal conduct, and the rehabilitation of offenders*. Cullompton, UK: Willan.

Pavlov, I. (1927/1960). *Conditioned reflexes: An investigation of the physiological activity of the cerebral cortex*. New York: Dover.

Piaget, J. (1932). *The moral judgment of the child*. London, UK: Routledge and Kegan Paul.

Piquero, A.R., Farrington, D.P., & Blumstein, A. (2003). The criminal career paradigm. *Crime and Justice, 30*, 359–506.

Pozzulo, J., Bennell, C., & Forth, A. (2015). *Forensic psychology* (4th ed.). Toronto: Pearson.

Rafter, N. (2008). *The criminal brain: Understanding biological theories of crime*. New York: New York University Press.

Redl, F., & Toch, H. (1979). Psychoanalytic perspective. In H. Toch (Ed.), *Psychology of crime and criminal justice* (pp. 183–197). New York: Holt, Rinehart, and Winston.

Redl, F., & Wineman, D. (1951). *Children who hate: The disorganization and breakdown of behavior controls*. New York: Free Press.

Reid, S., & Bromwich, R. (2017). Case study: Ashley Smith: A preventable prison homicide. In K. O'Regan & S. Reid, *Thinking about criminal justice in Canada* (2nd ed., pp. 355–361). Toronto: Emond Publishing.

Robinson, M.B., & Beaver, K.M. (2008). *Why crime? An interdisciplinary approach to explaining criminal behavior*. Durham, NC: Carolina Academic Press.

Robinson, M.B., & Scherlan, R.G. (2014). *Lies, damned lies, and drug war statistics: A critical analysis of claims made by the Office of National Drug Control Policy*. New York: State University of New York Press.

Ross, R.R., & Ross, R.D. (1995). *Thinking straight: The reasoning and rehabilitation program for delinquency prevention and offender rehabilitation*. Ottawa: Air Training.

Sampson, R.J. (2013). *Great American city*. Chicago: University of Chicago Press.

Serin, R., Forth, A., Brown, S., Nunes, K., Bennell, C., & Pozzulo, J. (2011). *Psychology of criminal behavior*. Toronto: Pearson.

Skinner, B.F. (1953). *Science and human behavior*. New York: Macmillan.

Sutherland, E. (1931). Mental deficiency and crime. In K. Young (Ed.), *Social attitudes* (pp. 357–375). New York: Henry Holt.

Williams, K.M., Paulhus, D.L., & Hare, R.D. (2007). Capturing the four-factor structure of psychopathy in college students via self-report. *Journal of Personality Assessment, 88*, 205–219.

Wilson, J.Q., & Herrnstein, R. (1985). *Crime and human nature*. New York: Simon and Schuster.

Yochelson, S., & Samenow, S. (1976). *The criminal personality*. New York: Jason Aronson.

Zlomislic, D. (2011, May 17). Ashley Smith charged over 500 times for behaviour in jail, court hears. *Toronto Star*. Retrieved from: https://www.thestar.com/news/canada/2011/05/17/ashley_smith_charged_over_500_times_for_behaviour_in_jail_court_hears.html

Chapter 9

Agnew, R. (1985). A revised strain theory of delinquency. *Social Forces, 64*(1), 151–167.

Agnew, R. (1992). Foundation for a general strain theory of crime and delinquency. *Criminology, 30*(1), 47–87.

Agnew, R. (1995). The contribution of social-psychological strain theory to the explanation of crime and delinquency. In F. Adler, W.S. Laufer, & R.K. Merton (Eds.), *The legacy of anomie theory* (pp. 113–137). New Brunswick, NJ: Transaction.

Agnew, R. (1997). The nature and determinants of strain: Another look at Durkheim and Merton. In N. Passas & R. Agnew (Eds.), *The future of anomie theory* (pp. 27–51). Boston: Northeastern University Press.

Agnew, R. (2010). Controlling crime: Recommendations from general strain theory. In H.D. Barlow & S.H. Decker (Eds.), *Criminology and public policy: Putting theory to work* (pp. 25–44). Philadelphia: Temple University Press.

Akers, R.L. (1998). *Social learning and social structure: A general theory of crime and deviance*. Boston: Northeastern University Press.

Akers, R.L. (2001). Social learning theory. In R. Paternoster & R. Bachman (Eds.), *Explaining criminals and crime: Essays in contemporary criminological theory* (pp. 192–210). Los Angeles: Roxbury.

Akers, R.L. (2011). The origins of me and social learning theory: Personal and professional recollections and reflections. In F.T. Cullen, C.L. Jonson, A.J. Myer, & F. Adler (Eds.), *The origins of American criminology: Advances in criminological theory* (Vol. 16, pp. 347–366). New Brunswick, NJ: Transaction.

Akers, R.L., & Matsueda, R.L. (1989). Donald R. Cressey: An intellectual portrait of a criminologist. *Sociological Inquiry, 59*(4), 423–438.

Akers, R.L., & Sellers, C.S. (2013). *Criminological theories: Introduction, evaluation, and application* (6th ed.). New York: Oxford University Press.

Andrews, D.A., & Bonta, J. (2010). *The psychology of criminal conduct* (5th ed.). Cincinnati, OH: Anderson.

Bartol, C.W. (1999). *Criminal behaviour: A psychosocial approach*. Upper Saddle River, NJ: Prentice Hall.

Beaver, K.M., Ratchford, M., & Ferguson, C.J. (2010). Evidence of genetic and environmental effects on the development of low self-control. *Criminal Justice and Behavior, 36*(11), 1158–1172.

Becker, H.S. (1963). *Outsiders: Studies in the sociology of deviance*. London, UK: Free Press of Glencoe.

Bernard, T.J. (1995). Merton versus Hirschi: Who is faithful to Durkheim's heritage? In F. Adler, W.S. Laufer, & R.K. Merton (Eds.), *The legacy of anomie theory* (pp. 81–90). New Brunswick, NJ: Transaction.

Bernard, T.J., Snipes, J.B., & Gerould, A.L. (2010). *Vold's theoretical criminology* (6th ed.). New York: Oxford University Press.

Brent, E., & Atkisson, C. (2011). Accounting for cheating: An evolving theory and emergent themes. *Research in Higher Education, 52*(6), 640–658. https://doi.org/10.1007/s11162-010-9212-1

Brezina, T., & Phipps, H.E. (2010). False news reports, folk devils, and the role of public officials: Notes on the social construction of law and order in the aftermath of Hurricane Katrina. *Deviant Behavior, 31*(1), 97–134. http://doi.org/10.1080/01639620902854803

Burgess, E.W. (1925/1967). The growth of the city: An introduction to a research project. In R.E. Park, E.W. Burgess, & R.D. McKenzie (Eds.), *The city* (pp. 47–62). Chicago: University of Chicago Press.

Burgess, R.L., & Akers, R.L. (1966). A differential association-reinforcement theory of criminal behavior. *Social Problems, 14*(2), 128–147.

Burns, R., & Crawford, C. (1999). School shootings, the media and public fear: Ingredients for a moral panic. *Crime, Law and Social Change, 32*(2), 147–168.

Burruss, G.W., Bossler, A.M., & Holt, T.J. (2013). Assessing the mediation of a fuller social learning model on low self-control's influence on software piracy. *Crime & Delinquency, 59*(8), 1157–1184. https://doi.org/10.1177/0011128712437915

Burtch, B.E. (2003). *The sociology of law: Critical approaches to social control* (2nd ed.). Toronto: Nelson Thomson.

Cartwright, B. (Ed.). (2011). *Sociological explanations of crime and deviance*. Boston: Pearson Learning Solutions.

City of Surrey. (2010). *Surrey city centre: The future lives here*. Surrey, BC: City of Surrey.

City of Surrey. (2012). *Sustainability charter: A commitment to sustainability*. Surrey, BC: City of Surrey.

Clinard, M.B. (1964). The theoretical implications of anomie and deviant behavior. In M.B. Clinard (Ed.), *Anomie and deviant behavior: A discussion and critique* (pp. 1–56). New York: Free Press of Glencoe.

Clinard, M.B., & Meier, R.F. (2004). *Sociology of deviant behaviour* (12th ed.). Belmont, CA: Thomson Wadsworth.

Cloward, R.A., & Ohlin, L.E. (1960). *Delinquency and opportunity: A theory of delinquent gangs*. New York: Free Press.

Cohen, A.K. (1955/1964). *Delinquent boys: The culture of the gang*. Glencoe, IL: Free Press of Glencoe.

Cohen, L.E., & Machalek, R. (1994). The normalcy of crime: From Durkheim to evolutionary ecology. *Rationality and Society, 6*(2), 286–308. https://doi.org/10.1177/1043463194006002007

Cohen, S. (1987). *Folk devils & moral panics: The creation of the mods and rockers.* Oxford, UK: Basil Blackwell.

Cohen, S., & Young, J. (Eds.). (1973). *The manufacture of news: Social problems, deviance and the mass media.* London, UK: Constable.

Cullen, F.T., & Messner, S.F. (2011). The making of criminology revisited: An oral history of Merton's anomie paradigm. In F.T. Cullen, C.L. Jonson, A.J. Myer, & F. Adler (Eds.), *The origins of American criminology: Advances in criminological theory: Vol. 16* (pp. 89–119). New Brunswick, NJ: Transaction.

Cullen, F.T., Wright, J.P., & Blevins, K.R. (Eds.). (2004). *Taking stock: The status of criminological theory.* New Brunswick, NJ: Transaction.

Cullen, F.T., Wright, J.P., Gendreau, P., & Andrews, D.A. (2003). What correctional treatment can tell us about criminological theory: Implications for social learning theory. In R.L. Akers & G.F. Jensen (Eds.), *Social learning theory and the explanation of crime: A guide for the new century* (pp. 339–362). New Brunswick, NJ: Transaction.

Curra, J. (2011). *The relativity of deviance* (2nd ed.). Thousand Oaks, CA: Sage.

Davies, S., & Tanner, J. (2003). The long arm of the law: Effects of labeling on employment. *Sociological Quarterly, 44*(3), 385–404. https://doi.org/10.1111/j.1533-8525.2003.tb00538.x

Deutschmann, L.B. (2002). *Deviance and social control* (3rd ed.). Toronto: Nelson Thomson Learning.

Durkheim, É. (1951). *Suicide: A study in sociology* (J.A. Spaulding & G. Simpson, Trans.). Glencoe, IL: Free Press.

Durkheim, É. (1964). In G.E.G. Catlin (Ed.), *The rules of sociological method* (J.H. Mueller & S.A. Solovay, Trans.) (8th ed.). New York: Free Press of Glencoe.

Durkheim, É. (1965). *The division of labor in society* (G. Simpson, Trans.). New York: Free Press.

Durkheim, É. (1895/1970). The normal and the pathological. In M. Wolfgang, L. Savitz, & N. Johnstone (Eds.), *The sociology of crime and delinquency.* London, UK: Wiley.

Ellis, L., & Walsh, A. (1997). Gene-based evolutionary theories in criminology. *Criminology, 35*(2), 229. https://doi.org/10.1111/j.1745-9125.1997.tb00876.x

Erikson, K.T. (1962). Notes on the sociology of deviance. *Social Problems, 9*(4), 307–314.

Erikson, K.T. (1964). Notes on the sociology of deviance. In H.S. Becker (Ed.), *The other side: Perspectives on deviance* (pp. 9–21). New York: Free Press of Glencoe.

Erikson, K.T. (2005). *Wayward puritans: A study in the sociology of deviance.* Boston: Allyn and Bacon.

Farrington, D.P., Coid, J.W., Harnett, L.M., Jolliffe, D., Soteriou, N., Turner, R.E., & West, D.J. (2006). *Criminal careers up to age 50 and life success up to age 48: New findings from the Cambridge study in delinquent development.* London, UK: Home Office Research, Development and Statistics Directorate.

Garland, D. (2001). *The culture of control: Crime and social order in contemporary society.* Chicago: University of Chicago Press.

Gelles, R.J. (1993). Through a sociological lens: Social structure and family violence. In R.J. Gelles & D. Loseke (Eds.), *Current controversies on family violence* (pp. 31–46). Thousand Oaks, CA: Sage.

Giddens, A. (1987). *Social theory and modern sociology.* Stanford, CA: Stanford University Press.

Gottfredson, M.R., & Hirschi, T. (1990). *A general theory of crime.* Stanford, CA: Stanford University Press.

Gove, W.R. (1980). The labelling perspective: An overview. In W.R. Gove (Ed.), *The labelling of deviance: Evaluating a perspective* (2nd ed.). Beverly Hills, CA: Sage.

Greenberg, D.F. (2010). *Building modern criminology: Forays and skirmishes.* Surrey, UK: Ashgate.

Hagan, J.A., Gillis, A.R., & Simpson, J. (1985). The class structure of gender and delinquency: Toward a power-control theory of common delinquent behavior. *American Journal of Sociology, 90*(6), 1151–1178.

Hayward, K., Maruna, S., & Mooney, J. (Eds.). (2010). *Fifty key thinkers in criminology.* London, UK: Routledge.

Hirschi, T. (1969). *Causes of delinquency.* Berkeley, CA: University of California Press.

Hoffman, J.P. (2010). Contemporary retrospective on general strain theory: The status of general strain theory. In H. Copes & V. Topalli (Eds.), *Criminological theory: Readings and retrospectives* (pp. 156–168). New York: McGraw-Hill.

Hutchings, A., & Clayton, R. (2016). Exploring the provision of online booter services. *Deviant Behavior, 37*(10), 1163–1178. https://doi.org/10.1080/01639625.2016.1169829

Immergluck, D. (2011). The local wreckage of global capital: The subprime crisis, federal policy, and high-foreclosure neighborhoods in the US. *International Journal of Urban and Regional Research, 35*(1), 130–146. https://doi.org/10.1111/j.1468-2427.2010.00991.x

Inderbitzen, M., Bates, K., & Gainey, R. (2013). *Deviance and social control: A sociological perspective.* Thousand Oaks, CA: Sage.

Kornhauser, R.R. (1978). *Social sources of delinquency: An appraisal of analytic models.* Chicago: University of Chicago Press.

Lamb, J. (1992, October 29). Living in Whalley now means having to say you're Surrey. *Vancouver Sun*, p. B1.

Laub, J.H., Nagin, D.S., & Sampson, R.J. (1998). Trajectories of change in criminal offending: Good marriages and the desistance process. *American Sociological Review, 63*(2), 225–238.

Laub, J.H., & Sampson, R.J. (1991). The Sutherland-Glueck debate: On the sociology of criminological knowledge. *American Journal of Sociology, 96*(6), 1402–1440.

Laub, J.H., & Sampson, R.J. (1993). Turning points in the life course: Why change matters to the study of crime. *Criminology, 31*(3), 301–325.

Laub, J.H., Sampson, R.L., & Allen, L.C. (2001). Explaining crime over the life course: Toward a theory of age-graded informal social control.

In R. Paternoster & R. Bachman (Eds.), *Explaining criminals and crime: Essays in contemporary criminological theory* (pp. 97–112). Los Angeles: Roxbury.

Lilly, J.R., Cullen, F.T., & Ball, R.A. (2015). *Criminological theory: Context and consequences* (6th ed.). Thousand Oaks, CA: Sage.

Lowenkamp, C.T., Cullen, F.T., & Pratt, T.C. (2003). Replicating Sampson and Groves's test of social disorganization theory: Revisiting a criminological classic. *Journal of Research in Crime and Delinquency, 40*(4), 351–373.

Matsueda, R.L. (1992). Reflected appraisals, parental labeling, and delinquency: Specifying a symbolic interactionist theory. *American Journal of Sociology, 97*(6), 1577–1611.

Matsueda, R.L. (2001). Labeling theory: Historical roots, implications, and recent developments. In R. Paternoster & R. Bachman (Eds.), *Explaining criminals and crime: Essays in contemporary criminological theory* (pp. 223–241). Los Angeles: Roxbury.

Merton, R.K. (1938). Social structure and anomie. *American Sociological Review, 3*(5), 672–682.

Messerschmidt, J.W. (1993). *Masculinities and crime: Critique and reconceptualization of theory.* Lanham, MD: Rowman & Littlefield.

Messerschmidt, J.W. (2005). Men, masculinities and crime. In M.S. Kimmel, J. Hearn, & R.W. Connell (Eds.), *Handbook of studies on men and masculinities* (pp. 196–212). Thousand Oaks, CA: Sage.

Messner, S.F., & Rosenfeld, R. (1994/2007). *Crime and the American dream* (4th ed.). Belmont, CA: Thomson Wadsworth.

Munro, H. (1998, February 3). Recapturing Whalley: This poor, crime-ridden section of Surrey has a tough reputation inside the RCMP. *Vancouver Sun,* p. B1.

Mutchnick, R.J., Martin, R., & Austin, T.W. (2009). *Criminological thought: Pioneers past and present.* Upper Saddle River, NJ: Prentice Hall.

O'Brian, A. (2003, January 25). Surrey's get-tough plan has backers: A-team will hit Whalley streets block by block. *Vancouver Sun,* p. B1.

Osgood, D.W., & Chambers, J.M. (2000). Social disorganization outside the metropolis: An analysis of rural youth violence. *Criminology, 38*(1), 81–115.

Park, R.E., & Burgess, E.W. (1967). *The city.* Chicago: University of Chicago Press.

Paternoster, R., & Bachman, R. (2001). Control theories of crime. In R. Paternoster & R. Bachman (Eds.), *Explaining criminals and crime: Essays in contemporary criminological theory* (pp. 80–191). Los Angeles: Roxbury.

Pfohl, S.J. (1985). *Images of deviance and social control: A sociological history.* New York: McGraw-Hill.

Plummer, K. (1979). Misunderstanding labelling perspectives. In D.M. Downes & P.E. Rock (Eds.), *Deviant interpretations* (pp. 85–121). Oxford, UK: Martin Robertson.

Pratt, T.C., & Cullen, F.T. (2000). The empirical status of Gottfredson and Hirschi's general theory of crime: A meta-analysis. *Criminology, 38*(3), 931–964. https://doi.org/10.1111/j.1745-9125.2000.tb00911.x

Pratt, T.C., Cullen, F.T., Sellers, C.S., Winfree, L.T., Madensen, T.D., Daigle, L.E., & Gau, J.M. (2010). The empirical status of social learning theory: A meta-analysis. *Justice Quarterly, 27*(6), 765–802.

Rafter, N.H. (1997). Psychopathology and the evolution of criminological knowledge. *Theoretical Criminology, 1*(2), 235–259. https://doi.org/10.1177/1362480697001002004

Ratner, R. (2006). Pioneering critical criminology in Canada. *Canadian Journal of Criminology and Criminal Justice, 48*(5), 647–662. https://doi.org/10.1353/ccj.2006.0055

Renzetti, C.M. (2013). *Feminist criminology.* London, UK: Routledge.

Rosenfeld, R., & Messner, S.F. (1995). Crime and the American dream: An institutional analysis. In F. Adler, W.S. Laufer, & R.K. Merton (Eds.), *The legacy of anomie theory* (pp. 159–181). New Brunswick, NJ: Transaction.

Sacco, V.F., & Kennedy, L.W. (2011). *The criminal event: An introduction to criminology in Canada* (5th ed.). Toronto: Nelson Education.

Sampson, R.J. (2002). Transcending tradition: New directions in community research, Chicago style. *Criminology, 4*(2), 213–230. https://doi.org/10.1111/j.1745-9125.2002.tb00955.x

Sampson, R.J., & Groves, W.B. (1989). Community structure and crime: Testing social-disorganization theory. *American Journal of Sociology, 94*(4), 774–802.

Sampson, R.J., & Laub, J.H. (1992). Crime and deviance in the life course. *Annual Review of Sociology, 18*(1), 63–84.

Schmalleger, F., MacAlister, D., & McKenna, P.F. (2004). *Canadian criminal justice today* (2nd ed.). Toronto: Pearson Prentice Hall.

Scully, D., & Marolla, J. (2003). Convicted rapists' vocabulary of motive. In P. Adler & P. Adler (Eds.), *Constructions of deviance: Social power, context and interaction* (4th ed., pp. 247–271). Belmont, CA: Thomson Wadsworth.

Sellin, T. (1938/1994). Culture conflict and crime. In J.E. Jacoby (Ed.), *Classics of criminology* (2nd ed., pp. 188–192). Prospect Heights, IL: Waveland Press.

Shaw, C.R., & McKay, H.D. (1969). *Juvenile delinquency and urban areas: A study of rates of delinquency in relation to differential characteristics of local communities in American cities* (Rev. ed.). Chicago: University of Chicago Press.

Skelton, C. (2004, February 6). Surrey's auto theft rate worst in English-speaking world: Mayor pledges tough new measures. *Vancouver Sun.*

Snodgrass, J. (2011). Clifford R. Shaw and Henry D. McKay: Chicago criminologists. In F.T. Cullen, C.L. Jonson, A.J. Myer, & F. Adler (Eds.), *The origins of American criminology: Advances in criminological theory* (Vol. 16, pp. 17–35). New Brunswick, NJ: Transaction.

Snyder, G.J. (2010). Howard Becker. In K. Hayward, S. Maruna, & J. Mooney (Eds.), *Fifty key thinkers in criminology* (pp. 163–168). London, UK: Routledge.

Sutherland, E.H. (1940). White-collar criminality. *American Sociological Review, 5*(1), 1–12.

Sutherland, E.H. (1949). *White collar crime.* New York: The Dryden Press.

Sutherland, E.H. (1937/1988). *The professional thief.* Chicago: University of Chicago Press.

Sutherland, E.H. (1947/1994). Differential association. In J.E. Jacoby (Ed.), *Classics of criminology* (2nd ed., pp. 226–227). Prospect Heights, IL: Waveland Press.

Sykes, G.M., & Matza, D. (1957). Techniques of neutralization: A theory of delinquency. *American Sociological Review, 22*(6), 664–670.

Taylor, I., Walton, P., & Young, J. (1973). *The new criminology: For a social theory of deviance.* London, UK: Routledge & Kegan Paul.

Taylor, I., Walton, P., & Young, J. (Eds.). (1975). *Critical criminology.* London, UK: Routledge & Kegan Paul.

Thompson, H. (2012). The limits of blaming neo-liberalism: Fannie Mae and Freddie Mac, the American state and the financial crisis. *New Political Economy, 17*(4), 399–419. https://doi.or g/10.1080/13563467.2011.595481

Thornberry, T. (1987). Toward an interactional theory of delinquency. *Criminology, 25*(4), 863–891.

Thornberry, T.P., & Krohn, M.D. (2005). Applying interactional theory to the explanation of continuity and change in antisocial behavior. In D.P. Farrington (Ed.), *Integrated developmental & life-course theories of offending* (pp. 183–209). New Brunswick, NJ: Transaction.

Tittle, C.R. (1980). Labelling and crime: An empirical evaluation. In W.R. Gove (Ed.), *The labelling of deviance: Evaluating a perspective* (2nd ed.). Beverly Hills, CA: Sage.

Traub, S.H., & Little, C.B. (1985). *Theories of deviance* (3rd ed.). Itasca, IL: F.E. Peacock.

Walsh, A. (2012). *Criminology: The essentials.* Thousand Oaks, CA: Sage.

Williams, F.P., & McShane, M.D. (2018). *Criminological theory* (7th ed.). Upper Saddle River, NJ: Pearson Prentice Hall.

Winfree, L.T., & Abadinsky, H. (2010). *Understanding crime: Essentials of criminological theory* (3rd ed.). Belmont, CA: Wadsworth, Cengage Learning.

Wolfgang, M.E., & Ferracuti, F. (1967). *The subculture of violence: Towards an integrated theory in criminology.* London, UK: Tavistock.

Wortley, R. (2011). *Psychological criminology: An integrative approach.* London, UK: Routledge.

Young, J. (2002). Critical criminology in the twenty-first century: Critique, irony and the always unfinished. In K. Carrington & R. Hogg (Eds.), *Critical criminology: Issues, debates and challenges* (pp. 251–274). Cullompton, UK: Willan.

Zeitlin, I.M. (2001). *Ideology and the development of sociological theory* (7th ed.). Upper Saddle River, NJ: Prentice Hall.

Zytaruk, T. (2009, February 20). "Time to stop the carnage": Politicians and police gather at Surrey city hall in search of gang violence fix. *Now,* 1.

Chapter 10

Adler, F. (1975). *Sisters in crime: The rise of the new female criminal.* New York: McGraw-Hill.

Agnew, R. (1985). A revised strain theory of delinquency. *Social Forces, 64*(1), 151–167.

Agnew, R. (2006). *Pressured into crime: An overview to general strain theory.* Los Angeles: Roxbury.

Agnew, R. (2013). When criminal coping is likely: An extension of general strain theory. *Deviant Behavior, 34,* 653–670.

Althoff, M. (2013). Multiple identities and crime: A study of Antillean women and girls in the Netherlands. *European Journal of Criminology, 10*(4), 394–407.

Arocho, R., & Kamp Dush, C.M. (2016). Anticipating the "ball and chain"? Reciprocal associations between marital expectations and delinquency. *Journal of Marriage and Family, 78,* 1371–1381.

Asay, S.M. DeFrain, J., Metzger, M., & Mayer B. (2016). Implementing a strengths-based approach to intimate partner violence worldwide. *Journal of Family Violence, 31*(3), 349–360.

Baron, S.W. (2017). It's more than the code: Exploring the factors that moderate the street code's relationship with violence. *Justice Quarterly, 34*(3), 491–516.

Beaver, K.M., Rowland, M.W., Schwartz, J.A., & Nedelec, J.L. (2011). The genetic origins of psychopathic personality traits in adult males and females: Results from an adoption-based study. *Journal of Criminal Justice, 39,* 426–432.

Bell, K.E. (2009). Gender and gangs: A quantitative comparison. *Crime & Delinquency, 55*(3), 363–387.

Bengtsson, T.T. (2012). Learning to become "gangster." *Journal of Youth Studies, 15*(6), 677–692.

Britton, D.M., Jacobsen, S.K., & Howard, G.E. (2018). *The gender of crime* (2nd ed.). Lanham, ML: Rowman and Littlefield.

Broidy, L., & Agnew, R. (1997). Gender and crime: A general strain perspective. *Journal of Research in Crime and Delinquency, 34*(3), 275–306.

Burgess-Proctor, A. (2006). Intersections of race, class, gender, and crime: Future directions for feminist criminology. *Feminist Criminology, 1*(1), 27–47.

Campbell, A. (1995). Girls, gangs, women and drugs. *Women and Criminal Justice, 7*(1), 107–110.

Castro, R.J., Cerellino, L.P., & Rivera, R. (2017). Risk factors of violence against women in Peru. *Journal of Family Violence, 32,* 807–815.

Chesney-Lind, M. (2006). Patriarchy, crime, and justice: Feminist criminology in an era of backlash. *Feminist Criminology, 1*(1), 6–26.

Cobbina, J.E., Like, T.Z., & Miller, J. (2016). Gender-specific conflicts among urban African-American youth: The roles of situational context and issues of contention. *Deviant Behavior, 37*(9), 1032–1051.

Copp, J.E., Kuhl, D.C., Giordano, P.C., Longmore, M.A., & Manning, W.D. (2015). Intimate partner violence in neighborhood context: The roles of structural disadvantage, subjective disorder, and emotional distress. *Social Science Research, 53,* 59–72.

Cudmore, R.M., Cuevas, C.A., & Sabina, C. (2017). The impact of polyvictimization on delinquency among Latino adolescents: A general strain perspective. *Journal of Interpersonal Violence, 32*(17), 2647–2667.

Cullen, P., Vaughan, G., Li, Z., Price, J., Yu, D., & Sullivan, E. (2018). Counting dead women in Australia: An in-depth case review of femicide. *Journal of Family Violence* (April). https://doi.org/ 10.1007/s10896-018-9963-6

Cutler, K.A. (2016). Beauty and care versus fun and flair: Applying a gendered theory of offending to college students' NMPDU. *Deviant Behavior, 37*(10), 1132–1151.

Descormiers, K., & Corrado, R.R. (2016). The right to belong: Individual motives and youth gang initiation rites. *Deviant Behavior, 27*(11), 1341–1359.

Dorais, M., & Corriveau, P. (2009). *Gangs and girls, understanding juvenile prostitution.* Montreal: McGill-Queen's University Press.

Dugan, L., Nagin, D.S., & Rosenfeld, R. (2003). Exposure reduction or retaliation? The effects of domestic violence resources on intimate-partner homicide. *Law & Society Review, 37*(1), 169–198.

Dunn, H.K., Clark, M.A., & Pearlman, D.N. (2017). The relationship between sexual history, bullying victimization, and poor mental health outcomes among heterosexual and sexual minority high school students: A feminist perspective. *Journal of Interpersonal Violence, 32*(22), 3497–3519.

Eitle, T.M., & Eitle, D. (2015). Explaining the association between gender and substance use among American Indian adolescents: An application of power-control theory. *Sociological Perspectives, 58*(4), 686–710.

Ellsberg, M., Jansen, H., Heise, L., Watts, C., & García-Moreno, C. (2008). Intimate partner violence and women's physical and mental health in the WHO multi-country study on women's health and domestic violence: An observational study. *Lancet, 371*, 1165–1172.

Elmquist, J., Wolford-Clevenger, C., Zapor, H., Febres, J, Shorey, R.C., Hamel, J., & Stuart, G.L. (2016). A gender comparison of motivations for physical dating violence among college students. *Journal of Interpersonal Violence, 31*(1), 186–203.

Esbensen, F.-A., Deschenes, E.P., & Winfree, L.T. (1999). Differences between gang girls and gang boys: Results from a multisite survey. *Youth and Society, 31*(1), 27–53.

Factor, R. (2017). A comparison of trans women, trans men, genderqueer individuals, and cisgender brothers and sisters on the BEM Sex-Role-Inventory: Ratings by self and siblings. *Journal of Homosexuality, 12*, 1872–1889.

Gaarder, E., & Belknap, J. (2002). Tenuous borders: Girls transferred to adult court. *Criminology, 40*, 481–518.

Gartner, R. (1990). The victims of homicide: A temporal and cross-national comparison. *American Sociological Review, 55*(1), 92–106.

Gartner, R., Dawson, M., & Crawford, M. (1999). Women killing: Intimate femicide in Ontario, 1974–1994. *Resources for Feminist Research, 26*, 151–173.

Giordano, P.C., Johnson, W.L., Manning, W.D., & Longmore, M.A. (2016). Parenting in adolescent and young adult intimate partner violence. *Journal of Family Issues, 37*(4), 443–465.

Goodlin, W.E., & Dunn, C.S. (2010). Three patterns of domestic violence in households: Single victimization, repeat victimization and co-occurring victimization. *Journal of Family Violence, 25*, 107–122.

Gottfredson, M.R., & Hirschi, T. (1990). *A general theory of crime.* Stanford, CA: Stanford University Press.

Guo, G., Roettger, M., & Cai, T. (2008). The integration of genetic propensities into social-control models of delinquency and violence among male youths. *American Sociological Review, 73*, 543–568.

Hagan, J., Gillis, A.R., & Simpson, J. (1985). Class in the household: A power-control theory of gender and delinquency. *American Journal of Sociology, 92*, 788–816.

Hagan, J., McCarthy, B., & Foster, H. (2002). A gendered theory of delinquency and despair in the life course. *Acta Sociologica, 45*, 37–46.

Hannah-Moffat, K., & Yule, C. (2011). Gaining insight, changing attitudes and managing "risk": Parole release decisions for women convicted of violent crimes. *Punishment & Society, 13*(2), 149–175.

Harper, S.B. (2017). Out of the shadows: Shedding light on intimate partner homicide among Latina women. *Sociology Compass, 11*, 1–15. https://doi.org/10.1111/soc4.12534

Haymos, S., & Gatti, U. (2010). Girl members of deviant youth groups, offending behaviour and victimisation: Results from the ISRD2 in Italy and Switzerland. *European Journal on Criminal Policy and Research* (September), 167–182.

Heimer, K., Lauritsen, J.L., & Lynch, J.P. (2009). The national crime victimization survey and the gender gap in offending: Redux. *Criminology, 47*(2), 427–438.

Heimer, K., Wittrock, S., & Ünal, H. (2006). The crimes of poverty: Economic marginalization and the gender gap in crime. In K. Heimer & C. Kruttschnitt (Eds.), *Gender and crime: Patterns of victimization and offending* (pp. 115–136). New York: New York University Press.

Helmer, A. (2017, November 24). Timeline: From 1982 to 2015, a history of Basil Borutski. *Ottawa Citizen.* Retrieved from https://ottawacitizen.com/news/local-news/timeline-from-1982-to-2015-a-history-of-basil-borutski

Hirschi, T. (1969). *Causes of delinquency.* Berkeley, CA: University of California Press.

Huck, J.L., Spraitz, J.D., Bowers, J.H., & Morris, C.S. (2017). Connecting opportunity and strain to understand deviant behavior: A test of general strain theory. *Deviant Behavior, 38*(9), 1009–1026.

Jennings, W.G., Piquero, N.L., Gover, A.R., & Pérez, D.M. (2009). Gender and general strain theory: A replication and exploration of Broidy and Agnew's gender/strain hypothesis among a sample of southwestern Mexican American adolescents. *Journal of Criminal Justice, 37*, 404–417.

Jung, H., Herrenkohl, T.I., Lee, J.O., Hemphill, S.A., Heerde, J.A., & Skinner, M.L. (2017). Gendered pathways from child abuse to adult crime through internalizing and externalizing behaviors in childhood and adolescence. *Journal of Interpersonal Violence, 32*(18), 2724–2750.

Kahle, L. (2018). Feminist and queer criminology: A vital place for theorizing LGBTQ youth. *Sociological Compass, 12*(3). https://doi.org/10.1111/soc4.12564

Kaufman-Parks, A.M., DeMaris, A., Giordano, P.C., Manning, W.D., & Longmore, M.A. (2018). Intimate partner violence perpetration from adolescence to young adulthood: Trajectories and the role of familial factors. *Journal of Family Violence, 33*, 27–41.

Knight, K.E., Ellis, C., Roark, J., Henry, K.L., & Huizinga, D. (2017). Testing the role of aspirations, future expectations, and strain on the development of problem behaviors across young and middle adulthood. *Deviant Behavior, 38*(12), 1456–1473.

Koon-Magnin, S., Bowers, D., Langhinrichsen-Rohling, J., & Arata, C. (2016). Social learning, self-control, gender, and variety of violent delinquency. *Deviant Behavior, 37*(7), 824–836.

LaFree, G., & Hunnicutt, G. (2006). Female and male homicide trends: A cross-national context. In K. Heimer & C. Kruttschnitt (Eds.), *Gender and crime: Patterns of victimization and offending* (pp. 195–229). New York: New York University Press.

Laub, J.H., & Sampson, R.J. (2003). *Shared beginnings, divergent lives: Delinquent boys to age 70.* Cambridge, MA: Harvard University Press.

Lauritsen, J.L., Heimer, K., & Lynch, J.P. (2009). Trends in the gender gap in violent offending: New evidence from the national crime victimization surveys. *Criminology, 47,* 361–399.

Li, Y., & Guo, G. (2016). Peer influence on aggressive behavior, smoking, and sexual behavior: A study of randomly-assigned college roommates. *Journal of Health and Social Behavior, 57*(3), 297–318.

Lombroso, C., & Ferrero, W. (1895/1958). *Female offender.* New York: Philosophical Press.

Lynch, K.R., & Logan, T.K. (2018). "You better say your prayers and get ready": Guns within the context of partner abuse. *Journal of Interpersonal Violence, 33*(4), 686–711.

MacKinnon, C.A. (1991). Difference and dominance: On sex discrimination. In K.T. Bartlett and R. Kennedy (Eds.), *Feminist legal theory* (pp. 81–94). Boulder, CO: Westview.

Macmillan, R.I., & Gartner, R. (1999). When she brings home the bacon: Labour force participation and spousal violence against women. *Journal of Marriage and the Family, 61,* 947–958.

Maghsoudi, A., Anaraki, N.R., & Boostani, D. (2018). Patriarchy as a contextual and gendered pathway to crime: A qualitative study of Iranian women offenders. *Quality Quantity, 52,* 355–370.

Mahony, T.H., Jacob, H., & Hobson, H. (2017). *Women and the criminal justice system.* Statistics Canada Catalogue no. 89-503-X. Retrieved from https://www150.statcan.gc.ca/n1/pub/89-503-x/2015001/article/14785-eng.htm

Mamayek, C., Paternoster, R., & Loughran, T.A. (2017). Self-control as self-regulation: A return to control theory. *Deviant Behavior, 38*(8), 895–916.

Massoglia, M., & Uggen, C. (2010). Settling down and aging out: Toward an interactionist theory of desistance and the transition to adulthood. *American Journal of Sociology, 116,* 543–582.

McCorkel, J.A. (2013). *Breaking women: Gender, race, and the new politics of imprisonment.* New York: New York University Press.

Menjivar, C., & Walsh S.D. (2017). The architecture of femicide: The state, inequalities, and everyday gender violence in Honduras. *Latin American Research Review, 52*(2), 221–240.

Merton, R. (1938). Social structure and anomie. *American Sociological Review, 3,* 672–682.

Messerschmidt, J.W. (2017). Masculinities and femicide. *Qualitative Sociology Review, 12*(3), 71–79.

Miller, J. (2008). *Getting played: African American girls, urban inequality, and gendered violence.* New York: New York University Press.

Morris, R.R. (1964). Female delinquency and relational problems. *Social Forces, 43*(1), 82–89.

Muller, H.J., Desmarais, S.L., & Hamel, J.M. (2009). Do judicial responses to restraining order requests discriminate against male victims of domestic violence. *Journal of Family Violence, 24,* 625–637.

Mullins, C.W., & Wright, R. (2003). Gender, social networks, and residential burglary. *Criminology, 41*(3), 813–840.

Oldehinkel, A.J. (2018). Let's talk about sex—The gender binary revisited. *Journal of Child Psychology and Psychiatry, 58*(8), 863–864.

Panno, A, Donati, M.A., Milioni, M. Chiesi, F., & Primi, C. (2018). Why women take fewer risks than men do: The mediating role of state anxiety. *Sex Roles, 78,* 286–294.

Powers, R.A., & Kaukinen, C.E. (2012). Trends in intimate partner violence: 1980–2008. *Journal of Interpersonal Violence, 27*(15), 2072–3090.

Schulz, N., Murphy, B., & Verona, E. (2016). Gender differences in psychopathy links to drug use. *Law and Human Behavior, 40*(2), 159–168.

Sherman, L.W., & Berk, R.A. (1984). The specific deterrent effects of arrest for domestic violence. *American Sociological Review, 49,* 261–272.

Sherman, L.W., Schmidt, J.D., Rogan, D.P., Cohn, P.R., Cohn, E.G., Collins, D., & Bacich, A.R. (1992). From initial deterrence to long-term escalation: Short-custody arrest for poverty ghetto domestic violence. *Criminology, 29*(4), 821–850.

Siegfried, C., & Woessner, G. (2016). The explanatory power of the general theory of crime: A comparative analysis of a general population and serious offender sample. *Deviant Behavior, 27*(5), 509–524.

Simon, R.J. (1975). *Women and crime.* Lexington, MA: Lexington Books.

Simpson, S.S., & Gibbs, C. (2006). Making sense of intersections. In K. Heimer & C. Kruttschnitt (Eds.), *Gender and crime: Patterns of victimization and offending* (pp. 269–302). New York: New York University Press.

Sokoloff, N.J., & Pearce, S.C. (2011). Intersections, immigration, and partner violence: A view from a new gateway—Baltimore, Maryland. *Women & Criminal Justice, 21,* 250–266.

Sprott, J.B. (2012). The persistence of status offences in the youth justice system. *Canadian Journal of Criminology and Criminal Justice, 55*(2), 279–292.

Steffensmeier, D., & Allan, E. (1996). Gender and crime: Toward a gendered theory of female offending. *Annual Review of Sociology, 22,* 459–487.

Steffensmeier, D., & Haynie, D. (2000). Gender, structural disadvantage, and urban crime: Do macrosocial variables also explain female offending rates? *Criminology, 38,* 403–438.

Steffensmeier, D., Schwartz, J., & Roche, M. (2013). Gender and twenty-first century crime: Female involvement and the gender gap in Enron-era corporate frauds. *American Sociological Review, 78*(3), 448–478.

Steffensmeier, D., Zhong, H., Ackerman, J., Schwartz, J., & Agha, S. (2006). Gender gap trends for violent crimes, 1980 to 2003. *Feminist Criminology, 1*(1), 72–98.

Sullivan, C.M. (2018). Understanding how domestic violence support services promote survivor well-being: A conceptual model. *Journal of Family Violence, 33*, 123–131.

Sutherland, E. (1947). *Principles of criminology*. Philadelphia: J.P. Lippincott.

Thomas, W.I. (1923/1969). *The unadjusted girl: With cases and standpoint for behavioral analysis*. Montclair, NJ: Patterson Smith.

Tolle, H. (2017). Gang affiliation as a measure of social structure in social structure social learning theory. *Deviant Behavior, 38*(8), 870–878.

Uggen, C. (2000). Work as a turning point in the life course of criminals: A duration model of age, employment and recidivism. *American Sociological Review, 65*(4), 529–546.

Wilhelm, C. (2018). Gender role orientation and gaming behavior revisited: Examining mediated and moderated effects. *Information, Communication & Society, 21*(2), 224–240.

Zorn, K.G., Wuerch, M.A., Faller, N., & Hampton, M.R. (2017). Perspectives on regional differences and intimate partner violence in Canada: A qualitative examination. *Journal of Family Violence, 32*, 633–644.

Chapter 11

Bowling, B., & Phillips, C. (2002). *Racism, crime and justice*. London, UK: Longman.

Brennan, S. (2012). *Police-reported crime statistics in Canada, 2011*. Ottawa: Statistics Canada.

Burgess-Proctor, A. (2006). Intersections of race, class, gender and crime: Future directions for feminist criminology. *Feminist Criminology, 1*(1), 27–47.

Canadian Press. (2018). Groups alleging racial profiling demand probe into Vancouver police street checks. *CBC News*. Retrieved from http://www.cbc.ca/news/canada/british-columbia/vpd-racial-profiling-street-checks-1.4706394

Caplow, T., & Simon, J. (1999). Understanding prison policy and population trends. In M. Tonry & J. Petersilia (Eds.), *Prisons* (pp. 63–120). Chicago: University of Chicago Press.

Chambliss, W., & Seidman, R. (1971). *Law, order, and power*. Reading, MA: Addison-Wesley.

Chesney-Lind, M. (2009). Feminism and critical criminology: Toward a feminist praxis. *Critical Criminology*. Retrieved from http://critcrim.org/chesney-lind1.htm

Christie, N. (1981/2007). *Limits to pain: The role of punishment in penal policy*. London: Wipf & Stock.

Christie, N. (1993/2002). *Crime control as industry*. London, UK: Routledge.

Christie, N. (2004). *A suitable amount of crime*. London, UK: Routledge.

Comack, E. (1996). *Women in trouble: Connecting women's law violations to their histories of abuse*. Halifax: Fernwood.

Correctional Investigator Canada. (2013). *Annual report of the Office of the Correctional Investigator, 2012–2013*. Ottawa: Government of Canada.

Daly, K., & Chesney-Lind, M. (1988). Feminism and criminology. *Justice Quarterly, 5*(4), 497–538.

DeKeseredy, W., Alvi, S., & Schwartz, M. (2006). An economic exclusion/male peer support model looks at "wedfare" and woman abuse. *Critical Criminology, 14*(1), 23–41.

Fanon, F. (1952/2008). *Black skin, white masks*. New York: Grove Press.

Federal Bureau of Investigation. (2011). FBI releases 2011 crime statistics. *FBI*. Retrieved from http://www.fbi.gov/about-us/cjis/ucr/crime-in-the-u.s/2011/crime-in-the-u.s.-2011/fbi-releases-2011-crime-statistics

Flavin, J. (2001). Feminism for the mainstream criminologist: An invitation. *Journal of Criminal Justice, 29*(4), 271–285.

Foucault, M. (1979). *Discipline and punish: The birth of the prison* (A. Sheridan, Trans.). New York: Vintage.

Garland, D. (2001). *The culture of control: Crime and social order in contemporary society*. Chicago: University of Chicago Press.

Glaze, L.E., & Herberman, E.J. (2013, December 19). *Correctional populations in the United States, 2012*. Washington, DC: Bureau of Justice Statistics. Retrieved from http://www.bjs.gov/content/pub/pdf/cpus12.pdf

Griffin, M. (2010). Feminist criminology: Beyond the slaying of dragons. In H.D. Barlow & S.H. Decker (Eds.), *Criminology and public policy: Putting theory to work* (pp. 215–232). Philadelphia: Temple University Press.

Hall, S., Critcher, C., Jefferson, T., Clarke, J., & Roberts, B. (1978). *Policing the crisis: Mugging, the state and law and order*. London, UK: Palgrave Macmillan.

Kable, D., & Glaze, L. (2016). *Correctional populations in the United States, 2015*. Washington, DC: Bureau of Justice Statistics. Retrieved from https://www.bjs.gov/content/pub/pdf/cpus15.pdf

Kitossa, T. (2012). Criminology and colonialism: Counter colonial criminology and the Canadian context. *The Journal of Pan African Studies, 4*(10), 204–226.

Lea, J., & Young, J. (1984). *What is to be done about law and order?* Harmondsworth, UK: Penguin.

Leman-Langlois, S. (2000). Mobilizing victimization: The construction of a victim-centred approach in the South African Truth and Reconciliation Commission. *Criminologie, 33*(1), 145–166.

Malone, G. (2016). Why Indigenous women are Canada's fastest growing prison population. *Vice*. Retrieved from https://www.vice.com/en_ca/article/5gj8vb/why-indigenous-women-are-canadas-fastest-growing-prison-population

Martinson, R. (1974). What works? Questions and answers about prison reform. *The Public Interest, 35*, 22–54.

Mawani, R. (2009). *Colonial perspectives: Crossracial encounters and juridical truths in British Columbia, 1871–1921*. Vancouver: UBC Press.

May, T. (1994). *The political philosophy of poststructuralist anarchism*. University Park, PA: Penn State University Press.

Maynard, R. (2017). *Policing black lives: State violence in Canada from slavery to the present*. Halifax: Fernwood.

Meyer, J., & O'Malley, P. (2005). Missing the punitive turn? Canadian criminal justice, "balance," and penal modernism. In J. Pratt, D. Brown, M. Brown, S. Hallsworth, & W. Morrison (Eds.), *The new punitiveness: Trends, theories, perspectives* (pp. 201–217). Cullompton, UK: Willan.

Milovanovic, D. (2002). *Critical criminology at the edge: Postmodern perspectives, integration and applications.* Westport, CT: Praeger.

Quinney, R. (1977). *Class, state and crime: On the theories and practices of criminal justice.* New York: David McKay.

Quinney, R. (1995). Socialist humanism and the problem of crime: Thinking about Erich Fromm in the development of critical/peacemaking criminology. *Crime, Law & Social Change, 23*(2), 147–156.

Reiman, J. (1979/2004). *The rich get richer and the poor get prison: Ideology, class, and criminal justice* (7th ed.). Boston: Allyn and Bacon/Pearson.

Reitano, J. (2016). *Adult correctional statistics in Canada, 2015/2016. Juristat, 37*(1). Statistics Canada Catalogue no. 85-002-X. Retrieved from https://www150.statcan.gc.ca/n1/pub/85-002-x/2017001/article/14700-eng.htm

Rigakos, G., & Ergul, A. (2011). Policing the industrial reserve army: An international study. *Crime, Law and Social Change, 56*(4), 329–371.

Simon, J. (2007). *Governing through crime: How the war on crime transformed American democracy and created a culture of fear.* New York: Oxford University Press.

Staples, R. (1975). White racism, Black crime, and American justice: An application of the colonial model to explain crime and race. *Phylon, 36*(1), 14–22.

Taylor, I., Walton, P., & Young, J. (1973). *The new criminology: For a social theory of deviance.* London, UK: Routledge.

Taylor, I., Walton, P., & Young, J. (1975). Critical criminology in Britain: Review and prospects. In I. Taylor, P. Walton, & J. Young (Eds.), *Critical criminology* (pp. 6–62). London, UK: Routledge and Kegan Paul.

Tonry, M. (2004). *Thinking about crime: Sense and sensibility in American penal culture.* New York: Oxford University Press.

Wacquant, L. (2009). *Punishing the poor: The Neoliberal government of social insecurity.* Durham, NC: Duke University Press.

Wagner, P., & Sawyer, W. (2018). Mass incarceration: The whole pie 2018. *Prison Policy Initiative.* Retrieved from https://www.prisonpolicy.org/reports/pie2018.html

Watkins, B. (2013). Rich, white kids have "affluenza," poor, Black kids go to prison. *Pittsburgh Courier.* Retrieved from https://newpittsburghcourieronline.com/2013/12/15/rich-white-kids-have-affluenza-poor-black-kids-go-to-prison

Woolford, A. (2009). *The politics of restorative justice: A critical introduction.* Halifax: Fernwood.

Young, J. (1999). *The exclusive society.* London, UK: Sage.

Young, J. (2002). Critical criminology in the twenty-first century: Critique, irony, and the always unfinished. In K. Carrington, R. Hogg, & D. Cullompton (Eds.), *Critical criminology: Issues, debates and challenges* (pp. 63–94). Devon, UK: Willan.

Chapter 12

Allen, M. (2018). Police-reported crime statistics in Canada, 2017. *Juristat, 38*(1). Statistics Canada Catalogue no. 85-002-X. Retrieved from https://www150.statcan.gc.ca/n1/pub/85-002-x/2018001/article/54974-eng.htm

Armitage, R. (2013). *Crime prevention through environmental design: Policy and practice.* London, UK: Springer.

Atkins, Charles. (n.d.). We are our choices. Retrieved from https://neologikonblog.wordpress.com/2016/05/18/we-are-our-choices

Barnett, B.S., Nesbit, A.E., & Sorrentino, R.M. (2018). The transgender bathroom debate at the intersection of politics, law, ethics, and science. *The Journal of the American Academy of Psychiatry and the Law, 46*(2), 232–241.

Beauregard, E., Proulx, J., Rossmo, K., Leclerc, B., & Allaire, J.F. (2007). Script analysis of the hunting process of serial sex offenders. *Criminal Justice and Behavior, 34*(8), 1069–1084.

Becker, G. (1968). Crime and punishment: An economic approach. *Journal of Political Economy, 76,* 169–217.

Bennett, T. (1986). A decision making approach to opioid addiction. In D. Cornish & R. Clarke (Eds.), *The reasoning criminal: Rational choice perspectives on offending.* New York: Springer-Verlag.

Brantingham, P.L., & Brantingham, P.J. (1980). *Environmental criminology.* Beverly Hills, CA: Sage.

Brantingham, P.L., & Brantingham, P.J. (1993). Nodes, paths and edges: Considerations on the complexity of crime and the physical environment. *Journal of Environmental Psychology, 13*(1), 3–28.

Brown, R. (2004). The effectiveness of electronic immobilisation: Changing patterns of temporary and permanent vehicle theft. In M.G. Maxfield & R.V. Clarke (Eds.), *Crime Prevention Studies* (Vol. 17, pp. 101–119). New York: Criminal Justice Press.

Clarke, R.V. (1997). *Situational crime prevention: Successful case studies* (2nd ed.). Guilderland, NY: Criminal Justice Press.

Clarke, R.V. (1999). Hot products: Understanding, anticipating and reducing demand for stolen goods. *Police Research Series, Paper 112.* London, UK: Home Office.

Clarke, R.V., & Cornish, D.B. (1985). Modeling offenders' decisions: A framework for research and policy. *Crime and Justice, 6,* 147–185.

Clarke, R.V., & Felson, M. (2011). The origins of the routine activity approach and situational crime prevention. In F.T. Cullen, C.L. Jonson, A.J. Myer, & F. Adler (Eds.), *The origins of American criminology: Vol. 16* (pp. 245–260). New Brunswick, NJ: Transaction.

Clarke, R.V., & Homel, R. (1997). A revised classification of situational crime prevention techniques. In S. Lab (Ed.), *Crime prevention at the crossroads* (pp. 17–30). Cincinnati, OH: Criminal Justice Press.

Clarke, R.V., & Lester, D. (1987). Toxicity of car exhausts and opportunity for suicide: A comparison between Britain and the United States. *Journal of*

Epidemiology and Community Health, 41(2), 114–120.

Clarke, R.V., & Mayhew, P. (1989). Crime as opportunity: A note on domestic gas suicide in Britain and the Netherlands. *The British Journal of Criminology, 29*(1), 35–46.

Clarke, R.V., & Weisburd, D. (1994). Diffusion of crime control benefits: Observations on the reverse of displacement. In R.V. Clarke (Ed.), *Crime Prevention Studies* (Vol. 2, pp. 165–182). Monsey, NY: Criminal Justice Press.

Cohen, L.E., & Felson, M. (1979). Social change and crime rate trends: A routine activities approach. *American Sociological Review, 44*(4), 588–608.

Cornish, D., & Clarke, R. (Eds.). (1986). *The reasoning criminal: Rational choice perspectives on offending.* New York: Springer-Verlag.

Cornish, D.B. (1994). The procedural analysis of offending and its relevance for situational prevention. In R.V. Clarke (Ed.), *Crime prevention studies: Vol 3* (pp. 91–107). Monsey, NY: Criminal Justice Press.

Cornish, D.B., & Clarke, R.V. (2003). Opportunities, precipitators and criminal decisions: A reply to Wortley's critique of situational crime prevention. In M.J. Smith and D.B. Cornish (Eds.), *Theory and practice in situational crime prevention: Vol 16* (pp. 41–96). Monsey, NY: Criminal Justice Press.

Darwin, C. (1859). *On the origin of species.* London, UK: John Murray.

Ekblom, P. (1991). Talking to offenders: Practical lessons for local crime prevention. In O. Nello (Ed.), *Urban crime: Statistical approaches and analyses* (pp. 29–43). Barcelona, Spain: Institut d'Estudis Metropolitans de Barcelona.

Ekblom, P. (2011). Crime prevention, security and community safety using the 5Is framework. New York: Palgrave Macmillan.

Ekblom, P. (2012). The private sector and designing products against crime. In B.C. Welsh & D.P. Farrington (Eds.), *Oxford handbook of crime prevention.* New York: Oxford University Press.

Farrell, G. (2010). Situational crime prevention and its discontents: Rational choice and harm reduction versus "cultural criminology." *Social Policy and Administration, 44*(1), 40–66.

Farrell, G., Tseloni, A., & Tilley, N. (2011). The effectiveness of car security devices and their role in the crime drop. *Criminology and Criminal Justice, 11*(1), 21–35.

Felson, M., & Boba, R. (2010). *Crime and everyday life.* Los Angeles: Sage.

Fennelly, L., & Crowe, T. (2013). *Crime prevention through environmental design.* Oxford, UK: Butterworth Heinemann.

Fujita, S., & Maxfield, M. (2012). Security and the drop in car theft in the United States. In J.J.M. van Dijk, A. Tseloni, & G. Farrell (Eds.), *The international crime drop: New directions in research.* London, UK: Palgrave Macmillan.

Gabor, T. (1994). *Everybody does it! Crime by the public.* Toronto: University of Toronto Press.

Goldstein, H. (1990). *Problem-oriented policing.* New York: McGraw-Hill.

Gottfredson, D.M., & Clarke, R.V. (1990). *Policy and theory in criminal justice: Essays in honour of Leslie T. Wilkins.* Brookfield, VT: Gower.

Guerette, R.T. (2009). *Analyzing crime displacement and diffusion.* Washington, DC: US Department of Justice, Office of Community Oriented Policing Services.

Guerette, R.T., & Bowers, K.J. (2009). Assessing the extent of crime displacement and the diffusion of benefits: A review of situational crime prevention evaluations. *Criminology, 47*(4), 1331–1368.

Hancock, G., & Laycock, G. (2010). Organised crime and crime scripts: Prospects for disruption. In K. Bullock, R.V. Clarke, & N. Tilley (Eds.), *Situational prevention of organised crimes* (pp. 172–192). Cullompton, UK and Portland, OR: Willan.

Hodgkinson, T., Andresen, M.A., & Farrell, G. (2016). The decline and locational shift of automotive theft: A local level analysis. *Journal of Criminal Justice, 44,* 49–57.

Jacobs, J. (1961). *Death and life of great American cities.* New York: Vintage Books.

James, S.E., Herman, J.L., & Rankin S. (2016). Executive summary of the report of the 2015 U.S. transgender survey. Washington, DC: National Center for Transgender Equality. Retrieved from https://transequality.org/sites/default/files/docs/usts/USTS-Executive-Summary-Dec17.pdf

Jeffery, C.R. (1971). *Crime prevention through environmental design.* Beverly Hills, CA: Sage.

Kirby, S., & Nailer, L. (2013). Reducing the offending of a UK organized crime group using an opportunity reducing framework: A three year case study. *Trends in Organized Crime, 16*(4), 397–412.

Knepper, P. (2012). An international crime decline: Lessons for social welfare crime policy. *Social Policy and Administration, 46*(4), 359–376.

Kriven, S., & Ziersch, E. (2007). New car security and shifting vehicle theft patterns in Australia. *Security Journal, 20*(2), 111–122.

Leddo, J., & Abelson, R.P. (1986). The nature of explanations. In J.A. Galambos, R.P. Abelson, & J.B. Black (Eds.), *Knowledge structures* (pp. 103–122). Hillsdale, NJ: Erlbaum.

Lester, A. (2001). Crime reduction through issues product design. *Trends and Issues in Crime and Criminal Justice, 206,* 1–6.

Linden, R., & Chaturvedi, R. (2005). The need for comprehensive crime prevention planning: The case of motor vehicle theft. *Canadian Journal of Criminology and Criminal Justice, 47*(2), 251–270.

MacDonald, A. (Producer), & Boyle, D. (Director). (1996). *Trainspotting* [Video file]. London, UK: Channel Four Films.

Mayhew, P.M., Clarke, R.V.G, Sturman, A., & Hough, J.M. (1976). *Crime as opportunity* (Home Office Research Study no. 34). London, UK: Her Majesty's Stationery Office.

Moffitt, T.E. (1993). Adolescence-limited and life-course persistent anti-social behavior: A developmental taxonomy. *Psychological Review, 100*(4), 674–701.

Perreault, S. (2013). Police reported crime statistics in Canada, 2012. *Juristat, 33*(1). Statistics Canada Catalogue no. 85-002-x. Retrieved from https://www150.statcan.gc.ca/n1/pub/85-002-x/2013001/article/11854-eng.htm

Simon, H. (1957). *Models of man: Mathematical models on rational human behaviour in a social setting.* New York: John Wiley.

Smith, M.J., & Cornish, D. (Eds.) (2003). *Theory for practice in situational crime prevention.* Boulder, CO: Lynne Rienner Publishers.

Statistics Canada. (2018). Police-reported crime statistics, 2017. *The Daily.* Retrieved from https://www150.statcan.gc.ca/n1/daily-quotidien/180723/dq180723b-eng.htm

Thaler, R., & Sunstein, C. (2008). *Nudge: Improving decisions about health, wealth, and happiness.* New Haven, CT: Yale University Press.

Tilley, N., & Farrell, G. (2013). *The reasoning criminologist: Essays in honour of Ronald V. Clarke.* New York: Routledge.

Tompson, L. (2011). *Crime script analysis* [PowerPoint presentation]. International Crime and Intelligence Analysis Conference. Retrieved from http://www.ucl.ac.uk/jdi/events/int-CIA-conf/ICIAC11_Slides/ICIAC11_5D_LTompson

Tseloni, A., Mailley, J., Farrell, G., & Tilley, N. (2010). Exploring the international decline in crime rates. *European Journal of Criminology, 7,* 375–394.

United Nations Office on Drugs and Crime. (2002). Action to promote effective crime prevention. Retrieved from https://www.un.org/en/ecosoc/docs/2002/resolution 2002-13.pdf

van Dijk, J. (2008). *The world of crime.* London, UK: Sage.

van Dijk, J., Tseloni, A., & Farrell, G. (2012). *The international crime drop: New directions in research.* Basingstoke, UK: Palgrave and McMillan.

van Ours, J.C., & Vollaard, B. (2013). The engine immobilizer: A non-starter for car thieves (CESifo working paper no. 4092). Retrieved from http://www.econstor.eu/bitstream/10419/69576/1/735723133.pdf

Weisburd, D., & Telep, C.W. (2012). Spatial displacement and diffusion of crime control benefits revisited: New evidence on why crime doesn't just move around the corner. In N. Tilley & G. Farrell (Eds.), *The reasoning criminologist* (pp. 142–159). New York: Routledge.

Wilkins, L.T. (1964). *Social policy, action, and research: Studies in social deviance.* London, UK: Tavistock.

Wilson, J.Q., & Herrnstein, R.J. (1985). *Crime and human nature.* New York: Simon and Schuster.

Wolfgang, M. (1996). Introduction. In C. Beccaria, *Of crimes and punishments.* New York: Marsilio.

Chapter 13

Allen, M. (2018). Police-reported crime statistics in Canada, 2017. *Juristat, 38*(1). Statistics Canada Catalogue no. 85-002-X. Retrieved from https://www150.statcan.gc.ca/n1/pub/85-002-x/2018001/article/54974-eng.htm

Allen, M., & McCarthy, K. (2018). Victims of police-reported violent crime in Canada: National, provincial and territorial fact sheets, 2016. *Juristat, 38*(1). Statistics Canada Catalogue no. 85-002-X. Retrieved from https://www150.statcan.gc.ca/n1/en/pub/85-002-x/2018001/article/54960-eng.pdf?st=jSMLoOiO

Anderson, E. (1999). *The code of the street: Decency, violence and the moral life of the inner city.* New York: W.W. Norton.

Bailey, W.C. (1984). Poverty, inequality, and city homicide rates: Some not so unexpected findings. *Criminology, 22,* 1–25.

Benson, M.L., Fox, G.L., DeMaris, A., & Van Wyk, J. (2003). Neighborhood disadvantage, individual economic distress, and violence against women in intimate relationships. *Journal of Quantitative Criminology, 19*(3), 207–235.

Blau, J.R., & Blau, P.M. (1982). The cost of inequality: Metropolitan structure and violent crime. *American Sociological Review, 47*(1), 114–129.

Blumstein, A. (1995). Violence by young people: Why the deadly nexus? *National Institute of Justice Journal, 229,* 2–9.

Brennan, S. (2011). Violent victimization of Aboriginal women in the Canadian provinces, 2009. *Juristat, 30*(1). Statistics Canada Catalogue no. 85-002-X. Retrieved from https://www150.statcan.gc.ca/n1/pub/85-002-x/2011001/article/11439-eng.pdf

Canadian Centre for Justice Statistics. (2018). Revising the classification of founded and unfounded criminal incidents in the Uniform Crime Reporting Survey. *Juristat, 38*(1). Statistics Canada Catalogue no. 85-002-X. Retrieved from https://www150.statcan.gc.ca/n1/pub/85-002-x/2018001/article/54973-eng.htm

Casteel, C., & Peek-Asa, C. (2000). Effectiveness of crime prevention through environmental design (CPTED) in reducing robberies. *American Journal of Preventative Medicine, 18*(4), 99–115.

Charron, M. (2009). *Neighbourhood characteristics and the distribution of police-reported crime in the City of Toronto.* Statistics Canada Catalogue no. 85-561-M, no. 18. Ottawa: Statistics Canada.

Cohen, A.K., & Felson, M. (1979). Social change and crime rate trends: A routine activity approach. *American Sociological Review, 44*(4), 588–608.

Cohen, J., Cork, D., Engberg, J., & Tita, G. (1998). The role of drug markets and gangs in local homicide rates. *Homicide Studies, 2*(3), 241–262.

Cohen, J., Gorr, W., & Singh, P. (2003). Estimating intervention effects in varying risk settings: Do police raids reduce illegal drug dealing at nuisance bars? *Criminology, 41*(2), 257–292.

Collins, J.J., & Messerschmidt, P.M. (1993). Epidemiology of alcohol-related violence. *Alcohol Health and Research World, 17,* 93–100.

Connell, R.W. (1987). *Gender and power: Society, the person and sexual politics.* Stanford, CA: Stanford University Press.

Connell, R.W. (2002). *Gender.* Cambridge, UK: Polity Press.

Cozens, P., Saville, G., & Hillier, D. (2005). Crime prevention through environmental design (CPTED): A review and modern bibliography. *Property Management, 23*(5), 328–356.

Cruise, K., Fernandez, K., McCoy, W., Guy, L., Colwell, L., & Douglas, T. (2008). The influence of psychosocial maturity on adolescent offenders' delinquent behaviour. *Youth Violence and Juvenile Justice, 6*(2), 178–194.

David, J.-D. (2017). Homicide in Canada, 2016. *Juristat, 37*(1). Statistics Canada

Catalogue no. 85-002-X. Retrieved from https://www150.statcan.gc.ca/n1/pub/85-002-x/2017001/article/54879-eng.htm

de Haan, W. (2008). Violence as an essentially contested concept. In S. Body-Gendrot & P. Spierenburg (Eds.), *Violence in Europe: Historical and contemporary perspectives* (pp. 27–40). New York: Springer.

Doob, A. (2004). Preventing violent offending in youth. In B. Kidd & J. Phillips (Eds.), *From enforcement and prevention to civic engagement: Research on community safety* (pp. 81–95). Toronto: Centre of Criminology.

Doolittle, R. (2017, February 3). Unfounded: Why police dismiss 1 in 5 sexual assault claims as baseless. *Globe and Mail*. Retrieved from https://www.theglobeandmail.com/news/investigations/unfounded-sexual-assault-canada-main/article33891309

Fagan, J., & Wilkinson, D. (1998). Guns, youth violence, and social identity in inner cities. In M. Tonry & M. Moore (Eds.), *Crime and justice: Vol. 24* (pp. 105–188). Chicago: University of Chicago Press.

Fajnzylber, P., Lederman, D., & Loayza, N. (2002). What causes violent crime? *European Economic Review, 46,* 1323–1357.

Farrington, D.P. (1986). Age and crime. In M. Tonry & N. Morris (Eds.), *Crime and justice: Vol. 7* (pp. 189–250). Chicago: University of Chicago Press.

Farrington, D.P., Piquero, A.R., & Jennings, W.G. (2013). *Offending from childhood to late middle age: Recent results from the Cambridge Study in Delinquent Development.* New York: Springer.

Fong, E., & Shibuya, K. (2000). The spatial separation of the poor in Canadian cities. *Demography, 37*(4), 449–459.

Gartner, R., & Thompson, S.K. (2004). Trends in homicide in Toronto. In B. Kidd & J. Phillips (Eds.), *From enforcement and prevention to civic engagement: Research on community safety* (pp. 28–39). Toronto: Centre of Criminology.

Greenland, J., & Cotter, A. (2018). Unfounded criminal incidents in Canada, 2017. *Juristat, 38*(1). Statistics Canada Catalogue no. 85-002-X. Retrieved from https://www150.statcan.gc.ca/n1/pub/85-002-x/2018001/article/54975-eng.htm

Grogger, J., & Willis, M. (1998). *The introduction of crack cocaine and the rise in urban crime rates* (NBER working paper no. 6353). Cambridge, MA: National Bureau of Economic Research.

Hampson, R. (2009, March 29). Anti-snitch campaign riles police, prosecutors. *USA Today*. Retrieved from http://usatoday30.usatoday.com/news/nation/2006-03-28-stop-snitching_x.htm

Hannon, L.E. (2005). Extremely poor neighbourhoods and homicide. *Social Science Quarterly, 86*(5), 1418–1434.

Henry, D.B., Tolan, P.H., & Gorman-Smith, D. (2001). Longitudinal family and peer group effects on violence and non-violent delinquency. *Journal of Clinical Child Psychology, 30*(2), 172–186.

Howell, J.C., & Hawkins, J.D. (1998). Prevention of youth violence. In M. Tonry & M. Moore (Eds.), *Youth violence: Crime and justice, a review of the research: Vol. 24* (pp. 263–315). Chicago: University of Chicago Press.

Huff-Corzine, L., Corzine, J., & Moore, D.C. (1986). Southern exposure: Deciphering the South's influence on homicide rates. *Social Forces, 64,* 906–924.

Jackman, M. (2002). Violence in social life. *Annual Review of Sociology, 28,* 387–415.

Kong, R., & AuCoin, K. (2008). Female offenders in Canada. *Juristat, 28*(1). Statistics Canada Catalogue no. 85-002-XIE. Retrieved from http://www.statcan.gc.ca/pub/85-002-x/85-002-x2008001-eng.pdf

La Prairie, C. (2002). Aboriginal over-representation in the criminal justice system: A tale of nine cities. *Canadian Journal of Criminology, 44*(2), 181–208.

Law Courts Education Society. (n.d.). Community crime prevention guide. Retrieved from https://www2.gov.bc.ca/assets/gov/public-safety-and-emergency-services/crime-prevention/community-crime-prevention/publications/crime-prevention.pdf

Loeber, R., & LeBlanc, M. (1990). Toward a developmental criminology. In M. Tonry & N. Morris (Eds.), *Crime and justice: Vol. 12* (pp. 375–437). Chicago: University of Chicago Press.

Ludwig, J. (2005). Better gun enforcement, less crime. *Criminology & Public Policy, 4*(4), 677–716.

Lynch, M.J., & Groves, W.B. (1989). *A primer in radical criminology* (2nd ed.). New York: Harrow and Heston.

Macmillan, R., & Gartner, R. (1999). When she brings home the bacon: Labor force participation and the risk of spousal violence against women. *Journal of Marriage and the Family, 61*(4), 947–958.

Mahony, T. (2011). Women and the criminal justice system. In Statistics Canada (Ed.), *Women in Canada: A gender-based statistical report.* Statistics Canada Catalogue no. 89-503-X (pp. 169–203). Retrieved from http://www.statcan.gc.ca/pub/89-503-x/2010001/article/11416-eng.htm

Merton, R. (1938). Social structure and anomie. *American Sociological Review, 3*(5), 672–682.

Messner, S. (1989). Economic discrimination and societal homicide rates: Further evidence on the cost of inequality. *American Sociological Review, 54,* 597–611.

Messner, S., & Tardiff, K. (1985). The social ecology of urban homicide: An application of the "routine activities" approach. *Criminology, 23*(2), 241–268.

Messner, S., & Zimmerman, G. (2012). Community-level influences on crime and offending. In B.C. Welsh & D.P. Farrington (Eds.), *The Oxford handbook of crime prevention* (pp. 155–171). New York: Oxford University Press.

Mullins, C.W., & Cardwell-Mullins, R.M. (2006). Bad ass or punk ass: The contours of street masculinity. *Universitas, 2*(2), 1–17.

Parker, R.N. (1989). Poverty, subculture of violence, and type of homicide. *Social Forces, 67*(4), 983–1007.

Patillo-McCoy, M. (1999). *Black picket fences: Privilege and peril among the black middle class.* Chicago: University of Chicago Press.

PeelRegionalPolice (2017, July 31). Considering re-landscaping your property this summer? … [Twitter Post]. Retrieved from https://

twitter.com/peelpolicemedia/status/892057771213848577

Perreault, S. (2013). Police-reported crime statistics in Canada, 2012. *Juristat, 33*(1). Statistics Canada Catalogue no. 85-002-x. Retrieved from http://www.statcan.gc.ca/pub/85-002-x/2013001/article/11854-eng.pdf

Perreault, S. (2015). Criminal victimization in Canada, 2014. *Juristat, 35*(1). Statistics Canada Catalogue no. 85-002-X. Retrieved from https://www150.statcan.gc.ca/n1/pub/85-002-x/2015001/article/14241-eng.htm

Perreault, S., & Brennan, S. (2010). Criminal victimization in Canada, 2009. *Juristat, 30*(2). Statistics Canada Catalogue no. 85-002-X. Retrieved from http://www.statcan.gc.ca/pub/85-002-x/2010002/article/11340-eng.htm

Piquero, A.R., Farrington, D.P., & Blumstein, A. (2007). *Key issues in criminal careers research: New analysis from the Cambridge Study in Delinquent Development.* Cambridge, MA: Cambridge University Press.

Roberts, J., & Doob, A. (1997). Race, ethnicity and criminal justice in Canada. *Crime and Justice, 21,* 469–522.

Rosenfeld, R., Fornango, R., & Baumer, E. (2005). Did Ceasefire, Compstat, and Exile reduce homicide? *Criminology and Public Policy, 4*(3), 419–450.

Sampson, R.J. (1995). The community. In J.Q. Wilson & J. Petersilia (Eds.), *Crime* (pp. 193–216). San Francisco: ICS Press.

Sampson, R.J., & Laub, J.H. (1990). Crime and deviance over the life course: The salience of adult social bonds. *American Sociological Review, 55*(5), 609–627.

Sampson, R.J., & Laub, J.H. (1993). *Crime in the making: Pathways and turning points through life.* Cambridge, MA: Harvard University Press.

Sampson, R.J., Raudenbush, S.W., & Earls, F. (1997). Neighbourhoods and violent crime: A multilevel study of collective efficacy. *Science, 277,* 918–924.

Sampson, R.J., & Wilson, W.J. (1995). Toward a theory of race, crime and urban inequality. In J. Hagan & R.D. Peterson (Eds.), *Crime and inequality* (pp. 37–54). Stanford, CA: Stanford University Press.

Saville, G. (1998). *New tools to eradicate crime places and crime niches.*

Conference on Safer Communities: Strategic Directions in Urban Planning convened jointly by the Australian Institute of Criminology and the Victorian Community Against Violence. Melbourne, Australia.

Silverman, R., & Kennedy, L. (2004). *Deadly deeds: Murder in Canada.* Toronto: Nelson.

Smith, C., Lizotte, A.J., & Thornberry, T.P. (1995). Resilient youth: Identifying factors that prevent high-risk youth from engaging in delinquency and drug use. *Current Perspectives on Aging and the Life Cycle, 4,* 217–247.

Statistics Canada. (2010). *Sub verbo* "violent crimes or offences/crimes against the person." Retrieved from http://www.statcan.gc.ca/pub/85-002-x/2010002/definitions-eng.htm

Statistics Canada. (2011). *Family violence in Canada: A statistical profile.* Statistics Canada Catalogue no. 85-224-X. Retrieved from http://www.statcan.gc.ca/pub/85-224-x/85-224-x2010000-eng.pdf

Stewart, E., & Simons, R. (2006). Structure and culture in African-American adolescent violence: A partial test of the code of the street thesis. *Justice Quarterly, 23,* 1–33.

Stolzenberg, L., Eitle, D., & D'Alessio, S. (2006). Race, economic inequality, and violent crime. *Journal of Criminal Justice, 34,* 303–316.

Sweeten, G., Piquero, A.R., & Steinberg, L. (2013). Age and the explanation of crime, revisited. *Journal of Youth and Adolescents, 42*(6), 921–938.

Thompson, S.K. (2009). *The social ecology and spatial distribution of lethal violence in Toronto, 1988–2003* (Doctoral dissertation). Centre of Criminology, University of Toronto.

Thompson, S.K. (2013). Case study: Black homicide victimization in Toronto, Ontario, Canada. In S. Bucerius & M. Tonry (Eds.), *The Oxford handbook of ethnicity, crime and immigration* (pp. 450–453). New York: Oxford University Press.

Thompson, S.K., & Bucerius, S. (2013). Unintended consequences of neighbourhood restructuring: Uncertainty, disrupted social networks and increased fear of violent victimization

among young adults. *British Journal of Criminology, 53*(5), 924–941.

Thompson, S.K., & Gartner, R. (2007). *Urban crime: The case of Toronto, Canada.* Case study prepared for Enhancing urban safety and security: Global report on human settlements 2007. London, UK: UN Habitat, Earthscan.

Thompson, S.K., & Gartner, R. (2014). The spatial distribution and social context of homicide in Toronto's neighbourhoods, 1988–2003. *Journal of Research in Crime and Delinquency, 51*(1), 88–118.

Tonry, M. (1995). *Malign neglect: Race, crime and punishment in America.* New York: Oxford University Press.

Tremblay, R., & Japel, C. (2003). Prevention during pregnancy, infancy, and the preschool years. In D.P. Farrington & J.W. Coid (Eds.), *Early prevention of adult antisocial behaviour* (pp. 202–242). New York: Cambridge University Press.

Vaillancourt, R. (2010). *Gender differences in police-reported violent crime in Canada, 2008.* Statistics Canada Catalogue no. 85F0033M, no. 24. Retrieved from http://www.statcan.gc.ca/pub/85f0033m/85f0033m2010024-eng.htm

Villarreal, A., & Silva, B. (2006). Social cohesion, criminal victimization and the perceived risk of crime in Brazilian neighbourhoods. *Social Forces, 84*(3), 1725–1753.

Wekerle, G., & Whitzman, C. (1995). *Safe cities: Guidelines for planning, design and management.* New York: Van Nostrand Reinhold.

White, H., & Gorman, D. (2000). Dynamics of the drug-crime relationship. In G. LaFree (Ed.), *The nature of crime: Continuity and change* (pp. 151–218). Washington, DC: Department of Justice.

Williams, K.R., & Flewelling, R.L. (1988). The social production of criminal homicide: A comparative study of disaggregated rates in American cities. *American Sociological Review, 53*(3), 421–431.

Wilson, W.J. (1987). *The truly disadvantaged: The inner city, the underclass, and public policy.* Chicago: University of Chicago Press.

Winnipeg Police Service. (2018). 2018 homicide crime map, City of Winnipeg.

Woldoff, R., & Weiss, K. (2010). Stop snitchin': Exploring definitions of the snitch and implications for urban black communities. *Journal of Criminal Justice and Popular Culture, 17*(1), 184–223.

Zimmerman, S. (1992). The revolving door of despair: Aboriginal involvement in the criminal justice system. *UBC Law Review, 26,* 367–427.

Chapter 14

Aggrawal, A. (2009). *Forensic and medico-legal aspects of sexual crimes and unusual sexual practices.* Boca Raton, FL: CRC Press.

American Psychiatric Association. (2013). *Diagnostic and statistical manual of mental disorders* (5th ed.). Washington, DC: American Psychiatric Association.

Bartol, C., & Bartol, A. (2016). *Criminal behaviour: A psychological approach* (11th ed.). Englewood Cliffs, NJ: Prentice Hall.

Bonta, J., & Andrews, D.A. (2007). Risk-need-responsivity model for offender assessment and rehabilitation (user report 2007-06). Ottawa: Public Safety Canada.

Boyd, N. (2012, June 7). Magnotta arrest telling illustration of power of Internet. *Globe and Mail.* Retrieved from http://www.theglobeandmail.com/globe-debate/magnotta-arrest-telling-illustration-of-power-of-internet/article4237414

Bradford, A., & Meston, C. (2014). Sex and gender disorders. In H. Barlow (Ed.), *The Oxford handbook of clinical psychology* (updated ed., pp. 452–475). New York: Oxford University Press.

Clarke, M., Brown, S., & Völlm, B. (2017). Circles of support and accountability for sex offenders: A systematic review of outcomes. *Sexual Abuse, 29*(5), 446–478.

Connelly, C., & Williamson, S. (2000). Review of the research literature on serious violent and sexual offenders. *Crime and Criminal Justice Research Findings, 46,* 1–121. Edinburgh, Scottish Executive Central Research Unit.

Craissati, J. (2004). *Managing high risk sex offenders in the community:*

A psychological approach. New York: Brunner-Routledge.

Delisi, M., Caropreso, D.E., Drury, A.J., Elbert, M.J., Evans, J.L., Heinrichs, T., & Tahja, K.M. (2016). The dark figure of sexual offending: New evidence from federal sex offenders. *Journal of Criminal Psychology, 6*(1), 3–15.

Doerner, W.G., & Lab, S.P. (2014). *Victimology* (7th ed.). New York, NY: Routledge.

Faust, E., Bickart, W., Renaud, C., & Camp, S. (2015). Child pornography possessors and child contact sex offenders: A multilevel comparison of demographic characteristics and rates of recidivism. *Sexual Abuse: A Journal of Research and Treatment, 27*(5), 460–478.

Fedoroff, J.P. (2008). Treatment of paraphilic sexual disorders. In D. Rowland & L. Incrocci (Eds.), *Handbook of sexual and gender identity disorders* (pp. 563–586). Hoboken, NJ: John Wiley and Sons.

Fedoroff, J.P. (2010). Paraphilic worlds. In S.D. Levine, C.B. Risen, & S.E. Althof (Eds.), *The handbook of clinical sexuality for mental health professionals* (2nd ed., pp. 401–424). New York: Routledge.

Fedoroff, J.P., Di Gioacchino, L., & Murphy, L. (2013a). Diagnostic dilemmas for the paraphilias. *Current Psychiatry Reports, 15*(363), 1–6.

Fedoroff, J.P., Fishell, A., & Fedoroff, B. (1999). A case series of women evaluated for paraphilic sexual disorders. *The Canadian Journal of Human Sexuality, 8*(2), 127–140.

Fedoroff, J.P., & Marshall, W.L. (2010). Paraphilias. In D. McKay, J.S. Abramowitz, & S. Taylor (Eds.), *Cognitive behavioural therapy for refractory cases.* Washington, DC: American Psychological Association.

Fedoroff, J.P., Ranger, R., & Murphy, L. (2013b). *Sexually violent predator programs: Who gets released?* Paper presented at the annual meeting of American Academy of Psychiatry and the Law (AAPL), San Diego, CA.

Freeman-Longo, R. (1996). Feel good legislation: Prevention or calamity. *Journal of Child Abuse & Neglect, 20*(2), 95–101.

Freund, K., & Blanchard, R. (1986). The concept of courtship disorder. *Journal of Sex & Marital Therapy, 12*(2), 79–92.

Greenfield, L. (1997). *Sex offences and offenders: An analysis of data on rape and sexual assault.* Washington, DC: US Department of Justice, Bureau of Justice Statistics.

Gudjonsson, G.H., & Young, S. (2007). The role and scope of forensic clinical psychology in secure unit provisions: A proposed service model for psychological therapies. *The Journal of Forensic Psychiatry & Psychology, 18*(4), 534–556.

Hanson, R.K., & Harris, A. (1998). *Dynamic predictors of sexual recidivism.* Ottawa: Public Works and Government Services Canada, Department of the Solicitor General of Canada.

Hanson, R.K., Harris, A., Helmus, L., & Thornton, D. (2014). High-risk sex offenders may not be high risk forever. *Journal of Interpersonal Violence, 29*(15), 2792–2813.

Hanson, R.K., Morton, K., & Harris, A. (2003). Sexual offender recidivism: What we know and what we need to know. In R. Prentky, E. Janus, & M. Seto (Eds.), *Sexually coercive behaviour: Understanding and management.* New York: New York Academy of Sciences.

Hanvey, S., Philpot, T, & Wilson, C. (2011). *A community-based approach to the reduction of sexual reoffending: Circles of support and accountability* (11th ed.). Philadelphia, PA: Jessica Kingsley Publishers.

Harris, A., & Hanson, K. (2004). *Sex offender recidivism: A simple question.* Ottawa: Public Safety and Emergency Preparedness.

Huey, L. (2016). Harm-focused policing. *Journal of Community Safety and Well-Being, 1*(3). Retrieved from https://journalcswb.ca/index.php/cswb/article/view/15/57

Jenkins, P. (2001). *Beyond tolerance: Child pornography on the Internet.* New York: New York University Press.

Kemshall, H., & Wood, J. (2007). Beyond public protection: An examination of community protection and public health approaches to high risk offenders. *Criminology and Criminal Justice, 7*(3), 203–222.

Knack, N., Murphy, L., & Fedoroff, J.P. (in press). Sadism and masochism. In B.J. Carducci (Editor-in-Chief), J.S. Mio

& R.E. Riggio (Vol. Eds.), *The Wiley-Blackwell encyclopedia of personality and individual differences: Vol. IV. Clinical, applied, and cross-cultural research.* Hoboken, NJ: John Wiley & Sons.

Ly, T., Murphy, L., & Fedoroff, J.P. (2016). Understanding online child sexual exploitation offences. *Current Psychiatry Reports, 18*(8), 1–9.

Makin, K. (2011, January 21). Why Canada's prisons can't cope with flood of mentally ill inmates. *Globe and Mail.* Retrieved from http://www.theglobeandmail.com/news/national/why-canadas-prisons-cant-cope-with-flood-of-mentally-ill-inmates/article563604

Mann, R.E., Hanson, R.K., & Thornton, D. (2010). Assessing risk for sexual recidivism: Some proposals on the nature of psychologically meaningful risk factors. *Sexual Abuse: A Journal of Research and Treatment, 22*(2), 191–217.

Marshall, W.L., Marshall, L., & Fernandez, Y. (2008). The Rockwood Preparatory Program for sexual offenders: Description and preliminary appraisal. *Sex Abuse, 20*(1), 25–42.

McAlinden, A.M. (2007). *The shaming of sex offenders: Risk, retribution and reintegration.* Portland, OR: Hart.

Morgan, R.E., & Kena, G. (2016). Criminal victimization, 2016: Revised. *The National Crime Victimization Survey.* U.S. Department of Justice. Retrieved from https://www.bjs.gov/content/pub/pdf/cv16.pdf

Murphy, L. (2013). *Ethics of sex offender management: Is there a right answer?* Paper presented at the annual meeting of American Academy of Psychiatry and the Law (AAPL), San Diego, CA.

Murphy, L., Bradford, J., & Fedoroff, J.P. (2014a). Treatment of paraphilias and paraphilic disorders. In G. Gabbard (Ed.), *Gabbard's treatment of psychiatric disorders* (5th ed.). New York: Oxford University Press.

Murphy, L., Brodsky, D., Brackel, J., Petrunik, M., Fedoroff, P., & Grudzinskas, A. (2009a). Community-based management of sex offenders: An examination of sex offender registries and community notification in the United States and Canada. In F.M., Saleh, A.J. Grudzinskas, J.M. Bradford,

& D.J. Brodsky (Eds.), *Sex offenders: Identification, risk assessment, treatment, and legal issues* (pp. 412–424). New York: Oxford University Press.

Murphy, L., & Fedoroff, J.P. (2013). Sexual offenders' views of Canadian sex offender registries: A survey of a clinical sample. *Canadian Journal of Behavioural Sciences* (Sex crime edition), *45*(3), 238–249.

Murphy, L., Fedoroff, P., & Martineau, M. (2009b). Canada's sex offender registries: Background, implementation, and social policy considerations. *Canadian Journal of Human Sexuality, 18*(1–2), 61–72.

Murphy, L., Ranger, R., & Fedoroff, J.P. (2014b). Legal and clinical issues in interpreting child pornography on the Internet. In F.M. Saleh, A. Grudzinskas Jr., & A. Judge (Eds.), *Adolescent sexual behavior in the digital age: Considerations for clinicians, legal professionals, and educators.* New York: Oxford University Press.

Parrish, J. (2013, August 2). Marek says posting grisly video was a public service, claims he's being persecuted. *CTVNews.ca.* Retrieved from http://edmonton.ctvnews.ca/marek-says-posting-grisly-video-was-a-public-service-claims-he-s-being-persecuted-1.1396322

Perreault, S. (2013). Police-reported crime statistics in Canada, 2012. *Juristat, 33*(1). Statistics Canada Catalogue no. 85-002-x. Retrieved from http://www.statcan.gc.ca/pub/85-002-x/2013001/article/11854-eng.pdf

Petrunik, M. (1982). The politics of dangerousness. *International Journal of Law and Psychiatry, 5,* 225–253.

Petrunik, M. (2002). Managing unacceptable risk: Sex offenders, community response, and social policy in the United States. *International Journal of Offender Therapy and Comparative Criminology, 46*(4), 483–511.

Petrunik, M. (2003). The hare and the tortoise: Dangerous and sex offender policy in the United States and Canada. *The Canadian Journal of Criminology and Criminal Justice, 45*(4), 43–72.

Petrunik, M. (2005). Dangerousness and its discontents: A discourse on the socio-politics of dangerousness. In S. Burns (Ed.), *Ethnographies of law and social*

control: The sociology of law, deviance and social control (Vol. 6, pp. 49–74). New York: Elsevier, JAI.

Petrunik, M., Murphy, L., & Fedoroff, P. (2008). American and Canadian approaches to sex offenders: A study of the politics of dangerousness. *Federal Sentencing Reporter, 21*(2), 111–123.

Quinsey, V., Harris, G., Rice, M., & Cormier, C. (1998). *Violent offenders: Appraising and managing risk.* Washington, DC: American Psychology Association.

Rice, S., Murphy, L., & Fedoroff, J.P. (2011). *Community correctional conditions imposed on sex offenders in Canada: Is more always better?* Paper presented at the annual meeting of American Academy of Psychiatry and the Law (AAPL), Boston.

Robbers, M.L.P. (2009). Lifers on the outside: Sex offenders and disintegrative shaming. *International Journal of Offender Therapy and Comparative Criminology, 53*(1), 5–28.

Seto, M. (2013). *Internet sex offenders.* Washington, DC: American Psychological Association.

Sinclair, R.L., & Sugar, D. (2005). *Internet-based child sexual exploitation environmental scan.* Ottawa: Royal Canadian Mounted Police.

Thomas, T. (2005). *Sex crime: Sex offending and society.* Devon, UK: Willan.

Webster, C., & Hucker, S. (2003). *Release decision making.* Hamilton, ON: St. Joseph's Healthcare.

Wilson, R., Cortoni, F., & McWhinnie, A. (2009). Circles of support and accountability: A Canadian national replication of outcome findings. *Sexual Abuse: A Journal of Research and Treatment, 21*(4), 412–430.

Wolak, J., Finkelhor, D., & Mitchell, K. (2011). Child pornography possessors: Trends in offender and case characteristics. *Sexual Abuse: A Journal of Research and Treatment, 23*(1), 22–42.

Worley, R.M., & Worley, V.B. (2013). The sex offender next door: Deconstructing the United States' obsession with sex offender registries in an age of neoliberalism. *International Review of Law, Computers & Technology, 27*(3), 335–344.

Wormith, J.S., & Hogg, S.M. (2011). The predictive validity of sexual offender recidivism with a general risk/needs assessment inventory. Research Report. Saskatoon: Program Effectiveness, Statistics and Applied Research Unit, Ministry of Community Safety and Correctional Services of Ontario.

Chapter 15

Allen, M. (2018). Police-reported crime statistics in Canada, 2017. *Juristat*, *38*(1). Statistics Canada Catalogue no. 85-002-X. Retrieved from https://www150.statcan.gc.ca/n1/pub/85-002-x/2018001/article/54974-eng.htm

Baron, S. (2013). Why street youth get involved in crime. In S. Gaetz, B. O'Grady, K. Buccieri, J. Karabanow, & A. Marsolais (Eds.), *Youth homelessness in Canada: Implications for policy and practice* (pp. 353–368). Toronto: Canadian Homelessness Research Network Press.

Beccaria, C. (1764/1995). *Essays on crime and punishment and other essays.* New York: Cambridge University Press.

Bennet, T., & Holloway, K. (2004). *Drug use and offending: Summary results of the first two years of the NEW-ADAM programme* (British Home Office report 179). London, UK: British Home Office.

Bentham, J. (1780/1973). *An introduction to the principals of morals and legislation.* Garden City, NY: Anchor Press Doubleday.

Bonger, W. (1916). *Criminology and economic conditions.* Boston: Little, Brown.

Buccieri, K. (2013). Back to the future for Canada's national anti-drug strategy: Homeless youth and the need for harm reduction. In S. Gaetz, B. O'Grady, K. Buccieri, J. Karabanow, & A. Marsolais (Eds.), *Youth homelessness in Canada: Implications for policy and practice* (pp. 199–216). Toronto: Canadian Homelessness Research Network Press.

Canadian Homelessness Research Network. (2012). *Canadian definition of homelessness.* Toronto: The Homeless Hub. Retrieved from http://www.homelesshub.ca/CHRNhomelessdefinition

Canadian Press. (2012, July 20). Livent co-founder Myron Gottlieb granted day parole. *CBCnews.ca.* Retrieved from http://www.cbc.ca/news/arts/livent-co-founder-myron-gottlieb-granted-day-parole-1.1167832

Chambliss, W., & Seidman, R. (1982). *Law, order and power* (2nd ed.). Reading, MA: Addison-Wesley.

Credit card fraud hits 20% of Canadians. (2010, September 15). *CBC News.* Retrieved from http://www.cbc.ca/news/credit-card-fraud-hits-20-of-canadians-1.900025

Durkheim, É. (1933). *The division of labor in society.* New York: Free Press.

Forster, H. (2015). Card fraud report 2015. Retrieved from https://www.paymentscardsandmobile.com/wp-content/uploads/2015/03/PCM_Alaric_Fraud-Report_2015.pdf

Gaetz, S., O'Grady, B., Buccieri, K., Karabanow, J., & Marsolais, A. (Eds.). (2013). *Youth homelessness in Canada: Implications for policy and practice.* Toronto: Canadian Homelessness Research Network Press.

Gaetz, S., O'Grady, B., & Vaillancourt, B. (1999). *Making money: The Shout Clinic report on homeless youth and employment.* Toronto: Central Toronto Community Health Centres. Retrieved from http://homelesshub.ca/sites/default/files/Making_Money.pdf

Hagan, J., & McCarthy, B. (1997). *Mean streets: Youth crime and homelessness.* Cambridge, UK: Cambridge University Press.

Hall, J. (1952). *Theft, law and society.* Indianapolis, IN: Bobbs-Merrill.

Keighley, K. (2017). Police-reported crime rates, Canada, 1962 to 2016. *Juristat*, *37*(1). Statistics Canada Catalogue no. 85-002-X. Retrieved from https://www150.statcan.gc.ca/n1/pub/85-002-x/2017001/article/54842-eng.htm

Kennedy, L., & Sacco, V. (1996). *Crime counts: A criminal event analysis.* Toronto: Nelson.

Lem, M., Coe, J.B., Haley, D.B., Stone, E., & O'Grady, W. (2013). Effects of companion animal ownership among Canadian street-involved youth: A qualitative analysis. *Journal of Sociology and Social Welfare*, *15*(4), 285–304.

Messerschmidt, J. (2006). *Criminology* (4th ed.). Los Angeles: Roxbury.

O'Grady, B. (n.d.). An analysis of property crime among homeless youth in Toronto. Unpublished raw data.

O'Grady, W. (2011). *Crime in Canadian context: Debates and controversies* (2nd ed.). Toronto: Oxford University Press.

Perreault, S. (2013). Police-reported crime statistics in Canada, 2012. *Juristat*, *33*(1). Statistics Canada Catalogue no. 85-002-x. Retrieved from http://www.statcan.gc.ca/pub/85-002-x/2013001/article/11854-eng.pdf

Public Health Agency of Canada (PHAC). (2006). Street youth in Canada: Findings from enhanced surveillance of Canadian street youth, 1999–2003. Retrieved from http://www.phac-aspc.gc.ca/std-mts/reports_06/pdf/street_youth_e.pdf

Quinney, R. (1975). *Criminology: Analysis and critique of crime in America.* Boston: Little, Brown.

Reasons, C., & Rich, R. (Eds.). (1978). *The sociology of law: A conflict perspective.* Toronto: Butterworths.

Royal Canadian Mounted Police (RCMP). (2011). Credit card fraud. Retrieved from http://www.rcmp-grc.gc.ca/scams-fraudes/cc-fraud-fraude-eng.htm

Tittle, C. (1969). Crime rates and legal sanctions. *Social Problems*, 16, 409–423.

Tonry, M. (2011). Less imprisonment is no doubt a good thing: More policing is not. *Criminology and Public Policy*, *10*(1), 137–152.

Tunnell, K. (2006). *Living off crime* (2nd ed.). Lanham, MD: Rowman and Littlefield.

Vago, S. (1997). *Law and society* (5th ed.). Upper Saddle River, NJ: Prentice Hall.

Chapter 16

Aldridge, J., Measham, F., & Williams, L. (2011). *Illegal leisure revisited: Changing patterns of alcohol and drug use in adolescents and young adults.* London: Routledge.

Alexander, P. (1987). Prostitution: A difficult issue for feminists. In F. Delacoste and P. Alexander (Eds.), *Sex work writing by women in the sex industry* (pp. 184–214). Pittsburgh: Cleis Press.

Bahr, S.J., Hoffmann, J.P., and Yang, X. (2005). Parental and peer influences on the risk of adolescent drug use. *Journal of Primary Prevention, 26*(6), 529–551.

Bell, L. (Ed.). (1987). *Good girls/bad girls.* Toronto: Women's Press.

Bentham, J. (1781/2007). *An introduction to the principles of morals and legislation.* Mineola, NY: Dover Philosophical Classics.

Beran, K. (2012). Revisiting the prostitution debate: Uniting liberal and radical feminism in pursuit of policy reform. *Law & Inequality, 30*, 19–55.

Boyd, N. (1991). *High society: Legal and illegal drugs in Canada.* Toronto: Key Porter.

CBC News. (2011, September 30). *Vancouver's Insite drug injection clinic will stay open.* CBC.ca/news. Reprinted by permission. Retrieved from http://www.cbc.ca/news/canada/british-columbia/vancouver-s-InSite-drug-injection-clinic-will-stay-open-1.1005044

Chapkis, W. (1997). *Live sex acts: Women performing erotic labor.* New York: Routledge.

Cohen, A.K. (1966). *Deviance and control.* Englewood Cliffs, NJ: Prentice Hall.

CTADS. (2015). *Canadian tobacco, alcohol and drugs survey: 2015 summary.* Ottawa: Statistics Canada.

Dalla, R. (2000). Exposing the "Pretty Woman" myth: A qualitative examination of the lives of streetwalking prostitutes. *The Journal of Sex Research, 37*(4), 344–354.

Davis, J. (2011, July 18). Prison costs soar 86% in past five years: Report. *National Post.* Retrieved from https://nationalpost.com/news/canada/prison-costs-soar-86-in-past-five-years

Davis, K. (1937). The sociology of prostitution. *American Sociological Review, 2*(5), 744–755.

Davis, N.J. (1980). *Sociological constructions of deviance: Perspectives and issues in the field* (2nd ed.). Dubuque, IA: William C. Brown.

Devlin, P. (1965). *The enforcement of morals.* London, UK: Oxford University Press.

Durkheim, É. (1933). *The division of labor in society* (G. Simpson, Trans.). New York: Macmillan.

Durkheim, É. (1938). *The rules of sociological method* (S.A. Solovay & J.H. Mueller, Trans.). Chicago: University of Chicago Press.

Dworkin, A. (1989). *Pornography.* New York: Dutton.

Engels, F. (1884/1942). *The origin of the family, private property, and the state.* New York: International.

Erikson, K.T. (1966). *Wayward puritans: A study in the sociology of deviance.* New York: John Wiley & Sons.

Fine, S. (2013, December 20). Supreme Court strikes down Canada's prostitution laws. *Globe and Mail.* Retrieved from http://www.theglobeandmail.com/news/national/supreme-court-rules-on-prostitution-laws/article16067485

Fisher, D.J. (1982). Reading Freud's Civilization and its discontents. *Journal Council for the Advancement of Psychoanalytic Education, 2*(2), 31–42.

Forum Research. (2015). More than half want prostitution legalized. Toronto: Forum Research Inc.

Freud, S. (1930/2002). *Civilization and its discontents.* London, UK: Penguin.

Gay, P. (Ed.). (1989). *The Freud reader.* New York: Norton & Company.

Giffen, P.J., Endicott, S.J., & Lambert, S. (1991). *Panic and indifference: The politics of Canada's drug laws.* Ottawa: Canadian Centre on Substance Abuse.

Hart, H.L.A. (1963). *Law, liberty and morality.* Stanford, CA: Stanford University Press.

Hughes, C.E., & Stevens, A. (2010). What can we learn from the Portuguese decriminalization of illicit drugs? *British Journal of Criminology, 50*, 999–1022.

Jenness, V. (1993). *Making it work: The prostitutes' rights movement in perspective.* New York: de Gruyter.

Johnson, H., & Rogers, K. (1993). A statistical overview of women in crime in Canada. In E. Adelberg & C. Currie (Eds.), *In conflict with the law: Women and the Canadian justice system* (pp. 95–116). Vancouver: Press Gang.

Lowman, J. (2000). Violence and the outlaw status of (street) prostitution in Canada. *Violence Against Women, 6*(9), 987–1011.

Matza, D. (1969). *Becoming deviant.* Englewood Cliffs, NJ: Prentice Hall.

Meil-Hobson, B. (1987). *Uneasy virtue.* New York: Basic Books.

Merton, R.K. (1957). *Social theory and social structure* (Rev. ed.). New York: Free Press.

Mill, J.S. (1859/2002). *On liberty.* Mineola, NY: Dover Philosophical Classics.

Miller, J.L. (1991). Prostitution in contemporary American society. In E. Grauerholz & M.A. Koralewski (Eds.), *Sexual coercion* (pp. 45–57). Lexington, MA: Lexington Books.

Office of Research and Data. (2011). *Memorandum to the chair of the United States Sentencing Commission.* Washington, DC: United States Sentencing Commission.

Overall, C. (1992). What's wrong with prostitution? Evaluating sex work. *Signs, 17*, 705–724.

Parsons, T. (1951). *The social system.* New York: Free Press.

Perkins, R. (1991). *Working girls: Prostitutes, their life and social control.* Canberra, Australia: Australian Institute of Criminology.

Phoenix, J. (2001). *Making sense of prostitution.* London, UK: Palgrave Macmillan.

Polsky, N. (1985). *Hustlers, beats and others.* Chicago: University of Chicago Press.

Prus, R.C., & Irini, S. (1980). *Hookers, rounders, and desk clerks: The social organization of the hotel community.* Toronto: Sage Publications.

Reitano, J. (2017). Adult correctional statistics in Canada, 2015/2016. *Juristat, 37*(1). Statitics Canada Catalogue no. 85-002-X. Retrieved from https://www150.statcan.gc.ca/n1/pub/85-002-x/2017001/article/14700-eng.htm

Richards, D.A.J. (1982). *Sex, drugs, death and the law: An essay on human rights and overcriminalization.* Totawa, NJ: Rowman & Littlefield.

Riley, D. (1998). *Drugs and drug policy in Canada: A brief review and commentary.* Ottawa: Report prepared for the Senate of Canada. Retrieved from https://sencanada.ca/content/sen/committee/371/ille/library/riley-e.htm

Roberts, N. (1992). *Whores in history: Prostitution in Western society.* London, UK: HarperCollins.

Rosen, F. (2003). *Classical utilitarianism from Hume to Mill*. London, UK: Routledge.

Rosen, R. (1982). *The lost sisterhood: Prostitution in America, 1900–1918*. Baltimore: John Hopkins University Press.

Schur, E.M. (1984). *Labeling women deviant: Gender, stigma, and social control*. Philadelphia: Temple University Press.

Senate Special Committee on Illegal Drugs. (2002). *Cannabis: Our position for a Canadian public policy*. Ottawa: Information Canada.

Stebbins, R.A. (1996). *Tolerable differences: Living with deviance*. Whitby, ON: McGraw-Hill Ryerson.

Tong, R. (1984). *Women, sex and the law*. Savage, MD: Rowman & Littlefield.

Tonry, M. (1995). *Malign neglect: Race, crime and punishment in America*. London, UK: Oxford University Press.

United Nations Office on Drugs and Crime (UNODC). (2017). *World drug report 2017*. (United Nations publication, Sales No. E.17.XI.6). Retrieved from https://www.unodc.org/wdr2017

Walkowitz, J. (1982). Male vice and feminist virtue: Feminism and the politics of prostitution in nineteenth-century Britain. *History Workshop, 13*, 79–83.

Chapter 17

Akers, R. (1997). *Criminological theories: Introduction and evaluation*. Los Angeles: Roxbury Press.

Anderson, E. (1999). *The code of the streets: Decency, violence and the moral life of the inner-city*. New York: Norton and Company.

Ball, R., & Curry, D. (1995). The logic of definition in criminology: Purposes and methods for defining gangs. *Criminology, 33*(2), 225–245.

Barrows, J., & Huff, R. (2009). Gangs and public policy: Constructing and deconstructing gang databases. *Criminology and Public Policy, 8*(4), 675–704.

Bennett, T., & Holloway, K. (2004). Gang membership, drugs and crime in the UK. *British Journal of Criminology, 44*, 305–323.

Bjerregaard, B. (2002). Self-definitions of gang membership and involvement in delinquent activities. *Youth & Society, 44*(1), 31–54.

Boyce, J., & Cotter, A. (2013). *Homicide in Canada, 2012. Juristat, 33*(1). Statistics Canada Catalogue no. 85-002-X. Retrieved from http://www.statcan.gc.ca/pub/85-002-x/2013001/article/11882-eng.pdf

Braga, A., Kennedy, D., & Tita, G. (2002). New approaches to the prevention of gang and group-involved violence. In C. Huff (Ed.), *Gangs in America* (3rd ed., pp. 271–286). Thousand Oaks, CA: Sage.

Braga, A., Pierce, G., McDevitt, J., Bond, B., & Cronin, S. (2008). The strategic prevention of gun violence among gang-involved offenders. *Justice Quarterly, 25*(1), 132–162.

Bridenhall, B., & Jesilow, P. (2005). Weeding criminals or planting fear: An evaluation of a weed and seed project. *Criminal Justice Review, 30*(1), 64–89.

Brownfield, D. (2006). A defiance theory of sanctions and gang membership. *Journal of Gang Research, 13*(4), 31–43.

Canadian Centre for Justice Statistics. (2008). *Uniform Crime Reporting Incident-Based Survey: CCJS reporting manual*. Ottawa: Statistics Canada.

Carr, R., Slothower, M., & Parkinson, J. (2017). Do gang injunctions reduce violent crime? Four tests in Merseyside, UK. *Cambridge Journal of Evidence-Based Policing, 1*(4), 195–210.

Chatterjee, J. (2006). *Gang prevention and intervention strategies*. Ottawa: Research and Evaluation Branch, Community, Contract and Aboriginal Policing Services, Royal Canadian Mounted Police.

Chettleburgh, M. (2007). *Young thugs: Inside the dangerous world of Canadian street gangs*. Toronto: Harper-Collins.

Cohen, A. (1955). *Delinquent boys: The culture of the gang*. New York: Free Press.

Craig, W., Vitaro, R., Gagnon, C., & Trembly, R.E. (2002). The road to gang membership: Characteristics of male gang and non-gang members from ages 10 to 14. *Social Development, 11*, 53–68.

Curry, G., & Decker, S. (1998). *Confronting gangs: Crime and community*. Los Angeles: Roxbury Press.

David, J.-D. (2017). Homicide in Canada, 2016. *Juristat, 37*(1). Statistics Canada Catalogue no. 85-002-X. Retrieved from https://www150.statcan.gc.ca/n1/pub/85-002-x/2017001/article/54879-eng.htm

Decker, S., & Curry, G. (2002). Gangs, gang members and gang homicides: Organized crimes or disorganized criminals. *Journal of Criminal Justice, 30*, 343–352.

Delaney, T. (2014). *American street gangs* (2nd ed.). Upper Saddle River, NJ: Pearson.

Denny, K., & Brownell, M. (2010). Taking a social determinants perspective on children's health and development. *Canadian Journal of Public Health, 101*(9), S4–S7.

Egley, A., Howell, J., & Moore, J. (2010, March). Highlights of the 2008 National Youth Gang Survey. OJJDP Fact Sheet.

Ellis, A. (2017). Memories of urban warfare: Trauma, PTSD and gang violence. *Journal of Community Corrections, 26*(2), 5–14(10).

Esbensen, F.-A., Osgood, D.W., Taylor, T., Peterson, D., & Freng, A. (2001). How great is G.R.E.A.T.? Results from a longitudinal quasi-experimental design. *Criminology and Public Policy, 1*(1), 87–118.

Esbensen, F.-A., Winfree, T., He, N., & Taylor, T. (2001). Youth gangs and definitional issues: When is a gang a gang, and why does it matter? *Crime and Delinquency, 47*(1), 105–130.

Ezeonu, I. (2014). Doing gang research in Canada: Navigating a different kaleidoscope. *Contemporary Justice Review, 17*(1), 4–22.

Farrington, D.P., & Welsh, B.C. (2007). *Saving children from a life of crime: Early risk factors and effective interventions*. Oxford, UK: Oxford University Press.

Fudge, Z.D. (2014). Gang definitions, how do they work?: What the Juggalos teach us about the inadequacy of current anti-gang law. *Marquette Law Review, 97*(4), 979–1037.

Gartner, R., & Thompson, S. (2004). Trends in homicide in Toronto. In B. Kidd & J. Phillips (Eds.), *From enforcement to prevention to civic engagement: Research on community safety* (pp. 28–42).

Toronto: Centre of Criminology, University of Toronto.

Gatti, U., Tremblay, R., Vitaro, F., & McDuff, P. (2005). Youth gangs: Delinquency and drug use—A test of the selection, facilitation and enhancement hypothesis. *Journal of Child Psychology and Psychiatry, 46*(11), 1178–1190.

Gordon, R. (2000, January). Criminal business organizations, street gangs and "wanna-be" groups: A Vancouver perspective. *Canadian Review of Criminology,* 39–60.

Gottfredson, M., & Hirschi, T. (1990). *A general theory of crime.* Stanford, CA: Stanford University Press.

Greene, J., & Pranis, K. (2007). *Gang wars: The failure of enforcement tactics and the need for effective public safety strategies.* Washington, DC: Justice Policy Institute.

Greenwood, P.W. (2006). *Changing lives: Delinquency prevention as crime-control policy.* Chicago: University of Chicago Press.

Hagedorn, J. (2008). *World of gangs: Armed young men and gangsta culture.* Minneapolis: University of Minnesota Press.

Hayden, T. (2004). *Street wars: Gangs and the future of violence.* New York: The New York Press.

Hemmati, T. (2006). *The nature of Canadian urban gangs and their use of firearms: A review of the literature and police survey.* Ottawa: Department of Justice Canada, Research and Statistics Division.

Hickson, M., & Roebuck, J. (2009). *Deviance and crime in colleges and universities: What goes on in the halls of ivy.* Springfield, IL: Charles C. Thomas.

Howell, J. (1998, August). Youth gangs: An overview. *Juvenile Justice Bulletin.*

Howell, J. (1999). Youth gang homicides: A literature review. *Crime and Delinquency, 45,* 208–241.

Huff, C.R. (2002). *Gangs in America* (3rd ed.). Thousand Oaks, CA: Sage.

Katz, C., & Webb, V. (2006). *Policing gangs in America.* New York: Cambridge University Press.

Kemp-North, M. (2007). Theoretical foundations of gang membership. *Journal of Gang Research, 14,* 11–26.

Kennedy, D. (2006). Old wine in new bottles: Policing and the lessons of pulling levers. In D. Weisburd & A. Braga (Eds.), *Police innovation: Contrasting perspectives* (pp. 155–170). New York: Cambridge University Press.

Kennedy, D. (2009). Comment on "Gangs and public policy: Constructing and deconstructing gang databases." *Criminology and Public Policy, 8*(4), 711–716.

Kerig, P., Wainryb, C., Twali, M.S., & Chaplo, S. (2013). America's child soldiers: Toward a research agenda for studying gang-involved youth in the United States. *Journal of Aggression, Maltreatment and Trauma, 22*(7), 773–795.

Klein, M., & Maxson, C. (2006). *Street gang patterns and policies.* Oxford, UK: Oxford University Press.

Lane, J., & Meeker, J. (2004). Social disorganization perceptions, fear of gang crime and behavioural precautions among Whites, Latinos and Vietnamese. *Journal of Criminal Justice, 32,* 49–62.

Langston, M. (2003). Addressing the need for a uniform definition of gang-involved crime. *FBI Law Enforcement Bulletin, 72*(2), 7–11.

Leschied, A.W. (2007). *The roots of violence: Evidence from the literature with emphasis on child and youth mental health disorder.* Prepared for and submitted to the Review of the Roots of Youth Violence by the Ministry of Children and Youth Services (Ontario).

Linden, R. (2010). Comprehensive approaches to address street gangs in Canada. *Public Safety Canada, 14,* 1–24. Retrieved from http://publications. gc.ca/collections/collection_2012/sp-ps/ PS4-113-2011-eng.pdf

Mares, D. (2010). Social disorganization and gang homicides in Chicago: A neighborhood-level comparison of disaggregated homicides. *Youth Violence and Juvenile Justice, 8*(1), 38–57.

Maxson, C., & Klein, M. (1995). Investigating gang structures. *Journal of Gang Research, 3,* 33–40.

McCabe, S., Schulenberg, J., Johnston, L., O'Malley, P., Bachman, J., & Kloska, D. (2005). Selection and socialization effects of fraternities and sororities on US college student substance use: A multi-cohort national longitudinal study. *Addiction, 100*(4), 512–524.

McClanahan, W.S. (2004). *Alive at 25: Reducing youth violence through monitoring and support.* Philadelphia: Public/Private Ventures.

Melde, C., Taylor, T., & Esbensen, F.-A. (2009). I got your back: An examination of the protective function of gang membership in adolescence. *Criminology, 47*(2), 565–594.

Merton, R. (1938). Social structure and anomie. *American Sociological Review, 3,* 672–682.

National Institute of Justice. (2011). Program profile: Indianapolis (Ind.) Violence Reduction Partnership (IVRP). Retrieved from http://www .crimesolutions.gov/ProgramDetails. aspx?ID=65

Papachristos, A., & Kirk, D. (2006). Neighbourhood effects on street gang behaviour. In J. Short & L. Hughes (Eds.), *Studying youth gangs* (pp. 63–83). Oxford, UK: Altamira Press.

Papachristos, A., Meares, T., & Fagan, J. (2007). Attention felons: Evaluating Project Safe Neighbourhoods in Chicago. *Journal of Empirical Legal Studies, 4,* 223–272.

Petersen, R.D. (2000). Definitions of a gang and impacts on public policy. *Journal of Criminal Justice, 28*(2), 139–149.

Public Safety Canada. (2018). Criminal gun and gang violence in Canada. Backgrounder. Retrieved from https:// www.canada.ca/en/public-safety- canada/news/2018/03/criminal-gun- and-gang-violence-in-canada.html

Rosenfeld, R., Bray, T., & Egley, A. (1999). Facilitating violence: A comparison of gang-motivated, and non-gang youth homicides. *Journal of Quantitative Criminology, 15*(4), 495–516.

Sanday, P. (1990). *Fraternity gang rape: Sex, brotherhood and privilege on campus.* New York: New York University Press.

Shaefer, D. (2004). Perceptual biases, graffiti and fraternity crime: Points of deflection that distort social justice. *Critical Criminology, 12*(2), 179–193.

Shaw, C., & McKay, H. (1942). *Juvenile delinquency and urban areas.* Chicago: University of Chicago Press.

Short, J. (2009). Gangs, law enforcement and the academy. *Criminology and Public Policy, 8*(4), 723–732.

Spano, R., Freilich, J., & Bolland, J. (2008). Gang membership, gun carrying and employment: Applying routine activities theory to explain violent victimization among inner city, minority youth living in extreme poverty. *Justice Quarterly, 25*(2), 381–410.

Spergel, I. (1995). *The youth gang problem.* New York: Oxford University Press.

Spergel, I. (2007). *Reducing youth gang violence: The little village gang project in Chicago.* Lanham, MD: Altamira Press.

Spergel, I. (2009). Gang databases: To be or not to be. *Criminology and Public Policy, 8*(4), 667–674.

Sullivan, M.L. (2005). Maybe we shouldn't study gangs: Does reification obscure youth violence? *Journal of Contemporary Criminal Justice, 21*(2), 170–190.

Sullivan, M.L. (2006). Are gang studies dangerous? Youth violence, local context and the problem of reification. In J. Short & L. Hughes (Eds.), *Studying youth gangs* (pp. 15–35). Oxford, UK: Altamira Press.

Sutherland, D., & Cressey, D. (1974). *Criminology.* New York: Lippincott.

Tanner, J., & Wortley, S. (2002). *The Toronto Youth Crime and Victimization Survey: Overview report.* Toronto: Centre of Criminology.

The Canadian Press. (2018). 75 per cent of shootings in Toronto are gang-related, Tory says. *Toronto Star.* Retrieved from https://www.thestar.com/news/gta/2018/07/03/75-per-cent-of-shootings-in-toronto-are-gang-related-tory-says.html

Thornberry, T., Huizinga, D., & Loeber, R. (2004, September). The causes and correlates studies: Findings and policy implications. *Juvenile Justice Journal, 9*(1), 3–19.

Thrasher, F.M. (1927/1963). *The gang: A study of one thousand three hundred thirteen gangs in Chicago.* (James F. Short Jr., Abridger, new introduction.) Chicago: University of Chicago Press.

United Nations. (2004). *Convention against transnational organized crime and the protocols thereto* (entered into force 29 September 2003). New York: Author.

Waller, I. (2006). *Less law, more order.* Westport, CT: Praeger.

Weerman, F.M., Maxson, C.L., Esbensen, F., Aldridge, J., Medina, J., & van Gemert, F. (2009). Eurogang program manual: Background, development, and use of the Eurogang instruments in multi-site, multi-method comparative research. Retrieved from https://www.umsl.edu/ccj/Eurogang/EurogangManual.pdf

Welford, C., Pepper, J., & Petrie, C. (2005). *Firearms and violence: A critical review.* Washington, DC: Committee to Improve Research Information and Data on Firearms and the National Academies Press.

Wheatley, J. (2008). The flexibility of RICO and its use on street gangs engaging in organized crime in the United States. *Policing, 2*(1), 82–91.

Wood, J., & Alleyne, E. (2010). Street gang theory and research: Where are we now and where do we go from here? *Aggression and Violent Behavior, 15*(2), 100–111.

Wortley, S. (2008). A province at the crossroads: Statistics on youth violence in Ontario. In R. McMurtry & A. Curling (Eds.), *The review of the roots of youth violence: Vol. 4* (pp. 1–64). Toronto: Queen's Printer for Ontario.

Wortley, S., Dorion, J., Levinsky, Z., Owusu-Bempah, A., Marshall, L., Adhopia, R., Samuels, K., … Boyce, A. (2008). Preventing youth crime and violence: A review of the literature. In R. McMurtry & A. Curling (Eds.), *The review of the roots of youth violence: Vol. 5* (pp. 229–561). Toronto: Queen's Printer for Ontario. Retrieved from http://www.children.gov.on.ca/htdocs/english/documents/youthandthelaw/rootsofyouthviolence-vol5.pdf

Wortley, S., & Tanner, J. (2007). *Youth gangs in Canada's largest city: Results of the Toronto youth gang pilot project.* Ottawa: Solicitor General of Canada.

Wortley, S., & Tanner, J. (2008). Money, respect and defiance: Explaining ethnic differences in gang activity among Canadian youth. In F. van Gemert, D. Peterson, & I.-L. Lien (Eds.), *Youth gangs, migration and ethnicity* (pp. 181–210). London, UK: Willan.

Chapter 18

Association of Certified Fraud Examiners. (2018). 2018 Report to the nations. Retrieved from https://www.acfe.com/rttn.aspx

Beare, M.E. (2003). *Critical reflections on transnational organized crime, money laundering, and corruption.* Toronto: University of Toronto Press.

Beare, M.E., & Schneider, S. (2007). *Money laundering: Chasing dirty money and dangerous dollars.* Toronto: University of Toronto Press.

Braithwaite, J. (2011). The essence of responsive regulation. *UBC Law Review, 44*, 475–520.

Brown, S.E., & Chiang, C.-P. (1995). Defining corporate crime: A critique of traditional parameters. In M.P. Blankenship (Ed.), *Understanding corporate criminality* (pp. 29–56). New York: Garland.

CBC News. (2013, September 17). Chocolate price-fixing costs candy makers $23M. Retrieved from https://www.cbc.ca/news/business/chocolate-price-fixing-costs-candy-makers-23m-1.1857642

Clinard, M.B., & Quinney, R. (1978). Corporate crime: Issues in research. *Criminology, 16*, 255–272.

Coffee, J.C., Jr. (1981). "No soul to damn, no body to kick": An unscandalized inquiry into the problem of corporate punishment. *Michigan Law Review, 79*, 386–459.

Competition Bureau. (2008, June 25). What does green really mean?: Competition Bureau and Canadian Standards Association seek greater accuracy in environmental claims [Press release]. Retrieved from http://www.marketwired.com/press-release/what-does-green-really-mean-competition-bureau-canadian-standards-association-seek-greater-872901.htm

Competition Bureau. (2018, February 14). List of charges and sentences for gasoline price-fixing. Retrieved from http://www.competitionbureau.gc.ca/eic/site/cb-bc.nsf/eng/03079.html

Cullen, F.T., Hartman, J.L., & Jonson C.L. (2009). Bad guys: Why the public supports punishing white-collar offenders. *Crime, Law & Social Change, 51*, 31–44.

Edmonds, O.P., & Edmonds, E.L. (1963). An account of the founding of H.M. Inspectorate of Mines and the work of the first inspector Hugh Seymour Tremenheere. *British Journal of Industrial Medicine, 20*, 210–217.

European Commission. (2001). *Green paper: Promoting a European framework for corporate social responsibility.* Retrieved from http://europa.eu/rapid/press-release_DOC-01-9_en.pdf

FBI. (2012, November 16). LCD price fixing conspiracy. *News.* Retrieved from https://www.fbi.gov/news/stories/lcd-price-fixing-conspiracy

First, H. (2010). Branch office of the prosecutor: The new role of the corporation in business crime prosecutions. *North Carolina Law Review, 89*, 23–98.

Fleury, S. (2010). Abusive tax planning: The problem and the Canadian context. Library of Parliament Background Paper no. 2010-22-E. Retrieved from https://lop.parl.ca/sites/PublicWebsite/default/en_CA/ResearchPublications/201022E

Government of Canada. (2018). Equality and Growth: A Strong Middle Class: Budget 2018. *Annex 2: Details of economic and fiscal projections: Section 3.2: Outlook for budgetary revenues: Table A.27.* (Tabled by the Hon William Francis Morneau, PC, MP, Minister of Finance.) Retrieved from https://www.budget.gc.ca/2018/docs/plan/anx-02-en.html#32-Outlook-for-Budgetary-Revenues

Green, B., & Podgor, E. (2013). Unregulated internal investigations: Achieving fairness for corporate constituents. *Boston College Law Review, 54*, 73–126.

Gustafson, J. (2007). Cracking down on white-collar crime: An analysis of the recent trend of severe sentences for corporate offenders. *Suffolk University Law Review, 40*, 685–701.

Holtfreter, K., Van Slyke, K., Bratton, J., & Gertz, M. (2008). Public perceptions of white-collar crime and punishment. *Journal of Criminal Justice, 36*, 50–60.

Kedia, S. (2012, September 19). Does the revolving door affect the SEC's enforcement outcomes? [Blog post]. *Harvard Law School Forum on Corporate Governance and Financial Regulation.* Retrieved from http://blogs.law.harvard.edu/corpgov/2012/09/19/does-the-revolving-door-affect-the-secs-enforcement-outcomes

Kochan, N., & Goodyear, R. (2011). *Corruption: The new corporation challenge.* New York: Palgrave Macmillan.

Leman-Langlois, S. (2008). Introduction: Technocrime. In S. Leman-Langlois (Ed.), *Technocrime: Technology, crime and social control* (pp. 1–13). Portland, OR: Willan.

Lozano, J.A. (2008, September 10). Enron investors to share $7.2 billion settlement. *Washington Post.* Retrieved from http://www.washingtonpost.com/wp-dyn/content/article/2008/09/09/AR2008090903144.html

Meeks, W. (2007). Corporate and white-collar crime enforcement: Should regulation and rehabilitation spell an end to corporate criminal liability? *Columbia Journal of Law & Social Problems, 40*, 77–124.

Murphy, P.B., & Dervan, L.E. (2005). Watching your step: Avoiding the pitfalls and perils of corporate and internal investigations. *Attorneys' Liability Assurance Society Loss Prevention Journal, 16*, 2–11.

Pecman, J. (2018, February 5). Shining a light into the shadows: What price-fixing investigations tell Canadians. Position Statement. Retrieved from http://www.competitionbureau.gc.ca/eic/site/cb-bc.nsf/eng/04335.html

Potter, G. (2010, November). What is green criminology? *Sociology Review, 8*–12.

Public Safety Canada. (2015). Integrated market enforcement teams. Retrieved from https://www.publicsafety.gc.ca/cnt/cntrng-crm/rgnzd-crm/ntgrtd-mrkt-nfrcmnt-en.aspx

Richard, P.K. (1997). *The Westray story: A predictable path to disaster: Report of the Westray Mine Public Inquiry.* Retrieved from http://novascotia.ca/lae/pubs/westray

Sabatini, P. (2007, March 25). Tax cheats cost U.S. hundreds of billions. *Pittsburgh Post-Gazette.* Retrieved from http://www.post-gazette.com/businessnews/2007/03/25/Tax-cheats-cost-U-S-hundreds-of-billions/stories/200703250264

Shapiro, S. (1990). Collaring the crime, not the criminal: Reconsidering the concept of white-collar crime. *American Sociological Review, 55*, 346–356.

Shapiro, S.P. (1985). The road not taken: The elusive path to criminal prosecution for white collar offenders. *Law and Society Review, 19*, 179–217.

Sher, J. (2011, May 24). Canada ranked worst of G7 nations in fighting bribery, corruption. *Globe and Mail.* Retrieved from http://www.theglobeandmail.com/news/politics/canada-ranked-worst-of-g7-nations-in-fighting-bribery-corruption/article592312

Shover, N., & Hochstetler, A. (2006). *Choosing white-collar crime.* New York: Cambridge University Press.

Snider, L. (1993). *Bad business: Corporate crime in Canada.* Scarborough, ON: Nelson Canada.

Spivack, P., & Raman, S. (2008). Regulating the "new regulators": Current trends in deferred prosecution agreements. *American Criminal Law Review, 45*, 159–193.

Stigler, G.J. (1971). The theory of economic regulation. *Bell Journal of Economics & Management Science, 2*, 3–21.

Sutherland, E.H. (1940). White-collar criminality. *American Sociological Review, 5*, 1–12.

Sutherland, E.H. (1945). Is "white-collar crime" crime? *American Sociological Review, 10*, 132–139.

Sutherland, E.H. (1949/1983). *White-collar crime: The uncut version.* New Haven, CT: Yale University Press.

White-collar crime in Canada: Too trusting. (2009, April 2). *The Economist.* Retrieved from http://www.economist.com/node/13415555

Chapter 19

Agnew, R. (2010). A general strain theory of terrorism. *Theoretical Criminology, 14*(2), 131–153.

Ahmed, S. (2015). The "emotionalization of the 'War on Terror'": Counter-terrorism, fear, risk, insecurity and helplessness. *Criminology & Criminal Justice, 15*(5), 545–560.

Akins, J.K., & Winfree, T. (2017). Social learning theory and becoming a terrorist: New challenges for a general theory. In G. LaFree & J.D. Freilich

(Eds.), *The handbook of the criminology of terrorism* (pp. 133–149). Chichester, UK: Wiley Blackwell.

Amirault, J., & Bouchard, M. (2015). A group-based sentencing premium? The role of context and cohort effects in the sentencing of terrorist offenders. *International Journal of Law, Crime, and Justice, 43*, 512–534.

Anderson, R., Barton, C., Böhme, R., Clayton, R., van Eeten, M.J.G., Levi, M., Moore, T., & Savage, S. (2012). Measuring the cost of cybercrime. In *Proceedings of the 11th workshop on the economics of information security.* Berlin, Germany: Berlin-Brandenburg Academy of Science.

Asal, V., Fair, C.C., & Shellman, S. (2008). Consenting to a child's decision to join a jihad: Insights from a survey of militant families in Pakistan. *Studies in Conflict and Terrorism, 31*(11), 973–994.

Australian Cyber Security Centre. (2016). *2016 cyber security survey.* Retrieved from https://www.acsc.gov.au/publications/ACSC_Cyber_Security_Survey_2016.pdf

B.C. Freedom of Information and Privacy Association. (2005). *PIPEDA and identity theft: Solutions for protecting Canadians.* Retrieved from https://fipa.bc.ca/wordpress/wp-content/uploads/2014/04/PIPEDA_and_Identity_Theft.pdf

Beech, A.R., Elliott, I.A., Birgden, A., & Findlater, D. (2008). The Internet and child sex offending: A criminological review. *Aggression and Violent Behavior, 13*(3), 216–228.

Bitcoin. (2018). Bitcoin: Open source P2P money. Retrieved from https://bitcoin.org/en

Bjørgo, T., & Horgan, J. (Eds.). (2009). *Leaving terrorism behind: Individual and collective disengagement.* London, UK: Routledge.

Blejwas, A., Griggs, A., & Potok, M. (2005). Almost 60 terrorist plots uncovered in the U.S. since the Oklahoma City bombing. *Intelligence Report* (Summer Issue). Southern Poverty Law Center. Retrieved from https://www.splcenter.org/fighting-hate/intelligence-report/2005/almost-60-terrorist-plots-uncovered-us-oklahoma-city-bombing

Borum, R. (2011). Radicalization into violent extremism I: A review of social science theories. *Journal of Strategic Security, 4*(4), 7–36.

Bouchard, M. (Ed.). (2015). *Social networks, terrorism, and counter-terrorism: Radical and connected.* New York: Routledge.

Brenner, S.W. (2002). Organized cybercrime: How cyberspace may affect the structure of criminal relationships. *North Carolina Journal of Law & Technology, 4*(1), 1–50.

Bubolz, B.F., & Simi, P. (2015). Leaving the world of hate: Life-course transitions and self-change. *American Behavioral Scientist, 59*(12), 1588–1608.

Bureau of Justice Statistics. (2017). *Stalking.* Retrieved from https://www.bjs.gov/index.cfm?ty=tp&tid=973

Butters, G. (2005, January 27). Your computer may be housing child porn. *Globe and Mail.* Retrieved from https://www.theglobeandmail.com/technology/your-computer-may-be-housing-child-porn/article1113613

CBC News. (2017, October 1). Terrorism charges pending in Edmonton attacks. *CBC.ca/news.* Retrieved from http://www.cbc.ca/news/canada/edmonton/edmonton-don-iveson-terrorism-attack-lone-wolf-1.4315693

Chase, A. (2000). Harvard and the making of the Unabomber. *The Atlantic.* Retrieved from https://www.theatlantic.com/magazine/archive/2000/06/harvard-and-the-making-of-the-unabomber/378239

Chertoff, M. (2017). A public policy perspective of the Dark Web. *Journal of Cyber Policy, 2*(1), 26–38.

Clough, J. (2015). *Principles of cybercrime* (2nd ed.). New York: Cambridge University Press.

Cohen, L. E., & Felson, M. (1979). Social change and crime rate trends: A routine activity approach. *American Sociological Review, 44*(4), 588–608.

Conway, M. (2006). Terrorism and the Internet: New media—new threat? *Parliamentary Affairs, 59*(2), 283–298.

Conway, M. (2012). From al-Zarqawi to al-Awlaki: The emergence of the Internet as a new form of violent radical milieu. *Combating Terrorism Exchange, 2*(4), 12–22.

Conway, M. (2016). Determining the role of the Internet in violent extremism and terrorism: Six suggestions for progressing research. *Studies in Conflict & Terrorism, 40*(1), 77–98.

Cooper, H.H.A. (2001). Terrorism: The problem of definition revisited. *American Behavioral Scientist, 44*(6), 881–893.

Criminal Intelligence Service Canada. (2014). Organized crime in Canada: Backgrounder. Retrieved from http://www.cisc.gc.ca/media/2014/2014-08-22-eng.htm

Davies, G., Bouchard, M., Wu, E., Joffres, K., & Frank, R. (2015). Terrorist organizations' use of the Internet for recruitment. In M. Bouchard (Ed.), *Social network, terrorism and counter-terrorism: Radical and connected* (pp. 105–127). New York: Routledge.

Davies, G., Neudecker, C., Ouellet, M., Bouchard, M., & Ducol, B. (2016). Toward a framework understanding of online programs for countering violent extremism. *Journal for Deradicalization, 6*, 51–86.

Dawson, L. (2017, November 28). How should we deal with foreign fighters who return to Canada? *Globe and Mail.* Retrieved from https://www.theglobeandmail.com/opinion/how-should-we-deal-with-foreign-fighters-who-return-to-canada/article37110307

Department of Justice Canada. (2015). Memorializing the victims of terrorism: Definitions of terrorism and the Canadian context. Retrieved from http://www.justice.gc.ca/eng/rp-pr/cj-jp/victim/rr09_6/p3.html

Department of Justice Canada. (2017). *A handbook for police and crown prosecutors on criminal harassment: Part 2: Guidelines for police: Investigating criminal harassment.* Retrieved from http://www.justice.gc.ca/eng/rp-pr/cj-jp/fv-vf/har/part2.html

Ducol, B., Bouchard, M., Davies, G., Ouellet, M., & Neudecker, C. (2015). *Assessment of the state of knowledge: Connections between research on the social psychology of the Internet and violent extremism.* Ottawa: Public Safety Canada.

Easson, J.J., & Schmid, A.P. (2011). Appendix 2.1. In A.P. Schmid (Ed.),

The Routledge handbook of terrorism research (pp. 99–157). New York: Routledge.

Europol. (2016, July 25). *No more ransom: Law enforcement and IT security companies join forces to right ransomware* [Press release]. Retrieved from https://www .europol.europa.eu/newsroom/news/ no-more-ransom-law-enforcement- and-it-security-companies-join-forces- to-fight-ransomware

Europol. (2018). Drug trafficking. Retrieved from https://www.europol.europa.eu/ crime-areas-and-trends/crime-areas/ drug-trafficking

Gartenstein-Ross, D., & Blackman, M. (2017). ISIL's virtual planners: A critical terrorist innovation. *War on the Rocks*. Retrieved from https://warontherocks .com/2017/01/isils-virtual-planners-a- critical-terrorist-innovation

Gill, P., Corner, E., Conway, M., Thornton, A., Bloom, M., & Horgan J. (2017). Terrorist use of the Internet by the numbers: Quantifying behaviors, patterns, and processes. *Criminology & Public Policy*, 16(1), 99–117.

Goldman, D. (2011, July 27). The cyber mafia has already hacked you. *CNN Money*. Retrieved from http://money .cnn.com/2011/07/27/technology/ organized_cybercrime/index.htm

Guitton, C. (2013). A review of the available content on Tor hidden services: The case against further development. *Computers in Human Behavior*, 29(6), 2805–2815.

Hamm, M.S. (2013). *The spectacular few: Prisoner radicalization and the evolving terrorist threat*. New York: New York University Press.

Hamm, M.S, & Spaaij, R. (2017). *The age of lone wolf*. New York: Columbia University Press.

Hao, S., Borgolte, K., Nikiforakis, N., Stringhini, G., Egele, M., Eubanks, M., Krebs, B., & Vigna, G. (2015). *Drops for stuff: An analysis of reshipping mule scams*. Proceedings of the 22nd ACM SIGSAC Conference on Computer and Communications Security. Denver, CO: CCS.

Harris-Hogan, S., Barrelle, K., & Zammit, A. (2015). What is countering violent extremism? Exploring CVE policy and practice in Australia. *Behavioral Sciences of Terrorism and Political Aggression*, 8(1), 6–24.

Hoffman, B. (2006). *Inside terrorism: Revised and expanded edition*. New York: Columbia University Press.

Holt, T.J., Blevins, K.R., & Burkert, N. (2010). Considering the pedophile subculture online. *Sexual Abuse: Journal of Research and Treatment*, 22, 3–24.

Holt, T.J., & Bossler, A.M. (2014). An assessment of the current state of cybercrime scholarship. *Deviant Behavior*, 35, 20–40.

Identity Theft Resource Center. (2005). *Identity theft: The aftermath 2004*. Retrieved from https://www. idtheftcenter.org/images/surveys_ studies/Aftermath2004.pdf

Identity Theft Resource Center. (2017). *Identity theft: The aftermath 2017*. Retrieved from https://www.ftc.gov/ system/files/documents/public_ comments/2017/10/00004-141444.pdf

International Labour Organization. (2012, June 1). New ILO Global Estimate of Forced Labour: 20.9 million victims. Retrieved from http://www.ilo.org/ global/about-the-ilo/newsroom/news/ WCMS_182109/lang—en/index.htm

International Telecommunication Union. (2017). ICT facts and figures 2017. Retrieved from https://www.itu.int/ en/ITU-D/Statistics/Documents/facts/ ICTFactsFigures2017.pdf

Interpol. (2018a). Cybercrime. Retrieved from https://www.interpol.int/ Crime-areas/Cybercrime/Cybercrime

Interpol. (2018b). People smuggling. Retrieved from https://www. interpol.int/Crime-areas/ Trafficking-in-human-beings/ People-smuggling

Interpol. (2018c). Trafficking in illicit goods and counterfeiting. Retrieved from https://www.interpol.int/Crime-areas/ Trafficking-in-illicit-goods-and- counterfeiting/Trafficking-in-illicit- goods-and-counterfeiting

Juniper Research. (2015, May 12). *Cybercrime will cost businesses over $2 trillion by 2019* [Press release]. Retrieved from https://www.juniperresearch.com/ press/press-releases/cybercrime-cost- businesses-over-2trillion

Koehler, D. (2016). *Understanding deradicalization: Methods, tools and programs for countering violent extremism*. London: Routledge.

Lenhart, A. (2010). *Cyberbullying 2010: What the research tells us*. Pew Research Center. Internet and Technology. Retrieved from http://www.pewinternet .org/2010/05/06/cyberbullying-2010- what-the-research-tells-us

Levi, M., & Reuter, P. (2006). Money laundering. *Crime and Justice*, 34(1), 289–375.

Lucas, G. (2017). *Ethics and cyber warfare: The quest for responsible security in the age of digital warfare*. New York: Oxford University Press.

Lusthaus, J. (2013). How organised is organised cybercrime? *Global Crime*, 14(1), 52–60.

McCauley, C., & Moskalenko, S. (2008). Mechanisms of political radicalization: Pathways toward terrorism. *Terrorism and Political Violence*, 20(3), 415–433.

McGuire, M., & Dowling, S. (2013a). *Cyber crime: A review of the evidence* [Research Report 75]. Chapter 1: Cyber-dependent crimes. Home Office. Retrieved from https://assets.publishing .service.gov.uk/government/uploads/ system/uploads/attachment_data/ file/246751/horr75-chap1.pdf

McGuire, M., & Dowling, S. (2013b). Chapter 4: Improving the cyber crime evidence base. In *Cyber crime: A review of the evidence: Research report 75*. Home Office. Retrieved from https:// assets.publishing.service.gov.uk/ government/uploads/system/uploads/ attachment_data/file/246756/horr75- chap4.pdf

Meiklejohn, S., Pomarole, M., Jordan, G., Levchenko, K., McCoy, D., Voelker, G.M., & Savage, S. (2013). *A fistful of bitcoins: Characterizing payments among men with no names*. Proceedings from the 13th ACM SIGCOMM Conference on Internet Measurement. New York: ACM.

Mitnick, K., & Simon, W.L. (2002). *The art of deception: Controlling the human element of security*. New York: John Wiley & Sons.

Moghadam, A. (2008). The Salafi-jihad as a religious ideology. *CTC Sentinel*, 1(3). Retrieved from https://ctc.usma

.edu/app/uploads/2010/06/Vol1Iss3-Art5.pdf

Moghaddam, F.M. (2005). The staircase to terrorism: A psychological exploration. *American Psychologist, 60*(2), 161–169.

Moore, D., & Rid, T. (2016). Cryptopolitik and the Darknet. *Survival, 58*(1), 7–38.

National Consortium for the Study of Terrorism and Responses to Terrorism (START). (2017). Global Terrorism Database. Retrieved from https://www.start.umd.edu/gtd

Newman, G., & Clarke, R. (2003). *Superhighway robbery: Preventing e-commerce crime.* Cullompton, UK: Willan Press.

Newton, M., & Newton, J.A. (1991). *Racial and religious violence in America: A chronology.* New York: Garland Publishers.

Office of the Law Revision Counsel of the United States House of Representatives. (2018). 18 USC Ch. 113B—Terrorism. Retrieved from http://uscode.house.gov/view.xhtml?path=/prelim@title18/part1/chapter113B&edition=prelim

Osterman Research. (2016, August). *Understanding the depth of the global ransomware problem.* Retrieved from https://www.malwarebytes.com/pdf/white-papers/UnderstandingTheDepthOfRansomwareIntheUS.pdf

Perry, B., & Scrivens, R. (2016). Uneasy alliances: A look at the right-wing extremist movement in Canada. *Studies in Conflict and Terrorism, 39*(9), 819–841.

Public Safety Canada. (2018). Human trafficking. Retrieved from https://www.publicsafety.gc.ca/cnt/cntrng-crm/hmn-trffckng/index-en.aspx

Roach, K. (2018, April 19). Why the Quebec City mosque shooting was terrorism. *Globe and Mail.* Retrieved from https://www.theglobeandmail.com/opinion/article-why-the-quebec-city-mosque-shooting-was-terrorism

Royal Canadian Mounted Police. (2013). National child exploitation coordination centre. Retrieved from http://www.rcmp-grc.gc.ca/ncecc-cncee/about-ausujet-eng.htm

Royal Canadian Mounted Police. (2017a). Bullying and cyberbullying. Retrieved

from http://www.rcmp-grc.gc.ca/cycp-cpcj/bull-inti/index-eng.htm

Royal Canadian Mounted Police. (2017b). Ransomware. Retrieved from http://www.rcmp-grc.gc.ca/scams-fraudes/ransomware-rancongiciels-eng.htm

Sageman, M. (2004). *Understanding terror networks.* Philadelphia, PA: University of Pennsylvania Press.

Sasso, M. (2018, April 5). Delta says data exposed for "several hundred thousand" customers. *Bloomberg Technology.* Retrieved from https://www.bnnbloomberg.ca/delta-says-data-exposed-for-several-hundred-thousand-customers-1.1047902

Scrivens, R., & Perry, B. (2017). Resisting the right: Countering right-wing extremism in Canada. *Canadian Journal of Criminology and Criminal Justice, 59*(4), 534–558.

Senate of Canada. (2012). *Cyberbullying hurts: Respect for rights in the digital age: A guide for parents.* Retrieved from http://www.cyberbullying.ca/wp-content/uploads/2017/02/AAA_Cyberbullying-Hurts-Respect-for-Rights-in-the-Digital-Age-Parent-Guide-English.pdf

Smith, B.L. (1994). *Terrorism in America: Pipe bombs and pipe dreams.* Albany, NY: State University of New York Press.

Stewart, M. (2017, November 29). Equifax says number of Canadians affected by hack passes 19,000. *Globe and Mail.* Retrieved from https://www.theglobeandmail.com/globe-investor/personal-finance/household-finances/number-of-canadians-affected-by-equifax-hack-passes-19000/article37122603

Tropina, T. (2010). Cyber crime and organized crime. *Freedom from Fear Magazine, 7.* Retrieved from https://www.slideshare.net/dondelillo69/freedom-from-fear-magazine-issue-7

Tsfati, Y., & Weimann, G. (2002). www.terrorism.com: Terror on the Internet. *Studies in Conflict & Terrorism, 25*(5), 317–332.

UNEP-Interpol. (2016). *The rise of environmental crime.* Retrieved from https://reliefweb.int/sites/reliefweb

.int/files/resources/environmental_crimes.pdf

United Nations Office on Drugs and Crime. (2018). The money-laundering cycle. Retrieved from https://www.unodc.org/unodc/en/money-laundering/laundrycycle.html

Vanian, J. (2016, March 16). This nasty new malware can infect your Apple iPhone or iPad. *Fortune.* Retrieved from http://fortune.com/2016/03/16/malware-infect-apple-iphone-ipad

Westlake, B., & Bouchard, M. (2016). Liking and hyperlinking: Community detection in online child exploitation networks. *Social Science Research, 59,* 23–36.

White, P. (2010, June 27). Vandalism a central part of anarchists' tactics. *Globe and Mail.* Retrieved from https://www.theglobeandmail.com/news/world/vandalism-a-central-part-of-anarchists-tactics/article4323075

Wikström, P.-O.H., & Bouhana, N. (2017). Analyzing radicalization and terrorism: A situational action theory. In G. LaFree & J.D. Freilich (Eds.), *The handbook of the criminology of terrorism* (pp. 175–186). Chichester, UK: Wiley Blackwell.

Williams, M. (2016). Guardians upon high: An application of routine activity theory to online identity theft in Europe at the country and individual level. *British Journal of Criminology, 56*(1), 21–48.

Young, R. (2006). Defining terrorism: The evolution of terrorism as a legal concept, international law and its influence on definitions in domestic legislation. *Boston College International and Comparative Law Review, 29*(1), 23–103.

Zelin, A.Z. (Ed.). (2017). *How Al-Qaeda survived drones, uprisings, and the Islamic State.* Washington, DC: The Washington Institute for Near East Policy.

Zetter, K. (2016, April). Hacker lexicon: What are white hat, gray hat, and black hat hackers? *Wired.* Retrieved from https://www.wired.com/2016/04/hacker-lexicon-white-hat-gray-hat-black-hat-hackers

Index

cybercrime, 423–436, *see also* Internet
  case study of, 423–424
  choice theory, and, 278–279
  computer crimes, 427, 433–436
  computer-facilitated crimes, 427, 429–433, 436
  computer-supported crimes, 427, 429
  defined, 84, 412, 426
  effect on crime measurement, 85–86, 426–427
  increase in, 65, 425
  increasing theoretical focus on, 137
  policing child pornography, 322
  simple *vs.* complex, 405
cyberstalking, 431–432
cyberterrorists, 434
cyberwarfare, 433–434

Damiens, Robert-François, 124
dangerous offenders (DOs), 131, 327
dangerousness, 314–315, 316
Danvers, R v, 372
Danzig Street shooting, 383, 384
dark figure of crime, 71, 290, 319
dark web, 428
Darwin, Charles, 121, 266, *see also* evolution, theory of
Davis, R.C., 111
Dawson, Myrna, 232
de Grood, Matthew, 141–142
de Montesquieu, Baron, 124, 125, 193
de Saint-Simon, Henri, 126, 193
death penalty, 8–9, 12, 51
decriminalization, 366, 367
deep web, 428
Deepwater Horizon, 406
deferred prosecution agreements (DPAs), 416, 418
DeKeseredy, Walter, 249
Delinquency and Opportunity, 204
Delinquent Boys, 204
DeLisi, Matt, 26
Delta Air Lines, 429
demographics, 9
demonology, 124–125
denunciation, 54–55
Department of Justice (US), 392
Department of the Environment, Food, and Rural Affairs (UK), 406
deradicalization, 444
Deschenes, Elizabeth, 228
Design Against Crime Centre, 275
designated victims, 104
designing-out, 272, 273–275
determinism, 129
deterrence, 54, 55, 126, 173, 392
deterrence theories, 123, 126, 207, 341
developmental and life-course criminology (DLC), 178–180, *see also* life-course-developmental theory
developmental psychology, 178
developmental taxonomy, 178, 179
deviance, 8, 11, 16, 31, 353, 358–359, *see also* sociology of deviance
deviant self-identification, 166–167
deviant sexual behaviours, 162, 315, 320–324, 327–329

Devlin, Lord, 355
Diagnostic and Statistical Manual of Mental Disorders (DSM), 108, 168, 320–321, 323, 324
"Dieselgate," 401, 406, 420
differential association-reinforcement theory, 199–200
differential association theory, 198–200
  as explanation for cause of gang-related crime, 387
  as integrated theory, 134
  as part of mainstream criminological thinking, 191–192
  defined, 123, 198
  influence on
    cultural transmission theory, 203
    Jeffery, 172
    social learning theory, 206
    Wolfgang and Ferracuti, 209
diffusion of preventive benefits, 276
direct victims, 100, 101, 102
Discipline and Punish, 124
discourses, 34, 251
disengagement, 444
displacement, 276
dispositional theories, 272
Ditton, Jason, 73
DNA, 18–19, 145
do-it-yourself (DIY) terrorism, 442
Dobson, R v, 423–424
Dobson, Scott, 423–424
Dodd-Frank Wall Street Reform and Consumer Protection Act, 419
Dollard, John, 172
domestic violence, 117–118, 229–231, 298, *see also* spousal violence
Doob, Leonard, 172
Doolittle, Robin, 72
dopamine, 148, 150, 152
Douglass, Frederick, 247
Dowds, Elizabeth, 79
Dowler, K., 30, 35, 36
Doyle, A., 36
Drabinsky, Garth, 336, 414
Drug and Crime Prevention Strategies Unit, 396
drug cartels, 373, 387
drugs, 362–368, *see also* cannabis
  alternatives to criminalizing, 366–368
  gang involvement in trade of, 385
  immigration, and, 8, 365
  in 1960s culture, 9
  in treatment of sex offenders, 328
  laws on, 352, 353, 364–366
  penalties for possession of, 3–4
  social learning and subcultural theories on, 363–364
  used by homeless youth, 345–346
  war on, 184, 246–247, 302–303, 366
Du Bois, W.E.B., 247
Duncan, Kashana, 371
Dunedin Multidisciplinary Health and Development Study, 179
Dunkley, Jermaine, 371
Dunn, Christopher, 229
duress, 52
Durkheim, Émile, 192–194
  consensus theories, and, 135, 138
  criticism of Positivist School, 132

Mitnick, K., 436
mixed methods approach, 20, 68
modelling, 123, 134, 173–174, 177, 192, 200
Mods, 31, 32
Moffitt, Terrie, 132, 134, 178, 179–180
money laundering, 407–408, 430–431
money mules, 431
Monney, R v, 372
monoamine oxidase A (MAOA), 152–153
monoamine oxidase B (MAOB), 152
Monstarz, 371
Moore, Michael, 28
moral absolutism, 355
moral development theory, 174–176
moral entrepreneurs, 31, 34, 201
moral panics, 30–32, 34, 202, 209, 244, 378
moral relativism, 355
morals, 351, *see also* crimes of morality
Morin, Guy Paul, 19
Mormons, 41
Morris, Michael H., 349
Morris, Ruth, 222–223
mosque shooting, 436, 437
motor vehicles, 271, 278, 337–338
Mowrer, O.H., 172
mugging, 30, 244
Mullins, Christopher, 228
Mulmat, D.H., 111
multi-causal (defined), 288
Muncie, J., 68
Munyaneza, Désiré, 47
Murphy, Emily, 3
Murray, Charles, 133, 164, 165
Muslims, 33
Mussolini, Benito, 128
Myers, Justice, 237, 238

Napoleon Bonaparte, 193
Narcotic Control Act of 1961, 3
Natapoff, Alexandra, 303
National Academy of Sciences, 178
National Child Exploitation Coordination Centre, 432
National Consortium for the Study of Terrorism and Responses to Terrorism (START), 443
National Crime Prevention Strategy, 275
National Crime Victimization Survey (NCVS), 221, 229
National Parole Board, 180
National Plan to Combat Human Trafficking, 433
National Public Radio, 27
National Rifle Association, 30
nature *vs.* nurture, *see* biographical approaches: *vs.* environmental and sociological
negligence, 411–412
neo-Marxism, 242–245, 249
nervous system, 150
Nestlé, 411
net widening, 18
neurotic (defined), 166
neuroticism (N), 171
neurotransmitters, 148, 150–152

neutralization, 199, 206
Never Again MSD, 30
New Criminology, The, 31, 202, 243
New Kind of Monster, A, 161
Newton, Isaac, 125
Nocella II, Anthony, 252
non-victims, 103
Nordheimer, Justice, 237
norepinephrine, 150, 152
no-snitch codes, 302–303, 377, 386
not criminally responsible, 141
novice hackers, 433, 434
nudge theory, 265

Obama, Barack, 69
O'Brien, Martin, 32
obtaining goods under false pretences, 335
Occupational Health and Safety Act, 411
offenders, *see also* sex offenders
    adolescent-limited, 132, 134, 179–180
    anti-social, 167, 168, 176–177
    as euphemism, 253
    dangerous, 131, 327
    finding biographies of, 91
    habitual criminals, 55–56
    intuitive criminals, 263
    life-course-persistent, 132, 134, 179, 180
    likely, 269
    long-term, 131, 327
    potential, 269
    research focus on, 99
    rights of victims *vs.*, 112
    risk of victimization, 102–103
    sex differences, and, 296
    study of, 15–17
Ohlin, Lloyd, 194, 204
Oler, James, 42
Olson, Clifford, 97, 167, 311
O'Malley, Pat, 251
omerta, 302
On Crimes and Punishments, 124, 125
On Criminal Man, 127
O'Neil, Casey, 216
Ong, A.D., 111
Ontario Court of Appeal, 117–118, 230, 237, 372
Ontario Superior Court, 237–238, 371–372
operant conditioning, 123, 134, 171–172, 177, 192, 200
Operation Ceasefire, 391–393
Operation Identification, 77
Opium Act, 1908, 364, 365
opportunity theory, 121
Order, The, 440
Organisation for Economic Co-operation and Development (OECD), 408
organized crime, *see* gangs and organized crime
Osgood, Wayne, 198
Osgoode Hall, 117
Osterman Research, 435
other (defined), 35
Ottawa Citizen, 215

Credits